COLLECTIVE SELF-DEFENCE IN INTERNATIONAL LAW

Collective self-defence can be defined as the use of military force by one or more states to aid another state that is an innocent victim of armed attack. However, it is a legal justification that is open to abuse and its exercise risks escalating conflict. Recent years have seen an unprecedented increase in the number of collective self-defence claims. It has been the main basis for US-led action in Syria (2014–) and was advanced by Russia in relation to its full-scale invasion of Ukraine (2022–). Yet, there has still been little analysis of collective self-defence in international law. This book crucially progresses the debate on various fundamental and under-explored questions about the conceptual nature of collective self-defence and the requirements for its operation. Green provides the most detailed and extensive account of collective self-defence to date, at a time when it is being invoked more than ever before.

JAMES A. GREEN is the author of *The Persistent Objector Rule in International Law* (2016), which won the ESIL Book Prize, and *The International Court of Justice and Self-Defence in International Law* (2010), which won ASIL's Lieber Prize. He is the Co-editor-in-Chief of the *Journal on the Use of Force and International Law* and co-rapporteur of the ILA's Use of Force Committee.

CAMBRIDGE STUDIES IN INTERNATIONAL AND COMPARATIVE LAW: 184

Established in 1946, this series produces high quality, reflective and innovative scholarship in the field of public international law. It publishes works on international law that are of a theoretical, historical, cross-disciplinary or doctrinal nature. The series also welcomes books providing insights from private international law, comparative law and transnational studies which inform international legal thought and practice more generally.

The series seeks to publish views from diverse legal traditions and perspectives, and of any geographical origin. In this respect it invites studies offering regional perspectives on core *problématiques* of international law, and in the same vein, it appreciates contrasts and debates between diverging approaches. Accordingly, books offering new or less orthodox perspectives are very much welcome. Works of a generalist character are greatly valued and the series is also open to studies on specific areas, institutions or problems. Translations of the most outstanding works published in other languages are also considered.

After seventy years, Cambridge Studies in International and Comparative Law sets the standard for international legal scholarship and will continue to define the discipline as it evolves in the years to come.

A list of books in the series can be found at the end of this volume.

COLLECTIVE SELF-DEFENCE IN INTERNATIONAL LAW

JAMES A. GREEN
University of the West of England, Bristol

CAMBRIDGE
UNIVERSITY PRESS

CAMBRIDGE
UNIVERSITY PRESS

Shaftesbury Road, Cambridge CB2 8EA, United Kingdom

One Liberty Plaza, 20th Floor, New York, NY 10006, USA

477 Williamstown Road, Port Melbourne, VIC 3207, Australia

314–321, 3rd Floor, Plot 3, Splendor Forum, Jasola District Centre, New Delhi – 110025, India

103 Penang Road, #05-06/07, Visioncrest Commercial, Singapore 238467

Cambridge University Press is part of Cambridge University Press & Assessment, a department of the University of Cambridge.

We share the University's mission to contribute to society through the pursuit of education, learning and research at the highest international levels of excellence.

www.cambridge.org
Information on this title: www.cambridge.org/9781009406383

DOI: 10.1017/9781009406420

First published 2024

A catalogue record for this publication is available from the British Library

Library of Congress Cataloging-in-Publication Data
Names: Green, James A., 1981- author.
Title: Collective self-defence in international law / James A. Green, University of the West of England, Bristol.
Other titles: Collective self-defense in international law
Description: Cambridge, United Kigndom ; New York, NY : Cambridge University Press, 2024. | Series: Cambridge studies in international and comparative law | Includes bibliographical references and index.
Identifiers: LCCN 2023033188 (print) | LCCN 2023033189 (ebook) | ISBN 9781009406383 (hardback) | ISBN 9781009406376 (paperback) | ISBN 9781009406420 (epub)
Subjects: LCSH: Self-defense (International law) | Aggression (International law) | Intervention (International law)
Classification: LCC KZ4043 .G725 2024 (print) | LCC KZ4043 (ebook) | DDC 341.6/3–dc23/eng/20230928
LC record available at https://lccn.loc.gov/2023033188
LC ebook record available at https://lccn.loc.gov/2023033189

ISBN 978-1-009-40638-3 Hardback

This book is for Logan.
I love you immeasurably.
Goggy you!

CONTENTS

Acknowledgements x
Table of Treaties xiii
Table of Cases and Arbitral Awards xvii

Introduction 1
0.1 The Subject of This Study and the Rationale for Undertaking It 1
0.2 A Focus on State Practice 9
0.3 The *Nicaragua* Case 15
0.4 A Brief Note on Terminology 18
0.5 The Structure of This Book 18

1 **Delineating Collective Self-Defence** 23
1.1 Introduction 23
1.2 The Many Faces of Collective Self-Defence 25
1.3 Collective Self-Defence as an Inherent Right 47
1.4 The Modality of Collective Self-Defence: Acts *Minoris Generis* 55
1.5 Conclusion 65

2 **The History and Development of Collective Self-Defence** 66
2.1 Introduction 66
2.2 The Concept of 'Collective Self-Defence' before the First World War 69
2.3 'Collective Self-Defence' during the Interwar Period and the Second World War 76
2.4 The Drafting of the UN Charter and the Conjoining of Individual and Collective Self-Defence 84
2.5 Conclusion 96

3 **The Requirements Shared by Individual and Collective Self-Defence** 98
3.1 Introduction 98
3.2 Armed Attack 100

3.3 Necessity and Proportionality 121
3.4 The Reporting Requirement 130
3.5 The 'Until Clause' 135
3.6 Conclusion 138

4 The Purported Declaration and Request Requirements for Collective Self-Defence 140
4.1 Introduction 140
4.2 The Declaration and Request Criteria in the Jurisprudence of the ICJ 142
4.3 Critique of the ICJ's Identification of Declaration and Request and Locating Them as a Matter of Law 147
4.4 The Requirements in State Practice/*Opinio Juris*: Request but Not Declaration 153
4.5 Conclusion 167

5 The Issuer of a Collective Self-Defence Request 169
5.1 Introduction 169
5.2 The Requirement of Statehood 170
5.3 A Requirement of UN Membership? 178
5.4 The De Jure Government as the Relevant Authority 183
5.5 Identifying the De Jure Government 185
5.6 Conclusion 203

6 The Manner and Form of a Collective Self-Defence Request 204
6.1 Introduction 204
6.2 The Addressee of the Request 204
6.3 Formalities and Inferred Requests 211
6.4 The Publicity of Requests 215
6.5 The Timing of the Request 222
6.6 Conclusion 231

7 Collective Self-Defence Treaty Arrangements 232
7.1 Introduction 232
7.2 The Variety of Collective Self-Defence Treaty Arrangements 234
7.3 The Nature and Strength of the Obligations within Collective Self-Defence Treaty Arrangements 238
7.4 Partially Overlapping Obligations and Disputes within Memberships 254

7.5 Geographical Limitations and the Relationship between Collective Self-Defence Treaty Arrangements and 'Regional Arrangements' 259
7.6 The Value of Collective Self-Defence Treaty Arrangements 268
7.7 Conclusion 274

8 The Relationship between Collective Self-Defence and Military Assistance on Request 276

8.1 Introduction 276
8.2 Collective Self-Defence and Military Assistance on Request at the Conceptual Level 280
8.3 Blurred State Argumentation 283
8.4 The Request Requirement 286
8.5 Armed Attack and the Possibility of an Equivalent for Counter-Intervention 291
8.6 Necessity and Proportionality 295
8.7 Reporting 297
8.8 Location and Simultaneousness 299
8.9 Conclusion 311

Conclusion 312

Bibliography 321
Index 349

ACKNOWLEDGEMENTS

I wrote this book while undertaking a British Academy Mid-Career Fellowship [MF21\210131]. The generous funding provided by the British Academy meant that I was able to produce it in a relatively short period of time (around a year), while also feeling like I had space to research and write at a civilised pace. That is a significant privilege, which academics rarely – if ever – enjoy. I fully acknowledge that financial support from the British Academy. I am so incredibly grateful for it. This book would have taken many years to write without it, if I ever would have been able to write it at all.

I would like to thank all of my colleagues at the University of the West of England (UWE), Bristol, for their tolerance of my sabbatical while undertaking the Fellowship. Particular thanks must go to Sarah Grabham, Shilan Shah-Davis, and Professor Noëlle Quénivet. I would also like to thank colleagues in the Research, Business and Innovation team at UWE – especially Alina Jaroszewicz-Czepulkowska – for helping me to administer the British Academy Fellowship in various ways. I owe thanks, too, to colleagues at my previous institution, the University of Reading, who supported me in preparing my application for the British Academy Fellowship: I moved academic home before it got underway, but I have not forgotten how important the support I had at Reading was in terms of me being awarded it in the first place.

I acknowledge that some aspects of Chapter 4 of this book were previously published as James A. Green, 'The "Additional" Criteria for Collective Self-Defence: Request but Not Declaration' (2017) 4 *Journal on the Use of Force and International Law* 4. However, the chapter included here significantly expands on, develops, and updates that work. Similarly, some aspects of a small part of Chapter 1, in Section 1.4, have appeared in a notably reworked form in James A. Green, 'The Provision of Weapons and Logistical Support to Ukraine and the *Jus ad Bellum*' (2023) 10 *Journal on the Use of Force and International Law* 3.

A paper including some of the material featured in Chapter 8 of this book was presented in Lisbon on 21 June 2022, at the International Law Association's Biennial Conference (during the working session of the Use of Force: Military Assistance on Request Committee). Many thanks go to all those who were present, and especially to those colleagues who asked questions: this was invaluable feedback. Thanks also go to Professor Guimei Bai for her helpful comments on the written version of that (unpublished) paper.

During the writing of this book, various colleagues have been kind enough to read draft chapters and provide me with comments to help improve them. I am so grateful for this. A *massive* thank you to Dr Max Brookman-Byrne, Professor Erika de Wet, Dr Luca Ferro, Dr Francis Grimal, Professor Daniel Joyner, Dr Ben Murphy, and Professor Noëlle Quénivet. I also would like to thank everyone at Cambridge University Press for their support of this project and the anonymous reviewers during the proposal stage for their invaluable suggestions.

Much of the writing of this book was soundtracked by the album 'They Fear Us' by the British metalcore band Ithaca. That album happened to be released while I was working on the book, and it is an astonishing musical achievement. I now consider it to be my favourite record of all time – among the thousands that I have played over the decades – and it helped drag me through a number of tough days grappling with UN verbatim records or staring at a blank screen struggling to write. Thanks, Ithaca, you made a masterpiece at just the right time.

A note of thanks goes to my friend Adam Wood, who kept me sane by discussing pop culture (and other things) with me via instant messages while I was writing this book. The helpful disconnect and recharge that our discussions provided me with during intermittent breaks meant that this book ended up being better than it would have otherwise been. Having said that, he likes *Top Gun* and *The Matrix* sequels far too much, and *Speed* far too little. Nobody is perfect, I guess.

Some people are not all that far off, though. The thanks that I owe to my wife, Dr Lia Emanuel – for her sense of humour, kindness, and patience with my perpetual nonsense – go far beyond what I can express in words. You are my partner, and you are my best friend. We reached ten years of marriage while I was in the middle of writing this book, and it has flown by. For me, at least. You're awesome, Lia. I love you very much indeed.

My final word of thanks is for our son, Logan, who, as I write this, has recently turned two. You didn't really help all that much with this book, little goblin. In fact, I'm pretty sure that the sleep deprivation and regular tantrums that you inflicted on us throughout the process made it harder. But you have also made me happier than I ever thought possible. And I was already pretty happy. So, that probably deserves a mention here. Thank you, my son. I love you so, *so* much.

Okay. Enough mushy stuff. Onwards.

All errors in this book are mine. You know the drill: my work = my screw-ups.

TABLE OF TREATIES

1680	A Defensive League betwixt Charles II. King of Spain and Charles II. King of Great Britain. Done at Windsor, June 10, 1680, reproduced in Charles Jenkinson (ed.), *A Collection of All the Treaties of Peace, Alliance, and Commerce, between Great-Britain and Other Powers* (London, J. Debrett, 1785), 257
1815	Treaty of Alliance and Friendship between Great Britain, Austria, Prussia, and Russia (1815) MET, vol. 1, 372
1882	Treaty of Alliance (Austria-Hungary, Germany, Italy) (1882), https://gspi.unipr.it/sites/st26/files/allegatiparagrafo/25-01-2016/triple_alliance.pdf (Treaty of Triple Alliance)
1912	Military Convention between the Kingdoms of Bulgaria and Servia (1912), reproduced in (1914) 8 *American Journal of International Law, Supplement: Official Documents* (January 1914), 5
1912	Military Convention between Bulgaria and Greece (1912), reproduced in (1914) 8 *American Journal of International Law, Supplement: Official Documents* (January 1914), 83
1919	Covenant of the League of Nations (1919) 225 CTS 195
1921	Defensive Alliance Convention between the Czechoslovak Republic (Czechoslovakia) and the Kingdom of Romania (1921) 13 LNTS 231
1928	International Treaty for the Renunciation of War as an Instrument of National Policy (1928), *The Avalon Project*, https://avalon.law.yale.edu/20th_century/kbpact.asp (Kellogg–Briand Pact/Treaty of Paris/Paris Peace Pact)
1935	France–USSR Treaty of Mutual Assistance (1935) reproduced in (1936) 30 *American Journal of International Law, Supplement: Official Documents* (October 1936), 177
1939	Agreement of Mutual Assistance between the United Kingdom and Poland (1939), *The Avalon Project*, https://avalon.law.yale.edu/wwii/blbk19.asp
1939	Pact of Mutual Assistance between the USSR and Estonia (1939), reproduced in (1968) 14 *Lituanus*, www.lituanus.org/1968/68_2_03Doc6.html

1940 Second Meeting of Ministers of Foreign Affairs of the American Republics, Havana (21–30 July 1940): Final Act and Convention, reproduced in (1941) 35 *Supplement to the American Journal of International Law* 1

1945 Charter of the United Nations (1945) 1 UNTS XVI (UN Charter)

1945 Statute of the International Court of Justice (1945) 33 UNTS 93

1945 Inter-American Reciprocal Assistance and Solidarity (1945), resolution approved by the Inter-American Conference on Problems of War and Peace at Mexico, 60 Stat. 1831 (Act of Chapultepec)

1946 Treaty of Alliance (with Annex and Exchange of Notes) (United Kingdom of Great Britain and Northern Ireland and Transjordan) (1946) 6 UNTS 143 (Treaty of London)

1947 Treaty of Alliance and Mutual Assistance between His Majesty in respect of the United Kingdom of Great Britain and Northern Ireland and the President of the French Republic (1947) 9 UNTS 121 (Treaty of Dunkirk)

1947 Treaty of Brotherhood and Alliance (Iraq/Transjordan) (1947) 23 UNTS 345

1948 Agreement of Friendship, Cooperation, and Mutual Assistance between The Union of Soviet Socialist Republics and The Republic of Finland (1948) 48 UNTS 149 (Finno–Soviet Treaty)

1948 Inter-American Treaty of Reciprocal Assistance (1948) 21 UNTS 77 (Rio Treaty)

1948 Treaty of Economic, Social and Cultural Collaboration and Collective Self-Defence (1948), *North Atlantic Treaty Organisation*, www.nato.int/cps/en/natohq/official_texts_17072.htm (Brussels Treaty) [NB: amended in 1954 by the WEU Treaty, see subsequent entry in this table]

1949 North Atlantic Treaty (1949) 34 UNTS 243

1950 Treaty of Friendship, Alliance and Mutual Assistance (China/USSR) (1950), reproduced in (1950) 44 *Supplement to the American Journal of International Law* 83

1950 Treaty of Joint Defense and Economic Cooperation between the States of the Arab League (1950), *The Avalon Project*, https://avalon.law.yale.edu/20th_century/arabjoin.asp

1951 Agreement between the Government of the United States and the Government of the Republic of Korea (1950), reproduced in (1951) 45 *American Journal of International Law Supplement: Official Documents* 73

1951 Mutual Defense Treaty between the Republic of the Philippines and the United States of America (1951) 177 UNTS 133

1951 Security Treaty between the United States and Japan (1951) 3 UST 3329

1952 Security Treaty between Australia, New Zealand, and the United States of America (1952) 131 UNTS 83 (ANZUS Treaty)

1954 Southeast Asia Collective Defense Treaty (with Protocol) (1954) 209 UNTS 28 (SEATO Treaty)

1954 Treaty of Alliance, Political Cooperation, and Mutual Assistance between the Turkish Republic, the Kingdom of Greece, and the Federal People's Republic of Yugoslavia (1954), *The Avalon Project*, text available at https://avalon.law.yale.edu/20th_century/eu002.asp (Balkan Pact)

1954 Treaty of Economic, Social and Cultural Collaboration and Collective Self-Defence (1948), as Amended by the 'Protocol Modifying and Completing the Brussels Treaty' (1954), FO 1093/575 (Western European Union Treaty /WEU Treaty)

1955 Pact of Mutual Cooperation between the Kingdom of Iraq, the Republic of Turkey, the United Kingdom, the Dominion of Pakistan, and the Kingdom of Iran (1955), *The Avalon Project*, text available at https://avalon.law.yale.edu/20th_century/baghdad.asp (Baghdad Pact)

1955 Treaty of Friendship, Cooperation and Mutual Assistance between the People's Republic of Albania, the People's Republic of Bulgaria, the Hungarian People's Republic, the German Democratic Republic, the Polish People's Republic, the Romanian People's Republic (1955) 219 UNTS 24 (Warsaw Pact)

1960 United Kingdom of Great Britain and Northern Ireland, Greece and Turkey and Cyprus, Treaty of Guarantee (1960) 382 UNTS 3

1969 Vienna Convention on the Law of Treaties (1969) 1155 UNTS 331 (VCLT)

1978 Treaty of Friendship and Co-operation between the Socialist Republic of Viet Nam and the Union of Soviet Socialist Republic (1978), annexed to Letter dated 7 November 1978 from the Permanent Representatives of the Union of Soviet Socialist Republics and Viet Nam to the United Nations addressed to the Secretary-General, UN Doc. A/33/362-S/12920 (8 November 1978)

1981 Economic Community of West African States (ECOWAS) Protocol relating to Mutual Assistance on Defence (1981) A/SP3/5/81

1981 Treaty Establishing the Organization of Eastern Caribbean States (1981) 20 ILM 1166 (OECS Treaty)

1996 Treaty Establishing the Regional Security System (1996), RSS, text available at www.rss.org.bb/wp-content/uploads/2020/02/Treaty-Establishing-the-RSS-.pdf (RSS Treaty)

2002 Traité destiné à adapter et à confirmer les rapports d'amitié et de coopération entre la République Française et la Principauté de Monaco (2002) (2006) *Journal de Monaco*, SO no. 407

2003 Southern African Development Community (SADC) Mutual Defence Pact (2003) 3156 UNTS

2005 African Union Non-Aggression and Common Defence Pact (2005), *African Union*, text available at https://au.int/sites/default/files/treaties/37292-treaty-0031_-_african_union_non-aggression_and_common_defence_pact_e.pdf (AU Pact)

2007 Consolidated Version of the Treaty on European Union (2007), reproduced in (2008) *OJ* C115/13 (TEU)

2012 Collective Security Treaty (1992), *Collective Security Treaty Organisation* (23 April 2012), text available at https://en.odkb-csto.org/documents/documents/dogovor_o_kollektivnoy_bezopasnosti/#loaded

2021 Agreement between the Government of the Hellenic Republic and the Government of the French Republic establishing a Strategic Partnership for Cooperation in Defence and Security (2021), titled in the authoritative French as 'un partenariat stratégique pour la coopération en matière de défense et de sécurité', text available at www.hellenicparliament.gr/Nomothetiko-Ergo/Anazitisi-Nomothetikou-Ergou?law_id=50f9990e-73f6-4015-b706-adb4013e7514) (Greek and French texts only: the treaty has not been translated into English) (Greek–French Treaty)

2022 Treaty of Friendship, Cooperation and Mutual Assistance between the Russian Federation and the Donetsk People's Republic (signed in Moscow, 21 February 2022), annexed to UN Doc. A/76/740–S/2022/179 (7 March 2022) (annex I) [NB: *purported* treaty]

2022 Treaty of Friendship, Cooperation and Mutual Assistance between the Russian Federation and the Lugansk People's Republic (signed in Moscow, 21 February 2022), annexed to UN Doc. A/76/740–S/2022/179 (7 March 2022) (annex II) [NB: *purported* treaty]

TABLE OF CASES AND ARBITRAL AWARDS

International Court of Justice/Permanent Court of International Justice

1969 *North Sea Continental Shelf Cases (Federal Republic of Germany v. Netherlands, Federal Republic of Germany v. Denmark)* (merits) [1969] ICJ Rep. 3

1970 *Barcelona Traction, Light and Power Company, Limited (Belgium v. Spain)* (judgment) [1970] ICJ Rep. 3

1985 *Continental Shelf (Libyan Arab Jamahiriya/Malta)* (merits) [1985] ICJ Rep. 13

1986 *Military and Paramilitary Activities in and against Nicaragua (Nicaragua v. United States of America)* (merits) [1986] ICJ Rep. 14

- *Military and Paramilitary Activities in and against Nicaragua (Nicaragua v. United States of America)* (application instituting proceedings) [1984] ICJ Plead., vol. I
- *Military and Paramilitary Activities in and against Nicaragua (Nicaragua v. United States of America)* (counter-memorial of the United States of America, questions of jurisdiction and admissibility) [1984] ICJ Plead., vol. II
- *Military and Paramilitary Activities in and against Nicaragua (Nicaragua v. United States of America)* (declaration of intervention of the Republic of El Salvador: intervention pursuant to Article 63 of the Statute of the International Court of Justice, filed in the Registry of the Court on 15 August 1984)
- *Military and Paramilitary Activities in and against Nicaragua (Nicaragua v. United States of America)* (jurisdiction of the court and admissibility of the application) [1984] ICJ Rep. 392

1994 *Territorial Dispute (Libyan Arab Jamahiriya/Chad)* (judgment) [1994] ICJ Rep. 6

- *Territorial Dispute (Libyan Arab Jamahiriya/Chad)* (memorial submitted by the Great Socialist People's Libyan Arab Jamahiriya) (26 August 1991)

1999 *Kasikili/Sedudu Island (Botswana/Namibia)* (judgment) [1999] ICJ Rep. 1045

2002 *Sovereignty over Pulau Litigan and Pulau Sipadan (Indonesia/Malaysia)* (judgment) [2002] ICJ Rep. 625

2003 *Case concerning Oil Platforms (Islamic Republic of Iran v. United States of America)* (merits) [2003] ICJ Rep. 161

- *Case concerning Oil Platforms (Islamic Republic of Iran v. United States of America* (preliminary objections) [1996] ICJ Rep. 803

2004 *Avena and Other Mexican Nationals (Mexico v. United States of America)* (judgment) [2004] ICJ Rep. 12

2004 *Legal Consequences of the Construction of a Wall in the Occupied Palestinian Territory* (advisory opinion) [2004] ICJ Rep. 135

2005 *Armed Activities on the Territory of the Congo (Democratic Republic of the Congo v. Uganda)* (judgment) [2005] ICJ Rep. 168

- *Armed Activities on the Territory of the Congo (Democratic Republic of the Congo v. Uganda)* (mémoire de la Republique Démocratique du Congo) (6 July 2000)
- *Armed Activities on the Territory of the Congo (Democratic Republic of the Congo v. Uganda)* (counter-memorial submitted by Uganda) (21 April 2001)

2012 *Jurisdictional Immunities of the State (Germany v. Italy: Greece intervening)* (merits) [2012] ICJ Rep. 99

Arbitral Awards

1923 *Tinoco Claims Arbitration (Great Britain v. Costa Rica)* (1923) 1 RIAA 369

1977 *Dispute between Argentina and Chile concerning the Beagle Channel* [1977] PCA, XXI RIAA, 53

Domestic Case Law

Ireland, Court of Criminal Appeal

1954 *The People (Attorney General) v. Keatley* [1954] IR 12

Senegal, Special Tribunal

2017 *Jugement rendu par la Chambre Africaine Extraordinaire d'Assises d'Appel dans l'affaire ministère public contre Hissein Habré*, Chambres Africaines Extraordinaires [2017], www.chambresafricaines.org/pdf/Arr%C3%AAt_int%C3%A9gral.pdf

United States of America, Court of Appeals of Virginia

1991 *Foster v. Commonwealth* [1991] 13 Va.App. 380, 383–384, 412 S.E.2d 198, 200

Introduction

This book examines collective self-defence in international law. Article 51 of the 1945 Charter of the United Nations (UN) sanctifies the modern legal concept of self-defence, setting out 'the inherent right of individual *or collective* self-defence if an armed attack occurs . . .'[1] The Charter thus designates individual and collective self-defence, together, as a single legal 'right', which is 'inherent'.[2] In so doing, it firmly established the place of collective self-defence within contemporary international law.[3]

0.1 The Subject of This Study and the Rationale for Undertaking It

The core concept of collective self-defence can be broadly defined as the use of military force by one or more states in response to an external attack[4] that has occurred or is occurring[5] against another state.

[1] Charter of the United Nations (1945) 1 UNTS XVI (UN Charter), Article 51 (emphasis added). In full, the article reads: '[n]othing in the present Charter shall impair the inherent right of individual or collective self-defence if an armed attack occurs against a Member of the United Nations, until the Security Council has taken measures necessary to maintain international peace and security. Measures taken by Members in the exercise of this right of self-defence shall be immediately reported to the Security Council and shall not in any way affect the authority and responsibility of the Security Council under the present Charter to take at any time such action as it deems necessary in order to maintain or restore international peace and security'.

[2] On the indivisible nature of self-defence as a single 'right' within Article 51, see, for example, Eugene V. Rostow, 'Until What? Enforcement Action or Collective Self-Defense' (1991) 85 *American Journal of International Law* 506, 510. For more on the status of collective self-defence as a *right* (and, indeed, as an *inherent* right), see Section 1.3. For discussion of the 'conjoining' of individual and collective self-defence that resulted from their inclusion in Article 51 of the UN Charter, see Section 2.4.

[3] See Section 2.4 for further discussion of the effect of Article 51 in this regard.

[4] This was traditionally considered to be an attack launched by a state. However, now, it arguably may also include attacks by non-state actors in certain circumstances. On the controversial question of collective self-defence against attacks by non-state actors, see Section 3.2.4.

[5] This arguably may also include attacks that will imminently occur. On the question of collective self-defence against imminent attacks, see Section 3.2.3.

Put even more simply: 'collective self-defence [exists] to assist third parties in countering an armed attack'.[6] This is, of course, in contrast to individual self-defence, which involves what one might more intuitively think of as 'self-defence' in the international context: that is, a state defending *itself* from attack.

While the basic notion of 'collective self-defence' can be relatively easily stated, delineating it any further quickly runs into problems.[7] Scholars who have scratched the surface of the concept, even tentatively, have described collective self-defence as being 'rather puzzling'[8] and 'not easily comprehensible'.[9] Despite its prominence in Article 51 of the UN Charter, 'collective self-defence' is not defined therein,[10] nor is it authoritatively defined elsewhere in international legal doctrine.

Moreover, it has often been claimed that collective self-defence had no historical 'pedigree' before 1945, and therefore that it was a new legal creation by the drafters of the UN Charter.[11] This can be contrasted to individual self-defence, many of the core features of which – it is widely accepted – can be traced back centuries.[12] For *individual* self-defence,

[6] Simona Ross, 'U.S. Justifications for the Use of Force in Syria through the Prism of the Responsibility to Protect' (2021) 8 *Journal on the Use of Force and International Law* 233, 237. See also A. J. Thomas Jr. and Ann Van Wynen Thomas, 'The Organization of American States and Collective Security' (1959) 13 *Southwestern Law Journal* 177, 186 ('collective self-defense is action taken by States not directly the victims of an armed attack').

[7] See Chapter 1 for discussion and for a detailed attempt to try to delineate the concept.

[8] Arthur Eyffinger, 'Self-Defence or the Meanderings of a Protean Principle', in Arthur Eyffinger, Alan Stephens and Sam Muller (eds.), *Self-Defence as a Fundamental Principle* (The Hague, Hague Academic Press, 2009), 103, 128.

[9] Yoram Dinstein, *War, Aggression and Self-Defence* (Cambridge, Cambridge University Press, 6th ed., 2017), 301.

[10] See Derek W. Bowett, 'Collective Self-Defence under the Charter of the United Nations' (1955–1956) 32 *British Yearbook of International Law* 130, 130.

[11] See, for example, *Military and Paramilitary Activities in and against Nicaragua* (*Nicaragua v. United States of America*) (merits) [1986] ICJ Rep. 14, dissenting opinion of Judge Jennings, 530–531; R. St. J. MacDonald, 'The *Nicaragua* Case: New Answers to Old Questions' (1986) 24 *Canadian Yearbook of International Law* 127, 143, 146; Rosalyn Higgins, *The Development of International Law through the Political Organs of the United Nations* (London, Oxford University Press, 1963), 208; Christian Henderson, *The Use of Force and International Law* (Cambridge, Cambridge University Press, 2018), 260; D.W. Greig, 'Self-Defence and the Security Council: What Does Article 51 Require?' (1991) 40 *International and Comparative Law Quarterly* 366, 373; Thomas M. Franck, *Recourse to Force: State Action against Threats and Armed Attacks* (Cambridge, Cambridge University Press, 2002), 48–49.

[12] See, for example, Stephen C. Neff, *War and the Law of Nations: A General History* (Cambridge, Cambridge University Press, 2005), 126–130.

there is a wealth of pre-UN doctrine and practice upon which one can draw to put legal 'meat' on the 'bones' of its central concept. This is not the case (at least, not in the same way or to the same extent) for collective self-defence. That said, the claim that collective self-defence was an entirely 'new' concept in 1945 is incorrect. In fact, it too has historical roots stretching back as far as recorded history.[13] It is true, though, that the notion of 'collective defence' in international law was substantially changed by the adoption of the UN Charter,[14] meaning that analysis of the historical development of the concept is indeed of less value in understanding the modern concept than is the case for its 'individual' twin.[15]

Another common assertion regarding collective self-defence is that it also 'has been little used in practice' *since* the creation of the United Nations in 1945.[16] There is a perception that for most of the UN era, collective self-defence has been an almost semi-dormant concept, invoked by states only extremely rarely. While a large number of collective self-defence treaty arrangements have continued to emerge,[17] this has 'not been matched by extensive state practice'.[18] This claim, too, is correct up to a point. Certainly, as compared to individual self-defence – which has been invoked by states almost ubiquitously since 1945[19] – collective self-defence has been advanced less often as a legal justification for the use of force in practice. There have been notably more examples of collective self-defence claims made by states in the UN era than is often perceived in the scholarship, however.[20]

13 M. A Weightman, 'Self-Defense in International Law' (1951) 37 *Virginia Law Review* 1095, 1110. See, generally, Chapter 2.

14 See Section 2.4.

15 This is certainly not to say that there is no value in so doing – as will be seen from the analysis in Chapter 2 – only that, in this writer's view, the 'history' of collective self-defence tells us less about the right today than does the 'history' of individual self-defence.

16 Christine Chinkin and Mary Kaldor, *International Law and New Wars* (Cambridge, Cambridge University Press, 2017), 140. See also, for example, Christine Gray, *International Law and the Use of Force* (Oxford, Oxford University Press, 4th ed., 2018), 176.

17 See Chapter 7.

18 Gray, n.16, 176.

19 See *ibid*, 121; Chris O'Meara, *Necessity and Proportionality and the Right of Self-Defence in International Law* (Oxford, Oxford University Press, 2021), 1: Rosalyn Higgins, 'The Legal Limits to the Use of Force by Sovereign States: United Nations Practice' (1961) 37 *British Yearbook of International Law* 269, 297.

20 See Jaemin Lee, 'Collective Self-Defense or Collective Security: Japan's Reinterpretation of Article 9 of the Constitution' (2015) 8 *Journal of East Asia and International Law* 373, 374 ('[i]t is *not uncommon* for a State (A) to invoke collective self-defense to justify their

Indeed, recent years have seen an unprecedented increase in the number of collective self-defence actions (or, at least, purported collective self-defence actions) undertaken by states. In particular, collective self-defence has been the primary legal justification advanced by the US-led coalition for ongoing military action in Syria since 2014 (on the basis that these states are acting in the defence of Iraq in response to attacks by the 'Islamic State of Iraq and the Levant' (ISIL)). This arguably represents the most extensive appeal to the legal notion of collective self-defence *ever*, with ten different coalition states separately invoking it.[21] In the years since, collective self-defence has continued to be used (and abused) as a

military actions against another State (B) that has invaded yet the third State (C)', emphasis added); Oscar Schachter, *International Law in Theory and Practice* (Dordrecht, Martinus Nijhoff, 1991), 155 (arguing that the right of collective self-defence has ultimately 'emerged as a major legal justification for military action by States outside of their own territories').

[21] See Letter dated 10 December 2015 from the Chargé d'affaires a.i. of the Permanent Mission of Germany to the United Nations addressed to the President of the Security Council, UN Doc. S/2015/946 (10 December 2015); Letter dated 11 January 2016 from the Permanent Representative of Denmark to the United Nations addressed to the President of the Security Council, UN Doc. S/2016/34 (13 January 2016); Letter dated 7 June 2016 from the Permanent Representative of Belgium to the United Nations addressed to the President of the Security Council, UN Doc. S/2016/523 (9 June 2016); Letter dated 9 September 2015 from the Permanent Representative of Australia to the United Nations addressed to the President of the Security Council, UN Doc. S/2015/693 (9 September 2015); Letter dated 10 February 2016 from the Chargé d'affaires a.i. of the Permanent Mission of the Netherlands to the United Nations addressed to the President of the Security Council, UN Doc. S/2016/132 (10 February 2016); Letter dated 3 June 2016 from the Permanent Representative of Norway to the United Nations addressed to the President of the Security Council UN Doc. S/2016/513 (3 June 2016); Identical letters dated 25 November 2014 from the Permanent Representative of the United Kingdom of Great Britain and Northern Ireland to the United Nations addressed to the Secretary-General and the President of the Security Council, UN Doc. S/2014/851 (26 November 2014); Letter dated 7 September 2015 from the Permanent Representative of the United Kingdom of Great Britain and Northern Ireland to the United Nations addressed to the President of the Security Council, UN Doc. S/2015/688 (8 September 2015); Letter dated 3 December 2015 from the Permanent Representative of the United Kingdom of Great Britain and Northern Ireland to the United Nations addressed to the President of the Security Council, UN Doc. S/2015/928 (3 December 2015); Letter dated 31 March 2015 from the Chargé d'affaires a.i. of the Permanent Mission of Canada to the United Nations addressed to the President of the Security Council, UN Doc. S/2015/221 (31 March 2015); Letter dated 23 September 2014 from the Permanent Representative of the United States of America to the United Nations addressed to the Secretary-General, UN Doc. S/2014/695 (23 September 2014); Identical letters dated 8 September 2015 from the Permanent Representative of France to the United Nations addressed to the Secretary-General and the President of the Security Council, UN Doc. S/2015/745 (9 September 2015).

legal justification by states more often than was previously the case. One might note, for example, Turkey alluding to the concept in relation to the military support it provided to Azerbaijan in the context of the Nagorno-Karabakh conflict in 2020,[22] the explicit invocation of the right by both the Collective Security Treaty Organisation (CSTO)[23] and Kazakhstan[24] in relation to the dispatch of troops by the former into the territory of the latter in January 2022,[25] and the appeal to collective self-defence made by Armenia in September 2022.[26] Another high-profile recent example, of course, is that Russia advanced collective self-defence as one of the purported legal justifications for its full-scale invasion of Ukraine in February 2022.[27] Collective self-defence is also arguably engaged by the *response* of the North Atlantic Treaty Organization (NATO) (and other states) to Russia's invasion[28] and certainly would be the basis for more

[22] See Statement of the Spokesperson of the Ministry of Foreign Affairs, Mr. Hami Aksoy, in Response to a Question Regarding the Armenian Attacks on Azerbaijan Which Started This Morning, Republic of Türkiye, Ministry of Foreign Affairs, QA-94 (27 September 2020), www.mfa.gov.tr/sc_-94_-ermenistan-in-azerbaycan-a-karsi-baslat tigi-saldiri-hk-sc.en.mfa. For discussion, see Ella Schönleben, 'Collective Self-Defence or Just Another Intervention?: Some Thoughts on Turkey Allegedly Sending Syrian Mercenaries to Nagorno-Karabakh', *Völkerrechtsblog* (2 November 2020), https://voelkerrechtsblog.org/de/collective-self-defence-or-just-another-intervention.

[23] See 'Session of CSTO Collective Security Council', Office of the President of the Russian Federation (10 January 2022), http://en.kremlin.ru/events/president/news/67568.

[24] See UNSC Verbatim Record, UN Doc. S/PV.8967 (16 February 2022), 20–21 (Kazakhstan).

[25] See, generally, Fyodor A. Lukyanov, 'Kazakhstan Intervention Sees Russia Set a New Precedent', *Russia in Global Affairs* (7 January 2022), https://eng.globalaffairs.ru/articles/kazakhstan-new-precedent.

[26] See 'Armenia Asked CSTO for Military Support to Restore Territorial Integrity Amid Azeri Attack – PM', *Armen Press* (14 September 2022), https://armenpress.am/eng/news/1092504.

[27] See 'Address by the President of the Russian Federation', Office of the President of the Russian Federation (24 February 2022), http://en.kremlin.ru/events/president/tran scripts/67843 (official English translation, as published by the Kremlin); Обращение Президента Российской Федерации, Президент России (24 февраля 2022 года), http://kremlin.ru/events/president/news/67843 (original Russian text, as published by the Kremlin). This address was also annexed (in a somewhat different English translation) to Letter dated 24 February 2022 from the Permanent Representative of the Russian Federation to the United Nations addressed to the Secretary-General, UN Doc. S/2022/154 (24 February 2022). For discussion, see James A. Green, Christian Henderson and Tom Ruys, 'Russia's Attack on Ukraine and the *Jus ad Bellum*' (2022) 9 *Journal on the Use of Force and International Law* 4, 17–21.

[28] For analysis, see Section 1.4.

'robust' NATO action to defend Ukraine, should it ever be taken.[29] Overall, it may be said that the right of collective self-defence – and how it is to be applied as a matter of international law – is of particular importance at the time of writing.

However, perhaps as a result of perceptions that it has been rarely used and has a limited historical pedigree, there has been relatively little academic analysis of the legal concept of collective self-defence throughout the UN era, and this remains the case today.[30] One might note, for example, the hugely impressive and influential *Oxford Handbook on the Use of Force in International Law*, which was published in 2015.[31] That volume has a whopping fifty-seven chapters covering the *jus ad bellum* in significant depth and from an array of perspectives but contains no chapter dedicated specifically to collective self-defence. There is certainly a lot of important scholarship examining collective self-defence, of course, but this has tended to form an aspect of a larger work on self-defence *in toto* or the wider *jus ad bellum*[32] or has focused on a particular aspect of the concept[33] rather than engaging with it more

[29] See Pavel Doubek, 'War in Ukraine: Time for a Collective Self-Defense?', *Opinio Juris* (29 March 2022), http://opiniojuris.org/2022/03/29/war-in-ukraine-time-for-a-collective-self-defense.

[30] This is in contrast to the law governing individual self-defence, where a vast literature has developed and is continually expanding. See Christopher Greenwood, 'Self-Defence', in Rüdiger Wolfrum (ed.), *Max Planck Encyclopaedia of Public International Law, vol. IX* (Oxford, Oxford University Press, 2012), 103, 113, para. 52 (providing a useful select bibliography of some of the key works, although it is important to be aware that the literature on the subject is truly huge).

[31] Marc Weller (ed.), *The Oxford Handbook of the Use of Force in International Law* (Oxford, Oxford University Press, 2015).

[32] See, for example, Dinstein, n.9, 301–327; Gray, n.16, 176–199; Henderson, n.11, 256–262; Tom Ruys, *'Armed Attack' and Article 51 of the UN Charter: Evolutions in Customary Law and Practice* (Cambridge, Cambridge University Press, 2010), 83–91; Derek W. Bowett, *Self-Defense in International Law* (Manchester, Manchester University Press, 1958), 200–248; Ian Brownlie, *International Law and the Use of Force by States* (Oxford, Oxford University Press, 1963), 328–331.

[33] See, for example, Sia Spiliopoulou Åkermark, 'The Puzzle of Collective Self-Defence: Dangerous Fragmentation or a Window of Opportunity? An Analysis with Finland and the Åland Islands as a Case Study' (2017) 22 *Journal of Conflict and Security Law* 249; Domingo E. Acevedo, 'Collective Self-Defense and the Use of Regional or Subregional Authority as Justification for the Use of Force' (1984) 78 *American Society of International Law Proceedings* 69; George K. Walker, 'Anticipatory Collective Self-Defense in the Charter Era: What the Treaties Have Said' (1998) 31 *Cornell International Law Journal* 321; Marko Svicevic, 'Collective Self-Defence or Regional Enforcement Action: The Legality of a SADC Intervention in Cabo Delgado and the

holistically.[34] As far as the present author is aware, there have been no monograph-length works devoted to collective self-defence prior to the present one.

More importantly, while states have advanced collective self-defence claims throughout the UN era, and *especially* over the last decade, there has been relatively little consideration of the nature and regulation of the concept by states themselves (or intergovernmental bodies/organisations) in a general sense. To the extent that states discuss collective self-defence, this has for the most part been restricted to arguments regarding the exercise of it (or purported exercise of it) in specific instances. As far back as 1965, the then chairperson of the UN General Assembly, Mr Abdullah El-Erian of the United Arab Republic, noted that '[t]he idea of legitimate collective self-defence deserves more thorough study'.[35] More than twenty-five years later, writing in the *American Journal of International Law*, Oscar Schachter made the same point, arguing that there was a:

> need for further consideration by the [UN Security] Council and other appropriate bodies of the requirements of legitimate collective self-defense and of the role of the Council under Article 51. Up to now, this subject has not received much attention.[36]

Yet, a further thirty plus years on, collective self-defence continues to be marginalised in state thinking about self-defence. One might, for

Question of Mozambican Consent' (2022) 9 *Journal on the Use of Force and International Law* 138; Patrick Terry, 'Germany Joins the Campaign against ISIS in Syria: A Case of Collective Self-Defence or Rather the Unlawful Use of Force?' (2016) 4 *Russian Law Journal* 26; James A. Green 'The "Additional" Criteria for Collective Self-Defence: Request but Not Declaration' (2017) 4 *Journal on the Use of Force and International Law* 4; Keisuke Minai, 'What Legal Interest Is Protected by the Right of Collective Self-Defense: The Japanese Perspective' (2016) 24 *Willamette Journal of International Law and Dispute Resolution* 105.

34 There have, of course, also been crucial works dedicated to collective self-defence in a general sense, but these have been relatively few in number and of much shorter length than the present book. See, for example, Bowett, n.10; Hans Kelsen, 'Collective Security and Collective Self-Defense under the Charter of the United Nations' (1948) 42 *American Journal of International Law* 783; Jane A. Meyer, 'Collective Self-Defense and Regional Security: Necessary Exceptions to a Globalist Doctrine' (1993) 11 *Boston University International Law Journal* 391; Russell Powell, 'The Law and Philosophy of Preventive War: An Institution-Based Approach to Collective Self-Defence' (2007) 32 *Australian Journal of Legal Philosophy* 67.

35 UNGA Summary Record, UN Doc. A/C.6/SR.877 (1 April 1966), para. 7.

36 Oscar Schachter, 'United Nations in the Gulf Conflict' (1991) 85 *American Journal of International Law* 452, 472.

example, note the 'Arria formula' meeting of the UN Security Council, which was convened by Mexico in February 2021.[37] The meeting was arguably the most substantial general discussion between states regarding the right of self-defence in international law since the mid-1970s.[38] However, states barely even took note of the concept of collective self-defence during those discussions.[39] This was, of course, despite the 'Arria formula' meeting taking place against the backdrop of a significant increase in the *exercise* (or purported exercise) of collective self-defence by states over the preceding ten years.

The relative lack of consideration of collective self-defence by both scholars and states (and intergovernmental bodies) has meant that it has long been under-theorised, and significant questions remain regarding how it operates – or, rather, *must* operate – in practice. This problem should not be overstated: given that individual and collective self-defence share multiple legal requirements, one can glean a significant amount of detail about the law governing collective self-defence from analysing the more extensive practice and scholarship relating to individual self-defence. However, consideration of the *application* of these requirements in the collective context has been negligible, and the close relation between individual and collective self-defence also means that the same controversies exist in relation to the exercise of both.[40] The 'shared' criteria are also far from the end of the story when it comes to the legal regulation of collective self-defence.[41]

With the increased number of collective self-defence claims that have been made in recent years, the implications of the general lack of engagement with the concept – in terms of guarding against its abusive invocation and providing a degree of clarity for any states seeking to exercise collective self-defence as to what is or is not permitted – can be said to have become more acute. Gray, for example, has argued that the recent increase in state invocation of collective self-defence in practice

[37] See Letter dated 8 March 2021 from the Permanent Representative of Mexico to the United Nations addressed to the President of the Security Council, UN Doc. S/2021/247 (16 March 2021).

[38] See Adil Ahmad Haque, 'The Use of Force against Non-State Actors: All Over the Map' (2021) 8 *Journal on the Use of Force and International Law* 278, 278.

[39] See UN Doc. S/2021/247, n.37.

[40] On the legal criteria (and controversies) that are shared between individual and collective self-defence, see Chapter 3.

[41] In particular, because of the existence of the request requirement, which only applies to collective self-defence. See Chapters 4–6.

has 'brought the right of collective self-defence back into prominence and has raised fundamental questions about the scope of the right'.[42] In a similar vein, Lee noted recently that:

> [g]iven the gravity of the concept of self-defense in international law and the importance of the role it plays in the present UN Charter regime ... any discussion of the issue of collective self-defense should be based on a thorough examination of the applicable jurisprudence and principles of international law.[43]

This book aims to respond to these calls by attempting to answer, or at least significantly progress debate on, the 'fundamental questions about the scope of the right', and do so 'based on a thorough examination of the applicable jurisprudence and principles of international law'. The intent is to provide the most detailed and extensive account of collective self-defence to date, at a time when it is being invoked in state practice more often than ever before.

0.2 A Focus on State Practice

This study is predominantly based on analytical, desk-based doctrinal research, premised on the traditional sources of international law set out in Article 38(1) of the Statute of the International Court of Justice (ICJ).[44] A key methodological focus herein is on the examination of *state*

[42] Gray, n.16, 176 (making this point specifically in relation to the use(s) of force in Syria since 2014). See also Elie Perot, 'The Art of Commitments: NATO, the EU, and the Interplay between Law and Politics within Europe's Collective Defence Architecture' (2019) 28 *European Security* 40, 41 (arguing in 2019 that collective self-defence has become a 'crucial domain'); Lee, n.20, 374 (arguing in 2015 that '[t]he concept of collective self-defense is now attracting increased global attention').

[43] Lee, n.20, 375.

[44] Statute of the International Court of Justice (1945) 33 UNTS 93, Article 38(1) ('The Court, whose function is to decide in accordance with international law such disputes as are submitted to it, shall apply: (a) international conventions, whether general or particular, establishing rules expressly recognized by the contesting states; (b) international custom, as evidence of a general practice accepted as law; (c) the general principles of law recognized by civilized nations; (d) subject to the provisions of Article 59, judicial decisions and the teachings of the most highly qualified publicists of the various nations, as subsidiary means for the determination of rules of law'). See Erika de Wet, *Military Assistance on Request and the Use of Force* (Oxford, Oxford University Press, 2020), 13 (characterising that author's approach – to the closely related concept of 'military assistance on request' – in a very similar way).

practice.[45] Despite its legal existence being starkly confirmed in Article 51 of the UN Charter, there is very little treaty law to indicate how collective self-defence is to be conceptualised and applied. Its nature and legal parameters therefore can only be ascertained from the analysis of its employment by states in practice and by the way in which they invoke it (and, perhaps more importantly, respond to the invocation of it), as evidence of *opinio juris*.[46] From these raw elements, an attempt can be made to establish the rules governing the exercise of collective self-defence under customary international law (and how they are to be applied), as well as a more developed picture of the nature and scope of the legal concept as a whole.

The primary approach of this book is therefore to examine in depth the (actual/avowed) instances of collective self-defence that have occurred, particularly in the UN era. As already noted, there is a general perception in the literature that collective self-defence has been rarely practiced since 1945.[47] One reason for this view is that states have often advanced collective self-defence claims in situations that do not appear to have met the legal requirements for the exercise of the right.[48] Indeed, a

[45] It is worth noting that, in addition, the practice of international organisations is also examined in depth, especially that of collective self-defence organisations (or organisations that include a collective self-defence function). See Wet, n.44, 14 (again, taking the same approach). See also ILC, *Conclusions on the Identification of Customary International Law, with Commentaries*, UN Doc. A/73/10 (2018), conclusion 4(2), 119 ('[i]n certain cases, the practice of international organizations also contributes to the formation, or expression, of rules of customary international law').

[46] Regarding the criteria of 'state practice' and '*opinio juris*' for the formation of customary international law, see UN Doc. A/73/10, n.45, particularly conclusions 2–10 (and commentaries), 124–142; *North Sea Continental Shelf Cases* (*Federal Republic of Germany v. Netherlands, Federal Republic of Germany v. Denmark*) (merits) [1969] ICJ Rep. 3, para. 77; *Continental Shelf* (*Libyan Arab Jamahiriya/Malta*) (merits) [1985] ICJ Rep. 13, para. 27; *Nicaragua* (merits), n.11, para. 207. The meanings of both state practice and *opinio juris* remain highly contentious among scholars. See, for example, Jörg Kammerhofer, 'Uncertainty in the Formal Sources of International Law: Customary International Law and Some of Its Problems' (2004) 15 *European Journal of International Law* 523, 525–536. However, these concepts are at least broadly accepted, and their content has been developed in the ICJ's jurisprudence to the extent that, in 2012, the Court noted that it needed to apply 'the criteria which it [the Court] *has repeatedly laid down* for identifying a rule of customary international law'. *Jurisdictional Immunities of the State* (*Germany v. Italy: Greece intervening*) (merits) [2012] ICJ Rep. 99, para. 55 (emphasis added).

[47] See nn.16–20 and accompanying text.

[48] See, for example, the use of force by the United States in Lebanon in 1958, which was justified both by Lebanon (UNSC Verbatim Record, UN Doc. S/PV.827 (15 July 1958), para. 84) and the United States (UN Doc. S/PV.827, n.48, para. 44) as an act of collective

significant proportion of the (purported) occurrences of collective self-defence that have occurred in the UN era can be said to have been of dubious legality:

> The cases of the use of force by a third State reveal how often this right has been abused: force in alleged collective self-defense has been used without there being an armed attack or even an external threat against the alleged 'victim State', or the 'victim State' has not considered itself attacked or threatened, and has not requested assistance. ... Most of the cases [of 'collective self-defence' in the UN era] have as the common denominator the blatant abuse of the right of collective self-defense.[49]

As such, it is perhaps unsurprising that many writers have concluded that there has been very little collective self-defence practice in the UN era, because *lawful* exercises of the right have indeed been rare. In a version of the well-worn apologist/utopian dilemma,[50] the question for the analyst thus is how much (if any) weight – in terms of the contribution to the interpretation or formation of legal standards – to ascribe to the claims made by states in instances where the invocation of collective self-defence was of questionable legality. To place too much weight on what states *say* when it comes to collective self-defence will inevitably result in an uncertain picture of its legal content,[51] because states themselves have not been shy in advancing dubious claims. In some instances, there is

self-defence, in circumstances where there obviously had been no armed attack whatsoever (nor any realistic threat of an imminent armed attack). On the armed attack requirement for collective self-defence, see Section 3.2. Much more recently, Russia claimed to be exercising collective self-defence at the request of the regions of Donetsk and Luhansk in Ukraine in 2022, despite the fact that these entities were not states and therefore could not request aid in collective self-defence. See 'Address by the President of the Russian Federation', n.27. On the requirement that collective self-defence requests must be made by states, see Section 5.2. These two examples – from either end of the UN era – are representative of a wider trend in practice towards dubious invocations of collective self-defence.

[49] Stanimir A. Alexandrov, *Self-Defence against the Use of Force in International Law* (The Hague, Kluwer Law International, 1996), 215. See also Abhimanyu George Jain, 'Rationalising International Law Rules on Self-Defence: The Pin-Prick Doctrine' (2014) 14 *Chicago-Kent Journal of International and Comparative Law* 23, 36, footnote 45; Eustace Chikere Azubuike, 'Probing the Scope of Self Defense in International Law' (2011) 17 *Annual Survey of International and Comparative Law* 129, 175; Gray, n.16, 178–179, 197.

[50] See, generally, Martti Koskenniemi, *From Apology to Utopia: The Structure of International Legal Argument* (Cambridge, Cambridge University Press, 2005 reissue).

[51] Andrew R. Willard, 'Incidents: An Essay in Method' (1984–1985) 10 *Yale Journal of International Law* 21, 24.

also a risk of giving credence to wholly spurious (and perhaps even abusive) legal arguments. Equally, to ignore the claims advanced by states and instead attempt to discern the nature of collective self-defence through a more principle-based, deductive method – while likely to produce a more coherent framework, aligned to conceptual clarity and underpinning values – risks having little relationship to reality.

Ultimately, the present author is inclined to recall the ICJ's famous statement in the 1986 *Nicaragua* case, that one cannot 'ascribe to States legal views which they do not themselves advance'.[52] The collective self-defence claims made by states have to be treated seriously, even when they are legally questionable. It is also worth noting that controversy among states over these collective self-defence claims has tended to centre on the facts and/or the application of the law to the facts in the relevant situation, rather than on the content of the law itself.[53] Thus, dubious legal justifications can contribute to the content of the law, particularly when assessed in combination with the reactions to them from other states. When a collective self-defence claim is considered by other states to be unlawful, this helps to identify the picture of what a lawful collective self-defence action must look like – especially when states advance their *reasons* for concluding that the action in question was unlawful. As Ferro has argued:

> it would be mistaken to ignore the repeated, public and explicit invocation of collective self-defence simply because its conditions under the *lex lata* have not been met. The expressed legal conviction of states must be taken seriously, regardless of commentators' evaluation of its accuracy under international law.[54]

On this basis, in this book, the claims made by states are taken at face value in the first instance and are referred to as 'examples of collective

[52] *Nicaragua* (merits), n.11, para. 207.

[53] Gray, n.16, 179.

[54] Luca Ferro, 'The Doctrine of "Negative Equality" and the Silent Majority of States' (2021) 8 *Journal on the Use of Force and International Law* 4, 25, footnote 109. See also Dino Kritsiotis, 'Intervention and the Problematisation of Consent', in Olivier Corten, Gregory H. Fox and Dino Kritsiotis, *Armed Intervention and Consent*, Max Planck Trialogues on the Law of Peace and War (Anne Peters and Christian Marxsen, series eds.), vol. IV (Cambridge, Cambridge University Press, 2023), 26, 79 (stating, in the context of discussing collective self-defence, that '[l]egally speaking, it therefore matters a great deal as to what legal justification (or set of justifications) are being pleaded for a given action: these should not be assumed or imagined because they come to define the normative minutiae that are to be applied in line with the respective justification').

self-defence', 'instances of relevant state practice', or similar terms. However, such shorthand phrases should not be taken as an indication that any given claim was correct on the legal merits. Context and – crucially – the reactions of other states are also considered throughout, to provide nuance.

As a result, the relevant 'pool' of collective self-defence practice to be assessed is perhaps larger than is commonly perceived. This is particularly the case following the unprecedented surge in the number of invocations of collective self-defence since 2014.[55] This practice is engaged with herein in significant depth. Indeed, this book is based – this author believes – on the most extensive review of collective self-defence practice ever conducted.[56] That said, this author makes no claims to total *comprehensiveness* as to the review of all (actual or asserted) instances of collective self-defence in the UN era. Every attempt has been made to review as many examples as possible, but it may well be the case that some have not been considered, especially as other scholars might have different views as to what instances of practice should rightly 'qualify'.

Care has been taken to ensure diversity in the sense of considering practice from geographically disparate regions, involving states from every continent and major legal system. Likewise, in considering collective self-defence organisations – especially in Chapter 7 – the analysis focuses not just on Global North organisations such as NATO but also on as many relevant organisations as possible from Africa, South America, and Asia. These attempts to ensure that the practice reviewed is suitably representative need to be qualified, however. There is, of course, likely to be an element of subconscious ethnocentricity in any selection and analysis of instances of state practice due to the intrinsic biases of the scholar (and other restrictions, such as language).[57] To an extent, this research is necessarily undertaken from a 'Western' perspective, and it is important to acknowledge that the attempts that have been made to offset that fact – while genuine and crucial – are, at best, only

55 See nn.21–29 and accompanying text.

56 See, as perhaps the most extensive review previously conducted, Aadhithi Padmanabhan and Michael Shih, 'Collective Self-Defense: A Report of the Yale Law School Center for Global Legal Challenges' (10 December 2012), https://law.yale.edu/sites/default/files/documents/pdf/cglc/GLC_Collective_SelfDefense.pdf.

57 See Willard, n.51, particularly 21–24; W. Michael Reisman, 'International Incidents: Introduction to a New Genre in the Study of International Law' (1984–1985) 10 *Yale Journal of International Law* 1, 13–14.

ever going to be partially successful. It is also always worth keeping in mind that international law itself remains an inherently 'Western' social construct, rooted in (neo)colonialism.[58] As such, states from other regions of the world have little choice but to engage with international law on the basis of the Global North's preoccupation with capitalist modernity.[59] Collective self-defence is no different from other areas of international law in this regard: its development has been skewed towards European and North American narratives, even in the context of its exercise or assessment by states from the Global South.

It also is the case that a disproportionate number of the examples of the avowed exercise of collective self-defence during the Cold War involved the superpowers of the time: the United States and the USSR. As such, despite attempts herein to ensure analysis of a diverse range of state practice, the available examples of collective self-defence from a large part of the UN era necessarily require greater consideration of the actions and statements of these powerful states (which are/were, of course, also nuclear powers). Further, the Cold War era examples must be reviewed with an eye to the climate of 'mutually assured rejection' of legal claims made across the iron curtain (in either direction) that defined international relations at the time.[60] Ideologically entrenched debates over collective self-defence actions were a key feature of the Cold War, meaning that one must be cautious in extracting legal meaning from them. It should additionally be said that the divisions between the world's major powers did not disappear with the fall of the Berlin Wall, either: as ongoing crises in both Syria and Ukraine (among others) demonstrate. Some of the same caution thus must be applied to the analysis of post–Cold War invocations of collective self-defence too.

[58] See, generally, Salvatore Caserta, 'Western Centrism, Contemporary International Law, and International Courts' (2021) 34 *Leiden Journal of International Law* 32; Brian-Vincent Ikejiaku, 'International Law Is Western Made Global Law: The Perception of Third-World Category' (2013) 6 *African Journal of Legal Studies* 337.

[59] See, generally, Ntina Tzouvala, *Capitalism as Civilisation: A History of International Law* (Cambridge, Cambridge University Press, 2020).

[60] See Gregory H. Fox, 'Intervention by Invitation', in Marc Weller (ed.), *The Oxford Handbook of the Use of Force in International Law* (Oxford, Oxford University Press, 2015), 816, 823–824 (noting that during the Cold War, the superpowers and their allies invariably took mutually opposed 'positions on the legitimacy of intervention depending on the political setting'); Masoud Zamani and Majid Nikouei, 'Intervention by Invitation, Collective Self-Defence and the Enigma of Effective Control' (2017) 16 *Chinese Journal of International Law* 663, 666.

Finally, in this section, it must be recalled that states are notorious for advancing blurred, 'mixed', or imprecise legal claims, especially in the context of the *jus ad bellum*.[61] For example, states sometimes combine individual and collective self-defence arguments without drawing clear distinctions between them.[62] They also have often mixed collective self-defence claims with references to so-called 'military assistance on request'.[63] So far as possible, care has been taken herein to 'unpick' these claims and focus on collective self-defence arguments only. However, in this book, it is important to be aware that assumptions and inferences are necessarily at times made about what a state has done or said, when the arguments it has made have not been as explicit or clear as one might have hoped. When this is the case, though, it is acknowledged.

0.3 The *Nicaragua* Case

Although the primary focus of much of this book is the analysis of practice, this is augmented by an extensive literature review and the analysis of relevant case law. With regard to the latter, there actually is relatively little case law that relates specifically to collective self-defence.[64] However, one key case is of notable importance, which is the famous 1986 *Nicaragua* decision of the ICJ. This case has had a huge impact on the understanding and development of the right of self-defence in general, albeit that a number of aspects of the Court's decision can be – and have been – critiqued.[65] Moreover, *Nicaragua* is of particular importance to the current study because the Court was specifically engaging with a collective self-defence claim and did so in significant detail. Much of the academic commentary that exists regarding collective self-defence has

61 See, generally, Dino Kritsiotis, 'Arguments of Mass Confusion' (2004) 15 *European Journal of International Law* 233.

62 See de Wet, n.44, 191. See, for example, Letter dated 7 October 2001 from the Chargé d'affaires a.i. of the Permanent Mission of the United Kingdom of Great Britain and Northern Ireland to the United Nations addressed to the President of the Security Council, UN Doc. S/2001/947 (7 October 2001) (the UK's self-defence claims following 9/11).

63 See Section 8.3.

64 That said, there are important references to collective self-defence in a number of ICJ cases that are considered in this book. For a detailed examination of the ICJ's case law relevant to the right of self-defence *in toto*, see James A. Green, *The International Court of Justice and Self-Defence in International Law* (Oxford, Hart Publishing, 2009).

65 See, generally, *ibid.*

therefore centred around the judgment.[66] It has been argued that, for good or ill, the *Nicaragua* case 'plays a crucial role' in relation to the contemporary law governing the exercise of collective self-defence.[67] The decision will be returned to at multiple points throughout this book. As such, it is worth briefly setting out the key facts, claims of the parties, and features of the case at this introductory stage.

In April 1984, Nicaragua made an application to the ICJ[68] alleging that the United States had supported, and was continuing to support, 'contra' forces opposing the Nicaraguan government,[69] as well as participating in more direct attacks against it.[70] Nicaragua asserted that these actions meant that the United States had violated, *inter alia*, the prohibition on the use of force under Article 2(4) of the UN Charter.[71]

Once the ICJ had ruled that it could entertain the dispute,[72] the United States made it clear that it would not participate further in the proceedings.[73] It filed no pleadings on the merits, nor was it represented at the oral proceedings in September 1985.[74] However, before withdrawing from the case, the United States had formally claimed that its actions were lawful instances of collective self-defence, in response to uses of force by Nicaragua against its neighbours. The United States alleged that Nicaragua had provided indirect support to the armed opposition groups

[66] See, for example, Zia Modabber, 'Collective Self-Defense: *Nicaragua v. United States*' (1988) 10 *Loyola of Los Angeles International and Comparative Law Journal* 449; R. St. J. MacDonald, 'The *Nicaragua* Case: New Answers to Old Questions' (1986) 24 *Canadian Yearbook of International Law* 127; Nicholas Rostow, '*Nicaragua* and the Law of Self-Defense Revisited' (1986) 11 *Yale Journal of International Law* 437; John Norton Moore, 'The Secret War in Central America and the Future of World Order' (1986) 80 *American Journal of International Law* 43; Paul S. Reichler and David Wippman, 'United States Armed Intervention in *Nicaragua*: A Rejoinder' (1986) 11 *Yale Journal of International Law* 462; John Lawrence Hargrove, 'The *Nicaragua* Judgment and the Future of the Law of Force and Self-Defence' (1987) 81 *American Journal of International Law* 135.

[67] Gray, n.16, 180. See also Gina Heathcote, *The Law on the Use of Force: A Feminist Analysis* (Abingdon, Routledge, 2012), 77 (arguing that the *Nicaragua* case 'affirm[ed] collective self-defence as an important component of the international right').

[68] *Military and Paramilitary Activities in and against Nicaragua* (*Nicaragua v. United States of America*) (application instituting proceedings) [1984] ICJ Plead., vol. I, 2.

[69] *Ibid*, particularly paras. 1–8.

[70] *Ibid*, particularly para. 10.

[71] *Ibid*, particularly paras. 9 and 15.

[72] See *Military and Paramilitary Activities in and against Nicaragua* (*Nicaragua v. United States of America*) (jurisdiction of the court and admissibility of the application) [1984] ICJ Rep. 392, especially para. 113.

[73] See *Nicaragua* (merits), n.11, para. 10.

[74] See *ibid*, para. 17.

in other states in Central America, particularly El Salvador,[75] while also participating in more direct forms of armed intervention in both Honduras and Costa Rica.[76]

A notable aspect of the *Nicaragua* case was the effect of a reservation entered by the United States when it declared its acceptance of the ICJ's jurisdiction under Article 36(2) of the Court's Statute. In the declaration, the United States included a reservation in relation to 'disputes arising under a multilateral treaty, unless . . . all parties to the dispute affected by the decision are also parties to the case before the Court'.[77] The ICJ took the view that any decision on the merits would necessarily 'affect' El Salvador,[78] in that this would reflect upon any measures El Salvador had taken in individual self-defence against Nicaragua.[79] As such, the Court concluded that the reservation precluded it from applying multilateral treaty law in the case.[80]

In the *Nicaragua* merits decision, the ICJ therefore outlined and applied to the dispute what it considered to be the *customary international law* on collective self-defence to the actions of the United States in and against Nicaragua.[81] It concluded that those actions did not meet the legal requirements for collective self-defence, and thus that the United States was indeed in violation of the prohibition on the use of force (albeit that prohibition as it exists in customary rather than conventional international law).[82] As noted at the start of this section, the Court's judgment – as well as the separate opinions of some of the judges

[75] *Military and Paramilitary Activities in and against Nicaragua (Nicaragua v. United States of America)* (counter-memorial of the United States of America, questions of jurisdiction and admissibility) [1984] ICJ Plead., vol. II, paras. 189–197.

[76] *Ibid*, paras. 198–201.

[77] United States of America, Declaration Recognizing as Compulsory the Jurisdiction of the Court, in Conformity with Article 36, Paragraph 2, of the Statute of the International Court of Justice (14 August 1946) (1946–1947) 1 UNTS 9.

[78] The United States argued that a decision by the Court would affect not only El Salvador but also Costa Rica and Honduras, *Nicaragua* (counter-memorial of the USA), n.75, vol. III, paras. 279–291. The ICJ only reached a conclusion on this question regarding El Salvador, but the Court made it clear that this was because it was unnecessary to examine the possible effect of a merits decision upon the other states, as its conclusion regarding El Salvador was enough in itself to mean that the US reservation was applicable: *Nicaragua* (merits), n.11, para. 48.

[79] *Nicaragua* (merits), n.11, paras. 42–56.

[80] See *ibid*.

[81] It is worth noting that the Court also could (and did) apply relevant *bilateral* treaties between the parties. See, for example, *ibid*, para. 271.

[82] See *ibid*, particularly para. 292.

that were appended to the decision – will be revisited in more detail at various points throughout this book.

0.4 A Brief Note on Terminology

The exercise of collective self-defence – at least, its *lawful* exercise – necessarily involves the relationship(s) between at least three states. These are 1) the state that has suffered an attack[83] and requests aid; 2) the state that responds to this request with defensive force; and 3) the state[84] that perpetrated the attack.[85] This is at a minimum, as there may be more than one state using defensive force, and there may be more than one state involved in perpetrating the armed attack.

To avoid confusion, it is worth stating the terminology employed herein regarding these different state actors in any given collective self-defence scenario. This book uses the same terms employed in the 1939 Draft Convention on Rights and Duties of States in Case of Aggression.[86] As per Article 1 of that document, a '"*defending State*" is a State which is the victim or object of aggression. … A "*co-defending State*" is a State which assists a defending State with armed force'.[87] As such, throughout this work, the state that has been attacked and is seeking aid is referred to as the *defending* state. The state (or states) using force in response to the defending state's appeal is referred to as the *co-defending* state (or states). In addition, the term 'aggressor state' is employed with regard to the state that perpetrated the original armed attack.

0.5 The Structure of This Book

Following the Introduction, this book begins with an attempt, in Chapter 1, to delineate the notion of collective self-defence. As already

83 This arguably may also include attacks that will imminently occur. See Section 3.2.3.

84 This arguably may also extend to a state from which a non-state actor has perpetrated an attack (or, perhaps, will imminently perpetrate an attack). See Sections 3.2.3 and 3.2.4.

85 Again, this arguably may include an imminent attack that has not yet occurred, see Section 3.2.3.

86 Harvard Research, *Draft Convention on Rights and Duties of States in Case of Aggression*, with Comment (1939), in (1939) 33 *Supplement to the American Journal of International Law* 819. The Draft was developed as part of a project undertaken by a group of (distinguished) researchers at Harvard University and was never adopted by states.

87 *Ibid*, 827, Article 1 (emphasis added).

noted,[88] while the core concept can be stated relatively easily, there has been persistent controversy regarding the nature of collective self-defence. It is possible to identify no fewer than five different 'conceptions' of collective self-defence that have been advanced in scholarship. These conceptions are explored in detail in the chapter. It also examines the question of whether collective self-defence is indeed an 'inherent right', as Article 51 of the UN Charter indicates. The status of collective self-defence as a right (and, moreover, as a right that is inherent) has also proved to be controversial, and so this requires theorisation and analysis of the views of states. Finally, Chapter 1 considers the modality of collective self-defence, and particularly the question of what action constitutes an instance of collective self-defence.

Chapter 2 then moves to an examination of the history and development of collective self-defence. It is argued that contrary to the common assertion that the concept was a new one in 1945[89] – in fact, its roots can be seen throughout history. The chapter maps that history, starting briefly with the alliances of ancient Greece and moving through to the influential writings of the seventeenth century, when recognisable characteristics of the modern concept truly began to emerge. There is then a notable focus on the developments in the interwar years and during the Second World War, which saw an increase in the number of collective defence treaties and more specificity in the drafting of those treaties. This period concluded with the emergence of a regional collective defence system in the Americas, which was extremely influential for the drafting of Article 51 in 1945. Chapter 2 concludes by analysing the drafting process and the changes to the concept of collective self-defence that the adoption of the UN Charter brought about. It is argued that Article 51 'conjoined' individual and collective self-defence in a way that had little basis in the previous historical development of collective defence arrangements under international law. This conjoining has had significant implications for how collective self-defence is understood today.

Chapters 3–6 represent the 'backbone' of this book, in that they identify and analyse the legal requirements for the operation of collective self-defence. Chapter 3 considers the criteria for collective self-defence that are shared with individual self-defence. It is uncontentious to say that the same criteria that apply to individual self-defence – armed attack, necessity, proportionality, etc. – also apply to collective self-

[88] See nn.4–10 and accompanying text.
[89] See n.11 and accompanying text.

defence. Indeed, this is an inevitable consequence of the conjoining of the concepts in Article 51. The nature and application of these criteria in the context of individual self-defence have been examined at great length in existing literature.[90] Chapter 3, therefore, does not provide in-depth analysis of all of their aspects. It is, however, necessary to include a brief overview of these requirements to ensure that this book presents a comprehensive picture of the operation of collective self-defence today. The chapter's primary focus, though, is to examine how the operation of these criteria works specifically in the context of collective self-defence actions, which is something that has been largely overlooked in scholarship.

Alongside the shared criteria with individual self-defence, the ICJ famously took the view in the *Nicaragua* case that two additional criteria exist for the lawful exercise of collective self-defence.[91] These criteria have been commonly repeated, as being rules of customary international law, in scholarship since.[92] First, it is said, the state that has been attacked must 'declare' that it has been attacked, and then it must 'request' aid in its defence. Chapter 4 sets out the manner in which the ICJ identified these requirements and whether it considered them to be legally determinative or merely evidentiary. It then goes on to examine state practice/ *opinio juris*, to test whether the requirements indeed can be identified as rules of customary international law. It is argued that the first of those asserted requirements (declaration), in fact, has no legal basis. However, the issuance of a request is, as the Court indicated, a binding requirement for the exercise of collective self-defence.

Yet, it is apparent that, under customary international law, a request in itself will be legally insufficient: the request must be *valid*. There are a range of factors that need to be considered that do (or, at least, may) have a bearing on the 'validity' of the request. Chapters 5 and 6, therefore, examine the application of the request requirement in significant detail, again by reference in particular to an extensive review of state practice and *opinio juris*. This is with the aim of identifying how that requirement operates, and when an alleged appeal for aid will be (or is likely to be) considered a legally valid collective self-defence request. Chapter 5 first examines the question of *who* can issue such a request. In so doing, it examines the view that only states can request aid in collective

[90] In relation to the huge literature on *individual* self-defence, see n.30.

[91] See *Nicaragua* (merits), n.11, particularly paras. 165–166, 195, 199, 231.

[92] See sources cited in Chapter 4, n.3.

self-defence and, indeed, further asks whether the issuer of the request must be a UN member state. The bulk of the chapter then examines how one identifies the de jure government of the state for the specific purpose of issuing a collective self-defence request.

Following on from the consideration in Chapter 5 of who can make a collective self-defence request, Chapter 6 examines *how* such a request needs to be issued. There are a number of unanswered questions about the necessary manner and form of collective self-defence requests. First, the chapter analyses whether 'open-ended' requests will suffice, or whether they must be targeted at the co-defending state(s). The chapter then considers whether collective self-defence requests must take any specific form and, in particular, queries whether they can be inferred. Similarly, it examines whether the request must even be made publicly (or, at least, be *publicised*), or whether secret/private requests can suffice. Finally, Chapter 6 engages with questions concerning the timing of the request.

Having analysed the requirements for collective self-defence in detail – especially the request requirement, which has previously received little attention in scholarship – Chapter 7 moves to a consideration of collective self-defence treaty arrangements. It engages with a diverse range of examples of the collective self-defence treaties (or treaties that contain collective self-defence aspects) that have emerged since 1945 to draw out common themes as to the nature, process, and role of such arrangements, as well as to establish notable variations. The aim is to contribute an overall picture of collective self-defence today specifically in the context of treaty relationships. The chapter argues that such relationships inevitably impose only weak obligations on their parties to defend each other and also can cause notable issues related to overlapping memberships, bureaucracy, and antagonism among members (among other difficulties). Equally, these arrangements – of which there are now hundreds – are concluded for good reason(s). They provide a range of notable benefits, especially in terms of their deterrent effect.

The final chapter of the book examines the relationship between collective self-defence and another legal basis for the use of force, which in scholarship is variously referred to as 'military assistance on request' or 'intervention by invitation'. Analysing the relationship between collective self-defence and military assistance on request is crucial because these concepts are, in some respects, strikingly similar. Indeed, it has been argued that they overlap. The chapter explores the extent to which the concepts can be differentiated at the 'doctrinal' or 'conceptual' level, before turning to the various legal requirements (actual or, in some cases, arguable) for collective self-defence and military assistance on request, with the aim of highlighting similarities or differences, as relevant, when it comes to the operation of these two concepts. The primary aim of the chapter – as with this book as a whole – is to advance the understanding of the concept of collective self-defence in international law.

1

Delineating Collective Self-Defence

1.1 Introduction

A fundamental initial question for a book focused on collective self-defence is to ask what 'collective self-defence' *is*. Of course, on one level, this can be answered very simply. As already set out in the Introduction, the concept of collective self-defence in international law involves an action by one or more states, which would otherwise be a violation of the prohibition on the use of force, in response to an external attack that has occurred or is occurring (or, perhaps, is demonstrably imminent) against *another* state.[1] It is axiomatic to say that 'collective self-defence' refers today to situations where State A (the defending state) is attacked, and yet it is State B, and maybe also States C, D, *et al.* (the co-defending state or states) that respond with defensive force.

However, as was also noted in the Introduction,[2] while the core concept of collective self-defence can be relatively easily stated, delineating the notion any further has proved to be problematic, and its meaning has been contested: 'the theory of collective self-defence has been controversial since debate over its express inclusion in the United Nations (UN) Charter'.[3] Uncertainty regarding the nature of the concept of collective self-defence in part[4] stems from the terminology that has been employed since 1945 – most notably in Article 51[5] – to identify it. For many cultures, the notion of the 'self' is intuitively an individual one. It is, for example, commonly argued (if not universally accepted) in

[1] Introduction, nn.4–6 and accompanying text.

[2] *Ibid*, nn.7–10 and accompanying text.

[3] Christine Gray, *International Law and the Use of Force* (Oxford, Oxford University Press, 4th ed., 2018), 179. See also Oscar Schachter, *International Law in Theory and Practice* (Dordrecht, Martinus Nijhoff, 1991), 155 ('[t]he right of "collective self-defense" recognized in Article 51 has given rise to much controversy among legal scholars').

[4] Another key reason is the similarity of collective self-defence to, and perhaps overlap with, the concept of 'military assistance on request'. See Chapter 8.

[5] Charter of the United Nations (1945) 1 UNTS XVI (UN Charter), Article 51.

psychology research that 'the individual self' takes primacy in the determination of human identity.[6] Thus, purely on an instinctive, psychological level, the term 'collective self-defence' can be perturbing, at least for some. More specifically, especially for lawyers from common law backgrounds where the concept of 'defence' is often intertwined with personhood and 'the self',[7] the term 'collective self-defence' might even sound oxymoronic.[8]

This has led to attempts in some quarters to make the *terminology* – so stark in Article 51[9] – 'fit' the *concept*, by locating the exercise of collective self-defence within the 'self' of the co-defending state.[10] However, while some of the debate over the nature of the concept may be rooted in terminology, the delimitation of collective self-defence is not purely a terminological matter, it is substantive. Since the inception of the United Nations, the nature of collective self-defence – and particularly who or what is *being defended* – has been debated, with a number of understandings of collective self-defence being advanced in scholarship.

There is also debate as to whether collective self-defence truly is an 'inherent right', as proclaimed in Article 51, and – if it is – whether it is a right held by the defending state, the co-defending state, or both. This

[6] See, for example, Jie Chen *et al.*, 'The Primacy of the Individual Versus the Collective Self: Evidence from an Event-Related Potential Study' (2013) 535 *Neuroscience Letters* 30. Equally, it is also clear that the psychology of identity is multifaceted, especially in the modern, online world. See, for example, Lia Emanuel *et al.*, 'Who am I? Representing the Self Offline and in Different Online Contexts' (2014) 41 *Computers in Human Behavior* 146. Indeed, three fundamental 'forms' of identity are commonly identified, of which 'the individual self' is but one, alongside 'the relational self' and, notably for this book, 'the collective self'. See Lowell Gaertner *et al.*, 'A Motivational Hierarchy Within: Primacy of the Individual Self, Relational Self, or Collective Self?' (2012) 48 *Journal of Experimental Social Psychology* 997. For a recent study focused on 'the collective self', see Garriy Shteynberg *et al.*, 'Agency and Identity in the Collective Self' (2022) 26 *Personality and Social Psychology Review* 35.

[7] See, for example, the law of personal defence in New South Wales, Australia, which entirely subsumes the concept of 'defence of others' within the criminal defence of 'self-defence'. See Crimes Act 1900 No 40, s.418 ('A person carries out *conduct in self-defence* if and only if the person believes the conduct is necessary . . . *to defend himself or herself or another person* . . .', emphasis added).

[8] See, for example, International Law Commission, Summary Record of the 20th meeting, *Fundamental Rights and Duties of States*, in (1949) I *Yearbook of the International Law Commission*, para. 59 (James L. Brierly); Hans J. Morgenthau, *Politics among Nations: The Struggle for Power and Peace* (New York, McGraw-Hill, 7th ed., revised by Kenneth W. Thompson and W. David Clinton, 2005), 311.

[9] At least, that is, in some of the official language versions of the text. See n.121 and accompanying text.

[10] See Section 1.2.

question is, on its face, largely theoretical, but in fact, the status of collective self-defence as an inherent right (and for whom) has potential implications for its operation in practice, notably the extent to which it can be limited. Ambiguity further exists in doctrine as to what exactly qualifies as an act of 'collective self-defence'. In particular, is the provision of weapons and logistical support to a state under attack, in itself, an instance of the exercise of the concept? This is an especially pertinent question at the time of writing, as Western allies continue to provide such aid to Ukraine following the full-scale invasion of it by Russia that began in February 2022.

This chapter is split into three main sections. Section 1.2, which is the longest section, identifies five different 'conceptions' of collective self-defence that have been advanced in scholarship. The first four of these are all unified by the underpinning claim that to exercise collective self-defence, the co-defending state must in some measure be defending an 'interest' of its own – albeit that each of the four versions of this idea conceives of the necessary interest differently. The fifth 'conception', in contrast, holds that 'collective self-defence' is the (misnamed) 'defence of another', and thus no 'interest' is required on the part of the state coming to the defending state's aid. Sections 1.2.1–1.2.5 analyse each of these five conceptions in turn. Section 1.3 then moves to the question of whether collective self-defence is indeed an inherent right. The language of Article 51 of the UN Charter seems clear that it is, but there are issues with this finding that need to be examined. Finally, Section 1.4 considers the modality of collective self-defence, and particularly the question of what action rises to the level of its exercise. In particular, it queries whether providing weapons and/or logistical support – but stopping short of actually supplying troops – amounts to collective self-defence.

1.2 The Many Faces of Collective Self-Defence

This section unpicks the theoretical conception(s) of collective self-defence, a range of which have been advanced. These can be grouped in different ways,[11] but, at the most basic level, there exist two fundamentally differing understandings of what collective self-defence 'is'.

[11] See, for example, Yoram Dinstein, *War, Aggression and Self-Defence* (Cambridge, Cambridge University Press, 6th ed., 2017), 301–303 (identifying four 'types' of self-defence, two of which he considers to be forms of collective self-defence); Keisuke Minai, 'What Legal Interest is Protected by the Right of Collective Self-Defense: The Japanese Perspective' (2016) 24 *Willamette Journal of International Law and Dispute Resolution* 105, 107–114 (identifying three distinct 'schools of thought' regarding collective self-defence).

The first of these, as was touched on in this chapter's introduction, is the view that collective self-defence requires that the co-defending state literally is using force to *defend itself* in some measure. This was, for example, the position taken by Judge Jennings in his dissenting opinion to the *Nicaragua* merits decision of the International Court of Justice (ICJ) in 1986:

> The assisting State surely must, by going to the victim State's assistance, be also, and *in addition* to other requirements, in some measure defending itself. There should even in 'collective self-defence' be some real element of self involved with the notion of defence.[12]

Judge Jennings did not go into specifics as to exactly what 'real element of self' needed, in his view, to be at issue for the co-defending state for collective self-defence to be exercised lawfully. Others sharing this general position, however, have articulated more precisely what interest – that is, what manifestation of 'the self' – they feel the co-defending state needs to be protecting. There has not been consistency among those taking this (broad) position, though, meaning that various understandings of the necessary 'interest' have been advanced. As such, the 'defence of the self' conception of collective self-defence actually needs to be broken down into no fewer than four different sub-categories. These will each be explored in turn.

The competing view to the (four) 'defence of the self' understandings of collective self-defence is the 'defence of another' conception. Here, it effectively is argued that collective *self*-defence is misnamed. This conceptualisation sees collective self-defence as not truly the defence of the 'self' at all, in that it does not require that any interest on the part of the co-defending state be affected. On this understanding, so long as the *defending* state is in a position where its right to individual self-defence is triggered, and it requests help, altruism (genuine or not) is a sufficient basis for co-defending states to respond to that request. This 'defence of another' conception will be returned to at the end of this section, following consideration of each of the four versions of the 'defence of the self' understanding.

[12] *Military and Paramilitary Activities in and against Nicaragua* (*Nicaragua v. United States of America*) (merits) [1986] ICJ Rep. 14, dissenting opinion of Judge Jennings, 528, 545 (emphasis in original, footnote omitted). See also, *ibid*, dissenting opinion of Judge Schwebel, para. 199.

1.2.1 Defence of the Self: Individual Self-Defence Collectively Exercised

The starkest iteration of the 'defence of the self' conceptualisation of collective self-defence has never been widely supported, but it did enjoy some prominence in the 1950s. Here, the 'defence of the self' notion is taken very literally: it is said that the co-defending state must, itself, be in a position lawfully to be able to exercise individual self-defence.[13] The 'collective' aspect of any such action thus is merely that the states concerned are exercising their respective rights of individual self-defence *in concert.*[14] This understanding of collective self-defence has been referred to as the 'collaborative-exercise-of-individual-self-defence doctrine',[15] or (with mercifully fewer hyphens) as 'individual self-defence collectively exercised'.[16]

The most famous advocate of this position was Derek Bowett, who took the view that:

> [t]he requirements of collective self-defence are ... two in number; first, *that each participating State has an individual right of self-defence*, and, second, that there exists an agreement between the participating states to exercise their rights collectively.[17]

At least based on the common understanding of the necessary trigger for individual self-defence, this would mean that *all of the states* acting in collective self-defence must each have suffered an armed attack,[18] or, perhaps, imminently be about to suffer one.[19] However, it is worth noting that for Bowett, the exercise of individual self-defence was not

[13] See, for example, Derek W. Bowett, 'Collective Self-Defence under the Charter of the United Nations' (1955–1956) 32 *British Yearbook of International Law* 130, in general, but particularly 137–140, 159–160; Rosalyn Higgins, *The Development of International Law through the Political Organs of the United Nations* (London, Oxford University Press, 1963), 208–209.

[14] International Law Commission, Summary Record of the 1619th meeting, *State Responsibility*, UN Doc. A/CN.4/SR.1619, in (1980) I *Yearbook of the International Law Commission*, para. 22 (Roberto Ago, referring to this understanding as the 'juxtaposition of a number of courses of conduct adopted in individual self-defence').

[15] Minai, n.11, 111.

[16] Dinstein, n.11, 301–302 (albeit considering this 'joint' exercise of individual self-defence to be distinct from truly so-called collective self-defence).

[17] Bowett, n.13, 139–140 (emphasis added).

[18] On the requirement of an 'armed attack' in the context of collective self-defence, see Section 3.2.

[19] On the controversial notion of using force in response to an armed attack that has not yet occurred – particularly in the collective self-defence context – see Section 3.2.3.

limited to instances where a state had suffered an armed attack. This is partly because he advocated for the lawfulness of 'anticipatory self-defence' and because he argued that other acts below the level of an armed attack could 'imperil [] a state's rights' to an extent that it could then use force in self-defence.[20] As such, Bowett's understanding of collective self-defence, too, is premised not on each state suffering an armed attack, but on each state facing a threat to its national security of this sort, which he saw as sufficient to trigger the right of individual self-defence for each and all of them.[21] Even though it was not exactly the argument that he advanced, Bowett's position was soon interpreted by others as being that all states involved – defending and co-defending – needed to have suffered an armed attack to engage in collective self-defence.[22]

In any event, there is a degree of intuitive appeal to the idea of 'individual self-defence exercised collectively'. This is not least because it describes a way in which self-defence can be legally exercised. It is clear that states can act in a defensive coalition in the exercise of their respective right(s) of individual self-defence, in instances where they all have been attacked.[23] Such cooperative action obviously can be seen as a feature of, for example, the two world wars of the twentieth century[24] and today is entirely uncontroversial (subject to the usual requirements for any exercise of individual self-defence).

As well as being evidently lawful, this understanding of collective self-defence was, and remains, terminologically appealing: there is certainly no problem with referring to this concept as one of 'self' defence. In more practical terms, the 'individual self-defence collectively exercised' approach would also make things easier when it came to identifying

[20] See Derek W. Bowett, *Self-Defense in International Law* (Manchester, Manchester University Press, 1958), in general, but particularly 187–193 and quoted at 192.

[21] For useful discussion of Bowett's position in this regard and how it shaped his view of collective self-defence, see Tom Ruys, *'Armed Attack' and Article 51 of the UN Charter: Evolutions in Customary Law and Practice* (Cambridge, Cambridge University Press, 2010), 85–86.

[22] See, for example, Roberto Ago, 'Addendum – Eighth Report on State Responsibility by Mr. Roberto Ago, Special Rapporteur – The Internationally Wrongful Act of the State, Source of International Responsibility (Part 1)', UN Doc. A/CN.4/318/Add.5–7, in (1980) I(1) *Yearbook of the International Law Commission* 13, 68, para. 118 (taking this view of Bowett's position and then rejecting it).

[23] Johanna Friman, *Revisiting the Concept of Defence in the* Jus ad Bellum*: The Dual Face of Defence* (Oxford, Hart Publishing, 2017), 94–95.

[24] See Dinstein, n.11, 302 (discussing the Second World War specifically).

the legal requirements for the exercise of collective self-defence, because they would be *identical* to those for individual self-defence, capable of being assessed on an individual and separable basis for every state using force as part of the collective.

However, the idea that the term 'collective self-defence' as it appears in Article 51 is merely a prosaic reference to aggregated individual self-defence was a highly improbable reading of Article 51 even when it was first advanced early in the UN era.[25] Pleasantly straightforward it may be but limiting collective self-defence only to 'individual self-defence collectively exercised' would make the notion normatively redundant. Its function would be merely to describe a way of exercising individual self-defence. Indeed, the concept becomes almost meaningless, to the point that there would be no reason for it to appear in Article 51 at all:

> [O]ne must dismiss the idea that 'collective' self-defence means nothing more than a plurality of acts of 'individual' self-defence committed collectively – or, better, concurrently – by different States, each of which has been the victim of an armed attack, for *there is no reason why the adjective 'collective' should be used to describe a situation* which is, in fact, only a purely fortuitous juxtaposition of several conducts adopted in 'individual' self-defence.[26]

Moreover, it is abundantly clear, when one considers state practice, that the exercise of collective self-defence is accepted as lawful in instances beyond merely those where the co-defending state itself would be permitted to exercise its right of individual self-defence.[27] Indeed, this is true even if one were to accept Bowett's more permissive threshold for the exercise of self-defence. Just a couple of examples here will suffice to illustrate this point, as they are replicated in this regard in the wider practice.

The use of force by the United States in Lebanon in 1958, for instance, was justified both by Lebanon[28] and the United States[29] as an act of collective self-defence, in circumstances where there obviously had been

[25] See Julius Stone, *Legal Controls of International Conflict: A Treatise on the Dynamics of Disputes and War-Law, Second impression, Revised with Supplement 1953–1958* (Sydney, Maitland Publications, 1959), 872–873; Ian Brownlie, *International Law and the Use of Force by States* (Oxford, Oxford University Press, 1963), 331.

[26] Ago, n.22, para. 118 (emphasis added).

[27] Patrick C. R. Terry, 'Afghanistan's Civil War (1979–1989): Illegal and Failed Foreign Interventions' (2011) 31 *Polish Yearbook of International Law* 107, 135.

[28] See, for example, UNSC Verbatim Record, UN Doc. S/PV.827 (15 July 1958), para. 84.

[29] See, for example, *ibid*, para. 44.

no attack (whether meeting the gravity threshold for an 'armed attack' or otherwise)[30] against the United States whatsoever. Nor was there any conceivable threat of attack to it stemming from the situation in Lebanon. The US action in Lebanon was far from uncontroversial, with the USSR in particular arguing, strenuously, that it was not a lawful exercise of self-defence. This was for various reasons,[31] but at no point was concern raised by the USSR, or any other state, that the United States was exercising collective self-defence when *it had not itself* suffered any attack (or, indeed, been faced with any notable threat to its security of any kind). That this might in some measure be a barrier to lawful collective self-defence was not even considered by other states, even those that were strongly opposed to the action.

A much more recent example is the intervention by the Collective Security Treaty Organisation (CSTO) – predominantly in the form of Russian forces – in Kazakhstan in January 2022.[32] The CSTO explicitly invoked collective self-defence as the basis for the intervention,[33] as did Kazakhstan itself.[34] The action was criticised by scholars[35] and, to a limited extent, by states.[36] However, the primary criticism (at least of the self-defence claim) was that it was dubious whether there had been any armed attack *against Kazakhstan* by 'terrorists', as was alleged.[37] The CSTO self-defence claim was thus viewed as a pretext.[38] Nonetheless, there was no suggestion that there was any need for Russia (or any other CSTO member aside from Kazakhstan itself) to have suffered an armed

[30] On the gravity requirement for an armed attack, see Section 3.2.2.

[31] See UN Doc. S/PV.827, n.28, paras. 95–123, particularly paras. 115–116 (variously arguing that there had been no armed attack against *Lebanon* (or threat thereof); that the request for aid was invalid; that the Security Council already had taken measures with respect to the situation; and that internal security matters could not give rise to the right of self-defence). For further discussion of some of these issues, see Chapters 4–6.

[32] See, generally, Fyodor A. Lukyanov, 'Kazakhstan Intervention Sees Russia Set a New Precedent', *Russia in Global Affairs* (7 January 2022), https://eng.globalaffairs.ru/articles/kazakhstan-new-precedent.

[33] See 'Session of CSTO Collective Security Council', Office of the President of the Russian Federation (10 January 2022), http://en.kremlin.ru/events/president/news/67568.

[34] See UNSC Verbatim Record, UN Doc. S/PV.8967 (16 February 2022), 20–21.

[35] See, for example, Seyfullah Hasar, 'Kazakhstan: Another Intervention by Invitation that Played Out as Expected', *Opinio Juris* (7 February 2022), http://opiniojuris.org/2022/02/07/kazakhstan-another-intervention-by-invitation-that-played-out-as-expected.

[36] See, for example, *Hansard*, HC Deb (6 January 2022), vol. 706, cols. 178, 206–207, 236, 245–246.

[37] See, for example, *ibid*, col. 178.

[38] See, for example, *ibid*, cols. 178, 206–207, 236, 245–246.

attack or any meaningful threat to its security that could conceivably give rise to the exercise of individual self-defence.

It is, therefore, clear that the co-defending state need not have suffered an armed attack to be able to exercise the right of collective self-defence at the request of the defending state.[39] Although 'individual self-defence collectively exercised' undoubtedly is a lawful way of acting in self-defence, it is perhaps inappropriate to consider it to be a manifestation of true 'collective self-defence'.[40] Instead, it is better to see it merely as describing linked instances of individual self-defence. Or, if one insists on categorising such action as a form of collective self-defence, as some writers still do,[41] then it is merely one form.

1.2.2 Defence of the Self: Protecting an Interest Established by Treaty Arrangement

Another version of the 'defence of the self' understanding of collective self-defence posits that, while the co-defending state need not itself be legally able to exercise individual self-defence, it still must have a demonstrable 'interest' in the act of defence. This, too, has its roots in the concept's terminological framing as '*self*-defence', albeit interpreted in a 'softer' form than the notion of 'individual self-defence collectively

[39] See Japan, Cabinet Legislation Bureau, interpretation of Article 9 (quoted in both Aurelia George Mulgan, 'Japan's Defence Dilemma' (2005) 1 *Security Challenges* 59, 60, footnote 2; and Shojiro Sakaguchi, 'Major Constitutional Developments in Japan in the First Decade of the Twenty-First Century', in Albert H. Y. Chen (ed.), *Constitutionalism in Asia in the Early Twenty-First Century* (Cambridge, Cambridge University Press, 2014), 52, 62 (Japan's 1981 definition of collective self-defence, summing this up nicely: '[i]t is recognized under international law that a state has the right of collective self-defense, which is the right to use actual force to stop an armed attack on a foreign country . . . *even when the [co-defending] state itself is not under direct attack*', emphasis added). See also Kevin Jon Heller, 'The Unlawfulness of a "Bloody Nose Strike" on North Korea' (2020) 96 *International Law Studies* 1, 15; George K. Walker, 'Anticipatory Collective Self-Defense in the Charter Era: What the Treaties Have Said' (1998) 31 *Cornell International Law Journal* 321, 353; Georg Nolte and Albrecht Randelzhofer, 'Article 51', in Bruno Simma, Daniel-Erasmus Khan, Georg Nolte, Andreas Paulus and Nikolai Wessendorf (eds.), *The Charter of the United Nations: A Commentary, vol. II* (Oxford, Oxford University Press, 3rd ed., 2012), 1397, 1420, para. 47; Stanimir A. Alexandrov, *Self-Defence against the Use of Force in International Law* (The Hague, Kluwer Law International, 1996), 102–103.

[40] See, for example, Dinstein, n.11, 303 ('[c]ollective self-defence has a different meaning' from 'individual self-defence collectively exercised').

[41] See, for example, Masoud Zamani and Majid Nikouei, 'Intervention by Invitation, Collective Self-Defence and the Enigma of Effective Control' (2017) 16 *Chinese Journal of International Law* 663, 676.

exercised'. Again, though, different scholars have presented the purported need for such an 'interest' in different ways.

The first of these involves a formalistic approach. A small number of scholars have argued that it is necessary that the shared interest between defending and co-defending states be sanctified via a collective self-defence treaty arrangement.[42] In other words, these writers have said that collective self-defence can *only* be exercised within the framework of a pre-existing treaty. Hundreds of collective self-defence treaty arrangements exist,[43] and since 1945, there have been various instances where states have acted – or at least claimed to be acting – in collective self-defence specifically under the framework of such arrangements.[44]

For example, the United States claimed in 1966[45] that its use of force in Vietnam was in part premised on the fulfilment of its obligations under the now defunct Southeast Asia Collective Defense Treaty – which created the Southeast Asia Treaty Organisation (SEATO) – or, to be wholly accurate, a combination of Article IV of that treaty and the Protocol thereto.[46] On the other side of the iron curtain at around the same time, the USSR, in relation to its 1968 intervention (along with various other communist states) in Czechoslovakia, claimed[47] to be acting in collective self-defence in fulfilment of the Warsaw Pact.[48]

[42] See, for example, Andrew Martin, *Collective Security: A Progress Report* (Paris, United Nations (UNESCO), 1952), 170; George Fletcher and Jens Ohlin, *Defending Humanity: When Force Is Justified and Why* (Oxford, Oxford University Press, 2008), 79 (albeit to an extent questioning this); J. E. S. Fawcett, 'Intervention in International Law: A Study of Some Recent Cases' (1961) 103 *Recueil des cours* 343, 369 (seemingly, although not explicitly, taking this view: '[t]his common interest in defence is clearly expressed in the principle that an attack upon any member *of a defined group of states* shall be deemed to be an attack upon all', emphasis added).

[43] Terry D. Gill, 'The Second Gulf Crisis and the Relation between Collective Security and Collective Self-Defense' (1989) 10 *Grotiana* 47, 72. For discussion of these treaty arrangements, see Chapter 7.

[44] See Gray, n.3, 188, footnote 350 (providing a list of examples).

[45] See 'The Legality of United States Participation in the Defense of Viet-Nam' (legal memorandum prepared by Leonard C. Meeker, Legal Adviser of the Department of State) (1966) 54 *Department of State Bulletin* 474, especially at 480–481.

[46] Southeast Asia Collective Defense Treaty (with Protocol) (1954) 209 UNTS 28 (SEATO Treaty), Article IV and Protocol.

[47] See, for example, UNSC Verbatim Record, UN Doc. S/PV.1441 (21 August 1968), para. 3.

[48] Treaty of Friendship, Cooperation and Mutual Assistance between the People's Republic of Albania, the People's Republic of Bulgaria, the Hungarian People's Republic, the German Democratic Republic, the Polish People's Republic, the Romanian People's Republic (1955) 219 UNTS 24 (Warsaw Pact).

A post–Cold War example is Australia's invocation[49] of the Security Treaty between Australia, New Zealand, and the United States of America (ANZUS Treaty)[50] in relation to its action in 2001/2002 to support the United States following 9/11.

Some collective self-defence treaty arrangements make it very clear that their members consider themselves as having a shared interest in their mutual defence, for example, by explicitly conceptualising an attack on one of their number as an attack on all.[51] Even for collective self-defence treaty arrangements that do not articulate a shared interest among their members quite so clearly, it is, of course, unlikely that a state would ever become party to such a treaty unless it viewed it as being in its interest – at least in some measure – to do so.[52] As such, the very existence of a collective self-defence treaty arrangement arguably acts to evidence such an interest.

There is, however, nothing in Article 51 to support a *requirement* that collective self-defence can only be exercised within the context of a pre-existing treaty.[53] There also seems no reason why the existence of such a treaty should be a prerequisite, even for those who take the view that an 'interest' on the part of the co-defending state is required for the exercise of collective self-defence. Surely, such an interest could emerge (and be demonstrated) in other ways: it is unclear why only treaty-based relationships would suffice.[54]

Most tellingly, while there are examples from the practice of states exercising collective self-defence via the prism of a pre-existing treaty relationship, there have also been many examples since 1945 where states have invoked collective self-defence in spite of the fact that no mutual defence treaty has existed between the co-defending state and defending

[49] See Letter dated 23 November 2001 from the Permanent Representative of Australia to the United Nations addressed to the President of the Security Council, UN Doc. S/2001/1104 (23 November 2001).

[50] Security Treaty between Australia, New Zealand, and the United States of America (1952) 131 UNTS 83 (ANZUS Treaty).

[51] See Section 7.3.3.

[52] Gill, n.43, 72.

[53] Indeed, the drafting of the provision suggests the opposite. See Chapter 2, nn.150–155 and accompanying text.

[54] W. W. Kulski, 'The Soviet System of Collective Security Compared with the Western System' (1950) 44 *American Journal of International Law* 453, 463.

state.[55] Importantly, in none of these instances was criticism levelled at the states making the claim – even from other states that were clearly opposed to the purported collective self-defence action – on the basis that no such treaty was in place.[56]

Again, just a couple of representative examples suffice to illustrate this. The claim that the United Kingdom was acting in the collective self-defence of Jordan in 1958,[57] for example, was wholly outside of a collective defence treaty framework. While the action was heavily criticised by some states,[58] no state appeared to have any concerns about the lack of a treaty relationship between the United Kingdom and Jordan. The same is true of Cuba's assertion to be acting in collective self-defence in Angola,[59] starting in 1975. States supportive of the action were clear that the presence of Cuban forces was, as Ethiopia put it, 'in full conformity with Article 51 of the Charter'.[60] Whereas states opposed to it – as most vividly illustrated by South Africa's extensive critique[61] – made no mention whatsoever of the lack of a pre-existing treaty relationship between Cuba and Angola.

Interestingly, there are also examples where even though a relevant collective defence treaty between the parties *did* exist, the co-defending state nonetheless chose not to invoke that treaty as its basis for acting in collective self-defence. For instance, while Australia, as noted, invoked the ANZUS Treaty when making its collective self-defence claim in 2001 following the attacks of 9/11,[62] New Zealand – also a party to ANZUS, of course – opted in 2002 simply to situate its collective self-defence argument in relation to its action in Afghanistan within the scope of Article 51, without any mention of the ANZUS Treaty.[63]

[55] See Eustace Chikere Azubuike, 'Probing the Scope of Self Defense in International Law' (2011) 17 *Annual Survey of International and Comparative Law* 129, 181; Gray, n.3, 188–189 (providing a list of some examples in footnote 351).

[56] See Gray, n.3, 188–189.

[57] UNSC Verbatim Record, UN Doc. S/PV.831 (17 July 1958), para. 24.

[58] See, for example, *ibid*, paras. 62–68.

[59] See, for example, 'Cuba-Angola Declaration' (4 February 1982), https://digitalarchive.wilsoncenter.org/document/118261#document-1; UNSC Verbatim Record, UN Doc. S/PV.2440 (24 May 1983), paras. 22–23.

[60] UNSC Verbatim Record, UN Doc. S/PV.2481 (20 October 1983), para. 23.

[61] *Ibid*, paras. 149–160.

[62] See n.49 and accompanying text.

[63] See Letter dated 17 December 2001 from the Permanent Representative of New Zealand to the United Nations addressed to the President of the Security Council, UN Doc. S/2001/1193 (18 December 2001). For more discussion of this trend, see Section 7.6.

Overall, it is unquestionably the case that there is no requirement that collective self-defence is conducted within a treaty-based framework.[64] There is no basis for this in state practice, Article 51, or elsewhere. Collective self-defence can be exercised in the fulfilment of obligations of a collective self-defence treaty arrangement, but it certainly need not be.[65]

1.2.3 *Defence of the Self: Protecting an Interest Established by 'Proximity'*

Less formalistically, therefore, some commentators have argued that while a demonstrable 'interest' on the part of the co-defending state must be established, this need not take the form of a treaty relationship. The required 'interest', for those taking this view, instead tends to be premised, more nebulously, on some degree of 'proximity'.[66] A defence treaty might be one way that such proximity could be ascertained,[67] but it also

[64] UN Doc. A/CN.4/SR.1619, n.14, para. 22 (a state can 'legitimately come to the defence of another State which suffered armed attack and invited or consented to help, *even outside the context of any regional mutual assistance agreement*', emphasis added).

[65] See Azubuike, n.55, 174 (stating, categorically, that a 'state may act in collective self defense in aid to a victim state, whether or not there is a treaty obligation between it and that other state'); C. H. M. Waldock, 'The Regulation of the Use of Force by Individual States in International Law' (1952) 81 *Recueil des cours* 451, 504 ('the word "collective" does not appear to have been intended to cover only contractual systems of self-defence and any assistance to a Member engaged in legitimate self-defence appears to be authorised by Article 51'); Ago, n.22, para. 118; Walker, n.39, 352–354; Alexandrov, n.39, 101–102; M. A. Weightman, 'Self-Defense in International Law' (1951) 37 *Virginia Law Review* 1095, 111; Gina Heathcote, *The Law on the Use of Force: A Feminist Analysis* (Abingdon, Routledge, 2012), 103; Emmanuel Roucounas, *l'Institut de droit international*, 10th Commission, 'Present Problems of the Use of Force in International Law Sub-group: Self-Defence' (2007) 72 *Annuaire de l'Institut de droit international* 75, para. 116; Nolte and Randelzhofer, n.39, 1421, para. 4; A.J. Thomas Jr. and Ann Van Wynen Thomas, 'The Organization of American States and Collective Security' (1959) 13 *Southwestern Law Journal* 177, 193.

[66] See, for example, Thomas and Thomas, n.65, 185, 193, 212; Josef Rohlik, 'Some Remarks on Self-Defense and Intervention: A Reaction to Reading Law and Civil War in the Modern World' (1976) 6 *Georgia Journal of International and Comparative Law* 395, 424; Patrick T. Egan, 'The Kosovo Intervention and Collective Self-Defence' (2001) 8 *International Peacekeeping* 39, 51.

[67] See, for example, D. W. Greig, 'Self-Defence and the Security Council: What Does Article 51 Require?' (1991) 40 *International and Comparative Law Quarterly* 366, 371–372 (noting that 'the most obvious [but not necessarily only] manifestation of a community of interest would have been a treaty alliance declaring the collective interest which each party had in the security of others').

could take a range of other forms: political alliances, geographical location, economic integration, etc.[68] The point being that the attack on the defending state must also be demonstrated to be, in some measure, an 'attack' on *the interests* of the co-defending state. For those making this argument, '[w]hatever the nexus is, it should be more than just a friendly desire to help another country ... [by] a Good Samaritan country'.[69]

The roots of this understanding – beyond the fact that it, again, fits the terminology of 'self' defence – can be found in an analogy to private law.[70] In particular, it can be traced back to the idea of 'defence of others' that emerged from the social hierarchies underpinning Roman law and to the subsequent medieval recognition of a master's privilege to defend and be defended by members of his household.[71] The analogy to private law here is weak and outdated, however. Although, historically, the use of force to protect another person was, in some domestic legal systems, 'limited to persons in a special relationship',[72] today, any such requirement has long been considered across most jurisdictions[73] to be both 'irrelevant'[74] and 'obsolete'.[75] It is notable that even Canada – which was one of the few states that had retained a historic 'proximity limitation' on the defence of others as an aspect of its criminal law into the twenty-first century[76] – repealed this provision in its Criminal Code in

[68] Bowett, n.20, 238.

[69] Jaemin Lee, 'Collective Self-Defense or Collective Security: Japan's Reinterpretation of Article 9 of the Constitution' (2015) 8 *Journal of East Asia and International Law* 373, 381.

[70] Arthur Eyffinger, 'Self-Defence or the Meanderings of a Protean Principle', in Arthur Eyffinger, Alan Stephens and Sam Muller (eds.), *Self-Defence as a Fundamental Principle* (The Hague, Hague Academic Press, 2009), 103, 128.

[71] See Larry C. Wilson, 'The Defence of Others – Criminal Law and the Good Samaritan' (1988) 33 *McGill Law Journal* 756.

[72] *The People (Attorney General) v. Keatley* [1954] IR 12, 17.

[73] See, for example, *Defences in Criminal Law*, Report of the Irish Law Reform Commission (December 2009), LRC 95–200, para. 2.50 (noting that '[i]n general ... the defence of others is not limited by any "special nexus" or relationship. Statutory provisions in New Zealand, Australia and in the American Law Institute's Model Penal Code do not require any special relationship between parties to justify the use of force to protect others' and setting out, in footnote 41, the numerous relevant provisions of domestic law from these legal systems).

[74] *Keatley*, n.72, 17.

[75] *Ibid* (quoting, with approval, W. T. S. Stallybrass, *Salmond's Law of Torts* (London, Sweet and Maxwell, 10th ed., 1945), 334).

[76] See, generally, Wilson, n.71; *Defences in Criminal Law*, n.73, para. 2.50, footnote 40.

2012.[77] Moreover, even if the analogy being advanced here was to current (rather than historical) private law, there is no particular reason why domestic criminal law should be considered an appropriate basis for aiding the understanding of the concept of collective self-defence at the international level.[78]

There have, admittedly, been occasional indications from states that they may view some form of 'interest' on the part of the co-defending state as being a requirement for the exercise of collective self-defence. One might note that the SEATO Treaty, for example, was at pains to make clear that the parties would act in collective self-defence in response to 'aggression by means of armed attack ... against any State or territory which the Parties by unanimous agreement may hereafter designate, would endanger *its own* peace and safety ...'[79] This would suggest that any collective self-defence taken under the auspices of the SEATO Treaty was premised upon a threat to the interests of all members, not just the defending state. Equally, though, while that proviso was a limiting factor on the treaty obligation being triggered, that does not necessarily imply that it was viewed by the parties as a requirement for the exercise of collective self-defence in general.

A more explicit indication of a state taking precisely that view, though, can be found in discussions from the 1966 Special Committee on Principles of International Law Concerning Friendly Relations. Ghana stated during those discussions that 'the principle [of collective self-defence] in Article 51 does not justify a third State not directly threatened intervening in a dispute'.[80] As such, Ghana was clear that the co-defending state needs to have an interest that is threatened by the act of the aggressor before it can use force in collective self-defence. Similarly, albeit in a softer form, the famous interpretation by Japan in 1981 of Article 9 of its own Constitution asserted that 'the right of

[77] Criminal Code (R.S.C., 1985, c. C-46), s.37 [repealed, 2012, c. 9, s. 2]. Under this now repealed provision, the ability to use force in the personal defence of another in Canada extended only to 'any one under his [the co-defender's] protection'.

[78] This is not to say that it is impossible for there to be value in analogising self-defence at the national and international levels in some respects. See, for example, Onder Bakircioglu, 'The Right to Self-Defence in National and International Law: The Role of the Imminence Requirement' (2009) 19 *Indiana International and Comparative Law Review* 1 (in relation to a shared imminence requirement).

[79] SEATO Treaty, n.46, Article IV (emphasis added).

[80] 1966 Special Committee on Principles of International Law Concerning Friendly Relations and Co-operation among States, Summary Record, UN Doc. A/AC.125/SR.15 (17 March 1966), para. 3.

collective self-defense . . . is the right to use actual force to stop an armed attack on a foreign country *with which it has close relations* . . .'[81] Even with the 2014 decision of Japan's Cabinet to adopt a more expansive understanding of Article 9 of its Constitution so as to allow Japan to use force in collective self-defence, this has still been reserved only for instances 'when an armed attack against a foreign country that is in a close relationship with Japan occurs and as a result threatens Japan's survival . . .'[82] However, Japan no longer views this as an account of the scope of collective self-defence under international law per se, as it seemingly did in 1981, but instead merely as a description of the extent to which *it* can exercise collective self-defence without violating its own Constitution.[83]

In any event, despite these few contrary indications, a review of state practice overall makes it pretty clear that there is no need for co-defending states to demonstrate some kind of 'proximity' to the defending state. As Ruys has noted,[84] one might, for example, consider the invocation of collective self-defence by a wide range of states in support of the United States following 9/11 in 2001,[85] claims that were widely accepted[86] and certainly were not contested on the basis of a lack

[81] Japan, interpretation of Article 9, n.39 (emphasis added).

[82] Japan, 'Cabinet Decision on Development of Seamless Security Legislation to Ensure Japan's Survival and Protect its People' (1 July 2014), www.cas.go.jp/jp/gaiyou/jimu/pdf/anpohosei_eng.pdf, para. 3(3).

[83] *Ibid*, para. 3(4) (the 'legal basis in international law and constitutional interpretation *need to be understood separately*. . . . Although [collective self-defence can be] triggered by an armed attack occurring against a foreign country, [the use of force is] permitted *under the Constitution* only when . . . measures for self-defense . . . are inevitable for ensuring Japan's survival and protecting its people . . .', emphasis added).

[84] Ruys, n.21, 87.

[85] See, for example, Lettre datée du 24 octobre 2001, adressée au Président du Conseil de sécurité par le Chargé d'affaires par intérim de la Mission permanente du Canada auprès de l'Organisation des Nations Unies, UN Doc. S/2001/1005 (24 October 2001); Lettre datée du 15 mars 2002, adressée au Président du Conseil de sécurité par le Représentant permanent de la Pologne auprès de l'Organisation des Nations Unies, UN Doc. S/2002/275 (15 March 2002); UN Doc. S/2001/1193, n.63; Letter dated 6 December 2001 from the Permanent Representative of the Netherlands to the United Nations addressed to the President of the Security Council, UN Doc. S/2001/1171 (6 December 2001).

[86] See Aadhithi Padmanabhan and Michael Shih, 'Collective Self-Defense: A Report of the Yale Law School Center for Global Legal Challenges' (10 December 2012), https://law.yale.edu/sites/default/files/documents/pdf/cglc/GLC_Collective_SelfDefense.pdf (noting that the collective self-defence claims made by states in 2001 in relation to the use of force in Afghanistan following 9/11 'were considered legitimate by large segments of the international community').

of proximity between the United States and the other states asserting collective self-defence. This, in Ruys' words, 'illustrates that a "proximity criterion" would merely constitute an empty shell'.[87] More recently, the invocation of collective self-defence by ten states as the basis for their use of force in Syria (in 2014 or since)[88] likewise illustrates the point. Here, although the collective self-defence claims have certainly not been uncontested,[89] they again have not been challenged on the basis of an insufficient degree of proximity between the coalition states and the defending state, Iraq.[90]

Even if a requirement of 'proximity' for the exercise of collective self-defence could be identified in state practice (which is not the case), any such requirement would come with notable problems of application. Unlike a formal requirement of a pre-existing treaty-based relationship, which can be objectively confirmed, a more nebulous understanding of 'proximity' as a condition for collective self-defence would invite an open-ended debate, in any given case, about exactly which (self) 'interest' of the co-defending state was threatened. It then would also require an assessment – with little or nothing to guide the assessor – as to whether that 'interest' was 'sufficient' in nature, and whether it was genuinely affected/threatened to an extent that would allow for the co-defending state to use force.[91] The result would be that collective self-defence would 'become a highly subjective and politicised concept' and would 'lead to

[87] Ruys, n.21, 87. See also Brownlie, n.25, 330.

[88] See Introduction, n.21.

[89] See, for example, Identical letters dated 17 September 2015 from the Permanent Representative of the Syrian Arab Republic to the United Nations addressed to the Secretary-General and the President of the Security Council, UN Doc. S/2015/719 (21 September 2015); 'Russia Condemns US Strikes on Islamic State without Syria's Approval', *The Moscow Times* (25 September 2014), www.themoscowtimes.com/news/article/russia-condemns-u-s-strikes-on-islamic-state-without-syria-s-approval/507784.html.

[90] See, for example, Letter dated 7 June 2016 from the Permanent Representative of Belgium to the United Nations addressed to the President of the Security Council, UN Doc. S/2016/523 (9 June 2016).

[91] See Kulski, n.54, 463 ('Article 51 leaves entirely to the good faith of Members the question of determining in each case whether an attack directed against another Member' would amount to an 'attack' on their 'interests' sufficient to permit them to use force in collective self-defence); Ruys, n.21, 87 ('the proximity criterion seems so vague and subjective that it can hardly be said to have any constraining effect at all'); Christian Henderson, *The Use of Force and International Law* (Cambridge, Cambridge University Press, 2018), 258; Gray, n.3, 188–189.

the danger of certain States being left unprotected ...'[92] Equally, the requirement of such an 'interest', if treated seriously, would risk denying a weaker state that has suffered an armed attack the ability to receive aid in collective self-defence, simply because the state that was willing to respond was unable to demonstrate a sufficient level of 'interest' in the situation.[93] Overall, therefore, a requirement of an 'interest'/'proximate relationship' can be said to be neither observable nor desirable in practice.

1.2.4 *Defence of the Self: Protecting International Peace and Security*

Understandably sidestepping such concerns, other commentators have argued that the 'interest' to be protected by the co-defending state is the wider goal of maintaining international peace and security, with the 'self' in question being the international community of states as a whole. Put differently, global peace is said to be an interest – shared by every state – that can be protected through the exercise of collective self-defence.[94] Friman illustrates this view, which she adopts, with the evocative metaphor of a fire:

> Collective self-defence may be likened to a fire in a terrace house. Unless curbed, fire – akin to aggression – has a tendency to spread rapidly. ... Thus, even if your own home has so far been spared the fire, it is still in your interest to try to put out the fire in the terrace house in order to prevent it from reaching your own home, under the banner of collective defence of the self. Likewise, every State has a demonstrable self-interest in the maintenance of international peace and security, for once aggression starts to spread there is no telling if, when, or where it will stop.[95]

In a similar vein, adopting a different – and now especially affecting metaphor, given the Covid-19 pandemic – Dinstein likens aggression to a

[92] Avra Constantinou, *The Right of Self-Defence under Customary International Law and Article 51 of the UN Charter* (Brussels, Bruylant, 2000), 187.

[93] Nolte and Randelzhofer, n.39, 1421, para. 47.

[94] See, for example, Myres S. McDougal and Florentino P. Feliciano, *Law and Minimum World Public Order: The Legal Regulation of International Coercion* (New Haven, Yale University Press, 1961), 248–253; Oscar Schachter, 'The Right of States to Use Armed Force' (1983–1984) 82 *Michigan Law Review* 1620, 1639; Walker, n.39, 353; Leland M. Goodrich, Anne Patricia Simons and Edvard Hambro, *Charter of the United Nations: Commentary and Documents* (New York, Columbia University Press, 3rd ed., 1969), 348.

[95] Friman, n.23, 95.

virus: 'an armed attack is like an infectious disease in the body politic of the family of nations. Every State has a demonstrable self-interest' in stopping that disease from spreading.[96]

It is certainly possible to conceive of collective self-defence as an act whereby a co-defending state is protecting the more nebulous 'interest' of global security.[97] Indeed, it is difficult to argue with the underpinning idea that all states have a stake in maintaining a global order whereby the aggressive use of force is responded to with defensive force (if absolutely necessary and proportionate to defensive goals, of course). The interconnected realities of the modern, globalised world are stark.[98]

Some writers have gone further than identifying a shared interest in global peace as the basis for collective self-defence and have suggested that such an interest is sufficient to establish a *duty* upon states to act in collective self-defence in response to an act of aggression against another state that cannot defend itself. Here, it is said that the international legal order, and particularly the UN Charter's commitment to 'save succeeding generations from the scourge of war',[99] creates an obligation for all states to act in collective self-defence in response to acts of aggression.[100]

96 Dinstein, n.11, 304.

97 One might note, for example, Covenant of the League of Nations (1919) 225 CTS 195, Article 11 ('[a]ny war or threat of war, whether immediately affecting any of the Members of the League or not, is hereby declared *a matter of concern to the whole League*', emphasis added).

98 One need only consider the rippling effects of Russia's 2022 invasion of Ukraine – ongoing at the time of writing – which has had wide-reaching implications for global economics, energy, health, food security, and defence. See, for example, Tim Benton, Antony Froggatt, and Laura Wellesley, 'Ukraine Crisis Could Trigger Cascading Risks Globally', *Chatham House* (16 March 2022), www.chathamhouse.org/2022/03/ukraine-crisis-could-trigger-cascading-risks-globally.

99 UN Charter, n.5, preamble.

100 See, for example, Robert Redslob, *Traité de droit des gens: l'évolution historique, les institutions positives, les idées de justice, le droit nouveau* (Paris, Recueil Sirey, 1950), 435 ('le devoir d'assurer la paix se résume dans le devoir d'association à la légitime défense. Ce même devoir découle, en cas d'agression manifeste, de l'obligation de sauvegarder la loi internationale par une interposition collective'); Sir W. Eric Beckett, *The North Atlantic Treaty, The Brussels Treaty, and the Charter of the United Nations* (London, Stevens & Sons, 1950), 35 (albeit reaching this conclusion tentatively). See also International Law Commission, Summary Record of the 14th meeting, *Fundamental Rights and Duties of States*, in (1949) I *Yearbook of the International Law Commission*, para. 67 (Georges Scelle: under 'the right of collective self-defence . . . [e]very State had the right, and *even the duty*, to intervene in order to protect the victim from the aggressor, under the supervision of the Security Council', emphasis added, albeit that for Scelle the (possible) duty is conceived as being owed more directly *to the defending state*, rather than to the international community at large); Maya Khater, 'The Legality of

Interestingly, during the process of the drafting of the UN Charter, New Zealand appeared to propose something that might be interpreted along the lines of such a collective defence obligation. It suggested that the following be inserted into the Charter: '[a]ll members of the Organisation undertake collectively to resist every act of aggression against any member'.[101] However, aside from this proposal being received positively by Peru,[102] it met with little support and was rejected.[103]

Today, it is clearly incorrect to say that states are under an *obligation* to act in collective self-defence to maintain international peace and security.[104] There is no basis for this in law,[105] and, indeed, it would be undesirable as a matter of policy. If states were bound to act in collective self-defence every time another state was the victim of an armed attack, international conflict would be on an unprecedented scale, with force being used *in abundantia*. Every single armed attack would have the

the Russian Military Operations Against Ukraine from the Perspective of International Law' (2022) 3 *Access to Justice in Eastern Europe* 1, 11 (discussing possible responses to Russia's 2022 invasion of Ukraine: '[t]he UN must implement the right of collective self-defence, according to the provisions of Art. 51 of the UN Charter, *obliging* the members of the UN to defend it [Ukraine] and sending military forces to support it …', emphasis added).

101 Documents of the United Nations Conference on International Organization, San Francisco, 1945 (London, United Nations Information Organization (United Nations), 22 volumes, 1945–1955), (UNCIO) vol. 3, 487; *ibid*, vol. 6, 342–343.

102 *Ibid*, vol. 6, 343.

103 *Ibid*, 721.

104 See Hans Kelsen, 'Collective Security and Collective Self-Defense under the Charter of the United Nations' (1948) 42 *American Journal of International Law* 783, 784; Constantinou, n.92, 174; Friman, n.23, 94–95; Brownlie, n.25, 375–376; Alfred Verdross, 'Austria's Permanent Neutrality and the United Nations Organization' (1956) 50 *American Journal of International Law* 61, 67; Joseph L. Kunz, 'Individual and Collective Self-Defence under Article 51 of the Charter of the United Nations' (1947) 41 *American Journal of International Law* 872, 875.

105 One might note that Dinstein, n.11, 304 points in this context to the fact that the ICJ, in 1970, determined that the prohibition of aggression gave rise to obligations *erga omnes*. While this is true (see *Barcelona Traction, Light and Power Company, Limited* (*Belgium v. Spain*) (judgment) [1970] ICJ Rep. 3, para. 34), the Court made this point in passing without providing any detail as to exactly what obligations were owed to the international community as a whole in relation to the prohibition of aggression (other than, as seems obvious, the obligation not to perpetrate it). See Maurizio Ragazzi, *The Concept of International Obligations* Erga Omnes (Oxford, Clarendon Press, 1997), 74–91 (discussing, generally, the *erga omnes* status of the prohibition of aggression). Of course, a state may have an obligation to act in collective self-defence by way of a multilateral or bilateral collective self-defence treaty arrangement (see Section 7.3), but this is not the situation under the general corpus of the *jus ad bellum*.

potential to risk a world war, and to do so outside the global collective security architecture of the United Nations at that. Such escalation of interstate force would run counter to the purposes of the United Nations,[106] not to mention all good sense. Moreover, the job of maintaining international peace and security is already taken by the UN Security Council, and – while the Council's failures in *doing* that job have meant self-defence (individual and collective) have taken on an important role in global security – the function of self-defence is ultimately defensive, not global security enforcement.[107]

Not only is there no duty to act in collective self-defence, but the assertion by both Friman and Dinstein in the above-quoted passages that states must have 'a *demonstrable* self-interest' in responding to specific armed attacks against other nations is also dubious. While some states might well be able to demonstrate a direct effect upon them as a result of an armed attack against a third party, for others it is likely in most cases that any such direct effect is – at least initially – only potential. To say that *all* states *always* have a 'demonstrable interest' in stopping acts of aggression would seem only to be true in the loosest sense: it is an interest demonstrated merely by virtue of being a fellow state of the world and based on hypothetical futures that can be envisaged in an ever-more interconnected global society.[108] So far as it goes, though, this loose understanding of the defence of a shared interest can be said to be correct. As the representative of the United States colourfully phrased this idea at a meeting of the First Committee of the UN General Assembly in 1949, 'peace [is] everybody's business'.[109]

1.2.5 Defence of Another

The final 'version' of collective self-defence differs from the previous conceptualisations already discussed in that it is not premised on any 'interest' on the part of the co-defending state. Here, collective self-defence is understood simply as the defence of the state attacked. This means that '[i]t is *not* self-defense, but defense of another state; it corresponds, in municipal law, not to self-defense, but to the defense of

[106] Stone, n.25, 264.
[107] Bowett, n.13, 140.
[108] *Ibid*, 135 ('this interest is no more than a general interest ... which members of any community have in the preservation of peace in that community').
[109] See UNGA Summary Record, UN Doc. A/C.1/SR.325 (14 November 1949), para. 35.

others'.[110] Under such a conception, the defending state is essentially exercising its right of individual self-defence through the co-defending state: the co-defender is, in effect, an altruistic facilitator of, and proxy for, an attacked state's own right of individual self-defence. The exercise of collective self-defence thus can be seen as 'parasitic' on the conditions for the exercise of the defending state's right of individual self-defence.

The 'defence of another' view would seem to be what the majority adopted in the ICJ's *Nicaragua* merits decision, where collective self-defence was famously at issue. Admittedly, the Court did not make this entirely explicit, but it can be inferred from the judgment.[111] As will be examined in later chapters,[112] in *Nicaragua*, the Court took the view that collective self-defence can be exercised only in instances where the defending state has declared that it has been the victim of an armed attack and explicitly requested aid in responding to it.[113] For some, including Judge Jennings in his dissent:

> this way of looking at collective self-defence . . . seems to be based almost upon an idea of vicarious defence by champions: that a third State may lawfully come to the aid of an authenticated victim of armed attack provided that the requirements of a declaration of attack and a request for assistance are complied with.[114]

In terms of state practice, examples have already been set out in earlier subsections that show that states do not feel that any demonstrable interest is required on the part of the co-defending state for the exercise of collective self-defence. Moreover, states themselves have – from the very start of the UN era – explicitly conceived of collective self-defence as the 'defence of another'. One might consider, for example, the definition of collective self-defence put forward by Peru's representative at the General Assembly in 1949, Manuel Maúrtua: collective self-defence being instances when states 'collectively ensured the defence of another State'.[115] Similarly, a year later, the United Kingdom characterised

[110] Kunz, n.104, 875 (emphasis added, footnotes omitted). See also Lee, n.69, 380; A.L. Goodhart, 'The North Atlantic Treaty of 1949' (1951) 79 *Recueil des cours* 182, 203 (referring to the concept as 'group defence').
[111] See Friman, n.23. 94.
[112] See Chapters 4–6.
[113] See *Nicaragua* (merits), n.12, *inter alia*, paras. 165–166, 195, 199.
[114] *Ibid*, dissenting opinion of Judge Jennings, 545.
[115] UNGA Summary Record, UN Doc. A/C.6/SR.173 (25 October 1949), para. 75.

collective self-defence as a situation where one state decided to 'go to the help of another State'.[116] Therefore, as Gray has stated:

> insistence on a third-state interest all seems rather far-fetched in the light of state practice since 1945 . . . [because] criticisms by states of the legality of actions taken in the name of collective self-defence have not mentioned the absence of a third-state interest.[117]

Given the relative clarity of state practice on the matter, it perhaps is unsurprising that the 'defence of another' conception has become the majority understanding of collective self-defence in UN era scholarship too.[118] There seems little question that this is the correct understanding of the concept.

One result of reaching this conclusion is that '[t]he term collective self-defense is not a happy one'.[119] Indeed, it 'is at the worst self-contradictory and at best clumsy and ambiguous'.[120] Disappointment at such terminological disutility is not something to dismiss out of hand, but it perhaps also is not something worth losing significant sleep over. This is not least because, while the Arabic ('دفاع عن الأنفس'), Chinese ('自卫'), and

[116] UNGA Summary Record, UN Doc. A/C.1/SR.360 (12 October 1950), para. 5.

[117] Gray, n.3, 188. See also Azubuike, n.55, 174 ('collective self defense is not merely the aggregate of individual right of self defense, since practice has shown that a third state may exercise the right of collective self defense even where it has no interest of its own to protect'). Of course, it is true that states – a breed of actor not exactly famous for their altruistic tendencies – are perhaps unlikely to intervene, *militarily*, in the affairs of other states entirely selflessly. All of the risks and costs that an interstate use of force inevitably entails will rarely, if ever, be borne by a state unless there is at least some self-interest (actual or perceived) in it doing so. See Josepeh Frankel, *National Interest* (London, Pall Mall Press, 1970), generally, though particularly at 24–26; Schachter, n.3, 156. Yet, this would fall a long way short of saying that a co-defending state must, legally, have such an interest, or that, if it does, that it needs to be articulated, demonstrated, or even legitimate.

[118] See, for example, Stuart Casey-Maslen, Jus ad Bellum: *The Law on Inter-State Use of Force* (Oxford, Hart Publishing, 2020), 75; Peter Haggenmacher, 'Self-Defence as a General Principle of Law and Its Relation to War', in Arthur Eyffinger, Alan Stephens and Sam Muller (eds.), *Self-Defence as a Fundamental Principle* (The Hague, Hague Academic Press, 2009), 3, 8–9; Helmut Rumpf, 'The Concepts of Peace and War in International Law' (1984) 27 *German Yearbook of International Law* 429, 440; Ruys, n.21, particularly 87–89; Henderson, n.91, 257–258; Brownlie, n.25, 328–331; Constantinou, n.92, 208; Gray, n.3, 188; Quincy Wright, 'United States Intervention in the Lebanon' (1959) 53 *American Journal of International Law* 112, 118; Azubuike, n.55, 174.

[119] Kunz, n.104, 875. See also Robert W. Tucker, 'The Interpretation of War under Present International Law' (1951) 4 *International Law Quarterly* 11, 29.

[120] Fawcett, n.42, 368.

Russian ('самооборону') texts of Article 51 all would seem to reflect the English terminology of 'self-defence', the equally authoritative French and Spanish texts notably refer, respectively, to 'légitime défense' and 'de legítima defensa'.[121] The qualifier – rooted, as it is, in common law thinking – that lawful defence need be of the 'self' thus is only present in *some* of the authoritative versions of the UN Charter, which hardly suggests that 'self' defence is a term that one must cling to in relation to collective defensive action.[122]

It is worth noting, too, that the term 'collective self-defence' is only problematic if one fixates on the perspective of the co-defending state. This is a common approach in scholarship: '[i]n the writings of highly qualified publicists collective self-defence *is defined* from the point of view of the assisting State rather than the victim State'.[123] There is no reason why this necessarily needs to be the case, however. Thus, although for the co-defender collective self-defence is, indeed, an unfortunate term to describe its action, from the perspective of the *defending* state, collective self-defence truly amounts to the defence of the self – albeit as exercised by the issuance of a request for aid rather than its own use of force.[124]

Another option to soften the terminological discomfort that some seem to feel regarding the label 'collective self-defence' is to revert to the 'protection of international peace and security' understanding outlined in Section 1.2.4. As discussed, there is merit in this conception: all states can be said to have a genuine interest in the maintenance of international peace and security, even if it will not in all instances be a direct and demonstrable interest. To the extent that this conceptualisation may make some feel more at ease with the terminology of *self*-defence,[125] and to the extent that it even may act to promote desirable values of a global community and the common good, it does no harm:

121 See *Nicaragua* (merits), n.12, dissenting opinion of Judge Oda, para. 93.

122 See, generally, Fletcher and Ohlin, n.42, 63–65.

123 Constantinou, n.92, 186 (emphasis added).

124 See Constantine Antonopoulos, 'Force by Armed Groups as Armed Attack and the Broadening of Self-Defence' (2008) 55 *Netherlands International Law Review* 159, 174 (implying that the request is part of the defending state exercising of its right of self-defence). Admittedly, when referring to the 'exercise of collective self-defence', states and scholars tend to be talking about the use of force by the co-defending state, not the defending state's request for help. See the state practice set out in Section 1.3.2 and the scholars cited at n.152.

125 Bowett, for example, felt that the idea of a universally shared interest in international peace and security already strayed too far from the notion of the 'self' for action taken in response accurately to be described as 'self-defence', see Bowett, n.13, 136.

> perhaps the most appropriate way to view the right [of collective self-defence] is as one permitting those who can exercise some means of defence to come to the aid of those who cannot, [but] it is *also possible* to view an invocation of the right of collective self-defence as a demonstration of solidarity against the attacks and the perpetrators of them.[126]

However, given that identifying a shared interest in defending 'peace and security' is both abstract and universal (thus meaning a state need do nothing to demonstrate it other than *be a state*), adopting this view does not result in any additional requirements for the exercise of collective self-defence. Ultimately, it is rather meaningless in legal terms. The better conclusion, it is argued, is simply that collective self-defence is, in the end, poorly named (at least in some languages, and at least when viewed from the perspective of the co-defending state).

Readers may therefore understandably question the use of the term 'collective self-defence' throughout this book and, indeed, as this book's very title. The label is adopted herein to reflect the existing terminology (as employed in Article 51 and now embedded well beyond it), alongside helping to ensure a degree of 'brand recognition'. More importantly, there is notable value in employing the term 'collective self-defence' in relation to the concept because it highlights the fact that, for good or ill, individual and collective self-defence have become fundamentally conjoined in the UN era. This is not in the sense that they both truly involve the defence of the 'self', but in the crucial sense that *the same legal requirements apply to both*, as will be discussed in later chapters.[127] The term therefore reflects the substance, at least on one level. These are pragmatic factors that have no bearing on the fact that scholarship, case law, and, most importantly, state practice, all establish – pretty clearly – that there is no need for the co-defending state to have any specific 'interest' in the act of defence itself, and, thus, that 'collective defence of another' (or a variation thereof) would be a more accurate term for the concept than 'collective self-defence'.

1.3 Collective Self-Defence as an Inherent Right

1.3.1 Querying the Status of Collective Self-Defence as an Inherent Right

Article 51 of the UN Charter refers to 'the inherent right of individual or collective self-defence if an armed attack occurs against a Member of the

[126] Henderson, n.91, 257 (emphasis added).

[127] On the 'conjoining' of individual and collective self-defence in the UN era, see Section 2.4. On the shared criteria for both individual and collective self-defence, see Chapter 3.

United Nations'.[128] The plain meaning of the text here indicates that both individual and collective self-defence are 'rights', and that the 'right' in each case is inherent. More accurately, in fact, given that they are spoken of in the same breath in Article 51 ('*the* . . . right'),[129] the text indicates that they are one single, indivisible 'right',[130] which is inherent.

It was argued in Section 1.2 that collective self-defence is, in actuality, a concept involving the 'defence of another' (or, if it does truly include an element of the defence of the 'self', this is only by way of a universal shared interest in international peace and security). However, this finding seems somewhat at odds with the idea that the collective self-defence is, as Article 51 proclaims, an 'inherent right'.

The legitimacy of defending *oneself* in some form or other has, over many centuries, been an intrinsic element of all major legal systems.[131] For some, the permissibility of defending oneself is a 'primary law of nature'.[132] It is on that basis that Article 51's qualification that self-defence is 'inherent' has been argued to be a reflection of a principle of 'natural law'.[133] In other words, it is said by those who take this view that Article 51 acknowledges that the right of self-defence *inheres* in statehood, in the same way that it is often said to inhere in personhood.[134]

One may question the extent to which conceptualising the notion of self-defence as a right that is 'natural' – and, thus, unimpeachable – is either accurate or desirable in the modern world. As Dinstein argues,

> a reference to self-defence as a 'natural' right or a right generated by 'natural law' . . . is unwarranted. It may be conceived of as an anachronistic residue from an era when international law was dominated by

[128] UN Charter, n.5, Article 51.

[129] *Ibid* (emphasis added).

[130] See, for example, Eugene V. Rostow, 'Until What? Enforcement Action or Collective Self-Defense' (1991) 85 *American Journal of International Law* 506, 510.

[131] See David B. Kopel, Paul Gallant and Joanne D. Eisen, 'The Human Right of Self-Defense' (2007) 22 *Brigham Young University Journal of Public Law* 43, 130 ('the right of self-defense has always been an essential part of international law, and has always been a principle of all major legal systems'); Bowett, n.20, 3.

[132] William Blackstone, *Commentaries on the Laws of England* (Oxford, Clarendon Press, 1765–1769), Book the Third – Chapter the First: Of the Redress of Private Wrongs by the Mere Act of Parties, Private Wrongs, 4.

[133] Weightman, n.65, 1108; Stephen C. Neff, *War and the Law of Nations: A General History* (Cambridge, Cambridge University Press, 2005), 326.

[134] Peter B. M. J. Pijpers, Hans J. F. R. Boddens Hosang, and Paul A. L. Ducheine, 'Collective Cyber Defence – The EU and NATO Perspective on Cyber Attacks' (2021) *Amsterdam Law School Legal Studies Research Paper* No. 2021–37, Amsterdam Center for International Law No. 2021–13, 6.

> ecclesiastical doctrines. . . . [Moreover] [i]t is not beyond the realm of the plausible that a day may come when States will agree to dispense completely with the use of force in self-defence, exclusively relying thenceforth on some central authority.[135]

If self-defence is considered part of the 'law of nature', this would risk foreclosing the possibility that the international community may, at some point in the future, become so committed to peace that it outlaws the unilateral use of force in all forms, including in self-defence.[136] It has been compellingly argued that the UN Charter's prohibition on the use of force 'must be regarded as the *beginning* of the outlawing of state violence', rather than as some kind of satisfactory conclusion.[137] It is important not to close off possible future progress by appealing to the dubious idea that any form of state-level violence has a natural law pedigree (whatever that even means in the modern context) and is thus 'sacrosanct'.

Even if it is argued that individual self-defence 'inheres' more prosaically in state sovereignty – rather than as part of dubious notions of 'the law of nature' – the same risk of embedding violence in perpetuity remains, at least to some extent.[138] Moreover, such a position is especially hard to sustain when it comes to collective self-defence:

> While article 51 of the UN Charter does not distinguish between individual and collective self-defence and qualifies both as inherent, this is difficult to justify in relation to the latter. Indeed, it does not seem to be a right without which sovereignty cannot exist or an essential means through which to defend the constitutive elements of statehood.[139]

None of the various conceptualisations of self-defence discussed in Section 1.2, other than 'individual self-defence collectively exercised', 'would automatically lead to the conclusion that the right of action is inherent'[140] for the co-defending state. Especially when collective self-defence is viewed as the 'defence of another', as was argued should be the

135 Dinstein, n.11, 198–199.
136 *Ibid*, 199.
137 Gina Heathcote, 'Feminist Perspectives on the Law on the Use of Force', in Marc Weller (ed.), *The Oxford Handbook of the Use of Force in International Law* (Oxford, Oxford University Press, 2015), 114, 125 (emphasis added).
138 Dinstein, n.11, 199; Heathcote, n.65, 79–85.
139 Marco Roscini, 'On the "Inherent" Character of the Right of States to Self-Defence' (2015) 4 *Cambridge Journal of International and Comparative Law* 634, 648.
140 Thomas and Thomas, n.65, 185.

case in the previous section, '[i]t is hardly possible to regard the right or duty of a state to assist another state as "inherent" . . .'[141]

Not all commentators see the term 'inherent' in Article 51 as a reference to a right inhering in all states, however. For some, it is read as a more positivistic reference to the law that pre-existed the Charter.[142] In effect, the argument here is that Article 51 simply notes that self-defence existed ('inhered') in earlier customary international law, rather than necessarily in the 'essence' of statehood itself, and that this pre-existing law is unaffected by the Charter. It is worth noting that these are not mutually exclusive understandings of the meaning of the term 'inherent' in Article 51. It could be referring both to a right inherent in statehood and to a pre-existing customary international law right to collective defence.

In any event, again, while there undoubtedly is significant historical pedigree to the modern concept of collective self-defence, particularly in the form of mutual defence alliances,[143] it is debatable whether – unlike individual self-defence – the modern 'right' of collective self-defence had a notable pre-Charter existence in customary international law, at least in the form in which it is now understood in the UN era.[144] As such, whether one sees the term 'inherent' in Article 51 as meaning 1) an intrinsic right of defence; 2) the pre-Charter law; or 3) both, it is difficult to see collective self-defence as qualifying.

Moreover, one might not only question whether collective self-defence is an inherent right, but also whether it is a 'right' at all. As Roscini argues, '[c]ollective self-defence *is not even a right*: . . . it is subordinated to the request of the victim state'.[145] Here, Roscini is referring to the requirement that a defending state must request aid, before the co-defending state lawfully can use force in collective self-defence. This

[141] Weightman, n.65, 1111. See also John S. Gibson, 'Article 51 of the Charter of the United Nations' (1957) 13 *India Quarterly* 121, 127–128.

[142] See, for example, Judith Gardam, *Necessity, Proportionality and the Use of Force by States* (Cambridge, Cambridge University Press, 2004), 200; R. St. J. MacDonald, 'The *Nicaragua* Case: New Answers to Old Questions' (1986) 24 *Canadian Yearbook of International Law* 127, 144; Constantinou, n.92, 174–176. This would also appear to be the understanding taken by the ICJ. See *Nicaragua* (merits), n.12, para. 193 ('the inherent right (or "droit naturel") which any State possesses . . . covers both collective and individual self-defence. Thus, the Charter itself testifies to the existence of the right of collective self-defence in customary international law').

[143] See Chapter 2.

[144] For further discussion, see *ibid.*

[145] Roscini, n.139, 648 (emphasis added).

requirement was identified by the ICJ in the *Nicaragua* case in 1986 and will be explored in Chapters 4–6 of this book. What suffices to note here is that it has been argued that if the exercise of collective self-defence is, for the co-defending state, subordinated to a request by – and thus to the whim of – another state, then it is difficult to see it as a *right* that is held by the co-defending state (inherent or otherwise). This is supported by the fact that permanent neutrality requires that a state refrain from using force as a co-defending state in collective self-defence,[146] as well as precluding its membership of collective self-defence organisations,[147] but does not stop a permanently neutral state from requesting aid in collective self-defence as a defending state if it suffers an armed attack.[148]

On the basis of all of the forgoing, Roscini concludes: '[t]he right of the victim state to ask for help may well be inherent, but the "right" of other states to come to its assistance is not'.[149] While Roscini's analysis has merit in itself, it is important to remember that it is focused only on the exercise of collective self-defence from the perspective of the *co-defending* state. It already has been noted that there is a tendency in scholarship to fixate on the co-defender(s) in this way, but it need not be so.[150] From the perspective of the *defending* state, collective self-defence is likely to be just as pivotal to the state's right to exist as would be the case for the state's exercise of individual self-defence. Leaving aside instances of pretext, collective self-defence is most likely to be engaged in circumstances where the defending state is faced with an armed attack (or imminent threat thereof) that it cannot, itself, abate. Faced with such a situation, the ability to request – and *receive* – aid surely can be seen as an aspect of that state's right to its own defence. One, therefore, could argue

[146] Michael Bothe, 'Neutrality, Concept and General Rules', in Rüdiger Wolfrum (ed.), *Max Planck Encyclopaedia of Public International Law, vol. VII* (Oxford, Oxford University Press, 2012), 617, 621, para. 18; Dinstein, n.11, 303.

[147] Marc Weller, 'Options for a Peace Settlement for Ukraine: Option Paper I – Neutrality and Related Concepts', *Opinio Juris* (31 March 2022), https://opiniojuris.org/2022/03/31/options-for-a-peace-settlement-for-ukraine-option-paper-i-neutrality-and-related-concepts. For discussion of such organisations, see Chapter 7.

[148] Bothe, n.146, para. 18; Dinstein, n.11, 303–304; Roscini, n.139, 648, footnote 104.

[149] Roscini, n.139, 648. A handful of other writers have also at least seemingly been a little wary of identifying collective self-defence as an inherent right. See, for example, Brownlie, n.25, 330 (referring to the 'right or, more precisely, a *power*, to aid third states which have become the object of an unlawful use of force', emphasis added); Gill, n.43, 49 (seemingly hedging his bets somewhat by referring to 'the principle or right of collective self-defense').

[150] See nn.123–124 and accompanying text.

that Roscini's critique can be supported without this conflicting with the ordinary meaning of Article 51: collective self-defence perhaps is therefore an inherent right, as therein proclaimed, held by the *defending* state but not the co-defender.[151]

However, it is notable that a clear majority of scholars view collective self-defence as a right held by the co-defending state as well as (and in some cases perhaps even instead of) the defending state.[152] If this is correct, it can only be because collective self-defence – for the co-defending state, at least – has the character of a *derivative* right.[153] The right to defend another only has meaning as a result of the right of that 'other' to defend themself. As has already been stated, this writer views collective self-defence as being parasitic on individual self-defence. Yet, the fact that collective self-defence is 'subordinated' to the request of the defending state does not preclude the possibility of collective self-defence amounting to a right for the co-defending state in this derivative sense.

151 Some writers do seem to conceive of collective self-defence as being (primarily or exclusively) a right held by the defending state, although this rarely is explicit. See, for example, Waldock, n.65, 504 (implicitly taking this view, in that he notes in context of discussing collective self-defence, that '[*t*]*he purpose of the article* [Article 51] *is to reserve a right of self-defence inherent in all States*', emphasis in original); Oscar Schachter, 'Self-Defense and the Rule of Law' (1989) 83 *American Journal of International Law* 259, 266 (implicitly taking this view, in that he notes that collective self-defence amounts to a recognition that 'the targets of aggression may require armed assistance by other states').

152 See, for example, Rein Müllerson, 'Self-Defence in the Contemporary World', in Lori Fisler Damrosch and David J. Scheffer (eds.), *Law and Force in the New International Order* (Boulder, Westview Press, 1991), 13, 23; Richard N. Gardner, 'Commentary on the Law of Self-Defence', in Lori Fisler Damrosch and David J. Scheffer (eds.), *Law and Force in the New International Order* (Boulder, Westview Press, 1991), 49, 50; Friman, n.23. 94 ('third states [have] the right to resort to force in collective self-defence'); Hans Kelsen, 'Is the North Atlantic Treaty in Conformity with the Charter of the United Nations?' (1950) 19 *University of Kansas City Law Review* 1, 14; Jun Okamoto, 'Legal Restrictions on the Actions of the Japan Air Self Defense Force' (2013) 40 *Reporter* 12, 15; Goodhart, n.110, 203–204, 208; Elvina Pothelet, 'U.S. Military's "Collective Self-Defense" of Non-State Partner Forces: What Does International Law Say?', *Just Security* (26 October 2018), www.justsecurity.org/61232/collective-self-defense-partner-forces-international-law-say (referring to 'the well-established UN Charter right of States *to defend other States*', emphasis in original).

153 Rohlik, n.66, 426 ('the exercise of that right [of collective self-defence] is wholly dependent on, and in its scope identical to, the individual right of the attacked state. In that sense the right of the assisting state is derivative or secondary. That has important consequences ...', footnotes omitted); Roda Mushkat, 'Who May Wage War – An Examination of an Old/New Question' (1987) 2 *American University Journal of International Law and Policy* 97, 149; Helen Michael, 'Covert Involvement in Essentially Internal Conflicts: United States Assistance to the Contras under International Law' (1990) 23 *Vanderbilt Journal of Transnational Law* 539, 580.

After all, individual self-defence, too, is subordinated to legal restrictions based on the circumstances in question (e.g. the occurrence of an armed attack), and yet few would suggest it is not a right of states.[154] It could be said that the request for aid (or lack thereof) is thus nothing but another 'circumstance', applicable in the collective context, which frames the boundaries of the exercise of the right.

The legal basis for the idea that collective self-defence is an inherent right can be open to question. As will be discussed in Chapter 2, this is not how the concept was historically conceived. However, it ultimately can be argued that – for good or ill – collective self-defence is a right that is inherent 'because the Charter bestows upon it the characteristics and requisites of being inherent'.[155] In other words, given that Article 51 plainly confirms that collective self-defence is an inherent right, without making a distinction as to which states (defending or co-defending) possess that right, *that confirmation in itself* can be said to establish that it is. This has then become embedded in the way in which states conceptualise collective self-defence.

1.3.2 *The Status of Collective Self-Defence as an Inherent Right in State Practice*

There are some examples in the UN era where states appear to have rejected the idea that collective self-defence is an inherent right vested in the co-defending state. For instance, in March 1966, Ghana concluded that it was 'extremely doubtful whether there could be said to be an inherent right of collective self-defence . . .'[156] Ghana left no room for doubt about its view in this regard, stating again, four months later, that although every state has the inherent right of individual self-defence, there is 'no inherent right of collective self-defence'.[157]

While not rejecting the idea that the co-defending state might possess a right of collective self-defence in the way that Ghana did, other states have occasionally implied that they see the holder of the right (or, at least,

[154] A rare example of someone making this (incorrect) argument is Weightman, n.65, 1110.

[155] Thomas and Thomas, n.65, 185, 189, quoted at 185. See also Gibson, n.141, 128; Murray Colin Alder, *The Inherent Right of Self-Defence in International Law* (Dordrecht, Springer, 2013), 117; Stone, n.25, 245. *Contra* Rumpf, n.118, 440.

[156] UN Doc. A/AC.125/SR.15, n.80, para. 3.

[157] 1966 Special Committee on Principles of International Law Concerning Friendly Relations and Co-Operation among States, Summary Record, UN Doc. A/AC.125/SR.16 (25 July 1966), para. 57.

the primary holder of the right) as being the defending state. For example, in 1977, India discussed a request for aid by Mozambique and was clear that it considered it to be a request made in the 'the exercise of' collective self-defence.[158] India therefore appeared to situate the right primarily with Mozambique – the (would be) defending state. More recently, in 2016, the Netherlands asserted that its action in Syria against the 'Islamic State of Iraq and the Levant' (ISIL) was 'in the exercise of the inherent right of collective self-defence *of Iraq*',[159] as opposed to indicating that it was exercising its own right of collective self-defence.

However, while such statements might chime with some of the analysis in the previous subsection, they are unusual among states. The vast majority of references to collective self-defence that have come from states indicate that they conceive of it as a right, held also *by the co-defending state*, and in many cases that this is an *inherent* right on the part of the co-defender to take action at the request of the defending state. Indeed, this has seemingly been the widespread understanding of states ever since the adoption of the UN Charter, with it being implicit in statements made throughout the 1950s.

In debates in the UN General Assembly in 1950, for example, the representative of the United Kingdom stressed that '[*i*]*ndependently of the Charter*, a State has the right of self-defence ... [to] help ... another State'.[160] The United Kingdom was thus clear that it viewed collective self-defence as a right held by the co-defending state. Indeed, it saw this as an inherent right, independent of and pre-dating the UN Charter. Similarly, in 1953, Peru referred to the 'inherent right of collective self-defence referred to in Article 51 of the Charter'.[161] This was in the context of a discussion regarding collective self-defence treaty arrangements, with Peru clearly seeing the 'inherent right' it spoke of as one vested in both the defending state and the co-defending state(s). Two years later, in 1955, the representative of Pakistan was clear that his state, too, saw collective self-defence as 'a right that exists independently of the Charter',[162] and that the ability to *provide aid* in collective self-defence

[158] UNSC Verbatim Record, UN Doc. S/PV.2018(OR) (30 June 1977), para. 78.
[159] Letter dated 10 February 2016 from the Chargé d'affaires a.i. of the Permanent Mission of the Netherlands to the United Nations addressed to the President of the Security Council, UN Doc. S/2016/132 (10 February 2016) (emphasis added).
[160] UN Doc. A/C.1/SR.360, n.116, para. 5 (emphasis added).
[161] UNGA Summary Record, UN Doc. A/C.1/SR.596 (10 April 1953), para. 13.
[162] UNGA Summary Record, UN Doc. A/C.1/SR.809 (9 December 1955), para. 6.

was 'one of the basic rights of a State under international law'.[163] The United States in 1958 argued that collective self-defence was something that 'the United Nations Charter regards as an inherent right, the right of *all nations to work together* to preserve their independence'.[164]

This view has been maintained, broadly, by states since the 1950s too, albeit that it arguably has been asserted less often. Thus, Japan referred in 1981 to collective self-defence as 'the *right* [of the co-defending state] to use actual force to stop an armed attack on a foreign country'.[165] Following 9/11 in 2001, New Zealand,[166] Canada[167] and Poland[168] were all explicit that they were exercising *their* inherent right/droit naturel by using force in response to the attack on the United States. Even more recently, unlike the Netherlands, Denmark was clear in 2016 in relation to its action against ISIL, that *it* was acting 'in exercise of the *inherent right* of collective self-defence'.[169] In 2022, collective self-defence was described in the UK Parliament as the 'democratic right' of co-defending states.[170]

Overall, then, it seems clear that states view collective self-defence as a right held by both defending and co-defending states. A combination of the text of Article 51 and the positions taken by states (and, to a lesser extent, scholars) have established that both actors hold this inherent right irrespective of the fact that this is perhaps logically (and certainly historically) debatable.

1.4 The Modality of Collective Self-Defence: Acts *Minoris Generis*

The final section of this chapter considers a rather more specific question about the delineation of the concept of collective self-defence than

163 *Ibid.*

164 UN Doc. S/PV.827, n.28, para. 44 (emphasis added).

165 Japan, interpretation of Article 9, n.39.

166 UN Doc. S/2001/1193, n.63 ('New Zealand has joined other States in the exercise of *its inherent right* of individual and *collective* self-defence following the terrorist attacks in the United States of America on 11 September 2001', emphasis added).

167 UN Doc. S/2001/1005, n.85 ('[l]e Canada agit ainsi dans *l'exercice de son droit naturel* de légitime défense individuelle *et collective*, conformément à l'Article 51 de la Charte des Nations Unies', emphasis added).

168 UN Doc. S/2002/275, n.85 ('... conformément *au droit naturel* de légitime défense, individuelle ou collective (Art. 51 de la Charte des Nations Unies) ...', emphasis added).

169 Letter dated 11 January 2016 from the Permanent Representative of Denmark to the United Nations addressed to the President of the Security Council, UN Doc. S/2016/34 (13 January 2016) (emphasis added).

170 *Hansard*, vol. 706, n.36, col. 231.

previous sections. This is the question of exactly what action on the part of a co-defending state will constitute an instance of collective self-defence. It has already been said that, simply put, collective self-defence can be defined as involving situations where the defending state is attacked, and the co-defending state (or states) responds with the use of force in their defence.[171] The response taken by the co-defending state(s) therefore will, itself, amount to a use of force, albeit a legally permissible one. Self-defence, including collective self-defence, 'almost by its very nature involves the use of armed force',[172] meaning that collective self-defence is fundamentally characterised by the fact that it is 'an exception to the prohibition against the use of force in international relations . . .'[173]

This conclusion begs the question of what constitutes a 'use of force' under the *jus ad bellum*, as prohibited by Article 2(4) of the UN Charter and customary international law. This question is not one that is specific to collective self-defence. It has been repeatedly explored throughout the UN era,[174] and that analysis has involved engaging with a number of sub-questions.[175] Indeed, it has been said that the meaning of 'force' in the *jus*

[171] See n.1 and accompanying text; Introduction, nn.4–6 and accompanying text.

[172] Report of the International Law Commission, 32nd sess., UN Doc. A/35/10 (1980).

[173] Text of the Draft Articles on Responsibility of States for Internationally Wrongful Acts, with commentaries, Report of the International Law Commission, 53rd sess., UN Doc. A/56/10 (2001), 74 (commentary to Article 21) (referring to self-defence in general, both individual and collective). Having said this, see *ibid* ('[s]elf-defence may justify non-performance of certain obligations other than that under Article 2, paragraph 4, of the Charter of the United Nations, provided that such non-performance is related to the breach of that provision'); Russell Buchan, 'Non-Forcible Measures and the Law of Self-Defence' (2023) 72 *International and Comparative Law Quarterly* 1 (arguing that actions in self-defence – including collective self-defence – can be non-forcible in nature); James A. Green and Francis Grimal, 'The Threat of Force as an Action in Self-Defense under International Law (2011) 44 *Vanderbilt Journal of Transnational Law* 285 (arguing that an otherwise unlawful *threat* of force could amount to a lawful action in self-defence).

[174] For discussion, see, for example, ILA, Use of Force Committee (2010–2018), Final Report on Aggression and the Use of Force, Sydney Conference (2018), https://ila.vettoreweb.com/Storage/Download.aspx?DbStorageId=11391&StorageFileGuid=6a499340-074d-4d4b-851b-7a56871175d6, 4–5; Henderson, n.91, 50–81; Andrzej Jacewicz, 'The Concept of Force in the United Nations Charter' (1977–1978) 9 *Polish Yearbook of International Law* 137.

[175] One might note, for example, the question of whether 'economic force' or 'political force' amounts to a violation of the prohibition of 'force' (see, e.g. James A. Delanis, '"Force" under Article 2(4) of the United Nations Charter: The Question of Economic and Political Coercion' (1979) 12 *Vanderbilt Journal of Transnational Law* 101; Tom J. Farer, 'Political and Economic Coercion in Contemporary International Law' (1985) 79 *American Journal of International Law* 40); the more recent equivalent question of whether 'cyber force' counts (see, e.g. Michael N. Schmitt, 'Computer Network Attack

ad bellum is 'the subject of controversy par excellence in international law'.[176] This is, therefore, certainly not the place to engage with the meaning of 'force' in international law in general.

However, it is necessary briefly to touch on the meaning of the use of force in the specific context of the actions that states take in the (avowed) defence of others, as this directly engages what has been referred to as the 'modality of collective self-defence'.[177] In particular, Gray has argued that the dispatch of 'other aid' by third-party states to an attacked state requesting help has been 'much more common than the use of . . . troops in actual fighting against an attacking state'.[178] In other words, co-defending states have at times – indeed, quite commonly – provided *minoris generis* assistance (e.g. supplying weapons, providing logistical support, etc.) to defending states, while stopping short of dispatching troops. The question is whether such *minoris generis* assistance to a state

and the Use of Force in International Law: Thoughts on a Normative Framework' (1999) 37 *Columbia Journal of Transnational Law* 885; James A. Green, 'The Regulation of Cyber Warfare under the *Jus ad Bellum*', in James A. Green (ed.), *Cyber Warfare: A Multidisciplinary Analysis* (Abingdon, Routledge, 2015), 96, 98–107); and the debate over whether there is, in general, a *de minimis* threshold for acts to qualify as 'force' (see, e.g. Tom Ruys, 'The Meaning of Force and the Boundaries of the *Jus ad Bellum*: Are Minimal Uses of Force Excluded from UN Charter Article 2(4)?' (2014) 108 *American Journal of International Law* 159; Mary Ellen O'Connell, 'The True Meaning of Force' (2014) 108 *AJIL Unbound* 141; Tom Ruys, 'The True Meaning of Force: A Reply to Mary Ellen O'Connell' (2014) 108 *AJIL Unbound* 148; Mary Ellen O'Connell, 'The True Meaning of Force: A Further Response to Tom Ruys in the Interest of Peace' (2014) 108 *AJIL Unbound* 153; Olivier Corten, *The Law against War: The Prohibition on the Use of Force in Contemporary International Law* (Oxford, Hart Publishing, 2nd ed., 2021), 62–90).

176 Pål Wrange, 'Law, Force and Contingency – Notes on a Bold Monograph on Article 2(4) and the Problems of Finding a Proper Basis for International Legal Reasoning' (1992–1993) 61 *Nordic Journal of International Law* 83, 83.

177 Dinstein, n.11, 321–323. It is worth noting that Dinstein is here referring to different 'modalities' to what is being discussed in this section. In particular, he claims that some of the actions that are permitted under individual self-defence, such as the protection of nationals abroad (see, generally, Thomas C. Wingfield, 'Forcible Protection of Nationals Abroad' (1999–2000) 104 *Dickinson Law Review* 447; Tom Ruys, 'The "Protection of Nationals" Doctrine Revisited' (2008) 13 *Journal of Conflict and Security Law* 233; James A. Green, 'Passportisation, Peacekeepers and Proportionality: The Russian Claim of the Protection of Nationals Abroad in Self-Defence', in James A. Green and Christopher P. M. Waters (eds.), *Conflict in the Caucasus: Implications for International Legal Order* (Basingstoke, Palgrave Macmillan, 2010), 54), are not permitted in the exercise of collective self-defence. There is no basis for this claim in practice and, indeed, the 'conjoining' of individual and collective self-defence in Article 51 (see Section 2.4) makes such distinctions conceptually untenable.

178 Gray, n.3, 177.

suffering an armed attack, amounts, *in itself*, to an instance of collective self-defence. As Kreß phrases this, what is:

> the point at which support for the use of force by another State amounts to a use of force by the supporting State. For as soon as a State uses force, it must be able to rely on an exception to the prohibition of the use of force [such as collective self-defence]. If, however, a State merely assists another State in that latter's use of force, this assistance is lawful without a need to rely on an exception, provided that the supported use of force itself is lawful. *The delineation in question is not crystal clear.*[179]

The 1986 *Nicaragua* decision suggests that *minoris generis* assistance would indeed be enough to qualify as an instance of collective self-defence. In *Nicaragua*, the ICJ was of the view that, while such activity did not constitute an 'armed attack' sufficient to trigger the right of self-defence, 'assistance to rebels in the form of the provision of weapons or logistical or other support … may be regarded as a threat or use of force'.[180] As a result, the ICJ concluded that 'the arming and training of the *contras* [by the US] can certainly be said to involve the threat or use of force against Nicaragua'.[181] It then went on to consider whether 'the acts in question of the United States are *justified by the exercise of its right of collective self-defence* …'[182] Although the Court concluded that such actions by the United States could not be justified in this way, this was on the basis that Nicaragua had not perpetrated an armed attack triggering the exercise of the right of self-defence.[183] The clear implication of all this being that the Court was of the view that if the other legal criteria *had* been met, the arming and training of the *contras* by the United States *would have* been justified as an action of collective self-defence.

The ICJ's conclusion that the provision of weapons or logistical support can qualify as a use of 'force' has not generally been controversial in the literature.[184] As with any view expressed by the Court, though, this

[179] Claus Kreß, 'The Ukraine War and the Prohibition of the Use of Force in International Law' (2022) *Torkel Opsahl Academic EPublisher, Occasional Paper Series* No. 13, 1, 15 (emphasis added).

[180] *Nicaragua* (merits), n.12, para. 195.

[181] *Ibid*, para. 228.

[182] *Ibid*, para. 229 (emphasis added).

[183] *Ibid*, paras. 229–238.

[184] See, for example, Louis B. Sohn, 'How New Is the New International Legal Order?' (1992) 20 *Denver Journal of International Law and Policy* 205, 210; Gill, n.43, 65; Azubuike, n.55, 178; Abdul Ghafur Hamid and Khin Maung Sein, 'Combating Terrorism and the Use of Force against a State: A Relook at the Contemporary World

reading of the law is not necessarily conclusive.[185] Indeed, it might be noted that elsewhere in the *Nicaragua* judgment,[186] the Court held that the *funding* of an insurgent group (as opposed to arming or training them) did *not* constitute a use of force.[187] For this author, drawing such a distinction between giving weapons to a group and giving them the money to buy weapons feels like splitting hairs, and there is no clear basis for it in practice.[188]

Some scholars have argued, *contra* the Court, that not only funding but also the provision of material assistance falls below the level of a use of force.[189] Indeed, the present writer himself has previously expressed scepticism of this aspect of the *Nicaragua* decision, stating, in an article co-authored with Francis Grimal, that:

> [i]t is unlikely that either the provision of weapons or other forms of logistical support involve the actual use of force. For example, if state A supplies machine guns to a paramilitary organization for use against state B, there has been no use of force by state A against state B, even indirectly.[190]

Others have pointed out that the Court's pronouncement in this regard relates specifically to the provision of such support to a non-state actor, in the context of a non-international armed conflict.[191] This is perhaps

Order' (2015) 8 *Journal of East Asia and International Law* 107, 111. To the extent that there has been critique of this aspect of the decision, it has largely been focused on the idea that the provision of weapons and logistical support should *not only* have been viewed as a use of force by the ICJ but *also* as an armed attack. See, for example, *Nicaragua* (merits), n.12, dissenting opinion of Judge Schwebel, para. 171; Nicholas Rostow, '*Nicaragua* and the Law of Self-Defense Revisited' (1986) 11 *Yale Journal of International Law* 437, 453; John Norton Moore, 'The Secret War in Central America and the Future of World Order' (1986) 80 *American Journal of International Law* 43, 89.

185 See Statute of the International Court of Justice (1945) 33 UNTS 93, Article 59 ('[t]he decision of the Court has no binding force except between the parties and in respect of that particular case'); James A. Green, *The International Court of Justice and Self-Defence in International Law* (Oxford, Hart Publishing, 2009), 24–25.

186 *Nicaragua* (merits), n.12, paras. 228, 242.

187 See discussion in Green, n.185, 36–37.

188 Henderson, n.91, 61.

189 See, for example, Paul S. Reichler and David Wippman, 'United States Armed Intervention in *Nicaragua*: A Rejoinder' (1986) 11 *Yale Journal of International Law* 462, 470–471; Green and Grimal, n.173, 293.

190 Green and Grimal, n.173, 293.

191 See, for example, Kreß, n.179, 16; Michael N. Schmitt, 'Providing Arms and Materiel to Ukraine: Neutrality, Co-Belligerency, and the Use of Force', *Articles of War* (7 March 2022), https://lieber.westpoint.edu/ukraine-neutrality-co-belligerency-use-of-force.

not a material difference in terms of the logic of the ICJ's analysis,[192] but state practice suggests that it is far less clear that material support by one state to another, in relation to an international armed conflict, is rightly to be considered a violation of Article 2(4) of the UN Charter. For example, Acevedo has noted that the logistical and military assistance that was provided by the United States to support the United Kingdom in its exercise of individual self-defence in the Falklands/Malvinas conflict of 1982 was not considered to amount to an exercise of collective self-defence.[193] Moreover, he took the view that it *could not have been*, as it did not amount to a use of force.[194] It also has been noted[195] that while the 1970 Friendly Relations Declaration makes it clear that support for non-state actors can constitute an indirect 'use of force',[196] there is no equivalent provision (therein, or elsewhere) in relation to assistance provided to another state.

This is not to say that practice in this regard is entirely clear, nor that it conclusively establishes that *minoris generis* assistance will fall short of being a measure of collective self-defence. For example, in 2008, the European Union, in the abstract, appeared to view the provision of 'military technology and equipment' as potentially amounting to an exercise of the right of self-defence, in that it concluded that '[s]tates have a right to transfer the means of self-defence, consistent with the right of self-defence recognised by the UN Charter'.[197] It is possible to

[192] Schmitt, n.191 (albeit noting that the Court's 'position on arming and training is not definitively settled', ultimately concluding that 'the logic of the court's holding arguably applies equally to IAC, for if arming and training a non-State group fighting a State is a use of force ... why would it not also be a use of force to provide arms to another State engaging in hostilities against that State? After all, the harm to the State could be much more severe, thereby meriting equal protection by international law').

[193] Domingo E. Acevedo, 'Collective Self-Defense and the Use of Regional or Subregional Authority as Justification for the Use of Force' (1984) 78 *American Society of International Law Proceedings* 69, 71.

[194] *Ibid.*

[195] Kreß, n.179, 16, footnote 73.

[196] Declaration on Principles of International Law Concerning Friendly Relations and Co-operation among States in Accordance with the Charter of the United Nations, UNGA Res. 2625 (XXV), UN Doc. A/RES/2625 (24 October 1970) annex.

[197] Council of the European Union, 'Council Common Position 2008/944/CFSP of 8 December 2008 defining common rules governing control of exports of military technology and equipment', *Official Journal of the European Union* (13 December 2008), recital 12.

read this as referring to the idea that the provider of the equipment merely is facilitating the defending state's right of individual self-defence, but it also certainly is possible to read it as a reference to the transfer of arms being an exercise, in itself, of collective self-defence.[198]

The question of whether the mere provision of weapons and/or logistical support to a defending state requesting aid in relation to an armed attack amounts to an exercise of collective self-defence thus remains unsettled. It is a question that has taken on a particular pertinence at the time of writing, following Russia's full-scale invasion of Ukraine, which began in February 2022, and currently is ongoing. Since that invasion started, the North Atlantic Treaty Organization (NATO) member states, the European Union, and other Western states have provided significant aid to Ukraine in the form, *inter alia*, of the supply of modern weapons and training.[199] This support, too, is ongoing at the time of writing.[200] Equally, and – again – as of the time of writing, NATO states have stopped short of imposing a no-fly zone, which would necessarily constitute a direct use of force against Russia.[201] They also have stopped *well* short of NATO boots on the ground. The question is thus whether NATO member states (and others) nonetheless are *already* acting in collective self-defence.[202]

198 See, for example, Tomas Hamilton, 'Defending Ukraine with EU Weapons: Arms Control Law in Times of Crisis' (2022) 1 *European Law Open* 635, 642; Kevin Jon Heller and Lena Trabucco, 'The Legality of Weapons Transfers to Ukraine Under International Law' (2022) 13 *Journal of International Humanitarian Legal Studies* 251, 254, footnote 14.

199 See, generally, Claire Mills, 'Military Assistance to Ukraine Since the Russian Invasion', *House of Commons Library*, Research Briefing (17 October 2022).

200 See David Brown, Jake Horton and Tural Ahmedzade, 'Ukraine Weapons: What Tanks and Other Equipment Are the World Giving?', *BBC News* (18 February 2023), www.bbc.co.uk/news/world-europe-62002218. It is also worth noting that, at the time of writing, it is clear that China has been providing 'non-lethal support' to Russia, and there have been suggestions that it may soon begin to provide 'lethal support', perhaps of closer equivalence to that being provided to Ukraine by NATO states and others. However, as of February 2023, this remains speculative. See 'Ukraine War: What Support is China Giving Russia?', *BBC News* (21 February 2023), www.bbc.co.uk/news/60571253.

201 See Mark Nevitt, 'The Operational and Legal Risks of a No-Fly Zone Over Ukrainian Skies', *Just Security* (10 March 2022), www.justsecurity.org/80641/the-operational-and-legal-risks-of-a-no-fly-zone-over-ukrainian-skies; Schmitt, n.191.

202 Some scholars certainly have taken the view that the actions of Western states in supporting Ukraine in 2022 amounted to the exercise of collective self-defence. See, for example, Agnieszka Szpak *et al.*, 'Reaction to the Russian Aggression against Ukraine: Cities as International Standards' Supporters' (2022) *Journal of Contemporary European*

The legal requirements for the collective self-defence – as will be discussed in future chapters – generally would seem to be present in relation to the situation in Ukraine in 2022. There is little question that Russia's invasion is an unlawful use of force[203] rising to the level of an armed attack.[204] The provision of support would seem necessary and proportionate.[205] Ukraine has *undoubtedly* requested aid.[206] Indeed, the only notable 'absentee' from the checklist for lawful collective self-defence would seem to be the failure of NATO states (and others) to report their actions in support of Ukraine to the UN Security Council.[207]

Of course, the fact that the states supporting Ukraine have not reported their acts as instances of collective self-defence is, itself, an indication that they do not consider themselves to be acting in collective self-defence in the first place.[208] Instead, their actions have been conceived of as support for Ukraine's right of individual self-defence. NATO has indicated that its members are 'helping [Ukraine] to uphold its fundamental right to self-defence',[209] rather than itself invoking collective self-defence. Individual member states have made the same point, with US President Joe Biden saying that the alliance has been 'delivering

Studies, advance access version, www.tandfonline.com/doi/full/10.1080/14782804.2022.2126445, 2; Hamilton, n.198, 637, 641–644, 654; Heller and Trabucco, n.198, 254–255. Others have taken the opposite view. See, for example, Kreß, n.179, 12–19; James A. Green, 'The Provision of Weapons and Logistical Support to Ukraine and the *Jus ad Bellum*' (2023) 10 *Journal on the Use of Force and International Law* 3; Pavel Doubek, 'War in Ukraine: Time for a Collective Self-Defense?', *Opinio Juris* (29 March 2022), http://opiniojuris.org/2022/03/29/war-in-ukraine-time-for-a-collective-self-defense.

203 See James A. Green, Christian Henderson and Tom Ruys, 'Russia's Attack on Ukraine and the *Jus ad Bellum*' (2022) 9 *Journal on the Use of Force and International Law* 4.

204 Heller and Trabucco, n.198, 254, 273. On the armed attack requirement for collective self-defence, see Section 3.2.

205 Doubek, n.202. On the necessity and proportionality requirements for collective self-defence, see Section 3.3.

206 See, for example, 'Ukraine's Zelenskiy Urges West to Consider No-Fly Zone for Russian Aircraft', *Reuters* (28 February 2022), www.reuters.com/world/europe/ukraines-zelenskiy-says-it-is-time-consider-no-fly-zone-russian-aircraft-2022-02-28. On the request requirement for collective self-defence, see Chapters 4–6.

207 On the reporting requirement for collective self-defence, see Section 3.4.

208 Kreß, n.179, 15–16 (making this point specifically with regard to Germany, but it applies to all of the states in question).

209 'NATO's response to Russia's invasion of Ukraine', *North Atlantic Treaty Organization*, statement (last updated 18 October 2022), www.nato.int/cps/en/natohq/topics_192648.htm.

critical military capabilities to Ukraine so it can defend itself',[210] while German Foreign Minister Annalena Baerbock stated that 'sei die Lieferung schwerer Waffen kein Kriegseintritt, weil damit das in der UN-Charta verbriefte Recht der Ukraine auf Selbstverteidigung unterstützt werde'.[211] Indeed, the German government has explicitly asserted that neither Germany nor its partners are acting in collective self-defence:

> Die Bundesrepublik Deutschland und ihre Partner unterstützen die Ukraine durch die Lieferung von Waffen bei der Ausübung ihres individuellen Selbstverteidigungsrechts gegen den völkerrechtswidrigen Angriffskrieg Russlands. Diese völkerrechtskonformen Unterstützungsmaßnahmen *überschreiten nicht die Schwelle zu einer kollektiven Ausübung des Selbstverteidigungsrechts.*[212]

This position is perhaps unsurprising, given the significant and inherent risks of any direct confrontation – actual or just perceived – between nuclear powers. Belligerent status to a conflict and the exercise of collective self-defence are differing legal considerations that do not necessarily overlap; indeed, the common view in scholarship is that the provision of weapons is, itself, insufficient to establish co-belligerency under International Humanitarian Law.[213] Therefore, even if one takes the view that such actions do amount to collective self-defence this would still not mean that states supplying weapons to Ukraine have thereby become parties to the conflict. However, in practice – and, crucially, in terms of perception – if a state can be said to be *using force* (even if it is doing so lawfully in collective self-defence) this certainly would provide an

[210] 'Statement from the President on Delivery of Air Defense Systems to Ukraine', *The White House*, Briefing Room, Statements and Releases (8 April 2022), www.whitehouse.gov/briefing-room/statements-releases/2022/04/08/statement-from-the-president-on-delivery-of-air-defense-systems-to-ukraine.

[211] 'Baerbock zur Hilfe für Ukraine: Panzerlieferung war "kein Schnellschuss"', *Tagesschau* (27 April 2022), www.tagesschau.de/inland/bundestag-baerbock-101.html.

[212] *Deutscher Bundestag*, Drucksache 20/1918, Susanne Baumann (Secretary of State at the Federal Foreign Office) (18 May 2022), 39 (response to question 56) (emphasis added).

[213] Heller and Trabucco, n.198, 265; Alexander Wentker, 'At War: When Do States Supporting Ukraine or Russia Become Parties to the Conflict and What Would that Mean?', *EJIL:Talk!* (14 March 2022), www.ejiltalk.org/at-war-when-do-states-supporting-ukraine-or-russia-become-parties-to-the-conflict-and-what-would-that-mean. See also James Upcher, *Neutrality in Contemporary International Law* (Oxford, Oxford University Press, 2020), 57–63 (albeit making this point in relation to indirect participation more generally and giving the example of logistical and financial support rather than the provisions of weapons specifically).

opposing belligerent state a greater basis to advance a case that it had become a party to the conflict (meaning, not least, that it could be targeted).[214] NATO states have understandably been extremely wary of any implication that they may have become parties to the conflict in Ukraine,[215] so it is hardly a shock that they have been keen to avoid, and in some instances have outright denied, any suggestion that they have been acting in collective self-defence.

Even in this context there have been some mixed messages, however. The European Parliament, for example, adopted a report in June 2022 that asserted that 'partners and allies should step up their military support to Ukraine and their provision of weapons, which is in line with Article 51 of the UN Charter that allows individual *and collective* self-defence'.[216] This at least implies that the European Union may already consider Western support for Ukraine to be an exercise in collective self-defence – although this is unclear and could just have been a rote reiteration of the wording of Article 51.

Ultimately, this author is of the view that the mere provision of *minoris generis* assistance does not constitute an exercise of collective self-defence, either in the case of Western support that is currently – at the time of writing – being provided to Ukraine or in general.[217] Predominantly, this is because there is little evidence that states themselves perceive such action in these terms: again, whether in the specific case of Ukraine in 2022 or in previous practice. This is not to say that the provision of weapons or logistical support to a defending state is an inherently lawful action irrespective of whether it complies with the requirements for collective self-defence. For example, it is likely to engage difficult questions regarding the law of neutrality.[218] However, such

[214] Jack Detsch and Robbie Gramer, 'Biden Administration Debates Legality of Arming Ukrainian Resistance', *Foreign Policy* (24 February 2022), https://foreignpolicy.com/2022/02/24/biden-legal-ukraine-russia-resistance; Kreß, n.179, 14.

[215] Lauren Turner, 'Ukraine Invasion: UK Troops Will Not Fight against Russia Says Wallace', *BBC News* (25 February 2022), www.bbc.co.uk/news/uk-60522745.

[216] European Parliament Resolution of 8 June 2022 on Security in the Eastern Partnership Area and the Role of the Common Security and Defence Policy (2021/2199(INI)), Texts adopted P9_TA(2022)0236, www.europarl.europa.eu/doceo/document/TA-9-2022-0236_EN.html, T. See also UNSC Provisional Verbatim Record, UN Doc. S/PV.9301 (10 April 2023), 21 (Poland, stating that it was 'proud to be a part of the world's collective self-defence against the trespasser trampling on the most fundamental principles of the United Nations Charter').

[217] See Green, n.202.

[218] Enzo Cannizzaro and Aurora Rasi, 'Europe at War' (2022), (2021) 6 *European Papers* 1523, 1523–1524; Schmitt, n.191; Heller and Trabucco, n.198, 255–263; Kreß, n.179, 16–19.

action is not in this author's view an unlawful use of force, and thus need not be (and, moreover, *cannot* be) an instance of collective self-defence. It must be accepted, though, that this conclusion is open to question, because of the position taken by the ICJ in 1986 (as well as the degree of support for it in scholarship since) and – more importantly – because the state practice can hardly be said to be entirely clear in this regard.

1.5 Conclusion

This chapter has explored the ways in which collective self-defence has been, and should be, conceived. Despite a wide range of claims that the co-defending state must possess some interest in engaging in collective self-defence, there is no basis for this in law. In particular, states have been very clear that collective self-defence can be exercised without any need for the co-defending state to have itself been attacked, be part of a treaty arrangement with the defending state or be able to demonstrate a degree of proximity (or other interest). Instead, collective self-defence actually should be conceived of as the 'defence of another' doctrine. This conclusion is reflected in both scholarship and practice.

This defence of another conception does, however, sit uneasily with the finding reached in Section 1.3 of this chapter, which is that collective self-defence is an inherent right not just for the defending state but also for the co-defending state. If some form of 'interest' was required, then it would be more logical that the state in question would possess the right to defend that interest. Absent the need for such an interest, it is not entirely clear why coming to the aid of another state should correctly be viewed as an inherent right, beyond the fact that Article 51 and the majority of states and scholars say that it is one. This is, however, perhaps enough, so long as this does not impinge on the requirement that any such 'right' is qualified by the need for a request on the part of the defending state.

Finally, it is argued that the mere provision of *minoris generis* assistance, such as weapons or logistical support, does not in itself constitute an action of collective self-defence. This conclusion is tentatively reached, and open to challenge, but state practice suggests that such assistance – as in the case of Western support for Ukraine in 2022 – will not be considered as rising to the level of a collective self-defence action.

Chapter 2 builds on the understanding of the modern right of collective self-defence that has been set out herein by considering the history and development of the concept.

2

The History and Development of Collective Self-Defence

2.1 Introduction

Having attempted to delineate the meaning of the modern concept of collective self-defence in Chapter 1, this chapter seeks to interrogate further its nature by exploring its history and development up to and including the adoption of the United Nations (UN) Charter in 1945.

Two claims are made about the historical origins of the modern right of collective self-defence that have been repeated so often in the literature since 1945 that both have become almost rote. The first of these claims is that collective self-defence – indeed, Article 51 and the right of self-defence *in toto* – was only included in the Charter *at all* in response to concerns raised by Latin American states that existing mutual defence treaties (notably, but not solely, the then freshly minted Act of Chapultepec)[1] might be incompatible with the collective security system being introduced by the Charter.[2] The second oft-repeated claim is that

[1] Inter-American Reciprocal Assistance and Solidarity (1945), resolution approved by the Inter-American Conference on Problems of War and Peace at Mexico, 60 Stat. 1831 (Act of Chapultepec).

[2] See, for example, Murray Colin Alder, *The Inherent Right of Self-Defence in International Law* (Dordrecht, Springer, 2013), 86–87; Joseph L. Kunz, 'Individual and Collective Self-Defence under Article 51 of the Charter of the United Nations' (1947) 41 *American Journal of International Law* 872, 872; Christian Henderson, *The Use of Force and International Law* (Cambridge, Cambridge University Press, 2018), 205–206; Terry D. Gill and Kinga Tibori-Szabó, 'Twelve Key Questions on Self-Defense against Non-state Actors' (2019) 95 *International Law Studies* 467, 474; Oscar Schachter, *International Law in Theory and Practice* (Dordrecht, Martinus Nijhoff, 1991), 155; Christian Wyse, 'The African Union's Right of Humanitarian Intervention as Collective Self-Defense' (2018) 19 *Chicago Journal of International Law* 295, 305; D. W. Greig, 'Self-Defence and the Security Council: What Does Article 51 Require?' (1991) 40 *International and Comparative Law Quarterly* 366, 370; C. H. M. Waldock, 'The Regulation of the Use of Force by Individual States in International Law' (1952) 81 *Recueil des cours* 451, 497, 503; Constantine Antonopoulos, 'Some Thoughts on the NATO Position in Relation to the Iraqi Crisis' (2004) 17 *Leiden Journal of International Law* 171, 175; Christine Gray, *International Law and the Use of Force* (Oxford, Oxford University Press, 4th ed., 2018),

the drafters of the UN Charter created a 'new' concept when they included collective self-defence in Article 51. As Judge Jennings phrased this view in his dissenting opinion to the International Court of Justice's 1986 *Nicaragua* merits decision, 'Article 51 … introduced a novel concept in speaking of "collective self-defence"'.[3]

These two common claims may appear mutually contradictory: the idea that the UN Charter 'invented' collective self-defence as a way of preserving pre-existing collective self-defence arrangements is, on its face at least, illogical. This incongruity feels especially stark in instances where the same scholar has made both claims in the same publication,[4] or even in the same sentence.[5] On a basic level, the contradiction here can be

179; A. L. Goodhart, 'The North Atlantic Treaty of 1949' (1951) 79 *Recueil des cours* 182, 211; Avra Constantinou, *The Right of Self-Defence under Customary International Law and Article 51 of the UN Charter* (Brussels, Bruylant, 2000), 173; Edward McWhinney, 'President Bush and the New U.S. National Security Strategy: The Continuing Relevance of the Legal Advisor and International Law' (2002) 1 *Chinese Journal of International Law* 421, 429–430; Robert W. Tucker, 'The Interpretation of War under Present International Law' (1951) 4 *International Law Quarterly* 11, 29; Zia Modabber, 'Collective Self-Defense: *Nicaragua v. United States*' (1988) 10 *Loyola of Los Angeles International and Comparative Law Journal* 449, 456; Jane A. Meyer, 'Collective Self-Defense and Regional Security: Necessary Exceptions to a Globalist Doctrine' (1993) 11 *Boston University International Law Journal* 391, 394; Thomas M. Franck, *Recourse to Force: State Action against Threats and Armed Attacks* (Cambridge, Cambridge University Press, 2002), 48; Dino Kritsiotis, 'A Study of the Scope and Operation of the Rights of Individual and Collective Self-Defence under International Law', in Nigel D. White and Christian Henderson (eds.), *Research Handbook on International Conflict and Security Law:* Jus ad Bellum, Jus in Bello *and* Jus Post Bellum (Abingdon, Routledge, 2013), 170, 171–172; John A. Perkins, 'The Right of Counterintervention' (1987) 17 *Georgia Journal of International and Comparative Law* 171, 198–199, 206; Aadhithi Padmanabhan and Michael Shih, 'Collective Self-Defense: A Report of the Yale Law School Center for Global Legal Challenges' (10 December 2012), https://law.yale.edu/sites/default/files/documents/pdf/cglc/GLC_Collective_SelfDefense.pdf, 5.

3 *Military and Paramilitary Activities in and against Nicaragua* (*Nicaragua v. United States of America*) (merits) [1986] ICJ Rep. 14, dissenting opinion of Judge Jennings, 530–531. See also, for example, R. St. J. MacDonald, 'The *Nicaragua* Case: New Answers to Old Questions' (1986) 24 *Canadian Yearbook of International Law* 127, 143, 146; Rosalyn Higgins, *The Development of International Law through the Political Organs of the United Nations* (London, Oxford University Press, 1963), 208; Stephen C. Neff, *War and the Law of Nations: A General History* (Cambridge, Cambridge University Press, 2005), 326; Henderson, n.2, 260; Greig, n.2, 373; Franck, n.2, 48–49; Gray, n.2, 179 (unsure '[w]hether or not collective self-defence was a *totally new concept*' in 1945, emphasis added); Stuart Casey-Maslen, Jus ad Bellum: *The Law on Inter-State Use of Force* (Oxford, Hart, 2020), 75 (albeit somewhat equivocal in expressing this view).

4 See, for example, Greig, n.2, 370, 373; Henderson, n.2, 205–206, 260.

5 Arthur Eyffinger, 'Self-Defence or the Meanderings of a Protean Principle', in Arthur Eyffinger, Alan Stephens, and Sam Muller (eds.), *Self-Defence as a Fundamental Principle*

explained by the fact that one of the two ubiquitous claims is incorrect. It *is* correct – albeit a little simplistic – to say that Article 51 was included in the Charter and drafted as it was (including the conceptualisation of collective self-defence therein) due 'in significant measure'[6] to the concerns expressed during drafting by Latin American states regarding the preservation of regional mutual defence agreements. However, it is *incorrect* to say that the drafters of the UN Charter 'invented' the concept of collective self-defence. In fact, it has a long history.

In fairness to the writers who initially appear to have advanced contradictory claims regarding the history of collective self-defence, it is clear that the concept was substantially altered by its appearance in Article 51. This was, in particular, in the way that it was 'conjoined' with individual self-defence. As such, assertions of 'newness' in 1945 are not entirely off the mark either, but they must be carefully nuanced. The blunt assertion that collective self-defence was a wholly new concept in 1945[7] is wrong.

This chapter starts, in Section 2.2, by mapping out the history of 'collective self-defence' prior to the First World War. The core concept can actually be traced back many centuries, although more of its modern contours are observable in the writings and – to a lesser extent – practice from the seventeenth century onwards. Section 2.3 considers developments in the interwar years (as well as during the Second World War itself). This period saw a notable increase in the number of collective defence treaties, trends towards increased specificity in their drafting, and, in the shape of the League of Nations, the first meaningful attempt to centralise some aspects of the 'collective defence' concept. The interwar years also saw some tentative indications of a growing association between collective defence and '*self*-defence' properly so called. The period concluded with the emergence of a regional collective defence system in the Americas, which, as already touched on, was soon to be hugely influential in the drafting of Article 51 of the UN Charter. Section 2.4 concludes this chapter by analysing the drafting process and the changes to the concept of collective self-defence that the UN Charter brought about. Most importantly, it is argued that Article 51 'conjoined'

(The Hague, Hague Academic Press, 2009), 103, 128 ('[p]revailing regional arrangements, notably in Latin-America, also lay at the base of that other puzzling novelty first introduced at San Francisco', collective self-defence).

6 Kritsiotis, n.2, 171.

7 See sources cited at n.3.

individual and collective self-defence in a way that had little basis in the previous historical development of the latter concept. This has had significant implications for how collective self-defence is understood today.

2.2 The Concept of 'Collective Self-Defence' before the First World War

2.2.1 *The Early History of 'Collective Self-Defence'*

As was briefly noted in Chapter 1, modern understandings of collective self-defence have, in part, been influenced by the 'defence of others' concept as it existed, historically, at the level of the individual citizen.[8] This was an element of Roman law,[9] as well as, later, an aspect of the medieval European recognition of a master's 'privilege' to defend those within his household.[10] The historic importance of the defence of others in the context of the actions of individual persons is nicely highlighted by the fact that, in the fourth century, St Augustine considered the defence of another citizen (or of one's 'city') to be a greater moral imperative on a person than the defence of themself.[11]

The development of the idea of the legitimate defence of another *nation* drew from – and to an extent paralleled – the defence of others concept in relation to the individual citizen. Far from being a new concept, the mutual defence of nations has been a prominent aspect of international relations for many centuries. Indeed, it has been argued that the 'notion of a defensive alliance or defensive treaty is as old as recorded history'.[12] One might note, as good examples of the long standing historical pedigree of 'collective self-defence',[13] the agreement for mutual

[8] See Chapter 1, nn.70–71 and accompanying text.

[9] See Derek W. Bowett, 'Collective Self-Defence under the Charter of the United Nations' (1955–1956) 32 *British Yearbook of International Law* 130, 133.

[10] See Larry C. Wilson, 'The Defence of Others: Criminal Law and the Good Samaritan' (1988) 33 *McGill Law Journal* 756.

[11] See, for example, St. Augustine (Augustine of Hippo), in 'Letter 47', in John E. Rotelle (ed.), *The Works of Saint Augustine: A Translation for the 21st Century, Part II – Letters*, vol. 1, Letters 1–99 (Hyde Park NY, New City Press, 2001) (398 CE) (Roland Teske, trans. and notes), 187, 190, para. 5.

[12] M. A. Weightman, 'Self-Defense in International Law' (1951) 37 *Virginia Law Review* 1095, 1110.

[13] See Nicholas Tsagourias and Nigel D. White, *Collective Security: Theory, Law and Practice* (Cambridge, Cambridge University Press, 2013), 3–5 (albeit conceptualising

defence reached between Rome and Messina – primarily to deter an attack by Carthage – in 241 BCE,[14] or the alliance concluded in 395 BCE between Athens, Boeotia, and Locris, providing for the mutual obligation 'that a state, coming to the aid of the other state, is to help *with full force*, according to what need the state who is under attack from another state has announced'.[15]

2.2.2 'Collective Self-Defence' in the Writings of the Seventeenth and Eighteenth Centuries

Although defensive military alliances of one form or another stretch back into ancient history, from the seventeenth century onwards something that began to look, in a number of respects, rather more specifically like the modern right of collective self-defence began to take shape, at least in scholarship. Some key elements of UN era collective self-defence can be identified in classic international law writings from the seventeenth and eighteenth centuries. For example, in 1625, Grotius wrote that:

> our Allies [are] to be defended, when such a Defence is stipulated in the Articles of Treaty; and this, whether they have entirely given themselves up on the Account of such a Protection, and so depend upon it, or whether it be agreed on for a mutual Help and Security.[16]

Indeed, even where there was not a pre-existing formal relationship between the 'Prince' and their 'allies', Grotius still argued that there remained a just cause to act in collective defence:

> A ... Reason for War is the Protection of our Friends, whom tho' not under any formal Promise, yet upon the Score of Friendship we are under

the practice of forming military alliances in Ancient Greece as a weak form of collective security rather than collective defence).

14 See Patrick T. Warren, 'Alliance History and the Future NATO: What the Last 500 Years of Alliance Behavior Tells Us about NATO's Path Forward', 21st Century Defense Initiative Policy Paper, Foreign Policy at Brookings (30 June 2010), www.brookings.edu/wp-content/uploads/2016/06/0630_nato_alliance_warren.pdf, 11.

15 Quoted (from translation) in Berhard Meiβner, 'Ancient Greek Coalition Warfare: Classical and Hellenistic Examples' (2012) 14 *Journal of Military and Strategic Studies* 1, 7 (emphasis in original).

16 Hugo Grotius, *On the Law of War and Peace* (*De juri belli ac pacis libri tres*) (Richard Tuck, ed./Jean Barbeyrac, original ed. and French trans., John Morrice, English trans., Indianapolis, Liberty Fund, 2005 (1625)), Book II, chapter XXV, 1155, para. IV.

> an Obligation of assisting, provided we bring not ourselves into any great Trouble, and Inconveniences by it.[17]

In a similar vein, Pufendorf asserted that:

> Amongst those, in whose Behalf it is not only lawful, but our Duty to make War, there ... are the Allies, with whom we have engaged to associate our Arms by Treaty: ... if they should chance to stand in need of Assistance at the same Juncture; but presupposing also, that the Allies have a just Cause, and begin the War with Prudence.
>
> After our Allies, our Friends deserve to be assisted by us, even without our Obligation to do it by a special Promise.[18]

Such conceptions from the seventeenth century became further embedded in future writings. For example, Vattel, who was working in the eighteenth century, noted that 'it is very usual for alliances to be purely defensive: and these are in general the most natural and lawful'.[19] Importantly, he also added that restrictions applied to the exercise of defensive obligations arising from such treaty-based alliances, which are reminiscent of the modern requirements of necessity[20] and proportionality.[21]

These various writings, taken together, sketch out an understanding of the 'just war of collective defence'.[22] This was considered a *right* (rather than a duty – unless a duty had additionally been established by way of a

[17] *Ibid*, Book II, chapter XXV, 1156, para. V.

[18] Samuel von Pufendorf, *The Whole Duty of Man According to the Law of Nature* (*De officio hominis & civis juxta legem naturalem libri duo*) (Ian Hunter and David Saunders, eds./Jean Barbeyrac, original ed. and French trans., Andrew Tooke, English trans., Indianapolis, Liberty Fund, 2003 (1673)), chapter XVI, 242, LNN l. 8. c.6., XI, para. 14. See also Grotius, n.16, Book II, chapter XXV, 1152, para. II ('[a] Prince is not always obliged to take up Arms [to defend another]').

[19] Emer de Vattel, *The Law of Nations* (*Droit des gens*) (Béla Kapossy and Richard Whatmore, eds., Thomas Nugent, trans., Indianapolis, Liberty Fund, 2008 (1758)), Book III, chapter VI, 512, para. 79.

[20] See, for example, *ibid*, Book III, chapter VI, 515, para. 90 ('[i]n a defensive alliance, the *casus fœderis* does not exist immediately on our ally being attacked. It is still our duty to examine whether he has not given his enemy just cause to make war against him: for we cannot have engaged to undertake his defence with the view of enabling him to insult others or to refuse them justice. If he is in the wrong, we must induce him to offer a reasonable satisfaction; and if his enemy will not be contented with it, – then, and not till then, the obligation of defending him commences').

[21] See, for example, *ibid*, Book II, chapter XVII, 422, para. 286 ('in case one of the allies happen to be attacked by an enemy of considerably superior strength, and more powerful in cavalry, the succours shall be furnished in cavalry, and not in infantry, – it appears that, in this case, the promised assistance ought to be ten thousand horse').

[22] Weightman, n.12, 1110.

treaty of alliance) to defend another nation,[23] either because it was unable to defend itself or more generally in the interests of 'mutual Help and Security',[24] so long as this was necessary and the response was of a similar proportion to the wrong being responded to. Such an understanding has some obvious similarities with the right of collective self-defence as we understand it today.

It is important to treat these similarities with some caution, however. This is, first, because the sweeping understandings of the classical writers as to what could be appropriately 'defended' and *how* – notwithstanding occasional illusions to necessity and proportionality – could hardly be said to map on to the modern *ad bellum* (or, indeed, *in bello*).[25] Second, there is little indication in these writings that the opinion of the nation being defended mattered a great deal: in other words, scholars in the seventeenth and eighteenth centuries do not appear to have advanced any equivalent to the modern 'request' criterion (at least, beyond the mere existence of a treaty relationship as a measure of indication of sovereign will, where such a treaty were present).[26] Finally, while Grotius did argue in general terms that the 'Reasons that can justify a Man in undertaking a War for himself [are] the very same [that] can justify those who espouse the Cause of others',[27] ultimately, the writers in the seventeenth and eighteenth centuries viewed this 'defence of another nation' idea as conceptually distinct from *self*-defence truly so called.[28] Indeed, they viewed it as having more in common with the defence of a nation's own citizens as distinct from the nation itself.[29]

[23] See Tsagourias and White, n.13, 7 (noting that Grotius, at least, considered the defence of others to be a right).

[24] Grotius, n.16, Book II, chapter XXV, 1155, para. IV.

[25] See, for example, von Pufendorf, n.18, 242, LNN l. 8. c.6., XI, para. 18 (arguing that war – including in defence of others – could extend to 'killing, plundering, and laying all Things waste', albeit that 'poisoning Fountains, or corrupting of Soldiers or Subjects to kill their Masters' would be 'base' and thus go too far for civilised nations).

[26] On the request requirement, see Chapters 4–6. Specifically in relation to the possibility under the modern law of *ex ante* requests, premised solely on a pre-existing treaty relationship, see Section 6.5.2.

[27] Grotius, n.16, Book II, chapter XXV, 1151, para. I.

[28] See Weightman, n.12, 1110 (noting that 'Grotius did not … confuse this [defence of other nations] with self-defense, properly speaking').

[29] For example, Grotius devoted an entirely different chapter of *De juri belli ac pacis libri tres* to self-defence, whereas he included defence of one's own citizens alongside defence of other nations. See Grotius, n.16, Book II, chapter II, 389–419 (examining self-defence) and chapter XXV, 1151–1166 (examining the defence of citizens and other nations). Von Pufendorf, on the other hand, did examine self-defence (in the sense of nations rather than individuals, at least) and defence of others in the same chapter but, nonetheless,

2.2.3 'Collective Self-Defence' in Practice from the Seventeenth Century to the First World War

While a notably developed (and strikingly recognisable) concept of 'collective self-defence' can be identified in writings from the seventeenth century onwards, it must be said that, in *practice*, most of the defence treaties from the seventeenth century right the way through to the start of the First World War did not possess quite the same level of nuance. For example, the 1815 Treaty of Alliance and Friendship – which included four of Europe's great powers at the time and was drafted following the defeat of Napoleon – only quite vaguely set out 'mutually obligatory' undertakings to 'maintain in full vigour, and, should it be necessary, [act] with the whole of their Forces' to ensure 'the safety and interest of Europe'.[30]

If and to the extent that collective defence treaties *were* prescriptive, this tended to be in terms of specifying the precise amount of aid that was to be given and when. Thus, the 1680 Treaty of Defence between Spain and Britain[31] was very specific that if either party was attacked, the other was permitted a three-month notice period before then needing to supply '8000 foot soldiers' to help the victim defend itself.[32] Almost 250 years later, the 1912 Treaty between Greece and Bulgaria committed each party, if the other were attacked:

> to aid ... [them] mutually, Greece with an effective force of at least one hundred and twenty thousand men, and Bulgaria with an effective force of at least three hundred thousand men. These forces must be equally well fitted to take the field upon the frontier.[33]

discussed them separately, while examining the defence of other nations along with the defence of citizens). See von Pufendorf, n.18, chapter XVI, 239, LNN l. 8. c.6., XI, para. 4 and 242, LNN l. 8. c.6., XI, para. 14, respectively. See also *ibid*, chapter XVI, 69 (examining personal self-defence, and as part of this wider conception of 'self-defence', in the context of an assessment of 'the duty of a man towards himself').

30 Treaty of Alliance and Friendship between Great Britain, Austria, Prussia, and Russia (1815) MET, vol. 1, 372, Article II.

31 A Defensive League betwixt Charles II. King of Spain and Charles II. King of Great Britain. Done at Windsor, June 10, 1680, reproduced in Charles Jenkinson (ed.), *A Collection of All the Treaties of Peace, Alliance, and Commerce, between Great-Britain and Other Powers* (London, J. Debrett, 1785), 257.

32 *Ibid*, para. IV. If the situation was considered to have attained the status of a full-blown war, however, then the obligation changed to assistance 'with all his force, by both sea and land', *ibid*, para. V.

33 Military Convention between Bulgaria and Greece (1912), reproduced in (1914) 8 *American Journal of International Law, Supplement: Official Documents* (January 1914), 83, Article 1.

Such 'technical' specifics belied a general lack of clarity in treaties of this period as to, in particular, the trigger for collective defence (*casus fœderis*) envisaged by the treaty in question. A lack of clarity in any given treaty as to exactly *when* a state was required to defend another party meant a notable amount of wiggle room for them to avoid actually ever having to do so in practice.[34]

One development of note that can be observed in many of the defence treaties that emerged from the nineteenth century onwards is that – despite still tending towards the same comparative vagueness overall – they often included a greater emphasis on consultation between the parties than did their predecessors from the seventeenth and eighteenth centuries.[35] Again, the 1815 Treaty of Alliance and Friendship is a useful example, in that it obliged parties to consult on 'the measures which . . . shall be considered'.[36] Other examples include the 1882 Treaty of Triple Alliance[37] and the (related) 1883 Austria-Hungary/Romania Treaty.[38] Although somewhat different in that these obligations were framed as mutual consultations rather than as deference to the sovereignty of the attacked state, such obligations can be viewed as early forerunners to the modern 'request' requirement.[39]

It is important to note that among the treaties that were concluded even up to the start of the First World War, a number continued to contain provision not only for defensive alliance if one of the parties were attacked, but also for *offensive* military alliance.[40] For example, the 1912 Bulgaria/Servia Treaty provided that parties 'may operate either offensively or defensively against Austria-Hungary'.[41] It is worth keeping in mind that no legal prohibition of the use of force in international

[34] It is worth noting that, at least to an extent, this trend has continued into the UN era. See Section 7.3.

[35] See George K. Walker, 'Anticipatory Collective Self-Defense in the Charter Era: What the Treaties Have Said' (1998) 31 *Cornell International Law Journal* 321, 326–327.

[36] Treaty of Alliance and Friendship, n.30, Article VI.

[37] Treaty of Alliance (Austria-Hungary, Germany, Italy) (1882), https://gspi.unipr.it/sites/st26/files/allegatiparagrafo/25-01-2016/triple_alliance.pdf (Treaty of Triple Alliance), Article 5.

[38] Quoted in Walker, n.35, 333.

[39] On the request requirement, see Chapters 4–6.

[40] See, for example, Walker, n.35, 327–329 (providing examples from the nineteenth century).

[41] Military Convention between the Kingdoms of Bulgaria and Servia (1912), reproduced in (1914) 8 *American Journal of International Law, Supplement: Official Documents* (January 1914), 5, 7, Article 3.

relations (or resort to war) existed until 1928 and, as such, the practice of forming military alliances considered so far in this chapter is in a context of *facilitation* – these arrangements enabled states to exercise their legal freedom to use force, whether that be in mutual defence or offensively. The offensive limb of the 1912 Bulgaria/Servia Treaty (and others like it) would, of course, be unlawful in the UN Charter framework and, prior to that, would be incompatible with the framework that was at least attempted in the interwar period, particularly following the 1928 Kellogg-Briand Pact.[42] This is a caveat that should be kept in mind when considering the extent to which the pre-First World War practice can be said to forebear the modern right of collective self-defence. Equally, it is worth noting that in just war theory, 'offensive alliances' were condemned by both Grotius[43] and Vattel[44] in their writings from centuries before this practice was proscribed as a matter of international law.

This amalgamation in some treaties of alliance between offensive and defensive action is, in part, also a reflection of the wider fact that such alliances were still not seen as having anything to do with *self*-defence at all, which remained the domain of individual states, 'essentially understood in a unilateralist manner'.[45] Despite pre-First World War treaties of mutual defence reflecting a number of aspects of the modern right of collective self-defence (albeit undoubtedly in a vaguer form and with some notable differences),[46] their parties considered the obligations contained within them as being separate from the notion of self-defence (whether it be their own right of self-defence or that of other nations). Mutual defence and military alliances on the one hand and self-defence on the other remained conceptually distinct at least until the interwar period.

Before turning to the interwar period, it is worth ending this section by recalling that it has focused almost entirely on *formal* alliances and mutual defence treaties. Some scholars writing in the modern era have

42 International Treaty for the Renunciation of War as an Instrument of National Policy (1928), *The Avalon Project*, https://avalon.law.yale.edu/20th_century/kbpact.asp (Kellogg–Briand Pact/Treaty of Paris/Paris Peace Pact). See Walker, n.35, 335.

43 See, for example, Grotius, n.16, Book II, chapter XVI, 866, para. XVI, 3.

44 See, for example, de Vattel, n.19, Book III, chapter I, 471, para. 5.

45 Sia Spiliopoulou Åkermark, 'The Puzzle of Collective Self-Defence: Dangerous Fragmentation or a Window of Opportunity? An Analysis with Finland and the Åland Islands as a Case Study' (2017) 22 *Journal of Conflict and Security Law* 249, 254. See also Tadashi Mori, *Origins of the Right of Self-Defence in International Law: From the* Caroline *Incident to the United Nations Charter* (Leiden, Brill Nijhoff, 2018), 124 ('[t]he right of self-defence recognised in the 19th century was the right of an individual state').

46 Walker, n.35, 335–336.

suggested that the historical development of 'collective self-defence' *exclusively* involved treaty relationships.[47] This is incorrect. It will be recalled that both Grotius[48] and Pufendorf[49] were of the view that the defence of other nations could occur without the existence of a pre-existing treaty relationship. In terms of practice, one might note, for example, the unwritten (and initially secret) mutual defence arrangement agreed between France and Sardinia in the summer of 1858.[50] There were also other examples.[51] Equally, such ad hoc arrangements were rare, at least in comparison to formalised treaty relationships. Thus, the focus in this section has been on such arrangements precisely because collective defence was, for centuries, predominantly framed by and exercised under them.

2.3 'Collective Self-Defence' during the Interwar Period and the Second World War

2.3.1 *Four 'Shifts' in Relation to 'Collective Self-Defence'*

It has been said that international relations in the interwar period (and during the Second World War itself) 'established a precursor of the contemporary right' of collective self-defence,[52] and that the period should be viewed as the 'legal adolescence'[53] of the modern concept of collective self-defence. In one respect these characterisations might be considered misleading, given the centuries worth of pre-First World War practice that has been discussed in the previous section. At the same

47 See, for example, Greig, n.2, 371 ('the notion of collective self-defence in 1945 . . . *related specifically* to . . . States enter[ing] into Alliances with whatever other States they wished', emphasis added).

48 See n.17 and accompanying text.

49 See n.18 and accompanying text.

50 This is the so-called Plombières Agreement. The agreement was not truly defensive in nature at all, in that it involved a decision to go to war so long as this could be presented as being defensive. However, it was couched in what today would be considered to be the language of collective self-defence (or something rather like it) – indeed, deliberately so. It is also worth noting that the agreement was formalised in a treaty the following January. For discussions, see Asa Briggs and Patricia Clavin, *Modern Europe, 1789–Present* (London, Routledge, 2nd ed., 2013), 94–95.

51 See Walker, n.35, 329–330 (providing examples).

52 Mori, n.45, 124–136, quoted at 125.

53 Johanna Friman, *Revisiting the Concept of Defence in the* Jus ad Bellum*: The Dual Face of Defence* (Oxford, Hart Publishing, 2017), 93.

time, as has already been noted,[54] the previous practice all occurred before there were any meaningful legal limitations – let alone a full-blown prohibition – on the resort to war. Alongside the move towards legally proscribing the use of force that occurred in the interwar years,[55] there also were notable developments in the emergence of the modern right of collective self-defence in that period.

The concept of collective defence still primarily coalesced around formal treaty arrangements for mutual protection during the interwar years (although, again, there were ad hoc examples that bucked that trend).[56] A development in this period of note, though, was that there was a significant influx in the *number* of such treaties that were concluded.[57] This perhaps is unsurprising, given the horrors of the Great War, and the desire for mutual security against any possible recurrence (especially as it became apparent at the end of the period that there was a growing risk of another global conflict).

A second point to note from this time is the creation of the League of Nations. Of course, the League was born from the same post-war context, but it is important to consider that it was deliberately conceived as a more centralised *alternative* to the patchwork of collective defence treaties that had existed before the First World War (treaties that, it was thought, especially in the US, in part led to it).[58] The Covenant of the League implicitly recognised the right of individual self-defence in Article 8, in that it allowed states to maintain armaments to the level 'consistent with national safety'.[59] More importantly for this book, though, is the fact that Article 10 stated:

[54] See n.42 and accompanying text.

[55] See, generally, Oona A. Hathaway and Scott J. Shapiro, *The Internationalists* (London, Penguin Books, 2018), 101–130.

[56] See, for example, Walker, n.35, 358–359 (referring to the example of the Netherlands' declaration of war against Japan during the Second World War, despite having no prior collective defence agreements with the Allies 'as evidence of informal collective self-defence, a concept recognized before and after the ratification of the Charter'). See also UNGA Summary Record, UN Doc. A/C.6/SR.411 (29 October 1954), para. 15 (Belarus, noting, in discussions in the Sixth Committee on question of defining aggression in 1954, that, during the Second World War, '[*a*]*ny State* that had not been directly attacked had nevertheless been justified in declaring war … as an act of collective self-defence', emphasis added); John S. Gibson, 'Article 51 of the Charter of the United Nations' (1957) 13 *India Quarterly* 121, 121 (noting that prior to the First World War, collective defence could be exercised 'by treaty *or understanding*', emphasis added).

[57] Gibson, n.56, 123; Goodhart, n.2, 205; Ian Brownlie, *International Law and the Use of Force by States* (Oxford, Oxford University Press, 1963), 328; Friman, n.53, 93.

[58] Gibson, n.56, 121–122.

[59] Covenant of the League of Nations (1919) 225 CTS 195, Article 8.

> The Members of the League undertake to respect and preserve as against external aggression the territorial integrity and existing political independence of all Members of the League. In case of any such aggression or in case of any threat or danger of such aggression the Council shall advise upon the means by which this obligation shall be fulfilled.[60]

A role of the Council of the League in the operation of Article 10 was clearly envisaged by the drafters, meaning, on its face, that the provision looks rather more like a centralised collective security mechanism, à la manière de Chapter VII of the UN Charter. Indeed, the League as a whole is commonly conceived of as an ambitious (although of course ultimately failed) exercise in collective security.[61]

However, Article 10 only gave the Council of the League an advisory function. The key role of responding to external aggression clearly was vested in its member states. It has been argued by various scholars that the Covenant therefore included something akin to the modern right of collective self-defence in Article 10 (as well as, to a lesser extent, Article 16), or, at least, that the League set up a system that was *closer* to what we would today understand as collective self-defence than to what we would today understand as 'true' collective security.[62] Nonetheless, the League involved a more centralised and process-based approach to mutual defence, and in that regard can be differentiated from previous collective defence treaties. It had the ambition of establishing something more sophisticated and unified.

It was previously noted that collective self-defence provisions prior to the First World War often tended to be vague as to, for example, the *casus fœderis* triggering their obligations.[63] To some extent, this can be said to have continued into the interwar years. It is worth noting, for example, that Article 10 of the League of Nations Covenant alluded to something that might be viewed as approaching an obligation rather than a right (members 'undertake to'), while at the same time setting that obligation out in decidedly 'soft' terms ('to respect and preserve' – which is a long way short of establishing a duty to use force in response). Another example from the period is the 1935 Treaty of Mutual

[60] *Ibid*, Article 10.

[61] Mary Ellen O'Connell, 'Preserving the Peace: The Continuing Ban on War between States' (2007) 38 *California Western International Law Journal* 41, 43.

[62] Hans Kelsen, 'The Future of Collective Security' (1951) 21 *Revista Juridica de la Universidad de Puerto Rico* 83, 84–88; Mori, n.45, 127; Åkermark, n.45, 254–255; Weightman, n.12, 1108; Brownlie, n.57, 328; Walker, n.35, 337–341; Friman, n.53, 93.

[63] See nn.30–34 and accompanying text.

Assistance between the USSR and France.[64] Article 2 of that treaty required, in the event of 'an attack on the part of a European State' upon either party, that the other 'shall immediately give each other aid and assistance'[65] without specifying in what form or to what extent.[66]

Notwithstanding such examples, a third 'shift' that can be discerned from the practice in the interwar period is that defence treaties began to include tighter drafting, leaving their parties less flexibility to escape the obligations that they contained. The 1921 Alliance Treaty between Czechoslovakia and Romania is a useful example of a collective defence agreement that presented a firmer statement of the *casus fœderis* that was to trigger it than did many of the equivalent pre-First World War treaties. It was specific in that it only related to action against one of the parties by Hungary, but more importantly also in relation to *what* action on thc part of Hungary would activate it: '[e]n cas d'une attaque non provoquée de la Hongrie contre l'une des Hautes Parties contractantes, l'autre Partie s'engage à concourir à la défense de la Partie attaquée'.[67]

This trend towards greater specificity appears to have increased towards the end of the interwar period. For example, the 1939 Treaty between the USSR and Estonia was much more precise than many of its predecessors, again particularly regarding its *casus fœderis*. It provided that the 'two Contracting Parties undertake to render each other assistance of every kind, including military assistance, in the event of direct *aggression* or threat of *aggression* [against the other party]'.[68] Similarly, the Mutual Assistance Pact between the UK and Poland in 1939[69] – hastily drafted to try to deter the advance of Nazi Germany, and then

64 France–USSR Treaty of Mutual Assistance (1935) reproduced in (1936) 30 *American Journal of International Law, Supplement: Official Documents* (October 1936), 177.

65 *Ibid*, 178, Article 2.

66 It is worth noting that softly worded hard obligations of this sort have remained a feature of some post-Charter collective self-defence arrangements too. See Section 7.3.

67 Defensive Alliance Convention between the Czechoslovak Republic (Czechoslovakia) and the Kingdom of Romania (1921) 13 LNTS 231, Article 1. Having said this, the treaty remained quite vague as to *what was then required* of the co-defending party once the treaty had been triggered. See *ibid*, Article 2.

68 Pact of Mutual Assistance between the USSR and Estonia (1939), reproduced in (1968) 14 *Lituanus*, www.lituanus.org/1968/68_2_03Doc6.html, Article 1 (emphasis added).

69 Agreement of Mutual Assistance between the United Kingdom and Poland (1939), *The Avalon Project*, https://avalon.law.yale.edu/wwii/blbk19.asp.

honoured by the UK when it failed to do so[70] – was similarly prescriptive as compared to many of its predecessors.[71] It was explicit that the *casus fœderis* for its activation was the occurrence of 'aggression',[72] it obliged parties to come to each other's aid 'at once', and required that the co-defending state had to provide 'all the support and assistance in its power'.[73] The treaty also established clear obligations for information exchange[74] and mutual communication.[75]

Finally, a fourth important – albeit relatively subtle – change in the interwar period, was that the idea of mutual defence in international relations gradually became more linked, conceptually, with the idea of self-defence in a manner not previously discernible. This was extremely tentative, but there were a few indications of the beginning of a trend in this regard among some states. The UK is the most notable example of this. For instance, although the Draft Treaty of Mutual Assistance of 1923[76] ultimately did not refer to self-defence,[77] during its development the UK argued that:

> [i]t could not be denied that if a State were attacked it had the right to defend itself. A group of States *should have* the *same right* and should be able to take action before any decision on the part of the Council [of the League of Nations].[78]

[70] See Yoram Dinstein, *War, Aggression and Self-Defence* (Cambridge, Cambridge University Press, 6th ed., 2017), 308.

[71] Although it still left some room for discretion. See UK–Poland Mutual Assistance Treaty, n.69, Article 4 ('[t]he methods of applying the undertakings of mutual assistance provided for by the present Agreement are established between the competent naval, military and air authorities of the Contracting Parties').

[72] *Ibid*, Article 1.

[73] *Ibid*.

[74] *Ibid*, Article 5.

[75] *Ibid*, Article 6(1).

[76] The Draft Treaty was developed under the auspices of the League of Nations, as part of its Fourth Assembly. See, generally, John H. Wigmore, 'The Work of the Fourth Assembly (1923) of the League of Nations: A Legislative Summary' (1924) 9 *The Virginia Law Register* 887. However, ultimately it was rejected by the Assembly and never formally adopted. See Mori, n.45, 88, 128–129.

[77] Mori, n.45, 88.

[78] League of Nations, Fourth Assembly, Minutes of the Third Committee (summary record), Ninth Meeting, Continuation of the Discussion on the Draft Treaty of Mutual Assistance (Article 8 and Article 4, paragraph 2) (19 September 1923), in (1923) 16 *League of Nations Official Journal, Special Supplement* 42, 44 (emphasis added). See also Andrew Martin, *Collective Security: A Progress Report* (Paris, United Nations (UNESCO), 1952), 131 (arguing that the Draft Convention was surprisingly similar to the system

This suggests that for the UK, at least, there was not yet a 'right' of collective self-defence in the same way that this existed for individual self-defence in 1923, but it felt there should be one. As Mori notes, '[t]he attempt here was to ground collective defence on the right of self-defence'.[79]

Five years later, in relation to the signing of the 1928 Kellogg-Briand Pact, the UK took a similar view, but went further, replacing the 'ought' with an 'is'. The UK argued that 'the right of self-defence [was] inalienable',[80] and that the use of force to protect certain regions around the world was 'a special and vital interest for *our* peace and safety' and therefore *amounted to* 'a measure of *self*-defence'.[81] The UK thus accepted the Kellogg-Briand Pact only on the understanding that the Pact did not 'prejudice their freedom of action in this respect'.[82] In doing so, it indicated that it saw individual self-defence and 'collective self-defence' as being aligned.

2.3.2 *The Pan-American Collective Defence Project*

The same tentative but growing conceptual link between individual self-defence and 'collective self-defence' in international relations can be observed in the emergence, towards the end of the 1930s, of an embryonic defence framework in the Americas. In 1938, for example, US President Franklin D. Roosevelt explicitly declared that American nations now 'represented a co-operative *self-defense* system'.[83] One might also note that the Declaration of Panama in 1939 held that,

> [a]s a measure of *continental self-protection*, the American Republics ... are *as of inherent right* entitled to have those waters adjacent to the American continent, which they regard as of primary concern and direct utility in their relations, free from the commission of any hostile act by

ultimately adopted by the UN Charter in 1945, including encompassing the same understanding of collective self-defence).

79 Mori, n.45, 128.

80 Letter from Sir Austen Chamberlain (UK Foreign Secretary) to Mr Houghton (US representative in London) (19 May 1928), No. 4, in 'United States Proposal for the Renunciation of War (Correspondence Respecting the)', *Appendix to the Journals of the House of Representatives of New Zealand* (1928) Session I, A-07, 12, 12, para. 4.

81 *Ibid*, 13, para. 10 (emphasis added).

82 *Ibid*.

83 Quoted in Gibson, n.56, 126 (emphasis added).

> any non-American belligerent nation, whether such hostile act be attempted or made from land, sea or air.[84]

Thus, although it did not explicitly link self-defence to collective defence, the Declaration of Panama clearly envisaged collective defence as synonymous with individual defence, using language reminiscent of what was soon to feature in Article 51 of the UN Charter.

Likewise, the Declaration of Havana a year later conceived the regional defence system as being based on the idea:

> [t]hat any attempt on the part of a non-American State against the integrity or inviolability of the territory, the sovereignty or the political independence of an American State shall be considered as an act of aggression against the states which sign this declaration.[85]

The Act of Chapultepec, which was adopted only a month before the UN Charter in 1945, went on to use almost identical wording:

> [E]very attack of a State against the integrity or the inviolability of the territory, or against the sovereignty or political independence of an American State, shall ... be considered as an act of aggression against the other States which sign this Act.[86]

This 'attack on one = attack on all' terminology, as found in the Havana Declaration and the Act of Chapultepec, later became more common in UN era collective defence arrangements.[87] In the early 1940s, though, it was indicative of a still unusual connection being made between concepts of self-defence and collective defence, implicitly conceiving of them as entwined.

[84] Declaration of Panama (1939), in United States Department of State, Foreign relations of the United States diplomatic papers (1939), *The American Republics*, vol. V (1939), 'Meeting of the foreign ministers of the American republics for consultation under the inter-American agreements of Buenos Aires and Lima, held at Panama' (23 September 1939), 15, 36 (emphasis added).

[85] Second Meeting of Ministers of Foreign Affairs of the American Republics, Havana (21–30 July 1940): Final Act and Convention, reproduced in (1941) 35 *Supplement to the American Journal of International Law* 1, part XV, 15–16. Admittedly, the Declaration then was quite vague as to what steps its signatories would actually need to *take* if one of their number was attacked. See *ibid*, 16 ('the nations signatory to the present declaration will consult among themselves in order to agree upon the measures it may be advisable to take').

[86] Act of Chapultepec, n.1, part I, Article 3.

[87] See Section 7.3.3.

The Pan-American collective defence 'project'[88] therefore contributed to an emerging conceptual link between collective and self-defence. This in part was due to the political roots of that regional initiative. It has been said that one can trace the collective defence system in the Americas back to the so-called 'Monroe doctrine',[89] and this is true to a point.[90] The doctrine long pre-dated the interwar period, of course, with US President James Monroe initially setting it out in 1823: in its simplest form, the rejection of European influence in the Americas.[91] An emerging corollary of that, though, was the perception in the US that its security was inherently tied to the security of the whole region.[92] It was not until the latter part of the interwar period that what had for more than a century been a unilateralist[93] – and deeply imperialistic[94] – doctrine morphed (in some respects, anyway) into something that looked rather closer to a true collective

[88] Alongside the aforementioned Declaration of Panama, n.84, Declaration of Havana, n.85, and Act of Act of Chapultepec, n.1, it is worth also noting that this Pan-American 'project' – which was a wider integration initiative stretching well beyond just collective defence – also emerged in the Declaration of Principles of Inter-American Solidarity and Cooperation (Declaration of Buenos Aires) (1936), *The Avalon Project*, https://avalon.law.yale.edu/20th_century/intam07.asp; and the Declaration of the Principles of the Solidarity of America (Declaration of Lima) (1938), Eighth International Conference of American States, in (1940) 34 *Supplement to the American Journal of International Law* 199. Both of these set out more general principles for regional cooperation (including collective defence), prioritising sovereign equality and consultation, that were later fleshed out. It also should be noted that this project continued into the UN era, with the entry into force of the Rio Treaty in 1948 (Inter-American Treaty of Reciprocal Assistance (1948) 21 UNTS 77 (Rio Treaty)). Indeed, this was as intended by the Act of Chapultepec, n.1, Part II. See A J. Thomas Jr. and Ann Van Wynen Thomas, 'The Organization of American States and Collective Security' (1959) 13 *Southwestern Law Journal* 177, 177 (noting that the Act set out plans for its own replacement by means of a permanent treaty).

[89] Derek W. Bowett, *Self-Defense in International Law* (Manchester, Manchester University Press, 1958), 107–112; Greig, n.2, 370–371; Mori, n.45, 125–127; Anne Orford, 'Regional Orders, Geopolitics, and the Future of International Law' (2021) 74 *Current Legal Problems* 149, 164–165; Charles G. Fenwick, 'The Monroe Doctrine and the Declaration of Lima' (1939) 33 *American Journal of International Law* 257.

[90] Other factors were also certainly at play, such as, for example, frustration in the Americas about the limitations and failures of the new League of Nations. See George Fletcher and Jens Ohlin, *Defending Humanity: When Force is Justified and Why* (Oxford, Oxford University Press, 2008), 72.

[91] See Charles E. Hughes, 'Observations on the Monroe Doctrine' (1923) 17 *American Journal of International Law* 611, 612–614.

[92] *Ibid.*

[93] *Ibid*, 615–617.

[94] See Alejandro Alvarez, 'The Monroe Doctrine from the Latin-American Point of View' (1917) 2 *St. Louis Law Review* 135.

defence doctrine.[95] This change resulted most notably from the reconceptualisation of the Monroe doctrine by Latin American states themselves, into an unlikely basis for Pan-Americanism as opposed to US influence.[96] The fact that the doctrine was, intellectually, one of *US* self-defence, as interpreted by a succession of US administrations, meant that its repurposing undoubtedly came with a residue of individual self-defence, blurring the line between the self and the collective.

In many ways, although it had some of its roots in the much older Monroe doctrine, the Pan-American 'project' for collective defence at the end of the interwar years was a culmination of many of the changes in that period discussed in this section and, as a result, had notable implications for the way in which collective self-defence ultimately was adopted in Article 51. The American nations had created a sophisticated collective self-defence system, at least as compared to what had gone before, featuring elements that could be seen as amounting to (quasi) collective security arrangements.[97] The importance of the emergence of the new system to Latin American states in particular led – famously – to the need to be explicit in the UN Charter that it remained unfettered. Less often noted is that, because the new regional defence framework in the Americas saw a subtle shift towards linking collective defence arrangements to the right of self-defence in international law, this provided a new conceptual context for the way in which Article 51 was drafted.

2.4 The Drafting of the UN Charter and the Conjoining of Individual and Collective Self-Defence

2.4.1 The Birth of Article 51

A fundamental aim of the new UN organisation was to centralise and limit the use of force.[98] This meant that, early in drafting the Charter,[99]

[95] Bowett, n.89, 210–212.

[96] See Juan Pablo Scarfi, 'Denaturalizing the Monroe Doctrine: The Rise of Latin American Legal Anti-Imperialism in the Face of the Modern US and Hemispheric Redefinition of the Monroe Doctrine' (2020) 33 *Leiden Journal of International Law* 541.

[97] See Modabber, n.2, 455 (arguing that the Act of Chapultepec in particular 'effectively created a collective security system for the region'); Thomas and Thomas, n.88, 177.

[98] Gary Wilson, 'The Legal, Military and Political Consequences of the "Coalition of the Willing" Approach to UN Military Enforcement Action' (2007) 12 *Journal of Conflict and Security Law* 295, 301–303.

[99] The key formulations on regional arrangements were a part of the initial Dumbarton Oaks Proposals. See, for example, Documents of the United Nations Conference on

restrictions were placed upon the activities of 'regional arrangements' in what became Chapter VIII: most notably requiring that any enforcement action that a regional arrangement/agency undertook must have been previously authorised by the Security Council.[100] As was noted at the start of this chapter, it has been often asserted[101] that self-defence (individual and collective) was only included explicitly in the UN Charter *at all* because of concerns expressed by Latin American states that the Charter's prohibition of force and requirement for Security Council approval of regional enforcement actions would override the embryonic regional defence project discussed in the previous section. This understanding is largely correct, if a little simplistic. It was not just Latin American states that were concerned that existing defence treaties might be overridden by the Charter: other states had the same fears with respect to other existing collective defence arrangements.[102] Thus, the claim that has been occasionally made[103] that the new Pan-American framework was the *only* reason for the existence of Article 51 is wrong. Equally, it must be acknowledged that the American states were the key drivers in this regard.[104]

In any event, following various drafts,[105] Article 51 (or, at least, an initial version of it) was ultimately proposed by the US to address such concerns.[106] It was devised as a compromise. On the one hand, the aim was to make it clear that the Charter did not impair the exercise of the

International Organization, San Francisco, 1945 (London, United Nations Information Organization (United Nations), 22 volumes, 1945–1955) (UNCIO), vol. 3, 18–19.

100 Charter of the United Nations (1945) 1 UNTS XVI (UN Charter), Article 53 ('no enforcement action shall be taken under regional arrangements or by regional agencies without the authorization of the Security Council . . .'). For further discussion, see Section 7.5.2.

101 See sources cited at n.2.

102 See, for example, UNCIO, n.99, vol. 12, 682 (Egypt, expressing concerns in relation to the position of the League of Arab States); *ibid*, 681 (France, expressing concerns as regards to existing bilateral arrangements in Europe); *ibid* (Uruguay, explicitly making the point that the introduction of 'collective self-defence' into the Charter was about more than solely the Act of Chapultepec). For discussion, see Bowett, n.89, 182–184; Kritsiotis, n.2, 172.

103 See, for example, McWhinney, n.2, 430.

104 UNCIO, n.99, vol. 11, 54–55 (Mexico); *ibid*, 55–56 (Venezuela).

105 See Franck, n.2, 51 (noting that the final text of Article 51 was 'the result of intense negotiation and uneasy compromise'). See, for example, UNCIO, n.99, vol. 12, 679–689, 723–724, 739–740, 857–858; *ibid*, vol. 17, 492, 532–533; *ibid*, vol. 18, 365; *ibid*, vol. 20, 371.

106 UNCIO, n.99, vol. 12, 674, 680.

obligations set out in collective defence treaties (especially, but, again, not solely, the Act of Chapultepec).[107] The main intent, and consequence, here being to ensure that a collective defensive action could be undertaken without the prior approval of the UN Security Council.[108] On the other hand, the US (and other drafting states, notably the UK) decided it was best to tie such collective action to self-defence in an attempt to maintain at least a degree of centralised authority for the new organisation. Some previous proposals attempting to address the concerns of Latin American (and other) states had suggested that the Charter should provide that – in instances where the Security Council failed to act – member states reserved an unfettered freedom to take whatever measures they considered necessary.[109] Such proposals, it was feared, would be a green light for the circumvention of the Security Council whensoever states wished and, thus, would 'smash ... the entire' UN project.[110] By linking collective action to self-defence – a right that *already* was considered to be exempt from the planned monopolisation of the lawful use of force by the Council[111] – the hope was that collective defence agreements could be preserved without this being viewed as a further erosion of the Council's authority. Self-defence was already permitted, so it was felt better simply to *consider collective action as self-defence*, rather than to punch another entirely new hole in the plan for the centralisation of the use of force.[112]

[107] Mori, n.45, 217. See, for example, UNCIO, n.99, vol. 12, 680–681 (Colombia, on behalf of itself and also fifteen other Latin American states: '[t]he Charter, in general terms, is a constitution, and it legitimizes the right of collective self-defense to be carried out in accord with ... regional pacts ... If a group of countries with regional ties declare[s] their solidarity for their mutual defense ... they will undertake such defense jointly if and when one of them is attacked. ... This is the typical case of the American system').

[108] See Thomas M. Franck, 'Who Killed Article 2(4)? or Changing the Norms Governing the Use of Force by States' (1970) 64 *American Journal of International Law* 809, 823–824; Fletcher and Ohlin, n.90, 73; Weightman, n.12, 1111.

[109] See, for example, UNCIO, n.99, vol. 3, 385 (France, proposing that '[s]hould the [Security] Council not succeed in reaching a decision, the members of the Organization reserve to themselves the right to act as they may consider necessary in the interest of peace, right and justice').

[110] Memorandum by Mr. Robert Hartley of the United States Delegation of a Conversation. Held at San Francisco (12 May 1945), quoted in Mori, n.45, 219.

[111] See, for example, UNCIO, n.99, vol. 6, 721; UNCIO, n.99, vol. 11, 514; UNCIO, n.99, vol. 12, 342. See also Mori, n.45, 215–217 (citing primary documents that confirm this perception).

[112] Mori, n.45, 221–223.

A decade or so after the adoption of the Charter, Bowett noted that the underpinning rationale here was that:

> since states were [prior to the Charter] formally free to conclude any defensive treaty of alliance and to act on the obligation of assistance contained therein, that freedom or right is still preserved to member states under Article 51.[113]

For Bowett, however, this could not be correct because this previous 'freedom' had existed at a time before there was any prohibition on the use of force (or, at least, when there only were limited legal restrictions on it, as in the interwar period), whereas the UN Charter changed that position.[114]

Yet leaving the pre-existing freedom to contract into defence arrangements untouched by the change wrought by the Charter was *precisely* what was intended by the inclusion of Article 51. It would seem from the *travaux préparatoires* that the states at San Francisco did not feel they were developing new law, but, rather, that they were merely preserving explicitly the existing law.[115] So far as states were concerned, the whole point of Article 51 was to acknowledge 'the *continuing* legitimacy of collective self-defence' so that the status quo in this regard was *not* altered by the Charter.[116]

2.4.2 *The Introduction of New Terminology*

As this chapter has demonstrated throughout, the core concept of 'collective self-defence' was not 'new' at all in 1945. One may therefore wonder why it has been so often claimed by scholars that it was

[113] Bowett, n.89, 217.
[114] *Ibid.*
[115] Padmanabhan and Shih, n.2, 3 ('the drafting history of Article 51 … shows that the Charter was merely intended to codify the existing law of collective self-defence and not to expand states' rights to invoke the doctrine'). See, for example, UNCIO, n.99, vol. 12, 681–682 (Czechoslovakia: 'the text [of Article 51] approved effectively reconciled the right of self-defense individual *and collective*, with the maintenance of a central authority capable of dealing with the problems of security as they arose', emphasis added. Thus, the Czechoslovakian delegate took the view that the right of collective self-defence was a pre-existing one, and that the difficulty when it came to drafting the Charter was about how to reconcile the preservation of that existing right with the new centralised Charter machinery); UNCIO, n.99, vol. 6, 400 ('[t]he use of arms in legitimate self-defence remains admitted and unimpaired', clearly in reference to both individual and collective self-defence).
[116] Alder, n.2, 87 (emphasis added). See also Walker, n.35, 359.

introduced by the UN Charter.[117] A simple explanation might be the fact that the *terminology* used in Article 51 in relation to this concept *was* new. It has been said that Article 51 introduced the 'language of "collective self-defence" into the *jus ad bellum*.'[118] The present author has found no use of the term 'collective self-defence' prior to 1945 that would contradict that assertion. Indeed, the novelty of this terminology was recognised by states themselves during the drafting of the Charter.[119]

Perhaps, then, writers have simply been mistaking the use of novel terminology for the creation of a novel legal concept. Given the fact that many of the features of the modern law of collective self-defence can be observed from a time before the adoption of the label 'collective self-defence' in 1945 (some of them stretching back centuries) it might be tempting to downplay the impact of the Charter on the concept, on the basis that any 'change' was merely terminological. As Kunz stated, quite simply: '[t]he term is new, but the thing was known previously'.[120]

Admittedly, this shift in terminology sowed conceptual uncertainty – particularly in the immediate post-war period, but which still persists – because collective self-defence is a wholly ill-fitting term for what was a long-standing 'defence of another' concept in international law. As was examined in Chapter 1, the term 'collective *self*-defence' has led to scholars arguing that the co-defending state must in some measure be defending itself – a requirement that has no basis in practice either before or after the drafting of the Charter – in an attempt to force the square peg of the 'defence of another' into the round hole of the new terminology ascribed to it.[121] However, it will also be recalled from Chapter 1 that the equally authoritative French and Spanish language versions of Article 51

[117] See n.3.

[118] Kritsiotis, n.2, 170–171. See also *Nicaragua* (merits), n.3, dissenting opinion of Judge Oda, para. 91 ('[t]he *term* "collective self-defence", [was] unknown before 1945 . . .', emphasis added); Hans J. Morgenthau, *Politics Among Nations: The Struggle for Power and Peace* (New York, McGraw-Hill, 7th ed., revised by Kenneth W. Thompson and W. David Clinton, 2005), 311; Mori, n.45, 124; Franck, n.2, 48; Thomas and Thomas, n.88, 185, 189; Gibson, n.56, 121, 126.

[119] See, for example, UNCIO, n.99, vol. 12, 680 (Colombia, speaking on behalf of 16 Latin American states: 'the *origin* of the *term* "collective self-defense" is identified with the necessity of preserving regional systems like the Inter-American one' in the new Charter framework, emphasis added).

[120] Kunz, n.2, 874. See also Gibson, n.56, 121 ('[t]his principle of collective defence, although couched in different phraseology in Article 51, is by no means new to international law . . .'), 126.

[121] See Section 1.2.

do not refer to collective *self*-defence at all, and instead refer, respectively, to 'légitime défense' and 'de legítima defensa'.[122] These terms far better reflect both the historical and modern concept of what is now, in English, called collective self-defence. This, again, might lead one to conclude that Article 51 did not involve any meaningful change to the legal *concept*, beyond a poorly worded attempt to describe it (and, even then, only in *some of* the authoritative versions of the text).[123] However, this would be a mistake.

2.4.3 *The Conjoining of Individual and Collective Self-Defence*

Article 51 certainly did not create the concept of 'collective self-defence' in international law, but it also did more than merely rename it.[124] The change in terminology (in some languages, at least) was indicative of a more pertinent, substantive shift. Influenced by the new Pan-American defence system[125] and, as noted, seeking a compromise between ensuring the continuance of collective defence arrangements and limiting the erosion of centralised Security Council authority,[126] the drafters of Article 51 formally *conjoined* the concepts of self-defence and collective defence.[127] As the representative of Colombia stated during the drafting of the Charter:

> [A]n aggression against one ... state constitutes an aggression against all ... and all of them exercise their right of legitimate defense by giving support to the state attacked, in order to repel such aggression. This is what is meant by the right of *collective self-defense*.[128]

This 'attack on one = attack on all' conception is reflected in the fact that Article 51 identifies individual and collective self-defence, together, as an

[122] See Chapter 1, n.121 and accompanying text.

[123] It will be recalled that the Arabic ('دفاع عن أنفس'), Chinese ('自卫') and Russian ('самооборону') texts of Article 51 all also seem to reflect the English terminology of 'self-defence'.

[124] Franck, n.2, 48 (noting that the change in terminology had a meaningful effect). See also Thomas and Thomas, n.88, 185.

[125] Padmanabhan and Shih, n.2, 5; Constantinou, n.2, 173–174.

[126] See nn.105–112 and accompanying text.

[127] *Ibid* (noting that Article 51 had the effect of individual and collective self-defence becoming almost indivisible).

[128] UNCIO, n.99, vol. 12, 687 (emphasis in original).

'inherent right' of states (singular).[129] Article 51 is also very clear that the requirements that apply to one equally apply to the other – as one would expect given that they are presented as one indivisible concept. The text does not discriminate between 'different invocations' of self-defence and applies equally to them.[130]

Although there were some indications, as discussed in Section 2.3, that certain states had begun to associate the defence of another concept more closely with the right of individual self-defence towards the end of the interwar period, the link between self and collective defence, at least in the stark way that this is set out in Article 51, is impossible to trace back meaningfully prior to 1945, and especially before the First World War.[131] Yet the fact that there is little historical basis for such a close (again, virtually *indivisible*) relationship between self and collective defence is ultimately immaterial as to the legal concept of collective self-defence as it exists today: the Charter has framed it thus, and so thus it is now framed.

One notable impact of this conjoining in Article 51 is that a degree of consistency emerged – almost overnight – between the legal regulation of the two concepts of individual and collective self-defence. There is a common theme across the criminal law of many jurisdictions that a person coming to the aid of a third party has no more right to defend that party than they would have had to defend themselves.[132] Sometimes referred to as the 'alter ego rule',[133] this idea has a long-standing historical pedigree in the private law of various domestic systems, as part of the 'defence of others' concept as applied to individual persons.[134] The UN Charter's conjoining of individual and collective self-defence for the first

129 UN Charter, n.100, Article 51.

130 Kritsiotis, n.2, 257.

131 Franck, n.108, 824 (referring to the link created by Article 51 between collective defence and self-defence as a 'new formulation').

132 See, for example, *Defences in Criminal Law*, Report of the Irish Law Reform Commission (December 2009), LRC 95–200, para. 2.51 ('lethal defensive force for the protection of a third party should only be lawful where the person who is being defended could also have used such force'); Marco F. Bendinelli and James T. Edsall, 'Defense of Others: Origins, Requirements, Limitations and Ramifications' (1995) 5 *Regent University Law Review* 153.

133 See, generally, Bendinelli and Edsall, n.132.

134 *Foster v. Commonwealth* [1991] 13 Va.App. 380, 383–384, 412 S.E.2d 198, 200, 201 ('[i]n a majority of jurisdictions, a person asserting a claim of defense of others may do so only where the person to whose aid he or she went would have been legally entitled to defend himself or herself').

time truly embedded a version of that understanding in the international law context. This is to say that it meant that the circumstances under which a state can lawfully be defended must mirror those under which it can defend itself.[135] As Colombia stated during the San Francisco conference, 'self-defense whether individual *or collective*, exercised as an inherent right, shall operate automatically within the provisions of the Charter'.[136] The resulting 'shared' criteria between individual and collective self-defence in the UN era will be explored in detail (with particular reference to the manner in which they apply in the collective context) in the next chapter.

It is sufficient here to note that Article 51 immediately put more 'meat on the bones' of the comparatively underdeveloped framework for collective defence,[137] which, in terms of practice, had been scattered across hundreds of differently worded treaties, the provisions of which had so often been left deliberately vague by the parties. The result is that the core legal framework for modern collective self-defence is more developed, and better established, than its historic 'defence of others' equivalent had

[135] Kevin Jon Heller, 'The Unlawfulness of a "Bloody Nose Strike" on North Korea' (2020) 96 *International Law Studies* 1, 10–11; Friman, n.53, 96, 193; Constantinou, n.2, 208; Richard N. Gardner, 'Commentary on the Law of Self-Defence', in Lori Fisler Damrosch and David J. Scheffer (eds.), *Law and Force in the New International Order* (Boulder, Westview Press, 1991), 49, 50; Richard A. Falk, 'The Cambodian Operation and International Law' (1971) 65 *American Journal of International Law* 1, 7, 13–14; Helen Michael, 'Covert Involvement in Essentially Internal Conflicts: United States Assistance to the Contras under International Law' (1990) 23 *Vanderbilt Journal of Transnational Law* 539, 580; Waldock, n.2, 505; Jaemin Lee, 'Collective Self-Defense or Collective Security: Japan's Reinterpretation of Article 9 of the Constitution' (2015) 8 *Journal of East Asia and International Law* 373, 377; Alexander Orakhelashvili, *Collective Security* (Oxford, Oxford University Press, 2011), 280; Thomas and Thomas, n.88, 185–186. See also *Nicaragua* (merits), n.3, para. 51 (referring to the inferential affect upon El Salvador's right of individual self-defence of a ruling upon the US' right of collective self-defence in the case, which shows the link between the two 'rights'); *ibid*, separate opinion of Judge Ni, 204 (stressing that in finding that the US had not acted in collective self-defence, it would necessarily indicate that El Salvador had no right of individual self-defence, given that the criteria effectively are the same).

[136] UNCIO, n.99, vol. 12, 687 (emphasis added).

[137] Brownlie, n.57, 329 ('[t]he express recognition of a right of collective self-defence in Article 51 of the UN Charter gave the right a precise legal status which it had perhaps lacked previously'); Gibson, n.56, 121 ('Article 51, in effect, *gives legal blessing* to the concept that one or more states may lend assistance to one or more other states, if the latter are being subjected to armed attack', emphasis added).

been for centuries.[138] As was noted in Chapter 1, this also turned collective self-defence into a *derivative* right.[139] It has become no longer a general freedom of action, but a right wholly dependent on the right of individual self-defence.

Yet, at the same time, the conjoining of 'the self-defences' also, of course, meant that collective self-defence became a right designated to be 'inherent'.[140] Article 51 was famously not included in the initial Dumbarton Oaks proposals during the drafting of the Charter.[141] This was because states were of the view that (individual) self-defence was a fundamental sovereign right, and this meant it would not be impaired by the Charter and thus it need not be spelled out explicitly.[142] The inclusion of Article 51 is a reflection of the fact that – while the state drafters of the Charter felt that they were merely acknowledging the pre-existing law, which already allowed for collective defence actions[143] – they did *not* feel at the time that collective defence was an 'inherent right' (or, at least, not one of the same pedigree as individual self-defence).[144] Otherwise, collective defence would have been considered to be self-evidently unimpaired in the same vein and, thus, an unnecessary inclusion. This was not the case, meaning that there was a need to articulate that 'nothing in the present Charter impair[ed]' any existing collective defence arrangements.

Irrespective of the centuries of practice of military alliances and defence pacts that preceded the adoption of the Charter, collective defence did not have the same kind of pedigree prior to 1945, in the sense of it being seen by states as 'inhering' in statehood.[145] States entered

[138] Seyfullah Hasar, *State Consent to Foreign Military Intervention during Civil Wars* (Leiden, Brill Nijhoff, 2022), 294 ('the right to collective self-defence and its contours are relatively well-addressed and established in the doctrine').

[139] See Chapter 1, nn.153–154 and accompanying text.

[140] For discussion of the modern status of collective self-defence as an 'inherent right', see Section 1.3.

[141] See Franck, n.108, 823; Waldock, n.2, 496–497.

[142] See Mori, n.45, 215–217 (citing primary documents that confirm this perception).

[143] See n.115–116 and accompanying text.

[144] See Gibson, n.56, 128; Harley A. Notter, *Postwar Foreign Policy Preparation, 1939–1945* (Washington DC, Greenwood Press, 1975), 444. See, for example, UNCIO, n.99, vol. 1, 661, 693 (China, emphasising the importance of including the right of self-defence explicitly in the Charter).

[145] See *Nicaragua* (merits), n.3, dissenting opinion of Judge Oda, para. 94 ('the idea that the right of collective self-defence is *inherent* is . . . not traceable up to 1928', i.e. the drafting of the Kellogg-Briand Pact, emphasis in original).

into collective defence agreements on a pragmatic basis, absent of any sense that the 'defence of others' was a crucial part of their statehood or that of the states they contracted to defend.[146] The 'conjoining' enacted by the UN Charter therefore moved collective self-defence beyond its safety-in-numbers origins, as developed through ad hoc treaty arrangements: instead, it became tied to the right, held most dear by states, that they be able to defend themselves.[147] Yet the fact that collective self-defence cannot boast the same philosophical pedigree during its history as can its individual counterpart,[148] again, no longer really matters. It gained the apparent trappings of 'natural law' lineage by association.[149]

The final consequence of the way in which collective self-defence was included in the UN Charter to note here is that it emphasised that the right could be exercised not only in the context of multilateral regional arrangements, but also in the context of bilateral agreements and ad hoc in the absence of any agreement.[150] This is perhaps an unexpected outcome given that the predominant focus throughout drafting was on formal regional arrangements.[151] Nonetheless, a review of the *travaux*

146 See Roda Mushkat, 'Who May Wage War – An Examination of an Old/New Question' (1987) 2 *American University Journal of International Law and Policy* 97, 146. A stark contrary example is, admittedly, the Declaration of Panama, n.84, which did explicitly designate collective defence in the Americas as an 'inherent right'. However, this was only six years prior to the drafting of the Charter, so is hardly evidence of a long-standing historical pedigree. It also perhaps is telling that this conception was not then replicated in the Act of Chapultepec, n.1. Going quite a bit further back, it is interesting that Vattel referred to the defence of other nations as '*natural* and lawful' in 1758 (see Vattel, n.19, Book III, chapter VI, 512, para. 79, emphasis added). However, there is no indication that this was how states perceived the concept at the time, nor does this understanding seem to have appeared in other scholarship of the era.

147 Alder, n.2, 1–23, quoted at 21. See also Neff, n.3, 126–130; David B. Kopel, Paul Gallant and Joanne D. Eisen, 'The Human Right of Self-Defense' (2007) 22 *Brigham Young University Journal of Public Law* 43, 130.

148 Greig, n.2, 371.

149 See Gibson, n.56, 128 ('[a]fter the inception of Article 51 ... collective self-defence apparently joined the inviolate ranks of natural law. The reason for this, of course, is that individual self-defence was considered as an inherent right and when the wording of Article 51 was hammered out, "self-defence by a group of nations" was joined on to individual self-defence as an inherent right').

150 Bowett, n.9, 131.

151 Mori, n.45, 217; Stanimir A. Alexandrov, *Self-Defence against the Use of Force in International Law* (The Hague, Kluwer Law International, 1996), 90. Some states had initially wanted to keep collective defence actions as being limited only to the context of regional arrangements. See, for example, UNCIO, n.99, vol. 17, 288 (France).

préparatoires confirms that this was the intent of states by the end of the drafting process.[152]

Individual self-defence can be exercised without the need for any existing treaty framework, and thus the Charter's conjoining of self and collective defence implicitly emphasised that the same was true for its new twin. It also is worth noting that Article 51 was originally added to Chapter VIII on regional arrangements[153] (perhaps unsurprisingly, given its initial *raison d'être*). However, extended debates ultimately led to it being moved to Chapter VII.[154] This 'sheering' of collective self-defence from the Charter rules for regional arrangements reinforced the fact that it could be exercised without the need for the same Security Council authorisation that was required for 'enforcement actions' by regional agencies. However, the article's final location in the Charter also further embedded the understanding that collective self-defence could be exercised without the need for any pre-existing treaty framework.[155]

2.4.4 *Summarising the Implications of Article 51 for Collective Self-Defence*

The way in which 'collective self-defence' was included in the UN Charter had far more to do with solving a practical problem of preserving regional defence arrangements within the Charter framework than it did in being an exercise in considered doctrinal positioning. Irrespective of this, Article 51's wording,[156] meaning and placement all have had significant implications for the nature of collective self-defence in the UN era.

First, Article 51 led to the law of individual self-defence (as it existed prior to 1945, as was set out in the article, and as it has developed since) being applied, wholesale, to collective defence actions. This has added

[152] See, for example, UNCIO, n.99, vol. 11, 53 (USA); *ibid*, vol. 12, 681 (France); *ibid*, vol. 12, 859–860 (Egypt); *ibid*, vol. 12, 860 (USA); *ibid*, vol. 17, 287 (Coordination Committee meeting).

[153] See UNCIO, n.99, vol. 3, 634–636; *ibid*, vol. 17, 532–533.

[154] See Gray, n.2, 179; Alexandrov, n.151, 90.

[155] See Alexandrov, n.151, 101–102; Waldock, n.2, 504.

[156] It is perhaps worth noting that Article 51 refers to 'the inherent right of individual *or* collective self-defence' (emphasis added), rather than to a right of individual *and* collective self-defence. The wording used suggests a right that is single and indivisible, but also one that exists as an *alternative*. However, this author found no indication within the drafting history that the grammatical choice was considered as notable, or to detract from the clear intent of conjoining the individual and collective self-defence.

'meat to the bones' of the law of collective self-defence and a notable degree of legal consistency as between the unilateral and collective use of defensive force.

Second, the conjoining of the self-defences has meant that, in the UN era, both defending states and co-defending states have been consistently clear that they possess an inherent right to exercise collective self-defence.[157] It may be recalled from Chapter 1 that it was argued that the occasional conceptualisation of self-defence as part of the 'law of nature' is an 'anachronistic residue' of international law's ecclesiastical past.[158] Moreover, it may be dangerous to conceive of even the right of individual self-defence as being an element of 'natural law', or as being intrinsic in sovereignty, because it could act to sanctify the legitimacy of a form of state violence in perpetuity.[159] As a result of the drafting of the UN Charter, collective self-defence, too, gained at least the appearance of possessing the same dubious Teflon coating. It has been argued on this basis that the decision by the drafters of the Charter to refer to collective self-defence as an 'inherent right' was a 'grave mistake', because it has meant that states have since ignored the legal requirements that restrict it, at least to a greater extent than otherwise would have been the case.[160] This is a difficult assertion to test as a counter-factual, but this author would agree that the provision of a 'natural law sheen' to collective self-defence ultimately was undesirable, particularly given the risk of escalation that collective military action can entail.[161]

Third, whereas previously it was rare – if not unheard of – for states to act in each other's defence in an ad hoc manner (i.e. absent any treaty relationship) in the pre Charter practice, this has no longer been the case in the UN era. Collective self-defence treaty arrangements remain crucial,[162] but there also have been numerous instances of collective self-defence being exercised (actually, or purportedly) absent any such relationship.[163] This has increased flexibility, in some respects desirably, but it also has led to inconsistency and – at times – reduced scrutiny.[164]

[157] See Section 1.3.2.

[158] Dinstein, n.70, 198. See Chapter 1, n.135 and accompanying text.

[159] See Chapter 1, nn.135–138 and accompanying text.

[160] Gibson, n.56, 128.

[161] On the potential for escalation in the context of collective self-defence actions, see, generally, Chapter 3, nn.32–33 and accompanying text.

[162] See, generally, Chapter 7.

[163] See Section 1.2.2.

[164] See Section 7.6.

Many of these themes will be returned to in subsequent chapters of this book, which examine the operation of the law governing collective self-defence in the UN era. For now, it is enough to note that, while it is wrong to say that collective self-defence was wholly new in 1945,[165] more nuanced claims in the literature to the effect that self-defence was 'expanded' or 'enlarged' to include collective action in a novel *way*[166] are entirely correct.

2.5 Conclusion

This chapter has examined the history of the concept of 'collective self-defence' and its development into the form it has now taken in the UN era. It is difficult to treat seriously any claim that the drafters of the UN Charter entirely 'invented' the modern law of collective self-defence in 1945 given that many of the key features of the current law were set out, in broad terms, in writings from 200–300 years prior. Indeed, the core concept of 'collective self-defence' at the international level stretches back as far as recorded history. This chapter has shown that, as Lee has phrased it, '"[c]ollective self-defence" has a long history in the international community'.[167] Yet Lee's use of inverted commas here is appropriate, and telling, because the *term* 'collective self-defence' has no such historical basis. The importance of that, in itself, is minimal, but what it reflects is of much greater note. The adoption of the UN Charter certainly resulted in major changes to the centuries-old concept. Article 51 tied collective defence to individual self-defence, sharing the applicable law between them, giving collective self-defence a 'natural law' sheen unwarranted by its past, and reinforcing the possibility for it to be exercised ad hoc.

[165] For examples of this claim being made, see sources cited at n.3. In response to it, see, for example, Bowett, n.89, 200 ('[t]he notion of a collective right of self-defence has long been accepted); Constantinou, n.2, 173 ('[t]he right of collective self-defence was entrenched in the practice of States long before the adoption of the UN Charter'); Walker, n.35, 324–325, 351–352; Lee, n.135, 374, 377; Quincy Wright, 'United States Intervention in the Lebanon' (1959) 53 *American Journal of International Law* 112, 118 ('[t]his right seems to have been formulated for the first time in the Charter, but the concept is implied by the common practice of making defensive alliances').

[166] See, for example, Eyffinger, n.5, 128; Perkins, n.2, 206–207; Hans Kelsen, 'Collective Security and Collective Self-Defense under the Charter of the United Nations' (1948) 42 *American Journal of International Law* 783, 792; Greig, n.2, 371, 373; Tucker, n.2, 29.

[167] Lee, n.135, 374.

Questions regarding the *desirability* of these outcomes, such as whether using force to aid another state should be conceived of as an inherent right or whether collective defence 'should be subsumed under the right of self-defense are debatable.'[168] There are advantages. For example, the fact that the more developed legal requirements for individual self-defence now also unquestionably apply to collective self-defence means there is greater scope for rigorous evaluation of purported defensive actions than otherwise might have been the case. Equally, the sense on the part of states (especially the most powerful) that collective self-defence may be a 'natural' right pulls the concept in the other direction, away from scrutiny and regulation and towards unilateralism.

In any event, irrespective of its different historical origin, by virtue of Article 51 states today *do* have an inherent right of collective self-defence, which is largely indivisible from individual self-defence.[169] This understanding of collective self-defence also has been fully accepted in practice – and thus has a basis in customary international law – since 1945.[170] The next four chapters of this book are dedicated to examining the modern legal requirements for the exercise collective self-defence in detail, starting, in Chapter 3, with the criteria that are shared between individual and collective self-defence.

[168] Weightman, n.12, 1111.

[169] *Ibid.*

[170] Gray, n.2, 179 ('the post-1945 practice has been crucial to its [collective self-defence's] crystallization').

3

The Requirements Shared by Individual and Collective Self-Defence

3.1 Introduction

As was discussed in Chapter 2, a notable consequence of the 'conjoining' of individual and collective self-defence – and the latter's resulting status as a derivative right – is that the legal requirements for the exercise of individual self-defence apply equally to collective self-defence.[1] It will be recalled that Article 51 refers to 'the inherent right of individual or collective self-defence' in the same breath.[2] This, in itself, makes it very clear that any requirements set out in Article 51 apply to both individual and collective self-defence.

Admittedly, the criteria for the lawful exercise of individual self-defence stem from a combination of conventional and customary international law.[3] However, the Charter's conjoining of self and collective defence was almost immediately reflected in state practice, meaning that it quickly influenced the customary international law as applicable to collective self-defence. It is now near-universally agreed that not only the requirements under Article 51 but also the criteria for the lawful exercise of individual self-defence under customary international law equally apply to collective self-defence.[4] As the US Army's *Operational Law Handbook* phrases this: '[t]o constitute a legitimate act of collective self-defense, *all conditions* for the exercise of an individual State's right

[1] See Chapter 2, nn.132–139 and accompanying text.

[2] Charter of the United Nations (1945) 1 UNTS XVI (UN Charter), Article 51.

[3] See James A. Green, *The International Court of Justice and Self-Defence in International Law* (Oxford, Hart Publishing, 2009), particularly 129–138; *Military and Paramilitary Activities in and against Nicaragua* (*Nicaragua v. United States of America*) (merits) [1986] ICJ Rep. 14, para. 34.

[4] See, for example, *Nicaragua* (merits), n.3, paras. 94, 195, 211, 237; Yoram Dinstein, *War, Aggression and Self-Defence* (Cambridge, Cambridge University Press, 6th ed., 2017), 317, 320–321; Louis Henkin, 'The Use of Force: Law and US Policy', in *Right v. Might* (New York, Council on Foreign Relations Press, 1991), 45.

of self-defense must be met . . .'[5] In subsequent chapters of this book, the analysis focuses on a customary international law requirement that *only* applies in the collective context: the need for the defending state to request aid. First, though, this chapter examines the requirements that are shared across both versions of the right.

The conjoining of self and collective defence means that the contours of the legal requirements for the lawful exercise of collective self-defence can be drawn in part from the more extensive state practice and scholarship relating to individual self-defence.[6] As a result, the criteria they share already have been significantly analysed in the context of the voluminous literature on the individual version of the right. This chapter deliberately only skirts the edges of many of these well-worn paths. Nevertheless, given that the shared criteria are crucial for determining the lawfulness of any collective self-defence action, it is necessary to revisit them at least briefly in a general sense here. The primary aim of this chapter, though, is to assess particular questions that arise in the context of the application of these criteria to collective self-defence actions.

Following this brief introduction, Section 3.2 considers the crucial 'armed attack' requirement for self-defence. In so doing, it confirms, first, that the requirement applies to collective self-defence actions, before also noting that the 'gravity threshold' for the application of the requirement likewise applies. The section also engages with difficult issues that continually plague the analysis and application of the right of self-defence more generally: the (un)lawfulness of preventative action and the (un)lawfulness of responses to armed attacks perpetrated by non-state actors. In both instances, the relevant debates are noted, and their particular impact in the collective self-defence context considered, but they are not fully engaged with as they run beyond the scope of this book. Section 3.3 then examines the other two primary criteria applicable to all self-defence actions: necessity and proportionality. Again, this is with particular focus on how they apply in the collective self-defence context. Sections 3.4 and 3.5 then consider two further, secondary, criteria relating to the Security Council: the reporting requirement and the so-called 'until clause'.

[5] *Operational Law Handbook*, National Security Law Department (The Judge Advocate General's Legal Center & School, U.S. Army, Charlottesville, Virginia, 2022 edn.), 5 (emphasis added).

[6] See Christopher Greenwood, 'Self-Defence', in Rüdiger Wolfrum (ed.), *Max Planck Encyclopaedia of Public International Law, vol. IX* (Oxford, Oxford University Press, 2012), 103, 113, para. 52 (providing a useful select bibliography of some of the key works).

3.2 Armed Attack

3.2.1 The Armed Attack Criterion Applies to Collective Self-Defence

The criterion of 'armed attack' is set out in Article 51 of the United Nations (UN) Charter, which holds, *inter alia*, that: '[n]othing in the present Charter shall impair the inherent right of individual or collective self-defence *if an armed attack occurs* against a Member of the United Nations'.[7] In the 1986 *Nicaragua* case, the International Court of Justice (ICJ) identified the occurrence of an 'armed attack' not just as a legal requirement but as 'the condition *sine qua non* for the exercise of the right of *collective self-defence*',[8] highlighting the criterion's place at the very heart of the legal exercise of the collective (as well as the individual) version of the right.[9] The Court elsewhere in the decision reiterated that the requirement was applicable in the context of collective self-defence:

> [i]n the case of individual self-defence, the exercise of this right is subject to the state concerned having been the victim of an armed attack. Reliance on collective self-defence of course does not remove the need for this.[10]

This conclusion also flows axiomatically from the wording of Article 51 itself, which, of course, clearly indicates that the armed attack criterion applies equally to individual and collective self-defence.

The armed attack criterion is a clear feature of collective self-defence state practice and *opinio juris*. There are numerous examples of states asserting,[11] in the abstract, that the requirement is applicable to collective self-defence.[12] The requirement is also explicitly referenced in various

[7] UN Charter, n.2, Article 51 (emphasis added).

[8] *Nicaragua* (merits), n.3, para. 237 (emphasis added).

[9] The Court has stressed the importance of the armed attack requirement to the law governing self-defence (whether individual or collective) throughout its jurisprudence. See *ibid*, paras. 35, 127, 191, 210, 211, 237; *Case Concerning Oil Platforms (Islamic Republic of Iran v. United States of America)* (merits) [2003] ICJ Rep. 161, paras. 51, 71; *Legal Consequences of the Construction of a Wall in the Occupied Palestinian Territory* (advisory opinion) [2004] ICJ Rep. 135, para. 139; *Armed Activities on the Territory of the Congo (Democratic Republic of the Congo v. Uganda)* (judgment) [2005] ICJ Rep. 168, paras. 143, 146.

[10] *Nicaragua* (merits), n.3, para. 195.

[11] It is worth noting that, terminologically, states have tended to mix the terms 'aggression' and 'armed attack', but when using the former term, they often clearly are referencing the latter concept. On the lack of terminological exactitude in relation to the law governing the right of self-defence in general, see Green, n.3, 115–119.

[12] See, for example, US Senate, Joint Resolution, Authorizing the President to employ the Armed Forces of the United States for protecting the security of Formosa, the Pescadores,

collective self-defence treaty provisions.[13] Similarly, when claiming to be acting in collective self-defence, states commonly point to the occurrence of (or, perhaps, threat of) an armed attack to which they are responding. For example, in relation to its 2014 collective self-defence claim in regard to its use of force in Syria, the United Kingdom was explicit that the 'Islamic State of Iraq and the Levant' (ISIL) was 'engaged in an *ongoing armed attack* against Iraq, and therefore action against ISIL in Syria is

and related positions and territories of that area (29 January 1955) H. J. Res. 159, *Public Law* 5–7 February 1955, 69 Stat. 7, www.govinfo.gov/content/pkg/STATUTE-69/pdf/STATUTE-69-Pg7.pdf (United States, in relation to a possible future attack by mainland China against Taiwan); UNGA Summary Record, UN Doc. A/C.6/SR.514 (7 October 1957), para. 29 (USSR, in the context of debates in the UN General Assembly Sixth Committee regarding the question of defining aggression, referring to 'armed aggression' as a requirement for the exercise of collective self-defence, but clearly meaning the 'armed attack' criterion by this); UNGA Summary Records, UN Doc. A/C.6/SR.720 (1 April 1962), para. 10 (Argentina, noting during discussions over the codification and development of international law that '[t]he right of collective self-defence permitted States to aid a country that was the object of aggression'); 1966 Special Committee on Principles of International Law Concerning Friendly Relations and Co-Operation among States, Summary Record of the Fifteenth Meeting held at Headquarters, New York, on Thursday, 17 March 1966, UN Doc. A/AC.125/SR.15 (1966), 5 (Ghana, 'Article 51 of the Charter authorized individual or collective self-defence in one specific circumstance, namely *in the event of an armed attack*; nothing was said in it about collective self-defence against "intervention"', emphasis added); UNGA Summary Record, UN Doc. A/C.6/SR.1076 (21 November 1968), para. 7 (Cuba, in debates surrounding the development of the definition of aggression, arguing that it is necessary to 'determine whether an act of armed aggression had occurred … to invoke the right to collective self-defence'); UNGA Summary Record, UN Doc. A/C.6/SR.1167 (3 December 1969), para. 40 (Cuba, making exactly the same point again a year later); Japan, Cabinet Legislation Bureau, interpretation of Article 9 (quoted in both Aurelia George Mulgan, 'Japan's Defence Dilemma' (2005) 1 *Security Challenges* 59, 60, footnote 2; and Shojiro Sakaguchi, 'Major Constitutional Developments in Japan in the First Decade of the Twenty-First Century', in Albert H. Y. Chen (ed.), *Constitutionalism in Asia in the Early Twenty-First Century* (Cambridge, Cambridge University Press, 2014), 52, 62) (Japan in 1981, defining 'the right of collective self-defense' as 'the right to use actual force to *stop an armed attack* on a foreign country', emphasis added).

13 See, for example, North Atlantic Treaty (1949) 34 UNTS 243, Article 5 ('The Parties agree that an armed attack against one or more of them … shall be considered an attack against them all'); Inter-American Treaty of Reciprocal Assistance (1948) 21 UNTS 77 (Rio Treaty), Article 3(1) ('The High Contracting Parties agree that an armed attack by any State against an American State shall be considered as an attack against all the American States'); Southeast Asia Collective Defense Treaty (with Protocol) (1954) 209 UNTS 28 (SEATO Treaty), Article IV (obliging parties to respond to 'aggression by means of armed attack').

lawful in the collective self-defence of Iraq'.[14] There are many other such examples.[15]

Even in instances where it was clear that no armed attack had occurred (or imminently was about to occur), states have nonetheless felt compelled to pay lip service to the requirement in making (dubious) collective self-defence claims. Thus, in 1968, for example, the USSR was keen to stress that it was responding to a threat to 'Czechoslovakia arising from counter-revolutionary forces which have entered into collusion with foreign powers hostile to socialism'.[16] Such tenuous claims of outside interference, alluding to – or more explicitly referring to – the occurrence of an armed attack can be observed elsewhere in the collective self-defence practice too.[17] Importantly, when there has been no (or limited) evidence that an armed attack has occurred (or is imminent), this has commonly been cited by *other states* as establishing the illegality of purported collective self-defence actions. For example, the USSR was very clear – and correct[18] – in 1958 that the United States' intervention in Lebanon was not a lawful exercise of collective self-defence, *inter alia*, on the basis that '[n]o one has attacked Lebanon and there is no threat of

[14] Letter dated 7 September 2015 from the Permanent Representative of the United Kingdom of Great Britain and Northern Ireland to the United Nations addressed to the President of the Security Council, UN Doc. S/2015/688 (8 September 2015) (emphasis added).

[15] See, for example, UNSC Verbatim Record, UN Doc. S/PV.2721 (19 November 1986), 19–20 (Zaire, arguing that it was entitled to use force under Article 51 to help 'Chad in resisting aggression against it' from Libya); Letter dated 9 August 1990 from the Permanent Representative of the United States of America to the United Nations addressed to the President of the Security Council, UN Doc. S/21492 (9 August 1990) (United States, claiming to be acting in the collective self-defence of Kuwait, following an armed attack by Iraq); Letter dated 15 July 1993 from the Permanent Representative of Tajikistan to the United Nations addressed to the Secretary-General, UN Doc. S/26092 (16 July 1993) (referring to its request to respond to an 'act of aggression'); Letter dated 10 December 2015 from the Chargé d'affaires a.i. of the Permanent Mission of Germany to the United Nations addressed to the President of the Security Council, UN Doc. S/2015/946 (10 December 2015) (Germany, 'ISIL has carried out, and continues to carry out, armed attacks against Iraq, France, and other States').

[16] UNSC Verbatim Record, UN Doc. S/PV.1441 (21 August 1968), para. 104.

[17] See, for example, UNSC Verbatim Record, UN Doc. S/PV.746 (28 October 1956), para. 155 (USSR, regarding its intervention in Hungary in 1956); UNSC Verbatim Record, UN Doc. S/PV.827 (15 July 1958), para. 45 (United States, regarding its intervention in Lebanon in 1958).

[18] Quincy Wright, 'United States Intervention in the Lebanon' (1959) 53 *American Journal of International Law* 112, particularly 119.

an armed attack against Lebanon'.[19] Again, this is but one example among many.[20]

It, therefore, is unquestionable that the armed attack criterion applies to collective self-defence just as it does to individual self-defence.[21] It is worth being clear, though, that the relevant requirement here is that the *defending state* must have suffered an armed attack (or, again, perhaps be faced with the imminent threat of an armed attack amounting to a grave use of force) for that collective self-defence action to be lawful. In case of any doubt – given occasional (incorrect) suggestions that the state using force in collective self-defence ultimately must be defending 'itself'[22] – it is worth reiterating, as was discussed in Chapter 1, that it is abundantly clear that there is no need for the *co-defending state* to have been, itself, the victim of an armed attack.[23] In contrast, the defending state must have suffered (or, perhaps, imminently be about to suffer) an armed attack against it, otherwise a purported collective self-defence action will be unlawful.

[19] UN Doc. S/PV.827, n.17, para. 116. It has been argued that the interventions of the United States and the United Kingdom in Lebanon and Jordan, respectively, in 1958 were aimed at supporting unpopular pro-Western governments against internal opposition movements, rather than responding to an armed attack. See F.A. Gerges, 'The Lebanese Crisis of 1958: The Risks of Inflated Self-Importance' (1993) 5 *Beirut Review* 83.

[20] See, for example, UNSC Verbatim Record, UN Doc. S/PV.831 (17 July 1958), paras. 65–68 (the USSR similarly arguing that the United Kingdom's intervention in Jordan, also in 1958, was not a lawful exercise of collective self-defence because there had been no armed attack against Jordan); UN Doc. A/C.6/SR.1076, n.12, para. 35 (the Netherlands, dismissing the Soviet claim to be acting in collective self-defence in relation to Czechoslovakia in 1968 on the basis that collective self-defence was lawful only in response to an armed attack, and no armed attack had occurred); UNSC Verbatim Record, UN Doc. S/PV.1442 (22 August 1968), para. 17 (China, likewise, dismissing the Soviet claim regarding Czechoslovakia in 1968 on the same basis).

[21] Roberto Ago, 'Addendum – Eighth Report on State Responsibility by Mr. Roberto Ago, Special Rapporteur – The Internationally Wrongful Act of the State, Source of International Responsibility (Part 1)', UN Doc. A/CN.4/318/Add.5–7, in (1980) I(1) *Yearbook of the International Law Commission* 13, 68, para. 118; Henkin, n.4, 45; Jaemin Lee, 'Collective Self-Defense or Collective Security: Japan's Reinterpretation of Article 9 of the Constitution' (2015) 8 *Journal of East Asia and International Law* 373, 379; A. J. Thomas Jr. and Ann Van Wynen Thomas, 'The Organization of American States and Collective Security' (1959) 13 *Southwestern Law Journal* 177, 188; Marko Svicevic, 'Collective Self-Defence or Regional Enforcement Action: The Legality of a SADC Intervention in Cabo Delgado and the Question of Mozambican Consent' (2022) 9 *Journal on the Use of Force and International Law* 138, 149.

[22] See Section 3.2.

[23] See *ibid* (setting out in detail the argument that an armed attack against the co-defending state is not required).

3.2.2 *The Meaning of Armed Attack in the Collective Self-Defence Context*

While it can be said that an 'armed attack' is a legal requirement for both individual and collective self-defence, nothing in Article 51 (or the Charter more generally) identifies exactly what an 'armed attack' *is*. However, the fact that the term 'armed attack' as used in Article 51 differs from the phrase 'use of force' in Article 2(4) indicates that the two concepts are not the same.[24]

Since the adoption of the Charter, the notion of an 'armed attack' has been interpreted – at least relatively consistently – to mean *a qualitatively grave use of force*.[25] As the ICJ famously phrased this in the *Nicaragua* case, an armed attack constitutes 'the most grave form of the use of force'.[26] It is worth recalling that the Court was, of course, advancing this understanding specifically in relation to collective self-defence.

A notable problem with the conclusion that an armed attack equates to a 'grave' use of force is that this leaves a 'gap' between violations of the prohibition of the use of force and action taken in defensive response. It is possible for an aggressor to perpetrate an unlawful use of force against another state that falls short of the required level of gravity to amount to an armed attack, meaning that the attacked party is unable to defend itself (or request that other states do so collectively).[27] Although

[24] See Lindsay Moir, *Reappraising the Resort to Force* (Oxford, Hart Publishing, 2010), 22; Dinstein, n.4, 205–206.

[25] See, for example, Olivier Corten, *The Law against War: The Prohibition on the Use of Force in Contemporary International Law* (Oxford, Hart Publishing, 2nd ed., 2021), 400; Avra Constantinou, *The Right of Self-Defence under Customary International Law and Article 51 of the UN Charter* (Brussels, Bruylant, 2000), 57; Christine Gray, *International Law and the Use of Force* (Oxford, Oxford University Press, 4th ed., 2018), 153–157. *Contra* Tarcisio Gazzini, *The Changing Rules on the Use of Force in International Law* (Manchester, Manchester University Press, 2005), 138; Elizabeth Wilmshurst (ed.), 'The Chatham House Principles of International Law on the Use of Force by States in Self-Defence' (2006) 55 *International and Comparative Law Quarterly* 963, 966.

[26] *Nicaragua* (merits), n.3, para. 191. This statement was also reiterated in *Oil Platforms* (merits), n.9, para. 51.

[27] See Chiara Redaelli, *Intervention in Civil Wars: Effectiveness, Legitimacy, and Human Rights* (Oxford, Hart Publishing, 2021), 55–56; Kevin Jon Heller, 'The Unlawfulness of a "Bloody Nose Strike" on North Korea' (2020) 96 *International Law Studies* 1, 9; Tom Ruys, 'The Meaning of "Force" and the Boundaries of the Jus ad Bellum: Are "Minimal" Uses of Force Excluded from UN Charter Article 2(4)?' (2014) 108 *American Journal of International Law* 159, 162–163; Green, n.3, 138–143; Natalia Ochoa-Ruiz and Esther Salamanca-Aguado, 'Exploring the Limits of International Law relating to the Use of Force in Self-Defence' (2005) 16 *European Journal of International Law* 499, 511;

this outcome is, itself, seemingly unjust,[28] the main rationale for a restrictive conception of armed attack is to limit escalation in uses of force, with comparatively minor incidents giving rise to spiralling responses.[29] In particular, and of relevance here, is the fact that it has been argued that the key reason that the ICJ asserted that an armed attack equates to 'the most grave form of the use of force' was to rule out large-scale uses of force involving multiple states avowedly acting in collective self-defence.[30] It is at least arguable that a higher triggering threshold for collective self-defence is more desirable than for individual self-defence,[31] as the potential for escalation of minor conflicts is greater when there is the possibility of multiple third-party states intervening,[32] as is the risk of abuse.[33]

Dinstein, n.4, 205–208; Thomas M. Franck, 'Who Killed Article 2(4)? or Changing the Norms Governing the Use of Force by States' (1970) 64 *American Journal of International Law* 809, 812–813; Edward Miller, 'Self-Defence, International Law and the Six Day War' (1985) 20 *Israeli Law Review* 49, 52–56; Gazzini, n.25, 138; William H. Taft IV, 'Self-Defence and the *Oil Platforms* Decision' (2004) 29 *Yale Journal of International Law* 295, 300; John Lawrence Hargrove, 'The *Nicaragua* Judgment and the Future of the Law of Force and Self-Defence' (1987) 81 *American Journal of International Law* 135, 139–140.

28 Hargrove, n.27, 139.

29 W. Michael Reisman, 'Old Wine in New Bottles: The Reagan and Brezhnev Doctrines in Contemporary International Law and Practice' (1988) 13 *Yale Journal of International Law* 171, 194–196.

30 See Tom J. Farer, 'Drawing the Right Line' (1987) 81 *American Journal of International Law* 112, 114; Gray, n.25, 156–157; John Norton Moore, 'The *Nicaragua* Case and the Deterioration of World Order' (1987) 81 *American Journal of International Law* 151, 152; R. St. J. MacDonald, 'The *Nicaragua* Case: New Answers to Old Questions' (1986) 24 *Canadian Yearbook of International Law* 127, 149; Abhimanyu George Jain, 'Rationalising International Law Rules on Self-Defence: The Pin Prick Doctrine' (2014) 14 *Chicago-Kent Journal of International and Comparative Law* 23, 36, footnote 45.

31 Eustace Chikere Azubuike, 'Probing the Scope of Self Defense in International Law' (2011) 17 *Annual Survey of International and Comparative Law* 129, 155.

32 Constantine Antonopoulos, 'Some Thoughts on the NATO Position in Relation to the Iraqi Crisis' (2004) 17 *Leiden Journal of International Law* 171, 177; C. H. M. Waldock, 'The Regulation of the Use of Force by Individual States in International Law' (1952) 81 *Recueil des cours* 451, 504; Green, n.3, 59 (a restrictive view of armed attack 'theoretically limits large conflicts, in that third party States will not be lawfully empowered to respond forcibly in instances involving uses of force of a comparatively minor nature').

33 *Nicaragua* (merits), n.3, dissenting opinion of Judge Jennings, 543 ('[i]t is of course a fact that collective self-defence is a concept that lends itself to abuse. One must therefore sympathize with the anxiety of the Court to define it in terms of some strictness'); Christine Chinkin and Mary Kaldor, *International Law and New Wars* (Cambridge, Cambridge University Press, 2017), 141; Constantine Antonopoulos, 'The Unilateral

The inherent 'conjoining' of the two manifestations of self-defence,[34] however, means that distinguishing two differing understandings of 'armed attack' – one applicable to individual and one, at a higher threshold, to collective self-defence – would be unworkable, and contrary to any reasonable interpretation of Article 51. Moreover, an assessment of the state practice regarding self-defence supports the view that the term 'armed attack' refers to a grave use of force in regard to both individual and collective self-defence. Application of a 'gravity threshold' for the armed attack criterion has admittedly not been entirely consistent in the UN era,[35] but, overall, '[i]t seems that in practice States still believe that self-defense can only be used as long as the original attack is of sufficient gravity'.[36]

This holds true when one considers the practice specific to collective self-defence.[37] As with individual self-defence, there is some inconsistency in the practice, but overall state support for the gravity threshold for armed attack can nonetheless be identified. Indeed, there is no discernible difference in the interpretation of the armed attack criterion in collective self-defence practice as compared to individual self-defence. Taking the intervention by the United States in Lebanon in 1958 as an example, although Lebanon initially claimed a right of self-defence based upon the 'intervention' of armed bands from the United Arab Republic (UAR) without indicating any level of gravity,[38] it ultimately was clear that it was facing 'aggression',[39] as contrasted to force below the level of aggression,[40] and was very keen to stress that there had been a 'massive intervention in the internal affairs of Lebanon'[41] despite there not being evidence to support this. For its part, the USSR also indicated that there was a gravity threshold for an armed attack, which it did not feel had

Use of Force by States after the End of the Cold War' (1999) 4 *Journal of Armed Conflict Law* 117, 127.

34 See Section 2.4.

35 For a detailed assessment of this state practice, see Green, n.3, 112–129.

36 Jean d'Aspremont, 'Mapping the Concepts Behind the Contemporary Liberalization of the Use of Force in International Law' (2010) 31 *University of Pennsylvania Journal of International Law* 1089, 1119.

37 Heller, n.27, 9; Svicevic, n.21, 150.

38 Letter dated 22 May 1958 from the Representative of Lebanon Addressed to the President of the Security Council, UN Doc. S/4007 (23 May 1958).

39 UNSC Verbatim Record, UN Doc. S/PV.825 (11 June 1958), para. 70.

40 *Ibid.*

41 UNSC Verbatim Record, UN Doc. S/PV.828 (15 July 1958), para. 54.

been met.[42] The UAR shared this view.[43] Sweden, as a non-aligned state, alluded to a gravity threshold too, albeit not especially clearly.[44] Overall, in relation to the Lebanon situation of 1958, a majority of states took the view that a level of force *beyond* a mere breach of Article 2(4) was a necessary legal trigger for collective self-defence.

Another example of note is Zaire's claim to be acting in the collective self-defence of Chad in 1986.[45] In making that claim, Zaire was at great pains to set out the scale and effects of the actions of the 'foreign forces occupying the northern part of Chad'[46] in significant detail. This was with the clear aim of establishing that these acts amounted to what it called 'aggression', rather than a use of force *simpliciter*.

In regard to the deployment of US troops to Honduras in 1988, avowedly in collective self-defence,[47] Honduras was very clear that it considered that it had suffered an 'aggression' by Nicaragua,[48] triggering its right to request aid in self-defence. For its part, Nicaragua conceded during the Security Council debate that it was engaged in cross-border military intervention in Honduras but argued that this did not rise to the level of 'aggression' because it had 'no intention of occupying' Honduran territory.[49] Peru, too, downplayed the scope of the situation, referring to 'armed clashes . . . in the Honduras-Nicaragua border area'.[50] It implied on that basis that it did not see Nicaragua's activity as reaching the level of an armed attack. Again, therefore, while there was disagreement as to the application of the criterion, states appeared to concur that a particular level of gravity was required.

A much more recent example highlighting the fact that states recognise the need for a degree of gravity for a use of force to qualify as an armed attack triggering collective self-defence is the coalition action taken against ISIL in Syria from 2014. Again, the states claiming to be

42 See, for example, UN Doc. S/PV.827, n.17, para. 118.

43 See, for example, UNSC Verbatim Record, UN Doc. S/PV.823 (6 June 1958), para. 103; UNSC Verbatim Record, UN Doc. S/PV.830 (16 July 1958), para. 7.

44 UN Doc. S/PV.830, n. 43, para. 48.

45 See, for example, UN Doc. S/PV.2721, n.15, 13–20.

46 *Ibid*, 19–20.

47 Letter dated 17 March 1988 from The Permanent Representative of Honduras to the United Nations addressed to the Secretary-General, UN Doc. A/42/931-S/19643 (17 March 1988), para. 6.

48 *Ibid*, paras. 2, 4, 6; UNSC Provisional Verbatim Record, UN Doc. S/PV.2802 (18 March 1988), 17, 22, 52.

49 *Ibid*, 41–45.

50 *Ibid*, 38.

acting in collective self-defence emphasised how serious the threat posed by ISIL was and referenced the scale and effects of its actions as justifying a forcible response. Denmark, for example, set out 'the horrifying terrorist attacks perpetrated by ISIL including in Sousse, Ankara, Beirut and Paris and over Sinai . . .'[51] Similarly, the United States stressed that 'ISIL and other terrorist groups in Syria are a threat not only to Iraq, but also to many other countries . . .',[52] which is especially notable given that the United States is one of the few states that generally is sceptical of a gravity requirement for armed attack.[53]

As with individual self-defence, therefore, the armed attack criterion requires the occurrence (or, perhaps, imminent occurrence) of a grave use of force against the defending state. This, of course, begs the question 'how grave is grave?'[54] There is no exact answer to that question. What constitutes 'sufficient gravity' will vary and is to be determined in a context-specific manner, based on the facts surrounding any given claim of collective self-defence.[55] What is clear, however, is that action causing actual harm to persons or property (or action that would have caused such harm), is necessary to trigger self-defence, whether individual or collective.[56]

3.2.3 *The Occurrence of an Armed Attack: Preventative Forms of Self-Defence*

There has been a significant amount of scholarship[57] concerning the contested lawfulness of what variously have been referred to as

[51] Letter dated 11 January 2016 from the Permanent Representative of Denmark to the United Nations addressed to the President of the Security Council, UN Doc. S/2016/34 (13 January 2016).

[52] Letter dated 23 September 2014 from the Permanent Representative of the United States of America to the United Nations addressed to the Secretary-General, UN Doc. S/2014/695 (23 September 2014).

[53] See, for example, United States, *Department of Defense Law of War Manual 2015* (updated May 2016) Office of General Counsel, Department of Defence, 47, para. 1.11.5.2.

[54] d'Aspremont, n.36, 1119 ('[g]ravity can ... be understood in various ways. ... This means that a lot of uncertainty remains as to how the gravity of the attack must be appraised', footnotes omitted); Heller, n.27, 10–11.

[55] See Tom Ruys, *'Armed Attack' and Article 51 of the UN Charter: Evolutions in Customary Law and Practice* (Cambridge, Cambridge University Press, 2010), 181; Keiichiro Okimoto, *The Distinction and Relationship between Jus ad Bellum and Jus in Bello* (Oxford, Hart Publishing, 2011), 46–51.

[56] Heller, n.27, 10–11.

[57] See, for example, Kinga Tibori-Szabó, *Anticipatory Action in Self-Defence: Essence and Limits under International Law* (The Hague, TMC Asser Press, 2011); Stefan Talmon,

anticipatory/pre-emptive/preventative[58] self-defence actions, without it leading to much in the way of resolution on the matter.[59] This book is not the place to (re)examine the deep and long-standing divisions that exist among states and scholars in this regard, but it is necessary briefly to sketch the key contours of the debate here.

Scholars who consider anticipatory action to be unlawful point to the fact that, as a matter of textual analysis, Article 51 is clear that an armed attack must have *occurred*.[60] This view is then supported further by reference to the fact that relatively few states have advanced a preventative justification for using force post-1945 and, even when they have, such claims have commonly been rejected by other states.[61] In contrast, those supporting preventative self-defence have argued that the use of force in self-defence in response to the threat of attack was lawful under pre-Charter customary international law, and that Article 51 explicitly preserves a state's 'inherent right' of self-defence (thus ensuring the

'Changing Views on the Use of Force: The German Position' (2005) 5 *Baltic Yearbook of International Law* 41, 60–63; Rainer Hofmann, 'International Law and the Use of Military Force against Iraq' (2002) 45 *German Yearbook of International Law* 9, 31; Noam Lubell, 'The Problem of Imminence in an Uncertain World', in Marc Weller (ed.), *The Oxford Handbook of the Use of Force in International Law* (Oxford, Oxford University Press, 2015), 697; Alex Bellamy, 'International Law and the War with Iraq' (2003) 4 *Melbourne Journal of International Law* 497, 515–517; Miriam Sapiro, 'Iraq: The Shifting Sands of Pre-Emptive Self-Defense' (2003) 97 *American Journal of International Law* 599; Christopher Greenwood, 'International Law and the Pre-Emptive Use of Force: Afghanistan, Al-Qaida, and Iraq' (2003) 4 *San Diego International Law Journal* 7; Abraham D. Sofaer, 'On the Necessity of Pre-Emption' (2003) 14 *European Journal of International Law* 209; Christine Gray, 'The US National Security Strategy and the New "Bush Doctrine" on Pre-emptive Self-Defence' (2002) 1 *Chinese Journal of International Law* 437; Christian Henderson, 'The 2006 National Security Strategy of the United States: The Pre-emptive Use of Force and the Persistent Advocate' (2007–2008) 15 *Tulsa Journal of Comparative and International Law* 1; James A. Green, 'The *Ratione Temporis* Elements of Self-Defence' (2015) 2 *Journal on the Use of Force and International Law* 97, 102–108.

58 These terms – and others – are used by different scholars to mean different things in this context, without consistency. See Green, n.57, 102–103.

59 See *ibid*, 106 (the present author, arguing that '[a] reasonable case can be made for either proposition', meaning that all that can be said with certainty 'is that self-defence in response to an imminent attack *may be* lawful at the current time', emphasis in original).

60 UN Charter, n.2, Article 51 ('[n]othing in the present Charter shall impair the inherent right of individual or collective self-defence if an armed attack *occurs*', emphasis added). See, for example, Ian Brownlie, *International Law and the Use of Force by States* (Oxford, Oxford University Press, 1963), particularly 275–278; Corten, n.25, 404–410.

61 See, for example, Corten, n.25, 414–419, 427–434; Gray, n.25, 170–175.

continued lawfulness of such action).[62] It has also been noted by some supporters of preventative self-defence that Article 51 says that self-defence is lawful if an armed attack occurs, but not 'if *and only if* an armed attack occurs'.[63] Another, more convincing, argument is that the equally authoritative French version of Article 51 appears to be less restrictive than the English text, in that it refers more generally to a UN member as being 'the object' of armed aggression, rather than an armed attack 'occurring' as such ('*dans le cas où un Membre des Nations Unies est l'objet d'une agression armée*').[64] Finally, it has been argued that it is illogical for a state to have to wait until it has been attacked before it can defend itself where it is clear that an attack is coming, especially when one considers modern weaponry and delivery systems.[65]

Thomas and Thomas have asserted that the collective self-defence context changes this well-worn 'preventative self-defence' debate.[66] This is said to be on the basis that, while customary international law allowed for anticipatory action in the case of self-defence (truly so-called), there was no right pre-exiting the Charter to use force in an anticipatory manner collectively.[67] Thus, irrespective of the fact that Article 51 had the effect of 'retrofitting' collective self-defence into an inherent right,[68] this did not act to preserve a right of 'anticipatory collective self-defence' because there was no such right: simply put, the Charter could not have 'impaired' something that did not exist. This means that the 'starting point' for collective – unlike individual – self-defence must be Article 51's restriction that an armed attack must have occurred.[69]

62 See, for example, Rosalyn Higgins, 'The Attitudes of Western States towards Legal Aspects of the Use of Force', in Antonio Cassese (ed.), *The Current Legal Regulation of the Use of Force* (Leiden, Martinus Nijhoff, 1986), 435, 442.

63 See, for example, *Nicaragua* (merits), n.3, dissenting opinion of Judge Schwebel, para. 173; Derek W. Bowett, *Self-Defense in International Law* (Manchester, Manchester University Press, 1958), 188.

64 See Rosalyn Higgins, *The Development of International Law through the Political Organs of the United Nations* (Oxford, Oxford University Press, 1963), 199; Waldock, n.32, 497.

65 See Rosalyn Higgins, *Problems and Process: International Law and How We Use It* (Oxford, Oxford University Press, 1994), 242–243; Noam Lubell, *Extraterritorial Use of Force against Non-state Actors* (Oxford, Oxford University Press, 2010), 57; Ashley S. Deeks, 'Taming the Doctrine of Pre-Emption', in Marc Weller (ed.), *The Oxford Handbook of the Use of Force in International Law* (Oxford, Oxford University Press, 2015), 661, 669–675.

66 Thomas and Thomas, n.21, 189.

67 *Ibid.*

68 See Section 2.4.

69 Thomas and Thomas, n.21, 189.

The argument advanced by Thomas and Thomas can be questioned. For one thing, while some pre-Charter collective defence arrangements were restricted purely to reactive actions,[70] many other such agreements clearly envisaged their parties acting collectively in an anticipatory manner, in relation to threats of future attack, and many 'collective defence' actions thus were preventative prior to 1945.[71] This was not widely conceived of as the exercise of an 'inherent right',[72] but it cannot be said to have been in any way restricted prior to the Charter and was widely practiced. As such, once Article 51 designated that collective self-defence *was* an inherent right that could not be impaired, the ability for states to continue this widespread practice would seem to have been preserved (assuming that one accepts the argument that the phrase 'nothing shall impair the inherent right' preserved the lawfulness of individual anticipatory self-defence actions).

It also would seem a logical consequence of the conjoining of the two manifestations of the right, as an indivisible whole,[73] that *if* a state can lawfully use force in individual self-defence in response to an imminent armed attack against it, then that state equally can request aid from other states in collective self-defence on the same basis (with the reverse also being true: if a state cannot act in this way to protect itself, nor can other states act in this way to protect it). As has already been noted, any attempt to 'sever' the law applicable to individual and collective self-defence is now conceptually untenable.[74] Even if Thomas and Thomas are correct that the notion of 'anticipatory collective self-defence' cannot have been preserved by Article 51 because it never existed in the first place, it is worth recalling that this only would remove one of the key arguments commonly advanced by those who support preventative self-defence: they also have advanced *other* arguments that would be unaffected by this point.[75]

[70] See George K. Walker, 'Anticipatory Collective Self-Defense in the Charter Era: What the Treaties Have Said' (1998) 31 *Cornell International Law Journal* 321, 374 (noting that some collective defence arrangements pre-1945 'had terms stating a reactive self-defense theory'). See also *ibid*, 335.

[71] *Ibid* (providing numerous examples throughout).

[72] See Chapter 2, nn.144–149 and accompanying text.

[73] See *ibid*, Section 2.4.

[74] See nn.31–37 and accompanying text, regarding the fact that the same 'gravity threshold' must apply to the armed attack requirement for both individual and collective self-defence.

[75] See nn.62–65 and accompanying text.

The present author is ultimately of the view that the debate over the (un)lawfulness of anticipatory self-defence is largely unchanged by the collective self-defence context.[76] However, it must be said that an anticipatory self-defence claim – which already is a legally controversial claim in itself – is likely to be especially controversial in the context of collective self-defence, because one of the key arguments used to indicate its lawfulness (i.e. the 'inherence' of the right of self-defence) can at least be brought into question in the collective context.[77] It is also possible that such a claim may be more politically, as well as legally, controversial. For example, Antonopoulos has suggested that the likelihood of greater scale and 'expansion' of the use of force when more states become involved may make third-party states more hostile to claims of collective self-defence in relation to an attack that has not yet occurred than they would have been in the context of an individual response.[78] Similarly, Walker notes that a possible difference between anticipatory self-defence in the individual and collective contexts could arise where states acting together in collective self-defence have differing views about the lawfulness or broader acceptability of preventative military action: that is, the more states that are involved, the more room there is for disagreement on controversial legal questions.[79] The points made by Antonopoulos and Walker are surely both correct, but they ultimately relate to the political (un)acceptability of the action in question for particular states, rather than being based on a normative distinction in the debate as between individual and collective actions.

In any event, it is worth noting that it is now the case that the majority view among both states and scholars is that a self-defence action *against*

[76] See Dino Kritsiotis, 'A Study of the Scope and Operation of the Rights of Individual and Collective Self-Defence under International Law', in Nigel D. White and Christian Henderson (eds.), *Research Handbook on International Conflict and Security Law:* Jus ad Bellum, Jus in Bello *and* Jus Post Bellum (Abingdon, Routledge, 2013), 170, 227 (implicitly reaching the same conclusion).

[77] On the controversy surrounding the idea of 'anticipatory collective self-defence' – as a matter of law – see Covey Oliver, 'International Law and the Quarantine of Cuba: A Hopeful Prescription for Legal Writing' (1963) 57 *American Journal of International Law* 373, 375; Edward McWhinney, *The September 11 Terrorist Attacks and the Invasion of Iraq in Contemporary International Law: Opinions on the Emerging New World Order System* (Leiden, Martinus Nijhoff Publishers, 2004), 52–53.

[78] Antonopoulos, n.32, 178.

[79] See Walker, n.70, 354.

a demonstrably imminent armed attack is lawful.[80] This is not an uncontroversial conclusion, with some writers continuing to assert that self-defence remains a possibility if, and only if, an armed attack has occurred or is occurring.[81] Less controversial, though, are situations involving more temporally remote threats. There undoubtedly is no legal basis to use force in self-defence against a non-imminent threat.[82] It is also worth being clear that *if* self-defence is lawful in response to an imminent attack, it is *only* lawful in response to an imminent *armed attack*: thus, 'armed attack' remains the relevant standard, irrespective of the side of the anticipatory self-defence debate on which one falls.[83]

Although most anticipatory self-defence claims since 1945 have related to purported acts of individual self-defence,[84] there are some instances where states have made what might be termed 'anticipatory collective self-defence' claims.[85] For example, the justification advanced in 1958 by the United Kingdom for its use of force at the request of Jordan was of an 'anticipatory' nature.[86] The United Kingdom argued that there was evidence of 'the *preparation* of a fresh attempt to overthrow the [Jordanian] regime and create internal disorder [including] the movements of Syrian forces toward the northern frontier of Jordan'.[87] It also

[80] See Anthony Garwood-Gowers, 'Israel's Airstrike on Syria's Al-Kibar Facility: A Test Case for the Doctrine of Preemptive Self-Defence?' (2011) 16 *Journal of Conflict and Security Law* 263, 279.

[81] See, for example, Johanna Friman, *Revisiting the Concept of Defence in the* Jus ad Bellum (Oxford, Hart Publishing, 2017), 60–66.

[82] See, for example, Joe Boyle, 'Making Sense of Self-Defence in the War on Terror' (2014) 1 *Journal on the Use of Force and International Law* 55, 62–65; Greenwood, n.57, 12–16; Christian Henderson, *The Persistent Advocate and the Use of Force: The Impact of the United States upon the* Jus ad Bellum *in the Post-Cold War Era* (Farnham, Ashgate, 2010), particularly 192–193; Heiko Meiertöns, *The Doctrines of US Security Policy: An Evaluation under International Law* (Cambridge, Cambridge University Press, 2010), particularly 221–224; James A. Green, Christian Henderson and Tom Ruys, 'Russia's Attack on Ukraine and the *Jus ad Bellum*' (2022) 9 *Journal on the Use of Force and International Law* 4, 12. *Contra* John Yoo, 'International Law and the War in Iraq' (2003) 97 *American Journal of International Law* 563, particularly 571–574.

[83] See *Nicaragua* (merits), n.3, paras. 35, 194; Terry D. Gill, 'The Law of Armed Attack in the Context of the *Nicaragua* Case' (1988) 1 *Hague Yearbook of International Law* 30, 35; Green, n.3, 28–30.

[84] Walker, n.70, 323.

[85] See Gray, n.25, 177 ('[s]tates have invoked collective self-defence as a justification for inviting foreign troops before any armed attack has occurred, in case collective self-defence is needed in the future').

[86] *Ibid*, 184.

[87] UN Doc. S/PV.831, n.20, para. 27 (emphasis added).

referred to a statement made on Bagdad radio: 'A revolution has started in Iraq and one in Lebanon, and *tomorrow* another revolution will start in Jordan.'[88] Ultimately, the United Kingdom asserted that:

> [t]here is nothing either in the Charter or in the established rules in international law to inhibit a Government from asking a friendly Government for military assistance as a defensive measure when it considers itself to be in danger. Nor is there anything to inhibit the Government thus appealed to from responding.[89]

While it was strongly opposed to the United Kingdom's action, it perhaps is notable that the USSR dismissed it on the basis that it felt that there was no imminent armed attack, not because it took the view that anticipatory self-defence was per se unlawful.[90] Similarly – while the United States did not make an *anticipatory* collective self-defence claim in regard to intervention in Lebanon (also in 1958) – as has already been noted in this section, the USSR took issue with the fact that '[n]o one has attacked Lebanon *and there is no threat of an armed attack against Lebanon*'.[91] This implies that although the United States was claiming that an armed attack had occurred,[92] for the USSR, even the *threat* of armed attack against Lebanon would have been sufficient.

Another example is the request for support from US troops by the King of Saudi Arabia, following the occupation of Kuwait in the early 1990s.[93] Saudi Arabia feared an imminent invasion itself,[94] with the United States concurring that 'Iraq may not stop using force to advance its ambitions [and had] ... massed an enormous war machine on the Saudi border capable of initiating hostilities with little or no additional preparation'.[95] Although this was not explicitly framed as an anticipatory

88 *Ibid* (emphasis added).

89 *Ibid*, para. 29.

90 See, for example, *ibid*, para. 68 (USSR: 'the specific purpose was not to help repel an imaginary threat ... hanging over Jordan, but to help ... crush the revolution in Iraq').

91 UN Doc. S/PV.827, n.17, para. 116 (emphasis added).

92 See, for example, *ibid*, para. 40 (United States, specifically citing 'the infiltration of arms and personnel into Lebanon from the United Arab Republic').

93 *Keesing's Record of World Events* (1990), 37635–37636, 37638; US Library of Congress – Federal Research Division, 'Country Profile: Saudi Arabia' (September 2006), www.marines.mil/Portals/1/Publications/Saudi%20Arabia%20Profile.pdf, 4.

94 See Constantine Antonopoulos, 'Force by Armed Groups as Armed Attack and the Broadening of Self-Defence' (2008) 55 *Netherlands International Law Review* 159, 175.

95 'Address to the Nation Announcing the Deployment of United States Armed Forces to Saudi Arabia', George Bush (8 August 1990), www.presidency.ucsb.edu/documents/

collective self-defence claim, it has been interpreted this way,[96] and the United States formally reported it to the Security Council, referencing Article 51 in so doing.[97] There was some concern expressed in scholarship as to whether the Saudi request may have been coerced,[98] as well as there being some internal discontent from more hard-line Islamist elements of Saudi society in relation to the US troop deployment.[99] However, other *states* did not seem to take issue with the action, either in general or on the basis that it was an 'anticipatory' deployment (despite it involving some cross-border elements). The United Kingdom, moreover, ultimately made a similar claim, formally reporting to the Security Council that it was responding to requests (which were 'pre-emptive', albeit that the United Kingdom did not make this point) from both Saudi Arabia and Bahrain.[100]

The United Kingdom also appeared to make an anticipatory collective self-defence claim following 9/11, in that it argued that its forces were:

> employed in exercise of the inherent right of individual and collective self-defence, recognized in Article 51, following the terrorist outrage of 11 September, *to avert the continuing threat of attacks* from the same source.[101]

This argument did somewhat blur individual and collective self-defence. The extent to which the anticipatory aspects of the United Kingdom claim related to individual self-defence (i.e. averting the continuing threat of attack against itself), to collective self-defence (i.e. averting the continuing threat of attack against the United States) or to both was not entirely clear. At least on one reading, though, this amounts to another example of an anticipatory collective self-defence argument.

address-the-nation-announcing-the-deployment-united-states-armed-forces-saudi-arabia.

96 Antonopoulos, n.94, 175.

97 UN Doc. S/21492, n.15.

98 Louisa Dris-Aït-Hamadouche and Yahia H. Zoubir, 'The US-Saudi Relationship and the Iraq War: The Dialectics of a Dependent Alliance' (2007) 24 *Journal of Third World Studies* 109, 109.

99 *Ibid*, 127.

100 Letter dated 13 August 1990 from the Permanent Representative of the United Kingdom of Great Britain and Northern Ireland to the United Nations addressed to the President of the Security Council, UN Doc. S/21501 (13 August 1990).

101 Letter dated 7 October 2001 from the Chargé d'affaires a.i. of the Permanent Mission of the United Kingdom of Great Britain and Northern Ireland to the United Nations addressed to the President of the Security Council, UN Doc. S/2001/947 (7 October 2001) (emphasis added).

Overall, therefore, it may be said that there are some indications in the specific context of collective self-defence practice that an imminent armed attack may be sufficient for the exercise of the right, but this practice is undoubtedly inconclusive. This reflects the practice regarding individual self-defence, which is much more extensive (but also, ultimately, inconclusive). Such an alignment in this regard is to be expected, given that – despite some suggestions to the contrary[102] – the 'anticipatory self-defence debate' is unchanged as between the individual or collective self-defence context. This book is certainly not the place to attempt definitively to resolve that debate. The most that can be said is that there is notable support for the idea that anticipatory action may be lawful where the armed attack being responded to is demonstrably imminent, and this remains true in the collective self-defence context.[103]

3.2.4 The Perpetrator of an Armed Attack: Non-state Actors

Finally, in this section, it is worth flagging – but then, again, not engaging fully with – the contentious debate that exists as to whether an armed attack must be perpetrated by a state, or whether an attack by non-state actors (where this cannot be attributed to a state) can be sufficient to trigger the right of self-defence.

The ICJ, for its part, has appeared to suggest that an armed attack must be authored by a state.[104] For example, in the *Wall* advisory opinion of 2004 it stated that 'Article 51 of the Charter thus recognises the existence of an inherent right of self-defence in the case of an armed attack *by one state* against another state.'[105] Pronouncements of the ICJ in other cases seem to echo this understanding,[106] although it must be said that the Court has never been especially clear on the matter.[107] In any event, some writers have understood the Court's jurisprudence as indicating the view that it is only when an attack by non-state actors is legally attributable to

102 See nn.66–79 and accompanying text.

103 Friman, n.81, 17 (acknowledging that the argument that anticipatory self-defence is lawful has 'gained momentum' – albeit that she takes the view that this is incorrect – and that this momentum relates to both individual and collective self-defence).

104 See Michael Byers, 'Geopolitical Change and International Law', in David Armstrong, Theo Farrell and Bice Maiguashca (eds.), *Force and Legitimacy in World Politics* (Cambridge, Cambridge University Press, 2005), 51, 56.

105 *Wall* (advisory opinion), n.9, para. 139 (emphasis added).

106 See *Nicaragua* (merits), n.3, 6, para. 195; *Armed Activities* (merits), n.9, para. 146.

107 Green, n.3, 44–51.

a state under the law of state responsibility that self-defence can be exercised in response.[108] This view is also held by many scholars[109] and accords with traditional understandings of self-defence as a purely interstate phenomena.[110]

The conclusion that the author of an armed attack must be a state can certainly be brought into question, however. First, one might note that while other related articles in the UN Charter explicitly apply to interstate action only (e.g. Article 2(4)'s reference to the threat or use of force 'against . . . any *state*'),[111] Article 51 merely affirms an inherent right of self-defence: 'if an armed attack occurs', without specifying that it must be perpetrated by a state.[112] Thus, Judge Higgins stated in her *Wall* separate opinion that '[t]here is, with respect, nothing in the text of Article 51 that . . . stipulates that self-defence is available only when an armed attack is made by a State'.[113] However, while it is true that Article 51 does not rule out the notion that a non-state actor can be the perpetrator of an armed attack, neither does it rule it 'in', at least not explicitly.

The issue therefore must turn on the interpretation of Article 51 in subsequent practice: in other words, reference must be made to the state practice concerning self-defence actions against non-state actors. This is not the place to engage with that practice, but it should be said that this is the point at which the debate stagnates. States have, on occasion, claimed to have been acting against non-state actors in self-defence for

108 See, for example, Antonopoulos, n.94,168.

109 See, for example, Niaz A. Shah, 'Self-Defence, Anticipatory Self-Defence and Pre-Emption: International Law's Response to Terrorism' (2007) 12 *Journal of Conflict and Security Law* 95, 108–111; Iain Scobbie, 'Words My Mother Never Taught Me: In Defence of the International Court' (2005) 99 *American Journal of International Law* 76, 80–81; Gazzini, n.25, 184–191; Patrick Terry, 'Germany Joins the Campaign against ISIS in Syria: A Case of Collective Self-Defence or Rather the Unlawful Use of Force?' (2016) 4 *Russian Law Journal* 26; Svicevic, n.21, 149–152.

110 See, for example, Hans Kelsen, 'Collective Security and Collective Self-Defense under the Charter of the United Nations' (1948) 42 *American Journal of International Law* 783, 791.

111 UN Charter, n.2, Article 2(4), emphasis added.

112 See Lubell, n.65, 31–32; Shah, n.109, 97.

113 *Wall* (advisory opinion), n.9, 7, separate opinion of Judge Higgins, para. 33. See also *ibid*, separate opinion of Judge Kooijmans, para. 35; *ibid*, declaration of Judge Buergenthal, para. 6; *Armed Activities* (merits), n.9, separate opinion of Judge Simma, paras. 4–15; *ibid*, declaration of Judge Koroma, para. 9; *ibid*, separate opinion of Judge Kooijmans, paras. 19–30.

centuries,[114] although there is no doubt since 9/11 that there have been an increased number of attempts by states to justify their uses of force as actions of self-defence against non-state actors. These instances of state practice, and responses to them, may suggest the beginnings of a paradigm shift in practice towards allowing responses in self-defence against non-state actors.[115] Indeed, some scholars have argued that such a shift has already occurred.[116] At the same time, many states – especially in the Global South – remain opposed to the idea that self-defence can be taken in response to attacks wholly perpetrated by non-state actors.[117]

Ultimately, this is an unsettled debate and one that has become notably polarised, with both sides claiming victory. Such absolutist assertions of legal clarity in either direction are difficult to treat seriously, not least because the extent of the division of opinion on the matter, in itself, suggests otherwise. This book is not the place to reopen or try to resolve the 'self-defence against non-state actors' debate, which is long-standing, and remains ongoing in scholarship with little end in sight.[118] It is important to be clear that this is not because the matter is unimportant

[114] See, for example, Craig Forcese, *Destroying the* Caroline*: The Frontier Raid that Reshaped the Right to War* (Toronto, Irwin Law, 2018), 35, 63, 74, 149–150, 157–158.

[115] Michael Byers, 'Terrorism, the Use of Force and International Law after 11 September' (2002) 51 *International and Comparative Law Quarterly* 401, 407–409.

[116] See Thomas M. Franck, 'Terrorism and the Right of Self-Defence' (2001) 95 *American Journal of International Law* 839, 840; Sean D. Murphy, 'Self-Defence and the *Israeli Wall* Advisory Opinion: An *Ipse Dixit* from the ICJ?' (2005) 99 *American Journal of International Law* 62, 67–70; Kimberley N. Trapp, 'Back to Basics: Necessity, Proportionality and the Right of Self-Defence against Non-state Terrorist Actors' (2007) 56 *International and Comparative Law Quarterly* 141, particularly 147–155; Ruth Wedgwood, 'Responding to Terrorism: Strikes against bin Laden' (1999) 24 *Yale Journal of International Law* 559, particularly 564; Ruth Wedgwood, 'The ICJ Advisory Opinion on the Israeli Security Fence and the Limits of Self-Defence' (2005) 99 *American Journal of International Law* 52, 57–59; Azubuike, n.31, 159; Peter B.M.J. Pijpers, Hans J. F. R. Boddens Hosang and Paul A. L. Ducheine, 'Collective Cyber Defence – The EU and NATO Perspective on Cyber Attacks' (2021) *Amsterdam Law School Legal Studies Research Paper* No. 2021–37, Amsterdam Center for International Law No. 2021–13, 10.

[117] See Ntina Tzouvala, 'TWAIL and the "Unwilling or Unable" Doctrine: Continuities and Ruptures' (2015) 109 *AJIL Unbound* 266.

[118] Some of the recent additions to the literature include: Said Mahmoudi, 'Self-Defence and "Unwilling or Unable" States' (2021) 422 *Recueil des cours* 249; Mary Ellen O'Connell, Christian J. Tams and Dire Tladi, *Self-Defence against Non-state Actors*, Max Planck Trialogues on the Law of Peace and War (Anne Peters and Christian Marxsen, series eds.) vol. I (Cambridge, Cambridge University Press, 2019); Terry D. Gill and Kinga Tibori-Szabó, 'Twelve Key Questions on Self-Defense against Non-state Actors' (2019) 95 *International Law Studies* 467; Craig Martin, 'Challenging and Refining the

to the collective self-defence context. Far from it: whether states can use force in self-defence in relation to attacks by non-state actors remains just as crucial a question for the operation of collective self-defence as it does for individual self-defence. However, as with the question of anticipatory action, the contours of this debate are not meaningfully altered by the collective context, and it is not the aim of this book to consider key issues of concern for self-defence as a whole, especially when those issues have been debated in depth elsewhere.

It suffices to note here, again, that the collective self-defence state practice reflects the wider individual self-defence practice in relation to the idea of armed attacks by non-state actors (absent attribution to a state). That is to say that states certainly have, at times, claimed to have been acting in collective self-defence in relation to attacks (or alleged attacks) by non-state actors in the UN era; equally, a review of the state practice is far from conclusive as to whether such action is *lawful*.

Just a couple of examples will serve here. First, it is useful again to consider the requests for aid in collective self-defence issued in 1958 by Lebanon[119] and Jordan.[120] Both states specifically alleged that external attacks were being perpetrated against them by irregular forces.[121] However, while, as Ruys notes: '[i]t does not appear from the [Security] Council debates that any State challenged the idea that [collective] self-defence could be exercised against irregulars sent from abroad per se';[122] Lebanon[123] and Jordan[124] both were careful to assert (more than once) that the force in question was indeed *sent* by Syria and the UAR, respectively. Thus, although they claimed to be requesting aid in relation to attacks by non-state actors, it is telling that ultimately Lebanon and

"Unwilling or Unable" Doctrine' (2019) 52 *Vanderbilt Law Review* 387; Federica Paddeu, 'Use of Force against Non-state Actors and the Circumstance Precluding Wrongfulness of Self-Defence' (2017) 30 *Leiden Journal of International Law* 93; Eliav Lieblich, 'Self-Defense against Non-state Actors and the Myth of the Innocent State', in Nehal Bhuta and Rodrigo Vallejo (eds.), *Global Governance and Human Rights* (Collected Courses of the Academy of European Law) (Oxford, Oxford University Press, forthcoming), *SSRN* version (13 May 2019), https://papers.ssrn.com/sol3/papers.cfm?abstract_id=3364163.

119 UN Doc. S/PV.827, n.17, para. 84.

120 UN Doc. S/PV.831, n.20, para. 24.

121 See, for example, *ibid*, paras. 18–24 (Jordan); UN Doc. S/PV.827, n.17, paras. 79, 82 (Lebanon).

122 Ruys, n.55, 397.

123 UN Doc. S/PV.827, n.17, para. 78; UNSC Verbatim Record, UN Doc. S/PV.833 (18 July 1958), para. 10.

124 UN Doc. S/PV.831, n.20, 18–24.

Jordan indicated that these attacks were attributable to a state actor (even in a situation where this was factually questionable).

As with individual self-defence, there has been increased support for collective self-defence actions against non-state actors since 9/11,[125] albeit that such action remains controversial. The key recent example is undoubtedly the collective self-defence claim(s) advanced by coalition states in regard to the use of force in Syria since 2014. These states have been very clear that their action is not directed at Syria and instead is an act of collective self-defence taken against ISIL, a non-state actor. The statement made by Australia in this regard is representative:

> States must be able to act in self-defence when the Government of the State where the threat is located is unwilling or unable to prevent attacks originating from its territory. The Government of Syria has, by its failure to constrain attacks upon Iraqi territory originating from ISIL bases within Syria, demonstrated that it is unwilling or unable to prevent those attacks.. . . These operations are not directed against Syria or the Syrian people[126]

It is notable that this aspect, at least, of the coalition's collective self-defence claim arguably received a measure of support among other states, although to the extent that statements of support were issued, they were vague endorsements of international efforts to combat ISIL rather than explicit endorsements of the coalition's use of force.[127] Chinkin and

[125] Olivia Flasch, 'The Legality of the Air Strikes against ISIL in Syria: New Insights on the Extraterritorial Use of Force against Non-state Actors' (2016) 3 *Journal on the Use of Force and International Law* 37, 48; Laurie O'Connor, 'Legality of the use of force in Syria against Islamic State and the Khorasan Group' (2016) 3 *Journal on the Use of Force and International Law* 70, 72; Masoud Zamani and Majid Nikouei, 'Intervention by Invitation, Collective Self-Defence and the Enigma of Effective Control' (2017) 16 *Chinese Journal of International Law* 663, 664.

[126] Letter dated 9 September 2015 from the Permanent Representative of Australia to the United Nations addressed to the President of the Security Council, UN Doc. S/2015/693 (9 September 2015). See also, in particular, Letter dated 31 March 2015 from the Chargé d'affaires a.i. of the Permanent Mission of Canada to the United Nations addressed to the President of the Security Council, UN Doc. S/2015/221 (31 March 2015) ('[i]n accordance with the inherent rights of individual and collective self-defence reflected in Article 51 of the United Nations Charter, States must be able to act in self-defence when the Government of the State where a threat is located is unwilling or unable to prevent attacks emanating from its territory').

[127] See, for example, UNSC Verbatim Record, UN Doc. S/PV.7316 (19 November 2014), 65 (Albania); UNSC Verbatim Record, UN Doc. S/PV.7565 (20 November 2015), 3 (China); *ibid*, 3 (Spain); *ibid*, 5 (Nigeria); *ibid*, 5–6 (Lithuania); *ibid*, 7 (Chile); *ibid*, 7 (Angola); *ibid*, 7–8 (Bolivia).

Kaldor have gone so far as to argue that the coalition's action in Syria has been 'a widely accepted example of collective self-defence, which accords with the conditions stipulated by the ICJ (even though the issue of whether self-defence can be claimed against non-state actors ... has hardly been raised at all)'.[128] In fact, though, while there certainly has been a degree of acceptance, the uses of force in Syria against ISIL (other than by states that had received explicit consent from Syria to do so) have not been without controversy,[129] and at least one reason for this is the 'self-defence against non-state actors' debate. Concern over legality here is evident from the fact that various states explicitly supported coalition action against ISIL in Iraq and then pointedly refrained from doing so when the action moved over the border into Syria.[130]

Without engaging fully with the debate here, it can ultimately be said the question of whether states can legally use force in collective self-defence in response to an armed attack by a non-state actor remains controversial, and any assertions that the matter is now beyond doubt seem premature.[131] Equally, the sheer number of states that have made this claim in relation to Syria is unprecedented and – when coupled with a degree of acquiescence among other states (if not, perhaps, unqualified support) – gives an indication as to how the law may be developing.[132]

3.3 Necessity and Proportionality

In addition to the criterion of an armed attack as set out in Article 51, there are two further crucial requirements for lawful self-defence under customary international law: the response taken must be both *necessary* and *proportional*. These intertwined criteria have a long-standing historical pedigree in the international legal system[133] but can be said to have

[128] Chinkin and Kaldor, n.33, 142.

[129] See Terry, n.109; Marko Milanovic, 'The Clearly Illegal US Missile Strike in Syria', *EJIL: Talk!* (7 April 2017), www.ejiltalk.org/the-clearly-illegal-us-missile-strike-in-syria (noting that the coalition claim to be acting in collective self-defence in Syria 'is hugely controversial').

[130] Flasch, n.125, 69; O'Connor, n.125, 94.

[131] O'Connor, n.125, 92–96.

[132] *Ibid*, 93.

[133] See, for example, Emer de Vattel, *The Law of Nations* (*Droit des gens*) (Béla Kapossy and Richard Whatmore, eds., Thomas Nugent, trans.), Indianapolis, Liberty Fund, 2008 (1758)), Book III, chapter VI, 515, para. 90.

appeared on the landscape of 'modern' international law[134] when they were referenced in a much-quoted letter of 1842 by Daniel Webster (then US Secretary of State), concerning the 1837 sinking of the steamship *Caroline*.[135] Since then, necessity and proportionality have crystallised into binding rules of customary international law.[136] It is now unquestionably the law that all actions in self-defence must be both necessary and proportional.[137]

The necessity criterion today requires that it would be unreasonable in the relevant circumstances to expect any attempt to be made by the attacked state (or, in the case of collective self-defence, its co-defenders) to take non-forcible measures of resolution.[138] The criterion does not procedurally require that other measures – such as negotiation – *must* be attempted prior to a resort to force,[139] only that any forcible response must be a 'last resort' in the sense that there existed no reasonable alternative to it.[140]

As for the proportionality requirement, this obliges the state to act in a manner that is proportional to the defensive necessity that has been

[134] See Byers, n.115, 159 (arguing that 'the modern law of self-defence was born' with the *Caroline* incident).

[135] Letter dated 27 July 1842, from Daniel Webster to Lord Ashburton (1841–1842) XXX *British and Foreign State Papers* 193–194 (extract taken from Webster's earlier letter to Henry S. Fox dated 24 April 1841, (1840–1841) XXIX *British and Foreign State Papers* 1137–1138) (a state claiming self-defence must: 'show a necessity of self-defence, instant, overwhelming, leaving no choice of means, and no moment for deliberation. It will be for it to show, also, that ... [it] did nothing unreasonable or excessive; since the act justified by the necessity of self-defence must be limited by that necessity, and kept clearly within it'). See, generally, Forcese, n.114.

[136] For a detailed examination of the developmental process of these criteria from their appearance in Webster's letter to elements of modern customary international law, see James A. Green, 'Docking the *Caroline*: Understanding the Relevance of the Formula in Contemporary Customary International Law Concerning Self-Defence' (2006) 14 *Cardozo Journal of International and Comparative Law* 429.

[137] Gray, n.25, 157 (noting that 'all states agree' that necessity and proportionality are required); Stanimir A. Alexandrov, *Self-Defence against the Use of Force in International Law* (The Hague, Kluwer Law International, 1996), 20; Judith Gardam, *Necessity, Proportionality and the Use of Force by States* (Cambridge, Cambridge University Press, 2004), particularly 6, 11; Oscar Schachter, 'Implementing Limitations on the Use of Force: The Doctrine of Proportionality and Necessity: Remarks' (1992) 86 *American Society of International Law Proceedings* 39.

[138] This interpretation of the necessity criterion can clearly be discerned from the state practice, see Green, n.136, 450–457; Ruys, n.55, 95–98.

[139] See Dinstein, n.4, 249–251; Green, n.3, 80–85.

[140] See Myra Williamson, *Terrorism, War and International Law: The Legality of the Use of Force against Afghanistan in 2001* (Farnham, Ashgate, 2009), 115.

established. This means that the proportionality criterion is not merely an obligation to ensure a numerical equivalence of scale or means as between the armed attack and the response taken.[141] Rather, it requires that the force employed must not be excessive with regard to the goal of abating or repelling the attack being responded to. In the context of individual self-defence, at least, this means that a state can use whatever force is required (in terms of scale and/or means) to abate the attack against it, but no more.[142] The proportionality criterion thus does not require that a state necessarily stop its response against an aggressor the instant that it is repelled to the territorial border. Otherwise, the aggressor simply can regroup and continue its attack from that location. The defensive action can continue into the territory of the aggressor, so long as this is a genuine defensive necessity to do so, and so long as it is not excessive to do so in relation to that defensive necessity.[143]

That the necessity and proportionality criteria apply specifically to collective self-defence actions is confirmed in scholarship[144] and was made explicit by the ICJ in the *Nicaragua* case.[145] This is also evident from a review of state practice.[146] One might note, for example, the fact

141 Sina Etezazian, 'The Nature of the Self-Defence Proportionality Requirement' (2016) 3 *Journal on the Use of Force and International Law* 260; Terry D. Gill, 'The Second Gulf Crisis and the Relation between Collective Security and Collective Self-Defense' (1989) 10 *Grotiana* 47, 67; Azubuike, n.31, 163.

142 See, for example, Chris O'Meara, *Necessity and Proportionality and the Right of Self-Defence in International Law* (Oxford, Oxford University Press, 2021), 97–171; Chatham House Principles, n.25, 968–969; Gardam, n.137, 142, 161; Green, n.3, 86–96; Ruth Wedgwood, 'Proportionality and Necessity in American National Security Decision Making' (1992) 86 *American Society of International Law Proceedings* 58, 59; Helen Michael, 'Covert Involvement in Essentially Internal Conflicts: United States Assistance to the Contras under International Law' (1990) 23 *Vanderbilt Journal of Transnational Law* 539, 576–577; Russell Powell, 'The Law and Philosophy of Preventive War: An Institution-Based Approach to Collective Self-Defence' (2007) 32 *Australian Journal of Legal Philosophy* 67, 85.

143 See Green, n.136, 462–463.

144 See, for example, Claus Kreß, 'The Ukraine War and the Prohibition of the Use of Force in International Law' (2022) *Torkel Opsahl Academic EPublisher, Occasional Paper Series* No. 13, 1, 13; Henkin, n.4, 45; Anne C. Cunningham, *Critical Perspectives on Government-Sponsored Assassinations* (New York, Enslow Publishing, 2018), 111; Thomas and Thomas, n.21, 189–190; MacDonald, n.30, 146, 151; Michael, n.142, 574; Christian Wyse, 'The African Union's Right of Humanitarian Intervention as Collective Self-Defense' (2018) 19 *Chicago Journal of International Law* 295, 327–328; Gill, n.141, 72; Lee, n.21, 377.

145 *Nicaragua* (merits), n.3, para. 194. See also *ibid*, dissenting opinion of Judge Schwebel, para. 7.

146 See Green, n.3, 83.

that, following the military action by various Warsaw Pact states in Czechoslovakia in 1968,[147] the USSR was extremely careful to stress that the action complied with the necessity criterion:

> Needless to say, the . . . military units [of the co-defending states] will be withdrawn from the territory of the Czechoslovak Socialist Republic as soon as the present threat to security is eliminated and the lawful authorities find that the presence of those units is no longer necessary.[148]

Across the iron curtain, the United States was similarly careful when it advanced its claim to be acting in the collective self-defence of Cambodia in 1970, which it claimed was in response to attacks by North Vietnamese forces against the South and Cambodia itself:

> The measures of collective self-defence being taken by United States and South Viet-Namese faces are restricted in extent, purpose and time. . . . These measures are limited and proportionate to the aggressive military operations of the North Viet-Namese forces and the threat they pose.[149]

Providing much more detail, with regard to US action in Honduras in 1988, both the defending state[150] and the co-defending state[151] were keen to emphasise that the deployment of US troops was necessary. In particular, they made much of the fact that the exercise of collective self-defence only occurred following the failure of active and notable steps to reach a peaceful resolution. More recently, of the ten states that have claimed to be acting in collective self-defence of Iraq since 2014, seven have been very explicit that they have been complying with the criteria of necessity and proportionality in exercising the right.[152]

147 See Kieran Williams, *The Prague Spring and Its Aftermath: Czechoslovak Politics, 1968–1970* (Cambridge, Cambridge University Press, 1997), 29–38.

148 UN Doc. S/PV.1441, n.16, para. 3. See also *ibid*, para. 214.

149 Letter dated 5 May 1970 from the Permanent Representative of the United States of America to the United Nations addressed to the President of the Security Council, UN Doc. S/9781 (5 May 1970).

150 UN Doc. A/42/931-S/19643, n.47, paras. 2, 8 (Honduras, stressing that it had engaged in multiple attempts to settle the matter peacefully before resorting to requesting aid in collective self-defence); UN Doc. S/PV.2802, n.48, 16 (Honduras, arguing that 'it has been and continues to be committed to the search for a solution to the present situation through diplomatic bilateral and regional channels').

151 UN Doc. S/PV.2802, n.48, 28–30 (United States, outlining the purported refusal of Nicaragua to engage with peaceful settlement options).

152 See Letter dated 7 June 2016 from the Permanent Representative of Belgium to the United Nations addressed to the President of the Security Council, UN Doc. S/2016/523 (9 June 2016); UN Doc. S/2016/34, n.51; UN Doc. S/2014/695, n.52; UN Doc. S/2015/693, n.126; Letter dated 3 June 2016 from the Permanent Representative of Norway to

Of course, *assertions* of compliance with the criteria of necessity and proportionality by states claiming to be acting in collective self-defence, while important, are nowhere near as important as *actual* compliance. It is noteworthy that, for all of the apparent deference to necessity and proportionality, it has too often been questionable whether the states claiming to be acting in collective self-defence have actually met these requirements. Take, for example, Honduras in 1988[153] or Syria since 2014.[154] Perhaps more important than what defending/co-defending states claim, therefore, is that at times states have taken issue with purported acts of collective self-defence by others on the basis that they did not comply with the necessity and/or proportionality requirements. For example, Yugoslavia questioned the lawfulness of the Soviet use of force in Hungary in 1956 on the basis that the action did not meet the necessity criterion. Yugoslavia indicated that it felt that the use of force was unnecessary because the Hungarian 'Government should be given the time and the possibility to restore peace, and its efforts to do so should not be impeded'.[155] With regard to the example of Honduras in 1988, already mentioned, one might note that Peru clearly saw the US action as both unnecessary and disproportional: 'this unjustified

the United Nations addressed to the President of the Security Council UN Doc. S/2016/513 (3 June 2016); UN Doc. S/2015/946, n.15; Letter dated 3 December 2015 from the Permanent Representative of the United Kingdom of Great Britain and Northern Ireland to the United Nations addressed to the President of the Security Council, UN Doc. S/2015/928 (3 December 2015); Identical letters dated 25 November 2014 from the Permanent Representative of the United Kingdom of Great Britain and Northern Ireland to the United Nations addressed to the Secretary-General and the President of the Security Council, UN Doc. S/2014/851 (26 November 2014); Letter dated 7 September 2015 from the Permanent Representative of the United Kingdom of Great Britain and Northern Ireland to the United Nations addressed to the President of the Security Council, UN Doc. S/2015/688 (8 September 2015).

153 See, for example, UN Doc. S/PV.2802, n.48, 3 (Nicaragua, unsurprisingly implying that it viewed the deployment of 3,200 US troops to be both unnecessary and disproportional); *ibid*, 32 (Argentina, suggesting that it saw the US action as unnecessary); *ibid*, 38 (Peru).

154 It is highly questionable whether the coalition's use of force in Syria since 2014 has in fact been 'necessary' to defend Iraq, and – particularly – whether that use of force has amounted to a proportional response to the attacks perpetrated by, and threat posed by, ISIL. See Simona Ross, 'U.S. Justifications for the Use of Force in Syria through the Prism of the Responsibility to Protect' (2021) 8 *Journal on the Use of Force and International Law* 233, 258 ('the actions [of the coalition in Syria] were . . . not in compliance with the international legal requirements of the necessity and proportionality principles').

155 UN Doc. S/PV.746, n.17, para. 34.

increased United States military presence in the area affects the political climate required for the fulfilment of the peace agreements . . .'[156]

Ultimately, '[i]t goes without saying that the requirements of necessity and proportionality . . . apply to any action undertaken in collective self-defense'.[157] Just as with individual self-defence, these requirements are not always complied with, but practice nonetheless shows that they are indeed legal benchmarks for collective self-defence, with both the states supporting and those critiquing purported exercises the right relying on them. That said, the operation of necessity and proportionality is extremely context-specific,[158] and they are based, to an extent, on nebulous notions of 'acceptability' and 'reasonableness'.[159] This means that their application to particular cases of self-defence – individual or collective – is never likely to be straightforward. Moreover, the collective self-defence context arguably adds additional complexity to the application of the necessity and proportionality criteria.

First, one might query who must make the determination of whether an action in self-defence is necessary and/or proportional. In particular, must the co-defending state assess independently the requirements of necessity and proportionality, or can it rely on the defending state's assessment alone? This writer would argue that there is no clear *opinio juris* to suggest that co-defending states are *legally required* to make their own assessments regarding the necessity and proportionality requirements, but in practice, it seems that they usually do so.[160] This is unsurprising: it is unlikely that a state would engage in the use of force in self-defence wholly on the basis of the determination by another state (even the state that it is intending to defend) without attempting to undertake some assessment of its own as to whether the legal requirements for that action would be met. Compliance with the necessity and proportionality criteria – however flexible they may be – are ultimately objective questions.[161] Co-defending states might well base determinations (at least in part) on information provided by the defending state,

[156] UN Doc. S/PV.2802, n.48, 38.

[157] Gill, n.141, 72.

[158] See Richard R. Baxter, 'The Legal Consequences of the Unlawful Use of Force under the Charter' (1968) 62 *American Society of International Law Proceedings* 68, 74.

[159] See Gardam, n.137, 21.

[160] See, for example, UN Doc. S/9781, n.149; UN Doc. S/PV.2802, n.48, 28–30; UN Doc. S/PV.1441, n.16, paras. 3, 214; UN Doc. S/2016/523, n.152.

[161] Oscar Schachter, 'United Nations in the Gulf Conflict' (1991) 85 *American Journal of International Law* 452, 471.

which is of course likely to have intimate knowledge of the attack that it is suffering. However, it would be unwise for a co-defending state to rely solely on the determination by another state that a response was necessary, or another state's view as to what level of response would be proportionate.[162]

Relatedly, collective self-defence increases the scope for disagreement among the states involved in a collective self-defence action as to the application of the (flexible) criteria of necessity and proportionality. This is because, especially in the context of large multilateral uses of force in collective self-defence involving multiple co-defenders, there are more 'interpreters' involved in trying to reach the relevant determinations. As noted in the previous paragraph, all of the co-defending states involved would be wise to reach their own conclusions, and if those differ, this can lead to functional issues for military alliances or coalitions. For example, there were 'sharp differences of opinion over the necessity and proportionality of the military action taken by the coalition' in defence of Kuwait in 1991, causing divisions as between the co-defending states involved.[163]

Although the collective self-defence context may make the process of applying the necessity criterion more complex in practice, the present writer would argue that, at the substantive level, the criterion operates identically as between individual and collective self-defence. As noted, compliance with that criterion turns on whether there exists a situation of defensive necessity for the state that has suffered the armed attack in question (or, arguably, the imminent threat of armed attack), and whether force taken in response is thus a last resort. That this force is deployed by a co-defending state or states on behalf of the victim – rather than by the victim itself – is immaterial to the determination of whether the use of force per se is, in the circumstances, a defensive necessity (or whether a non-forcible response may be a reasonable alternative).

As regards proportionality, however, there is an additional substantive question in the collective context, in terms of how the relevant calculation is to be made. It is relatively straightforward to say that the proportionality requirement means that the 'intervening state may, at a maximum, deploy the level of force the requesting state would be

162 For a similar discussion of the importance of co-defending states being able to make their own determination as to whether an 'armed attack' had occurred, see Section 7.3.4 (which approaches the question in the context of treaty arrangements).

163 Schachter, n.161, 471–472.

permitted to deploy were it acting for itself'.[164] But in situations where multiple states are responding in collective self-defence in relation to the same armed attack, it might be asked whether 'proportionality' is to be calculated singly or cumulatively. In other words, is a separate proportionality calculation to be made in relation to each co-defending state's use of force, or are the collective actions of a coalition of co-defending states to be assessed together?

Interestingly, the way that states themselves have referred to the proportionality requirement would, at times, suggest that they envisage an individual calculation being made. Again, the positions taken by the states claiming to be acting in collective self-defence in Syria since 2014 are illustrative. Belgium, for example, was clear that '*the Kingdom of Belgium is taking* ... proportionate measures ... in the exercise of the right of collective self-defence'.[165] Denmark likewise argued that *it* was taking 'proportionate measures against the so-called Islamic State in Iraq and the Levant (ISIL, also known as Da'esh) in Syria',[166] not that these measures were part of a wider action that was proportional overall. A number of statements by other coalition states are similarly phrased.[167]

One might also take the view, at first glance, that undertaking multiple separate proportionality calculations is the appropriate approach, especially if it is accepted that collective self-defence is an inherent right not just for the defending state but also for co-defending states.[168] This is because it could be argued that if one state party to a collective self-defence coalition were to act disproportionately in its exercise of

[164] Aadhithi Padmanabhan and Michael Shih, 'Collective Self-Defense: A Report of the Yale Law School Center for Global Legal Challenges' (10 December 2012), https://law.yale.edu/sites/default/files/documents/pdf/cglc/GLC_Collective_SelfDefense.pdf, 1.

[165] UN Doc. S/2016/523, n.152 (emphasis added).

[166] UN Doc. S/2016/34, n.51.

[167] See, for example, UN Doc. S/2014/695, n.52 ('the United States has initiated ... proportionate military actions in Syria in order to eliminate the ongoing ISIL threat to Iraq'); UN Doc. S/2015/693, n.126 ('Australia is ... undertaking ... proportionate military operations against ISIL in Syria in the exercise of the collective self-defence of Iraq'); UN Doc. S/2016/513, n.152 ('Norway is taking ... proportionate measures against the terrorist organization Islamic State in Iraq and the Levant (ISIL, also known as Da'esh) in Syria in the exercise of the right of collective self-defence'); UN Doc. S/2015/928, n.152 ('the United Kingdom of Great Britain and Northern Ireland is taking ... proportionate measures ... in exercise of the inherent right of individual and collective self-defence').

[168] See Section 1.3.

collective self-defence, a cumulative or holistic appraisal of proportionality could act unilaterally to strip other states of their *inherent right* to defend the victim.

However, individual proportionality calculations could lead to absurd and abusive outcomes. The goal of the proportionality requirement is to limit escalation and ensure that self-defence measures truly are defensive in nature.[169] No more can be done than can be justified by the defensive necessity faced by the defending state. In other words, the 'inherent right' to defend another state in collective self-defence only exists when and to the extent that there remains a defensive necessity for that state. A response by one member of a coalition that was disproportionate would act to alleviate that necessity (indeed, by definition it would go beyond what was required to alleviate it). This would mean that there was no ongoing defensive necessity against which further collective self-defence action by other members of the coalition could be balanced in making a proportionality calculation.

If calculations were made individually – balancing each state in a coalition's use of force against the armed attack that the defending state is facing – then the cumulative response could well end up being wildly disproportionate in relation to the armed attack suffered. Of course, as noted, there need not be exact equivalence of scale between the armed attack and the response,[170] but it nonetheless holds that the aggregated gravity of a response allowed by a series of individual calculations could quickly end up being disproportional to the defensive necessity that the armed attack established. This would be a licence for coalitions of 'co-defending' states to circumvent the *raison d'être* of the proportionality requirement. It surely must be the case, therefore, that irrespective of the fact that states may have *phrased* their claims to act proportionally in collective self-defence as being about their actions alone, it is the collective self-defence action as a whole that is assessed when applying the proportionality requirement. That action, overall, cannot go beyond what

[169] As this author has previously argued, this means that the proportionality requirement is an essential – arguably the *most* essential – legal restriction on the use of force in self-defence. See Green, n.3, 137–138. See also Kevin C. Kenny, 'Self-Defence', in Rüdiger Wolfrum and Christiane E. Philipp (eds.), *United Nations: Law, Policies and Practice, vol. II* (Dordrecht, Martinus Nijhoff, 1995), 1162, 1168; Brownlie, n.60, 261; Mary Ellen O'Connell, 'Review: *Necessity, Proportionality and the Use of Force by States* by Judith Gardam' (2006) 100 *American Journal of International Law* 973, 975.

[170] See n.141 – and n.143 and accompanying text.

is required to alleviate the defensive necessity felt by the defending state.[171]

It, therefore, is worth noting that – in the envisaged scenario of one coalition party acting disproportionately – it is not the case that the other coalition states would be legally responsible for the breach of the prohibition on the use of force that this disproportionate action entailed. Another coalition state might be responsible for providing aid or assistance to facilitate it, however, if it did so with knowledge of the disproportionality of the 'defensive' force used.[172] In such instances, though, the state would only 'be responsible to the extent that its own conduct has caused or contributed to the internationally wrongful act'.[173] In any event, at the very least, it would be the case that the application of the proportionality requirement would mean other coalition states would be barred from taking any *further* action in collective self-defence themselves.

3.4 The Reporting Requirement

In addition to the three primary criteria of armed attack, necessity, and proportionality are two secondary legal requirements for the exercise of self-defence (individual or collective). Both of these additional requirements are set out in Article 51 of the UN Charter, and both of them concern the relationship between the right of self-defence and the UN Security Council. The first of these criteria is the so-called reporting requirement. Article 51 provides that '[m]easures taken by members in exercise of this right of self-defence shall be immediately reported to the Security Council'.[174]

[171] See Roda Mushkat, 'Who May Wage War – An Examination of an Old/New Question' (1987) 2 *American University Journal of International Law and Policy* 97, 149 (referring to proportionality in the context of collective self-defence as a cumulative calculation); Bowett, n.63, 238 (implicitly understanding proportionality this way in the collective self-defence context without going so far as to state it).

[172] See Text of the Draft Articles on Responsibility of States for Internationally Wrongful Acts, with commentaries, Report of the International Law Commission, 53rd sess., UN Doc. A/56/10 (2001), 65–67 (Article 16 and commentary); Vladyslav Lanovoy, *Complicity and Its Limits in the Law of International Responsibility* (Oxford, Hart Publishing, 2016), particularly 92–161. See also Miles Jackson, *Complicity in International Law* (Oxford, Oxford University Press, 2015), 136–147 (regarding, specifically, complicity in relation to an act of aggression).

[173] UN Doc. A/56/10, n.172, 66, para. 2.

[174] UN Charter, n.2, Article 51.

There is no question that this requirement applies to collective self-defence as well as to individual self-defence.[175] It is notable that the obligation to report to the UN Security Council is explicitly reiterated in many collective self-defence treaties.[176] Indeed, if anything, some treaties have gone further in terms of their reporting obligations than what is required by Article 51.[177] For example, Article 5 of the 1948 Rio Treaty states:

> The High Contracting Parties shall immediately send to the Security Council of the United Nations, in conformity with Articles 51 and 54 of the Charter of the United Nations, *complete information* concerning the activities undertaken or in contemplation in the exercise of the right of self-defense[178]

Whereas, while Article 6(4) of the 2003 Southern African Development Community (SADC) Mutual Defence Pact much more closely mirrors Article 51 in relation to reporting to the UN Security Council, the

[175] See Anthony Clark Arend and Robert J. Beck, *International Law and the Use of Force* (London, Routledge, 1993), 31; Josef Rohlik, 'Some Remarks on Self-Defense and Intervention: A Reaction to Reading Law and Civil War in the Modern World' (1976) 6 *Georgia Journal of International and Comparative Law* 395, 426–427; Roman Kwiecień, 'The *Nicaragua* Judgment and the Use of Force – 30 Years Later' (2016) 36 *Polish Yearbook of International Law* 21, 31; Kreß, n.144, 15; Kritsiotis, n.76, 227; Stuart Casey-Maslen, Jus ad Bellum: *The Law on Inter-State Use of Force* (Oxford, Hart Publishing, 2020), 75; Joseph L. Kunz, 'Individual and Collective Self-Defence under Article 51 of the Charter of the United Nations' (1947) 41 *American Journal of International Law* 872, 879.

[176] See, for example, North Atlantic Treaty, n.13, Article 5; Treaty of Friendship, Cooperation and Mutual Assistance between the People's Republic of Albania, the People's Republic of Bulgaria, the Hungarian People's Republic, the German Democratic Republic, the Polish People's Republic, the Romanian People's Republic (1955) 219 UNTS 24 (Warsaw Pact), Article 4; Treaty of Economic, Social and Cultural Collaboration and Collective Self-Defence (1948), as Amended by the 'Protocol Modifying and Completing the Brussels Treaty' (1954), FO 1093/575 (Western European Union Treaty / WEU Treaty), Article V.

[177] See Sir W. Eric Beckett, *The North Atlantic Treaty, The Brussels Treaty, and the Charter of the United Nations* (London, Stevens & Sons, 1950), 20–21; A. L. Goodhart, 'The North Atlantic Treaty of 1949' (1951) 79 *Recueil des cours* 182, 214. See also Harvard Research, *Draft Convention on Rights and Duties of States in Case of Aggression*, with Comment (1939), in (1939) 33 *Supplement to the American Journal of International Law* 819, 829, Article 9 ('[a] State assumes the status of a co-defending State by giving notice of that fact *to all other States*', emphasis added).

[178] Rio Treaty, n.13, Article 5 (emphasis added).

provision also requires collective self-defence reporting to the Peace and Security Council of the African Union.[179]

Despite the apparently mandatory language in Article 51 (and the collective self-defence treaty arrangements that reflect or expand it), it is generally accepted that a failure to meet this requirement – whether in the context of individual or collective action – does not, in itself, turn an otherwise lawful use of force in self-defence into an unlawful use of force.[180] The failure to report,[181] or to report in a timely manner,[182] can, however, form part of the evidence establishing the unlawfulness of military action. While compliance with the reporting requirement was poor in the early period of the United Nations, in recent decades it has improved.[183] Interestingly, compliance throughout the UN era has been better in cases of states invoking collective (as opposed to individual) self-defence.[184]

Specific to the collective self-defence context is the additional question of exactly who should be doing the reporting.[185] Article 51 itself offers no

179 Southern African Development Community (SADC) Mutual Defence Pact (2003) 3156 UNTS, Article 6(4). See Svicevic, n.21, 157–158.

180 See James A. Green, 'The Article 51 Reporting Requirement for Self-Defense Actions' (2015) 55 *Virginia Journal of International Law* 463, 592–596; Dinstein, n.4, 258–260; Gazzini, n.25, 154–155; D. W. Greig, 'Self-Defence and the Security Council: What Does Article 51 Require?' (1991) 40 *International and Comparative Law Quarterly* 366, 387–388; Lee, n.21, 378. See also *Nicaragua* (merits), n.3, para. 200; Azubuike, n.31, 148–149. *Contra* Bowett, n.63, 197–199.

181 See *Nicaragua* (merits), n.3, para. 200. However, the ICJ reached this conclusion on the basis of customary international law and not Article 51 itself: the legal implications of the reporting requirement therefore remain somewhat unclear. See Greig, n.180, particularly 367–388; Lee, n.21, 378; Gray, n.25, 128, 189–190.

182 Nick van der Steenhoven, 'Conduct and Subsequent Practice by States in the Application of the Requirement to Report under UN Charter Article 51 (2019) 6 *Journal on the Use of Force and International Law* 242, 257–260; Green, n.180, 596–599.

183 Green, n.180, 573–585.

184 See Gray, n.25, 189 (setting out state practice to demonstrate this).

185 Rostow, for example, noted in the context of the First Gulf War in 1990–1991 that the Security Council rather vaguely indicated that 'the States concerned' were required to report, without specifying further. See Eugene V. Rostow, 'Until What? Enforcement Action or Collective Self-Defense' (1991) 85 *American Journal of International Law* 506, 508–509. Rostow specifically was referring to UNSC Res. 678, UN Doc. S/RES/678 (29 November 1990), para. 4. It is worth noting that the coalition action in the Gulf could be viewed as having its legal basis in Security Council authorisation – by virtue of *ibid* – rather than collective self-defence. Rostow himself viewed it as a collective self-defence action, but a credible case can be made for either. See Henderson, n.82, 53–55; Alexandrov, n.137, 263–278; Schachter, n.161, 457–462; Sir Michael Wood, 'Self-Defence and Collective Security', in Marc Weller (ed.), *The*

guidance as to who is supposed to report, simply stating that self-defence actions 'shall be reported'.[186] In the case of individual actions, reporting is generally understood to be the responsibility of the state defending itself,[187] but in the collective context, it is unclear whether *both* the defending state and the co-defending state need to report.[188] And if the co-defending state is required to report, a related question is, when *multiple* co-defenders act in a coalition, do *all of them* need to report?

It has been suggested that the requirement to report ultimately lies with the state using force (i.e. the co-defending state rather than the defending state).[189] It has also been argued that where there are multiple co-defending states, the obligation to report falls 'upon each State rendering assistance'.[190] However, while it makes a good deal of sense that a state actually using force is charged with reporting it, ultimately so long as the self-defence action is reported that would seem to comply with the requirement as set out in Article 51. Given that a failure to report is not going to be terminal for a self-defence action, at least in itself, it seems unlikely that it would be viewed as especially problematic by the Security Council if the defending state rather than the co-defending state reported, or if only one co-defending state from a coalition reported on behalf of them all.

Although negative inference has occasionally been drawn from the failure to report by a co-defending state,[191] as stated, for the most part

Oxford Handbook of the Use of Force in International Law (Oxford, Oxford University Press, 2015), 649, 650–653.

186 UN Charter, n.2, Article 51.

187 Greig, n.180, 386.

188 Kelsen, n.110, 792–793.

189 Emmanuel Roucounas, *l'Institut de droit international*, 10th Commission, 'Present Problems of the Use of Force in International Law Sub-group: Self-Defence' (2007) 72 *Annuaire de l'Institut de droit international* 75, para. 117.

190 Russell Buchan and Nicholas Tsagourias, *Regulating the Use of Force in International Law: Stability and Change* (Cheltenham, Edward Elgar, 2021), 73.

191 For example, both the USSR (see UNSC Verbatim Record, UN Doc. S/PV.1106 (2 April 1964), para. 77) and the United States (see UNSC Verbatim Record, UN Doc. S/PV.1108 (6 April 1964), para. 67) took the view that the United Kingdom's 1963–1964 action against Yemen was not a genuine instance of self-defence, in part on the basis that the United Kingdom did not report to the Security Council until almost a year after it first used force. Admittedly, whether the UK action could have been conceived of as collective self-defence in any event may be debated, given that it was highly questionable whether the Federation of South Arabia – which the United Kingdom was purportedly defending – was a state under international law. On the requirement that the requester be a state, see Section 5.2.

reporting in the collective self-defence context has actually been notably better than in the individual self-defence context. Indeed, in recent practice – where self-defence reporting has become much more 'belt and braces' than it used to be – it has become most common for *both* defending state and co-defending state to report. Where there have been multiple co-defending states, at times only one coalition state has submitted a report, but, if so, it has tended formally to do so on behalf of others. One might note, for example, the 2015 letter reporting action in support of the Hadi regime in Yemen (asserted to be in collective self-defence) by Qatar.[192] This was explicitly submitted on behalf of itself, Bahrain, Saudi Arabia, the United Arab Emirates, and Kuwait.[193] Increasingly, though, in situations involving (at least purported) collective self-defence coalitions, it is the case that *all* states report separately. The most obvious example of this is the fact that ten different coalition states formally reported acting in the collective self-defence of Iraq from 2014 to 2016, in relation to attacks from ISIL.[194] Iraq itself also reported.[195] Each of these reporting letters was separate and individualised to the state concerned, albeit that there were a large number of similarities between many of them.

This approach is perhaps an example of what some have referred to, with a degree of concern, as 'over-reporting'.[196] Even if this is a correct characterisation, though, in this author's view, it nonetheless is to be welcomed in the collective self-defence context, given that the implications of escalation arguably are greater than in relation to individual self-defence.[197] One might note that in 1948, the Commission to Study the

[192] Identical letters dated 26 March 2015 from the Permanent Representative of Qatar to the United Nations addressed to the Secretary-General and the President of the Security Council, UN Doc. S/2015/217 (27 March 2015), 4.

[193] *Ibid*, 2.

[194] See Letter dated 10 February 2016 from the Chargé d'affaires a.i. of the Permanent Mission of the Netherlands to the United Nations addressed to the President of the Security Council, UN Doc. S/2016/132 (10 February 2016); Identical letters dated 8 September 2015 from the Permanent Representative of France to the United Nations addressed to the Secretary-General and the President of the Security Council, UN Doc. S/2015/745 (9 September 2015); UN Doc. S/2015/946, n.15; UN Doc. S/2016/34, n.51; UN Doc. S/2016/523, n.152; UN Doc. S/2015/693, n.126; UN Doc. S/2016/513, n.152; UN Doc. S/2014/851, n.152; UN Doc. S/2015/221, n.126; UN Doc. S/2014/695, n.52.

[195] Letter dated 20 September 2014 from the Permanent Representative of Iraq to the United Nations addressed to the President of the Security Council, UN Doc. S/2014/691 (22 September 2014).

[196] Gray, n.25, 129–131.

[197] See nn.32–33 and accompanying text.

Organisation of Peace argued that while all self-defence actions must be reported to the Security Council as per Article 51, an additional requirement should be created that measures in collective self-defence must also be reported to the General Assembly.[198] This suggestion was never implemented, of course, but it is illustrative of the importance of reporting – and the resulting scrutiny and objective assessment that it affords – in the collective self-defence context. In any event, while reporting collective self-defence actions (or not) is not legally determinative, it is legally relevant, and the fact that there is widespread and general compliance with the requirement in the collective context is positive. Equally, as with the reporting of individual self-defence actions, the length and substantive quality of those reports still could be improved.[199]

3.5 The 'Until Clause'

In addition to the reporting requirement, Article 51 holds that the right of self-defence can be exercised only 'until the Security Council has taken measures necessary to maintain international peace and security'.[200] This so-called 'until clause'[201] requires that the use of force in self-defence must stop once the Security Council has taken action in response to the armed attack in question.

It has been said that the until clause applies to collective self-defence just as it does to individual self-defence.[202] There is plenty of reason to support this conclusion, not least being the fact that Article 51 itself sets out the requirement in relation to both manifestations of self-defence. Numerous collective self-defence treaties are explicit that the exercise of the right that they envisage is limited to circumstances where the Council has not (or has not yet) taken necessary measures to abate the relevant armed attack.[203] It is also worth noting that the rationale for the until clause – which, along with the reporting requirement, is to centralise uses of force within the collective security framework of the United Nations,

198 Commission to Study the Organisation of Peace, 6th Report (1948), 13.

199 Green, n.180, 602–606.

200 UN Charter, n.2, Article 51.

201 A term used, for example, by Ruys, n.55, 74.

202 Henkin, n.4, 45; Antonopoulos, n.32, 179.

203 See, for example, Security Treaty between Australia, New Zealand, and the United States of America (1952) 131 UNTS 83 (ANZUS Treaty), Article IV; Rio Treaty, n.13, Article 3 (4); Warsaw Pact, n.176, Article 4; WEU Treaty, Article V; North Atlantic Treaty, n.13, Article 5.

as pre-eminently embodied by the Security Council[204] – holds equally for collective and individual self-defence.

It has commonly been said that it is only when the Security Council adopts 'effective' measures to bring about the end of the relevant armed attack that the until clause kicks in and the self-defence action must cease.[205] For example, the United Kingdom argued in regard to the Falklands/Malvinas conflict in 1982 that the until clause 'can only be taken to refer to measures which are actually effective to bring about the stated objective'.[206] From a policy perspective, it is difficult to argue that a state's right to defend itself should be limited before the Security Council has actually abated the defensive necessity in question.[207] Otherwise, any measure on the Council's part, however insufficient, could leave an attacked state helpless.

This interpretation of the until clause would also seem to be reflected specifically in the collective self-defence state practice, although this has not always been entirely consistent. One might note, for example, that both the UAR[208] and the USSR[209] objected to the US action in Lebanon in 1958 on the basis that the Security Council was already seized of the matter, without meaningful consideration of 'effectiveness'. However, the United States was clear that it would continue to take military action 'only until the United Nations itself is able to assume the necessary responsibility *for ensuring* the continued independence of Lebanon'.[210]

[204] Kelsen, n.110, 785; O'Meara, n.142, 41; Azubuike, n.31, 149.

[205] Malvina Halberstam, 'The Right to Self-Defense Once the Security Council Takes Action' (1996) 17 *Michigan Journal of International Law* 229; Jane A. Meyer, 'Collective Self-Defense and Regional Security: Necessary Exceptions to a Globalist Doctrine' (1993) 11 *Boston University International Law Journal* 391, 399; Christian Henderson, *The Use of Force and International Law* (Cambridge, Cambridge University Press, 2018), 266–271; Marco Roscini, 'On the "Inherent" Character of the Right of States to Self-Defence' (2015) 4 *Cambridge Journal of International and Comparative Law* 634, 655; Greig, n.180, 389–399; Shah, n.109, 120–122; Rostow, n.185, 511; Wood, n.185, 656; Ruys, n.55, 74–83. *Contra* Abram Chayes, 'The Use of Force in the Persian Gulf', in Lori Fisler Damrosch and David J. Scheffer (eds.), *Law and Force in the New International Order* (Boulder, Westview Press, 1991), 3, 5–6; Tadashi Mori, 'Collective Self-Defence in International Law and in the New Japanese Legislation for Peace and Security (2015)' (2017) 60 *Japanese Yearbook of International Law* 158, 165.

[206] Letter dated 30 April 1982 from the Permanent Representative of the United Kingdom of Great Britain and Northern Ireland to the United Nations addressed to the President of the Security Council, UN Doc. S/15016 (4 April 1982).

[207] Halberstam, n.205, 238–239.

[208] UN Doc. S/PV.828, n.41, para. 36.

[209] UN Doc. S/PV.827, n.17, para. 116.

[210] *Ibid*, para. 44 (emphasis added).

Likewise, Lebanon itself stressed that Council action taken to that point was insufficient, and that it would only consider that the United States must stop providing aid in collective self-defence if those measures were effective:

> In view of this situation, my Government would again appeal to the Security Council and urge it to take some more effective emergency measure than the one it has already taken, and one more likely to achieve the Council's purpose; to prevent any illegal infiltration of personnel or any supply of arms or other material across the Lebanese borders. The Lebanese Government would like to reaffirm here, today, before the Security Council, that it is always anxious to ensure that the assistance it needs to protect Lebanon's independence and integrity should be obtained through the United Nations and within the framework of the United Nations Charter.[211]

It is unlikely that the US action was indeed a lawful exercise of the right of collective self-defence,[212] but on the application of the until clause, there was general support among other states for the US/Lebanon position that measures on the part of the Council needed to be effective before self-defence was precluded. For example, the representative of Canada stressed that 'there is no reason why the action reported to the Council by the representative of the United States should not be considered as complementary to the mission which the United Nations has already inaugurated'.[213]

One also might note that in August 1990, some states argued following Iraq's invasion of Kuwait that the Security Council had taken non-forcible measures in response, and thus that the until clause precluded the initiation of any military action in collective self-defence.[214] This view

[211] *Ibid*, para. 83. See also *ibid*, para. 84 ('[i]t is clearly understood that this assistance [provided by the US] is strictly temporary and will continue only until such time as the measure we have asked of the Security Council is carried into effect').

[212] Particularly due to the lack of an armed attack. See n.19 and accompanying text.

[213] UN Doc. S/PV.828, n.41, para. 17. See also *ibid*, paras. 2–12 (France).

[214] See UNSC Verbatim Record, UN Doc. S/PV.2937 (18 August 1990), 6 (Yemen: '[w]e believe that utilization of this military blockade by one State without taking into consideration the role assumed by the Security Council for the safeguarding of international peace and security is an act that is not defensive in character'); *ibid*, 13 (China: 'to solve the present serious crisis in the Gulf, it is necessary to implement the three relevant resolutions of the Security Council in a serious and effective manner'); *ibid*, 31 (Cuba: 'the Charter is being used deceitfully, as something to be implemented unilaterally by one State after the Security Council has taken the decisions it deems appropriate. . . . Does it [the US] believe that the Security Council have not taken the steps it should? Or, contrary to Article 51, does it feel that it has the right to infringe the

was expressed even though the Council's measures undeniably had been insufficient, at that point at least, to abate Iraq's occupation of Kuwait, which lasted until February 1991. This suggests an interpretation of the until clause on the part of some states that saw *any* Council action as sufficient to bar the initiation or continuance of self-defence measures. Ultimately, though, as the United States[215] and United Kingdom[216] themselves pointed out, the resolution of the Council that some states[217] saw as triggering the until clause – resolution 661 – itself affirmed the inherent right of individual and collective self-defence in relation to the situation.[218] Thus, in the very act of taking measures, the Security Council acknowledged that the exercise of self-defence could continue, implicitly reflecting the view that a condition of 'effectiveness' is inherent in the until clause.[219]

It is therefore argued that, as with individual self-defence, states can take measures in collective self-defence only up to the point that the Council takes *effective* measures to abate the relevant armed attack.

3.6 Conclusion

This chapter examines the criteria that apply equally to individual and collective self-defence. The most important of these criteria are armed attack, necessity, and proportionality, with the reporting requirement and the until clause having additional, secondary roles. The three primary criteria, in particular, are crucial for the lawful exercise of collective self-defence. As such, it was important that they be set out in this book. Equally, these criteria have been much discussed in the individual self-defence context, and so they have not been analysed in depth here. The goal of this chapter was more modest: to assess these criteria particularly in relation to collective self-defence actions. In that regard, it ultimately

authority and responsibility of the Security Council?'); *ibid*, 42–45 (Iraq: '... Article 51 grants the right of individual or collective self-defence "until the Security Council has taken measures necessary to maintain international peace and security". The Security Council took such measures by its hasty and unjust resolution 661 (1990) requesting all states to respect that Article').

215 *Ibid*, 34–35; UNSC Verbatim Record, UN Doc. S/PV.2934 (9 August 1990), 8.

216 UN Doc. S/PV.2934, n.215, 17–18.

217 See, for example, UN Doc. S/PV.2937, n.214, 42–45 (Iraq).

218 UNSC Res. 661, UN Doc. S/RES/661 (6 August 1990) (the Security Council '[a]ffirm[ed] the inherent right of individual or collective self-defence, in response to the armed attack by Iraq against Kuwait, in accordance with Article 51 of the Charter').

219 Gray, n.25, 132.

can be said that the collective self-defence practice at least broadly reflects the individual self-defence practice as to both the applicability and the application of these criteria. Simply put, they apply, and for the most part, they apply in the same way. This provides a notable degree of consistency to the law governing the right of self-defence as a whole. It also means that problematic debates regarding individual self-defence – such as whether it can be exercised pre-emptively, and whether it can be exercised in response to attacks by non-state actors – are equally problematic, and equally unresolved, in the collective self-defence context.[220]

220 Antonopoulos, n.32, 175 (making this point with regard to the exercise of collective self-defence specifically by NATO, although it holds true to any exercise of collective self-defence).

4

The Purported Declaration and Request Requirements for Collective Self-Defence

4.1 Introduction

The previous chapter examined the legal criteria for the exercise of collective self-defence that are shared with individual self-defence. In addition to these criteria, it is often said that two further requirements exist that are specific to collective self-defence only: 'declaration' and 'request'. The majority view is that the defending state must 1) declare that it has been the victim of an armed attack and 2) request that another state or states come to its aid in response to that attack. These two 'additional' criteria for collective self-defence were most famously articulated by the International Court of Justice (ICJ) in the 1986 *Nicaragua* merits decision.[1] The ICJ's endorsement of these criteria has faced notable critique.[2] Nonetheless, since *Nicaragua*, they have been repeatedly identified by scholars as requirements for the lawful exercise of collective self-defence.[3]

[1] See Section 4.2.

[2] See Section 4.3.

[3] See, for example, Sir Michael Wood, 'Self-Defence and Collective Security', in Marc Weller (ed.), *The Oxford Handbook of the Use of Force in International Law* (Oxford, Oxford University Press, 2015), 649, 654; Johanna Friman, *Revisiting the Concept of Defence in the* Jud ad Bellum: *The Dual Face of Defence* (Oxford, Hart Publishing, 2017), 94, 193; Dino Kritsiotis, 'A Study of the Scope and Operation of the Rights of Individual and Collective Self-Defence under International Law', in Nigel D. White and Christian Henderson (eds.), *Research Handbook on International Conflict and Security Law:* Jus ad Bellum, Jus in Bello *and* Jus Post Bellum (Abingdon, Routledge, 2013), 170, 185–187; Alexander Orakhelashvili, *Collective Security* (Oxford, Oxford University Press, 2011), 280; Johan D. van der Vyver, 'Military Intervention in Syria: The American, British and French Alternatives and the Russian Option' (2015) 48 *De Jure* 36, 42, footnote 20; Eustace Chikere Azubuike, 'Probing the Scope of Self Defense in International Law' (2011) 17 *Annual Survey of International and Comparative Law* 129, 174, 180; Zia Modabber, 'Collective Self-Defense: *Nicaragua v. United States*' (1988) 10 *Loyola of Los Angeles International and Comparative Law Journal* 449, 462; Christopher Greenwood, 'Self-Defence', in Rüdiger Wolfrum (ed.), *Max Planck Encyclopaedia of Public International Law, vol. IX* (Oxford, Oxford University Press, 2012), 103, 110, para. 39; Josef Mrázek, 'Prohibition of the Use and Threat of Force: Self-Defence

Thus, Greenwood stated in 2012 that while the declaration and request requirements 'attracted some criticism at the time, the approach of the Court has generally been followed since the judgment [*Nicaragua*] was given in 1986'.[4] This statement certainly is correct when it comes to *scholars*.[5] However, whether the ICJ's approach has been 'followed' by *states* – and thus whether 'declaration' and 'request' can be identified as binding requirements in customary international law – is very much open to question, at least with regard to the declaration criterion.

This chapter examines whether 'declaration' and 'request' are indeed legal limitations on collective self-defence, as has been indicated by the ICJ and a majority of scholarship. Following this introduction, Section 4.2 examines the identification and conception of 'declaration' and 'request' in the jurisprudence of the ICJ, including asking whether the Court advanced these criteria as legally determinative requirements for collective self-defence or merely as evidentiary factors. Section 4.3 then explores critiques of the ICJ's identification of the criteria. These include the arguments that 1) in identifying these criteria, the Court misconceived the nature of collective self-defence; 2) the criteria act as unnecessary formal barriers to the exercise of a defensive right; and, crucially, 3) the Court presented almost no evidence to establish the criteria as a matter of law. The section goes on to explore the possible legal source of the criteria, concluding that if they exist, they can only exist as rules of customary international law. Section 4.4 examines state practice and *opinio juris* to determine whether the criteria can, in fact, be identified

and Self-Help in International Law' (1989) 27 *Canadian Yearbook of International Law* 81, 93; Ella Schönleben, 'Collective Self-Defence or Just Another Intervention?: Some Thoughts on Turkey Allegedly Sending Syrian Mercenaries to Nagorno-Karabakh', *Völkerrechtsblog* (2 November 2020), https://voelkerrechtsblog.org/de/collective-self-defence-or-just-another-intervention; Pavel Doubek, 'War in Ukraine: Time for a Collective Self-Defense?', *Opinio Juris* (29 March 2022), http://opiniojuris.org/2022/03/29/war-in-ukraine-time-for-a-collective-self-defense. It should be acknowledged that, like many other commentators, in the past, the present author has been guilty of accepting uncritically the existence in law of the two additional criteria for collective self-defence. See Christopher P. M. Waters and James A. Green, 'International Law: Military Force and Armed Conflict', in George Kassimeris and John Buckley (eds.), *The Ashgate Research Companion to Modern Warfare* (Farnham, Ashgate Publishing, 2010), 289, 297.

4 Greenwood, n.3, para. 39.

5 See n.3 and accompanying text. Albeit that there is also a growing trend for scholars to accept 'request' while ignoring, or even rejecting 'declaration'. See nn.136–138 and accompanying text.

in custom. Given that these criteria have been reiterated so often in scholarship (while at the same time being notably critiqued by other writers), it is strange that few attempts have been made to establish their existence (or not) in custom: this is remedied here. It is ultimately argued that there is, indeed, clearly a requirement in customary international law that the defending state must request aid. In the absence of such a request, even if the criteria discussed in Chapter 3 are met, any ostensible collective self-defence action amounts to an unlawful use of force. In contrast, it is argued that there is no basis in international law for the purported 'declaration' requirement advanced by the ICJ. The continued reference to such a criterion in scholarship is both incorrect and unhelpful.

4.2 The Declaration and Request Criteria in the Jurisprudence of the ICJ

4.2.1 The Court's Identification of the Declaration and Request Criteria

In its 1986 *Nicaragua* merits decision, the ICJ indicated that for collective self-defence to be exercised, first, 'the State which is the victim of an armed attack ... must form and *declare* the view that it has been so attacked'.[6] The Court reinforced this by stating that:

> [t]here is no rule in customary international law permitting another State to exercise the right of collective self-defence on the basis of its own assessment of the situation. Where collective self-defence is invoked, it is to be expected that the State for whose benefit this right is used *will have declared itself to be the victim of an armed attack*.[7]

Second, the ICJ held in *Nicaragua* that the defending state must not only declare itself to be the victim of an armed attack but must then also *request* military aid in response to that attack:

> [T]he Court finds that in customary international law ... there is no rule permitting the exercise of collective self-defence *in the absence of a request* by the State which regards itself as the victim of an armed attack.[8]

6 *Military and Paramilitary Activities in and against Nicaragua (Nicaragua v. United States of America)* (merits) [1986] ICJ Rep. 14, para. 195 (emphasis added).
7 *Ibid* (emphasis added).
8 *Ibid*, para. 199 (emphasis added). See also *ibid*, paras. 165–166.

The Court was clear that it viewed these declaration and request criteria as being located in customary international law.[9] Moreover, while the Court was not entirely explicit on this point, it seems that it did not derive these requirements from 'other' customary international law obligations. In other words, the Court saw declaration and request as being separate from the criteria, discussed in Chapter 3, which are applicable to both individual and collective self-defence. For example, having considered the question of the occurrence of an armed attack in the *Nicaragua* case, the Court referred to the declaration and request criteria as '*other considerations* which justify [reaching a conclusion regarding] … the exercise of the right of collective self-defence'.[10] Thus, declaration and request were conceived of by the ICJ as 'stand-alone' criteria, specific to collective self-defence.

The ICJ was also clear in *Nicaragua* that it saw the declaration and request criteria as separate from each other:

> The Court concludes that the requirement of a request by the State which is the victim of the alleged attack *is additional* to the requirement that such a State should have declared itself to have been attacked.[11]

In this understanding, declaration and request are two sequential 'steps' to be taken by the co-defending state. This means that, in the view of the ICJ in *Nicaragua*, at least, a declaration that a state has suffered an armed attack cannot be inferred from its request for aid in response to it. This conceived separation of the criteria should be borne in mind in the later sections of this chapter.

Since the *Nicaragua* case, the requirement of a request has been referred to by the ICJ again in more recent decisions. For example, in the 2003 *Oil Platforms* judgment, the Court noted the existence of the request requirement,[12] albeit that, unlike in *Nicaragua*, the United States did not advance the claim of collective self-defence in *Oil Platforms*, and so the Court's reference to the need for a request was hardly pertinent to its decision. Nonetheless, the Court quoted its earlier judgment in holding that *had* the United States 'claimed to have been exercising collective self-defence … this would have required the existence of a request …

[9] *Ibid*, paras. 34, 195, 199.
[10] *Ibid*, para. 231.
[11] *Ibid*, para. 199 (emphasis added).
[12] *Case Concerning Oil Platforms (Islamic Republic of Iran v. United States of America)* (merits) [2003] ICJ Rep. 161, para. 51.

"by the State which regards itself as the victim of an armed attack"'.[13] Two years later, in the 2005 *Armed Activities* decision, the Court similarly endorsed – albeit rather less explicitly – the 'request' requirement for collective self-defence by holding that 'a State may *invite* another State to assist it in using force in self-defence'.[14]

The ICJ has thus been consistent in its jurisprudence in identifying the request requirement for the exercise of collective self-defence, having done so in *Nicaragua*, *Oil Platforms* and *Armed Activities*. It is notable, however, that in neither *Oil Platforms* nor *Armed Activities* did the Court make any reference to a separate, corresponding requirement that the defending state first declare that it has suffered an armed attack. Admittedly, in neither decision did the ICJ explicitly *reject* its earlier statement that a separate declaration was required. It may be seen as telling nevertheless that it was only in the *Nicaragua* case that the Court identified such a requirement.[15] This is particularly the case in *Armed Activities*, where collective self-defence once again was at issue (at least in part). If a declaration really were legally required by the Democratic Republic of the Congo in the context of that case, one might expect that the Court would have at least mentioned it (as it did the request requirement). Even in *Oil Platforms*, where collective self-defence was not at issue, the Court saw fit to reiterate the request requirement, while staying silent on declaration. Thus, it may be said that the purported declaration criterion has been notable by its absence in ICJ jurisprudence other than in *Nicaragua* itself.

4.2.2 Did the Court Present Declaration and Request as Legally Determinative Requirements?

Despite the seemingly clear indication by the ICJ of the need for a request (in *Nicaragua*, *Oil Platforms* and *Armed Activities*) and a declaration (in *Nicaragua* only), it has been suggested that the Court may not, in fact, have seen these 'requirements' as being essential for the lawful exercise of collective self-defence. Instead, it is said, the language used by the Court indicates that it viewed the criteria that it was identifying as being merely

13 *Ibid* (in part quoting from *Nicaragua* (merits), n.6, references omitted).

14 *Armed Activities on the Territory of the Congo* (*Democratic Republic of the Congo v. Uganda*) (merits) [2005] ICJ Rep. 223, para. 128 (emphasis added).

15 See Tom Ruys, *'Armed Attack' and Article 51 of the UN Charter: Evolutions in Customary Law and Practice* (Cambridge, Cambridge University Press, 2010), 91.

evidentially beneficial in determining the lawfulness of a collective self-defence action.[16] In adopting this reading of the Court's position in 2009, the Report of the Independent International Fact-Finding Mission on the Conflict in Georgia (IIFFMCG), which was set up by the Council of the European Union to investigate the 2008 Russia–Georgia conflict,[17] concluded that:

> [t]he International Court seems not to consider a declaration and request as a legal condition. The ICJ merely takes the absence of such a declaration and request as a confirmation that there had been no armed attack.[18]

It is true that the Court was far from as clear in *Nicaragua* as one might have hoped regarding the legal consequences of complying (or, more pertinently, *not* complying) with the criteria of declaration and request.[19] For example, it will be recalled that the Court in *Nicaragua* stated that 'it is *to be expected* that the State for whose benefit this right is used will have declared itself to be the victim of an armed attack',[20] and that elsewhere in the judgment it referred to declaration and request as '*considerations* which justify the Court' reaching a decision on collective self-defence.[21] It further stated that:

> it is evident that it is the victim State, being the most directly aware of that fact, which *is likely* to draw general attention to its plight. It is also evident that if the victim State wishes another State to come to its help in the exercise of the right of collective self-defence, *it will normally* make an express request to that effect.[22]

Such language is more equivocal than would be expected in relation to legally mandatory requirements. One might also note that a declaration

16 See D. W. Greig, 'Self-Defence and the Security Council: What Does Article 51 Require?' (1991) 40 *International and Comparative Law Quarterly* 366, 376–378. See also Yoram Dinstein, *War, Aggression and Self-Defence* (Cambridge, Cambridge University Press, 6th ed., 2017), 20 (implying this, at least in some circumstances).

17 See Council Decision 2008/901/CFSP of 2 December 2008 Concerning an Independent International Fact-finding Mission on the Conflict in Georgia (2008) 323 *Official Journal of the European Union* 66.

18 Report of the Independent International Fact-Finding Mission on the Conflict in Georgia (IIFFMCG) (2009), vol. II, 281 (references omitted).

19 James A. Green, *The International Court of Justice and Self-Defence in International Law* (Oxford, Hart Publishing, 2009), 53–54.

20 *Nicaragua* (merits), n.6, para. 195 (emphasis added).

21 *Ibid*, para. 231 (emphasis added).

22 *Ibid*, para. 232 (emphasis added).

by a state to the effect that it has suffered an armed attack and/or its request for aid in repelling that attack could be indicative evidence that might help to strengthen the conclusion that such an attack had occurred. Or, perhaps of more probatory value, the *absence* of a declaration and/or request by an attacked state could act as useful evidence supporting the conclusion that no armed attack had occurred (albeit that the absence of declaration/request alone could not establish the non-occurrence of such an attack). Similar evidentiary benefits might also be possible to the effect that a declaration and request (or lack thereof) could help to establish the necessity (or lack thereof) of a response. As such, perhaps the Court really was just referring to the value of declaration and request in helping to assess other, legally determinative criteria.

However, at least regarding the request requirement, the Court also has used much more mandatory language. For example, in *Nicaragua*, it referred more than once to 'the *requirement* of a request'.[23] In *Oil Platforms*, the ICJ asserted that collective self-defence '*required* the existence of a request'.[24] Indeed, the Court's discussion of the request requirement in 2003 can also be read as the ICJ indicating, counterfactually, that *had* the United States made a collective self-defence claim – which the Court implied it could have at least tried to do, given that it 'referred to attacks on vessels and aircraft of other nationalities'[25] – then that claim would not have been accepted by the Court purely on the basis that there had not been a request for aid. It is also worth noting that, at times, the Court has used mandatory language even in relation to the declaration requirement: for example, the defending state '*must* form and declare the view that it has been . . . attacked'.[26]

One might note that in his separate opinion to the *Nicaragua* judgment, Judge Ruda appeared to interpret the majority's view as being that *both* declaration and request are mandatory requirements for collective self-defence.[27] It has also already been noted that the Court took the view that declaration and request are distinct from other legal criteria for the

[23] *Ibid*, paras. 198, 199 (emphasis added).

[24] *Oil Platforms* (merits), para. 51 (emphasis added).

[25] *Ibid*.

[26] *Nicaragua* (merits), n.6, para. 195 (emphasis added). See also *ibid*, para. 199.

[27] *Ibid*, separate opinion of Judge Ruda, para. 12. It should be noted, however, that Judge Ruda saw the discussion of the possible 'additional' requirements of collective self-defence by the majority in *Nicaragua* as unnecessary, given that the Court had already concluded that there had been no armed attack upon El Salvador *et al*.

exercise of self-defence,[28] which would strongly suggest that it did not see them merely as ways of helping to establish compliance with such other criteria.

Ultimately, it is fair to say that the Court gave somewhat mixed messages as to whether it considered compliance with the declaration and request requirements to be legally determinative for the exercise of collective self-defence, or merely evidentially relevant. It is submitted, however, that the best reading of the jurisprudence is that the ICJ identified 'request', at least, as legally essential. This is probably also the view that the Court took of 'declaration', although that is rather less clear.[29]

4.3 Critique of the ICJ's Identification of Declaration and Request and Locating Them as a Matter of Law

4.3.1 The (Un)Desirability of Declaration and Request and Critique of the Court's Position

It is worth noting that the purported criteria of 'request' and 'declaration' have a compelling policy goal underpinning them. It is undesirable for 'white knight' states to make the decision to intervene unilaterally and 'ride in' to other sovereign states' territories unneeded and/or unwanted.[30] The criteria aim to stop states from employing collective self-defence as a pretext for the use of force for other purposes,[31] and to

[28] See nn.9–10 and accompanying text.

[29] See R. St. J. MacDonald, 'The *Nicaragua* Case: New Answers to Old Questions' (1986) 24 *Canadian Yearbook of International Law* 127, 150 (interpreting the Court's position as being that a lack of either declaration or request 'renders illegal an otherwise legitimate use of force'). See also Greig, n.16, 377–378.

[30] *Nicaragua* (merits), n.6, dissenting opinion of Judge Sir Robert Jennings, 544–545; Yoram Dinstein, 'The Jurisprudence of the Court in the *Nicaragua* Decision: Remarks' (1987) 81 *American Society of International Law Proceedings* 266, 268; Christine Gray, *International Law and the Use of Force* (Oxford, Oxford University Press, 4th ed., 2018), 185; Rein Müllerson, 'Self-Defence in the Contemporary World', in Lori Fisler Damrosch and David J. Scheffer (eds.), *Law and Force in the New International Order* (Boulder, Westview Press, 1991), 13, 20; Derek W. Bowett, 'Collective Self-Defence under the Charter of the United Nations' (1955–1956) 32 *British Yearbook of International Law* 130, 138; Helen Michael, 'Covert Involvement in Essentially Internal Conflicts: United States Assistance to the Contras under International Law' (1990) 23 *Vanderbilt Journal of Transnational Law* 539, 596–597.

[31] Emmanuel Roucounas, *l'Institut de droit international*, 10th Commission, 'Present Problems of the Use of Force in International Law Sub-group: Self-Defence' (2007) 72 *Annuaire de l'Institut de droit international* 75, para. 113; Christian Henderson, *The Use*

protect the sovereign autonomy of the defending state. As Wright has argued, the existence of a request for aid is important because '[i]f a state could invade another's territory merely by alleging that the latter had been attacked . . . the way would be open to unlimited aggression'.[32]

Despite their apparent desirability, however, the identification of the declaration and request criteria in 1986 by the ICJ faced a degree of criticism,[33] including from within the Court itself at the time.[34] This has been for several reasons. First – for those who take the view that collective self-defence must be viewed as involving an element of defending the 'self' – the Court's assertion that declaration and request are required acts to situate collective self-defence, conceptually, as defence of the 'other'.[35] If, so this argument goes, collective self-defence is an inherent right of the co-defending state to defend itself (on the basis that, in responding to an armed attack against another state, the co-defending state must, in some measure, necessarily be protecting an interest of its own), then the exercise of collective self-defence surely cannot be premised on the 'whim' of the defending state. This would therefore mean that the declaration and request criteria cannot be good law.[36] However, this criticism can be dismissed. As was argued in Chapter 1, it is abundantly clear today that the co-defending state need not possess a particular interest in the act of defence (or, at least, not a demonstrable one going beyond the interest that all states share in a peaceful global order). Collective self-defence is best understood as the defence of another, and, as such, its conceptual basis reinforces rather than undermines the value of the defending state being the 'gatekeeper' for such operations.

of Force and International Law (Cambridge, Cambridge University Press, 2018), 260; Christine Chinkin and Mary Kaldor, *International Law and New Wars* (Cambridge, Cambridge University Press, 2017), 142.

32 Quincy Wright, 'United States Intervention in the Lebanon' (1959) 53 *American Journal of International Law* 112, 118.

33 See Greig, n.16, 370–379; Ruys, n.15, 83–91.

34 See, for example, *Nicaragua* (merits), n.6, dissenting opinion of Judge Sir Robert Jennings, 545–546; *ibid*, dissenting opinion of Judge Schwebel, paras. 191, 221–227.

35 See, for example, Dinstein, n.16, 319; *Nicaragua* (merits), n.6, dissenting opinion of Judge Sir Robert Jennings, 545–546.

36 Greig, n.16, 372–373. See also Marco Roscini, 'On the "Inherent" Character of the Right of States to Self-Defence' (2015) 4 *Cambridge Journal of International and Comparative Law* 634, 648 (discussing this view, albeit reaching the inverse conclusion – i.e. that the request requirement means that collective self-defence cannot be an inherent right for the state using force).

Second, the requirements of declaration and request have been seen as overly formal/impractical, and, thus, as unnecessary and unhelpful procedural restrictions on the exercise of the inherent right of self-defence.[37] There is some merit in this critique, certainly in regard to the need for two separate steps, declaration and *then* request, which does, indeed, seem unnecessarily formalistic. The rationale advanced for the two requirements – to ensure that aid is truly needed/wanted, and that collective self-defence is not used as a pretext – surely is fulfilled by the request requirement alone.[38] When the requirement of an armed attack is coupled with the requirement for a request for aid, then the need for the defending state *also* formally to declare that the armed attack has occurred seems superfluous (and, indeed, as critics of this aspect of *Nicaragua* have stressed, overly formalistic/impractical). One might even take the view that a separate declaration would be needlessly antagonistic.[39] As such, while the request requirement can be viewed as a desirable protection against abuse, the additional declaration requirement can be seen as an undesirable burden on the exercise of a defensive right, where time to respond may be limited.[40]

A third criticism that has been levelled at the ICJ's identification of declaration and request is that – in *Nicaragua* and subsequent decisions – the Court has provided almost no evidence in support of the existence of these requirements. This is said to bring the status of the criteria as rules of international law into question.[41] It is this critique that 'bites' the deepest, because, while important, neither the policy desirability nor the undesirability of the criteria have a direct bearing on their existence as *lex*

[37] See, for example, Fred L. Morrison, 'Legal Issues in the *Nicaragua* Opinion' (1987) 81 *American Journal of International Law* 160, 163; *Nicaragua* (merits), n.6, dissenting opinion of Judge Sir Robert Jennings, 544–545; *ibid*, dissenting opinion of Judge Schwebel, para. 191.

[38] Avra Constantinou, *The Right of Self-Defence under Customary International Law and Article 51 of the UN Charter* (Brussels, Bruylant, 2000), 182; James A. Green, 'The "Additional" Criteria for Collective Self-Defence: Request but not Declaration' (2017) 4 *Journal on the Use of Force and International Law* 4, 11.

[39] MacDonald, n.29, 151 ('[i]n certain circumstances it is conceivable that such a declaration will escalate tensions').

[40] Müllerson, n.30, 20.

[41] See for example, Omar Abubakar Bakhashab, 'The Relationship between the Right of Self-Defence on the Part of States and the Powers of the Security Council' (1996) 9 *Journal of King Abdulaziz University: Economics and Administration* 3, 9–10; Greig, n.16, 375–376; Tadashi Mori, 'Collective Self-Defence in International Law and in the New Japanese Legislation for Peace and Security (2015)' (2017) 60 *Japanese Yearbook of International Law* 158, 162–163.

lata. If these criteria exist, as the ICJ asserted in 1986, then they need to be established in law.

4.3.2 The Possible Legal Source of the Requirements

As a matter of treaty interpretation, it would be a significant stretch to try to identify 'declaration' and/or 'request' as being required under Article 51 of the United Nations (UN) Charter in general, or as an aspect of the armed attack criterion therein more specifically.[42] The 1969 Vienna Convention on the Law of Treaties (VCLT)[43] of course requires, in Article 31, that a treaty be 'interpreted in good faith in accordance with the ordinary meaning to be given to the terms of the treaty in their context and in the light of its object and purpose'.[44] It is difficult to see how one could interpret the ordinary meaning of 'if an armed attack occurs' as somehow incorporating the need for that occurrence to be declared. And it is even more difficult to decipher a request requirement in the wording of Article 51. This holds true even when considering, as is required, the ordinary meaning of Article 51 in the wider teleological context of the Charter.[45]

42 Müllerson, n.30, 20.

43 Vienna Convention on the Law of Treaties (1969) 1155 UNTS 331 (VCLT).

44 *Ibid*, Article 31(1).

45 The relevance of the VCLT's rules of treaty interpretation to Article 51 might be queried for two reasons. First, the VCLT only applies to treaties concluded after its own entry into force (January 27, 1980). See *ibid*, Article 4 (on the inapplicability of the VCLT to pre-existing treaties); *ibid*, Article 84 (on the VCLT's own entry into force). The UN Charter of course was concluded well prior to this date. Second, not all states are party to the VCLT. However, many of the VCLT's provisions, including those on treaty interpretation, are mirrored in customary international law. See, for example, *Territorial Dispute (Libyan Arab Jamahiriya/Chad)* (judgment) [1994] ICJ Rep. 6, para. 41; *Case Concerning Oil Platforms (Islamic Republic of Iran v. United States of America* (preliminary objections) [1996] ICJ Rep. 803, para. 12; *Legal Consequences of the Construction of a Wall in the Occupied Palestinian Territory* (advisory opinion) [2004] ICJ Rep. 136, para. 94; *Avena and Other Mexican Nationals (Mexico v. United States of America)* (judgment) [2004] ICJ Rep. 12, para. 83; Ulf Linderfalk, 'Is Treaty Interpretation an Art or a Science? International Law and Rational Decision Making' (2015) 26 *European Journal of International Law* 169, 169; Panos Merkouris, 'Introduction: Interpretation Is a Science, Is an Art, Is a Science', in Malgosia Fitzmaurice, Olufemi Elias and Panos Merkouris (eds.), *Treaty Interpretation and the Vienna Convention on the Law of Treaties: 30 Years On* (Leiden, Martinus Nijhoff, 2010), 1, 5. The ICJ has applied the customary equivalents of these provisions to treaties concluded long before the VCLT entered into force. See *Kasikili/Sedudu Island (Botswana/Namibia)* (judgment) [1999] ICJ Rep. 1045, para. 20 (applying the VCLT interpretation rules to a treaty from 1890); *Sovereignty over Pulau*

Elsewhere in treaty law, a request requirement is (or was) a feature of some regional collective self-defence treaty arrangements. The obligations of the 1948 Rio Treaty,[46] for example, are triggered only '[o]n the request of the State or States directly attacked'.[47] The now-defunct Southeast Asia Treaty Organization likewise made it clear 'that no action . . . shall be taken except at the invitation or with the consent of the Government concerned'.[48] However, the presence of such a requirement in a collective self-defence treaty does not in itself act to establish a general requirement of this kind for the exercise of collective self-defence. Instead, it only establishes such a requirement for the parties thereto, and – even then – only with regard to triggering the relevant treaty's obligation to act in collective self-defence rather than a requirement for the exercise of collective self-defence per se. At most, cameo appearances of request criteria in some collective self-defence treaty arrangements could form a part of the raw material for identifying customary international law, but they certainly cannot establish a request requirement in and of themselves, whether as a matter of treaty law or custom. It is also worth noting that there are (or have been) more collective self-defence treaties that are *silent* on the need for any kind of request than there are such treaties that include a reference to it.[49] Moreover, no declaration criterion can be found in any such treaty.

Litigan and Pulau Sipadan (Indonesia/Malaysia) (judgment) [2002] ICJ Rep. 625, para. 38 (applying the VCLT interpretation rules to a treaty from 1891). Similarly, the Permanent Court of Arbitration has used the general rule under VCLT Article 31 to interpret a treaty from 1881, see *Dispute between Argentina and Chile concerning the Beagle Channel* [1977] PCA, XXI RIAA, 53, para. 15. The ICJ has also applied the customary equivalents of the VCLT interpretation provisions to treaties between states that are not themselves VCLT parties. See, for example, *Sovereignty over Pulau Litigan and Pulau Sipadan*, n.45, para. 37 (Indonesia not being a VCLT state party). It is, thus, relatively uncontentious that the VCLT treaty interpretation provisions apply, indirectly as a matter of customary international law, to treaties to which any states are party, including the UN Charter.

46 Inter-American Treaty of Reciprocal Assistance (1948) 21 UNTS 77 (Rio Treaty).

47 *Ibid*, Article 3(2).

48 Southeast Asia Collective Defense Treaty (with Protocol) (1954) 209 UNTS 28 (SEATO Treaty), Article IV(3).

49 See, for example, North Atlantic Treaty (1949) 34 UNTS 243, Articles 4 and 5; Security Treaty between Australia, New Zealand, and the United States of America (1952) 131 UNTS 83 (ANZUS Treaty), Articles IV and V; Treaty of Friendship, Cooperation and Mutual Assistance between the People's Republic of Albania, the People's Republic of Bulgaria, the Hungarian People's Republic, the German Democratic Republic, the Polish People's Republic, the Romanian People's Republic (1955) 219 UNTS 24 (Warsaw Pact), Article 4.

Declaration and request – at least as general criteria for the exercise of collective self-defence – are not rules of treaty law, meaning that the ICJ was surely correct in indicating that, if they exist as legal criteria, they must be identified as rules of customary international law. Moreover, it is difficult to see how they could be derived from *other* customary international law requirements, such as necessity. It was previously noted that a request for aid, for example, could contribute to establishing that there was a need for such aid,[50] but that is a long way from saying that defensive action is unnecessary unless it is requested. Thus, the Court was also correct that the criteria would need to be 'stand-alone' customary international law requirements.

The critique that the Court then provided almost no evidence to establish those requirements in customary international law is correct too, however. In relation to the 'request' requirement, the sole piece of evidence that the Court advanced was a reference to the Rio Treaty.[51] As already noted, the occasional appearance of a reference to the need for a request in some collective self-defence treaty arrangements is a wholly insufficient basis upon which to establish that the request requirement exists as general customary international law, and – in any event – the Court referred only to one such treaty.[52] In relation to the 'declaration' criterion, the ICJ offered no support whatsoever for its claim that this constituted a rule of customary international law.[53] Given that collective self-defence treaties are silent on declaration, this perhaps is no surprise.

That the ICJ did not provide sufficient evidence supporting the existence of the criteria in custom in 1986 does not, of course, mean that no such evidence existed at the time. And even if the criteria were not in custom in 1986, that does not mean that they could not have crystallised into binding customary international law requirements since. The key question is whether sufficient state practice and *opinio juris* can be identified to conclude that the requirements of declaration and request exist in customary international law today. Given that they have been regularly reiterated by a majority in scholarship since 1986 while also being heavily critiqued by a minority, it is notable that very few serious attempts have been made to establish their existence (or not) in custom.[54]

[50] See n.22 and accompanying text.
[51] See *Nicaragua* (merits), n.6, paras. 197–199.
[52] MacDonald, n.29, 150.
[53] See *ibid*; Gray, n.30, 185.
[54] See, for example, *ibid*, 185–188; Green, n.38, 6–10; Ruys, n.15, 81–91.

The next section considers the practice and *opinio juris* of states in the UN era to do precisely this.

4.4 The Requirements in State Practice/*Opinio Juris*: Request but Not Declaration

4.4.1 Examining the Relevant State Practice

Contrary to what has been suggested by some writers,[55] the notion that the defending state requests aid in collective self-defence was not 'invented' by the ICJ in 1986. This is true in spite of the fact that it is not present in Article 51. However, it is also true that in the early years of the UN system, it is at least debatable whether such a requirement was established as part of customary international law.[56] It is notable that the Commission to Study the Organisation of Peace concluded in 1948 that there were no customary international law restrictions upon collective self-defence beyond those relevant to individual self-defence.[57] It perhaps also should be said, though, that the Commission raised this as a matter of concern, stressing that further legal restrictions would be desirable.[58]

Although it seems unlikely that either declaration or request were customary international law requirements for collective self-defence at the start of the post–Second World War period, the premising of collective self-defence actions on a request for aid from the defending state quickly became common in state practice right from the inception of the UN onward, that is, long before the 1986 *Nicaragua* decision. Whereas, in complete contrast, a separate declaration by the defending state seems never to have been a meaningful feature of practice in the UN era (before or since *Nicaragua*).

One of the earliest relevant post-1945 examples is the request for aid by the Republic of Korea (ROK) to support it against the proclaimed Democratic People's Republic of Korea (DPRK) in the north.[59] The United States made much of the ROK's request in defending its decision

[55] See, for example, MacDonald, n.29, 143, 150.
[56] Ian Brownlie, *International Law and the Use of Force by States* (Oxford, Oxford University Press, 1963), 330.
[57] Commission to Study the Organisation of Peace, 6th Report (1948), 13.
[58] *Ibid.*
[59] UNSC Verbatim Record, UN Doc. S/PV.473 (25 June 1950), 8.

to intervene.[60] The Korean War, thus, can be seen as an early instance in the UN era of a request for aid, and a corresponding reliance on that request to support a claim of collective self-defence.[61] At the same time, while the ROK 'declared' that it was the victim of an 'act of aggression' on the part of the DPRK, this was merely subsumed within its request for help rather than in any way being a separate act.[62]

Following its military action in Hungary in 1956, the USSR was careful in the Security Council to outline the Hungarian request for its assistance and stressed that its action was in response to that request.[63] Whereas, no mention was made by the USSR of a corresponding declaration by Hungary that it had been the victim of an armed attack. Hungary,[64] when publicly announcing, via Budapest radio, that it had requested Soviet aid, stated that this was in response to 'a treacherous armed assault',[65] which was as close as it got to making a formal declaration that it had suffered an armed attack.[66]

[60] UNSC Verbatim Record, UN Doc. S/PV.474 (27 June 1950), 4. See also UNSC Verbatim Record, UN Doc. S/PV.475 (30 June 1950), 10.

[61] Having said this, it is contestable as to whether the legal basis of the action taken in the Korean War was Security Council authorisation or collective self-defence. See Nigel D. White, 'The Korean War – 1950–53', in Tom Ruys and Olivier Corten (with Alexandra Hofer) (eds.), *The Use of Force in International Law: A Case-Based Approach* (Oxford, Oxford University Press, 2018), 17, particularly 31–32; Julius Stone, *Aggression and World Order* (Berkeley and Los Angeles, University of California Press, 1958), 189; Dinstein, n.16, 326; Wood, n.3, 650–651. For further discussion, see Chapter 5, nn.66–70 and accompanying text.

[62] UN Doc. S/PV.473, n.59, 8.

[63] UNSC Verbatim Record, UN Doc. S/PV.746 (28 October 1956), para. 156.

[64] That is to say, *one of* the entities claiming to be the de jure government of Hungary at the time. See Chapter 5, nn.105–115 and accompanying text.

[65] UN Doc. S/PV.746, n.63, para. 157.

[66] It should be noted that it can be questioned whether the Soviet action was an exercise of collective self-defence at all. The lack of anything looking even remotely like an 'armed attack' could mean that it is better viewed as a (controversial) exercise of 'military assistance on request' in relation to an internal uprising. See Eliav Lieblich, 'The Soviet Intervention in Hungary – 1956', in Tom Ruys and Olivier Corten (with Alexandra Hofer) (eds.), *The Use of Force in International Law: A Case-Based Approach* (Oxford, Oxford University Press, 2018), 48 (assessing the intervention against the requirements for military assistance on request). For the relationship between collective self-defence and military assistance on request, see Chapter 8. The USSR itself did not explicitly state that it was acting in collective self-defence. However, it did situate its legal claim in the obligations established by the Warsaw Pact, which, of course, was a collective self-defence treaty explicitly premised on the occurrence of an armed attack. See UN Doc. S/PV.746, n.63, para. 156; Warsaw Pact, n.49, Article 4; Lieblich, n.66, 61. The USSR also argued, dubiously, that it was responding to external interference in Hungary. See UNSC Verbatim Record, UN Doc. S/PV.754 (4 November 1956), paras. 49–50. The United

In 1958, Jordan made it very clear that it had formally requested that the United Kingdom and the United States 'come to its immediate aid', in response to an alleged threat from the United Arab Republic.[67] While Jordan made sure that its request was front and centre, it was rather less clear as to what the request that it made was in relation to.[68] Certainly, it did not label the 'threat' it faced an armed attack or make any sort of formal declaration. The United Kingdom – which sent troops to Jordan – made a great deal of the 'appeal from a Government which felt certain that the independence and integrity of its country was imperilled' in justifying its use of force.[69] In rejecting the United Kingdom's claim of collective self-defence, the USSR, *inter alia*, questioned the *validity* of Jordan's request,[70] thereby indicating that it felt that a request was necessary.[71] However, it made no mention of any need for a Jordanian declaration of the occurrence of an armed attack, let alone the failure to meet such a requirement.

Also in 1958, the United States was very careful to state that its avowed collective self-defence action in Lebanon was undertaken at the request of the Lebanese government,[72] with the importance of this request additionally being stressed by Lebanon itself.[73] Interestingly, in what is an extremely rare (possible) example, Lebanon also *separately* communicated to the UN Security Council a list of the acts that it alleged constituted 'intervention' against it by the United Arab Republic.[74] These included – but were not limited to – support for 'the infiltration of armed bands ... [and] the destruction of Lebanese life and property by such bands ...'[75] Lebanon here made no mention of an 'armed attack', nor did it specifically tie its list of allegations to its request for aid in

Kingdom, Cuba, and Peru certainly saw the Soviet claim as being one of collective self-defence on this basis. See UN Doc. S/PV.746, n.63, paras. 78–79 (UK), 108 (Cuba), 116 (Peru). Some scholars have also taken this view since. See, for example, Chinkin and Kaldor, n.31, 146; Wright, n.32, 119; Keisuke Minai, 'What Legal Interest Is Protected by the Right of Collective Self-Defense: The Japanese Perspective?' (2016) 24 *Willamette Journal of International Law and Dispute Resolution* 105, 110.

67 UNSC Verbatim Record, UN Doc. S/PV.831 (17 July 1958), para. 24.

68 See, for example, *ibid.*

69 *Ibid*, paras. 27–32.

70 *Ibid*, paras. 62–68.

71 On the 'validity' of requests, see Chapters 5 and 6.

72 See, for example, UNSC Verbatim Record, UN Doc. S/PV.827 (15 July 1958), para. 44.

73 See, for example, *ibid*, para. 84.

74 Letter dated 22 May 1958 from the Representative of Lebanon Addressed to the President of the Security Council, UN Doc. S/4007 (23 May 1958).

75 *Ibid.*

response.[76] Nonetheless, this letter to the Council arguably could be seen as a 'declaration' by Lebanon that it had been attacked, distinguishable from its request for aid. However, even if it were interpreted this way, it is of note that neither the United States nor Lebanon made any further reference to this 'declaration'; more importantly, nor did any other state. In contrast, a key criticism[77] of the collective self-defence claim by the USSR was that the *request* by Lebanon was invalid.[78] Thus not only was a request made, but it was also relied upon by states evaluating the legality of the action (in both directions).

In relation to the military action by various Warsaw Pact states in Czechoslovakia in 1968,[79] the USSR stressed repeatedly that it was acting in collective self-defence following a request for aid.[80] Conversely, the US,[81] Canada[82] and Denmark[83] all rejected the Soviet legal justification on the basis that the request was not valid.[84] Again, therefore, the request was a key reference point for states assessing the legality of the action. Czechoslovakia 1968 did involve another rare formal 'declaration' by the victim state, but this was to the effect that the intervention by the states *claiming to be acting in collective self-defence on its behalf* amounted to an 'illegal occupation'.[85] As such, this was not a declaration that was tied to a claim of collective self-defence, but one precisely used to refute such a claim. None of the states that contributed to the Security Council debates on the intervention mentioned any form of declaration requirement for collective self-defence.

[76] *Ibid.*

[77] The USSR raised various criticisms of the claim. See UN Doc. S/PV.827, n.72, paras. 95–123 (arguing that the request for aid was invalid; that there had been no armed attack against Lebanon (or threat thereof); that the Security Council already had taken measures with respect to the situation; and that internal security matters could not give rise to the right of self-defence).

[78] *Ibid*, para. 114.

[79] See Kieran Williams, *The Prague Spring and Its Aftermath: Czechoslovak Politics, 1968–1970* (Cambridge, Cambridge University Press, 1997), 29–38.

[80] UNSC Verbatim Record, UN Doc. S/PV.1441 (21 August 1968), paras. 3, 75, 104, 216.

[81] *Ibid*, paras. 11–12, 30, 36, 40, 248.

[82] *Ibid*, paras. 51, 171.

[83] *Ibid*, para. 185.

[84] For further discussion of 'validity' in this regard, see Chapters 5 and 6.

[85] UN Doc. S/PV.1441, n.80, para. 138 (Czechoslovakian representative, quoting from Declaration of the Ministry of Foreign Affairs, with the endorsement of the President of the Czechoslovak Socialist Republic and on behalf of the Government of the Republic (21 August 1968)).

During the Vietnam War, the South Vietnamese (Republic of Vietnam, RVN) made repeated requests for aid against the North,[86] upon which the United States relied heavily in its formal collective self-defence claim, particularly in the mid-1960s.[87] The need for a valid request itself was unquestioned in the context of the US support for the RVN, albeit controversy again surrounded what constituted 'validity' in this context, and whether such a standard had been met.[88] Also seemingly unquestioned was the fact that – while the United States argued that an armed attack had occurred,[89] again controversially[90] – the South appeared to make no separate 'declaration' that it had suffered such an attack.

The USSR's 1979 intervention in Afghanistan, which the USSR asserted was at the request of the government of Afghanistan,[91] was criticised by a number of states, for a range of reasons related to the validity of the purported request.[92] However, it was clear that the USSR, the states that supported its action, and the states that were critical of it all saw 'request' as a necessary requirement. In contrast, again, there was no separate declaration by the (purported) representatives of the government of Afghanistan, and nothing was made of that fact by other states.

[86] See *Report on the War in Vietnam (as of 30 June 1968)*, Section 1: Report on Air and Naval Campaigns against North Vietnam and Pacific Command-wide Support of the War, June 1964–July 1968. Section 11: Report on Operations in South Vietnam, January 1964 – June 1968 (United States, Army Department, Pacific Command, U.S. Government Printing Office, 1969), 4.

[87] See 'The Legality of United States Participation in the Defense of Viet-Nam' (legal memorandum prepared by Leonard C. Meeker, Legal Adviser of the Department of State) (1966) 54 *Department of State Bulletin* 474, repeatedly throughout. See also USA, Congressional Record – House (24 February 1966) (U.S. Government Printing Office, 1966), 4029.

[88] See Richard A. Falk, 'International Law and the United States Role in the Viet Nam War' (1966) 75 *Yale Law Journal* 1122, 1127.

[89] Meeker, n.87, repeatedly throughout.

[90] Falk, n.88, particularly 1135–1137.

[91] UNSC Verbatim Record, UN Doc. S/PV.2186 (5 January 1980), paras. 15–23 (USSR). See also *ibid*, paras. 120–122 (Poland); UNSC Verbatim Record, UN Doc. S/PV.2187 (6 January 1980), para. 142 (Hungary).

[92] These included the legitimacy of the 'requester' and the timing of the request. See UN Doc. S/PV.2186, n.91, para. 37 (China); UN Doc. S/PV.2187, n.91, paras. 17, 21–22 (USA), 43 (Singapore), 61 (Norway), 87 (Malaysia), 94–96 (Costa Rica), 119–121 (Liberia).

When the United States deployed troops to Honduras in 1988, avowedly in collective self-defence,[93] Honduras stressed on multiple occasions that it had made a valid request for aid against what it characterised as 'aggression' on the part of Nicaragua.[94] The United States, too, was clear that this request was the ultimate basis of its action: 'President Reagan has responded to an explicit request of the Government of Honduras by ordering the immediate deployment of an Infantry Brigade Task Force …'[95] Again, though, there was no separate 'declaration' by Honduras, and no state made any mention of the lack of one.

In 1990, following the invasion by Iraq, Kuwait requested military aid repeatedly, both formally[96] and informally.[97] For its part, the United States relied on these requests by Kuwait, as well as requests for military aid by other states, notably Saudi Arabia. The United States explicitly linked these requests to Article 51 and stressed that they underpinned its exercise of collective self-defence.[98] The United Kingdom similarly made repeated reference to Kuwait's requests for aid (as well as to separate requests by Saudi Arabia and Bahrain), linked these directly to the exercise of collective self-defence, and implied strongly that the various requests acted to validate its military action.[99]

[93] Letter dated 17 March 1988 from The Permanent Representative of Honduras to the United Nations addressed to the Secretary-General, UN Doc. A/42/931-S/19643 (17 March 1988), para. 6.

[94] *Ibid*, para. 4; UNSC Provisional Verbatim Record, UN Doc. S/PV.2802 (18 March 1988), 21–22.

[95] *Ibid*, 27.

[96] See, for example, Letter dated 12 August 1990 from the Permanent Representative of Kuwait to the United Nations addressed to the President of the Security Council, UN Doc. S/21498 (13 August 1990).

[97] See, for example, Sheik Jabir al-Ahmad al-Jabir Al Sabah, the Amir of Kuwait, letter to President George H. W. Bush (12 August 1990) (referred to in Statement by Press Secretary Fitzwater on the Persian Gulf Crisis (12 August 1990), www.presidency.ucsb.edu/documents/statement-press-secretary-fitzwater-the-persian-gulf-crisis).

[98] See *ibid*; Letter dated 9 August 1990 from the Permanent Representative of the United States of America to the United Nations addressed to the President of the Security Council, UN Doc. S/21492 (10 August 1990); UNSC Verbatim Record, UN Doc. S/PV.2934 (9 August 1990), 7–8; UNSC Verbatim Record, UN Doc. S/PV.2938 (25 August 1990), 29–30. It is worth recalling that there remains uncertainty as to whether the coalition action in the Gulf was truly an act of collective self-defence. See Chapter 3, n.185.

[99] See UN Doc. S/PV.2938, n.98, 48; UN Doc. S/PV.2934, n.98, 17–18; Letter dated 13 August 1990 from the Permanent Representative of the United Kingdom of Great Britain and Northern Ireland to the United Nations addressed to the President of the

As was the case during the Cold War, detractor states also focused on the request requirement at the start of the First Gulf War. For example, Cuba asserted that the United States' military action was unlawful, based on a range of arguments concerning both Security Council resolution 661 and Article 51.[100] Of note for current purposes, though, is the fact that one of the issues that Cuba (counterfactually) stressed in asserting the unlawfulness of the action was that force had been used 'without any request from any quarter'.[101]

Interestingly, a little like Lebanon's (arguable) 'declaration' in 1958, Kuwait's representative in the Security Council did formally – and separately from its request for aid – stress that it had 'been subjected to attack in an armed military invasion'.[102] While Kuwait did not explicitly refer to this as an 'armed attack',[103] this 'declaration' did look rather like what seemingly was envisaged by the ICJ in *Nicaragua*. However, while this represents a rare example in collective self-defence practice of a defending state making an express – and notably formal – declaration that it had been attacked, neither the states that intervened on its behalf nor those that debated the intervention went on to refer to this declaration at all.

To move to a much more recent example of post–Cold War state practice, it is worth considering the ongoing military operations in Syria against the 'Islamic State of Iraq and the Levant' (ISIL) since 2014. Ten different states justify (or have justified) their uses of force in Syria as collective self-defence actions in support of Iraq.[104] As the defending state in this context, Iraq requested military aid on various occasions, including at the Paris Conference on 15 September 2014[105] and, more formally, in letters addressed to the President of the Security Council[106]

Security Council, UN Doc. S/21501 (13 August 1990); *Hansard*, HC Deb (6 September 1990), vol. 177, cols. 734–735, 738.

100 UNSC Verbatim Record, UN Doc. S/PV.2937 (18 August 1990), 29–31.

101 *Ibid*, 29.

102 UNSC Verbatim Record, UN Doc. S/PV.2932 (2 August 1990), 4–5.

103 As noted by Kritsiotis, n.3, 187, footnote 91.

104 See Introduction, n.21 and accompanying text.

105 See 'ISIS: World Leaders Give Strong Backing for Iraq at Paris Conference – as It Happened', *The Guardian* (last updated 15 September 2014), www.theguardian.com/world/live/2014/sep/15/isis-leaders-hold-crisis-meeting-on-isis-in-paris-live-coverage?page=with:block-5416c62ae4b0691640d60091#block-5416c62ae4b0691640d60091.

106 Letter dated 20 September 2014 from the Permanent Representative of Iraq to the United Nations addressed to the President of the Security Council, UN Doc. S/2014/

and UN Secretary-General.[107] However, while – when making these requests for aid – Iraq referred, for example, to ISIL's actions in 'terrorizing citizens, carrying out mass executions, persecuting minorities and women, and destroying mosques, shrines and churches',[108] it did not come close to declaring itself to be the victim of an armed attack formally. It simply was contextualising its request for help.

Most of the states that invoked collective self-defence as the basis of their military action against ISIL referred to Iraq's request for aid, without, at the same time, making any reference to a declaration requirement.[109] Thus, Belgium, for example, asserted that it was using force 'in Syria in the exercise of the right of collective self-defence, in response to the request from the Government of Iraq',[110] but did not mention any declaration by Iraq (or, more accurately, the *need for* any declaration by Iraq, given that there was not one). Similarly, Australia,[111] the Netherlands,[112] Norway,[113] and the United Kingdom[114] were all explicit

691 (22 September 2014) (this letter not only requested military aid but also referred to previous requests of this nature).

107 Letter dated 25 June 2014 from the Permanent Representative of Iraq to the United Nations addressed to the Secretary-General, UN Doc. S/2014/440 (25 June 2014).

108 *Ibid.*

109 It should be said that a small number of the states that asserted collective self-defence in relation to action in Syria since 2014 made no reference to either the request criterion or the declaration criterion. See, for example, Letter dated 10 December 2015 from the Chargé d'affaires a.i. of the Permanent Mission of Germany to the United Nations addressed to the President of the Security Council, UN Doc. S/2015/946 (10 December 2015); Letter dated 11 January 2016 from the Permanent Representative of Denmark to the United Nations addressed to the President of the Security Council, UN Doc. S/2016/34 (13 January 2016).

110 Letter dated 7 June 2016 from the Permanent Representative of Belgium to the United Nations addressed to the President of the Security Council, UN Doc. S/2016/523 (9 June 2016).

111 Letter dated 9 September 2015 from the Permanent Representative of Australia to the United Nations addressed to the President of the Security Council, UN Doc. S/2015/693 (9 September 2015).

112 Letter dated 10 February 2016 from the Chargé d'affaires a.i. of the Permanent Mission of the Netherlands to the United Nations addressed to the President of the Security Council, UN S/2016/132 (10 February 2016).

113 Letter dated 3 June 2016 from the Permanent Representative of Norway to the United Nations addressed to the President of the Security Council UN Doc. S/2016/513 (3 June 2016).

114 Identical letters dated 25 November 2014 from the Permanent Representative of the United Kingdom of Great Britain and Northern Ireland to the United Nations addressed to the Secretary-General and the President of the Security Council, UN Doc. S/2014/851 (26 November 2014).

that they were acting in collective self-defence on the basis of Iraq's request for aid; yet, in so doing, none of these states mentioned a declaration criterion. Only Canada referred to anything even close to such a requirement, stating that Iraq had made it 'clear that it was facing a serious threat of continuing attacks', before – like most other states asserting collective self-defence – going on to make much of Iraq's corresponding request for aid.[115]

Similarly telling is that, when formally asserting that the coalition's actions were unlawful, Syria made it clear that the request of Iraq was insufficient to legally justify the use of force, and that such a request needed to have come from Syria itself.[116] This raises crucial questions about who validly can request aid in collective self-defence. These questions will be examined in detail in Chapter 5, but for the purposes of the analysis in this chapter, it is enough to note that the request criterion was again – for a state that was rejecting the collective self-defence claims of others – fundamental. It is also worth noting that, while being less explicit in regard to the insufficiency of Iraq's request and the wider claim of collective self-defence, Russia made a similar point, arguing that the intervention required the 'unequivocal permission' of Syria.[117] Neither Russia nor Syria made any mention of a declaration criterion.

Finally, as an even more recent example, one might note that among a range of *ad bellum* arguments seeking to justify its 2022 full-scale invasion of Ukraine,[118] Russia asserted that it was acting in the collective self-defence of two separatist-leaning regions in the Donbas (Donetsk and

[115] See Letter dated 31 March 2015 from the Chargé d'affaires a.i. of the Permanent Mission of Canada to the United Nations addressed to the President of the Security Council, UN Doc. S/2015/221 (31 March 2015)

[116] Identical letters dated 17 September 2015 from the Permanent Representative of the Syrian Arab Republic to the United Nations addressed to the Secretary-General and the President of the Security Council, UN Doc. S/2015/719 (21 September 2015).

[117] See 'Russia Condemns US Strikes on Islamic State without Syria's Approval', *The Moscow Times* (25 September 2014), www.themoscowtimes.com/news/article/russia-condemns-u-s-strikes-on-islamic-state-without-syria-s-approval/507784.html.

[118] These arguments were set out in 'Address by the President of the Russian Federation', Office of the President of the Russian Federation (24 February 2022), http://en.kremlin.ru/events/president/transcripts/67843 (official English translation, as published by the Kremlin); Обращение Президента Российской Федерации, Президент России (24 февраля 2022 года), http://kremlin.ru/events/president/news/67843 (original Russian text, as published by the Kremlin). President Putin's address was also annexed (in a somewhat different English translation) to Letter dated 24 February 2022 from the Permanent Representative of the Russian Federation to the United Nations addressed to the Secretary-General, UN Doc. S/2022/154 (24 February 2022).

Luhansk). Just prior to the invasion, these entities were recognised by Russia as independent states: the 'Donetsk People's Republic' and the 'Luhansk People's Republic', respectively.[119] Following their recognition by Moscow, the regions immediately signed treaties of friendship and mutual assistance with Russia,[120] and both then formally requested its military support.[121]

However, while those requests for aid made references to '[m]ilitary aggression on the part of Ukraine'[122] and 'ongoing military aggression by the Armed Forces of Ukraine',[123] respectively, neither included an explicit declaration that an armed attack had occurred nor was imminent. To the extent that the separatist regions referred to what they were requesting aid in relation to, this was subsumed within the issuance of that request. Certainly, neither the 'Donetsk People's Republic' nor the 'Luhansk People's Republic' made any *separate* declaration. Russia explicitly relied on the requests made by these regions as the basis of its collective self-defence claim without referring to any related declaration requirement.[124] Russia's collective self-defence argument was widely rejected by other states.[125] However, among all of the criticism of

[119] See Presidential Decree of the Russian Federation, No. 71, 'About recognition of the Donetsk People's Republic' (21 February 2022); Presidential Decree of the Russian Federation, No. 72, 'About recognition of the Luhansk People's Republic' (21 February 2022).

[120] Treaty of Friendship, Cooperation and Mutual Assistance between the Russian Federation and the Donetsk People's Republic (signed in Moscow, 21 February 2022); Treaty of Friendship, Cooperation and Mutual Assistance between the Russian Federation and the Lugansk People's Republic (signed in Moscow, 21 February 2022). These documents were subsequently annexed to Letter dated 3 March 2022 from the Permanent Representative of the Russian Federation to the United Nations addressed to the Secretary-General, UN Doc. A/76/740–S/2022/179 (7 March 2022) (annexes I and II, respectively).

[121] The respective documents requesting aid initially were released (in Russian) by the Kremlin and published by Russian news agencies on social media sites such as Telegram; for example, TACC, *Telegram* (23 February 2022), https://t.me/tass_agency/111840. They were subsequently annexed (in English) to UN Doc. A/76/740–S/2022/179, n.120 (annexes III and IV, respectively).

[122] UN Doc. A/76/740–S/2022/179, n.120, annex III.

[123] *Ibid*, annex IV.

[124] 'Address by the President of the Russian Federation', n.118 (President Putin, phrasing the collective self-defence claim, '[t]he people's republics of Donbass . . . asked Russia for help', and so it responded 'in execution of the treaties of friendship and mutual assistance with the Donetsk People's Republic and the Lugansk People's Republic, ratified by the Federal Assembly on February 22').

[125] For discussion, see Chapter 5, nn.38–44 and accompanying text.

Russia's invasion, one might note that no state raised any concerns – or even took note of the fact – that the regions had not declared that they had suffered an armed attack.

4.4.2 *Analysis of the State Practice*

A request for aid – actual or avowed – has been a defining feature of collective self-defence claims throughout the UN era, including well before the *Nicaragua* judgment. Invocations of collective self-defence almost always have been coupled with a request on the part of the victim.[126] Indeed, this author has only been able to identify one instance of a claim of collective self-defence in the UN era where the co-defending state did not purport to be premising its action on an underpinning request for aid. This was the claim by the United States to be acting in the collective self-defence of Cambodia in 1970. Cambodia did not make an explicit request, and the United States did not refer to any request on the part of Cambodia when it set out its collective self-defence claim.[127] Having said this, it is possible to infer a request for aid from Cambodia,[128] and it is also true that – after the initial operation ended – the United States stated that it was going to act in the collective self-defence of Cambodia again, and this time it was clear that it was to do so at its request.[129] So even this example is hardly an overwhelming

[126] See Gray, n.30, 187 ('[i]n *every case* where a third state has invoked collective self-defence it has based its claim on the request of the victim state . . .', emphasis added). See also Constantinou, n.38, 178, footnote 27 ('[t]he instances where request for assistance has been invoked to justify claims of collective self-defence *are very numerous*', emphasis added).

[127] Letter dated 5 May 1970 from the Permanent Representative of the United States of America to the United Nations addressed to the President of the Security Council, UN Doc. S/9781 (5 May 1970).

[128] Letter dated 18 June 1970 from the Permanent Representative of Cambodia to the United Nations addressed to the President of the Security Council, UN Doc. S/9842 (19 June 1970), 2 (noting with approval the 'military operations of the United States' against North Vietnamese forces on Cambodian territory). On the possibility of inferring collective self-defence requests, see Section 6.3.2.

[129] Letter dated 1 July 1970 from the Permanent Representative of the United States to the United Nations addressed to the President of the Security Council, UN Doc. S/9854 (1 July 1970), 1–2 ('the United States will conduct – *with the approval of the Cambodian Government* – air interdiction missions against North Viet-Namese forces . . . These air interdiction missions are appropriate and limited measures of collective self-defence . . .', emphasis added).

abrogation of the request requirement. In any event, if it is viewed as an exception, it is the exception that proves the rule.

Crucially, it is not merely the case that defending states regularly make requests for aid: co-defending states *rely* on those requests. Collective self-defence actions are legally premised on the defending state's request, even in circumstances where that request is or might be of dubious validity. Requests are repeatedly stressed in communications and debates concerning the co-defending state's action and its related collective self-defence claim.

It will be recalled that the ICJ has not been entirely clear as to whether it views the request requirement as legally determinative for the exercise of collective self-defence, or merely evidentially important, albeit it was argued that the former is a better reading of the jurisprudence.[130] Even in spite of the ubiquity of requests in relation to collective self-defence claims, one perhaps might still take the view that the practice of states is similarly inconclusive on the question of whether the lack of a valid request – in itself – would turn an otherwise lawful collective self-defence action into an unlawful one. Defending states request aid, and co-defending states rely on those requests. Yet, while this indicates that requests have an important role in relation to collective self-defence actions, it could be argued that this practice does not necessarily establish that such requests are legally essential, because it does not demonstrate the necessary *opinio juris*. In the virtual absence of action taken in collective self-defence in the UN era where there has *not* been a request, it is perhaps hard to assess the legal implications of an 'un-requested' collective self-defence action.

However, this would be an incomplete reading of the practice. Tellingly, as the examples in this section have shown, the perceived absence of a (valid) request has been a common reason that states have argued that purported collective self-defence claims have been unlawful. It has been a common feature of the practice for states to disagree as to whether the relevant request was 'valid', but those very debates on validity highlight the shared view that there was a need for a request for aid on the part of the defending state. The factors that influence the 'validity' of the request will be returned to in Chapters 5 and 6, but at this juncture, it is enough to note that states have been consistent in indicating that the lack of (valid) request means that a purported exercise of

[130] See Section 4.2.2.

collective self-defence in fact is unlawful. This view, often repeated and by different states, demonstrates sufficient *opinio juris* to establish that a request is mandatory for the exercise of collective self-defence as a matter of customary international law. It is arguable that the ICJ may have further 'solidified' the importance of the collective self-defence request requirement in subsequent practice, but, in any event, while the Court was likely already correct that the request requirement was binding custom in 1986, there is no question that it is now. A valid request is undoubtedly a legal requirement for collective self-defence.[131]

In stark contrast, there is almost no evidence to indicate that a separate 'declaration' criterion has any basis in state practice or *opinio juris*. This is not to say that defending states never declare, in the context of collective self-defence actions, that they have suffered an armed attack (or – more commonly – made such a declaration using broadly comparable terminology, such as 'aggression'). However, this is almost never done in a formal manner. Declarations on the part of the defending state, if made, are informal and/or are almost always incorporated into its request for aid: alerting other states to the occurrence of the armed attack being subsumed within the request for help in responding to it. Indeed, the very act of requesting aid implies that the state making that request has determined for itself that it is the victim of an armed attack.

There are one or two examples that buck the trend of no meaningful declaration being issued – such as Lebanon in 1958,[132] where a separate declaration was (arguably) made, and, in particular, Kuwait in 1990, where a more formal declaration was present (although even then, no mention was made of an armed attack).[133] However, such examples are extremely scarce, and not especially clear as instances of 'declaration' at least in the way the ICJ conceived. More importantly, there appear to be *no* instances in practice where the *absence* of a declaration that an armed attack has occurred was even noted (let alone seen as determinative) by other states that were considering the lawfulness of a collective

131 Constantinou, n.38, 181. See also Modabber, n.3, 450, footnote 10 (a request 'is a *crucial prerequisite* to successfully invoking collective self-defense', emphasis added). *Contra* IIFFMCG, n.18, vol. II, 281 (a 'request is only one factor to be taken into account in the assessment of the legal grounds for collective self-defence: it is not a *conditio sine qua non*').

132 UN Doc. S/4007, n.74. See nn.74–76 and accompanying text.

133 UN Doc. S/PV.2932, n.102, 4–5. See nn.102–103 and accompanying text.

self-defence claim.[134] It is clear that other states have derived no meaning whatsoever from the lack of a declaration.

While, as has been noted, the *Nicaragua* 'declaration + request' formulation still commonly is repeated by a majority of writers in the literature,[135] it is notable that there is a growing tendency for commentators to identify the request criterion but not the declaration criterion. This has, most often, involved an acceptance of the request requirement with simply no mention being made of the declaration requirement (rather than an explicit rejection of it).[136] As a good example, one might note the 2007 resolution of the Institut de droit International (IDI) on self-defence. In Article 8 of the resolution, the IDI was unequivocal that '[c]ollective self-defence may be exercised only at the request of the target State',[137] while making no reference to any separate declaration

[134] Green, n.38, 11.

[135] See n.3 and accompanying text.

[136] See, for example, Stuart Casey-Maslen, Jus ad Bellum: *The Law on Inter-State Use of Force* (Oxford, Hart Publishing, 2020), 75; Kevin Jon Heller, 'The Unlawfulness of a "Bloody Nose Strike" on North Korea' (2020) 96 *International Law Studies* 1, 15; Olivier Corten, *The Law against War: The Prohibition on the Use of Force in Contemporary International Law* (Oxford, Hart Publishing, 2nd ed., 2021), 401, 467; Mary Ellen O'Connell, 'Preserving the Peace: The Continuing Ban on War between States' (2007) 38 *California Western International Law Journal* 41, 54; Gina Heathcote, *The Law on the Use of Force: A Feminist Analysis* (Abingdon, Routledge, 2013), 77, 103; Aadhithi Padmanabhan and Michael Shih, 'Collective Self-Defense: A Report of the Yale Law School Center for Global Legal Challenges' (10 December 2012), https://law.yale.edu/sites/default/files/documents/pdf/cglc/GLC_Collective_SelfDefense.pdf, 4; Roscini, n.36, 648; James A. Green, Christian Henderson and Tom Ruys, 'Russia's Attack on Ukraine and the *Jus ad Bellum*' (2022) 9 *Journal on the Use of Force and International Law* 4, 17; Michael Byers, 'Geopolitical Change and International Law', in David Armstrong, Theo Farrell and Bice Maiguashca (eds.), *Force and Legitimacy in World Politics* (Cambridge, Cambridge University Press, 2005), 51, 56; Terry D. Gill, 'The Second Gulf Crisis and the Relation between Collective Security and Collective Self-Defense' (1989) 10 *Grotiana* 47, 72; Aurel Sari, 'The Mutual Assistance Clauses of the North Atlantic and EU Treaties: The Challenge of Hybrid Threats' (2019) 10 *Harvard National Security Journal* 405; A. J. Thomas Jr. and Ann Van Wynen Thomas, 'The Organization of American States and Collective Security' (1959) 13 *Southwestern Law Journal* 177, 184, 190; Jaemin Lee, 'Collective Self-Defense or Collective Security: Japan's Reinterpretation of Article 9 of the Constitution' (2015) 8 *Journal of East Asia and International Law* 373, 377; Josef Rohlik, 'Some Remarks on Self-Defense and Intervention: A Reaction to Reading Law and Civil War in the Modern World' (1976) 6 *Georgia Journal of International and Comparative Law* 395, 426.

[137] 'Present Problems of the Use of Armed Force in International Law: Self-Defence', *Institut de droit international*, Session of Santiago, Resolution (2007), Article 8. However, one might note that the Sub-Group's Rapporteur appeared to identify both declaration and request as requirements in his report. See Roucounas, n.31, para. 116.

requirement. In addition, a few scholars have begun to *explicitly* reject the idea that there is any legal 'declaration' requirement for collective self-defence:

> the requirement of an official declaration that a State has been the victim of an armed attack does not have the position of a prerequisite for the lawfulness of the use of force in collective self-defence nor does it affect the substance of claims of collective self-defence.[138]

Overall, customary international law requires that the defending state make a request for aid in the context of any collective self-defence action; there is no requirement that it also makes a separate declaration that it has been attacked.

4.5 Conclusion

This chapter has argued that there is no legal requirement for the defending state to 'declare' that it has been the victim of an armed attack – at least, beyond this being implicit in its request for aid. Indeed, the continued repetition in the scholarship of the need for a declaration is both inaccurate and unhelpful. In contrast, there exists a customary international law requirement that the defending state requests aid in collective self-defence. This is well established in case law, scholarship, and, most importantly, state practice. As the 2022 edition of the US Army's *Operational Law Handbook* succinctly states:

> To constitute a legitimate act of collective self-defense, all conditions for the exercise of an individual State's right of self-defense must be met, *along with the additional requirement that the victim State must consent to the assistance.*[139]

The conclusion that collective self-defence is necessarily premised on a request for aid begs a number of further (crucial) questions about how the request requirement must be *applied*, however. It is clear from the

[138] Constantinou, n.38, 178–183, quoted at 183. See also Ruys, n.15, 91; Green, n.38; Henderson, n.31, 260–262; Marko Svicevic, 'Collective Self-Defence or Regional Enforcement Action: The Legality of a SADC Intervention in Cabo Delgado and the Question of Mozambican Consent' (2022) 9 *Journal on the Use of Force and International Law* 138, 155–156 (explicitly querying the need for a declaration, but not going so far as to outright reject it).

[139] *Operational Law Handbook*, National Security Law Department (The Judge Advocate General's Legal Center & School, U.S. Army, Charlottesville, Virginia, 2022 edn.), 5 (emphasis added).

practice discussed in Section 4.4 of this chapter that not any 'request' will suffice: the request must be *valid*.[140] Factors that influence 'validity' include who can make a request for aid, to whom that request must be addressed, the form of the request (e.g. whether it must be made publicly and/or formally), and the timing of the request. It is to such questions that this book now turns, in Chapters 5 and 6.

[140] Constantinou, n.38, 181 ('the practice of States shows that the lawful exercise of the right of collective self-defence is contingent upon the validity of the request for assistance').

5

The Issuer of a Collective Self-Defence Request

5.1 Introduction

It was argued in the previous chapter that it is a customary international law requirement for the exercise of collective self-defence that the defending state issues a request for aid. It has almost invariably been the case in practice that when states claim to be acting in collective self-defence, they premise this on a request (actual or at least purported) by the defending state.[1] However, nearly as ubiquitous as the reliance on requests has been dispute over their validity. As Gray has stated, 'in almost all the cases of collective self-defence . . . there has been controversy over the existence or the genuineness of the request'.[2] It is clear that not any request will suffice: the request must be 'valid'.

There are a range of factors that need to be considered that do (or at least may) have a bearing on the validity of the request. The next two chapters thus examine the *application* of the request requirement, with the aim of identifying how it operates, and when a request will be (or will be likely to be) considered a 'valid' basis for a collective self-defence action. It is worth noting that because the request requirement is not found in Article 51 and instead is binding in custom, the analysis in the next two chapters is necessarily an exercise in customary international law interpretation.

Chapter 6 considers *how* a collective self-defence needs to be issued, but this chapter first examines the question of *who* can issue such a request. Section 5.2 tests the widely held view that only states can issue a collective self-defence request. It is concluded that this view is correct. An additional question is whether the issuer need not only be a state but

[1] See Chapter 4, nn.126–129 and accompanying text; Avra Constantinou, *The Right of Self-Defence under Customary International Law and Article 51 of the UN Charter* (Brussels, Bruylant, 2000), 178, footnote 27; Christine Gray, *International Law and the Use of Force* (Oxford, Oxford University Press, 4th ed., 2018), 187.

[2] Gray, n.1, 187.

also be a United Nations (UN) member – Section 5.3 considers this. Section 5.4 briefly notes that the authority entitled to represent the state in making a collective self-defence request must be its de jure government. The bulk of this chapter, however, is to be found in Section 5.5, which is dedicated to an assessment of how one *identifies* the de jure government for the specific purpose of issuing a collective self-defence request. It is argued, based predominately on an extensive consideration of state practice, that multiple factors influence this determination. However, the effective control of territory – which has been the traditional starting point for the recognition of governments generally[3] – is not especially important among those factors in the collective self-defence context. In any event, it ultimately appears that the relevant factors are not legal criteria but, rather, are political considerations, which will be applied by other states in a context-specific manner.

5.2 The Requirement of Statehood

It is widely agreed by scholars that only a state can request aid in collective self-defence. Indeed, for most writers, this appears to be taken as self-evident. It is much more common for the requirement of statehood to be implicit in the language used by scholars in relation to collective self-defence than it is for 'statehood' to be explicitly acknowledged as a requirement.[4] Equally, on occasion writers do explicitly identify a requirement of statehood in relation to the necessary

[3] See Section 5.5.1.

[4] Scholars almost invariably use language that makes it clear that they perceive the 'state' as the executor of the request. See, for example, Laurie R. Blank, 'Irreconcilable Differences: The Thresholds for Armed Attack and International Armed Conflict' (2020–2021) 96 *Notre Dame Law Review* 249, 252 (referring to collective self-defence as action taken 'in response to another state's request for assistance'); Paola Diana Reyes Parra, 'Self-Defence against Non-state Actors: Possibility or Reality?' (2021) 9 *Revista de la Facultad de Jurisprudencia* 151, 168 (collective self-defence is exercisable 'on the request of the victim State'); Marco Roscini, 'On the "Inherent" Character of the Right of States to Self-Defence' (2015) 4 *Cambridge Journal of International and Comparative Law* 634, 648 (collective self-defence is 'subordinated to the request of the victim state'); Johanna Friman, *Revisiting the Concept of Defence in the* Jus ad Bellum*: The Dual Face of Defence* (Oxford, Hart Publishing, 2017), 193 (collective self-defence requires a 'request by the victim State'); Anthony Clark Arend and Robert J. Beck, *International Law and the Use of Force* (London, Routledge, 1993), 31 ('the victim state may receive assistance' in collective self-defence); Stuart Casey-Maslen, Jus ad Bellum*: The Law on Inter-State Use of Force* (Oxford, Hart Publishing, 2020), 75 ('the state . . . must seek action in self-defence'); Dino Kritsiotis, 'A Study of the Scope and Operation of the Rights of Individual and Collective

'requester' in collective self-defence. Haque, for example, has unequivocally asserted that '[t]here is no right of collective self-defense of non-state actors . . .'[5] For its part, as will be recalled from the previous chapter, the International Court of Justice (ICJ) identified the legal requirement of a 'request *by the State* which regards itself as the victim of an armed attack' in the 1986 *Nicaragua* case.[6] Other references to this requirement

Self-Defence under International Law', in Nigel D. White and Christian Henderson (eds.), *Research Handbook on International Conflict and Security Law:* Jus ad Bellum, Jus in Bello *and* Jus Post Bellum (Abingdon, Routledge, 2013), 170, 185 (a 'request for collective self-defence must be made by the victim state'); Zia Modabber, 'Collective Self-Defense: *Nicaragua v. United States*' (1988) 10 *Loyola of Los Angeles International and Comparative Law Journal* 449, 462 ('the attacked state . . . must . . . request' aid in collective self-defence). Indeed, this has already been the case throughout this book, of course: for example, by the repeated use of the term 'defending *state*'.

[5] Adil Ahmad Haque, 'On the Precipice: The U.S. and Russia in Syria', *Just Security* (19 June 2017), www.justsecurity.org/42297/precipice-u-s-russia-syria. See also Yoram Dinstein, *War, Aggression and Self-Defence* (Cambridge, Cambridge University Press, 6th ed., 2017), 317; Laura Visser, 'Intervention by Invitation and Collective Self-Defence: Two Sides of the Same Coin?' (2020) 7 *Journal on the Use of Force and International Law* 292, 307; Christine Chinkin and Mary Kaldor, *International Law and New Wars* (Cambridge, Cambridge University Press, 2017), 146; Andrea Spagnolo, 'The Armed Attack against Ukraine and the Italian Reaction from a *Ius ad Bellum* Perspective' (2022) 2 *The Italian Review of International and Comparative Law* 443, 450; Maya Khater, 'The Legality of the Russian Military Operations against Ukraine from the Perspective of International Law' (2022) 3 *Access to Justice in Eastern Europe* 1, 4; Christian Henderson, 'A Countering of the Asymmetrical Interpretation of the Doctrine of Counter-Intervention' (2021) 8 *Journal on the Use of Force and International Law* 34, 63; Richard A. Falk, 'The Cambodian Operation and International Law' (1971) 65 *American Journal of International Law* 1, 12; Elizabeth Wilmshurst, 'Ukraine: Debunking Russia's Legal Justifications', *Chatham House* (24 February 2022), www.chathamhouse.org/2022/02/ukraine-debunking-russias-legal-justifications; James A. Green, Christian Henderson and Tom Ruys, 'Russia's Attack on Ukraine and the *Jus ad Bellum*' (2022) 9 *Journal on the Use of Force and International Law* 4, 18–22; Claus Kreß, 'The Ukraine War and the Prohibition of the Use of Force in International Law' (2022) *Torkel Opsahl Academic EPublisher, Occasional Paper Series* No. 13, 1, 7; International Law Commission, Summary Record of the 2348th meeting, held on Thursday, 2 June 1994, 46th sess., extract from the *Yearbook of the International Law Commission* (1994), vol. 1, UN Doc. A/CN.4/SR.2348 (1 January 1996), para. 16; 'American Policy vis-a-vis Vietnam, in Light of our Constitution, the United Nations Charter; the 1954 Geneva Accords, and the Southeast Asia Collective "Defense Treaty"', Memorandum of Law (prepared by Lawyers Committee on American Policy Toward Vietnam, Hon. Robert W. Kenny, Honorary Chairman), reprinted in 112(23) US Congressional Record, 89th Congress, 2nd sess. (9 February 1966), 2666, 2668.

[6] *Military and Paramilitary Activities in and against Nicaragua* (*Nicaragua v. United States of America*) (merits) [1986] ICJ Rep. 14, para. 199 (emphasis added). See also *ibid*, para. 196 ('the lawfulness of the use of collective self-defence by the third State for the

by the Court in later judgments – *Oil Platforms* in 2003[7] and *Armed Activities* in 2005[8] – likewise explicitly identify the necessary author of the request as being a state.

The near ubiquity of the view that only a state can request aid in collective self-defence perhaps is not surprising, given that there are strong policy reasons to support it. Allowing non-state actors to request aid would risk escalation in both the number and the severity of armed conflicts and would be notably open to abuse.[9] Indeed, as the present author has argued previously, in a piece co-written with Christian Henderson, this:

> would be extremely damaging to international peace and security. States could forcibly aid any entity that requested help; the scope for the (increased) abuse of the right of self-defence would be huge.[10]

The 'statehood' requirement is also a logical consequence of the fact that collective self-defence is directly tied to individual self-defence, in the sense that it can only be exercisable in instances where the defending state could itself legally act in individual self-defence.[11] Although some arguments have been advanced regarding at least the desirability of a right of self-defence for some non-state entities in some circumstances,[12] especially for contested states,[13] the fact remains that only states can act

benefit of the attacked State also depends on a request addressed by that State to the third State').

[7] See *Case Concerning Oil Platforms* (*Islamic Republic of Iran v. United States of America*) (merits) [2003] ICJ Rep. 161, para. 51.

[8] *Armed Activities on the Territory of the Congo* (*Democratic Republic of the Congo v. Uganda*) (merits) [2005] ICJ Rep. 223, para. 128.

[9] Chinkin and Kaldor, n.5, 160; Report of the Independent International Fact-Finding Mission on the Conflict in Georgia (IIFFMCG) (2009), vol. II, 281.

[10] Christian Henderson and James A. Green, 'The *Jus ad Bellum* and Entities Short of Statehood in the Report on the Conflict in Georgia' (2010) 59 *International and Comparative Law Quarterly* 129, 137.

[11] Helen Michael, 'Covert Involvement in Essentially Internal Conflicts: United States Assistance to the Contras under International Law' (1990) 23 *Vanderbilt Journal of Transnational Law* 539, 580 ('[t]he right of collective self-defense is derived from the right of the *state* requesting assistance to employ force in response to an act of aggression. Therefore, no state may employ force in collective self-defense unless the *state* requesting help is entitled to employ force in individual self-defense', emphasis added).

[12] See, for example, Eliav Lieblich, 'Internal *Jus ad Bellum*' (2016) 67 *Hastings Law Journal* 687.

[13] See, for example, Ryan M. Fisher, 'Defending Taiwan: Collective Self-Defense of a Contested State' (2020) 32 *Florida Journal of International Law* 101, 119–122, 140–145;

in individual self-defence under existing international law.[14] This means, in turn, that only states can request aid in collective self-defence. Similarly, the use of force by a state against an internal rebel group – while this could well be unlawful – would not be an 'armed attack',[15] and thus any response at the request of that group could not constitute an action in collective self-defence.[16]

When one considers state practice, though, it is apparent that there have been recent instances where states have claimed to have been responding in collective self-defence to a request made by a non-state entity. Of note in particular is the justification advanced by the US-led coalition in Syria in June 2017 to the effect that it had shot down a Syrian fighter jet 'in collective self-defense of Coalition partnered forces' (a reference to the Syrian Democratic Forces (SDF)).[17] Leaving aside heated debates as to the SDF's legitimacy as an opposition force,[18] none would consider the SDF to be (or have been) the de jure representative of the Syrian state.[19] The United States certainly did not make such a claim, nor did it come anywhere close even to implying it. Therefore, in this instance, the United States advanced the argument that it could act in collective self-defence at the request of a non-state actor. It is worth stressing just how novel this claim was in 2017:

> This was the first time any UN Member State openly invoked collective self-defense, which is generally understood as the right of states to defend

Christian Henderson, 'Contested States and the Rights and Obligations of the *Jus ad Bellum*' (2013) 21 *Cardozo Journal of International and Comparative Law* 367, 394–406.

14 See, for example, Paul Cliteur, 'Self-Defence and Terrorism', in Arthur Eyffinger, Alan Stephens and Sam Muller (eds.), *Self-Defence as a Fundamental Principle* (The Hague, Hague Academic Press, 2009), 67, 83, 86 ('[a]ccording to the law of nations, a *state* is an entity that is allowed to defend itself' and therefore self-defence is only triggered when 'a state (and not a group of people) is physically attacked', emphasis in original).

15 On the armed attack requirement, see Section 3.2.

16 Dinstein, n.5, 317–318.

17 US Central Command, 'Coalition Defends Partner Forces from Syrian Fighter Jet Attack', CJTFOIR, press release #20170618-02 (18 June 2017), www.centcom.mil/MEDIA/PRESS-RELEASES/Press-Release-View/Article/1217892/coalition-defends-partner-forces-from-syrian-fighter-jet-attack.

18 See Wladimir van Wilgenburg, 'Syrian Democratic Forces (Syria)', in Guns and Governance: How Europe Should Talk with Non-state Armed Groups in The Middle East the Middle East and North Africa', *European Council on Foreign Relations*, https://ecfr.eu/special/mena-armed-groups/syrian-democratic-forces-syria.

19 *Ibid.*

> *other states* under international law, to justify an attack on another state *in defense* of a non-state actor.[20]

However, this position was strongly rejected by scholars[21] and, notably, by some states.[22] The United States nonetheless made the same claim again in relation to a further strike in February 2018 (i.e. that it was acting in the collective self-defence of the SDF).[23] This has been viewed similarly as being unlawful.[24] That the United States has been willing to make this claim explicitly, twice, is nonetheless of note.

Russia's primary *ad bellum* claim in relation to its use of force in Georgia in 2008 was individual self-defence, specifically in relation to the protection of Russian nationals in Georgian territory.[25] However, Russia also later claimed – albeit rather tentatively – to be acting in response to a request by the de facto autonomous South Ossetia region, in collective

[20] Annie Himes and Brian J. Kim, 'Self-Defense on Behalf of Non-state Actors' (2021) 43 *University of Pennsylvania Journal of International Law* 241, 243 (emphasis in original). While this was indeed, so far as this author can tell, the first time that a UN member state *openly* invoked collective self-defence based on the request of a non-state actor, it is worth noting that the United States had toyed with a similar argument more than fifty years earlier, when it argued that even if the Republic of Vietnam (RVN) was not a state (which the United States contended it was), this would not preclude action being taken to defend it in collective self-defence. See n.76. It is also the case that states have argued that entities that are not states *are* states, so as to try to legally validate their collective self-defence request. See, for example, the other examples set out in this section.

[21] See Himes and Kim, n.20, particularly 278–279; Kinga Tibori-Szabó, 'The Downing of the Syrian Fighter Jet and Collective Self-Defence', *Opinio Juris* (23 June 2017), http://opiniojuris.org/2017/06/23/the-downing-of-the-syrian-fighter-jet-and-collective-self-defence; Haque, n.5; Kevin Jon Heller, 'The Coming Attack on Syria will be Unlawful', *Opinio Juris* (12 April 2018), http://opiniojuris.org/2018/04/12/the-coming-attack-on-syria-will-be-unlawful (the United States 'claimed that the attack on the militia was "self-defence" – as if collective self-defence somehow permitted the US to come to the aid of a rebel group').

[22] See, for example, 'Russia Cuts Deconfliction Channel with Washington after US Downs Syrian Jet', *TASS* (19 June 2017), https://tass.com/defense/952119 (quoting Russia's Defense Ministry: '[t]he shooting down of a Syrian Air Force jet in Syria's airspace is a cynical violation of Syria's sovereignty … [it is part of an action] against the legitimate armed forces of a UN member-state [and is] a flagrant violation of international law, in addition to being actual military aggression against the Syrian Arab Republic').

[23] US Department of Defense, 'Press Briefing by Lieutenant General Jeffrey Harrigian, commander, U.S. Air Forces Central Command (via teleconference from Al Udeid Airbase, Qatar)' (13 February 2018), https://perma.cc/P9PA-TRL8.

[24] See, for example, Himes and Kim, n.20, particularly 278.

[25] See Letter dated 11 August 2008 from the Permanent Representative of the Russian Federation to the United Nations addressed to the President of the Security Council, UN Doc. S/2008/545 (11 August 2008).

self-defence.[26] In making this claim, Russia was careful to stress that it had taken the step of formally recognising South Ossetia as a state (along with fellow autonomous region Abkhazia).[27] However, South Ossetia certainly was not widely recognised as a state, and it is fairly clear that it did not meet the requirements for statehood, irrespective of its de facto autonomous status.[28] Scholars certainly took the view that the Russian action in Georgia was not a lawful action in collective self-defence, *inter alia*, because South Ossetia was not a state.[29] Other states, while not meaningfully engaging with the collective self-defence argument specifically, were still predominately of the view that South Ossetia and Abkhazia were not states, and that the Russian use of force was unlawful.[30] The North Atlantic Treaty Organization (NATO) took a similar view.[31]

Interestingly, the Independent International Fact-Finding Mission on the Conflict in Georgia (IIFFMCG) – having rightly concluded that

[26] Although Russia did not use the term 'collective self-defence', it argued that it 'helped South Ossetia to repel . . . aggression' and then explicitly linked this to Article 51, which would strongly suggest it was making a collective self-defence claim. See UNGA Verbatim Record, UN Doc. A/63/PV.14 (27 September 2008), 2. This was certainly how the Russian position was interpreted by the IIFFMCG. See IIFFMCG, n.9, vol. II, 280 ('Sergey Lavrov, Foreign Minister of the Russian Federation . . . thereby claimed that Russia relied on collective self-defence, defending South Ossetia against an armed attack by Georgia'). *Contra* Kristi Land, 'Legal Aspects of the Conflict in Georgia and Post-Conflict Developments' (2008–2009) *Estonian Ministry of Foreign Affairs Yearbook* 49, 52 (arguing that 'Russia never justified its actions with collective self-defence').

[27] See UN Doc. A/63/PV.14, n.26, 2. For the statement of recognition itself, see 'Statement by President of Russia Dmitry Medvedev', Office of the President of the Russian Federation (26 August 2008), http://en.kremlin.ru/events/president/transcripts/1222. It is worth noting that, while this act of recognition preceded the assertion of a collective self-defence *claim*, it actually occurred *after* the Russian use of force had begun – as well as after the issuance of a request for aid from South Ossetia (which, itself, came after the initiation of forcible action). See Chapter 6, nn.136–145 and accompanying text.

[28] IIFFMCG, n.9, vol. II, 127–135.

[29] Tamás Hoffmann, 'The International Legal Aspects of the Georgia-Russia Conflict' (December 2008) *Foreign Policy Review* 80, 80; Land, n.26, 52; Alexander Lott, 'The Tagliavini Report Revisited: *Jus ad Bellum* and the Legality of the Russian Intervention in Georgia' (2012) 28 *Merkourios – International and European Security Law* 4, 13.

[30] See, for example, UNSC Verbatim Record, UN Doc. S/PV.5961 (19 August 2008), 9–10 (UK); UN Doc. A/63/PV.14, n.26, 32 (Czech Republic); Statement of President George W. Bush, video link, *BBC News* (11 August 2008), http://news.bbc.co.uk/2/hi/europe/7554507.stm.

[31] 'NATO Chief Deplores "Disproportionate" Force in Georgia', *The Age* (11 August 2008), www.theage.com.au/world/nato-chief-deplores-disproportionate-force-in-georgia-20080811-3t3z.html.

South Ossetia was not a state – controversially[32] then asserted that entities short of statehood, including South Ossetia, possess a right of *individual* self-defence.[33] In the view of the present writer, this conclusion is incorrect,[34] but, in any event, even the IIFFMCG was unwilling to extend this to collective self-defence.[35] It concluded that, although it felt that some non-state actors could act in individual self-defence, such entities could not request external aid in collective self-defence.[36] Such a distinction between individual and collective self-defence is entirely illogical.[37] Nonetheless, it ultimately was the case that the IIFFMCG, too, was clear that only states can request aid in collective self-defence.

In 2022, Russia claimed to be exercising collective self-defence at the request of the regions of Donetsk and Luhansk in Ukraine.[38] These entities undoubtedly were not states at the time of the Russian use of force.[39] However, as it had done in relation to South Ossetia fourteen

[32] Henderson and Green, n.10, 134–135.

[33] IIFFMCG, n.9, vol. II, 241–242, 262–263.

[34] See nn.11–14 and accompanying text.

[35] This was primarily due to policy concerns, see IIFFMCG, n.9, vol. II, 281.

[36] *Ibid*, 281–282.

[37] Henderson and Green, n.10, 136–137; Dinstein, n.5, 318.

[38] For Russia's claim, see 'Address by the President of the Russian Federation', Office of the President of the Russian Federation (24 February 2022), http://en.kremlin.ru/events/president/transcripts/67843 (official English translation, as published by the Kremlin); Обращение Президента Российской Федерации, Президент России (24 февраля 2022 года), http://kremlin.ru/events/president/news/67843 (original Russian text, as published by the Kremlin). President Putin's address was also annexed (in a somewhat different English translation) to Letter dated 24 February 2022 from the Permanent Representative of the Russian Federation to the United Nations addressed to the Secretary-General, UN Doc. S/2022/154 (24 February 2022). For the respective requests for aid from the purported representatives of Donetsk and Luhansk, see Letter dated 3 March 2022 from the Permanent Representative of the Russian Federation to the United Nations addressed to the Secretary-General, UN Doc. A/76/740–S/2022/179 (7 March 2022) (annexes III and IV, respectively).

[39] See Terry D. Gill, 'The *Jus ad Bellum* and Russia's "Special Military Operation" in Ukraine' (2022) 25 *Journal of International Peacekeeping* 121, 125; Green, Henderson and Ruys, n.5, 17–21; Kreß, n.5, 7–8; Sofia Cavandoli and Gary Wilson, 'Distorting Fundamental Norms of International Law to Resurrect the Soviet Union: The International Law Context of Russia's Invasion of Ukraine' (2022) 69 *Netherlands International Law Review* 383, 399–400; 'Statement by Members of the International Law Association Committee on the Use of Force', *Just Security* (4 March 2022), www.justsecurity.org/tag/statement-by-members-of-ila-committee-on-use-of-force (available, at the time of writing, in twenty-nine languages) ('[t]he right to self-determination is no legal basis for the creation of the Ukrainian territories Donetsk and Luhansk as "states". Therefore, their recognition by the Russian Federation is a flagrant violation of Ukraine's territorial integrity, and as such without legal effect. Since these territories are

years prior,[40] Russia recognised these entities as states[41] and emphasised their 'resulting' statehood in the context of their requests for aid (upon which Russia then based its collective self-defence claim).[42] These acts of recognition were seen by other states as illegal,[43] and Russia's reliance on the request for aid by these purported 'states' was viewed merely as a pretext for the unlawful use of force.[44]

Yet, unlike the United States' more brazen claims in relation to the SDF in 2017/2018, where the United States ignored (but implicitly accepted) the lack of statehood of the entity it was co-defending, the very fact that Russia took the step of recognising South Ossetia in 2008 and Donetsk and Luhansk in 2022 is perhaps telling. This suggests that Russia, at least, has viewed the statehood of the requester(s) as a prerequisite for making a collective self-defence claim, to the point that it has preferred to advance improbable assertions of statehood rather than

not states, the Russian Federation cannot invoke collective self-defense on behalf of these territories in order to justify its attack on Ukraine').

40 Unlike in 2008, however, these acts of recognition occurred *before* the use of force was initiated. On the timeliness of the request, see Section 6.5.

41 See Presidential Decree of the Russian Federation, No 71, 'About recognition of the Donetsk People's Republic' (21 February 2022); Presidential Decree of the Russian Federation, No 72, 'About recognition of the Luhansk People's Republic' (21 February 2022).

42 This can be seen from the Treaty of Friendship, Cooperation and Mutual Assistance between the Russian Federation and the Donetsk People's Republic (signed in Moscow, 21 February 2022) and the Treaty of Friendship, Cooperation and Mutual Assistance between the Russian Federation and the Lugansk People's Republic (signed in Moscow, 21 February 2022), both of which refer explicitly to the regions as states. These documents were subsequently annexed to UN Doc. A/76/740–S/2022/179, n.38 (annexes I and II, respectively). Russia specifically invoked these treaties in the context of the requests for aid and its response. See 'Address by the President of the Russian Federation', n.38 (arguing that Russia responded 'in execution of the treaties of friendship and mutual assistance with the Donetsk People's Republic and the Lugansk People's Republic, ratified by the Federal Assembly on February 22').

43 See, for example, UNGA Res. ES-11/1, UN Doc. A/RES/ES-11/1 (2 March 2022) para. 5 (the UN General Assembly denouncing in unequivocal terms the Russian recognition of the Donetsk and Luhansk regions 'as a violation of the territorial integrity and sovereignty of Ukraine and [as] inconsistent with the principles of the Charter'). See also *ibid*, para. 6 (further demanding that 'the Russian Federation immediately and unconditionally reverse the decision' to recognise them). This position is surely correct. See Hersch Lauterpacht, 'Recognition of States in International Law' (1944) 53 *Yale Law Journal* 385, 390–396.

44 See, for example, UNGA Verbatim Record, UN Doc. A/76/PV.58 (23 February 2022), 26–27 (New Zealand); UNGA Verbatim Record, UN Doc. A/ES-11/PV.2 (28 February 2022), 2–3 (Slovakia); *ibid*, 3 (Belgium); *ibid*, 6 (Liechtenstein); UNGA Verbatim Record, UN Doc. A/ES-11/PV.4 (1 March 2022); *ibid*, 5 (South Korea); *ibid*, 10 (Germany).

claiming that force can be used in collective self-defence to protect 'state-like' entities.

Overall, it seems pretty clear that – while the United States has recently tried to claim differently – the widely held view that the requester must be a state remains correct as a matter of customary international law.

5.3 A Requirement of UN Membership?

Article 51 of the UN Charter holds that '[n]othing in the present Charter shall impair the inherent right of individual or collective self-defence if an armed attack occurs *against a Member of the United Nations*'.[45] Given that it is the state that has suffered the armed attack that must request aid in relation to it,[46] Article 51 apparently indicates that the requester needs to be not only a state but also a UN member.[47]

On this basis, in relation to the collective self-defence claim made by Russia in 2022 with regard to the separatist-leaning regions of Donetsk and Luhansk, Ezechi *et al.* have suggested that there was no need to grapple with inherently contestable questions of statehood when assessing Russia's collective self-defence claim. Given that it was an objective and demonstrable fact that neither Donetsk nor Luhansk was a member of the United Nations in February 2022, Ezechi *et al* indicate that those entities could not issue a self-defence request whether they were states or not.[48] Other commentators have made a similar argument about the need for the 'requester' to be a UN member.[49]

[45] Charter of the United Nations (1945) 1 UNTS XVI (UN Charter), Article 51 (emphasis added).

[46] See, for example, *Nicaragua* (merits), n.6, para. 199 (identifying the legal requirement of a 'request by the State which regards itself as the victim of an armed attack'). See also *ibid*, para. 196.

[47] See M. A. Weightman, 'Self-Defense in International Law' (1951) 37 *Virginia Law Review* 1095, 1111–1112 (noting but questioning the appropriateness of this implication).

[48] K. C. Ezechi, A. U. Onyishi, W. O. Okonkwo and Ikenna Ogbuka, 'Maintenance of International Peace and Security and Great Power Hypocrisy: Insights from the Iraqi and Ukrainian Invasions' (2022) 4 *Sapientia Foundation Journal of Education, Sciences and Gender Studies* 237, 246.

[49] See, for example, Andrew Martin, *Collective Security: A Progress Report* (Paris, United Nations (UNESCO), 1952), 170–171; Cavandoli and Wilson, n.39, 17 (arguing, like Ezechi *et al.*, that Donetsk and Luhansk would have needed to have been UN members); Memorandum of Law, n.5, 2667 (arguing that because South Vietnam was not a UN member, it could not request aid from the United States in collective self-defence at the start of the Vietnam War); Aadhithi Padmanabhan and Michael Shih, 'Collective Self-Defense: A Report of the Yale Law School Center for Global Legal Challenges' (10

However, the majority of scholars have taken the opposite view and have argued that the defending state need not be a UN member.[50] This has usually been for (one or both of) two intertwined reasons. The first of these is based on the object and purpose of Article 51 – which, of course, must be considered as part of any process of treaty interpretation[51] – to the extent that its *raison d'être* is to *preserve* the right of states to defend themselves (or be defended) against aggression. Waldock, for example, has argued that it does not:

> seem legitimate, on the principle *expressie unius exclusio alterius*, to interpret the express reference to Members in Article 51 as only authorising defence of another Member but not of a Non-Member. *The purpose of the article is to reserve a right of self-defence inherent in all States* and it can hardly have the effect of precluding, for no reason whatever, defensive aid to a Non-Member State defending itself against an aggressor.[52]

Second, it has been pointed out[53] that collective self-defence exists as a justification for the use of force under customary international law, independently of the Charter,[54] and thus the Charter cannot limit its exercise to UN members only. Admittedly, whether – and, if so, the extent to which – collective self-defence existed as an aspect of customary

December 2012), https://law.yale.edu/sites/default/files/documents/pdf/cglc/GLC_Collective_SelfDefense.pdf, 1 (making the same point implicitly: collective self-defence 'permits a member state to intervene *in the defence of another member state*', emphasis added); Weightman, n.47, 1111–1112 (noting this as a *potential* requirement).

50 See, for example, Ian Brownlie, *International Law and the Use of Force by States* (Oxford, Oxford University Press, 1963), 331; Derek W. Bowett, *Self-Defense in International Law* (Manchester, Manchester University Press, 1958), 193–195; Stanimir A. Alexandrov, *Self-Defence against the Use of Force in International Law* (The Hague, Kluwer Law International, 1996), 103–104; Falk, n.5, 12; Dinstein, n.5, 305; Casey-Maslen, n.4, 75; C. H. M. Waldock, 'The Regulation of the Use of Force by Individual States in International Law' (1952) 81 *Recueil des cours* 451, 504; Quincy Wright, 'Legal Aspects of the Viet-Nam Situation' (1966) 60 *American Journal of International Law* 750, 751, footnote 4; Eberhard P. Deutsch, 'The Legality of the United States Position in Vietnam' (1966) 52 *American Bar Association Journal* 436, 438; William E. Holder, 'The Legality of United States Participation in Vietnam: An Appraisal' (1966) 2 *Australian Yearbook of International Law* 67, 76; John Norton Moore and James L. Underwood, 'The Lawfulness of United States Assistance to the Republic of Viet Nam' (1966) 5 *Duquesne Law Review* 235, 304–305; A. L. Goodhart, 'The North Atlantic Treaty of 1949' (1951) 79 *Recueil des cours* 182, 203, 232.

51 See Vienna Convention on the Law of Treaties (1969) 1155 UNTS 331 (VCLT), Article 31 (1).

52 Waldock, n.50, 504 (emphasis in original, the Latin maxim used in the quote translates as 'the expression of one thing is the exclusion of the other').

53 See, for example, Dinstein, n.5, 305.

54 See, for example, *Nicaragua* (merits), n.6, paras. 34, 195, 199.

international law at the time of the adoption of the Charter is debatable,[55] but there is no question as to its customary status today.[56]

State practice in the UN era indicates that there is no requirement that the requesting state be a UN member.[57] Various scholars have noted that non-UN members were party to collective self-defence treaty arrangements in the early period of the UN era without this being viewed as in any way controversial at the time.[58] Italy,[59] West Germany,[60] and Portugal[61] were all members of NATO[62] prior to joining the United Nations, for example. Other collective self-defence treaties have had members such as the People's Republic of China,[63] Jordan[64] and the Republic of Korea (ROK)[65] – again, in all cases before these states had joined the United Nations – and the treaties in question all clearly situated their respective obligations within the framework of Article 51 of the UN Charter without this being seen as controversial.

Regarding the ROK in particular, one might also note the United States' claim that its participation in the Korean War was in response to the ROK's request for aid in defending itself against the proclaimed

55 See, generally, Chapter 2.

56 Dinstein, n.5, 305.

57 Eustace Chikere Azubuike, 'Probing the Scope of Self Defense in International Law' (2011) 17 *Annual Survey of International and Comparative Law* 129, 174.

58 See, for example, Bowett, n.50, 193; Wright, n.50, 751, footnote 4; Brownlie, n.50, 331, footnote 3; Norton Moore and Underwood, n.50, 304.

59 See, for example, Bowett, n.50, 193; Brownlie, n.50, 331, footnote 3; Norton Moore and Underwood, n.50, 304; Goodhart, n.50, 218.

60 Wright, n.50, 751, footnote 4.

61 *Ibid*; Norton Moore and Underwood, n.50, 304; Goodhart, n.50, 218.

62 North Atlantic Treaty (1949) 34 UNTS 243.

63 Treaty of Friendship, Alliance and Mutual Assistance (China/USSR) (1950), reproduced in (1950) 44 *Supplement to the American Journal of International Law* 83, particularly Article I ('[i]n the event of one of the High Contracting Parties being attacked by Japan or states allied with it, and thus being involved in a state of war, the other High Contracting Party will immediately render military and other assistance with all the means at its disposal').

64 Treaty of Alliance (with Annex and Exchange of Notes) (United Kingdom of Great Britain and Northern Ireland and Transjordan) (1946) 6 UNTS 143 (Treaty of London), particularly Article 5 (which refers to 'armed attack' and 'collective self-defence').

65 Agreement between the Government of the United States and the Government of the Republic of Korea (1950), reproduced in (1951) 45 *American Journal of International Law Supplement: Official Documents* 73, particularly Article I.1 ('such assistance as may be authorized by either party hereto shall be consistent with the Charter of the United Nations').

Democratic People's Republic of Korea (DPRK) in the north.[66] There is no question that the ROK was an established state at the outbreak of the Korean War,[67] but it was not yet a UN member. Admittedly, there has long been debate as to whether the US action in Korea can be classed as an action of collective self-defence at all, or whether it should rightly be viewed as a UN-authorised collective security action.[68] There are some strong indications that the action was one of collective self-defence,[69] but this is not clear. In any event, to the extent that the Korean War can be viewed as an example of self-defence – while the US action was legally controversial[70] – the ROK's lack of UN membership was not raised as an issue even by the states that strongly opposed US presence on the peninsula.

Another potentially useful example is the US claim to be acting in the collective self-defence of the Republic of Vietnam (RVN) at the start of the Vietnam War. A case can be made that the RVN had achieved independent statehood prior to the start of the 1960s,[71] although this

[66] UNSC Verbatim Record, UN Doc. S/PV.474 (27 June 1950), 4; UNSC Verbatim Record, UN Doc. S/PV.475 (30 June 1950), 10.

[67] See, for example, UNGA Res. 195 (III), UN Doc. A/RES/195(III) (12 December 1948) (recognising the Republic of Korea as the lawful government of the state). That said, there remains doubt as to whether the DPRK had yet separated from the ROK as a sovereign state or whether the Korean War was in fact an internationalised non-international armed conflict. See Nigel D. White, 'The Korean War – 1950–53', in Tom Ruys and Olivier Corten (with Alexandra Hofer) (eds.), *The Use of Force in International Law: A Case-Based Approach* (Oxford, Oxford University Press, 2018), 17, 30.

[68] See, for example, White, n.67, particularly 31–32; Julius Stone, *Aggression and World Order* (Berkeley and Los Angeles, University of California Press, 1958), 189; Dinstein, n.5, 326; Sir Michael Wood, 'Self-Defence and Collective Security', in Marc Weller (ed.), *The Oxford Handbook of the Use of Force in International Law* (Oxford, Oxford University Press, 2015), 649, 650–651.

[69] For example, relevant Security Council resolutions referred to the occurrence of an 'armed attack', and to states 'assisting the Republic of Korea in defending itself'. See UNGA Res. 84 (1950), UN Doc. S/1588 (7 July 1950). See also UNGA Res. 82 (1950), UN Doc. S/1501 (25 June 1950) (again using the term 'armed attack'). See Alexandrov, n.50, 252–263. Moreover, as was noted in the Introduction to this book, the very fact that a collective self-defence claim is *made* is enough for that claim to be of value in terms of assessing the legal parameters of collective self-defence, even if the claim itself does not hold up to legal scrutiny. See Introduction, nn.50–54 and accompanying text.

[70] See, for example, UNGA Verbatim Record, UN Doc. A/PV.294 (7 October 1950), paras. 1-35 (Ukraine); *ibid*, 118–121, 189 (Czechoslovakia); *ibid*, paras. 170–175 (USSR); *ibid*, paras. 179–186 (Poland).

[71] For a detailed presentation of the arguments supporting the conclusion that the RVN was an independent state by the start of the Vietnam War, see Norton Moore and Underwood, n.50, 239–262. See also Deutsch, n.50, 437–438.

was hotly debated.[72] However, while a handful of communist bloc states argued that the RVN had not acquired statehood,[73] for the most part, the question of RVN statehood (or lack thereof) remained a scholarly debate.[74] Tellingly, the scholars holding either position were all in agreement as to the fact that the RVN needed to be a state to be able to issue a valid collective self-defence request.[75] They just disagreed on the application of that requirement to the facts.[76]

Whereas, it was the alleged requirement *itself* that was controversial when it came to the question of whether UN membership was needed in addition to statehood. Again, though, this was primarily an academic controversy.[77] As for states, the United States was explicit that the RVN was entitled to request aid in collective self-defence irrespective of the fact that it was not a UN member:

> Protection against aggression and self-defense against armed attack are important elements in the whole charter scheme for the maintenance of international peace and security. To deprive nonmembers of their inherent right of self-defense would not accord with the principles of the organization, but would instead be prejudicial to the maintenance of peace.[78]

Apart from the United States itself, the present writer was unable to find instances where other states raised the fact that RVN was not a UN

[72] See, for example, Richard A. Falk, 'International Law and the United States Role in the Viet Nam War' (1966) 75 *Yale Law Journal* 1122, particularly 1128–1133; Memorandum of Law, n.5, 2668; Holder, n.50, 69–70; Wright, n.50, 756–764.

[73] See, for example, UNSC Verbatim Record, UN Doc. S/PV.1118 (19 May 1964), paras. 3–7 (USSR); *ibid*, paras. 11–12 (Czechoslovakia); Letter dated 11 May 1972 from the Representative of Cuba to the Secretary-General, UN Doc. S/10642 (11 May 1972) (Cuba).

[74] See sources cited in n.71 and n.72.

[75] *Ibid*.

[76] Having said this, the United States itself – while explicitly arguing that the RVN was a state – went on to claim that even if the RVN was *not* a state, it still could request aid in collective self-defence: '[t]here is nothing in the charter to suggest that United Nations members are precluded from participating in the defense of a recognized international entity against armed attack merely because the entity may lack some of the attributes of an independent sovereign state'. See 'The Legality of United States Participation in the Defense of Viet-Nam' (legal memorandum prepared by Leonard C. Meeker, Legal Adviser of the Department of State) (1966) 54 *Department of State Bulletin* 474, 478. This is, quite simply, incorrect. See Section 5.2.

[77] See, for example, Wright, n.50, 751, footnote 4; Deutsch, n.50, 438; Holder, n.50, 76; Norton Moore and Underwood, n.50, 304–305; Memorandum of Law, n.5, 2667.

[78] Meeker, n.76, 476.

member in the context of the US collective self-defence claim, with the exception of a statement made by Cambodia in 1964.[79] Interestingly, Cambodia had written to the Security Council earlier that year to complain of spillover 'acts of aggression by United States–South Vietnamese forces'.[80] In that context, it explicitly argued that the *jus ad bellum* regime was applicable to 'South Viet-Nam, although not a Member of the United Nations . . .'[81] Although this statement did not directly affirm the applicability of *the right of collective self-defence* to the RVN, the Cambodian position did this by implication.

It is worth noting that, for the few states that argued that the RVN was not a state, their silence specifically regarding its lack of UN membership should be viewed as inconclusive. This is because – for these states – UN membership would perhaps have been a moot point because only states can be members. However, even the USSR primarily took issue with what it considered to be the absence of an armed attack rather than questions of statehood or UN membership.[82] The majority of states thus were apparently unperturbed by the fact that the RVN was not a UN member, for all the legal controversy that surrounded other aspects of the Vietnam War.

It seems apparent overall that, while the requester needs to be a state, it does not also need to be a UN member. Of course, given that the United Nations now has near-universal membership, at least among uncontested states, this conclusion has less resonance today than it once would have.

5.4 The De Jure Government as the Relevant Authority

It has been argued that an entity requesting aid in collective self-defence must be a state (although it need not be a UN member state). The difficulty with this, of course, is identifying the authority that is entitled to represent the state for the purposes of making such a request. There are a number of ways in (and extents to) which entities may 'represent' the state as a matter of international law. These range from, for example,

79 UN Doc. S/PV.1118, n.73, para. 24.

80 Letter dated 13 May 1964 from the Permanent Representative of Cambodia addressed to the President of the Security Council, UN Doc. S/5697 (13 May 1964).

81 UN Doc. S/PV.1118, n.73, para. 24.

82 See, for example, Letter dated 11 May 1972 from the representative of the Union of Soviet Socialist Republics to the President of the Security Council, UN Doc. S/10643 (11 May 1972).

instances where the actions of that entity are sufficiently attributable to the state to give rise to its legal responsibility for international wrongs[83] to the power to consent to treaties on behalf of the state.[84] Such differing forms of 'representing the state' do not necessarily coalesce in the same actor(s) or remain fixed in different circumstances.[85]

De Wet has argued that there is a 'well-established principle in international law that the competence to request either direct military assistance or indirect military assistance … rests with the *de jure* government'.[86] Thus, she holds that in the context of requesting military aid, the relevant authority is the state's lawful government. Although de Wet made this point in relation to so-called military assistance on request,[87] it also would seem to be the correct starting point for collective self-defence.[88] It is notable that most domestic systems vest state power to use force, including in self-defence, with the executive (albeit that some jurisdictions have additional constitutional hurdles and/or a degree

[83] See, for example, Text of the Draft Articles on Responsibility of States for Internationally Wrongful Acts, with commentaries, Report of the International Law Commission, 53rd sess., UN Doc. A/56/10 (2001).

[84] See, for example, VCLT, n.51, Article 7.

[85] See, generally, Jean Salmon, 'Representatives of States in International Relations', in Rüdiger Wolfrum (ed.), *Max Planck Encyclopaedia of Public International Law, vol. VIII* (Oxford, Oxford University Press, 2012), 919.

[86] Erika de Wet, *Military Assistance on Request and the Use of Force* (Oxford, Oxford University Press, 2020), 21.

[87] On the relationship between collective self-defence and military assistance on request, see Chapter 8.

[88] Some writers have noted that the requester must be the defending state's government specifically in the context of collective self-defence but have not tended then to back up this assertion. See, for example, Josef Rohlik, 'Some Remarks on Self-Defense and Intervention: A Reaction to Reading Law and Civil War in the Modern World' (1976) 6 *Georgia Journal of International and Comparative Law* 395, 426 (arguing that a legal requirement for collective self-defence is the 'request of the attacked state, which *can be made only by the legitimate government* of the attacked state', emphasis added); Quincy Wright, 'United States Intervention in the Lebanon' (1959) 53 *American Journal of International Law* 112, 118 (asking '[w]hat *government* of an attacked state is competent to make such a [collective self-defence] request?', emphasis added); Sia Spiliopoulou Åkermark, 'The Puzzle of Collective Self-Defence: Dangerous Fragmentation or a Window of Opportunity? An Analysis with Finland and the Åland Islands as a Case Study' (2017) 22 *Journal of Conflict and Security Law* 249, 263 ('the constitutionally responsible authorities decide upon whether there is an aggression and ask for assistance'). See also Inger Österdahl, 'Sweden's Collective Defence Obligations *or* this is Not a Collective Defence Pact (or Is It?): Considerations of International and Constitutional Law' (2021) 90 *Nordic Journal of International Law* 127, 152.

of legislature oversight or input).[89] An extension of the power to authorise force on behalf of the state is the power to request forcible aid on behalf of the state. This is inherently an executive function. It is unsurprising, therefore, that in practice, states themselves have commonly referred to the collective self-defence request requirement as involving requests by the *government* of the defending state.[90] As the 2022 edition of the US Army's *Operational Law Handbook* notes, a collective self-defence request must be made 'by the *de jure* government for assistance'.[91]

5.5 Identifying the De Jure Government

5.5.1 The Recognition of Governments Generally

The conclusion that it is the de jure government of the state that can request aid in collective self-defence obviously begs the question of how one identifies the de jure government in this context. Issues persist in international law generally when it comes to the identification and recognition of governments.[92] The traditional starting point has long been the effective control of territory and the (closely linked) ability to perform executive functions.[93] Effective control has the benefit of being a question of objective fact, albeit one that prompts inevitably subjective

[89] See Michael Wood, 'International Law and the Use of Force: What Happens in Practice?' (2013) 53 *Indian Journal of International Law* 345, especially 345–346.

[90] See, for example, UNSC Verbatim Record, UN Doc. S/PV.746 (28 October 1956), paras. 14, 15, 142, 145, 148 (USSR, in relation to Hungary 1956); *ibid*, para. 34 (Yugoslavia, in relation to Hungary 1956, referring to 'the sovereign and legal Government of Hungary'); UNSC Verbatim Record, UN Doc. S/PV.831 (17 July 1958), paras. 27–31 (United Kingdom, in relation to Jordan 1958); UNGA Verbatim Record, UN Doc. A/ES-6/PV.6 (14 January 1980), para. 29 (Belarus, in relation to Afghanistan 1979); Letter dated 17 January 1991 from the Permanent Representative of the United States of America to the United Nations Addressed to the President of the Security Council, UN Doc. S/22090 (17 January 1991) (United States, regarding Kuwait 1990).

[91] *Operational Law Handbook*, National Security Law Department (The Judge Advocate General's Legal Center & School, U.S. Army, Charlottesville, Virginia, 2022 edn.), 6.

[92] See, generally, Stefan Talmon, *Recognition of Governments in International Law: With Particular Reference to Governments in Exile* (Oxford, Clarendon Press, 1998); Anne Schuit, 'Recognition of Governments in International Law and the Recent Conflict in Libya' (2012) 14 *International Community Law Review* 381, 388–393.

[93] See, as the classic example, the *Tinoco Claims Arbitration* (*Great Britain v. Costa Rica*) (1923) 1 RIAA 369. See also Hersch Lauterpacht, 'Recognition of Governments: I' (1945) 45 *Columbia Law Review* 815.

sub-questions of degree.[94] The 'effective control test' is also, of course, notably pragmatic: it attaches the wielding of governmental power to the entity that is likely to be best placed to wield it,[95] and it allows de facto and de jure status to be helpfully aligned. However, the test is also agnostic to questions of value or legitimacy.[96] It has, admittedly, been argued that if an entity has achieved a level of effective control, then this can be viewed as a reflection of the will of the people of the state, at least in some instances.[97] This is questionable: 'effective control' is at best a blunt tool for gauging the exercise of a people's right to self-determination[98] and at worst can amount to a mask for despotism.[99] It has also been seen to be an indeterminate test, and one open to being 'skewed by foreign involvement'.[100] As such, other concerns have been increasingly emphasised, particularly democratic legitimacy. Factors such as legal/constitutional origin, compliance with external legal obligations, and external recognition all have also been advanced.[101] However, effective control remains a core point of focus, and the weight to be given to other possible factors is unclear.[102]

The question of identifying the government in relation to a collective self-defence request specifically has been left almost entirely

94 Masoud Zamani and Majid Nikouei, 'Intervention by Invitation, Collective Self-Defence and the Enigma of Effective Control' (2017) 16 *Chinese Journal of International Law* 663, 664, 670–674.

95 Schuit, n.92, 390.

96 *Ibid* ('the effective control test ... [is] of practical rather than moralistic value'); W. Michael Reisman, 'Sovereignty and Human Rights in Contemporary International Law' (1990) 84 *American Journal of International Law* 866, 870.

97 See Brad R. Roth, 'The Enduring Significance of State Sovereignty' (2004) 56 *Florida Law Review* 1017, 1024 (referring to 'the venerable legal presumption that "effective control through internal processes" reflects the sovereign political community's will'). See also John Hursh, 'International Humanitarian Law Violations, Legal Responsibility, and US Military Support to the Saudi Coalition in Yemen: A Cautionary Tale' (2020) 7 *Journal on the Use of Force and International Law* 122, 130–131.

98 Christopher J. Le Mon, 'Unilateral Intervention by Invitation in Civil Wars: The Effective Control Test Tested' (2003) 35 *New York University Journal of International Law and Politics* 741, 746.

99 Zamani and Nikouei, n.94, 670.

100 Brad R. Roth, *Governmental Illegitimacy in International Law* (Oxford, Oxford University Press, 1999), 253.

101 Lauterpacht, n.93, 826.

102 See Schuit, n.92, 388; Thomas M. Franck, 'Who Killed Article 2(4)? Or: Changing Norms Governing the Use of Force by States' (1970) 64 *American Journal of International Law* 809, 817.

unexamined.[103] However, it is clear that there is a strong policy reason that effective control *cannot* be viewed as the primary or determining factor in establishing the entity that can request aid in collective self-defence.[104] If, for example, the incumbent government of State A loses effective control as a result of an armed attack by State B, which now occupies its territory, it cannot thereby have lost its right to exercise collective self-defence: it is not barred from asking State C to come and aid it in ousting the aggressor. Otherwise, the wrong would preclude the remedy.

5.5.2 *Examining the Relevant State Practice*

State practice, too, would suggest that effective control should not be considered the determinative factor in identifying the lawful 'requester' for collective self-defence actions. However, it must also be said that the practice is far from clear on this matter.

An early example is the USSR's use of force in Hungary in 1956.[105] Here, the de jure status of the requesting authority was viewed as being premised on a degree of democratic legitimacy, at least in the sense of

103 Having said this, scholarship exists that has examined the possible criteria for establishing whether a purported 'government' can lawfully make a 'use of force' request of another state in the context of 'military assistance on request'. See, for example, Olivier Corten, *The Law against War: The Prohibition on the Use of Force in Contemporary International Law* (Oxford, Hart Publishing, 2nd ed., 2021), 278–291; ILA, Use of Force Committee (2010–2018), *Final Report on Aggression and the Use of Force*, Sydney Conference (2018), https://ila.vettoreweb.com/Storage/Download.aspx?DbStorageId=11391&StorageFileGuid=6a199340-074d-4d4b-851b-7a56871175d6, 19; de Wet, n.86, 21–73; Gerhard Hafner, *l'Institut de droit international*, 10th Commission, 'Present Problems of the Use of Force in International Law Sub-group: Intervention by Invitation' (2009) 73 *Annuaire de l'Institut de droit international* 299, 320–325; Seyfullah Hasar, *State Consent to Foreign Military Intervention during Civil Wars* (Leiden, Brill Nijhoff, 2022), 68–123. On the relationship between collective self-defence and military assistance on request, see Chapter 8.

104 See Dino Kritsiotis, 'Intervention and the Problematisation of Consent', in Olivier Corten, Gregory H. Fox and Dino Kritsiotis, *Armed Intervention and Consent*, Max Planck Trialogues on the Law of Peace and War (Anne Peters and Christian Marxsen, series eds.), vol. IV (Cambridge, Cambridge University Press, 2023), 26, 79, 81, footnote 334 (alluding to this).

105 It is worth recalling that it can be debated whether the use of force in Hungary can be seen as an example of collective self-defence (actual or claimed), although the USSR at least implicitly made the argument that it was, and a number of other states assessed it on that basis at the time. See Chapter 4, n.66.

emphasising the importance of the 'will of the people'. This held true both for states that supported the intervention and those that opposed it.

It is interesting that within the USSR, it appears that there was concern expressed internally, among members of the Presidium of the Communist Party, that the legality of the action might be questionable because the request did not come from the appropriate Hungarian officials.[106] Externally, however, USSR stressed that:

> a regime has been established in Hungary on the basis of principles providing for the democratization of the country. This regime is founded on the will of the Hungarian workers, who are building a socialist society. It is founded on the freely expressed democratic will of the Hungarian workers, and on the historic successes they have achieved in the struggle for the building of a new society.[107]

Thus, the USSR made much of what it argued were the democratic credentials of the entity making the request upon which it relied.

In contrast, the states objecting to the action[108] focused on what they saw as the illegitimacy, and particularly *electoral* illegitimacy, of the entity claiming to be the government of Hungary that was making the request. For example, France,[109] Cuba[110] and Peru[111] all saw the uprising in Hungary as an exercise of the right of self-determination, implying that this meant that any request for aid from the purported authorities could not be seen as valid. In this context, states opposed to the Soviet intervention referred to the lack of free elections in Hungary.[112] This, ultimately, reflected the majority position as adopted by the General Assembly in resolution 1131 (XI). Therein, the Assembly:

> [c]ondemn[ed] the violation of the Charter of the United Nations by the Government of the Union of Soviet Socialist Republics in depriving

106 This is reported in Joel H. Westra, *International Law and the Use of Armed Force: The UN Charter and the Major Powers* (Abingdon, Routledge, 2007), 104.

107 UN Doc. S/PV.746, n.90, para. 21.

108 See, for example, Letter dated 27 October 1956 from the representatives of France, the United Kingdom of Great Britain and Northern Ireland and the United States of America to the President of the Security Council concerning 'the situation in Hungary', UN Doc. 3690 (27 October 1956).

109 UNSC Verbatim Record, UN Doc. S/PV.752 (2 November 1956), paras. 110, 122.

110 *Ibid*, para. 66.

111 *Ibid*, paras. 79–101.

112 See, for example, *ibid*, paras. 91, 96. See also UN Doc. S/PV.746, n.90, para. 66 (UK).

> Hungary of its liberty and independence and the Hungarian people of the exercise of their fundamental rights.[113]

Democratic legitimacy was thus invoked as a fundamental standard both by the USSR and by the states opposed to its action – which, in the end, amounted to a majority of UN members – albeit that, unsurprisingly, they took directly contrary views as to whether such legitimacy had been established by the requester in the Hungarian case.[114] States on the western side of the iron curtain were even more specific that legitimacy needed to stem from free and fair elections. It is, however, worth keeping in mind that there was a notable element of pragmatism at play in the views expressed by states as to the de jure government of Hungary in 1956. The United Kingdom, for example, was unwilling to recognise – de jure – either the new government that emerged from the Hungarian uprising or the government installed by Moscow to replace it following the Soviet intervention: the United Kingdom viewed it as 'premature' to make any determination in late 1956.[115] For all the rhetoric regarding the 'will of the people' from the Western bloc, the United Kingdom's caution here was seemingly based on uncertainty as to who had (or would have) effective control (and to what extent and for how long) in Hungary.

Just over a decade later, following the ascension of Alexander Dubček to the position of First Secretary of the Communist Party of Czechoslovakia at the start of 1968, the USSR became increasingly uneasy with Dubček's liberal reformist agenda.[116] By August, the USSR, along with three other Warsaw Pact states, had invaded Czechoslovakia.[117] The USSR repeatedly claimed that this was an act of collective self-defence at the request of the Czechoslovakian government,[118] whereas the representatives of Dubček's

[113] UNGA Res. 1131 (XI), UN Doc. A/RES/11/1131 (12 December 1956). See also UNGA Res. 1127 (XI), UN Doc. A/RES/11/1127 (21 November 1956); UNGA Res. 1128 (XI), UN Doc. A/RES/11/1128 (21 November 1956); UNGA Res. 1129 (XI), UN Doc. A/RES/11/1129 (21 November 1956); UNGA Res. 1130 (XI), UN Doc. A/RES/11/1130 (4 December 1956); UNGA Res. 1132 (XI), UN Doc. A/RES/11/1132 (10 January 1957).

[114] Wright, n.88, 119 ('[t]he issue in this case was whether the proper government of Hungary had made such a request, and the United Nations General Assembly decided it had not').

[115] *Hansard*, HC Deb (14 November 1956), vol. 560, col. 946.

[116] See Kieran Williams, *The Prague Spring and Its Aftermath: Czechoslovak Politics, 1968–1970* (Cambridge, Cambridge University Press, 1997), 63–111.

[117] See *ibid*, 29–38.

[118] See, for example, UNSC Verbatim Record, UN Doc. S/PV.1441 (21 August 1968), paras. 3, 75, 104, 216.

government explicitly denied this[119] and labelled the action an 'illegal occupation'.[120]

The Soviet *et al.* action was widely condemned,[121] including even by some other Warsaw Pact states.[122] A key feature of this criticism, *inter alia*, was that the purported request for aid was seen as invalid because it did not come from the de jure government of Czechoslovakia. Various reasons were advanced to highlight this point. For example, the United States stressed the need for external recognition. Indeed, it noted the recognition of Dubček's government *by the USSR itself*, pointing out that only a few days before the invasion, Soviet leaders had formally met with its representatives, which 'they clearly recognized as the authoritative leaders of Czechoslovakia'.[123] The United States further indicated the importance of formal *internal* processes, arguing that the purported request came from 'vague and unnamed individuals',[124] and that these 'shadow figures'[125] were demonstrably not the 'duly constituted leaders of the Czechoslovak government'.[126] Canada,[127] Senegal[128] and Yugoslavia[129] all took similar positions, viewing internal constitutional process as key.

[119] See, for example, *ibid*, para. 142 (quoting from a session of the Czechoslovak Government).

[120] *Ibid*, para. 138 (quoting from Declaration of the Ministry of Foreign Affairs, with the endorsement of the President of the Czechoslovak Socialist Republic and on behalf of the Government of the Republic (21 August 1968)).

[121] See, for example, the vast majority of the statements made by states during debates on the matter at the UN Security Council (UN Doc. S/PV.1441, n.118; UNSC Verbatim Record, UN Doc. S/PV.1442 (22 August 1968); UNSC Verbatim Record, UN Doc. S/PV.1443 (22 August 1968); UNSC Verbatim Record, UN Doc. S/PV.1444 (23 August 1968); UNSC Verbatim Record, UN Doc. S/PV.1445 (24 August 1968)).

[122] Both Romania and Albania were publicly opposed to the intervention. Regarding Romania, see, for example, 'Record of the Meeting of the Executive Committee of the CC of the RCP concerning the situation in Czechoslovakia' (21 August 1968), History and Public Policy Program Digital Archive, National Central Historical Archives (ANIC), Fund CC of the RCP – Chancellery, File No. 133/1968, 6–26 (trans. Delia Razdolescu), http://digitalarchive.wilsoncenter.org/document/110451. Regarding Albania, see, for example, Ana Lalaj, '1968: The Prague Spring and the Albanian "Castle"', in Kevin McDermott and Matthew Stibbe (eds.), *Eastern Europe in 1968* (Cham, Palgrave Macmillan, 2018), 235.

[123] UN Doc. S/PV.1441, n.118, para. 12. See also *ibid*, para. 30.

[124] *Ibid*. See also *ibid*, para. 36.

[125] *Ibid*, para. 40.

[126] *Ibid*. See also *ibid*, para. 248.

[127] *Ibid*, para. 169.

[128] UN Doc. S/PV.1443, n.121, para. 18.

[129] UN Doc. S/PV.1444, n.121, para. 102.

For its part, China indicated that the Dubček regime represented the people of Czechoslovakia and emphasised the legitimacy of that regime through reference to concepts such as freedom, equal rights, and self-determination.[130] Senegal, too, emphasised the right of self-determination in this context,[131] as did Pakistan,[132] whereas Yugoslavia pointed to the Dubček regime's democratic credentials (albeit arguably overstating them).[133] Similarly, the United States suggested that Dubček's government was the only entity entitled to make a collective self-defence request on behalf of Czechoslovakia, as it was a manifestation of the will of 'the Czechoslovak peoples'.[134] Unsurprisingly, Dubček's government itself was also keen to indicate that it was 'the legally elected constitutional representative [] [and] the true representative [] of the Czechoslovak Socialist Republic *and its people*'.[135]

Overall, therefore, a mixed picture emerges from the invasion of Czechoslovakia, but it may be said that it was not a picture that was especially centred around the importance of effective control. External recognition, internal constitutional process, and at least some measure of representation of the people were all emphasised by the states discussing the (il)legitimacy of the request for aid; these factors were all emphasised by multiple states and to a similar degree.

Another useful example is Cuba's dispatch of troops to Angola in the 1970s and 1980s. In 1975, the Movimento Popular de Libertação de Angola (MPLA) – which had the same year secured a significant degree of de facto control over the territory of Angola and later became widely recognised as its de jure government[136] – requested aid from Cuba in response to South African involvement in the initial stages of the Angolan Civil War.[137] Despite the MPLA's de facto control of much of Angola at the time, states were very keen to premise either their support or their criticism of the Cuban intervention on the (il)legitimacy of the

[130] UN Doc. S/PV.1442, n.121, para. 17.
[131] UN Doc. S/PV.1443, n.121, para. 19.
[132] UN Doc. S/PV.1445, n.121, para. 192.
[133] UN Doc. S/PV.1444, n.121, para. 102.
[134] UN Doc. S/PV.1441, n.118, para. 36.
[135] UN Doc. S/PV.1443, n.121, para. 10 (emphasis added).
[136] 'Angola: Civil War', in *Mass Atrocity Endings*, World Peace Foundation (7 August 2015), https://sites.tufts.edu/atrocityendings/2015/08/07/angola-civil-war.
[137] Nathaniel Sheppard Jr., 'Cuban Troops in Angola Aid U.S.', *Chicago Tribune* (4 December 1986), www.chicagotribune.com/news/ct-xpm-1986-12-04-8603310808-story.html (discussing the 1975 request for aid).

MPLA as the representative of the will of the Angolan people, rather than on its control of territory. Thus, Cuba itself stressed that its collective self-defence action was on behalf of and at the request of the people of Angola.[138] Other states supportive of the Cuban action similarly stressed that Angola's request was valid and linked this to the legitimacy of the Angolan government, on the basis that it was giving effect to its people's right of self-determination.[139]

In contrast, South Africa – which was the alleged aggressor state and so was vociferously against the presence of Cuban troops[140] – appeared to question the legitimacy of the Angolan request. South Africa was not especially clear in this regard, but it took issue with the idea that the MPLA could be viewed as the lawful representative of the state of Angola.[141] In particular, it argued that the MPLA, and especially the Forças Armadas Populares de Libertação de Angola – which was acting as the armed forces of the MPLA by 1975 – was merely a proxy for the USSR, and thus could not be seen as truly representing the Angolan people.[142]

Ultimately, the extent to which the MPLA could be viewed as a genuine representative for the people of Angola in the late 1970s and 1980s can be questioned given that multi-party and (mostly) free and fair elections were not held until 1992.[143] Irrespective of the validity of the request and thus the lawfulness of Cuba's use of force, though, what is of

138 See, for example, UNSC Verbatim Record, UN Doc. S/PV.2440 (24 May 1983), para. 25 ('[t]he Angolan people are not prepared to allow their territory to be attacked and occupied by the Pretoria racists and their counter-revolutionary followers').

139 See, for example, UNSC Verbatim Record, UN Doc. S/PV.2481 (20 October 1983), paras. 23–24 (Ethiopia: 'the presence of Cuban forces was requested by the *legitimate Government of Angola*, for the clear and express objective of repulsing the open and flagrant invasion by South Africa. Even though the first invasion was repulsed in time *by the Angolan people*, with the assistance of Cuban troops, we should not forget that South Africa's acts of aggression have continued since. . . . Hence the continued need for the assistance of Cuban forces, which is in full conformity with Article 51 of the Charter. . . . The presence of Cuban forces in Angola, therefore, is not only *legitimate and legal*; it is also a positive element in the continuing struggle for the maintenance of the sovereignty and territorial integrity of Angola', emphasis added).

140 *Ibid*, paras. 149–160.

141 *Ibid*, paras. 151.

142 *Ibid*, paras. 152–153.

143 See *The Path Toward Democracy in Angola*, Hearing before the Subcommittee on Africa of the Committee on International Relations, House of Representatives, 104th Congress, 1st sess. (13 July 1995), vol. 4 (Washington DC, U.S. Government Printing Office, 1995) (Gerald J. Bender), 34, 35–36.

note is that both the states that supported and those that opposed the action indicated that the determining factor was whether the 'requester' represented the will of people of the state that it purported to speak for, rather than this being premised on effective control of territory. It is worth specifying, though, that so far as this can be seen as an endorsement of a democratic legitimacy test, this is only in a limited sense. Again, given that elections did not occur in Angola until the 1990s, it at best speaks to an illiberal and procedurally flawed form of democratic representation and at worst suggests the mere payment of lip service to it.

Around a similar time, elsewhere in Africa, various states intervened in Chad following the end of the first Chadian Civil War.[144] From the late 1970s onwards, Libya deployed increasing numbers of troops in support of the Gouvernement d'Union Nationale de Transition (GUNT), which held a degree of effective control in Chad from 1979 to 1982.[145] By 1986, France and Zaire had sent troops (with additional backing from the United States and others) in support of Hissène Habré, whose forces had wrestled effective control of much of the territory from the GUNT in 1982.[146] It is worth noting that it is unclear whether Libya's use of force in Chad should be considered an example of collective self-defence – it does not appear that Libya made that claim explicitly; its action perhaps is better understood as a (still highly controversial) instance of military assistance on request.[147] Nonetheless, some commentators have interpreted the Libyan intervention as a possible example of collective self-defence.[148] In contrast, France[149] and Zaire[150] *were* explicit that they were acting in collective self-defence in response to a request from the Habré regime to help Chad repel Libyan forces from the north of the state. Chad itself (as represented at the United Nations by the Habré

[144] See, for example, *The Yearbook of the United Nations* 1981, 222–223; *The Yearbook of the United Nations* 1983, 180–187.

[145] See Alex Rondos, 'Civil War and Foreign Intervention in Chad' (1985) 84 *Current History* 209; Nathaniel K. Powell, *France's Wars in Chad: Military Intervention and Decolonisation in Africa* (Cambridge, Cambridge University Press), 263–301.

[146] See Michael Brecher, *A Century of Crisis and Conflict in the International System* (Cham, Palgrave Macmillan, 2017), 152.

[147] See Le Mon, n.98, 768–777.

[148] See, for example, Gray, n.1, 189, footnote 354.

[149] UNSC Verbatim Record, UN Doc. S/PV.2721 (19 November 1986), 22.

[150] *Ibid*, 17–18.

regime)[151] and the United States[152] also emphasised that France was acting in collective self-defence.

Even though both the GUNT and the Habré regime had at least a measure of effective control at different times (1979–1982 and 1982–1990, respectively), the states supporting them did not, for the most part, emphasise this in relation to the requests for aid that were issued. Libya stressed, instead, the importance of representative legitimacy: referring to the GUNT as the 'legitimate government' of the people of Chad and stressing conversely that the Habré regime was 'not recognized by the people of Chad'.[153] Libya also pointed to the external recognition of the GUNT by, for example, the Organisation of African Unity (OAU).[154] Moreover, Libya acknowledged that the GUNT no longer had effective control over the territory but stressed, more than once, that this fact was not enough to alter its status as the de jure government.[155]

In a similar vein, albeit from the other direction, France was keen to paint Habré very much as the champion of the Chadian people.[156] Zaire likewise asserted that Habré made his collective self-defence request 'on behalf of the people of Chad',[157] and premised the view that his regime was 'the rightful government of Chad'[158] on the basis that he 'expressed his absolute willingness to create conditions that would allow Chad, *with the help of all its people* ... to ensure its development'.[159] Of the states

[151] Letter dated 18 February 1986 from the Permanent Representative of Chad to the United Nations addressed to the President of the Security Council, UN Doc. S/17837 (18 February 1986).

[152] UN Doc. S/PV.2721, n.149, 24–25.

[153] *Ibid*, 32. See also *Territorial Dispute* (*Libyan Arab Jamahiriya/Chad*) (memorial submitted by the Great Socialist People's Libyan Arab Jamahiriya) (26 August 1991), paras. 6.78–6.80 (Libya, later emphasising the right of self-determination in relation to its presence in the north part of Chad).

[154] UN Doc. S/PV.2721, n.149, 32.

[155] Letter dated 24 November 1981 from the Charge d'affaires a.i. of the Permanent Mission of the Libyan Arab Jamahiriya to the United Nations addressed to the President of the Security Council, UN Doc. S/14767 (24 November 1981), para. 3; Letter dated 17 March 1983 from the Permanent Representative of the Libyan Arab Jamahiriya to the United Nations addressed to the President of the Security Council, UN Doc. S/15645 (17 March 1983), 2.

[156] UN Doc. S/PV.2721, n.149, 22.

[157] *Ibid*, 18.

[158] *Ibid*.

[159] *Ibid* (emphasis added).

involved,[160] the United States was something of an outlier, in that it appeared to see effective control as the determining factor. The United States seemed to take the view – albeit not especially clearly – that the GUNT's request was invalid because it had collapsed as an effective government, with the de jure status of the Habré government correspondingly being established by its control of Chad.[161]

Overall, the predominant focus from the parties involved in the conflict in Chad in the 1980s was on the legitimacy of the requester as premised on its (alleged) representation of the people. However, external recognition was also explicitly referenced, and there is no question that once the Habré government was recognised de facto at the OAU and the United Nations, this ended any serious debate on the question of de jure status.[162] Effective control was also seen as a factor, at least by the United States. Thus, the picture that emerges from the example of Chad regarding the identification of the 'requester' is unclear. It is also important to note that what the intervening states *said* regarding the democratic legitimacy of the requester was not reflected in reality. For example, the claim that Habré had widespread popular support among the people of Chad at the time of requesting outside aid was questionable,[163] and once firmly in power, Habré was a notorious despot: his government was brutal in its violations of human rights,[164] and it also was conspicuously anti-democratic.[165]

160 It should be noted that the United States openly provided economic support and covertly provided forms of paramilitary support via the CIA, but it did not go so far as to send US troops. See Human Rights Watch, 'Enabling a Dictator: The United States and Chad's Hissène Habré 1982–1990' (June 2016), www.hrw.org/sites/default/files/report_pdf/ushabre0616web.pdf.

161 UN Doc. S/PV.2721, n.149, 26.

162 See George Joffe, 'Turmoil in Chad' (1990) 89 *Current History* 157, 177.

163 Kofi Oteng Kufuor, 'The OAU and the Recognition of Governments in Africa: Analyzing its Practice and Proposals for the Future' (2002) 17 *American University International Law Review* 369, 383.

164 See, for example, Habré's 2016 conviction for a range of human rights abuses (subsequently upheld on appeal a year later) by a Special Tribunal in Senegal, see *Jugement rendu par la Chambre Africaine Extraordinaire d'Assises d'Appel dans l'affaire ministère public contre Hissein Habré*, Chambres Africaines Extraordinaires [2017], www.chambresafricaines.org/pdf/Arr%C3%AAt_int%C3%A9gral.pdf.

165 See, generally, William F. S. Miles, 'Tragic Tradeoffs: Democracy and Security in Chad' (1995) 33 *The Journal of Modern African Studies* 53.

Moving to examples from the post–Cold War era, Kritsiotis cites Kuwait's request for aid in the early 1990s,[166] as evidence that 'effective control' is not the key factor in relation to identifying the 'requester' in collective self-defence.[167] He notes that 'whether the crown prince had authority or effective control never became a point on which the validity of the requests was challenged'.[168] Kritsiotis' reading is correct. Indeed, some states – such as Italy[169] and the United Kingdom[170] – expressed the opposite view: that is, that the status of the de jure government of Kuwait remained unchanged by the lessening of its effective control. States did not make it clear what they *did see* as establishing the legitimate authority of the requester in this instance, but even the states that were critical of the action taken by the United States and its allies in the region did not appear to take issue with the power of the government of Kuwait to make a collective self-defence request.[171] Iraq was alone in questioning the legitimacy of the Kuwaiti regime that it sought to displace, but it did not argue that this alleged lack of legitimacy was in any way linked to the question of effective control, at least not explicitly.[172]

The request by Tajikistan for support in repelling what it labelled an 'attack carried out from the territory of the Islamic State of Afghanistan' in 1993[173] (in the context of the Tajik Civil War) is another useful example. Russia/the Commonwealth of Independent States (CIS) responded with force and justified that action *inter alia* as collective

[166] Kuwait requested military aid repeatedly, both formally (see, e.g. Letter dated 12 August 1990 from the Permanent Representative of Kuwait to the United Nations addressed to the President of the Security Council, UN Doc. S/21498 (13 August 1990)) and informally (see, e.g. Sheik Jabir al-Ahmad al-Jabir Al Sabah, the Amir of Kuwait, letter to President George H. W. Bush (12 August 1990) (referred to in Statement by Press Secretary Fitzwater on the Persian Gulf Crisis (12 August 1990), www.presidency .ucsb.edu/documents/statement-press-secretary-fitzwater-the-persian-gulf-crisis). It is worth recalling that there exists some debate as to whether the coalition action in the Gulf was truly an act of collective self-defence. See Chapter 3, n.185.

[167] Kritsiotis, n.104, 79.

[168] *Ibid.*

[169] UNSC Verbatim Record, UN Doc. S/PV.2937 (18 August 1990), 53–55.

[170] *Ibid*, 21; UNSC Verbatim Record, UN Doc. S/PV.2938 (25 August 1990), 49–50.

[171] See, for example, UN Doc. S/PV.2937, n.169, 18–20 (USSR); *ibid*, 24–33 (Cuba); UN Doc. S/PV.2938, n.170, 10–11 (Yemen); *ibid*, 11–21 (Cuba); *ibid*, 41–45 (USSR).

[172] See UN Doc. S/PV.2937, n.169, 42–45.

[173] Letter dated 15 July 1993 from the Permanent Representative of Tajikistan to the United Nations addressed to the Secretary-General, UN Doc. S/26092 (16 July 1993).

self-defence.[174] At the point of making its request, however, the effectiveness of the Tajik government was in serious question, and it has been argued that it only survived because of Russian/CIS intervention.[175] However, other states appeared to take no issue with the position of the Tajik government to make the request, and it continued to be treated as the de jure authority at the United Nations during the crisis. The legality of CIS intervention also was not questioned by other states.[176] Indeed, members of the Security Council went as far as to commend Russia and other CIS members for their efforts to restore peace.[177] Of course, the response (or lack thereof) of the international community has to be read in the context of the shared perception of the importance of the stability of the new states emerging from the breakup of the USSR. Nonetheless, the Tajikistan example again highlights that effective control may not be the primary factor in identifying the entity that can make a collective self-defence request.

A more recent example to consider is the French intervention in Mali in 2013 ('Operation Serval), which was *inter alia* justified as collective self-defence.[178] The request for aid upon which France relied[179] was issued by Mali's interim leader, Dioncounda Traoré, who was instated under a brokered deal following the 2012 coup.[180] Traoré's temporary administration certainly did not have control over Mali at the point at which the request was made, with most of the north of the country held

[174] Letter dated 15 July 1993 from the Permanent Representative of the Russian Federation to the United Nations addressed to the Secretary-General, UN Doc. S/26110 (19 July 1993).

[175] Bess A. Brown, 'The Civil War in Tajikistan, 1992–1993', in Mohammad-Reza Djalili, Frédéric Grare and Shirin Akiner (eds.), *Tajikistan: The Trials of Independence* (Richmond, Curzon Press, 1998), 86, 94–95.

[176] See, for example, the debates on the situation in Tajikistan in UNSC Verbatim Record, UN Doc. S/PV.3482 (16 December 1994).

[177] Note by the President of the Security Council, UN Doc. S/26341 (23 August 1993).

[178] See Press conference given by M. Laurent Fabius, Minister of Foreign Affairs – excerpts, Paris (11 January 2013), http://ambafrance-us.org/spip.php?article4216. It should be noted that some have argued that Operation Serval cannot be considered a collective self-defence action and is better understood as an instance of 'military assistance on request'. See Theodore Christakis and Karine Bannelier, 'French Military Intervention in Mali: It's Legal but . . . Why? Part I', *EJIL:Talk!* (24 January 2013), www.ejiltalk.org/french-military-intervention-in-mali-its-legal-but-why-part-i.

[179] See John R. Crook (ed.), 'Contemporary Practice of the United States relating to International Law' (2013) 107 *American Journal of International Law* 431, 468.

[180] See 'Mali Junta Says Power Transfer "Within Days"', *Al Jazeera* (7 April 2012), www.aljazeera.com/news/2012/4/7/mali-junta-says-power-transfer-within-days.

by various non-state groups.[181] Traoré was acting in an interim role, was unelected – at least, that is, to the role of president – and there were concerns regarding his 'legitimacy and "representativeness"'.[182] However, despite a lack of effective control and shaky democratic legitimacy on the part of the requester:

> France did not receive a single protest on the legality of Operation Serval. On the contrary, the number of expressions of support has been overwhelming: many individual states, regional organizations, the UN Secretary-General, and the UNSC itself . . . expressed their total support and understanding.[183]

The Security Council, for example, explicitly 'welcom[ed] the swift action by the French forces, at the request of the transitional authorities of Mali'.[184]

It has been suggested that the key factor in the perceived legitimacy of the requester – and thus the request – was external recognition, given that the Traoré government was the only externally recognised representative of Mali at the time.[185] To this might be added that there was also undoubtedly an element of pragmatism involved, with Traoré being seen as a 'safe pair of hands' and thus the best prospect for Mali to be able to move towards peace and stability.[186]

A final example worthy of note in this subsection is the (Saudi-led) coalition intervention in Yemen in 2015 (Operation Decisive Storm). The increasingly violent armed insurrection by Houthi forces in Yemen eventually resulted, in early 2015, in the democratically elected President Abdo Rabbo Mansour Hadi fleeing Sana'a.[187] Hadi's government first

[181] 'New Mali Leader Dioncounda Traore Warns Rebels of War', *BBC News* (7 April 2012), www.bbc.co.uk/news/world-africa-17686468; Zamani and Nikouei, n.94, 679–680; Karine Bannelier and Theodore Christakis, 'Under the UN Security Council's Watchful Eyes: Military Intervention by Invitation in the Malian Conflict' (2013) 26 *Leiden Journal of International Law* 855, 856–857.

[182] Bannelier and Christakis, n.181, 865–866.

[183] *Ibid*, 857 (references omitted).

[184] UNSC Res. 2100, UN Doc. S/RES/2100 (25 April 2013).

[185] Bannelier and Christakis, n.181, 859, 865.

[186] See Tiemoko Diallo and Adama Diarra, '"Safe Hand" Traore Must Put Mali Back on Track', *Reuters* (11 April 2012), www.reuters.com/article/us-mali-president-idUSBRE83A10020120411.

[187] See Saeed al-Batati, 'Yemen's Houthi Rebels Say Former President Has Fled Capital', *The Guardian* (21 February 2015), www.theguardian.com/world/2015/feb/21/yemen-houthi-rebels-president-hadi-fled-capital.

retreated to the port city of Aden,[188] before ultimately being forced to leave the country entirely, taking refuge in Saudi Arabia.[189] Just prior to departing Yemen, though, Hadi had requested foreign military aid, explicitly in exercise of the right of collective self-defence.[190] It may be said that at least at the point that he left the capital, Hadi's legitimacy 'could hardly be challenged', given the notable electoral mandate he received from the Yemeni people in 2012 to lead the transitional process in Yemen.[191] Equally, Hadi's 'government had lost much effective control over Yemen by the time it issued a request for foreign military assistance'.[192]

The resulting coalition intervention was widely supported by other states,[193] and even the few that argued that the action was unlawful did not appear to take any issue with the legitimacy of Hadi's request, per se.[194] A number of states explicitly stressed the continued legitimacy of the Hadi government,[195] and Security Council resolution 2216 even went

188 Mohamed Ghobari and Mohammed Mukhashaf, 'Yemen's Hadi Flees to Aden and Says He Is Still President', *Reuters* (21 February 2015), www.reuters.com/article/us-yemen-security-idUSKBN0LP08F20150221.

189 de Wet, n.86, 107.

190 Identical letters dated 26 March 2015 from the Permanent Representative of Qatar to the United Nations addressed to the Secretary-General and the President of the Security Council UN Doc. S/2015/217 (27 March 2015), 4.

191 Benjamin Nußberger, 'Military Strikes in Yemen in 2015: Intervention by Invitation and Self-Defence in the Course of Yemen's "Model Transitional Process"' (2017) 4 *Journal on the Use of Force and International Law* 110, 142.

192 Tom Ruys and Luca Ferro, 'Weathering the Storm: Legality and Legal Implication of the Saudi-Led Military Intervention in Yemen' (2016) 65 *International and Comparative Law Quarterly* 61, 84.

193 See, for example, Japan, 'Statement by Foreign Press Secretary Yasuhisa Kawamura on the Military Action by Saudi Arabia and Other Countries in Yemen' (31 March 2015), www.mofa.go.jp/press/release/press4e_000703.html; United States, 'Statement by NSC Spokesperson Bernadette Meehan on the Situation in Yemen' (25 March 2015), www.whitehouse.gov/the-press-office/2015/03/25/statement-nsc-spokesperson-bernadette-meehan-situation-yemen; United Kingdom, 'Yemen – in-year update July 2015' (15 July 2015), www.gov.uk/government/publications/yemen-in-year-update-july-2015/yemen-in-year-update-july-2015.

194 See, for example, Letter dated 17 April 2015 from the Permanent Representative of the Islamic Republic of Iran to the United Nations addressed to the Secretary-General, UN Doc. S/2015/263 (17 April 2015).

195 See, for example, UNSC Verbatim Record, UN Doc. S/PV.7426 (14 April 2015), 7 (France, referring to Hadi as 'Yemen's legitimate President'); *ibid* (Chad, noting 'the legitimacy represented by President Abdrabuh Mansour Hadi Mansour'); *ibid*, 8 (Jordan, noting that Hadi's 'legitimacy is reiterated … by the [UN Security] Council, which has also expressed its support for him').

so far as to take note of the request for aid from 'the President of Yemen'.[196] It has been said that Hadi remained undisputed as the de jure President of Yemen in the view of the international community.[197] The exiled government's 'democratic credentials' and the importance of constitutional due process were important factors in this widespread perception of continued legitimacy.[198] It is worth noting, though, that while Hadi had lost control over the majority of Yemeni territory, his government still retained at least *some* control, particularly in the south.[199] Thus, a measure of 'effective control' may still have been of some residual relevance to perceived de jure status – at least when combined with the factors of democratic legitimacy and international recognition – although it is difficult to say this conclusively.

In any event, the example of Yemen in 2015 must be treated with care. While Hadi explicitly characterised his request as one issued in collective self-defence,[200] as did the Arab League,[201] the co-defending states largely steered clear of justifying their intervention on this basis.[202] The characterisation of the intervention as one of collective self-defence is ultimately highly dubious, not least because of the lack of any armed attack.[203] The action is perhaps more appropriately characterised as an instance of

[196] UNSC Res. 2216, UN Doc. S/RES/2216 (14 April 2015).
[197] Ruys and Ferro, n.192, 85.
[198] See, for example, UN Doc. S/PV.7426, n.195, 7 (Chad). It is worth noting that Yemen itself also made much of the question of its embattled government's democratic and constitutional legitimacy, see *ibid*, 9.
[199] See, for example, UNSC Verbatim Record, UN Doc. S/PV.7411 (22 March 2015), 3 (Jamal Benomar, Special Adviser of the Secretary-General on Yemen: '[i]t would be an illusion to think that the Houthis could mount an offensive and succeed in taking control of the entire country, including Mareb, Taiz and the south. It would be equally false to think that President Hadi could assemble sufficient forces to liberate the country from the Houthis').
[200] UN Doc. S/2015/217, n.190, 4.
[201] See Tom Ruys, Nele Verlinden and Luca Ferro (eds.), 'Digest of State Practice: 1 January–30 June 2015' (2015) 2 *Journal on the Use of Force and International Law* 257, 276.
[202] For discussion, see Nußberger, n.191, 119–121.
[203] See *ibid*, 156–158; Luca Ferro, 'The Doctrine of "Negative Equality" and the Silent Majority of States' (2021) 8 *Journal on the Use of Force and International Law* 4, 30; Zachary Vermeer, 'The *Jus ad Bellum* and the Airstrikes in Yemen: Double Standards for Decamping Presidents?', *EJIL:Talk!* (30 April 2015), www.ejiltalk.org/the-jus-ad-bellum-and-the-airstrikes-in-yemen-double-standards-for-decamping-presidents; Ruys and Ferro, n.192, 71–77.

'military assistance on request', therefore.[204] Even if it is accepted that the fact that the intervention was *claimed to be* one of collective self-defence is enough for it to be of relevance to the present discussion,[205] as with the previous examples reviewed in this subsection, there was very little clarity from states as to precisely why Hadi's request was widely perceived to be legitimate. That said, in the view of this author, it is notable that 'effective control' (or lack thereof) again appeared to be of little, if any, relevance. Democratic legitimacy and, particularly, continued recognition by other states were seemingly far more important.

5.5.3 *Analysis of the State Practice*

The previous subsection set out quite a large number of examples of state practice for readers to wade through. However, this has been necessary, because – when it comes to the question of identifying the legitimate government for the purposes of issuing a collective self-defence request – the practice is far from clear. As such, as wide a pool as possible of potentially relevant examples has been considered, in the hope of somewhat offsetting that lack of clarity and building a more nuanced picture.

What does seem clear, at least, is that the primary factor is not the effective control of territory. As was previously argued, pure reliance on an effective control test not only is wholly agnostic to value but also would result in situations where the remedy is deprived by the wrong.[206] Other factors would seem to be more crucial in the determination, particularly democratic legitimacy/self-determination and external recognition: what we might perhaps think of as a combination of 'internal' and 'external' legitimacy.[207]

Thus, Norton Moore and Underwood have argued that the self-determination of the peoples of the defending state is the ultimate basis

[204] See, generally, Ruys and Ferro, n.192, 79–96. For discussion of the relationship between collective self-defence and military assistance on request, see Chapter 8.

[205] See Introduction, nn.50–54 and accompanying text (arguing that if a collective self-defence claim is made, this is enough for that claim to be of value in terms of assessing the legal parameters of collective self-defence, even if the claim is legally dubious).

[206] See n.104 and accompanying text.

[207] See Jean d'Aspremont, 'Legitimacy of Governments in the Age of Democracy' (2006) 38 *New York University Journal of International Law and Politics* 877, 882–883 (albeit using these terms in a somewhat different manner).

of validity for any collective self-defence claim,[208] whereas Wright has asserted that:

> [i]t seems clear that the *generally recognized government* of a state can properly make a request for military assistance for collective self-defense, even if foreign invasion has driven it from much of its territory, and perhaps even if it has been driven entirely from its territory and has become a government in exile.[209]

However, while these factors – and others, such as constitutional due process – are often advanced, they are applied inconsistently. Indeed, assertions of, for instance, a requester's democratic credentials have too often occurred in instances where those credentials are actually absent.

It would also be a mistake entirely to dismiss the relevance of effective control to the question of who is able to request aid in collective self-defence. While it cannot be the sole or determinative criterion in itself, and is de-emphasised in practice, it nonetheless has been a factor for some states in the collective self-defence context. It can be seen as being intertwined with other concerns, such as recognition, which may then be sufficient even once that effective control is lost.

Overall, there has not been a consistent approach in state practice as to how to identify the entity that is empowered to make a collective self-defence request on the part of the state. While drawing firm legal conclusions in this regard is difficult, however, it seems evident that a range of factors will underpin the determination of de jure status. These include effective control, but that is not the determinative criterion, at least in the short term. Instead, democratic legitimacy and external recognition emerge as key factors (although there are others). Exactly how these various criteria are likely to be applied, though, would seem to be dependent on the circumstances. Therefore, in a similar way to the recognition of governments in general,[210] perhaps the identification of the valid 'requester' in collective self-defence is ultimately more political than legal in operation: '[w]hether a request . . . has emanated from a legitimate authority within the state in question must always be context-specific'.[211]

[208] Norton Moore and Underwood, n.50, 308–309.

[209] Wright, n.88, 119.

[210] See John Bassett Moore, 'The New Isolation' (1933) 27 *American Journal of International Law* 607, 613; Lauterpacht, n.93, 816–817.

[211] Chinkin and Kaldor, n.5, 145.

5.6 Conclusion

This chapter has argued that the widely held view that only states can issue a request for aid in collective self-defence is, indeed, correct. However, contrary to some assertions, there is no requirement that the requester be a UN member state.

The authority empowered to make a collective self-defence request on behalf of the state is its de jure government. Identifying the de jure government in instances where this is unclear or disputed can be extremely difficult, however. While the effective control of territory is the traditional starting point for the recognition of governments in international law generally, this does not appear to be the test for identifying a collective self-defence requester. Or, at least, it is not the primary or determinative test. Other factors are crucial, including the democratic credentials of the requester (actual or at least purported), external recognition, and internal constitutional (or other formal) process. The extent to which these factors are considered and applied is context specific. Ultimately, there does not appear to be binding criteria in customary international law as to how this must be determined. Instead, these factors are likely to influence the (political) decision of other states as to whether a collective self-defence 'requester' is indeed competent to issue a collective self-defence request on behalf of the defending state.

Having examined questions surrounding the issuer of a collective self-defence request, Chapter 6 considers the necessary manner and form of such requests.

6

The Manner and Form of a Collective Self-Defence Request

6.1 Introduction

Having examined *who* can make a collective self-defence request in Chapter 5, this chapter concludes the analysis of the 'request requirement' by examining *how* that request must be made. There are a number of questions – that have been largely undiscussed in the literature – as to the operation of the request requirement, especially concerning the manner and form of its issuance.

This chapter begins, in Section 6.2, by considering who the necessary addressee of the request must be. In particular, it is asked whether the request needs to be made of the state(s) that respond, or whether 'open ended' requests suffice. Section 6.3 then considers whether collective self-defence requests must take any specific form and, in particular, queries whether they can be inferred, rather than formally articulated. Relatedly, Section 6.4 then goes on to analyse if the request must even be made publicly (or, at least, be *publicised*), or whether secret/private requests can suffice. Finally, Section 6.5 examines two questions related to the timing of the request. First, it is asked whether the request must be made before the use of force in response to it has begun, as one would assume. Second, the section considers whether *ex-ante* consent, given previously in the abstract (e.g. via a collective self-defence treaty arrangement), is sufficient, or whether contemporaneous consent, specific to the armed attack in question, is legally required.

6.2 The Addressee of the Request

This section engages with the question of whether the defending state must request the aid of the state (or states)[1] that *actually respond* to that

[1] It is worth noting that at least one writer has implied – in a mirroring of the argument examined in Section 5.3 – that the *co-defending* state must be a United Nations (UN)

request, or whether a general request for aid is legally acceptable. Must the defending state submit a request to the state or states that it hopes then will act, or is it enough (assuming the other necessary criteria all are met) for an open request to be issued to the international community at large, to which a specific co-defending state then elects to respond?

As the current author has noted in previous writings, it is not entirely clear from the 1986 *Nicaragua* merits judgment what position the International Court of Justice (ICJ) took on this matter.[2] There are some possible indications in the decision as to the Court's view, however. For example, it noted that the lawfulness of collective self-defence 'depends on a request *addressed* by that State to *the* third State'.[3] Elsewhere in the judgment, the Court noted 'the lack of direct evidence of a formal request for assistance from any of the three States concerned [Honduras, Costa Rica or El Salvador] *to the United States*'.[4] More recently, the ICJ asserted in the 2003 *Oil Platforms* merits decision that *had* the United States 'claimed to have been exercising collective self-defence ... this would have required the existence of a request *made to the United States* ...'[5] All of this suggests that the ICJ has taken the view that a collective self-defence request must be directed at the state (or states) that ultimately

member (this, again, being premised on the wording of the Charter of the United Nations (1945) 1 UNTS XVI (UN Charter), Article 51: '[n]othing in the present Charter shall impair the inherent right of individual or collective self-defence if an armed attack occurs *against a Member of the United Nations*', emphasis added). See Hans Kelsen, 'Collective Security and Collective Self-Defense under the Charter of the United Nations' (1948) 42 *American Journal of International Law* 783, 792. The same rebuttals apply to this argument as were set out in Section 5.3. The purpose of Article 51 is to *preserve* states' right to defence and collective self-defence, which are sanctified in customary international law. This strongly indicates that the right of collective self-defence, for defending or co-defending states, is not limited only to UN members. There is no indication in state practice that the co-defending state must be a UN member either. See Andrew Martin, *Collective Security: A Progress Report* (Paris, United Nations (UNESCO), 1952), 170 (arguing that the question of whether the co-defending state is a UN member 'is immaterial'). Of course, given the current membership of the UN, the chances of a non-member state being in a position to act as a co-defending state are slim in any event.

2 James A. Green, *The International Court of Justice and Self-Defence in International Law* (Oxford, Hart, 2009), 52–53.

3 *Military and Paramilitary Activities in and against Nicaragua* (*Nicaragua v. United States of America*) (merits) [1986] ICJ Rep. 14, para. 196 (emphasis added).

4 *Ibid*, para. 166 (emphasis added).

5 *Case concerning Oil Platforms* (*Islamic Republic of Iran v. United States of America*) (merits) [2003] ICJ Rep. 161, para. 51 (in part quoting from *Nicaragua* (merits), n.3, references omitted, emphasis added).

provides that aid, rather than being open and general in nature. This can only, at best, be inferred from the judgments though.

There is little in the way of explicit guidance in scholarship concerning the question of the necessary addressee of the request either. However, one arguably can identify an implicit position in the writings of some scholars. Lee, for example, asserts that there must be 'an affirmative request by a victim State *directed to a State* exercising its right of collective self-defence'.[6] Kritsiotis, too, argues that the request 'must be made by the victim state *to the states* purporting to act in collective self-defence',[7] whereas Modabber writes that 'the attacked state ... must ... request the help *of the intervening state*'.[8] Other writers have used similar language, all without explicitly asserting that there exists a requirement that the request be 'targeted' in the way that their language implies.[9] Therefore, as with the ICJ, there are arguably some suggestions from scholarship that the request must be specifically directed to the state(s) that respond to it; also like the ICJ, however, scholars do not seem to have justified this conclusion or even been explicit in reaching it.

State practice too is far from clear on the matter. Indeed, the (arguably) relevant practice must be treated with care. This is both because there is so little of it and because the potential examples are controversial and/or can be read in different ways. To the extent that one might draw

[6] Jaemin Lee, 'Collective Self-Defense or Collective Security: Japan's Reinterpretation of Article 9 of the Constitution' (2015) 8 *Journal of East Asia and International Law* 373, 377 (emphasis added).

[7] Dino Kritsiotis, 'A Study of the Scope and Operation of the Rights of Individual and Collective Self-Defence under International Law', in Nigel D. White and Christian Henderson (eds.), *Research Handbook on International Conflict and Security Law:* Jus ad Bellum, Jus in Bello *and* Jus Post Bellum (Abingdon, Routledge, 2013), 170, 185 (emphasis added).

[8] Zia Modabber, 'Collective Self-Defense: *Nicaragua v. United States*' (1988) 10 *Loyola of Los Angeles International and Comparative Law Journal* 449, 462 (emphasis added).

[9] See, for example, Russell Buchan and Nicholas Tsagourias, *Regulating the Use of Force in International Law: Stability and Change* (Cheltenham, Edward Elgar, 2021), 73 ('it is only those States that are the recipients of the invitation that can invoke the right of self-defence'); Sia Spiliopoulou Åkermark, 'The Puzzle of Collective Self-Defence: Dangerous Fragmentation or a Window of Opportunity? An Analysis with Finland and the Åland Islands as a Case Study' (2017) 22 *Journal of Conflict and Security Law* 249, 263 (arguing that when a collective self-defence request is issued, 'it is up to the ... government recipients of such a request ...' to decide whether or not to respond); Tadashi Mori, 'Collective Self-Defence in International Law and in the New Japanese Legislation for Peace and Security (2015)' (2017) 60 *Japanese Yearbook of International Law* 158, 164 ('the exercise of this right [of collective self-defence] is limited to a state that is asked for assistance').

inferences from the practice as to the addressee of a collective self-defence request, however, they seem to point in the opposite direction to the case law and scholarship.

One example of possible relevance is the 1950 request for aid made by the Republic of Korea (ROK). The ROK's representative in the Security Council, Mr Chang, made the request in question by stating:

> The invasion of my country is an act of aggression, and a threat to international peace and security. I appeal to the Security Council to act forthwith in removing this threat to international peace.[10]

At least as explicitly presented, therefore, the ROK's request was directed at the Security Council *ut totum*, rather than at any individual state or states. The United States nonetheless cited this request as the basis for its participation in the Korean War.[11] Indeed, the United States even acknowledged that the ROK's request was directed at the Council, without seeming to view this as a concern: '[t]he Republic of Korea has appealed *to the United Nations* for protection. ... [and] the United States is prepared ... to furnish assistance ...'[12] States critical of the US action,[13] perhaps more importantly, did not raise this as an issue either.

One must be cautious as to the precedential value of the Korean War in relation to the required addressee of a collective self-defence request, however. It has already been noted that there is a lack of clarity as to whether the US action in Korea was an action of collective self-defence or an action authorised by the United Nations (UN) Security Council.[14] The case certainly can be made that it was a collective self-defence action,[15] but specifically in relation to the question of the necessary addressee of the request, it is noteworthy that the objections of the states that were critical of the US action at the time were focused on the validity of the purported 'authorising' Security Council resolutions, not the criteria for

10 UNSC Verbatim Record, UN Doc. S/PV.473 (25 June 1950), 8.

11 UNSC Verbatim Record, UN Doc. S/PV.474 (27 June 1950), 4. See also UNSC Verbatim Record, UN Doc. S/PV.475 (30 June 1950), 10.

12 UN Doc. S/PV.474, n.11, 4.

13 See, for example, UNGA Verbatim Record, UN Doc. A/PV.294 (7 October 1950), paras. 1–35 (Ukraine); *ibid*, 118–121, 189 (Czechoslovakia); *ibid*, paras. 170–175 (USSR); *ibid*, paras. 179–186 (Poland).

14 See Chapter 4, n.61 and accompanying text.

15 See Chapter 5, n.69 and accompanying text.

collective self-defence.[16] Thus, it may be unwise to read too much into the fact that these states did not take issue with the request being directed at the Security Council rather than the United States, given that – at that point, at least – they apparently viewed it precisely as being the *Council* that was responding to that request (albeit, these states alleged, unlawfully).

An example from practice that perhaps has a little more value here concerns the complaint made by Mozambique in 1977 – at what, it would turn out, was the outset of the so-called Mozambican Civil War – over 'armed aggressions' against it by apartheid Rhodesia.[17] Mozambique made an 'open' request for aid in 1977, appealing to the UN Security Council and, explicitly, 'the international community' at large.[18] Admittedly, Mozambique was not clear this was a *collective self-defence* request specifically, with its primary emphasis being on the need for weapons and logistical support.[19] However, other states interpreted the request as amounting to an exercise of Mozambique's right of collective self-defence, even though that request was not addressed to any particular state or states.[20]

The USSR ultimately responded to Mozambique's request; indeed, it did so on an ongoing basis for years. However, for the most part, this was restricted to economic support,[21] and the USSR did not claim to be acting in collective self-defence. This example must again, therefore, be treated cautiously. Yet, the fact that some states saw the Mozambican plea for aid as a lawful collective self-defence request, even though it was issued to the world at large, again at least suggests that such requests do not need to be targeted at a specific addressee.

Interestingly, while the ICJ in the *Nicaragua* case seemed to take the view that for the request to have been valid it would have needed to have

[16] See, for example, UN Doc. A/PV.294, n.13, paras. 170–175 (USSR); *ibid*, para. 185 (Poland).

[17] Letter dated 22 June 1977 from the Permanent Representative of Mozambique to the United Nations addressed to the President of the Security Council, UN Doc. S/12350 (23 June 1977).

[18] See UNSC Verbatim Record, UN Doc. S/PV.2014(OR) (28 June 1977), paras. 8–51 (referring specifically to the need for aid from 'the international community' at para. 44).

[19] See, for example, *ibid*, para. 44. For the argument that such action falls below the level of a measure of collective self-defence, see Section 1.4.

[20] UNSC Verbatim Record, UN Doc. S/PV.2018(OR) (30 June 1977), para. 78 (India).

[21] See William Gehrke, 'The Mozambique Crisis: A Case for United Nations Military Intervention' (1991) 24 *Cornell International Law Journal* 135, 138.

been addressed specifically to the United States, the United States itself claimed that 'El Salvador, Honduras and Costa Rica have each sought outside assistance, *principally from* the United States ... [and] the United States has responded to these requests.'[22] If this were indeed the case – noting that the Court was sceptical about whether such requests had been made[23] – then it perhaps would fall somewhere between an 'open call' for support and a request specifically aimed at the ultimate co-defending state. The United States here suggested that it was asked to provide aid, but also it was not the only addressee of this request. Similarly, at least one of the alleged defending states, El Salvador, argued before the Court that it:

> requested support and assistance *from abroad*. [And] ... that President Duarte, during a recent visit to the United States and in discussions with United States congressmen, reiterated the importance of this assistance for our defence *from the United States and the democratic nations of the world*.[24]

This too, identifies the United States as a specific addressee of the request but indicates that it was also a standing request for other states to provide aid.

One might similarly note that Chad's request for aid in the 1980s was initially directed at a single state: 'in accordance with Article 51 of the Charter concerning the inherent right of self-defence of States, [Chad has] requested military intervention *from France* to repel the Libyan attack'.[25] However, in addition, Chad later 'issued an appeal to all nations' to come to its aid in collective self-defence.[26] It was to this

[22] *Military and Paramilitary Activities in and against Nicaragua* (*Nicaragua v. United States of America*) (counter-memorial of the United States of America, questions of jurisdiction and admissibility) [1984] ICJ Plead., vol. II, para. 202 (emphasis added). Albeit that, elsewhere in the same counter-memorial, the United States referred more directly to the right of the relevant states involved to 'self-defense and their right to request assistance *from the United States* to that end'. *Ibid*, para. 25 (emphasis added).

[23] *Nicaragua* (merits), n.3, paras. 165–166.

[24] *Military and Paramilitary Activities in and Against Nicaragua* (*Nicaragua v. United States of America*) (declaration of intervention of the Republic of El Salvador: intervention pursuant to Article 63 of the Statute of the International Court of Justice, filed in the Registry of the Court on 15 August 1984), para. XII (emphasis added).

[25] Letter dated 18 February 1986 from the Permanent Representative of Chad to the United Nations addressed to the President of the Security Council, UN Doc. S/17837 (18 February 1986) (emphasis added).

[26] UNSC Verbatim Record, UN Doc. S/PV.2721 (19 November 1986), 18.

second 'open' request that Zaire responded and upon which Zaire relied to seek to legalise its use of force.[27]

More recently, the 2014 request for aid against the 'Islamic State of Iraq and the Levant' (ISIL) made by Iraq follows a similar pattern. Iraq noted that it 'requested the United States of America to lead international efforts to strike ISIL sites and military strongholds, with our express consent',[28] and that this was the basis for the 'military assistance it is receiving, *including* the assistance provided by the United States of America'.[29] Once again, therefore, the United States was identified as an addressee of the request, but it was also made clear that the request extended to other states. And, of course, that request was then the basis for *multiple* states' claims to be using force in collective self-defence.[30]

Overall, therefore, while states do sometimes specify the addressee (or addressees) of a collective self-defence request very clearly,[31] there is not sufficient *opinio juris* to support the idea that there is a requirement that they do so. The practice in this regard is mixed, but states have made entirely open requests, or requests directed at a specific state as well as more generally to additional unspecified states without this being a point of controversy for other states. There is also no policy reason why open requests should be considered insufficient. As such, it may be tentatively concluded that there is no requirement that a collective self-defence request be directed at a particular state (or states): this would be a restriction upon the way in which states can comply with the request that cannot be established in customary international law. Defending states would thus seem free to meet the requirement in the least restrictive way, meaning that 'open' requests suffice.

27 *Ibid.*

28 Letter dated 20 September 2014 from the Permanent Representative of Iraq to the United Nations addressed to the President of the Security Council, UN Doc. S/2014/691 (22 September 2014).

29 *Ibid* (emphasis added).

30 See Introduction, n.21 and accompanying text.

31 See, for example, UNSC Verbatim Record, UN Doc. S/PV.831 (17 July 1958), para. 24 (Jordan, indicating that it had 'requested the Governments of the United Kingdom and the United States of America to come to its immediate aid'); Letter dated 17 March 1988 from The Permanent Representative of Honduras to the United Nations addressed to the Secretary-General, UN Doc. A/42/931-S/19643 (17 March 1988), para. 4 (Honduras, reporting that it had decided to '*ask the United States Government* for the effective and immediate assistance which Honduras needs in order to maintain its territorial sovereignty and integrity', emphasis added).

6.3 Formalities and Inferred Requests

6.3.1 Formalities and Form

The next question that must be considered in this chapter is whether there are any particular formalities required for the issuance of a collective self-defence request. In the *Nicaragua* judgment, for example, the ICJ referred to the need for 'a *formal* request for assistance'[32] as the basis for collective self-defence action. The majority was unclear as to what would qualify as being sufficiently 'formal', however. It is also, perhaps, worth noting that – while the Court appeared to require an element of *formality* – it gave no indication of there being any required *format* for collective self-defence requests.[33] Both Judge Jennings[34] and Judge Schwebel[35] suggested in their dissenting opinions to *Nicaragua* that a requirement of formality, as suggested by the majority, was overly procedural and unrealistic in practice.[36]

Such concerns perhaps have been a little overstated, however, because 'states do not seem to have found [the request requirement] to be either onerous or inconvenient to their actions'.[37] This is, in part, precisely because they have *not* concerned themselves with particular formalities when it comes to making self-defence requests. There is no basis in practice to support either a requirement for the observation of any particular formalities when issuing a collective self-defence request or a requirement that such requests be made in a specific format. Requests have been made in various forms and with differing levels of formality, without any issue being taken by other states in this regard. For example, collective self-defence requests have been made[38] in letters to the UN Secretary-General[39] or President of the Security

[32] *Nicaragua* (merits), n.3, para. 166 (emphasis added).

[33] Kritsiotis, n.7, 187, footnote 189 (making this point regarding the Court's jurisprudence).

[34] *Nicaragua* (merits), n.3, dissenting opinion of Judge Jennings, 545.

[35] *Ibid*, dissenting opinion of Judge Schwebel, para. 191.

[36] See also George Fletcher and Jens Ohlin, *Defending Humanity: When Force Is Justified and Why* (Oxford, Oxford University Press, 2008), 70–71; Fred L. Morrison, 'Legal Issues in the *Nicaragua* Opinion' (1987) 81 *American Journal of International Law* 160, 163; Kritsiotis, n.7, 186.

[37] Kritsiotis, n.7, 187.

[38] Or, at least, 'reported' by the defending state and/or co-defending state. See nn.96–105 and accompanying text.

[39] Letter dated 15 July 1993 from the Permanent Representative of Tajikistan to the United Nations addressed to the Secretary-General, UN Doc. S/26092 (16 July 1993) (Tajikistan,

Council,[40] in debates at the Security Council[41] or General Assembly,[42] in independent press releases,[43] at conferences,[44] via radio broadcasts[45] and now – inevitably – on social media.[46] That requests have been communicated in these different ways has not, in itself, been of any concern to other states. As such, it seems clear that requests need not be in a particular format or be accompanied with any particular formalities.[47]

6.3.2 *Inferred/Implied Requests*

This conclusion raises the question of whether requests even need to be explicit.[48] It has been suggested that the fact that customary international law requires the defending state's 'approval' for the exercise of a collective self-defence action does not mean that such 'approval' cannot be inferred.[49] This reasoning is sometimes based on the policy goals

requesting aid in relation to an 'attack carried out from the territory of the Islamic State of Afghanistan').

40 UN Doc. S/17837, n.25 (Chad, requesting aid 'to repel the Libyan attack').

41 UN Doc. S/PV.831, n.31, para. 24 (Jordan, requesting aid in response to an alleged threat from the United Arab Republic).

42 See, for example, UNGA Verbatim Record, UN Doc. A/63/PV.14 (27 September 2008), 2 (Russia, in relation to the request by the 'state' of South Ossetia – although it should be noted that here the collective self-defence claim was only implicit).

43 See, for example, Sheik Jabir al-Ahmad al-Jabir Al Sabah, the Amir of Kuwait, letter to President George H. W. Bush (12 August 1990) (in Statement by Press Secretary Fitzwater on the Persian Gulf Crisis (12 August 1990), www.presidency.ucsb.edu/documents/statement-press-secretary-fitzwater-the-persian-gulf-crisis) (Kuwait, in relation to the invasion by Iraq).

44 See, for example, 'ISIS: World Leaders Give Strong Backing for Iraq at Paris Conference – As It Happened', *The Guardian* (last updated 15 September 2014), www.theguardian.com/world/live/2014/sep/15/isis-leaders-hold-crisis-meeting-on-isis-in-paris-live-coverage?page=with:block-5416c62ae4b0691640d60091#block-5416c62ae4b0691640d60091 (Iraq, making a collective self-defence request in response to the actions of ISIL).

45 See, for example, UNSC Verbatim Record, UN Doc. S/PV.746 (28 October 1956), para. 156 (USSR, quoting from a statement read on a Budapest radio station on 24 October 1956 on behalf of an entity claiming to be the de jure government of Hungary, requesting aid under the Warsaw Pact).

46 See, for example, TACC, *Telegram* (23 February 2022), https://t.me/tass_agency/111840 (requests by the 'states' of Donetsk and Luhansk).

47 See *Nicaragua* (merits), n.3, dissenting opinion of Judge Schwebel, para. 191; Stuart Casey-Maslen, Jus ad Bellum: *The Law on Inter-State Use of Force* (Oxford, Hart, 2020), 75 (arguing the request 'does not need to be overly formal in nature').

48 See Tom Ruys, *'Armed Attack' and Article 51 of the UN Charter: Evolutions in Customary Law and Practice* (Cambridge, Cambridge University Press, 2010), 89.

49 *Ibid*, 91; Christian Henderson, *The Use of Force and International Law* (Cambridge, Cambridge University Press, 2018), 260; John Norton Moore, 'The *Nicaragua* Case and

underpinning the request criterion, which are to ensure that aid is truly needed/wanted (protecting the defending state's sovereign autonomy), and prevent abuse.[50] Thus, Ruys, for example, has suggested that:

> the request criterion is primarily aimed at securing the approval of the victim State. If this approval can be established in some other way, for example, if it is clear that the States' military actions are closely coordinated or if the States jointly submit a report to the Security Council, a flexible interpretation should arguably prevail.[51]

In 2009, the Independent International Fact-Finding Mission on the Conflict in Georgia (IIFFMCG) concluded that there was no formal element to the request criterion and that such a request could be implicit. Indeed, it stated that the 'prevailing opinion is that such a request can . . . be informal and implicit'.[52] Whether this is the 'prevailing opinion' is debatable, but as noted, there is support in practice at least for the view that requests can be informal.[53]

Interestingly, in a 2008 letter to the UN Secretary-General related to alleged aggression by Armenia, Azerbaijan seemed to see the acceptability of 'inferred requests' as being dependant on where the defending state's use of force was going to occur:

> if a third State sends troops into the territory of the direct victim of the armed attack . . ., uninvited yet allegedly in order to offer military assistance against the armed attack underway by the attacking State . . . this will be viewed as another armed attack against the [defending state]. . . . On the contrary, the third State does have the right to take forcible action against [the aggressor] . . . in exercise of the collective right of self-defence conferred directly on the third State by both Article 51 and customary international law. Still, the third State can proceed into action . . . only in a manner consistent with the sovereign rights of the [defending state].[54]

Azerbaijan here appeared to argue that if the use of force to protect the defending state occurs on the defending state's territory (even if only in

the Deterioration of World Order' (1987) 81 *American Journal of International Law* 151, 155.

[50] See Chapter 4, nn.38–40 and accompanying text.

[51] Ruys, n.48, 91.

[52] Report of the Independent International Fact-Finding Mission on the Conflict in Georgia (IIFFMCG) (2009), vol. II, 281.

[53] See nn.39–46 and accompanying text (citing examples).

[54] Letter dated 22 December 2008 from the Permanent Representative of Azerbaijan to the United Nations addressed to the Secretary-General, UN Doc. A/63/662–S/2008/812 (24 December 2008), para. 32.

part), then an express request is necessary, but if it takes place wholly on the territory of the aggressor, then the request can be inferred. However, this statement aside, there is little indication that a line is drawn by states between different 'manifestations' of collective self-defence in this way.[55]

It will be recalled from Chapter 4 that when states claim to be acting in collective self-defence, this has almost always been premised on an explicit request from the defending state (actual, or at least alleged).[56] There is thus insufficient evidence to allow us definitively to conclude that an 'implicit' request will be enough to comply with the request requirement, because states almost always make their requests explicit. However, the limited evidence that does exist might suggest that requests could be inferred. For example, it may be recalled[57] that when the United States claimed to be acting in the collective self-defence of Cambodia in 1970, this was initially in the absence of an explicit Cambodian request for aid, and the United States made no indication that it saw this as being necessary.[58] However, a month later, Cambodia referred, with strong approval, to the 'devastating' effect of the 'military operations of the United States' against North Vietnamese forces on its territory.[59] One could reasonably infer a 'request' from this. There is no evidence that other states were critical of a lack of compliance with the request criterion in this instance, which might suggest that other states would accept alternative factors implicitly indicating a defending state's approval as being sufficient to satisfy the requirement to ensure that such approval is present. More importantly, this author has identified no *opinio juris* suggesting that a requirement of 'explicitness' has emerged under customary international law. Again, if it cannot be established that a legal restriction exists on the manner in which a state can comply with the request requirement, then the least restrictive approach would seem to be available.

[55] Although, see Yoram Dinstein, *War, Aggression and Self-Defence* (Cambridge, Cambridge University Press, 6th ed., 2017), 320 (making a similar point – in fact, suggesting that perhaps no request is required *at all* if the action takes place wholly outside the defending state's territory).

[56] See Chapter 4, nn.126–129 and accompanying text.

[57] See *ibid.*

[58] Letter dated 5 May 1970 from the Permanent Representative of the United States of America to the United Nations addressed to the President of the Security Council, UN Doc. S/9781 (5 May 1970).

[59] Letter dated 18 June 1970 from the Permanent Representative of Cambodia to the United Nations addressed to the President of the Security Council, UN Doc. S/9842 (19 June 1970), 2.

It therefore may be argued, tentatively, that it is correct that requests can be inferred as a matter of *law*. However, the absence of a clearly expressed request is likely to be hugely problematic for the co-defending state when it looks to *evidence* that the (legally essential) requirement of 'request' has been met. The easiest way for a state to establish that it wants help is to ask for it unequivocally. Failure to do so may understandably be viewed as indicative of abuse or coercion – which would bring the validity of the request into question – or may simply be taken as evidence that the defending state did not approve of the actions of the co-defending state. At the very least, it may be said that co-defending states would be wise to secure an explicit request from the state that they intended to co-defend or risk the legality of their action being brought into question.

6.4 The Publicity of Requests

This section follows closely on from Section 6.3, in that it examines whether the request must be made publicly, or whether it can be covert (i.e. communicated only to the state or states that then respond(s)). It seems that it might be acceptable for requests to be inferred as a matter of law (although this is not without its problems), but what if requests are not just implied but wholly *secret*?

Disagreement exists in scholarship as to whether states can exercise the right of self-defence covertly.[60] Some scholars take the view that 'intervention is not prima facie … unlawful simply because it is covert',[61] whereas others argue that '[c]laims of self-defense need to be publicly asserted, just as actions in self-defense need to be publicly performed'.[62] Much of this debate has focused on the fact that the Article 51 reporting requirement[63] might present an issue for self-defence being exercised

[60] On the implications of covert uses of force for the application and development of international law, see, generally, Marie Aronsson-Storrier, *Publicity in International Law-Making: Covert Operations and the Use of Force* (Cambridge, Cambridge University Press, 2020).

[61] Catherine Lotrionte, 'The Just War Doctrine and Covert Responses to Terrorism' (2002) 3 *Georgetown Journal of International Affairs* 85, 92.

[62] Paul W. Kahn, 'From Nuremburg to The Hague: The United States Position in *Nicaragua v. United States* and the Development of International Law' (1987) 12 *Yale Journal of International Law* 1, 29.

[63] UN Charter, n.1, Article 51.

covertly.[64] That, of course, would hold true whether the exercise of self-defence was individual or collective, as the reporting requirement applies to both.[65] In the collective self-defence context, though, the request requirement also could have comparable implications for the covert exercise of the right.

It may be recalled that in the *Nicaragua* decision, the ICJ referred to the need for the defending state to 'make an *express* request' for collective self-defence.[66] This would perhaps suggest that the Court saw a need for the request to be public. In his dissenting opinion to the decision, Judge Schwebel interpreted the majority's position as being that 'the only kind of request for assistance that appears to count [for the lawful exercise of collective self-defence] is one formally and publicly made'.[67] Similarly, in an article published at the time, MacDonald read the judgment as saying that 'in order to render assistance a state must receive a *formal and public request* for aid from the victim'.[68] These readings put words in the Court's mouth, however.[69] It was nowhere near so explicit.[70]

The question of whether a collective self-defence request can be issued secretly or privately has largely been ignored in the literature. A few writers have implicitly indicated that they believe that there is a requirement that a public request be made,[71] while others – including the present author in previous writings – have explicitly mused on whether this might be the case but have not then attempted to provide an

[64] See, for example, James P. Rowles, 'Secret Wars, Self-Defense and the Charter – A Reply to Professor Moore' (1986) 80 *American Journal of International Law* 568, 577; Dinstein, n.55, 251; James A. Green, 'The Article 51 Reporting Requirement for Self-Defense Actions' (2015) 55 *Virginia Journal of International Law* 463, 617–619.

[65] See Section 3.4 for discussion of the reporting requirement's application to collective self-defence.

[66] *Nicaragua* (merits), n.3, para. 232 (emphasis added).

[67] *Ibid*, dissenting opinion of Judge Schwebel, para. 191.

[68] R. St. J. MacDonald, 'The *Nicaragua* Case: New Answers to Old Questions' (1986) 24 *Canadian Yearbook of International Law* 127, 150 (emphasis added).

[69] See Patrick C. R. Terry, 'Afghanistan's Civil War (1979–1989): Illegal and Failed Foreign Interventions' (2011) 31 *Polish Yearbook of International Law* 107, 138, footnote 135 (making this point specific in relation to the interpretation of the majority's position by Judge Schwebel).

[70] Indeed, if anything, a close reading of the *Nicaragua* judgment would suggest that 'publicity' was only seen as evidentiarily important by the Court, rather than legally determinative. See *Nicaragua* (merits), n.3, para. 236; discussion at nn.112–120 and accompanying text.

[71] See, for example, Johanna Friman, *Revisiting the Concept of Defence in the* Jus ad Bellum: *The Dual Face of Defence* (Oxford, Hart, 2017), 193 (collective self-defence requires 'an *explicit* request by the victim State', emphasis added).

answer.[72] However, there has been a notable amount of scholarship considering whether military assistance on request can be premised on covert consent.[73] Brookman-Byrne, for example, provided a detailed consideration of this question in a 2020 article.[74] He argued therein that:

> [t]here are clear reasons in favour of a publicity requirement for the production of valid consent. . . . [S]uch a requirement would allow greater transparency and public scrutiny of the extraterritorial uses of force [. . . and, perhaps, a reduction in] the likelihood that states will engage in forcible intervention . . . From a more practical perspective, the lawfulness of an intervention that has been invited is contingent upon it remaining within the parameters and scope of the invitation, and so making clear the contours of consent will make it easier to assess whether a state has gone beyond the limits of what has been permitted.[75]

As will be discussed in detail in Chapter 8, one must be careful in drawing conclusions regarding the operation of collective self-defence based on an analogy to military assistance on request.[76] However, the policy arguments for supporting a publicity requirement that Brookman-Byrne advances would seem to be equally appropriate to the collective self-defence context. There is no question that 'clandestine' acts of self-defence provide notable scope for abuse, given the impossibility of external scrutiny.[77] Relatedly, covert self-defence also acts to circumvent the primacy of the Security Council in relation to international peace and security.[78] Just as is the case with the reporting requirement,[79] a

[72] See, for example, Anthony Clark Arend and Robert J. Beck, *International Law and the Use of Force* (London, Routledge, 1993), 36; James A. Green, 'The "Additional" Criteria for Collective Self-Defence: Request but Not Declaration' (2017) 4 *Journal on the Use of Force and International Law* 4, 7.

[73] See, for example, Seyfullah Hasar, *State Consent to Foreign Military Intervention during Civil Wars* (Leiden, Brill Nijhoff, 2022), 59–61; Sean D. Murphy, 'The International Legality of US Military Cross-border Operations from Afghanistan into Pakistan' (2009) 85 *International Legal Studies* 109, 118–120; ILA, Use of Force Committee (2010–2018), *Final Report on Aggression and the Use of Force*, Sydney Conference (2018), https://ila.vettoreweb.com/Storage/Download.aspx?DbStorageId=1391&StorageFileGuid=6a499340-074d-4d4b-851b-7a56871175d6, 19; Max Brookman-Byrne, 'Intervention by (Secret) Invitation: Searching for a Requirement of Publicity in the International Law on the Use of Force with Consent' (2020) 7 *Journal on the Use of Force and International Law* 74.

[74] Brookman-Byrne, n.73.

[75] *Ibid*, 86.

[76] See, generally, Chapter 8.

[77] Kahn, n.62, 29.

[78] Rowles, n.64, 577; Dinstein, n.55, 259.

[79] Green, n.64, 569.

transparent request for aid in collective self-defence (even if implicit, so long as it is clear) can act to alleviate concerns of abuse. Open requests girder the objective determination of whether the requirements for the lawful exercise of self-defence – particularly armed attack, necessity, and proportionality – have been met.

Of course, as Brookman-Byrne acknowledges in the military assistance on request context,[80] there are also policy arguments *against* a publicity requirement. In particular, there may be operational implications regarding the sharing of information with opposition forces. It is also worth noting the unjust asymmetry of potentially requiring an overt defensive response to a covert aggressive attack.[81]

Due to such concerns, Judge Schwebel asked, in his dissent in *Nicaragua*, 'where is it written that, where one State covertly promotes the subversion of another by multiple means tantamount to an armed attack, the latter may not informally and quietly seek foreign assistance?'[82] As Judge Schwebel himself immediately acknowledged (although did not endorse),[83] one might respond to this question by saying that it in fact *is* written: Article 51 of the UN Charter holds that self-defence actions must be reported to the Security Council.[84] To be clear, this is not to say that the Article 51 reporting requirement directly implicates the operation of the request requirement as a matter of law. The request requirement is not found in Article 51: it exists in customary international law. However, *if* Article 51 indeed means that a state exercising collective self-defence must meet the reporting requirement – a separate obligation from the request requirement – by *reporting publicly*, then the covert status of any operation is already going to be 'blown'. This would indirectly affect the operation of the request requirement because keeping the request covert would become moot.

It is therefore perhaps not surprising that, in practice, the reporting of collective self-defence actions commonly is also used as a way to publicise the request upon which that claim is premised. In other words, these two acts of publicising the action – to demonstrate fulfilment of two different

80 Brookman-Byrne, n.73, 86.

81 See *Nicaragua* (merits), n.3, dissenting opinion of Judge Schwebel, paras. 221–230 (making these points specifically in relation to collective self-defence, albeit predominantly focusing on the reporting requirement rather than the request requirement).

82 *Ibid*, para. 191.

83 *Ibid*.

84 UN Charter, n.1, Article 51.

criteria – are often done together. For example, in 1986, in a letter to the President of the Security Council, the representative of Chad wrote:

> I have the honour to inform you that . . . in accordance with Article 51 of the Charter concerning the inherent right of self-defence of States, [Chad has] requested military intervention from France to repel the Libyan attack.[85]

Chad's letter thus was designed both to fulfil the Article 51 reporting requirement *and* to publicise that it had requested aid in collective self-defence.

Nonetheless, it is generally accepted by both states and scholars that a failure to meet the reporting requirement does not turn an otherwise lawful use of force in self-defence into an unlawful use of force.[86] Thus, the existence of the reporting requirement in Article 51 cannot be seen – in itself – as establishing a legal obligation of publicity,[87] in general for self-defence actions or with regard to collective self-defence in particular.

The question instead is whether a 'public request' requirement for collective self-defence can be identified in customary international law. It is extremely difficult to assess state practice and *opinio juris* regarding any such requirement (or – especially – a lack thereof), given that wholly covert conduct obviously will not be known of.[88] States undoubtedly do sometimes act in self-defence in a clandestine manner (or at least later claim to have done so). Norton Moore provides a useful list of examples.[89] However, it is perhaps noteworthy that the examples on his list either were instances of individual self-defence or were collective self-defence actions (at least allegedly) that had covert *elements* but were not entirely covert even at the time. As Aronsson-Storrier notes, on occasion, uses of force are entirely unacknowledged by the state(s)

[85] UN Doc. S/17837, n.25.

[86] See, for example, Ruys, n.48, 68–74; Green, n.64, 592–596. See also Chapter 3, nn.180–183 and accompanying text.

[87] Green, n.64, 618–619.

[88] See, for example, ILC, *Conclusions on the Identification of Customary International Law, with Commentaries*, UN Doc. A/73/10 (2018), commentary to conclusion 5, 133 ('[i]n order to contribute to the formation and identification of rules of customary international law, practice must be known to other States. Indeed, it is difficult to see how confidential conduct by a State could serve such a purpose unless and until it is known to other States', footnotes omitted). See also Aronsson-Storrier, n.60, particularly 37–87.

[89] John Norton Moore, 'The Secret War in Central America and the Future of World Order' (1986) 80 *American Journal of International Law* 43, 89–90.

conducting them,[90] but at other times, the conduct is partially acknowledged or 'quasi-covert'.[91] Norton Moore's list shows that there are examples of collective self-defence actions (actual or claimed) that fall into the latter category. Again, it will be recalled that states have invariably relied on requests in the collective self-defence context,[92] and this includes all of the listed 'quasi-covert' examples. Whether there also exist entirely unacknowledged actions that otherwise would meet the requirements for collective self-defence – including the issuance of a wholly private request – is impossible to know. But the present writer would hypothesise that this is perhaps unlikely, and if there are some such examples, there probably are not many.

In any event, there is no meaningful *opinio juris* indicating that states believe that, as a matter of law, a request in collective self-defence must be public. This means that – as with the possible 'explicitness' requirement discussed in the previous section – it is difficult to identify a requirement of publicity embedded in the request criterion as a matter of customary international law.[93] Perhaps, therefore, it may be that – again as with 'explicitness',[94] and as has been argued in relation to the issuance of consent in the military assistance on request context[95] – even if a failure to make the request publicly is not legally terminal in itself, it would make *evidencing* the request extremely difficult for the co-defending state.

It is worth noting that if there is a 'publicity requirement' for collective self-defence requests, it is not a requirement that the request be *public*, but that it be *publicised*. States do sometimes make their request publicly. One might note, for example, Iraq's 'request' for aid in collective self-defence in relation to attacks by ISIL in 2014, which, in fact, involved

[90] Aronsson-Storrier, n.60, particularly 130–161. In the case of 'unacknowledged' uses of force, no legal justification is provided at all, of course. See Terry, n.69, 130.

[91] Aronsson-Storrier, n.60, 88–129.

[92] See n.56.

[93] See, for example, IIFFMCG, n.52, vol. II, 280 (seemingly taking the view that there is no legal requirement of publicity: '[c]ollective self-defence in favour of South Ossetia presupposes … that South Ossetia at least implicitly and *covertly* requested Russian help').

[94] See n.59 and accompanying text.

[95] See, for example, Mary Ellen O'Connell, 'Unlawful Killing with Combat Drones: A Case Study of Pakistan, 2004–2009', in Simon Bronitt, Miriam Gani and Saskia Hufnagel (eds.), *Shooting to Kill: Socio-Legal Perspectives on the Use of Lethal Force* (Oxford, Hart, 2012), 263, 282; Brookman-Byrne, n.73, 88–90; Hasar, n.73, 60–61; Murphy, n.73, 118; ILA, *Final Report on Aggression and the Use of Force*, n.73, 19.

multiple requests, all of which were themselves openly communicated or published.[96] It is more common, though, for states making a collective self-defence claim to *refer to* their request in a public document or forum, with the *request itself* remaining a communication only between the states concerned. For example, Michael has suggested that, in 1958, 'the Lebanese Government apparently requested privately that the United States unilaterally employ armed force on its behalf' in collective self-defence.[97] This is true only to the extent that the letter sent to the United States requesting aid was not published. But it was not a 'private' request: in the UN Security Council, Lebanon explicitly stated that relying 'on Article 51 of the Charter . . . the Lebanese Government has asked for direct assistance from friendly countries'.[98] The United States referenced the Lebanese request at the same meeting.[99] Although the legality of the US action was questioned by other states for a range of reasons,[100] the fact that the request *itself* was not made public was not one of them.

One might similarly recall the letter sent by Chad to the Security Council in 1986,[101] already discussed in this section,[102] which only referred to the request that Chad had made. Chad also mentioned in Security Council meetings that it had issued a request.[103] However, the request itself was never published. This approach was made explicit in

[96] These included a request made at the Paris conference in September that year (see 'ISIS: World Leaders', n.44), and various letters addressed to the UN Secretary-General (see, e.g. Letter dated 20 September 2014 from the Permanent Representative of Iraq to the United Nations addressed to the President of the Security Council, UN Doc. S/2014/691 (22 September 2014) (this letter not only requested military aid but also referred to previous requests of this nature); Letter dated 25 June 2014 from the Permanent Representative of Iraq to the United Nations addressed to the Secretary-General, UN Doc. S/2014/440 (25 June 2014)). Another example is the requests made by the 'states' of Donetsk and Luhansk in 2022. These were published in full on social media sites such as Telegram, for example, TACC, *Telegram*, n.46. They then subsequently were annexed – again in full but also translated into English – to Letter dated 3 March 2022 from the Permanent Representative of the Russian Federation to the United Nations addressed to the Secretary-General, UN Doc. A/76/740–S/2022/179 (7 March 2022) (annexes III and IV, respectively).

[97] Helen Michael, 'Covert Involvement in Essentially Internal Conflicts: United States Assistance to the Contras under International Law' (1990) 23 *Vanderbilt Journal of Transnational Law* 539, 592.

[98] UNSC Verbatim Record, UN Doc. S/PV.827 (15 July 1958), para. 84.

[99] *Ibid*, para. 44.

[100] See, for example, *ibid*, paras. 95–123 (USSR).

[101] UN Doc. S/17837, n.25.

[102] See n.85 and accompanying text.

[103] See, for example, UN Doc. S/PV.2721, n.26, 18.

relation to the deployment of US troops to Honduras in 1988, which was avowedly an action in collective self-defence.[104] The United States stressed that 'the request from Honduras *was reported* in the 16 March *press statement* . . . [which was then] circulated a General Assembly and Security Council document. . .'[105] The Honduran request itself, though, was not published, and other states did not seem to take issue with that fact. That it has been relatively common practice for states merely to confirm that a request has been made rather than necessarily disseminating the request itself – and that this has seemingly not been questioned by other states – might further support the idea that 'publicity' is of evidentiary importance rather than being legally necessary in itself.

Overall, as a policy matter, there are both pros and cons to requiring that collective self-defence requests be publicised. This author would err on the side of emphasising the pros, but that does not mean that the cons should be ignored. In any event, as a matter of *law*, it is difficult to establish that publicity is a determinative requirement. Even if it is not, though, it is always worth keeping in mind that the request itself *is* a determinative requirement, meaning that if that request is not publicised at all, then the states in question will have a tricky time evidencing that this requirement has been complied with.

6.5 The Timing of the Request

6.5.1 Ex Post Facto *Requests*

Scholars have argued that a collective self-defence action will be unlawful if the 'request for assistance is made after the intervening State's assistance has commenced'.[106] This position has at times been defended in the

[104] UN Doc. A/42/931-S/19643, n.31, para. 6.

[105] UNSC Provisional Verbatim Record, UN Doc. S/PV.2802 (18 March 1988), 27 (emphasis added).

[106] Avra Constantinou, *The Right of Self-Defence under Customary International Law and Article 51 of the UN Charter* (Brussels, Bruylant, 2000), 180. See also Eustace Chikere Azubuike, 'Probing the Scope of Self Defense in International Law' (2011) 17 *Annual Survey of International and Comparative Law* 129, 180–181; Henderson, n.49, 259; Christine Gray, *International Law and the Use of Force* (Oxford, Oxford University Press, 4th ed., 2018), 185; D. W. Greig, 'Self-Defence and the Security Council: What Does Article 51 Require?' (1991) 40 *International and Comparative Law Quarterly* 366, 378 (albeit making this point conditional on whether a request is in fact legally essential, which he queries).

literature[107] on the basis that for consent to preclude the wrongfulness of an act under the law of state responsibility, it must be given in advance.[108] Strictly speaking, a request for aid in collective self-defence is not the issuance of 'consent'[109] but the analogy here nonetheless seems reasonable. The rationale behind the request requirement – sovereign autonomy and protection against abuse[110] – would surely be undermined if the request is only made *ex post facto*. Retroactive requests raise serious concerns about the 'genuineness' of the request, due to either the possibility of coercion or the installation of a 'puppet' government by the purported defending state.[111]

In the *Nicaragua* case, the ICJ took issue with the fact that – when the United States referenced[112] purported requests by Honduras, Costa Rica, and El Salvador – it gave no indication of when those requests were made.[113] When El Salvador first asserted that it had, more than once, requested aid, this was in the context of its declaration of intervention to the *Nicaragua* proceedings, in August 1984.[114] The Court similarly noted that '[a]gain, no dates [were] given' by El Salvador in its declaration for when these alleged requests occurred,[115] and saw it as telling that, despite a number of obvious opportunities, El Salvador had not previously publicly mentioned that it had requested help.[116] On this basis, the Court concluded that:

> the request of El Salvador, made publicly for the first time in August 1984, do[es] not support the contention that in 1981 there was an armed attack

[107] Constantinou, n.106, 180, footnote 38.

[108] See Text of the Draft Articles on Responsibility of States for Internationally Wrongful Acts, with commentaries, Report of the International Law Commission, 53rd sess., UN Doc. A/56/10 (2001), 73 (commentary to Article 20) ('[c]onsent to the commission of otherwise wrongful conduct may be given by a State in advance or even at the time it is occurring'). Having said this, subsequent consent can act as a form of waiver, precluding a claim: see *ibid*, 121–123 (Article 45 and commentary).

[109] See Chapter 8, nn.48–51 and accompanying text.

[110] See Chapter 4, nn.38–40 and accompanying text.

[111] For example, the collective self-defence claim made by the USSR in 1979 in relation to its intervention in Afghanistan was disputed specifically on this basis. See nn.134–135 and accompanying text; Constantinou, n.106, 180, footnote 37.

[112] *Nicaragua* (counter-memorial of the USA), n.22, vol. II, para. 202.

[113] *Nicaragua* (merits), n.3, paras. 165–166. Indeed, the Court was sceptical about whether such requests had been made at all.

[114] *Nicaragua* (declaration of intervention of El Salvador), n.24, paras. XII, XIV.

[115] *Nicaragua* (merits), n.3, para. 165.

[116] *Ibid*, para. 233.

> capable of serving as a legal foundation for United States activities which began in the second half of that year.[117]

This might suggest that the ICJ was of the view that a timely request was legally required.[118] However, the Court actually stopped short of doing so. This can be seen from the fact that it also stated that:

> while *no strict legal conclusion may be drawn* from the date of El Salvador's . . . official request addressed to the United States concerning the exercise of collective self-defence . . . [that date has] significance as evidence of El Salvador's view of the situation.[119]

As such, the Court in fact took the view that the timing of El Salvador's *public acknowledgement* that it had requested aid was not, in itself, legally determinative. Whether this was because the Court took the view that there is no legal requirement for a prior request, because it could not rule out that an implicit/secret request had been made prior to the use of force (and accepted that such covert requests could satisfy the request requirement),[120] or *both*, is unclear. What is clear, though, is that the Court nonetheless drew negative legal inference from the fact that the first indications by either defending or co-defending that a request had been made came after the United States had used force, at least when this was coupled with the fact that no clear evidence was advanced to establish that such a request had been made (even privately) before that use of force began.

This suggests that the Court may have seen the publicity of requests as evidentiarily important – as was, indeed, argued to be the case in Section 6.4 – and that it also took the same view of the timing of requests. In other words, it appears that the Court was of the view that a 'late' request would *suggest* that a collective self-defence action was unlawful, but that it did not necessarily confirm this. Kritsiotis thus was appropriately cautious in his choice of language when he concluded that 'the Court considered the timing of [a collective self-defence request] to be *of some relevance*'.[121] That much is clear.

The importance of the timing of a collective self-defence request certainly has been a feature of the state practice. For example, in the

[117] *Ibid*, para. 236.
[118] Henderson, n.49, 259–260.
[119] *Nicaragua* (merits), n.3, para. 236 (emphasis added).
[120] See Section 6.4.
[121] Kritsiotis, n.7, 186 (emphasis added). See also Greig, n.106, 378–379.

context of the highly controversial intervention in Hungary by the USSR,[122] it is noteworthy that the relied upon[123] request by Hungary – or, at least, by *one of* the entities claiming to be the de jure government of Hungary at the time[124] – was not made (explicitly, anyway) until 24 October 1956.[125] This was after the Soviet use of force had commenced during the night of 23 October.[126] That the relevant request was issued *ex post facto* was seen by other states as one of the factors that established that the Soviet action was unlawful. Thus, speaking in the Security Council, the representative of France, Mr Cornut-Gentille, stated that:

> there is every reason to believe that the foreign intervention was spontaneous and that it occurred before any appeal was made by the Hungarian Government. Moreover, that appeal was not made until after the night of 23 to 24 October, when the Soviet troops intervened. There was therefore no justification in the Warsaw Pact for their intervention[127]

Making the same point in the opposite direction across the iron curtain, the USSR rejected the United Kingdom's claim[128] to be acting in collective self-defence at the request of Jordan[129] in 1958 – *inter alia* – because it saw Jordan's request itself as being invalid. And a key reason for this was because that request was issued after (or, at least, at exactly the same time as) the United Kingdom's military operation began.[130] The USSR saw this as confirmation that the request was not genuine.

The need for a timely request can also be observed when the positions of the Cold War protagonists were again reversed in relation to the USSR's intervention in Afghanistan, which began in 1979. That action was explicitly justified by the USSR as an act of collective self-defence based on a request by Afghanistan.[131] This was criticised by other states

[122] It is again worth recalling that it is not entirely clear whether the use of force in Hungary was even claimed to be – let alone met the criteria for being – an instance of collective self-defence. However, the USSR at least implicitly made the argument that it was, and various other states assessed it on that basis at the time. See Chapter 4, n.66.

[123] See, for example, UN Doc. S/PV.746, n.45, para. 156.

[124] See Chapter 5, nn.105–115 and accompanying text.

[125] UN Doc. S/PV.746, n.45, para. 156 (USSR, quoting from the Budapest radio broadcast of the request).

[126] See Constantinou, n.106, 180, footnote 38.

[127] UN Doc. S/PV.746, n.45, para. 90.

[128] UN Doc. S/PV.831, n.31, paras. 27–32.

[129] *Ibid*, para. 24.

[130] *Ibid*, paras. 62–64.

[131] UNSC Verbatim Record, UN Doc. S/PV.2186 (5 January 1980), paras. 15–23.

for various reasons, but notably, again, because the request was issued *ex post facto*.[132] Malaysia, for example, stated that:

> [i]t has been claimed that the Soviet troops had been invited into Afghanistan to assist the Government and the people of that country to face alleged interference and provocation by external enemies. ... My delegation finds it difficult to accept such a claim, in the light of available evidence to the contrary, in that the request was made only after, the armed intervention[133]

Indeed, the alleged 'requester' was, in fact, a puppet government that was installed by the USSR as a result of its intervention.[134] As Singapore noted:

> the Soviet Union brought an Afghan, Babrak Karmal, from exile in Eastern Europe and made him the new President of Afghanistan. The *important fact* is that *at the time of the Soviet intervention*, Babrak Karmal was not part of the Government of Afghanistan and therefore had no authority to request the intervention by Soviet troops.[135]

More recently, it is worth noting that Russia's (tentative) claim to be acting in the collective self-defence of South Ossetia[136] was made in relation to a formal request that was issued after – albeit not all that much after – Russia had already begun to use force in Georgian territory. Accounts differ, but Russia's extra-territorial use of force began at some point between 02:00 and 06:00 on 8 August 2008,[137] whereas South Ossetian authorities only formally requested aid at around 11:00 the same day.[138]

Leaving aside the fact that any collective self-claim in this context necessarily failed because South Ossetia was not a state,[139] it is worth noting that some scholars argued that the *ex post facto* nature of the South Ossetian request was an additional confirmation of the

[132] See, for example, UNSC Verbatim Record, UN Doc. S/PV.2187 (6 January 1980), paras. 17, 21 (USA), 61 (Norway), 94–96 (Costa Rica), 119–121.
[133] *Ibid*, para. 87.
[134] Terry, n.69, 139–140.
[135] UN Doc. S/PV.2187, n.132, para. 43 (emphasis added).
[136] See UN Doc. A/63/PV.14, n.42, 2.
[137] IIFFMCG, n.52, vol. II, 230, footnote 2.
[138] *Ibid*, 281.
[139] See Chapter 5, nn.25–37 and accompanying text.

unlawfulness of Russia's use of force in the Caucasus in 2008.[140] As for other states, a number expressed the view that the action was unlawful,[141] but none engaged with the question of the timing of the request specifically. For its part, when examining the legal aspects of the intervention in detail, the IIFFMCG did note in 2009 that the formal request by South Ossetia came a number of hours after the fact.[142] The Mission seemingly was of the view that this delay *would have meant* that the use of force was unlawful,[143] were it not that it also concluded that collective self-defence requests could be inferred,[144] and felt that there was (unspecified) evidence of an implicit Ossetian 'request' prior to the Russian use of force.[145] For the IIFFMCG, it was only the *explicit* request that was issued after the intervention was underway – not necessarily any request – and, thus, any possible requirement of timeliness nevertheless was met.

It is clear that collective self-defence claims have been disputed by other states in the UN era on the ground that the request was issued after the relevant use of force was already underway. It is unclear, however, whether 'late requests' have been viewed – in themselves – as legally terminal for the exercise of collective self-defence, or whether they are commonly taken as part of a wider pattern of evidence that requests were coerced, manufactured, or issued by an inappropriate authority. It is worth noting that all of the relevant examples discussed in this subsection were legally controversial on other grounds too, which hardly helps one to try to unpick their implications for tardy requesting specifically.

This author is of the view that, on balance, the timeliness of requests is viewed as a fundamental matter for states, which indicates that if the request is not issued until after the use of force is underway, then it simply *will not meet* the request requirement and, thus, the action purportedly taken in collective self-defence will be unlawful. There are

140 See, for example, Alexander Lott, 'The Tagliavini Report Revisited: *Jus ad Bellum* and the Legality of the Russian Intervention in Georgia' (2012) 28 *Merkourios – International and European Security Law* 4, 13.

141 See, for example, UNSC Verbatim Record, UN Doc. S/PV.5961 (19 August 2008), 9–10 (UK); UN Doc. A/63/PV.14, n.42, 32 (Czech Republic); Statement of President George W. Bush, video link, *BBC News* (11 August 2008), http://news.bbc.co.uk/2/hi/europe/7554507.stm.

142 IIFFMCG, n.52, vol. II, 281.

143 *Ibid.*

144 *Ibid*, 280–281. See Section 6.4.

145 IIFFMCG, n.52, vol. II, 281.

also policy reasons to support a mandatory timeliness element so that the request requirement serves the purposes that it is supposed to serve.

However, this reading is certainly open to challenge. Even if it is correct that a timely request is not only evidentiarily important but legally mandatory, that is not the end of the story. This is because, as already has been argued, it appears that implicit and even covert 'requests' may be permissible as a matter of law – albeit that they are problematic in terms of evidencing that the request requirement has been met.[146] In this regard, the present author is inclined to concur with the IIFFMCG to the effect that a request *must* occur prior to the use of force commencing, but that this need not – as a strict legal matter – be an explicit, public request. However, a legally determinative timeliness requirement is undoubtedly extremely difficult to apply in practice if it can be complied with in secret. Again, then, the line between legal requirements and evidencing legal requirements becomes effectively blurred in the context of collective self-defence requests.

6.5.2 Ex-Ante *Requests*

It was tentatively argued in the previous subsection that the defending state's request for aid in collective self-defence must have been issued before force is used by the co-defending state. However, another question relating to the 'timeliness' of the request is whether there is any limitation on *how long* before. More specifically, one might ask whether a pre-existing collective self-defence treaty commitment is, in the abstract, sufficient to amount to the necessary 'request' for force to be used in collective self-defence once an armed attack occurs against a party to the relevant treaty. Sari and Nasu, for example, have suggested that a pre-existing collective self-defence treaty arrangement might, itself, 'not only impose an *obligation*' on the defending state but also establish for it 'a *right* to take forcible action without the need for a specific . . . request to this effect' from the defending state.[147] In other words, they consider that a standing *ex-ante* 'request' is sufficient.[148]

In contrast, it has been convincingly argued that 'military assistance on request' requires more than just a general *ex-ante* authorising treaty:

[146] See Sections 6.3 and 6.4.

[147] Aurel Sari and Hitoshi Nasu, 'Collective Self-Defense and the "Bloody Nose Strategy": Does It Take Two to Tango?', *Just Security* (26 January 2018), www.justsecurity.org/51435/collective-self-defense-bloody-nose-strategy-tango (emphasis in original).

[148] See also Morrison, n.36, 163 (taking the same view, at least by implication).

additional *ad hoc* consent is necessary in relation to the specific use of force in question.[149] The recurring caveats in this book about using caution in analogising collective self-defence and military assistance on request again apply here,[150] but, in this context, the analogy seems appropriate. As a matter of policy in both instances, requiring a targeted *ad hoc* request aims to protect against abuse. Indeed, it would seem even more important in regard to collective self-defence that a request be issued specific to the circumstances in question, because – unlike military assistance on request – collective self-defence is both 1) necessarily premised on the occurrence of a *particular* armed attack and 2) can allow for the use of force on the territory of a *non-consenting* state.

State practice also suggests that the existence of a collective self-defence treaty arrangement will not be sufficient to constitute a 'request' in itself. Indeed, it will be recalled that some such treaties explicitly indicate that the obligation of mutual defence that they set out is only triggered by the request of the attacked state.[151] This obviously demonstrates that at least *those* treaties are insufficient evidence of a 'request' in themselves. It equally will be recalled, though, that there are (or have been) more collective self-defence treaties that do not include any reference to a request requirement than there are such treaties that do.[152] The North Atlantic Treaty Organization (NATO)[153] falls into the latter group, as did the now defunct Warsaw Pact.[154]

It is telling, therefore, that, in relation to its intervention in Hungary in 1956, the USSR explicitly argued that it was acting in collective self-defence under the auspices of the Warsaw Pact, while also accepting that an additional request from Hungary was a necessary requirement.[155]

[149] Erika de Wet, 'Military Assistance Based on *Ex-Ante* Consent: A Violation of Article 2 (4) UN Charter?' (2020) 93 *Die Friedens-Warte* 413.

[150] See Chapter 8 for more detail.

[151] See Chapter 4, nn.46–48 and accompanying text. Examples include the Inter-American Treaty of Reciprocal Assistance (1948) 21 UNTS 77 (Rio Treaty), Article 3(2) and the Southeast Asia Collective Defense Treaty (with Protocol) (SEATO Treaty) (1954) 209 UNTS 28, Article IV(3).

[152] See Chapter 4, n.49 and accompanying text.

[153] North Atlantic Treaty (1949) 34 UNTS 243, Articles 4 and 5.

[154] Treaty of Friendship, Cooperation and Mutual Assistance between the People's Republic of Albania, the People's Republic of Bulgaria, the Hungarian People's Republic, the German Democratic Republic, the Polish People's Republic, the Romanian People's Republic (1955) 219 UNTS 24 (Warsaw Pact), Article 4.

[155] See Quincy Wright, 'United States Intervention in the Lebanon' (1959) 53 *American Journal of International Law* 112, 119.

Indeed, it made this point in the abstract in relation to any use of force taken under the banner of the Pact:

> [T]he Soviet Government proceeds from the general principle that the stationing of troops of one state that is a party to the Warsaw Pact ... [must be] with the agreement of the state on whose territory these troops are stationed or are planned to be stationed *at its request*.[156]

In a similar vein, during the months leading up to it joining NATO in 1949, and then during the initial years of its membership, Norway received a series of notes from the USSR (which sought to deter Norwegian integration with the Western bloc). With the aim of easing Soviet fears, Norway responded on more than one occasion by making it clear that – NATO membership notwithstanding – any foreign military action on or from Norwegian territory could only be actioned if Norway had first suffered an armed attack *and* had expressly and contextually requested aid from other NATO states.[157] Although these responses were not entirely satisfactory for the USSR, it did not take issue with Norway's reading of the request requirement in the NATO context, only with the implications of that reading for Soviet security.[158] Similarly, other NATO states did not appear to dispute Norway's assertion of the necessity of an additional *ad hoc* request.

Thus, even where the collective self-defence treaty in question is silent on the need for a request, it seems relatively clear that an additional ad hoc request is required.[159] Given the conclusions in previous sections, as a matter of law, this perhaps can be implicit or even private. Nevertheless, an additional ad hoc request must be made, and it must be temporally proximate to, and linked to, the armed attack being responded to. This tallies with the equivalent requirement for military assistance on request and is – this author would contend – desirable from a policy perspective.

156 Soviet Statement on Hungary, Moscow Radio, 30 October 1956, transcript available at https://soviethistory.msu.edu/1956-2/hungarian-crisis/hungarian-crisis-texts/soviet-statement-on-hungary.

157 See Robert K. German, 'Norway and the Bear: Soviet Coercive Diplomacy and Norwegian Security Policy' (1982) 7 *International Security* 55, 59–60; Wright, n.155, 119; John van Oudenaren, *Détente in Europe: The Soviet Union and the West since 1953* (Durham, Duke University Press, 1991), 113.

158 See van Oudenaren, n.157.

159 Kevin Jon Heller, 'The Unlawfulness of a "Bloody Nose Strike" on North Korea' (2020) 96 *International Law Studies* 1, 16–17; Craig Martin, 'Japan's Definition of Armed Attack and "Bloody Nose" Strikes against North Korea', *Just Security* (1 February 2018), www.justsecurity.org/51678/japans-definition-armed-attack-bloody-nose-strikes-north-korea.

6.6 Conclusion

This chapter has engaged with questions related to the manner and form of collective self-defence requests. It argued, first, that the request need not be directed specifically at the state or states that ultimately respond to it: requests can be an 'open call' for aid in response to an armed attack. It was then concluded that there is no required format for collective self-defence requests, with these having been issued in a range of ways during the UN era. Similarly, there are no particular formalities required.

Perhaps more controversially, it was then concluded that – at least as a legal matter – it may be possible for the 'request' to be inferred and even for it to be entirely private. However, given that the occurrence of a request itself is legally essential, where the request is not explicit, there will be significant difficulties for the co-defending state in establishing that the request requirement has been complied with. Clear, explicit, public requests are preferable both on policy grounds and as a procedural matter. It is worth noting that they are also the norm in practice. None of which establishes that such elements are legally essential.

This chapter further argues that the request must be issued before the relevant use of force commences (albeit that this requirement is complicated by the possibility of it being complied with implicitly or covertly). It was also noted herein that a pre-existing *ex-ante* request in a collective defence treaty is insufficient to comply with the request requirement. The request must be *ad hoc* and specific to the armed attack that it relates to.

It is worth noting that the lack of clarity in the state practice has meant that many of the conclusions reached in this chapter are necessarily tentative, and it is acknowledged that alternative credible readings are in some instances possible. Nonetheless, the overall picture that emerges is one where a great deal of flexibility can be observed in the way that collective self-defence requests are made and received. The need for a request (or some form of approval) by the defending state is clearly crucial to the lawfulness of collective self-defence, but *how that is established* is much less so. This flexibility has benefits in terms of prioritising the reason that requests are required rather than unnecessary procedure or formality relating to them. Equally, though, it has negative implications for certainty when it comes to the legal assessment of a purported collective self-defence action.

7

Collective Self-Defence Treaty Arrangements

7.1 Introduction

Collective defence treaty arrangements have existed throughout recorded history.[1] Despite the changes to the concept of collective self-defence that were occasioned by the adoption of the United Nations (UN) Charter in 1945,[2] it did not remove the long-standing power for states to enter into these arrangements.[3] Indeed, it will be recalled from Chapter 2 that Article 51 was designed precisely to ensure that states retained the ability to maintain and create such treaty relationships under the new UN collective security system.[4]

It will also be recalled that there was a notable influx in the number of collective defence treaties in the interwar years and during the Second World War itself.[5] This trend continued after the adoption of the Charter too: in fact, the first two decades immediately following the war saw an even greater explosion in the number of such treaties being concluded.[6] Although fewer collective self-defence treaty arrangements have emerged since that initial 'burst' at the start of the UN era, there has nonetheless been a steady flow of them, which has continued after the end of the Cold

[1] See Chapter 2, especially Section 2.2.

[2] See Section 2.4.

[3] Louis Henkin, 'The Use of Force: Law and US Policy', in *Right v. Might* (New York, Council on Foreign Relations Press, 1991), 45 ('[i]t is generally accepted . . . that states are permitted to organize themselves in advance in bona fide collective self-defense arrangements (such as the North Atlantic Treaty Organization) for possible response if one of the members should become the victim of an armed attack'); UNGA Summary Record, UN Doc. A/C.6/SR.877 (1 April 1966), para. 7 (United Arab Republic).

[4] See Section 2.4.

[5] See Chapter 2, n.57 and accompanying text.

[6] Ian Brownlie, *International Law and the Use of Force by States* (Oxford, Oxford University Press, 1963), 328 ('[s]ince 1945 . . . treaties providing for mutual assistance, primarily in the form of military aid in case of unlawful use of force against a party, have been numerous'). See also *ibid*, 129–127 (providing a list of forty-nine relevant treaties created between 1945 and 1961).

War[7] right through the Covid-19 pandemic.[8] As such, there are now hundreds of collective self-defence treaty arrangements.[9]

This chapter maps the collective self-defence treaty arrangements that have emerged since 1945. The aim is not to be comprehensive as to the coverage of these arrangements – there are far too many of them for that to be worthwhile, and the exercise would just descend into a (long) list. Instead, the intent here is to refer to examples to draw out common themes as to the nature, process, and role of such arrangements, as well as to establish notable variations. In so doing, this chapter seeks to contribute an overall picture of collective self-defence today specifically in the context of treaty relationships.

Section 7.2 highlights the variety of collective self-defence treaty arrangements that have emerged in the UN era. Section 7.3 then considers the nature and scope of the obligations that these arrangements place upon their parties. It first sets these arrangements within the context of the collective security system created by the UN Charter. The section then assesses the implications of variations in the trigger (*casus fœderis*) employed within different treaties and notes the common (but not universal) feature of reciprocity inherent in these arrangements. The argument is then made that the obligations contained within collective self-defence treaty arrangements are invariably 'soft' in nature, leaving a great deal of scope for parties to avoid having to commit forces in collective self-defence should the relevant treaty arrangement's *casus*

[7] See, for example, Collective Security Treaty (1992), *Collective Security Treaty Organisation* (23 April 2012), https://en.odkb-csto.org/documents/documents/dogovor_o_kollektivnoy_bezopasnosti/#loaded; Treaty Establishing the Regional Security System (1996), RSS, www.rss.org.bb/wp-content/uploads/2020/02/Treaty-Establishing-the-RSS-.pdf (RSS Treaty); Southern African Development Community (SADC) Mutual Defence Pact (2003) 3156 UNTS, Article 15(4); African Union Non-Aggression and Common Defence Pact (2005), African Union, https://au.int/sites/default/files/treaties/37292-treaty-0031_-_african_union_non-aggression_and_common_defence_pact_e.pdf (AU Pact), Article 4; Consolidated Version of the Treaty on European Union (2007), reproduced in (2008) *OJ* C115/13 (TEU), Article 42(7).

[8] See, for example, Agreement between the Government of the Hellenic Republic and the Government of the French Republic establishing a strategic partnership for cooperation in defence and security (2021), titled in the authoritative French as 'un partenariat stratégique pour la coopération en matière de défense et de sécurité', www.hellenicparliament.gr/Nomothetiko-Ergo/Anazitisi-Nomothetikou-Ergou?law_id=50f9990e-73f6-4015-b706-adb4013e7514) (Greek and French texts only: the treaty has not been translated into English) (Greek–French Treaty).

[9] See Christine Gray, *International Law and the Use of Force* (Oxford, Oxford University Press, 4th ed., 2018), 176, footnote 277.

fœderis occur. Some of the problems that have emerged from the network of such arrangements are examined in Section 7.4, which engages with 'overlapping memberships' and tensions within collective self-defence organisations. Section 7.5 then examines geographical limitations that are often self-imposed by collective self-defence bodies, as well as considering the distinction between 'collective self-defence arrangements' on the one hand and 'regional arrangements' as regulated by Chapter VIII of the UN Charter on the other. Finally, the role and, ultimately, *value* of collective self-defence treaty arrangements are analysed in Section 7.6.

7.2 The Variety of Collective Self-Defence Treaty Arrangements

The creation of collective self-defence treaty arrangements has been a 'very widespread practice among States of differing ideology and geographical location'.[10] That diversity is reflected in the fact that there is no single 'approach' taken by states with regard to the collective self-defence treaty arrangements that they have developed, meaning that a 'patchwork' of differing, and, at times, overlapping, collective self-defence relationships exist today. Modern collective treaty arrangements come in innumerable forms and shapes.

Some collective self-defence treaty arrangements have, for example, created major international organisations, such as the North Atlantic Treaty Organization (NATO). In other instances, collective self-defence merely forms one point of focus for an organisation or initiative that has a much wider remit.[11] This has at times been 'built in' from the start; such was the case with the 1981 Treaty Establishing the Organisation of Eastern Caribbean States (OECS), albeit that it only listed 'mutual defence and security' as one of eighteen different areas that fell under the auspices of the new organisation.[12] In contrast, existing organisations, not previously having had any collective self-defence focus, sometimes later venture into that realm. One might note the South African Development Community (SADC) as an example. SADC emerged from the Southern African Development Coordination Conference in

10 Terry D. Gill, 'The Second Gulf Crisis and the Relation between Collective Security and Collective Self-Defense' (1989) 10 *Grotiana* 47, 71–72.

11 Jaemin Lee, 'Collective Self-Defense or Collective Security: Japan's Reinterpretation of Article 9 of the Constitution' (2015) 8 *Journal of East Asia and International Law* 373, 387.

12 Treaty Establishing the Organization of Eastern Caribbean States (1981) 20 ILM 1166 (OECS Treaty), Article 3(2)(q).

1992 and then – more than a decade later – developed its 2003 Mutual Defence Pact, establishing that one aspect of the organisation's function was to act as a collective self-defence body (which hardly can be said to have been SADC's original *raison d'être*). Another example here is the European Union (EU). The European Union only evolved to adopt something that could truly be considered a 'collective self-defence' provision with the Treaty of Lisbon in 2007,[13] and collective self-defence still remains a relatively small point of focus for the organisation.[14] Given examples of this kind, it is worth noting that the use of the label 'collective self-defence treaty *arrangements*' in this chapter (rather than just 'collective self-defence *treaties*') is deliberate. Many such arrangements are to be found in provisions *within* treaties that cannot correctly be described as 'collective self-defence treaties' *ut totum*.[15] Alongside multilateral collective self-defence organisations and alliances (large and small) exist hundreds of bilateral treaties establishing more specific arrangements.[16] Such bilateral agreements have continued to emerge throughout the UN era, from the Treaty of Dunkirk between the United Kingdom and France in 1947[17] to the alliance treaty between Greece and France in 2021.[18]

Faced with such a plethora of collective self-defence treaty arrangements, Dinstein has sought to impose some conceptual order by drawing a distinction between what he calls 'mutual assistance treaties' and

13 TEU, n.7, Article 42(7).

14 See Sia Spiliopoulou Åkermark, 'The Puzzle of Collective Self-Defence: Dangerous Fragmentation or a Window of Opportunity? An Analysis with Finland and the Åland Islands as a Case Study' (2017) 22 *Journal of Conflict and Security Law* 249, 259–263.

15 It is also perhaps worth noting that occasionally states reach explicitly non-binding agreements that – aside from their lack of binding status – otherwise are very similar to collective self-defence treaty arrangements. See, for example, Declaration of the Inviolability of Frontiers, annexed to Letter dated 10 August 1993 from the representatives of the Permanent Missions of Kazakhstan, Kyrgyzstan, the Russian Federation, and Tajikistan to the United Nations addressed to the Secretary-General, UN Doc. A/48/304 (11 August 1993) (signed by Russia, Kazakhstan, Kyrgyzstan, Tajikistan, and Uzbekistan).

16 Gray, n.9, 176, footnote 277 (there are ... hundreds of bilateral treaties that provide for collective self-defence); Avra Constantinou, *The Right of Self-Defence under Customary International Law and Article 51 of the UN Charter* (Brussels, Bruylant, 2000), 174.

17 Treaty of Alliance and Mutual Assistance between His Majesty in respect of the United Kingdom of Great Britain and Northern Ireland and the President of the French Republic (1947) 9 UNTS 121 (Treaty of Dunkirk).

18 Greek–French Treaty, n.8.

'military alliances'.[19] The former – which can be multilateral or bilateral in nature – are described as treaties that set out a mutual obligation whereby when one party is attacked, the other(s) will come to its aid. Military alliances do the same, but go further, moving 'beyond an abstract commitment for mutual assistance in the event of an armed attack'.[20] The key distinction is that, in so doing, military alliances also require their member states to take active steps of preparedness. For example, such alliances often develop much more sophisticated and integrated architecture for collective self-defence (such as, say, creating an integrated high command).[21] They also may well include features like a standing organisational structure,[22] a standing deployment of forces[23] and/or shared bases.[24] 'Military alliances' therefore perhaps can be thought of as 'military assistance treaties *plus*'.

The distinction that Dinstein makes between these two categories is descriptively valuable, as it illustrates notable differences between existing collective self-defence treaty relationships, as well as features that are common between some of them. Equally, the distinction is quite artificial. In practice, the line between 'mutual assistance treaties' and 'military alliances' is blurred, with some arrangements being difficult to place in one category or another with any certainty. The Security Treaty between

[19] Yoram Dinstein, *War, Aggression and Self-Defence* (Cambridge, Cambridge University Press, 6th ed., 2017), 306–312.

[20] *Ibid*, 309.

[21] See, for example, Treaty of Economic, Social and Cultural Collaboration and Collective Self-Defence (1948), as Amended by the 'Protocol Modifying and Completing the Brussels Treaty' (1954), FO 1093/575 (Western European Union Treaty/WEU Treaty), Protocol No. II on Forces of Western European Union (1954). See also Thomas M. Franck, 'Who Killed Article 2(4)? or Changing the Norms Governing the Use of Force by States' (1970) 64 *American Journal of International Law* 809, 829 (discussing the integrated high commands of NATO and the Warsaw Pact).

[22] See, for example, Anatoliy A. Rozanov and Alena F. Douhan, *Collective Security Treaty Organisation, 2002–2012* (Geneva/Minsk, The Geneva Centre fort the Democratic Control of Armed Forces, 2013), 47–48 (discussing the CSTO Permanent Council).

[23] See, for example, 'NATO Response Force', *North Atlantic Treaty Organisation* (last updated 11 July 2022), www.nato.int/cps/en/natolive/topics_49755.htm; Alan Johnston, 'Arab League Agrees to Create Joint Military Force', *BBC News* (29 March 2015), www.bbc.co.uk/news/world-middle-east-32106939. See also John S. Gibson, 'Article 51 of the Charter of the United Nations' (1957) 13 *India Quarterly* 121, 136 (discussing the standing forces – at least as they were at the end of the 1950s – across a number of different collective self-defence organisations).

[24] See, for example, Jan Eichler, *NATO's Expansion after the Cold War: Geopolitics and Impacts for International Security* (Cham, Springer, 2021), 103 (discussing NATO shared bases).

Australia, New Zealand and the United States of America (ANZUS Treaty)[25] serves as an example. It created *some* elements of an integrated infrastructure – such as a standing Council, 'organized as to be able to meet at any time'[26] – but stopped well short of including many of the other features that Dinstein identifies as characteristic of military alliances. It is also the case that, as Dinstein himself notes,[27] states certainly do not make it clear that any given agreement represents one 'type' of arrangement or the other: 'mutual assistance treaties' and 'military alliances' are not terms of art.[28] The reality of collective self-defence treaty arrangements is perhaps better conceived of as a spectrum of agreements of various sorts rather than as falling into two neat categories.

That this 'spectrum' exists perhaps should not be surprising, because pros and cons can be observed at all of the points along it. For example, the more sophisticated a collective self-defence arrangement is, the better placed it should be to respond quickly and effectively to an armed attack: the infrastructure, operational alignment, and resources all will be in place for a coordinated response at scale. Equally, virtually all large multilateral defence arrangements include some form of consultation requirement,[29] and some have centralised consensus decision-making.[30] While such processes provide important checks and balances, they are also inevitably bureaucratic, which can lead to delays and deadlock.[31] For example, it has been argued that the nature of NATO decision-making by consensus means that a single member can veto any action being taken under Article 5 even if all other member states were willing to respond to

[25] Security Treaty between Australia, New Zealand, and the United States of America (1952) 131 UNTS 83 (ANZUS Treaty)

[26] *Ibid*, Article VII.

[27] Dinstein, n.19, 310.

[28] Having said this, these terms were used as terms of art by the UN Secretary-General in 1952, in his report on aggression. See 'Question of Defining Aggression', Report by the Secretary-General, UN Doc. A/2211 (3 October 1952), para. 171.

[29] Derek W. Bowett, *Self-Defense in International Law* (Manchester, Manchester University Press, 1958), 224; Leland M. Goodrich, Anne Patricia Simons and Edvard Hambro, *Charter of the United Nations: Commentary and Documents* (New York, Columbia University Press, 3rd ed., 1969), 351.

[30] See, for example, 'Consensus Decision-Making at NATO', *North Atlantic Treaty Organisation* (last updated 14 June 2022), www.nato.int/cps/en/natohq/topics_49178.htm.

[31] Dinstein, n.19, 308; Bruno Tertrais, 'Article 5 of the Washington Treaty: Its Origins, Meaning and Future' (2016) *NATO Defense College*, Research Paper No. 130, 5, 8 (discussing NATO specifically).

the armed attack in question.[32] One might also note Article 8 of the OECS treaty, which required the unanimous decision of the organisation's Defence and Security Committee before any collective self-defence action could be taken under the auspices of the organisation.[33] Concern over the restrictive nature of OECS security decision-making was a driver in the adoption of a subsequent collective self-defence treaty arrangement in the Caribbean in 1996: the Treaty Establishing the Regional Security System (RSS).[34] The RSS avoided unanimous decision-making[35] and was explicit that the decision to take collective self-defence measures was vested in individual members,[36] but it retained consultation obligations.[37]

A less integrated arrangement of this sort provides valuable flexibility, as well as costing the parties less than taking more sophisticated and permanent steps towards preparedness. However, these advantages come with increased scope for parties to shirk their obligations under the treaty in question when push comes to shove – as will be discussed in the next section. In any event, it may ultimately be said that the considerable variety that can be observed across the extensive network of 'collective self-defence treaty arrangements' that now exist[38] is a result of different needs (or perceived needs) on the part of the states party, and choices they have made about the pros and cons of different approaches.

7.3 The Nature and Strength of the Obligations within Collective Self-Defence Treaty Arrangements

7.3.1 The Subordination of Collective Self-Defence Treaty Arrangements to the UN Collective Security System

While states retain a good deal of freedom to design their collective self-defence treaty arrangements as they wish – resulting in the variety

[32] Zbigniew Brzezinski, 'An Agenda for NATO – Toward a Global Security Web' (2009) 88 *Foreign Affairs* 2, 15. Of course, this would not preclude those states from acting in collective self-defence (individually or collectively) outside the framework of NATO (subject to the lawful requirements for such action being met).

[33] OECS Treaty, n.12, Article 8.

[34] RSS Treaty, n.7.

[35] *Ibid*, Article 6(1).

[36] *Ibid*, Article 4(5).

[37] *Ibid*, Article 4(4).

[38] Christine Chinkin and Mary Kaldor, *International Law and New Wars* (Cambridge, Cambridge University Press, 2017), 140.

discussed in the previous section – it is ultimately the case that all such arrangements must stay within the legal parameters afforded to them by the UN collective security system. The primacy of the UN Charter in relation to other legal obligations is famously articulated by Article 103, which provides:

> In the event of a conflict between the obligations of the Members of the United Nations under the present Charter and their obligations under any other international agreement, their obligations under the present Charter shall prevail.[39]

For collective self-defence treaty arrangements, this means, as the representative of the United Arab Republic stated at a meeting of the UN General Assembly in 1965, that states are entitled to:

> strengthen their security by means of mutual assistance agreements *concluded in accordance with the Charter* and in observance of their international obligations. Likewise, common defence arrangements [are] lawful as long as they [are] ... *in accordance with the provisions of the Charter.*[40]

Put differently, *all* collective self-defence treaty arrangements 'are ultimately grounded in Article 51 of the United Nations Charter'.[41] The requirements for the lawful exercise of collective self-defence, as examined in Chapters 3–6, must be complied with by collective self-defence organisations just as in instances involving the ad hoc exercise of the right.[42] Alliances do not acquire any greater legal freedom in this regard than is possessed by their members.[43]

[39] Charter of the United Nations (1945) 1 UNTS XVI (UN Charter), Article 103.

[40] UN Doc. A/C.6/SR.877, n.3, para. 7 (emphasis added). See also Bruno Simma, 'NATO, the UN and the Use of Force: Legal Aspects' (1999) 10 *European Journal of International Law* 1, 19; Bowett, n.29, 225; Nicholas Tsagourias and Nigel D. White, *Collective Security: Theory, Law and Practice* (Cambridge, Cambridge University Press, 2013), 125.

[41] Ruth C. Lawson, *International Regional Organizations: Constitutional Foundations* (New York, Praeger, 1962), vi. See also Goodrich, Simons and Hambro, n.29, 350. It is worth noting that force can otherwise be used by regional arrangements or agencies, in the form of an 'enforcement action' under UN Charter, n.39, Article 53, but this is distinct from the exercise of collective self-defence and is lawful only with the authorisation of the Security Council. See Section 7.5.2.

[42] Alexander Orakhelashvili, *Peremptory Norms in International Law* (Oxford, Oxford University Press, 2006), 76; Lee, n.11, 384; Tsagourias and White, n.40, 130; Aurel Sari, 'The Mutual Assistance Clauses of the North Atlantic and EU Treaties: The Challenge of Hybrid Threats' (2019) 10 *Harvard National Security Journal* 405, 412, 453.

[43] See Roda Mushkat, 'Who May Wage War – An Examination of an Old/New Question' (1987) 2 *American University Journal of International Law and Policy* 97, 148; Simma, n.40, 19 (making this point specifically in relation to NATO).

As a result, the drafters of post-Charter collective self-defence treaty provisions have been at pains to signpost their deference to the UN system. The vast majority of such arrangements[44] have 'expressly subordinated themselves to the Charter of the United Nations'.[45] The Warsaw Pact, for example, was clear that action taken under its Article 4 involved collective self-defence 'in accordance with Article 51 of the Charter of the United Nations Organization'.[46] Article 5 of the North Atlantic Treaty employs near-identical wording,[47] as does Article 4 of the Collective

[44] See, for example, Treaty of Dunkirk, n.17, Article II; Inter-American Treaty of Reciprocal Assistance (1948) 21 UNTS 77 (Rio Treaty), Article 3(1); ANZUS Treaty, n.25, Article VII; Treaty of Joint Defense and Economic Cooperation between the States of the Arab League (1950), text available at *The Avalon Project*, https://avalon.law.yale.edu/20th_century/arabjoin.asp, Article 2; Mutual Defense Treaty between the Republic of the Philippines and the United States of America (1951) 177 UNTS 133, Article I; WEU Treaty, n.21, Article V; Treaty of Alliance, Political Cooperation, and Mutual Assistance Between the Turkish Republic, the Kingdom of Greece, and the Federal People's Republic of Yugoslavia (1954), *The Avalon Project*, https://avalon.law.yale.edu/20th_century/eu002.asp (Balkan Pact) Article II; Pact of Mutual Cooperation Between the Kingdom of Iraq, the Republic of Turkey, the United Kingdom, the Dominion of Pakistan, and the Kingdom of Iran (1955), *The Avalon Project*, https://avalon.law.yale.edu/20th_century/baghdad.asp (Baghdad Pact); SADC Pact, n.7, Article 15(4); TEU, n.7, Article 42(7); Greek–French Treaty, n.8, Article 2.

[45] Dinstein, n.19, 312 (making this point specifically regarding NATO and the Warsaw Pact). See also Christian Henderson, *The Use of Force and International Law* (Cambridge, Cambridge University Press, 2018), 103 (arguing that collective self-defence organisations are not framed as an alternative to the UN framework to the point that their constituting treaties usually explicitly 'expressed allegiance to the UN framework of collective security'); C. H. M. Waldock, 'The Regulation of the Use of Force by Individual States in International Law' (1952) 81 *Recueil des cours* 451, 504; Hans Kelsen, 'The Future of Collective Security' (1951) 21 *Revista Juridica de la Universidad de Puerto Rico* 83, 86; M. A. Weightman, 'Self-Defense in International Law' (1951) 37 *Virginia Law Review* 1095, 1112, 1114; Gill, n.10, 49; Eustace Chikere Azubuike, 'Probing the Scope of Self Defense in International Law' (2011) 17 *Annual Survey of International and Comparative Law* 129, 175; A. L. Goodhart, 'The North Atlantic Treaty of 1949' (1951) 79 *Recueil des cours* 182, 219 (making this point specifically in relation to NATO); Åkermark, n.14, 262 (making this point specifically in relation to NATO); Zia Modabber, 'Collective Self-Defense: *Nicaragua v. United States*' (1988) 10 *Loyola of Los Angeles International and Comparative Law Journal* 449, 457 (making this point specifically in relation to the Rio Treaty); Bowett, n.29, 227 (making this point specifically in relation to the Warsaw Pact); Simma, n.40, 3 (making this point specifically in relation to NATO).

[46] Treaty of Friendship, Cooperation and Mutual Assistance between the People's Republic of Albania, the People's Republic of Bulgaria, the Hungarian People's Republic, the German Democratic Republic, the Polish People's Republic, the Romanian People's Republic (1955) 219 UNTS 24 (Warsaw Pact), Article 4.

[47] North Atlantic Treaty (1949) 34 UNTS 243, Article 5 (providing for the 'exercise of … collective self-defence recognised by Article 51 of the Charter of the United Nations'). See

Security Treaty Organisation (CSTO)'s founding treaty from 1992.[48] The drafters of the Southeast Asia Treaty Organisation (SEATO)'s constituent treaty went even further, grandly proclaiming its members' 'faith in the purposes and principles set forth in the Charter of the United Nations'.[49]

It is worth stressing that the explicit deference to the UN collective security system found across the majority of collective self-defence treaty arrangements is, by virtue of a combination of Articles 2(4), 51, 53, and 103 of the UN Charter,[50] ultimately declaratory.[51] It might be noted that in the early years of the UN era, some collective self-defence treaties did not acknowledge their subordination to the UN system. This was the case, for example, with both the 1947 Treaty of Brotherhood and Alliance between Iraq and Transjordan[52] and the 1950 Sino-Soviet Treaty of Friendship, Alliance and Mutual Assistance.[53] Neither of these treaties made any mention of the United Nations, and they also did not replicate any of the 'language' of the Charter so as to implicitly indicate that they operated within its terms. Yet, such silence on the matter does not change the fact that treaty provisions legally cannot provide for the use of force absent the requirements for collective self-defence being fulfilled (unless authorisation from the Security Council is forthcoming). This has not stopped the general trend towards proclaiming conformity with the Charter, though: indeed, the failure to do so appears to be a historic phenomenon from the initial post-war years. The now ubiquitous trend

also *ibid*, Article 7 ('[t]his Treaty does not affect, and shall not be interpreted as affecting in any way the rights and obligations under the Charter of the Parties which are members of the United Nations, or the primary responsibility of the Security Council for the maintenance of international peace and security'); UNGA Summary Record, UN Doc. A/C.1/SR.596 (10 April 1953), para. 7 (USA, arguing that there is 'no conflict between the purposes of the United Nations and those of NATO. It was, and would continue to be, the duty of free nations to encourage regional defence pacts in conformity with the Purposes and Principles of the United Nations Charter').

48 Collective Security Treaty, n.7, Article 4 ('. . . in accordance with the right to collective defence pursuant to article 51 of the UN Charter').

49 Southeast Asia Collective Defense Treaty (with Protocol) (1954) 209 UNTS 28 (SEATO Treaty), preamble. For discussion, see John Norton Moore and James L. Underwood, 'The Lawfulness of United States Assistance to the Republic of Viet Nam' (1966) 5 *Duquesne Law Review* 235, 305–308.

50 Tsagourias and White, n.40, 131.

51 Bowett, n.29, 224.

52 Treaty of Brotherhood and Alliance (Iraq/Transjordan) (1947) 23 UNTS 345.

53 Treaty of Friendship, Alliance and Mutual Assistance (China/USSR) (1950), reproduced in (1950) 44 *Supplement to the American Journal of International Law* 83.

to announce deference to the UN system presumably has been adopted to avoid any possible suggestion to the contrary.[54]

7.3.2 *The* Casus Fœderis *for Collective Self-Defence Treaty Arrangements*

Collective defence agreements prior to 1945 contained a range of different triggers for their operation, with no standard *casus fœderis* emerging in practice.[55] In contrast, the need for modern agreements to defer to the UN Charter system, as discussed in the previous subsection, has meant that there has been much more standardisation, with a notable majority of agreements mirroring Article 51 in setting their activating trigger as the occurrence of an 'armed attack'.[56]

However, there still has not been complete consistency in this regard in the UN era.[57] Just a few examples are sufficient to show this. The 1978 Treaty of Friendship and Co-operation between Vietnam and the USSR went simply for 'attack' (dropping the 'armed' qualifier).[58] Article 42(7) of the Treaty on European Union (TEU), introduced in 2007, designates 'armed aggression' as the relevant *casus fœderis* for EU members to act in collective self-defence.[59] The Economic Community of West African States (ECOWAS) Protocol relating to Mutual Assistance on Defence from 1981, for its part, is notably open ended, setting the trigger as '*any* armed *threat* or aggression'.[60]

[54] Bowett, n.29, 224.

[55] See Chapter 2, nn.30–34 and accompanying text; *ibid*, nn.63–75 and accompanying text.

[56] See, for example, North Atlantic Treaty, n.47, Article 5; Treaty of Dunkirk, n.17, Article II; Rio Treaty, n.44, Article 3(1); Agreement of Friendship, Cooperation, and Mutual Assistance between The Union of Soviet Socialist Republics and The Republic of Finland (1948) 48 UNTS 149 (Finno–Soviet Treaty), Article 1; WEU Treaty, n.21, Article V; Warsaw Pact, n.46, Article 4; Mutual Defense Treaty (Philippines/USA), n.44, Article IV; SEATO Treaty, n.49, Article IV(1); ANZUS Treaty, n.25, Article IV; SADC Pact, n.7, Article 6(1).

[57] See, for example, UN Doc. A/2211, n.28, paras. 177–201 (providing a list of various different triggers found in treaties agreed up to 1952 – this includes pre-Charter treaties, but also a large number drafted following the adoption of the Charter); Bowett, n.29, 225.

[58] Treaty of Friendship and Co-operation between the Socialist Republic of Viet Nam and the Union of Soviet Socialist Republic (1978), annexed to Letter dated 7 November 1978 from the Permanent Representatives of the Union of Soviet Socialist Republics and Viet Nam to the United Nations addressed to the Secretary-General, UN Doc. A/33/362-S/12920 (8 November 1978), Article 6.

[59] TEU, n.7, Article 42(7).

[60] Economic Community of West African States (ECOWAS) Protocol relating to Mutual Assistance on Defence (1981) A/SP3/5/81, Article 3 (emphasis added).

It can, though, be argued that the terminology used in these treaties for their triggering *casus fœderis* – that is, 'armed attack', 'aggression', 'armed threat', etc. – may not ultimately make a meaningful difference to the operation of respective treaty arrangements in practice.[61] States are notorious for blurring the terminology of armed attack and aggression in particular, and yet the meaning – a grave use of force – is usually clear whichever term is used.[62] To take a recent example, when the CSTO dispatched troops into Kazakhstan avowedly in collective self-defence in 2022, that organisation's Chairman was clear that it was acting in response to 'aggression from outside' of Kazakhstan.[63] Similarly, Kazakhstan itself stated that it had been the victim of an 'act of aggression'.[64] Both assertions were clearly made in reference to the armed attack requirement, irrespective of the differing terminology used. And while criticism of the CSTO action did include the view that no armed attack had occurred,[65] it certainly did not draw the conclusion that this was because of a distinction between armed attack and aggression. Indeed, the CSTO's founding treaty itself is explicit in blurring these concepts, setting its triggering *casus fœderis* as 'aggression (armed attack menacing to safety, stability, territorial integrity and sovereignty)'.[66]

It is also worth recalling that even the treaties that use the term 'aggression' still tend to show explicit deference to the UN system and Article 51,[67] making it pretty clear that while they might *say* 'aggression', they actually *mean* 'armed attack'.[68] In any event, while a treaty can set a higher threshold than an armed attack to trigger its collective self-defence obligations for its members, it cannot set a lower threshold, because that would be contrary to Article 51 and thus a violation of Article 2(4).[69]

[61] Derek W. Bowett, 'Collective Self Defence under the Charter of the United Nations' (1955–1956) 32 *British Yearbook of International Law* 130, 150; Sari, n.42, 122–423.

[62] See James A. Green, *The International Court of Justice and Self-Defence in International Law* (Oxford, Hart, 2009), 115–119.

[63] 'Statement by Nikol Pashinyan, the Chairman of the CSTO Collective Security Council – Prime Minister of the Republic of Armenia', *Collective Security Treaty Organisation* (6 January 2022), https://en.odkb-csto.org/news/news_odkb/zayavlenie-predsedatelya-soveta-kollektivnoy-bezopasnosti-odkb-premer-ministra-respubliki-armeniya-n/#loaded.

[64] UNSC Verbatim Record, UN Doc. S/PV.8967 (16 February 2022), 20.

[65] See, for example, *Hansard*, HC Deb (6 January 2022), vol. 706, col. 178.

[66] Collective Security Treaty, n.7, Article 4.

[67] See, for example, Balkan Pact, n.44, Article II; Treaty of Joint Defense and Economic Cooperation, n.44, Article 2; TEU, n.7, Article 42(7).

[68] Bowett, n.29, 226.

[69] *Contra* Rozanov and Douhan, n.22, 31 (arguing that the use of the term 'aggression' as the trigger for collective self-defence treaty obligations provides 'a wide possibility for abuse' because aggression is a concept that is 'much broader than "armed attack"').

Finally, it is worth noting that in some (rare) instances, no triggering *casus fœderis* is set out in the relevant treaty *at all*. An example is the now defunct Baghdad Pact of 1955,[70] which left it entirely up to its members to determine what would activate their shared commitment to act in collective self-defence in the future, seemingly on a case-by-case basis. Again, though, while the parties to a treaty without a *casus fœderis* have *notable* freedom as to when they act,[71] whatever threshold they select in relation to any given case cannot be below the level of an armed attack.

7.3.3 *Reciprocity as an Aspect of Collective Self-Defence Treaty Arrangements and 'Treaties of Guarantee'*

It has been commonly stated in the literature that collective self-defence treaty relationships are characterised by their reciprocal nature.[72] Most collective self-defence treaty arrangements are, indeed, designed to establish, pre-emptively, a framework of mutual assurance: states party to the relevant treaty contract to exercise collective self-defence, as co-defending states, in the aid of any their number. As such, these treaty provisions represent a form of what might be considered 'collective security lite' – that is, possessing the same reciprocal nature as a collective security mechanism, but absent the centralised mechanism and wide enforcement powers of a true collective security system.[73]

It is worth noting, though, that 'reciprocity' is arguably not an accurate characterisation of *all* collective self-defence treaty arrangements. This is because of the existence of what are sometimes are called 'treaties of guarantee'.[74] These are treaties whereby one party (or, perhaps, more than one) agrees to defend another party (or parties), but that obligation is *not* reciprocal. Such 'unidirectional' arrangements[75] include,

[70] Baghdad Pact, n.44, particularly Articles 1 and 2.

[71] See Section 7.3.4.

[72] Elie Perot, 'The Art of Commitments: NATO, the EU, and the Interplay between Law and Politics within Europe's Collective Defence Architecture' (2019) 28 *European Security* 40, 41; Dinstein, n.19, 312; Bowett, n.61, 150; Constantinou, n.16, 173.

[73] Kelsen, n.45, 96; Lee, n.11, 382; Tsagourias and White, n.40, 83; A. J. Thomas Jr. and Ann Van Wynen Thomas, 'The Organization of American States and Collective Security' (1959) 13 *Southwestern Law Journal* 177, 177. See also Sir Michael Wood, 'Self-Defence and Collective Security', in Marc Weller (ed.), *The Oxford Handbook of the Use of Force in International Law* (Oxford, Oxford University Press, 2015), 649 (arguing that there is a clear distinction between collective self-defence and collective security).

[74] See, for example, Dinstein, n.19, 312–316.

[75] *Ibid*, 313.

for example, the notorious 1960 Treaty of Guarantee, whereby the United Kingdom, Greece, and Turkey all undertook to 'recognise and guarantee the independence, territorial integrity, and security of the Republic of Cyprus'[76] without any reciprocal requirement.[77] Another example from the immediate post-war period is the 1951 Security Treaty between the United States and Japan, which obliged the United States to protect 'the security of Japan against armed attack from without', absent any corresponding obligation upon Japan.[78] More recently, in a 2002 treaty, France (re)pledged to defend Monaco, without – unsurprisingly – any reciprocal requirement incumbent on the microstate: 'La République française assure à la Principauté de Monaco la défense de son indépendance et de sa souveraineté . . .'[79]

Some commentators have taken the view that 'treaties of guarantee' are not rightly to be considered collective self-defence treaties at all, precisely on the basis that they lack the characteristic element of reciprocity.[80] However, the present author would disagree. The action that these treaties oblige of their parties is one of collective self-defence – that is, the use of force to defend a party that has suffered an armed attack – and the fact that this obligation is only incumbent upon some, and not all, of those parties does not, in this writer's view, change the nature of that obligation. Instead, it perhaps is more accurate to view treaties of

[76] United Kingdom of Great Britain and Northern Ireland, Greece and Turkey and Cyprus, Treaty of Guarantee (1960) 382 UNTS 3, Article II.

[77] See, generally, Costas M. Constantinou, 'Revising the Treaty of Guarantee for a Cyprus Settlement', *EJIL:Talk!* (21 June 2017), www.ejiltalk.org/revising-the-treaty-of-guarantee-for-a-cyprus-settlement/#:~:text=The%20existing%20Treaty%20of%20Guarantee,led%20military%20coup%20in%201974 (noting that the 1960 Treaty of Guarantee 'has failed in so many respects. It has been violated by the Greek side, which suspended basic articles of the Constitution under the doctrine of necessity in the 1960s and sought to unite the island with Greece following the junta-led military coup in 1974. It has also been violated by the Turkish side, which used it to militarily intervene in 1974').

[78] Security Treaty between the United States and Japan (1951) 3 UST 3329, Article I.

[79] Traité destiné à adapter et à confirmer les rapports d'amitié et de coopération entre la République Française et la Principauté de Monaco (2002) (2006) *Journal de Monaco*, SO no. 407, Article 1.

[80] See, for example, Shigenori Matsui, *The Constitution of Japan: A Contextual Analysis* (London, Hart, 2011), 248–249. See also Agata Kleczkowska, 'The Meaning of Treaty Authorisation and *Ad Hoc* Consent for the Legality of Military Assistance on Request' (2020) 7 *Journal on the Use of Force and International Law* 270, 273–276 (not explicitly setting out this reasoning, but conceiving of treaties of guarantee as providing for 'military assistance on request' as opposed to collective self-defence).

guarantee as a (relatively uncommon) 'lopsided' form of collective self-defence treaty arrangement.[81]

For the majority of collective self-defence treaty arrangements, which *are* premised on reciprocity, it may be noted that they sometimes conceive of the nature of their mutual interrelation in different ways. The 'classic' formulation is the idea that an attack on one of the parties equates to an attack on them all, to which all therefore are required to respond.[82] A number of multilateral treaties take this approach. The North Atlantic Treaty is probably the most famous example of this trend, holding that '[t]he Parties agree that an armed attack against one or more of them . . . *shall be considered an attack against them all*'.[83]

This 'attack on one = attack on all' underpinning to some treaties may be said to be a fiction,[84] at least in terms of a real and specific 'interest' being engaged by all parties in all cases where one of their number is attacked. There might be instances where an attack on one state party to a collective self-defence treaty can be seen as an attack (or, more accurately, a genuine *threat* of attack) against all of its other parties. Equally, it is clear that this will not always be the case. The context-specific and asymmetrical nature of shared security interests in this regard has been neatly highlighted by Gill, who uses the example of Turkey and the United States (both of which are, of course, NATO states).[85] As he notes, an attack on Alaska, say, is rather unlikely to pose a direct security threat to Turkey; whereas, in contrast, an attack against Turkey may conceivably amount to such a threat to the security of the United States.[86] Even

[81] Dinstein, n.19, 312–316.

[82] See Bowett, n.29, 150.

[83] North Atlantic Treaty, n.47, Article 5 (emphasis added). See also, for example, Rio Treaty, n.44, Article 3(1) ('an armed attack by any State against an American State shall be considered as an attack against all the American States'); ECOWAS Protocol, n.60, Article 2 ('any armed threat or aggression directed against any Member State shall constitute a threat or aggression against the entire Community').

[84] Keisuke Minai, 'What Legal Interest Is Protected by the Right of Collective Self-Defense: The Japanese Perspective' (2016) 24 *Willamette Journal of International Law and Dispute Resolution* 105, 108; Bowett, n.61, 150, 152; Bowett, n.29, 234. *Contra Military and Paramilitary Activities in and against Nicaragua* (*Nicaragua v. United States of America*) (merits) [1986] ICJ Rep. 14, dissenting opinion of Judge Jennings, 545 ('[t]his [the 'attack on one = attack on all' concept expressed in many defence treaties], I believe, should not be regarded as a mere contractual arrangement for collective defence – a legal fiction used as a device for arranging for mutual defence – it is to be regarded as an organized system of collective security by which the security of each member is made really and truly to have become involved with the security of the others').

[85] Gill, n.10, 72.

[86] *Ibid.*

then, though, an attack on Turkey surely could not be considered an 'attack' on the United States, in and of itself.

Avoiding the hyperbole inherent in the 'attack on one = attack on all' conceptualisation, other collective self-defence treaty arrangements instead identify an attack on one party as a threat to peace that effects all members in a more general (and more realistic) sense. The SEATO Treaty, for example, stressed that an attack on one party 'would endanger [each other party's] own peace and safety',[87] without equating an attack on one as an attack on all. More recently, the SADC Mutual Defence Pact stated that an 'armed attack against a State Party shall be considered a threat to regional peace and security'.[88]

It was argued in Chapter 1 that there is no legal requirement for any kind of demonstrable shared 'interest' for the exercise of collective self-defence.[89] This remains the case whether or not an action of collective self-defence occurs within the context of a treaty framework. It therefore should not be surprising that some treaties do not 'justify' the collective self-defence obligation that they incorporate by reference to any interest *at all*. For example, while the Western European Union (WEU) Treaty noted that its members had a 'close community of . . . interests',[90] it did not tie this in any way to its collective self-defence obligation.[91]

In any event, despite some variations in both the triggering *casus fœderis* and the mutual interest it engages, it is evident that collective self-defence treaty arrangements post-1945 have usually been built around the idea of a reciprocal obligation to use defensive force should an armed attack occur against one of their number.

7.3.4 'Soft' Obligations in Collective Self-Defence Treaty Arrangements

It is often said that another notable feature of collective self-defence treaty arrangements is that they fundamentally change the legal 'dynamic' of collective self-defence. This is because – for their members – they turn the exercise of what otherwise is a right into an *obligation*.[92]

87 SEATO Treaty, n.49, Article IV(1).
88 SADC Pact, n.7, Article 6(1).
89 See Section 1.2.
90 WEU Treaty, n.21, Article I.
91 *Ibid*, Article V.
92 See Joseph L. Kunz, 'Individual and Collective Self-Defence under Article 51 of the Charter of the United Nations' (1947) 41 *American Journal of International Law* 872,

This is exactly what collective self-defence treaties purport to do, of course, and it is how states refer to them.[93] The idea that parties are obliged to defend one another, reciprocally, has already been noted in the previous subsection. However, the characterisation of collective self-defence treaties as creating 'obligations', truly described, can be queried. It will be recalled from Section 7.3.2 that in some instances, no triggering *casus fœderis* is set out in the relevant treaty, as was the case in the 1955 Baghdad Pact.[94] Treaties such as the Baghdad Pact, which do not articulate any 'trigger', fairly obviously impose only a very weak obligation on their members to act in collective self-defence.

It was also noted in Section 7.3.2 that most UN era arrangements do set out a pretty clear trigger, though, and that this usually is the occurrence of an armed attack. However, the drafters of collective self-defence treaty provisions have been very careful to avoid the 'automation' of obligations if the relevant trigger is 'activated'.[95] The existence of an armed attack does not, itself, usually trigger any obligation to respond even when such an attack is explicitly the relevant treaty's *casus fœderis*. Instead, collective self-defence treaty provisions have

875; George K. Walker, 'Anticipatory Collective Self-Defense in the Charter Era: What the Treaties Have Said' (1998) 31 *Cornell International Law Journal* 321, 355, 359; Åkermark, n.14, 253, 264; Josef Rohlik, 'Some Remarks on Self-Defense and Intervention: A Reaction to Reading Law and Civil War in the Modern World' (1976) 6 *Georgia Journal of International and Comparative Law* 395, 426; Kelsen, n.45, 86; Thomas and Thomas, n.73, 183–184; Azubuike, n.45, 174–175; Constantinou, n.16, 175; George Fletcher and Jens Ohlin, *Defending Humanity: When Force Is Justified and Why* (Oxford, Oxford University Press, 2008), 177–178.

93 See, for example, United States, Affidavit of Secretary of State George P. Shultz, dated 14 August 1984, annexed to *Military and Paramilitary Activities in and Against Nicaragua* (*Nicaragua v. United States of America*) (counter-memorial of the United States of America, questions of jurisdiction and admissibility) [1984] ICJ Plead., vol. II, Annex 1, 177, 178, para. 7 (arguing – in relation to the actions that were the subject of dispute in the *Nicaragua* case – that it was using force '[p]ursuant to the inherent right of collective self-defense, and in accord with *its obligations* under the Inter-American Treaty of Reciprocal Assistance', emphasis added); UNSC Verbatim Record, UN Doc. S/PV.1441 (21 August 1968), para. 3 (USSR, arguing that Warsaw Pact states acted 'in conformity with mutual treaty *obligations*', emphasis added); Försvarsberedningen, *Värnkraft – Inriktningen av säkerhetspolitiken och utformningen av det militära försvaret 2021–2025*, Ds 2019:8, 88 (Sweden, referring to '*de försvarsförpliktelser* som återfinns i Natofördragets artikel 5 och i artikel 42.7 i EU:s Lissabonfördrag', emphasis added).

94 Baghdad Pact, n.44, particularly Articles 1 and 2.

95 Constantinou, n.16, 175; Sari, n.42, 428; Michael A. Goldberg, 'Mirage of Defense: Reexamining Article Five of the North Atlantic Treaty after the Terrorist Attacks on the United States' (2003) 26 *Boston College International and Comparative Law Review* 77, 86–87, 90.

deliberately[96] included discretion for their parties as to whether and/or how they are required to respond. The North Atlantic Treaty, for example, states that when Article 5 is triggered, each party must take 'such action *as it deems necessary*'.[97] Replicating this almost exactly, the defunct Warsaw Pact only required a party to respond with 'such means as it deem[ed] necessary'.[98] Taking more recent examples, the Collective Security Treaty vaguely obliges members to provide 'necessary help . . . as well as provide support by the means at their disposal'.[99] The SADC Pact of 2003 likewise requires a state party only to take part in collective action 'in any manner it deems appropriate'.[100]

These explicit qualifications leave notable room for reluctant states to sidestep the obligations apparent in a collective self-defence treaty to which they are party if another member is attacked. This establishes an 'apparent conflict between duty and choice'.[101] The extent of such flexibility will depend on the exact treaty arrangement in question.[102] For more sophisticated and integrated collective self-defence arrangements, for example, there is perhaps less likelihood of members shirking their obligation to act in collective self-defence, due to the influence of factors such as collective decision-making and the collective political pressure to contribute.[103] Even in the case of some organisations with binding consensus decision-making processes, though, discretion is still commonly built in.[104] The Rio Treaty, for example, was clear that each party could 'determine the immediate measures which it may individually take' in collective self-defence,[105] but *also* – where the Organ of Consultation took a joint decision, which would normally be binding on parties – there was an exception to the effect that no party could 'be required to use armed force without its consent'.[106]

[96] Tertrais, n.31, 2 (referring to the wording of the North Atlantic Treaty, n.47, Article 5 in this regard as 'deliberately ambiguous').
[97] North Atlantic Treaty, n.47, Article 5 (emphasis added).
[98] Warsaw Pact, n.46, Article 4.
[99] Collective Security Treaty, n.7, Article 4.
[100] SADC Pact, n.7, Article 6(3).
[101] Goodhart, n.45, 223.
[102] See, for example, Perot, n.72, 51 (making this point by comparing the North Atlantic Treaty, n.47, Article 5 with TEU, n.7, Article 42(7)).
[103] Dinstein, n.19, 310.
[104] Bowett, n.29, 232–233.
[105] Rio Treaty, n.44, Article 3(2).
[106] *Ibid*, Article 20.

Given the foregoing, it is sometimes argued that collective self-defence treaty provisions are not actually 'obligations' at all.[107] Some scholars have, for example, questioned the extent to which Article 5 of the North Atlantic Treaty is legally binding.[108] This is both because of the caveat within Article 5 that a NATO member only ever needs to take action 'as it deems necessary' in response to an armed attack[109] and because of other factors such as the restrictive nature of consensus decision-making.[110] Similar views have been expressed regarding TEU Article 42 (7).[111] That article only provides a basis for EU members to cooperate in collective self-defence on an intergovernmental basis: it does not provide for a role for the organisation itself.[112] Moreover, political commitments to collective self-defence within the European Union have, overall, been limited.[113] As such, the provision certainly can be considered a 'weak' one legally, although that should not necessarily diminish its political importance.[114] It is possible that some states also take the view that TEU Article 42(7) is not a binding mutual assistance clause. For example, Sweden seems to have implicitly indicated that it feels that Article 42(7) is not binding upon it, despite its membership of the European Union.[115] Sweden asserted in both 2016[116] and

[107] See, generally, Michael J. Glennon, 'United States Mutual Security Treaties: The Commitment Myth' (1986) 24 *Columbia Journal of Transnational Law* 509.

[108] Brzezinski, n.32, 14–16; J. E. S. Fawcett, 'The Legal Character of International Agreements' (1953) 30 *British Yearbook of International Law* 381, 392–393; Goldberg, n.95, 90–91.

[109] North Atlantic Treaty, n.47, Article 5.

[110] See n.31 and accompanying text.

[111] See, for example, Jean-Claude Piris, *The Lisbon Treaty: A Legal and Political Analysis* (Cambridge, Cambridge University Press, 2010), 275; Jan Wouters, Frank Hoffmeister, Geert de Baere and Thomas Ramopoulos, *The Law of EU External Relations: Cases, Materials, and Commentary on the EU as an International Legal Actor* (Oxford, Oxford University Press, 3rd ed., 2021), 415–416; Panos Koutrakos, *The EU Common Security and Defence Policy* (Oxford, Oxford University Press, 2013), 68–70; Panos Koutrakos, 'The Role of Law in Common Security and Defence Policy: Functions, Limitations and Perceptions', in Panos Koutrakos (ed.), *European Foreign Policy: Legal and Political Perspectives* (Cheltenham, Edward Elgar, 2011), 235, 237–239.

[112] See Gray, n.9, 193; Sari, n.42, 433.

[113] *Ibid*, 455.

[114] Piris, n.111, 275.

[115] See Inger Österdahl, 'Sweden's Collective Defence Obligations *or* This Is Not a Collective Defence Pact (or Is It?): Considerations of International and Constitutional Law' (2021) 90 *Nordic Journal of International Law* 127, 145.

[116] *Förutsättningar enligt regeringsformen för fördjupat försvarssamarbete*, Statens Offentliga Utredningar (SOU) 2016:64, 106 ('[d]et finns som har framgått i dagsläget

2018[117] that there is no legal obligation incumbent upon it to deploy its armed forces abroad,[118] which would strongly suggest it does not view Article 42(7) as a binding obligation.[119]

In any event, this author is of the view that even if a mutual assistance clause in a treaty can be characterised as a 'weak obligation' – which they generally can be, to one degree or other – this does not mean the provision is not binding on states party.[120] A provision's status as a legally binding obligation and the strength of that obligation are different things. This distinction reflects the wider way in which scholars have conceptualised the flexibility inherent in most collective self-defence treaty arrangements.[121]

That said, even where a lack of 'automaticity' is not explicitly spelled out in the treaty in question, which is rare,[122] discretion ultimately can still be seen as an inherent feature of the operation of the treaty in question.[123] This is because even when there is no explicit flexibility as

inte någon internationell förpliktelse för Sverige som kräver att svensk väpnad styrka sätts in eller sänds till utlandet').

[117] *En lag om operativt militärt stöd mellan Sverige och Finland*, Statens Offentliga Utredningar (SOU) 2018:31, 83 ('... det i dagsläget inte finns någon internationell förpliktelse som kräver att Sverige sänder väpnade styrkor till Finland till stöd för Finland').

[118] See Österdahl, n.115, 145.

[119] Sweden has not set out its reasoning for the view that it is not bound by TEU, n.7, Article 42(7), given that it has argued this only implicitly.

[120] See Österdahl, n.115, particularly 135–137; Sari, n.42, 428–430.

[121] See, for example, Dino Kritsiotis, 'A Study of the Scope and Operation of the Rights of Individual and Collective Self-Defence under International Law', in Nigel D. White and Christian Henderson (eds.), *Research Handbook on International Conflict and Security Law:* Jus ad Bellum, Jus in Bello *and* Jus Post Bellum (Abingdon, Routledge, 2013), 170, 184 (concluding that Article 5 of the North Atlantic Treaty is binding, but 'cast in the language of a soft obligation').

[122] See Österdahl, n.115, 137. An example of a treaty which *prima facie* appears to create an automatically triggered obligation is the WEU Treaty, n.21, Article 5, which states, without obvious qualifiers, its collective self-defence obligation in the following manner: '[i]f any of the High Contracting Parties should be the object of an armed attack in Europe, the other High Contracting Parties will, in accordance with the provisions of Article 51 of the Charter of the United Nations, afford the party so attacked all the military and other aid and assistance in their power'.

[123] See, for example, Sir W. Eric Beckett, *The North Atlantic Treaty, The Brussels Treaty, and the Charter of the United Nations* (London, Stevens & Sons, 1950), 28–29; Louis B. Sohn, 'Western European Treaty for Collaboration and Collective Self-Defence' (1948) 34 *American Bar Association Journal* 406, 406 (arguing that although the Treaty of Economic, Social and Cultural Collaboration and Collective Self-Defence (1948), *North Atlantic Treaty Organisation*, www.nato.int/cps/en/natohq/official_texts_17072.htm (Brussels Treaty) – which preceded and was amended by the WEU Treaty,

to how parties to a collective self-defence treaty arrangement are to respond, they 'retain unfettered discretion'[124] to act as a co-defending state only after their own prior determination of whether the *casus fœderis* has indeed been triggered.[125] As a matter of law, the occurrence of an armed attack is an objective question,[126] but in practice, there is notable scope for interpretation.[127] Genuine differences of opinion as to the existence of an armed attack can occur within alliances,[128] and any member state wishing not to commit its forces in defence of another 'will not have to contrive to find an ingenious escape clause in the text'.[129]

It has been argued that the inherent discretion that can be observed – to at least some extent – across all collective self-defence treaty arrangements 'could be disastrous' for a defending state in a case where it suffers an armed attack.[130] However, it seems extremely unlikely that states would ever enter into a treaty arrangement that resulted in the automatic commitment of their forces simply on the basis of the determination of a fellow party or even based on some form of 'objective' third-party assessment.[131]

States will inevitably retain the ability to make their own assessment of whether the *casus fœderis* has been met, for various reasons.[132] For one, they could find themselves engaged in a violation of Article 2(4), because – for example – it turned out that there had in fact not been

n.21 – appeared to create an automatic obligation, that 'each party will have to decide for itself').

124 Franck, n.21, 829.

125 Hans Kelsen, 'Collective Security and Collective Self-Defense under the Charter of the United Nations' (1948) 42 *American Journal of International Law* 783, 90.

126 See Mary Ellen O'Connell, 'Rules of Evidence for the Use of Force in International Law's New Era' (2006) 100 *American Society of International Law Proceedings* 44, 46; Sari, n.42, 414; James A. Green, 'Fluctuating Evidentiary Standards for Self-Defence in the International Court of Justice' (2009) 58 *International and Comparative Law Quarterly* 163, 164.

127 Sari, n.42, 447; Kelsen, n.45, 795; Sohn, n.123, 406 (making this point regarding the Brussels Treaty, n.123, which preceded and was amended by the WEU Treaty, n.21).

128 Sari, n.42, 415.

129 Dinstein, n.19, 307.

130 Sohn, n.123, 406.

131 Broderick C. Grady, 'Article 5 of the North Atlantic Treaty: Past, Present, and Uncertain Future' (2002) 31 *Georgia Journal of International and Comparative Law* 167, 179 (making this point in relation to the United States, but it can be extended to any state).

132 For a similar discussion of the importance of co-defending states being able to make their own determination as to whether the requirements of 'necessity' and 'proportionality' have been complied with, see Chapter 3, nn.160–162 and accompanying text.

an armed attack against the defending state.[133] Again, before using force, a state will inevitably wish to verify and self-assess the need for it to do so rather than relying on another state's assessment of the facts, even an ally. It is also worth noting that in the case of large multilateral arrangements with multiple members, an 'automatic trigger' could be especially problematic for ensuring compliance with the proportionality requirement. It will be recalled that it was argued in Chapter 3 that the proportionality calculation must be aggregated across all co-defending states.[134] Therefore, if all members of a large collective self-defence alliance were separately compelled to use defensive force immediately and automatically upon the occurrence of an armed attack, this could quickly result in a disproportionate overall response.[135] Or it at least could make balancing compliance with the treaty obligation and compliance with the proportionality requirement difficult, with each state needing to use a minimal amount of force (rather than allowing some states to act while others do not, which likely will be more practical in some instances).

Moreover, if a collective self-defence treaty were to oblige its parties to commit their forces automatically, governments could face a choice between violating the collective self-defence treaty in question or violating their own constitutional requirements for the authorisation to use force.[136] Such requirements may include internal processes and approval that can take time and, of course, may not ultimately result in the constitutional authority to act at all.

States may also wish simply to be able to avoid engaging in a foreign conflict (especially if that might involve troop deployment and resulting domestic political opposition),[137] making flexible treaty arrangements desirable. Finally, it has been argued that exactitude in collective self-defence treaty arrangements has the potential to limit the range of lawful responses available[138] and may even indicate to hostile states exactly what they can 'get away with' before action was taken.[139] In contrast,

[133] Constantinou, n.16, 175; Bowett, n.29, 231–232.

[134] Chapter 3, nn.164–173 and accompanying text.

[135] Bowett, n.29, 238.

[136] Grady, n.131, 179; Goldberg, n.95, 91; Fawcett, n.108, 392. See North Atlantic Treaty, n.47, Article 11 (spelling out that '[t]his Treaty shall be ratified *and its provisions carried out* by the Parties in accordance with their respective constitutional processes', emphasis added).

[137] Sari, n.42, 426.

[138] *Ibid*, 410–411, 426.

[139] *Ibid*, 410–411.

less precise obligations could in fact increase the deterrent effect,[140] because it will be unclear to a potential aggressor exactly how far it can 'go' before a defensive response is triggered.

Despite this inherent flexibility – and the various reasons for it – this author would not go so far as to conclude that the reciprocal obligations at the heart of (most) collective self-defence treaty arrangements are not 'obligations' after all. It is worth recalling that international law requires that obligations contained within treaties are to be complied with in good faith.[141] This is a requirement that holds parties to the spirit of collective self-defence treaty arrangements, at least residually.[142] However, it is clear that mutual assistance clauses in collective self-defence treaty arrangements are, to varying degrees, all relatively weak obligations. There are arguably good reasons for that fact, but it does ultimately mean that it is questionable whether such arrangements offer the level of security – especially for less powerful states – as it might first appear.[143]

7.4 Partially Overlapping Obligations and Disputes within Memberships

The fact that a plethora of collective self-defence treaties have emerged in the UN era has inevitably resulted in states adopting concurrent obligations by being party to multiple arrangements. This can increase security (actual, perceived) for weaker states and can increase influence for powerful states. However, it also can lead to complex interactions between collective self-defence regimes.[144] States have been aware of this issue since the inception of the United Nations[145] and have taken steps to address it. For example, the 1948 Brussels Treaty was amended in 1954 and transformed into the WEU Treaty, with NATO having been created in the interim. As such, the drafters of the amending protocol were careful to make clear that the WEU was intended to work alongside

140 *Ibid.*

141 See Vienna Convention on the Law of Treaties (1969) 1155 UNTS 331 (VCLT), Article 26.

142 Rohlik, n.92, 425; Sari, n.42, 430.

143 It may be recalled that this 'wiggle room' was a common feature of the pre-Charter treaties too. See Chapter 2, nn.30–34 and accompanying text; *ibid*, nn.63–75 and accompanying text. Ultimately, this trend can be said to have continued into the UN era. See Gibson, n.23, 123.

144 Perot, n.72, 54.

145 See Simma, n.40, 14–16.

and complement NATO. The amended treaty stated that the parties and organs of the WEU:

> shall work in close co-operation with the North Atlantic Treaty Organisation. Recognising the undesirability of duplicating the military staffs of NATO, the Council and its Agency will rely on the appropriate military authorities of NATO for information and advice on military matters.[146]

More recently, also in Europe, since 2007, members of both the European Union and NATO have found themselves bound by collective self-defence provisions of Article 42(7) TEU and Article 5 of the North Atlantic Treaty simultaneously.[147] These are provisions that, despite slight differences, on their face are substantively the same.[148] However, TEU Article 42(2) explicitly defers to NATO:

> Commitments and cooperation in this area [defence and security] shall be consistent with commitments under the North Atlantic Treaty Organisation, which, for those States which are members of it, remains the foundation of their collective defence and the forum for its implementation.[149]

This would suggest that the relationship between the obligations is clear, with NATO remaining the 'primary framework' for collective self-defence for those states party to both the North Atlantic Treaty and the TEU.[150] Yet, France then famously invoked – for the first (and still only) time ever – the collective defence clause in the TEU Article 42(7) in 2015 following the Paris attacks, while at the same time choosing not to invoke Article 5 of the North Atlantic Treaty.[151] This decision brought

[146] WEU Treaty, n.21, Article IV.

[147] Perot, n.72, 41. See also Sari, n.42, 409 (noting that around two-thirds of the membership overlaps as between the two organisations).

[148] Sari, n.42, 409–410, 422; Österdahl, n.115, 132.

[149] TEU, n.7, Article 42(7).

[150] EU High Representative, Shared Vision, Common Action: A Stronger Europe (A Global Strategy for the European Union's Foreign and Security Policy) (2016), www.eeas.europa.eu/eeas/global-strategy-european-unions-foreign-and-security-policy_en, 20; Sari, n.42, 435.

[151] Council of Ministers of the European Union, 'Outcome of the Council Meeting', Brussels (16–17 November 2015), 14120/15, 6. See also Tom Ruys, Luca Ferro and Nele Verlinden (eds.), 'Digest of State Practice, 1 July–31 December 2015' (2016) 3 *Journal on the Use of Force and International Law* 126, 127–128; Olivier Corten, *The Law against War: The Prohibition on the Use of Force in Contemporary International Law* (Oxford, Hart, 2nd ed., 2021), 460; Gray, n.9, 193.

the avowed primacy of NATO over the European Union in relation to collective self-defence into some doubt.

It is also, of course, worth keeping in mind that not all members of NATO are in the European Union and vice versa.[152] On this basis, Perot envisages a direct conflict between the two regimes:

> [I]t is possible to foresee a contradiction between EU and NATO commitments in the hypothesis of a conflict between a non-NATO EU member state and a non-EU NATO ally. In this case, the members of both the EU and NATO could be subject to conflicting requests for assistance – leaving aside the logical problem of both warring countries claiming to be the aggressed party.[153]

Although Perot makes this point specifically as regards NATO and the European Union, such mutually contradictory collective self-defence requests could potentially arise between many other overlapping collective self-defence treaty arrangements too. Dinstein gives the example of the Balkan Pact from 1954, between Greece, Turkey, and Yugoslavia, where the first two states were members of NATO while Yugoslavia was not. In that context, '[p]ressures on Yugoslavia could have produced a suction process, drawing in non-Contracting Parties belonging to NATO (through the pipeline of Greece and Turkey)'.[154] The same could be possible for a major power straddling multiple arrangements.[155] Following 9/11, Article 5 of the North Atlantic Treaty[156] and Article 3 of the Rio Treaty[157] were activated – the United States, of course, being a party to both. It does not take much, therefore, to envisage a scenario where the United States found itself responding to a European NATO member's request for aid, which then led to the United States itself requesting aid, thereby pulling other non-NATO American states into a European conflict by virtue of the Rio Treaty.[158]

Taking this idea further, Weightman has conceptualised the bilateral collective self-defence treaties concluded between the USSR and other states immediately after the Second World War – of which there were no

[152] Perot, n.72, 56.
[153] *Ibid*, 52.
[154] Dinstein, n.19, 311.
[155] *Ibid.*
[156] See Constantine Antonopoulos, 'Some Thoughts on the NATO Position in Relation to the Iraqi Crisis' (2004) 17 *Leiden Journal of International Law* 171, 174.
[157] See Organization of American States, OEA/Ser.F/II.24, RC.24/RES.1/01, Terrorist Threat to the Americas (21 September 2001).
[158] Dinstein, n.19, 311.

fewer than nineteen – as effectively amounting to a single collective self-defence treaty arrangement at the start of the Cold War, on the basis of this same 'suction' process.[159] In other words, with the USSR as the unifying 'pipeline', an attack on a party to any one of those bilateral treaties could have cascaded into triggering obligations on them all.

While this 'suction effect' is possible, it is unlikely in practice and arguably has been overstated a little by the writers who have identified it.[160] Perhaps a greater risk is the more straightforward situation of one member of an alliance drawing other members into a conflict over a comparatively small-scale dispute. For example, in 2015, Turkey shot down a Russian fighter jet, which it claimed was flying over Turkish airspace (a claim that Russia rejected).[161] Turkey then called a meeting of NATO, and there was fear among other NATO states at the time that this risked direct conflict between the organisation and Russia.[162] Yet, even the likelihood of this type of occurrence should not be overstated, given the consensus decision-making structures of organisations such as NATO, and the scope for states to sidestep their collective self-defence treaty obligations, as discussed in Section 7.3.4.

In any multilateral collective self-defence treaty arrangement, there is also always the potential for members to be antagonistic towards *each other* despite their membership.[163] This can lead to fissures and can cause notable issues for effective consensus decision-making. One example is Uzbekistan's relationship with the CSTO – an organisation that it has suspended membership of, and then rejoined, on multiple occasions.[164] This has undoubtedly caused instability within the CSTO.[165] Another notable example is the relationship between Greece and Turkey, which has been tense for decades despite both states being members of NATO. Issues between the two 'allies' recently became evident again at the

159 Weightman, n.45, 1112.
160 Perot, n.72, 56.
161 See Report of the Secretary-General on the Implementation of Security Council Resolutions 2139 (2014), 2165 (2014) and 2191 (2014), UN Doc. S/2015/962 (11 December 2015), para. 9.
162 'Statement by the NATO Secretary General after the Extraordinary NAC Meeting', North Atlantic Treaty Organization, Press Release (2015) 169 (25 November 2015). See Gray, n.9, 195–196.
163 Dinstein, n.19, 311.
164 'Uzbekistan Suspends Its Membership in CSTO', *Gazette of Central Asia* (29 June 2012), http://gca.satrapia.com/uzbekistan-suspends-its-membership-in-csto.
165 Rozanov and Douhan, n.22, 17–18.

adoption of the 2021 Greek–French Treaty.[166] Greek Prime Minister Kyraikos Mitsotakis was not subtle in implying that the agreement was directed at Turkey.[167] And while France attempted to ease tensions by stating that this was not in fact the case,[168] Turkey responded with concerning rhetoric of its own.[169]

The inevitability of such tensions means that the constituting treaties of some military alliances have gone so far as to oblige explicitly their members not to attack each other.[170] It is also worth noting that, while 'it would hardly conform to the concept of an alliance' for a collective self-defence treaty to be activated against one of its own parties,[171] this does not mean it is legally impossible:

> [N]othing in the wording of [Article 51 of the UN Charter] can be interpreted to mean that ... action taken in the exercise of collective self-defense must not be directed against an aggressor who is a party to the treaty organizing the collective self-defense.[172]

Overall, it may be said that collective self-defence treaty arrangements create notable complexities for their members, both because of overlapping obligations and because of different views or even outright antagonism between members. Before turning to the *benefits* of such arrangements in

166 Greek–French Treaty, n.8. See Patrick M. Butchard and Jasmin Johurun Nessa (eds.), 'Digest of State Practice, 1 July–31 December 2021' (2022) 9 *Journal on the Use of Force and International Law* 171, 179–180.

167 Lefteris Papadimas, Michele Kambas and George Georgiopoulos, 'Greek Parliament Approves Defence Pact with France', *Reuters* (7 October 2021), www.reuters.com/world/europe/greece-france-defence-pact-protects-against-third-party-aggression-greek-pm-2021-10-07 (Kyraikos Mitsotakis: 'for the first time it is clearly stipulated that there be military assistance in the event of a third party attacking one of the two states. And we all know who is threatening whom with a *casus belli* [cause for war] in the Mediterranean').

168 *Ibid.*

169 Turkey, Ministry of Foreign Affairs, 'Statement of the Spokesperson of the Ministry of Foreign Affairs, Ambassador Tanju Bilgiç, in Response to a Question Regarding the Statement of Greek Defence Minister Concerning the Inclusion of Maritime Jurisdiction Areas to the Defence Agreement Signed with France' (1 October 2021), www.mfa.gov.tr/sc_-42_-yunanistan-savunma-bakani-nin-aciklamasi-hk-sc.en.mfa.

170 See, for example, WEU Treaty, n.21, Article VII; Treaty of Joint Defense and Economic Cooperation, n.44, Article 1.

171 Antonopoulos, n.156, 175.

172 Hans Kelsen, 'Is the North Atlantic Treaty a Regional Arrangement?' (1951) 45 *American Journal of International Law* 162, 165. *Contra* Tertrais, n.31, 3 (arguing that '[l]ogically, no government of a member State could invoke [a collective self-defence treaty provision] if attacked by another member state').

Section 7.6, the next section first considers the geographical features of these arrangements, and, as part of that analysis, the relationship between collective self-defence treaty arrangements and 'regional arrangements' under Chapter VIII of the UN Charter.

7.5 Geographical Limitations and the Relationship between Collective Self-Defence Treaty Arrangements and 'Regional Arrangements'

7.5.1 Geographical Limitations in Collective Self-Defence Treaty Arrangements

Collective self-defence treaty arrangements are 'often regional in the geographic sense'.[173] This is in a number of respects. First, some multilateral treaty arrangements are only open to states within a defined geographical region. For example, the 1996 RSS Treaty is explicit that Eastern Caribbean states alone can become party to it.[174] It has occasionally been argued that collective self-defence treaty parties *must* be exclusively from a defined region.[175] However, this claim is impossible to support. Nothing in Article 51 of the UN Charter suggests such a limitation, and, as was argued in Chapter 1, there is no requirement of 'proximity' – geographical or otherwise – for the lawful exercise of collective self-defence.[176] Moreover, some collective self-defence treaties are explicit that any state can be considered for membership – without this being a point of controversy for other states. The CSTO's founding treaty serves as an example here: '[t]his Treaty shall be open for accession of all interested states sharing its goals and principles'.[177]

Many collective self-defence organisations (or organisations that include a collective self-defence function) appear to be formed based on regional membership but, in fact, this is not required by the

[173] Dinstein, n.19, 308. See also Goodrich, Simons and Hambro, n.29, 350; Stanimir A. Alexandrov, *Self-Defence against the Use of Force in International Law* (The Hague, Kluwer Law International, 1996), 234.

[174] RSS Treaty, n.7, Article 2.

[175] See, for example, 'American Policy vis-a-vis Vietnam, in Light of Our Constitution, the United Nations Charter; the 1954 Geneva Accords, and the Southeast Asia Collective "Defense Treaty"', Memorandum of Law (prepared by Lawyers Committee on American Policy Toward Vietnam, Hon. Robert W. Kenny, Honorary Chairman), reprinted in 112 (23) US Congressional Record, 89th Congress, 2nd sess. (9 February 1966), 2666, 2668.

[176] See Section 1.2.

[177] Collective Security Treaty, n.7, Article 10.

constituting treaty, which has led to members joining from outside the relevant region. SEATO – that is, the *Southeast Asia* Treaty Organisation – did not require that its members be Southeast Asian states, for example, and it had the United States and the United Kingdom as members from the outset. NATO itself has members, such as Turkey and Greece, that would be difficult to consider to be geographically part of the 'North Atlantic' region, even as broadly defined. However, the North Atlantic Treaty does not proscribe membership in this way, irrespective of the name of the organisation, and there is no reason why it would need to do so. There is certainly no requirement that collective self-defence treaty arrangements need to restrict members to states from a particular geographical region.[178] As the United Kingdom stressed in a meeting of the UN General Assembly in 1950, states can 'enter into defensive agreements for collective self-defence on a bilateral, regional or world-wide basis', as suits their needs.[179]

Of greater note is the fact that collective self-defence treaty arrangements commonly self-impose geographical restrictions on their operation in the sense that 'many of them are restricted *in their application* to defined regions'.[180] For example, the Rio Treaty indicates that its obligations are triggered only by an armed attack that 'takes place within the region ... or within the territory of an American State'.[181] The 'region' is then defined extremely precisely by reference to longitude and latitude.[182] The SEATO Treaty was similarly prescriptive with regard to its designation of the relevant area of Southeast Asia wherein an attack would trigger it.[183] In contrast, the WEU Treaty was limited only to 'an armed attack *in Europe*',[184] without going so far as to specify coordinates defining the precise boundaries of that continent.

[178] See Weightman, n.45, 1113 (noting that nothing in Article 51 defines or restricts the groups that are able to invoke collective self-defence); William E. Holder, 'The Legality of United States Participation in Vietnam: An Appraisal' (1966) 2 *Australian Yearbook of International Law* 67, 77 (giving US membership of SEATO as an example); Constantinou, n.16, 173; Goodhart, n.45, 206–207.

[179] UNGA Summary Record, UN Doc. A/C.1/SR.360 (12 October 1950), para. 5.

[180] Bowett, n.61, 151 (emphasis added).

[181] Rio Treaty, n.44, Article 3(3).

[182] *Ibid*, Article 4.

[183] SEATO Treaty, n.49, Article VIII ('the "treaty area" is the general area of Southeast Asia, including also the entire territories of the Asian Parties, and the general area of the Southwest Pacific not including the Pacific area north of 21 degrees 30 minutes north latitude').

[184] WEU Treaty, n.21, Article V (emphasis added).

Bearing in mind the phenomenon of states being parties to multiple arrangements discussed in the previous section, it is worth noting that geographical limitations on the trigger for different treaties have led to some complicated, partially overlapping regimes. For example, Article 5 of the North Atlantic Treaty is triggered by an armed attack on the territory of a member, including 'Islands under the jurisdiction of any of the Parties in the North Atlantic area north of the Tropic of Cancer', as well as the forces of members either in the same region or in the Mediterranean Sea.[185] This means that, for example, the United Kingdom could not have invoked Article 5 in relation to the Falklands/Malvinas conflict in 1982, as the islands lie outside this defined area.[186] It also means that 'NATO's Article 5 could not be invoked in case of an armed attack taking place on the US state of Hawaii or against Guam and other US islands in the Pacific, for instance in the event, of a military conflict with China or North Korea'.[187] Article 42(7) of the TEU is, in contrast, triggered where an EU member state 'is the victim of armed aggression *on its territory*',[188] without further limiting this geographically, but unlike NATO does not provide for action in response to an attack against its members' forces. As a result, states that are members of both NATO and the European Union could find that an attack against them might trigger TEU Article 42(7) but not NATO Article 5[189] or vice versa.[190] This, again, adds complexity to the relationship between NATO and TEU Article 42(7) in terms of the current structures for collective self-defence for many European nations: it is certainly not as simple as NATO primacy.

Notwithstanding complexity resulting from overlapping regimes, it is worth ending this subsection by reiterating that the geographical limitations[191] within collective self-defence treaties (of whatever sort) are self-

[185] North Atlantic Treaty, n.47, Article 6.

[186] Tertrais, n.31, 2; Perot, n.72, 56.

[187] Perot, n.72, 50. See also Thomas and Thomas, n.73, 192 (making a very similar point with regard to the geographical limitations of the Rio Treaty).

[188] TEU, n.7, Article 42(7).

[189] Perot, n.72, 50; Peter B. M. J. Pijpers, Hans J. F. R. Boddens Hosang and Paul A. L. Ducheine, 'Collective Cyber Defence – The EU and NATO Perspective on Cyber Attacks' (2021) *Amsterdam Law School Legal Studies Research Paper* No. 2021-37, Amsterdam Center for International Law No. 2021-13, 8.

[190] Sari, n.42, 424–425.

[191] Some treaties have gone even further than limiting their trigger only to attacks in particular territorial or geographical locations, to limit also the *ratione personae* of the aggressor. For example, a number of treaties concluded immediately following the

imposed by the parties to the treaty in question. Moreover, they limit only the scope of the trigger for the activation of the respective treaty's collective self-defence *obligations*. States party (whether acting individually or collectively) of course remain able to use force ad hoc in defence of a state that has suffered an armed attack outside the relevant region, so long as the legal requirements for exercising collective self-defence are met.[192]

7.5.2 Collective Self-Defence Treaty Arrangements and 'Regional Arrangements'

The fact that collective self-defence treaty arrangements have commonly been organised along regional lines begs the question of the relationship between such arrangements and 'regional arrangements' as a term of art employed under Chapter VIII of the UN Charter. This is especially important because Article 53 of the Charter states that:

> [t]he Security Council shall, where appropriate, utilize such regional arrangements or agencies for enforcement action under its authority. But *no enforcement action shall be taken under regional arrangements or by regional agencies without the authorization of the Security Council*[193]

This means that for 'regional arrangements' or 'regional agencies',[194] any enforcement measure must have been previously authorised by the Council; of course, the exercise of collective self-defence is not subject to Security Council sanction in the same way.[195] In this sense, 'collective defense action under Article 51 is entirely different from "enforcement action" . . .'[196]

Second World War restricted the obligation incumbent on their parties to mutual defence *only* in response to a future attack by Germany. See Walker, n.92, 348–349 (discussing some of these treaties). Examples include the Treaty of Dunkirk, n.17, Article I and the Finno–Soviet Treaty, n.56, Article 1.

192 Thomas and Thomas, n.73, 196.

193 UN Charter, n.39, Article 53 (emphasis added).

194 Some scholars have argued that 'regional arrangements' are ad hoc, whereas 'regional agencies' are characterised by a degree of permanence. See Andrew Martin, *Collective Security: A Progress Report* (Paris, United Nations (UNESCO), 1952), 171; Dinstein, n.19, 306. This is a very reasonable reading of the different terms as used in Article 53, although ultimately it is speculative.

195 Bowett, n.29, 221.

196 Norton Moore and Underwood, n.49, 304, footnote 197. See also Richard H. Heindel, Thorsten V. Kalijarvi and Francis O. Wilcox, 'The North Atlantic Treaty in the United States Senate' (1949) 43 *American Journal of International Law* 633, 639; Lord Ismay,

One might therefore conclude that establishing a sharp distinction between 'collective self-defence arrangements' and 'regional arrangements' is imperative. Indeed, particularly in the initial decades of the UN era, concerns that NATO might find itself beholden to the whims of the Soviet veto meant that the organisation went to some lengths to be explicit that it was purely a collective self-defence organisation and not a regional arrangement: notwithstanding the undeniable fact that the organisation's activity is restricted to responses to armed attacks within a defined 'region'.[197] The UK Foreign Secretary, Ernest Bevan, expressed the NATO position clearly in 1949:

> The [North Atlantic] Treaty is not a regional arrangement under Chapter VIII of the Charter. The action which it envisages is not enforcement action in the sense of Article 53 at all. The Treaty is an arrangement between certain States for collective self-defence as foreseen by Article 51 of the Charter.[198]

Scholars have also often expressed the view that NATO is a 'pure' collective self-defence organisation and not a 'regional arrangement',[199] on the basis that none of the provisions of the North Atlantic Treaty itself envisage the sort of activity ascribed to regional arrangements under Chapter VIII of the UN Charter.[200] The same could have been said[201] previously for the similarly worded Warsaw Pact.[202] There is little question that the *raison d'être* for both is/was collective self-defence.[203]

Yet, many other collective self-defence treaty arrangements are less obviously of such a singular purpose. It was noted in Section 7.2 that collective self-defence treaty arrangements take a wide range of forms, and many of them are but one aspect of a much wider arrangement or organisation. Take the Organisation of American States (OAS), which

NATO: The First Five Years, 1949–1954 (Paris, North Atlantic Treaty Organisation, 1955), 12–13.

197 See Henderson, n.45, 119.

198 *Hansard*, HC Deb (12 May 1949), vol. 464, cols. 218–219.

199 See, for example, Simma, n.40, 10; Grady, n.131, 184; Antonopoulos, n.156, 175; Goodhart, n.45, 207–208, 214, 233–234; Beckett, n.123, 26, 30–31, 34; Oscar Schachter, *International Law in Theory and Practice* (Dordrecht, Martinus Nijhoff, 1991), 156.

200 See, generally, North Atlantic Treaty, n.47.

201 Schachter, n.199, 156.

202 Warsaw Pact, n.46.

203 Anne Orford, 'Regional Orders, Geopolitics, and the Future of International Law' (2021) 74 *Current Legal Problems* 149, 166; Alexander Orakhelashvili, *Collective Security* (Oxford, Oxford University Press, 2011), 80 (making this point regarding NATO only).

absorbed the Rio Treaty. The OAS clearly has collective self-defence as a key aspect of its function,[204] but its field of activity also extends to wider regional security, as well as undertaking social and economic work.[205] Likewise, Deutsch argues that SEATO was very deliberately constituted to have a dual function: both 'collective self-defence arrangement' and 'regional arrangement'.[206] That this 'mixing' of roles sometimes can be observed is perhaps unsurprising, given that the concept of a 'regional arrangement' in the sense of Chapter VIII is nowhere authoritatively delineated, and 'inter-state security arrangements', as broadly conceived, are essentially self-defining in terms of membership and objectives.[207] It is clearly possible for the functions of collective self-defence and regional 'enforcement action' (and other activities associated with 'regional arrangements') to be vested in the same organisation.[208]

Indeed, irrespective of whether an organ is designated as a 'regional arrangement' or not, it can act in collective self-defence without Security Council authorisation, because Article 51 is clear that '[n]othing in the present Charter shall impair' the exercise of collective self-defence,[209] and that includes the requirements found in Chapter VIII.[210] This holds true even if the organisation *self-defines* as a regional organisation. For example, the OAS Charter is unequivocal in stating that 'the Organization of American States is a regional agency'.[211] However, as already noted, OAS states are bound by collective self-defence obligations by virtue of their membership, and there is no question that the OAS could lawfully defend one of its members that had suffered an armed attack.[212]

The reverse also holds: if an organisation such as NATO – which has traditionally self-defined as a 'pure' collective self-defence body – *behaves*

[204] Charter of the Organization of American States (1948) 119 UNTS 3 (OAS Charter), Article 28.

[205] Antonopoulos, n.156, 175; Tsagourias and White, n.40, 115; Goodhart, n.45, 213.

[206] See Eberhard P. Deutsch, 'The Legality of the United States Position in Vietnam' (1966) 52 *American Bar Association Journal* 436, 437.

[207] Tsagourias and White, n.40, 116.

[208] Dinstein, n.19, 306; Schachter, n.199, 156.

[209] UN Charter, n.39, Article 51.

[210] See Kelsen, n.45, 90; Kelsen, n.172, 163; Thomas and Thomas, n.73, 197; Bowett, n.61, 140; Bowett, n.29, 223; Tsagourias and White, n.40, 132; Nader Iskandar Diab, 'Enforcement Action by Regional Organisations Revisited: The Prospective Joint Arab Forces' (2017) 4 *Journal on the Use of Force and International Law* 86, 95.

[211] OAS Charter, n.204, Article 1.

[212] Beckett, n.123, 20; Schachter, n.199, 156.

in the manner of a 'regional arrangement', then it is difficult to see how the requirements of Chapter VIII would not apply to that activity. This has taken on greater pertinence since the end of the Cold War, given that NATO has undeniably expanded its focus and activity beyond only collective self-defence preparedness.[213] Even during the Cold War, though, there was nothing that would have stopped NATO undertaking an 'enforcement action' with authorisation from Security Council.[214] Writing as early as 1949, Heindel *et al* stressed that:

> it is not necessary to define the organization of the North Atlantic community as exclusively one or the other. It *can* be utilized as a regional arrangement, subject to the pertinent provisions of the Charter, if the members so desire.[215]

In short, an organ that is predominantly – or even exclusively – designed as a collective self-defence arrangement can undertake wider 'enforcement action' as a 'regional arrangement' so long as it is authorised to do so by the Security Council.[216]

It has been argued on the basis of the foregoing that the line between a 'collective self-defence arrangement' and a 'regional arrangement' has 'been blurred to the point that such a distinction is obsolete'.[217] This author would agree with this in the sense of drawing any kind of hard distinction based on the form of the organisation: no given treaty arrangement can be said to be exclusively one thing or the other. However, it is not the case that the drawing of any distinction at all is 'obsolete', because the applicable law is different depending on the determination. Crucially, of course, there is the question of whether Security Council authorisation is required for the use of force, but there is also another practical difference. This is the fact that Article 54 of the UN Charter requires that '[t]he Security Council shall at all times be kept fully informed of activities undertaken or in contemplation under regional arrangements or by regional agencies for the maintenance of international peace and security'.[218] This would seem more onerous than

213 See nn.268–269 and accompanying text.
214 Bowett, n.61, 154; Bowett, n.29, 239; Kelsen, n.172.
215 Heindel, Kalijarvi and Wilcox, n.196, 639 (emphasis in original).
216 Bowett, n.29, 223.
217 Christian Wyse, 'The African Union's Right of Humanitarian Intervention as Collective Self-Defense' (2018) 19 *Chicago Journal of International Law* 295, 305.
218 UN Charter, n.39, Article 54.

the Article 51 reporting requirement for self-defence.[219] In any event, it is clear that a distinction between collective self-defence and the activities of 'regional arrangements' matters in identifying the applicable law.

Given that this distinction cannot be drawn based on the *form* of the organisation, it instead must be drawn based on the *function* that it is exercising:

> [C]ontroversy arises from an attempt to characterize organizations by form rather than function, as being either organizations in collective self-defence or regional arrangements. If . . . we start from the premiss that members of the organization, whether regional or not, can always exercise this right of self-defence, then the relevant question becomes not 'What sort of organization is this?' but rather 'What function is it exercising?' Once the latter question is answered it is then possible to define the obligations which are incumbent on members according to whether they are exercising their right of self-defence, or are purporting to take enforcement action[220]

While NATO member states in particular have tended to draw a much firmer line to distinguish that organisation from 'regional arrangements',[221] other states have often been clear that there is no neat distinction in this way, instead adopting the 'functional' approach.[222] Cuba, for example, twice has made the point that a 'regional agency' could act in collective self-defence (in 1968 and 1969).[223] Also in the late 1960s, Syria made the same point,[224] whereas Uruguay argued that a 'regional' organisation of whatever kind could lawfully use military force in compliance

[219] Goodhart, n.45, 233. On the reporting requirement for collective self-defence, see Section 3.4.

[220] Bowett, n.29, 222. See also Azubuike, n.45, 176, footnote 237 (arguing that the applicable law is dependent on 'a determination of the action taken'); Alexandrov, n.173, 234.

[221] See nn.197–203 and accompanying text.

[222] Although see, *contra*, 1966 Special Committee on Principles of International Law Concerning Friendly Relations and Co-Operation among States, Summary Record of the Fifteenth Meeting held at Headquarters, New York, on Thursday, 17 March 1966, UN Doc. A/AC.125/SR.15 (1966), 5 (Ghana, '. . . under Article 53, no enforcement action could be taken under regional arrangements or by regional agencies without the authorization of the Security Council; it thus seemed clear that no group of States could take it upon itself to intervene in the affairs of another State on the pretext of "collective self-defence"').

[223] UNGA Summary Record, UN Doc. A/C.6/SR.1076 (21 November 1968), para. 7; UNGA Summary Record, UN Doc. A/C.6/SR.1167 (3 December 1969), para. 40.

[224] Special Committee on the Question of Defining Aggression, UNGA Summary Record, UN Doc. A/AC.134/SR.l-24 (30 September 1968), 186.

with either Article 51 or following Security Council authorisation as per Article 53.[225]

It is worth noting that although an organisation can act as both a collective self-defence arrangement and a regional arrangement,[226] it is unlikely that an organisation will be able to act as both *at the same time*, because the respective functions are different. This means that, in practice, an organisation can 'fluctuate' between one designation or the other depending on the function that it is exercising, but it is unlikely to be both a collective self-defence arrangement and a regional arrangement simultaneously.

Drawing this kind of functional distinction, which can 'fluctuate' depending on the activity undertaken at any given point, is not without difficulty. This is not least because of the complexity involved in unpicking exactly what measures are being taken by an organisation. For example, an organisation could begin by trying to resolve a dispute through pacific settlement, as a 'regional arrangement' under Article 52 of the UN Charter, before then transitioning into a use of force in collective self-defence (assuming this became necessary and was in response to an armed attack).[227] The applicable law would change significantly in such a case, which would be undesirable in terms of both legal and practical clarity.

It has further been argued that the 'dual character' of some treaty arrangements in this regard might open up the possibility of abuse, because 'under the guise of exercising the right of collective self defense pursuant to Article 51 [an organisation may] take enforcement action . . . without obtaining the consent of the Security Council'.[228] This is certainly a reasonable concern, although perhaps ultimately is an argument in favour of drawing a careful distinction at the functional level in each individual case, rather than a reason to try to impose artificial distinctions based on form. Ultimately, one must ask whether 1) the legal requirements for the exercise of collective self-defence have been met or 2) the Security Council has authorised the action. If the answer to both 1 and 2 is 'no', then any use of force by an organisation or

225 *Ibid*, 206.

226 Azubuike, n.45, 176; Franck, n.21, 826–827; Beckett, n.123, 26; Kelsen, n.172, 164; Thomas and Thomas, n.73, 178 (making this point specifically in relation to the OAS and the Rio Treaty).

227 Thomas and Thomas, n.73, 197.

228 Azubuike, n.45, 176.

arrangement – however, it self-defines and irrespective of its wider role(s) – will be a violation of Article 2(4) of the UN Charter.[229]

7.6 The Value of Collective Self-Defence Treaty Arrangements

It was noted in the introduction to this chapter that collective self-defence treaty arrangements have been created throughout the UN era and that there are now hundreds of them.[230] At the same time, there have been various instances since 1945 where states have invoked collective self-defence in spite of the fact that no collective self-defence treaty existed between the defending state and co-defending state.[231] The survey of state practice conducted for this book suggests that there actually have been *more* invocations of collective self-defence in the UN era that have not been made in the context of a pre-existing treaty relationship than those that have.[232] This is in clear contrast to the pre-Charter practice, where 'ad hoc collective defence' – while legal and occasionally practiced – was extremely rare.[233] Contrastingly, far more collective self-defence treaty arrangements have emerged in the UN era than have occurred actual invocations of collective self-defence under the auspices of those arrangements.[234] This is obviously no bad thing: it is significantly preferable for there to be a plethora of agreements preparing for the use of defensive force than there to be a plethora of instances where such preparations need to be actioned.[235]

229 See UN Doc. A/AC.134/SR.l-24, n.224, 206.

230 See nn.6–9 and accompanying text.

231 See Section 1.2.2. See also many of the examples of UN era state practice that have been discussed throughout Chapters 3–6.

232 This cannot be said with complete certainty, as this author makes no claims to total comprehensiveness as to a review of all (actual or asserted) instances of collective self-defence. However a this book's underpinning study of state practice indicates that states act in collective self-defence ad hoc more commonly than they invoke a treaty relationship. *Contra* Azubuike, n.45, 174 ('in a *majority of cases*, there is a treaty relationship or arrangement between the third state and the state being defended', emphasis added). See also Lee, n.11, 374.

233 See Chapter 2, nn.47–51 accompanying text; *ibid*, n.56 and accompanying text. However, one also might recall that it was argued in Section 2.4 that the way in which the right of collective self-defence was framed in Article 51 of the UN Charter reinforced the idea that collective defence need not necessarily involve a treaty relationship.

234 Azubuike, n.45, 176.

235 This trend may even suggest valuable deterrent effect on the part of the treaties in question. See nn.251–264 and accompanying text.

Nonetheless, it remains the case that throughout the UN era, states have more often than not preferred to invoke the right of collective self-defence ad hoc rather than trigger collective self-defence treaty provisions.[236] Even when collective force has been used by a larger number of states, there has been an increasing tendency for this to be done through temporary 'coalitions' of the willing rather than existing collective self-defence organisations or frameworks.[237] One might note, for example, that Article 5 of the North Atlantic Treaty was never activated during the Cold War,[238] and even when it was activated for the first time following 9/11, the avowed self-defence action taken in Afghanistan was ultimately not undertaken by NATO but by the United States and its allies acting in coalition.[239]

This general preference not to activate collective self-defence treaty provisions perhaps can be explained, at least in part, by a cautiousness about risking any direct confrontation between large groupings of 'opposing' military alliances,[240] especially once the world moved into the nuclear age. Ad hoc action may be less likely to trigger the 'suction' effect discussed in Section 7.4, or immediately to pit large numbers of states against each other. This fear was, of course, exemplified by the Cold War but undoubtedly has continued beyond it. On a more prosaic level, it also has been persuasively postulated that the major powers have preferred the flexibility and lack of scrutiny afforded them by 'going it alone', which had resulted in a degree of disuse of collective self-defence treaty arrangements in practice.[241]

236 See Section 1.2.2.

237 Chinkin and Kaldor, n.38, 141.

238 Antonopoulos, n.156, 173. See also Patrick T. Egan, 'The Kosovo Intervention and Collective Self-Defence' (2001) 8 *International Peacekeeping* 39, 40 (noting that NATO action in Kosovo in 1999 'was the first campaign to which all NATO member states contributed and only the second time in its entire history that alliance forces had engaged in battle'. The first use of force at all under the auspices of NATO occurred in 1994, in Bosnia. See David S. Yost, 'NATO and the Anticipatory Use of Force' (2007) 83 *International Affairs* 39, 50.

239 Antonopoulos, n.156, 174; Tsagourias and White, n.40, 81; Grady, n.131, 169, 189, 197; Tertrais, n.31, 4.

240 See, discussing the potential for an armed conflict between two defence organisations, both avowedly claiming to be acting in collective self-defence, Kelsen, n.125, 795; Waldock, n.45, 504–505; Orakhelashvili, n.203, 281. See also Documents of the United Nations Conference on International Organization, San Francisco, 1945 (London, United Nations Information Organization (United Nations), 22 volumes, 1945–1955) (UNCIO), vol. 12, 682 (New Zealand).

241 Antonopoulos, n.156, 174 (making this point in relation to the United States).

When the trend towards ad hoc action is considered in the context of various other factors discussed in this chapter – for example, the fact that collective self-defence treaties cannot provide additional legal basis for the use of force beyond that proclaimed in Article 51, the 'soft' nature of most collective self-defence treaty obligations, or the potential issues that can arise from overlapping memberships – one might reasonably question what 'value' these arrangements actually have post-1945. Collective self-defence treaties seem to have notable value to states, because they have repeatedly concluded them, across all regions of the world and up until the time of writing.[242] It is clear that a collective self-defence treaty is 'more than [just] an abstract framework within which to discuss the theory of collective self-defense'.[243]

In fact, there are various potential benefits that might stem from the creation of collective self-defence treaties. Given that they cannot regulate the merits of the right of collective self-defence,[244] treaty arrangements instead create additional legal structures for their parties (which, while needing to be consistent with the existing *jus ad bellum*, can obviously go beyond it).[245] This means that they have a *facilitating* function.[246] The existence of a treaty arrangement can act to clarify and frame a specific exercise of collective self-defence.[247] It can also be a crucial first step towards meaningful preparedness – operational and strategic – as it can codify how and when these steps are to be taken, and by whom,[248] as well as facilitating training and security capacity-building for states that might not otherwise receive such support. It has been argued on that basis that at least the more sophisticated of collective self-defence treaty arrangements, for all their limitations, are ultimately more likely to be able to

[242] Gill, n.10, 75 ('[b]oth large and small States have a clear interest in their continuance – otherwise it would be difficult to understand why there are so many such agreements in existence').

[243] Norton Moore and Underwood, n.49, 307.

[244] Constantinou, n.16, 175. This is necessarily done by Article 51 of the UN Charter and customary international law.

[245] Bowett, n.29, 231–232.

[246] Kelsen, n.45, 86; Bowett, n.61, 151; Grady, n.131, 185; Mushkat, n.43, 148.

[247] W. W. Kulski, 'The Soviet System of Collective Security Compared with the Western System' (1950) 44 *American Journal of International Law* 453, 463; Federica Paddeu, 'The Rio Treaty: Paving the Way for Military Intervention in Venezuela?', *Just Security* (29 October 2019), www.justsecurity.org/66758/the-rio-treaty-paving-the-way-for-military-intervention-in-venezuela (describing the Rio Treaty as providing 'a *legal framework* for the exercise of collective self-defense by States in the Americas', emphasis added).

[248] Lee, n.11, 384; Gill, n.10, 75.

underpin the effective and timely response to an armed attack than the UN Security Council can.[249] It is also worth noting that the obligatory framework provided by a collective self-defence treaty can provide a useful basis upon which states can seek to justify their use of force in collective self-defence *internally*, helping to establish compliance with national constitutional requirements.[250]

These various benefits notwithstanding, this author would argue that the importance that states have attached to collective self-defence treaties in the UN era at least began as a consequence of the Cold War. The emergence of these treaties in the decades immediately following the creation of the United Nations – which saw the largest 'boom' in such agreements – must be viewed in the context of the disillusionment with the UN system that quickly followed its inception and, especially, with the ability of the Security Council to act effectively to maintain international peace and security in the face of entrenching superpower opposition.[251] This had a lasting impact on the importance ascribed by states to collective self-defence, and particularly the perceived value of formal collective self-defence arrangements.[252] As Australia stressed at a meeting of the First Committee of the UN General Assembly in 1950, states were coming to the view that 'if the Security Council was paralysed in its action', then setting up architecture to ensure that states could effectively act in each other's 'collective self-defence was an *imperative measure*'.[253]

Collective self-defence treaty arrangements thus formed a key aspect of the global security system during the Cold War.[254] However, the primary

249 Gill, n.10, 75.

250 See Perot, n.72, 42; Patrick Terry, 'Germany Joins the Campaign against ISIS in Syria: A Case of Collective Self-Defence or Rather the Unlawful Use of Force?' (2016) 4 *Russian Law Journal* 26, 29, footnote 9 (giving the example of the German Government's reliance, in 2015, on TEU, n.7, Article 42(7) to justify its actions under German constitutional law).

251 Jane A. Meyer, 'Collective Self-Defense and Regional Security: Necessary Exceptions to a Globalist Doctrine' (1993) 11 *Boston University International Law Journal* 391, 392; Rohlik, n.92, 427; Gill, n.10, 73; Marina Salvin, 'The North Atlantic Pact' (1949) 27 *International Conciliation* 375, 415.

252 See Kelsen, n.45, 88–91; Henderson, n.45, 103; Goodhart, n.45, 211–212; Antonopoulos, n.156, 175; Waldock, n.45, 496.

253 UNGA Summary Record, UN Doc. A/C.1/SR.364 (16 October 1950), para. 63 (emphasis added).

254 See Gill, n.10, 49 ('the foreign and defense policies of the United States and its allies and the U.S.S.R. and its (former) allies in Central Europe and elsewhere were based *in large measure* upon the N.A.T.O. and Warsaw Treaty systems and numerous similar

value of the Cold War era collective self-defence arrangements, and thus the importance that states placed on them, may be found in signalling and mutual deterrence rather than the actual use of force.[255] Effective deterrence requires not just military capability but also the projection and communication of an intention to employ that military capability if required.[256] On that basis, collective self-defence treaty arrangements arguably are, first and foremost, sophisticated mechanisms for signalling intent:

> [T]he solemn commitments in which countries enter when they subscribe to collective defence treaties is precisely such an instrument to [project and communicate] ... one's intentions and to influence those of other parties effectively, or at least more effectively than if those commitments had not been formalised into legal documents.[257]

For nuclear weapons-possessing states, keen to emphasise to others that, if it came to it, they actually would use such weapons (thereby ensuring the deterrent effect that is the *raison d'être* of nuclear weapons possession in the first place), this analysis has particular pertinence. By legally committing to a treaty that might, at least potentially, *oblige* them to act is a powerful means of demonstrating intent, while also providing the security of a 'nuclear umbrella' for allied non-nuclear weapons states without engaging in nuclear proliferation.[258] It has therefore been said that nuclear weapons have 'long been considered the fulcrum of collective defence'.[259]

Of course, some collective self-defence arrangements do not involve nuclear powers (including some that are notably large in scope).[260] A strong case can still be made, though, that – irrespective of whether they have nuclear weapons-possessing member states or not – almost all

multilateral and bilateral treaty regimes', emphasis added); Goodhart, n.45, 187 (hailing the North Atlantic Treaty as 'the most important international agreement with has been entered into since the United Nations came into being'); Gibson, n.23, 130.

255 Tertrais, n.31, 4; Antonopoulos, n.156, 173, 183; Gray, n.9, 198; Chinkin and Kaldor, n.38, 457 (giving the example of the Pan-American system and arguing it was motivated more by the desire to deter the spread of communism than ensuring effective regional defence); Dinstein, n.19, 307 (although arguably then contradicting this conclusion at 323).

256 Thomas Schelling, *Arms and Influence* (New Haven, Yale University Press, 1966 (Veritas paperback ed., 2020)), 35–91.

257 Perot, n.72, 42. See also Rohlik, n.92, 428.

258 Rohlik, n.92, 429; Antonopoulos, n.156, 178.

259 Perot, n.72, 59.

260 See, for example, AU Pact, n.7.

collective self-defence treaty arrangements can be viewed as being more about deterrence than about the actual exercise of collective self-defence. Moreover, this remains the case post–Cold War. Despite some suggestions in the 1990s that collective self-defence organisations/arrangements might become *relics* of the Cold War,[261] this has not proven to be the case. Although some of the Cold War era collective self-defence architecture fell away – most notably the Warsaw Pact[262] – other Cold War era collective defence organisations/arrangements have endured. The most notable of these is obviously NATO. To an extent, NATO has sought to evolve its functions beyond purely collective self-defence since the 1990s,[263] with a particular focus on forms of crisis management.[264]

Equally, the stagnation of the UN collective security system – and, thus, the perception of the need for effective security alternatives – did not end with the fall of the Berlin Wall,[265] meaning that the importance of collective self-defence arrangements has continued. This has been fuelled in particular by the threat of international terrorism.[266] For example, it has been said that when France invoked TEU Article 42(7) following the Paris attacks of 2015, 'collective self-defence in the EU took a new turn'.[267] Despite a period of discontent within the NATO alliance and a sense of wavering commitment to mutual defence amongst some of its members (especially during the Trump presidency in the United States),[268] the organisation has renewed its focus on its original *raison d'être* – that is, collective self-defence as a traditional deterrent to other states – in light of an increasingly aggressive Russia.[269] Indeed, following the full-scale invasion of Ukraine, which began in 2022 and is ongoing at

261 See, for example, Donald Daniel and Bradd Hayes, 'Toward a West European Navy: Organizational and Operational Issues', in Gert de Nooy (ed.), *The Role of European Naval Forces after the Cold War* (The Hague, Kluwer Law International, 1996), 73, 92; Grady, n.131, 197–198.

262 See Walker, n.92, 376; Chinkin and Kaldor, n.38, 140.

263 Gray, n.9, 45; Simma, n.40, 14–16, 19; Antonopoulos, n.156, 172, 182; Walker, n.92, 376; Dinstein, n.19, 310–311; Henderson, n.45, 119–120; Chinkin and Kaldor, n.38, 140; Orford, n.203, 172–174.

264 Perot, n.72, 43; Orakhelashvili, n.203, 80–81.

265 See, for example, Wyse, n.217, 297, 309 (arguing that the emergence of the African Union's collective self-defence structure in the early 2000s was a direct result of the failures of the UN Security Council in the 1990s, especially in relation to Rwanda).

266 Tertrais, n.31, 5; Perot, n.72, 46.

267 Åkermark, n.14, 270.

268 Österdahl, n.115, 136; Pijpers, Boddens Hosang and Ducheine, n.189, 3; Perot, n.72, 40, 44; Sari, n.42, 408.

269 Sari, n.42, 408, 440–441; Tertrais, n.31, 1; Perot, n.72, 44.

the time of writing, NATO is more united and focused on its core collective self-defence role than it has been at any point since the end of the Cold War.

It is worth recalling that 2022 also saw the first ever invocation of Article 4 of the Collective Security Treaty, and the resulting deployment of CSTO troops, in Kazakhstan in January.[270] Article 4 was then again invoked, this time by Armenia, in September 2022,[271] albeit that the CSTO did not ultimately respond with force.[272] While the CSTO is far from a direct successor to the Warsaw Pact in all respects,[273] its 'awakening' as a collective self-defence organisation precisely as NATO is mobilising in response to Russia's full-scale invasion of Ukraine is unlikely to be coincidental.

Despite the modern context, unforeseen in 1945, of hybrid threats, sophisticated armed non-state actors and technological interconnectivity, collective self-defence treaty arrangements retain notable importance within the UN collective security system.[274] Indeed, in this author's view, this is, unfortunately, clearer at the time of writing than it has been for at least three decades.

7.7 Conclusion

This chapter has sought to map out the nature and scope of the hundreds of collective self-defence treaty arrangements that have emerged in the UN era. These arrangements have a facilitating function, and are, of course, in no way required for the lawful exercise of collective self-defence. As such, states have had great freedom to devise them as suits their needs, leading to a wide range of types of arrangement. Across this diversity, some common themes can be identified.

[270] See Fyodor A. Lukyanov, 'Kazakhstan Intervention Sees Russia Set a New Precedent', *Russia in Global Affairs* (7 January 2022), https://eng.globalaffairs.ru/articles/kazakhstan-new-precedent.

[271] See 'Armenia Asked CSTO for Military Support to Restore Territorial Integrity Amid Azeri Attack – PM', *Armen Press* (14 September 2022), https://armenpress.am/eng/news/1092504.

[272] See 'CSTO Did Not Take Definitive Action to Assist Armenia', *Asbarez* (29 October 2022), https://asbarez.com/csto-did-not-take-definitive-action-to-assist-armenia.

[273] See Dmitry Gorenburg, 'Russia and Collective Security: Why CSTO Is No Match for Warsaw Pact', *Russia Matters* (27 May 2020), www.russiamatters.org/analysis/russia-and-collective-security-why-csto-no-match-warsaw-pact.

[274] Sari, n.42, 451.

Modern collective self-defence treaty arrangements generally coalesce – unsurprisingly – around Article 51, with a focus on the reciprocal commitment to respond to an armed attack. It was argued in this chapter that these arrangements generally have 'weak' or 'soft' obligations, and they also can cause complexity due to multiple memberships resulting in overlapping but different requirements, tensions between members, convoluted decision-making and geographical limitations. Given these features, it was argued that the ultimate value of these treaty arrangements has generally been in their deterrent effect rather than their actual activation. However, it was also noted that the importance of collective self-defence treaty arrangements has endured beyond the Cold War and, indeed, there has been something of a renewed sense of their importance at the time of writing, given East–West tensions over, in particular, Russian aggression against Ukraine.

8

The Relationship between Collective Self-Defence and Military Assistance on Request

8.1 Introduction

The final chapter of this book examines the relationship between collective self-defence and another legal basis for the use of force, which in scholarship is variously referred to as 'military assistance on request' or 'intervention by invitation' (as well as, less commonly, by other names).[1] All these terms refer to military activity undertaken on a consenting state's territory. The presumptive *ad bellum*[2] legality of such action is 'a truth universally acknowledged'.[3]

[1] See Laura Visser, 'What's in a Name? The Terminology of Intervention by Invitation' (2019) 79 *Zeitschrift für Ausländisches Öffentliches Recht und Völkerrecht* 651.

[2] It is always important to recall that a request of this kind cannot set aside other obligations under international law, such as provisions of international humanitarian law or international human rights law. See, for example, Max Byrne, 'Consent and the Use of Force: An Examination of "Intervention by Invitation" as a Basis for US Drone Strikes in Pakistan, Somalia and Yemen' (2016) 3 *Journal on the Use of Force and International Law* 97, 120–124.

[3] Laura Visser, 'May the Force Be with You: The Legal Classification of Intervention by Invitation' (2019) 66 *Netherlands International Law Review* 21, 21 (employing a literary turn of phrase). See also Michael N. Schmitt, 'Drone Attacks under the *Jus as Bellum* and *Jus in Bello*: Clearing the "Fog of Law"' (2010) 13 *Yearbook of International Humanitarian Law* 311, 315 ('[i]t is *indisputable* that one state may employ force in another with the consent of that state', emphasis added). The legality of military assistance on request is well established in the case law of the International Court of Justice (ICJ). See *Military and Paramilitary Activities in and against Nicaragua (Nicaragua v. United States of America)* (merits) [1986] ICJ Rep 14, para. 246; *Armed Activities on the Territory of the Congo (Democratic Republic of the Congo v. Uganda)* (judgment) [2005] ICJ Rep 168, especially paras. 39–54). It is also well established in state practice. See Christian Henderson, *The Use of Force and International Law* (Cambridge, Cambridge University Press, 2018), 352 (noting that '[hi]story is replete with examples of states intervening upon the justification that there has been an invitation to intervene by the government of a state' and going on to provide a long list of examples). There is also significant scholarship devoted to this legal basis for the use of force. See, for example, Erika de Wet, *Military Assistance on Request and the Use of Force* (Oxford, Oxford University Press, 2020); Seyfullah Hasar, *State Consent to Foreign Military Intervention during Civil Wars* (Leiden, Brill Nijhoff, 2022);

Mapping the relationship between collective self-defence and military assistance on request is important because these concepts are, in some respects, strikingly similar.[4] They both involve a *prima facie* unlawful use of force[5] by one state, undertaken at the request of another, which can be[6] rendered lawful as a result of that request. The similarity between the concepts is perhaps even more pronounced between collective self-defence and a particular manifestation of military assistance on request, sometimes known as 'counter-intervention' (i.e. military assistance at the request of a government specifically in response to external support for rebels/insurrectionists).[7] This is because both collective self-defence and counter-intervention are exercised in response to some measure of 'external intervention'.[8]

It is perhaps unsurprising, therefore, that when one begins to examine instances of state invocation of collective self-defence and/or military assistance on request, it quickly becomes clear that these claims are often blurred or mixed.[9] Equally, it is relatively uncontroversial to say that

Chiara Redaelli, *Intervention in Civil Wars: Effectiveness, Legitimacy, and Human Rights* (Oxford, Hart, 2021); Eliav Lieblich, *International Law and Civil Wars: Intervention and Consent* (Abingdon, Routledge, 2013); Karine Bannelier-Christakis, 'Military Interventions against ISIL in Iraq, Syria and Libya, and the Legal Basis of Consent' (2016) 29 *Leiden Journal of International Law* 74.

[4] Laura Visser, 'Intervention by Invitation and Collective Self-Defence: Two Sides of the Same Coin?' (2020) 7 *Journal on the Use of Force and International Law* 292, 292 ('these two notions of public international law seem quite alike').

[5] It will be recalled that collective self-defence, by its very nature, almost necessarily involves the use of force. See Chapter 1, nn.172–173 and accompanying text. Military assistance on request as, for example, defined by the International Law Association's current Use of Force Committee, also amounts to the use of force. See ILA, Use of Force: Military Assistance on Request Committee, *Interim Report* (2022), www.ila-hq.org/index.php/committees, section III.B. However, unlike collective self-defence, 'military assistance on request' does not have a specific legal meaning, and thus the concept could be interpreted more narrowly, to only include more 'direct' uses of force (e.g. 'Present Problems of the Use of Force in International Law: Military Assistance on Request', *Institut de droit international*, Session of Rhodes, Resolution (2011)) or, more broadly, so as to extend to other forms of 'military assistance' that would not *prima facie* amount to a violation of the prohibition on the use of force at all (e.g. 'The Principle of Non-Intervention in Civil Wars', *Institut de droit international*, Session of Wiesbaden, Resolution (1975) (albeit that this is limited to the context of civil wars)).

[6] Subject, of course, to compliance with respective legal requirements.

[7] On counter-intervention generally, as well as its similarities to collective self-defence, see John A. Perkins, 'The Right of Counterintervention' (1987) 17 *Georgia Journal of International and Comparative Law* 171.

[8] See Section 8.5.2.

[9] See Section 8.3.

collective self-defence and military assistance on request are conceptually distinct and have (some) different requirements for their lawful exercise. The concepts commonly are distinguished in scholarship, whether or not the reasons for making that distinction are explicit and irrespective of whether or not the similarities between them are acknowledged. This can be seen from the fact that the leading works that examine the law on the use of force *in toto* (and thus provide commentary on both concepts in the same work) tend to consider their legal content separately.[10] A clear boundary between collective self-defence and military assistance on request is also sometimes drawn more explicitly in scholarship.[11]

It is worth noting that the Independent International Fact-Finding Mission on the Conflict in Georgia (IIFFMCG) saw a difference between *practice* and *theory* when it came to considering the relationship between collective self-defence and military assistance on request. The IIFFMCG took the view that '[i]n doctrinal terms, the two concepts are distinct', but that '[i]n practice, collective self-defence overlaps with military intervention upon invitation'.[12] This conclusion is, admittedly, a little simplistic, but it is nonetheless a useful framing device for some of the analysis in this chapter.

Given that there are clearly similarities, and perhaps even some 'overlap' between collective self-defence and military assistance on request, it is notable that relatively few academic works have directly explored their relationship.[13] This chapter aims to build upon that small pocket of

[10] See, for example, Yoram Dinstein, *War, Aggression and Self-Defence* (Cambridge, Cambridge University Press, 6th ed., 2017) (at 125–130 examining military assistance on request; at 301–327 examining collective self-defence); Henderson, n.3 (at 349–378 examining military assistance on request; at 256–262 examining collective self-defence); Christine Gray, *International Law and the Use of Force* (Oxford, Oxford University Press, 4th ed., 2018) (at 75–119 examining military assistance on request; at 176–199 examining collective self-defence – albeit acknowledging their similarities at 177); Ian Brownlie, *International Law and the Use of Force by States* (Oxford, Oxford University Press, 1963) (at 318–327 examining military assistance on request; at 328–331 examining collective self-defence).

[11] See, for example, de Wet, n.3, 181 (describing them as 'two separate legal constructs under international law'); Hasar, n.3, 296 (describing them as 'two distinct principles').

[12] Report of the Independent International Fact-Finding Mission on the Conflict in Georgia (IIFFMCG) (2009), vol. II, 282. See also Gray, n.10, 177 ('although in theory there is a distinction between collective self-defence and assistance in reply to an invitation by a government to respond to internal intervention against the government, in practice the line may not be a clear one').

[13] A key exception is Visser, n.4. See also Dino Kritsiotis, 'Intervention and the Problematisation of Consent', in Olivier Corten, Gregory H. Fox and Dino Kritsiotis,

existing literature, and – in so doing – further delineate the concept of collective self-defence in particular. It starts, in Section 8.2, by exploring the relationship between the concepts at the 'doctrinal' or 'conceptual' level, that is, where the IIFFMCG felt that a clear distinction could be drawn. Section 8.3 then turns to the claims that have been advanced in the United Nations (UN) era by states, where – as already noted – the reverse is true. States have, for the most part, been unhelpfully unclear when advancing legal claims related to uses of force, making drawing a clear distinction in practice difficult.

The remainder of this chapter examines various legal requirements (actual or, in some cases, arguable) for collective self-defence and military assistance on request, with the aim of highlighting similarities or differences as they arise in the discussion. Section 8.4 considers the shared 'request' criterion, building on the analysis in Chapters 4–6 and comparing the collective self-defence 'request' requirement as set out therein to the equivalent requirement for military assistance on request; Section 8.5 explores whether any equivalent tigger to 'armed attack' may exist for military assistance on request. Section 8.6 asks whether the self-defence criteria of necessity and proportionality likewise apply to military assistance on request. Section 8.7, in a similar vein, examines whether the reporting requirement for self-defence is reflected in an equivalent requirement for military assistance on request. Finally, Section 8.8 examines the territorial location of the force used under each claim – something that has been said to amount to 'the key difference between the two concepts' of collective self-defence and military assistance on request.[14] The section also considers whether the same use of force can simultaneously be an instance of both collective self-defence and military assistance on request.

Armed Intervention and Consent, Max Planck Trialogues on the Law of Peace and War (Anne Peters and Christian Marxsen, series eds.), vol. IV (Cambridge, Cambridge University Press, 2023), 26, especially 76–94; Claus Kreß, 'The Fine Line between Collective Self-Defense and Intervention by Invitation: Reflections on the Use of Force against "IS" in Syria', *Just Security* (17 February 2015), www.justsecurity.org/20118/claus-kreb-force-isil-syria; Hasar, n.3, 294–298; Irène Couzigou, 'Respect for State Sovereignty: Primacy of Intervention by Invitation over the Right to Self-Defence' (2019) 79 *Zeitschrift für Ausländisches Öffentliches Recht und Völkerrecht* 695; de Wet, n.3, 181–217 (albeit as part of exploring the relationship between military assistance on request and the right of self-defence *in toto*).

[14] Visser, n.4, argued throughout, quoted at 315.

8.2 Collective Self-Defence and Military Assistance on Request at the Conceptual Level

Even at the theoretical or conceptual level, there exist at least some similarities between collective self-defence and military assistance on request. Both concepts very clearly have their roots in state sovereignty, for example. Of course, this is neither an especially profound conclusion (given the significant range of meanings that are/have been ascribed to 'sovereignty'),[15] nor is it revelatory (given that 'sovereignty' can be seen as a key underpinning to much of the content of the international legal system).[16]

More specifically, then, it can be said that both collective self-defence and military assistance on request can be considered sovereign *rights* and – indeed – as *inherent* sovereign rights. As has been noted throughout this book, Article 51 of the UN Charter proclaims that nothing therein impairs the 'inherent right of individual or collective self-defence'.[17] Despite the fact that some have questioned – irrespective of this unequivocal language – whether the right to use military force in collective self-defence truly amounts to a 'right' that 'inheres' in the co-defending state,[18] it will be recalled that states themselves have expressed the view that collective self-defence is a right held by both the defending state and the co-defending relatively consistently.[19] In any event, collective self-defence is undoubtedly an inherent right for the defending state at least.[20]

As for military assistance on request, the UN Security Council was no less unequivocal than the text of Article 51 when it recalled in 1976 'the *inherent* and lawful *right* of every State, in the exercise of its sovereignty,

[15] Winston P. Nagan and Craig Hammer, 'The Changing Character of Sovereignty in International Law and International Relations' (2004) 43 *Columbia Journal of Transnational Law* 141.

[16] See Samantha Besson, 'Sovereignty', in Rüdiger Wolfrum (ed.), *Max Planck Encyclopaedia of Public International Law*, vol. IX (Oxford, Oxford University Press, 2012), 366, 387, para. 150.

[17] Charter of the United Nations (1945) 1 UNTS XVI (UN Charter), Article 51.

[18] See, for example, Marco Roscini, 'On the "Inherent" Character of the Right of States to Self-Defence' (2015) 4 *Cambridge Journal of International and Comparative Law* 634, 648.

[19] See Section 1.3.2 and accompanying text (setting out examples of relevant state practice and providing discussion).

[20] See C. H. M. Waldock, 'The Regulation of the Use of Force by Individual States in International Law' (1952) 81 *Recueil des cours* 451, 504.

to request assistance from any other State or group of States'.[21] The International Court of Justice (ICJ),[22] scholars[23] and (occasionally) states[24] all also have explicitly conceived of military assistance on request as a sovereign right.

The respective inherent rights to request military assistance and to request defensive aid do come from somewhat different manifestations of sovereignty, however. The ability to provide military assistance on request flows most directly from a state's exclusive territorial jurisdiction, resulting in a wide (albeit, of course, far from unlimited)[25] right to consent to external military activity on its territory.[26] It is thus premised, at its core, on sovereign notions of jurisdiction, control, and autonomy. This is conceptually distinct, at least to an extent, from collective self-defence. For good or ill, the wagon of collective self-defence was irrevocably hitched to the horse of individual self-defence by Article 51 of the UN Charter.[27] As such, while military assistance on request has its roots in the control of territory and the exercise of jurisdiction flowing therefrom, collective self-defence, at least in the UN era, is a corollary of the state's entitlement to exist.

Relatedly, the rights that are affected by the exercise of military assistance on request and collective self-defence can be said to be implicated in different ways too. In the case of military assistance on request, the implicated right is that of the requesting state not to have another state use force on its territory. The issue is, thus, whether that state (validly and genuinely) 'renounces the protection that the law affords

21 UNSC Res. 387, UN Doc. S/RES/387 (31 March 1976) (emphasis added).

22 *Nicaragua* (merits), n.3, para. 195 (referring to military assistance at the request of the state as a 'general *right* of intervention', emphasis added).

23 See, for example, Michael Byers, 'Still Agreeing to Disagree: International Security and Constructive Ambiguity' (2021) 8 *Journal on the Use of Force and International Law* 91, 105; Geir Ulfstein and Hege Føsund Christiansen, 'The Legality of the NATO Bombing in Libya' (2013) 62 *International and Comparative Law Quarterly* 159, 169; Gregory H. Fox, 'Invitations to Intervene after the Cold War: Toward a New Collective Model', in Olivier Corten, Gregory H. Fox and Dino Kritsiotis, *Armed Intervention and Consent*, Max Planck Trialogues on the Law of Peace and War (Anne Peters and Christian Marxsen, series eds.), vol. IV (Cambridge, Cambridge University Press, 2023), 179, 179, 196.

24 See, for example, Special Committee on Principles of International Law Concerning Friendly Relations and Co-operation among States: Summary Record, 28th mtg., 21 September 1964, UN Doc. A/AC.119/SR.28 (23 October 1964), 6 (Argentina).

25 See, for example, Hasar, n.3, 154–181; Byrne, n.2, 120–124.

26 Hasar, n.3, 33–34.

27 See Section 2.4.

to one of its rights in a specific set of circumstances'.[28] However, in the context of collective self-defence, the interrelated rights involved are more complex, in that the rights of at least three states are engaged (the defending state, co-defending state, and aggressor).[29] As between the defending and co-defending state (where the force is used on the territory of the former),[30] the effected right remains the same as it does in the case of military assistance on request: the right of the defending state not to have another use force on its territory. The request in either case is acting to renounce the required performance of that right in the particular instance in question.[31] But an action in collective self-defence also implicates the rights of the *aggressor* state, certainly if force is used beyond the territory of the defending state. Again, this predominantly concerns the right of the aggressor not to have force used against it, but that right is not being renounced. Rather, it is forfeited – in an appropriately limited and non-punitive manner – as a result of the aggressor's own armed attack.[32] The appropriate limitations to be placed on that forfeiture are premised not on the scope of the defending state's request for aid but on the parameters of that state's defensive need, and what is necessary and proportional in responding to it.

Another fundamental conceptual distinction is that the exercise of collective self-defence is an act that remains a legal wrong, *prima facie*, albeit an excused one.[33] In contrast, military assistance of request is

[28] Federica Paddeu, *Justification and Excuse in International Law: Concept and Theory of General Defences* (Cambridge, Cambridge University Press, 2018), 131–134, 170–172, quoted at 170. See also David Wippman, 'Military Intervention, Regional Organizations, and Host-State Consent' (1996) 7 *Duke Journal of Comparative and International Law* 209, 209–212.

[29] Of course, this is at a minimum, as there often will be more than one co-defending state, and – indeed – there could be more than one aggressor too.

[30] See Section 8.8 (arguing that a collective self-defence action can occur on the territory of the defending state, extra-territorially, or both).

[31] Wippman, n.28, 220–221.

[32] Paddeu, n.28, 218–222.

[33] Text of the Draft Articles on Responsibility of States for Internationally Wrongful Acts, with commentaries, Report of the International Law Commission, 53rd sess., UN Doc. A/56/10 (2001), 177 (commentary to Article 21) ('the existence of a general principle admitting self-defence [individual or collective] *as an exception* to the prohibition against the use of force in international relations is undisputed', emphasis added). See also Christian J. Tams, 'Self-Defence against Non-State Actors: Making Sense of the "Armed Attack" Requirement', in Mary Ellen O'Connell, Christian J. Tams and Dire Tladi, *Self-Defence against Non-State Actors*, Max Planck Trialogues on the Law of Peace and War (Anne Peters and Christian Marxsen, series eds.), vol. I (Cambridge, Cambridge University Press, 2019), 90, 100–101; Jaemin Lee, 'Collective Self-Defense or Collective

widely (and in this author's view, correctly) regarded as not being a legal justification or defence. Instead, the majority view is that the (valid) request has the effect of circumventing the prohibition on the use of force in the first instance, meaning that the action falls without the boundary of the primary norm.[34] Thus, it may be said that while both stem from sovereignty, only collective self-defence is a violation of sovereignty (albeit an excused one), whereas military assistance on request is not.

It ultimately can be said that the line between a justified intervention that is intertwined with the right of states to defend themselves (collective self-defence) and an act stemming from jurisdictional autonomy that is *not even an intervention* (military assistance on request) is 'perfectly clear from the juridical point of view'.[35] Collective self-defence and military assistance on request are, at their conceptual core, indisputably distinct. They both are inherent rights, and both stem from state sovereignty (albeit in different ways), but it is clear that they function as doctrinally independent legal claims.

8.3 Blurred State Argumentation

Section 8.2 argued that, while there are some similarities, a fairly clear distinction can be drawn between collective self-defence and military assistance on request at the conceptual or doctrinal level. However, as

Security: Japan's Reinterpretation of Article 9 of the Constitution' (2015) 8 *Journal of East Asia and International Law* 373, 378.

34 ILA, Use of Force Committee (2010–2018), *Final Report on Aggression and the Use of Force*, Sydney Conference (2018), https://ila.vettoreweb.com/Storage/Download.aspx?DbStorageId=11391&StorageFileGuid=6a499340-074d-4d4b-851b-7a56871175d6, 18; Byrne, n.2, 99–101; Benjamin Nußberger, 'Military Strikes in Yemen in 2015: Intervention by Invitation and Self-Defence in the Course of Yemen's "Model Transitional Process"' (2017) 4 *Journal on the Use of Force and International Law* 110, 125–126; Tom Ruys and Luca Ferro, 'Weathering the Storm: Legality and Legal Implication of the Saudi-Led Military Intervention in Yemen' (2016) 65 *International and Comparative Law Quarterly* 61, 79–80. *Contra* Federica I. Paddeu, 'Military Assistance on Request and General Reasons against Force: Consent as a Defence to the Prohibition of Force' (2020) 7 *Journal on the Use of Force and International Law* 227 (making some convincing arguments as to the *desirability* of consent being considered a defence in this regard, but not – for this author – establishing this as *lex lata*).

35 Rein Müllerson, 'Intervention by Invitation', in Lori Fisler Damrosch and David J. Scheffer (eds.), *Law and Force in the New International Order* (Boulder, Westview Press, 1991), 127, 127. See also Antonio Tanca, *Foreign Armed Intervention in Internal Conflict* (Dordrecht, Martinus Nijhoff, 1993), 25.

has already been noted at the start of this chapter,[36] at the *practical* level, the division between the concepts is less evident. One key reason for this is that in the cut and thrust of legal argumentation 'on the ground', states have been far from clear or consistent in distinguishing collective self-defence and military assistance on request claims.[37] Of course, states are notorious for advancing blurred, 'mixed', or imprecise legal claims, especially in the context of the *jus ad bellum*,[38] but this trend is even more pronounced in relation to force deployed in response to a request (or alleged request) for aid.[39]

It is true that states have sometimes drawn a very clear distinction between collective self-defence and military assistance on request in their legal arguments.[40] In other instances, such a distinction has been implicit, but still relatively clear: for example, where a state refers to a 'request' as the basis for forcible action while tellingly avoiding using any of the 'language' of self-defence.[41]

However, it has also been common in the UN era for states to argue explicitly that the very same use of force is justified *both* as an instance of collective self-defence *and* as military assistance on request.[42] This

[36] See nn.9–12 and accompanying text.

[37] See, for example, Tanca, n.35, 24–25; de Wet, n.3, 95, 107.

[38] See, generally, Dino Kritsiotis, 'Arguments of Mass Confusion' (2004) 15 *European Journal of International Law* 233.

[39] See Anne Peters, 'Armed Intervention and Consent: Principle and Practice', in Olivier Corten, Gregory H. Fox and Dino Kritsiotis, *Armed Intervention and Consent*, Max Planck Trialogues on the Law of Peace and War (Anne Peters and Christian Marxsen, series eds.), vol. IV (Cambridge, Cambridge University Press, 2023), 1, 19; Larissa van den Herik, 'Replicating Article 51: A Reporting Requirement for Consent-Based Use of Force?' (2019) 79 *Zeitschrift für Ausländisches Öffentliches Recht und Völkerrecht* 707, 709; Agata Kleczkowska, 'The Misconception about the Term "Intervention by Invitation"' (2019) 79 *Zeitschrift für Ausländisches Öffentliches Recht und Völkerrecht* 1, 1–2; Hasar, n.3, 295–298.

[40] See, for example, Prime Minister of Australia, 'Interview with Fran Kelly', *ABC Radio National* (16 September 2014), www.abc.net.au/radionational/programs/breakfast/tony-abbott/5746376 (the then Prime Minister of Australia, Tony Abbott, asserting in relation to the use of force against 'Islamic State' in 2014 that '[t]he legalities of operating inside Syria . . . are quite different from the legalities of operating inside Iraq').

[41] See, for example, Letter dated 15 October 2015 from the Permanent Representative of the Russian Federation to the United Nations addressed to the President of the Security Council, UN Doc. S/2015/792 (15 October 2015).

[42] Examples include Russian/Commonwealth of Independent States intervention in Tajikistan in 1993 (justified as military assistance on request: Letter dated 20 October 1993 from the Permanent Representative of the Russian Federation to the United Nations addressed to the Secretary-General, UN Doc. S/26610 (21 October 1993), appendix I, para. 2; and as collective self-defence: Letter dated 15 July 1993 from the Permanent

approach has been particularly perplexing in some instances, where the criteria for one of the two claims (say, collective self-defence) had clearly not been met on the facts.[43] This begs the question why states have, on a number of occasions in the UN era, opted to invoke both collective self-defence and military assistance of request in relation to the same use of force. In part, this probably can be explained by the fact that 'relying on additional grounds for intervention' in this way means 'not putting all one's eggs in the [same] basket'.[44] Yet, this would seem an unsatisfactory explanation in circumstances where one claim is notably weaker than the other. Some commentators therefore have mused whether the reason for this approach may relate to some states' domestic contexts.[45] If the internal requirements for the executive to use force internationally in 'self-defence' are less onerous than for using force in other circumstances, this might influence a state's decision to advance multiple claims.[46]

Whatever the reason, the mixing of collective self-defence and military assistance on request claims in practice is a barrier to clarifying the relationship between the concepts[47] and also can pose problems for identifying and interpreting their respective legal content. The difficulty

Representative of the Russian Federation to the United Nations addressed to the Secretary-General, UN Doc. S/26110 (19 July 1993)); French intervention in Mali (justified as military assistance on request: Identical letters dated 11 January 2013 from the Permanent Representative of France to the United Nations addressed to the Secretary-General and the President of the Security Council, UN Doc. S/2013/17 (14 January 2013); and as collective self-defence: Press conference given by M. Laurent Fabius, Minister of Foreign Affairs – excerpts, Paris (11 January 2013), http://ambafrance-us.org/spip.php?article4216); the justifications advanced for interventions in Yemen since 2015 (asserting both military assistance on request and collective self-defence: Identical letters dated 26 March 2015 from the Permanent Representative of Qatar to the United Nations addressed to the Secretary-General and the President of the Security Council UN Doc. S/2015/217 (27 March 2015)).

43 The interventions in Yemen since 2015 provide a good example here. For discussion, see Nußberger, n.34, 156–158; Luca Ferro, 'The Doctrine of "Negative Equality" and the Silent Majority of States' (2021) 8 *Journal on the Use of Force and International Law* 4, 30. It will be recalled from the Introduction to this book that this reflects a wider trend in relation to collective self-defence argumentation, whereby a notable proportion of collective self-defence *claims* in the UN era have been legally dubious. See Introduction, nn.50–54 and accompanying text.

44 'Military Intervention by Consent' (2017) 111 *American Society of International Law Proceedings* 221 (Remarks by Robert Taylor, 227), 228.

45 Oona Hathaway and Luke Hartig, 'Still at War: The United States in Somalia', *Just Security* (31 March 2022), www.justsecurity.org/80921/still-at-war-the-united-states-in-somalia.

46 *Ibid* (considering specifically the US context).

47 Tanca, n.35, 25.

of unpicking state claims in this regard should be borne in mind throughout the remainder of this chapter.

8.4 The Request Requirement

8.4.1 A Shared Request Requirement

This section examines what is perhaps the starkest *similarity* between collective self-defence and military assistance on request: both are necessarily premised on the existence (and continuance) of a valid 'request'. This is a straightforward conclusion in itself. For collective self-defence, it will be recalled from Chapter 4 that, despite occasional suggestions to the contrary in the literature,[48] there is no question that a valid request is indeed a requirement for collective self-defence under customary international law. As for military assistance on request, the need for a valid 'request' effectively amounts to its *sine qua non*: it can be said to be the defining feature of the legal claim.

It therefore is patently clear that both collective self-defence and military assistance on request are premised on a request. However, it is perhaps worth noting that the function of the request is somewhat different in the two instances.[49] In the case of military assistance on request, the 'request' is effectively an expression of *consent*.[50] By making a request for aid, the state in question is consenting to another state using force on its territory, whereas, in the collective self-defence context, this only holds true where (and in relation to the fact that) force is used on the territory of the requesting state.[51] When force is used extra-territorially against a non-consenting sovereign state in collective self-defence, the defending state obviously cannot 'consent' to the use of force by one state (the co-defender) against another (the aggressor). As noted previously,[52] the way that rights are implicated by military assistance on

[48] See for example, Omar Abubakar Bakhashab, 'The Relationship between the Right of Self-Defence on the Part of States and the Powers of the Security Council' (1996) 9 *Journal of King Abdulaziz University: Economics and Administration* 3, 9–10.

[49] See, generally, Christian Henderson, 'Book Review: Erika de Wet, *Military Assistance on Request and the Use of Force*' (2022) 33 *European Journal of International Law* 1037, 1042 (alluding to the idea that the request requirement might not function identically as between the two concepts).

[50] See, generally, Byrne, n.2.

[51] See Section 8.8 (arguing that a collective self-defence action can occur on the territory of the defending state, extra-territorially, or both).

[52] See nn.28–32 and accompanying text.

request and collective self-defence differ: one involves the renunciation of rights and the other involves a renunciation and/or a forfeiture, depending on the context. This means that a collective self-defence request, primarily, is not an act of 'consent', but, rather, is an act of self-help. That said, for all practical purposes, this is a vanishingly thin distinction. A request in collective self-defence is an expression of sovereign will by the state and is a legal requirement for force to be used, just as is the case for military assistance on request. It is ultimately entirely uncontroversial to say that both require a request.

8.4.2 *The Issuer of the Request*

The similarities in this regard go further, however, in that it is also clear that the request must come from a state; more specifically – in both instances – it must stem from the de jure government of the state.[53] This undoubtedly is the case for collective self-defence.[54] Likewise, it is widely accepted that there is no right for a non-state actor to request military assistance in a struggle against the incumbent government.[55]

It has been suggested, however, that a distinction can be drawn between collective self-defence and military assistance on request when it comes to who is rightly to be viewed as the 'legitimate government' for the purposes of making such a request.[56] The primary factor in identifying the actor with the authority to request military assistance has often been said to be the effective control of territory.[57] However, as was examined in Chapter 5, the effective control of territory is not the primary test for establishing the entity that can act as the valid 'requester' for collective self-defence. The state practice examined in that chapter indicated that effective control had a marginal role (if any) in that determination.[58] Moreover, it was also argued that if an incumbent government loses effective control as the result of an external armed

[53] See, respectively, *Nicaragua* (merits), n.3, para. 246; Dinstein, n.10, 317–318.

[54] See Section 5.4.

[55] de Wet, n.3, 24–31.

[56] See Kritsiotis, n.13, 79, 81, footnote 334; Masoud Zamani and Majid Nikouei, 'Intervention by Invitation, Collective Self-Defence and the Enigma of Effective Control' (2017) 16 *Chinese Journal of International Law* 663, 677 (albeit focusing rather more on the different extent or way in which effective control may apply).

[57] Hasar, n.3, 71–106.

[58] See Section 5.5.

attack, this cannot thereby mean it also loses the ability to request aid to repel that same attack.[59]

This rationale (i.e. that the wrong must not preclude the remedy) does, it must be said, also hold true[60] for one well-established 'type' of military assistance on request – instances of so-called counter-intervention.[61] However, it may perhaps be contrasted to at least some other types of military assistance on request, where 'effective control' as internally manifested has been seen, at least by some, as acting as a degree of useful shorthand for the self-determination of the people of the state.[62] However, it certainly cannot be said that 'effective control' can be seen as indicating the will of a state's people in instances where that control has been seized by an external actor.[63] As such, a distinction can – possibly – be drawn between collective self-defence and counter-intervention on one hand and other types of military assistance on request on the other.

In terms of state practice, one can identify a degree of support for the continued primacy of effective control in relation to who can request internal military assistance (again, outside situations of counter-intervention).[64] This should not be overstated, however. The state practice in this regard has been inconsistent, to the extent that it is perhaps difficult to argue that there is an established approach as to who can invite outside military assistance on behalf of the state.[65] Other factors – for example, democratic credentials or external recognition – have also been viewed as being significant for military assistance on request throughout the UN era, both by states and by scholars.[66] These approaches and their

59 See Chapter 5, n.104 and accompanying text; *ibid*, n.206 and accompanying text.

60 See Christian Henderson, 'A Countering of the Asymmetrical Interpretation of the Doctrine of Counter-Intervention' (2021) 8 *Journal on the Use of Force and International Law* 34, 39; Lieblich, n.3, 169.

61 See, generally, Perkins, n.7.

62 See Brad R. Roth, 'The Enduring Significance of State Sovereignty' (2004) 56 *Florida Law Review* 1017, 1024; John Hursh, 'International Humanitarian Law Violations, Legal Responsibility, and US Military Support to the Saudi Coalition in Yemen: A Cautionary Tale' (2020) 7 *Journal on the Use of Force and International Law* 122, 130–131.

63 See Henderson, n.60, 39; Lieblich, n.3, 169.

64 Brad R. Roth, *Governmental Illegitimacy in International Law* (Oxford, Oxford University Press, 1999), 253–320 (setting out practice that suggests that effective control remains the 'go to' test, but also that this is not settled and that other factors can influence the determination). See also Hasar, n.3, 71–106.

65 See Roth, n.64, 253–320.

66 See, generally, de Wet, n.3, 21–73 (including examples from state practice).

variations, especially those related to demonstrations of some form of 'legitimacy', are also seen by many as being preferable on policy grounds (albeit that they come with their own problems).[67]

It will also be recalled from Chapter 5 that, while effective control is not the primary test for identifying 'the requester' for collective self-defence, it equally is not entirely clear what the correct test *is*.[68] Some of the very same factors (democratic credentials, external recognition, etc.) appear to be relevant to the equivalent determination in the context of both collective self-defence and military assistance on request. As such, despite a few suggestions to the contrary,[69] it is difficult to draw a clear distinction between the concepts based on the respective test(s) for identifying who can represent the government for the purposes of making the necessary request. Both, ultimately, are necessarily premised on a valid request from the de jure government – and while there is uncertainty as to how one is to *determine* the de jure government, that uncertainty is, itself, also common to both concepts.

8.4.3 *The Implications of Terminological Choices*

To conclude this section, it is worth considering that the shared 'request' requirement between collective self-defence and military assistance on request may have implications for the desirability of the terminology applied to the latter concept.

There is no legally authoritative term for what is referred to as 'military assistance on request' in this chapter; indeed, traditionally, the most commonly adopted term probably has been 'intervention by invitation'.[70] In recent years, however, the suitability of the label 'intervention by invitation' has been critiqued,[71] and instead 'military assistance on

67 See, generally, Jean d'Aspremont, 'Legitimacy of Governments in the Age of Democracy' (2006) 38 *New York University Journal of International Law and Politics* 877; Roth, n.64, 121–199.

68 See Section 5.5.

69 See n.56 and accompanying text.

70 See, for example, Louise Doswald-Beck, 'The Legal Validity of Military Intervention by Invitation of the Government' (1985) 56 *British Yearbook of International Law* 189; Anne Peters, 'Intervention by Invitation: Impulses from the Max Planck Trialogues on the Law of Peace and War' (2019) 79 *Zeitschrift für Ausländisches Öffentliches Recht und Völkerrecht* 635; Gregory H. Fox, 'Intervention by Invitation', in Marc Weller (ed.), *The Oxford Handbook of the Use of Force in International Law* (Oxford, Oxford University Press, 2015), 816.

71 See, for example, Kleczkowska, n.39; Visser, n.1.

request' has been used with increasing prominence.[72] For those who have adopted it, the term 'military assistance on request' is preferable both because of its higher degree of specificity (to 'uses of force' rather than any form of intervention)[73] and because 'intervention by invitation' can be viewed as a contradiction in terms (i.e. if 'intervention' is invited, then it is not an intervention).[74]

These reasons are valid and explain the recent shift in the scholarship from the use of 'intervention by invitation' to 'military assistance on request' – a trend continued in this book. However, it is worth keeping in mind that the term 'military assistance on request' is *also* a wholly accurate description of the right of collective self-defence. The exercise of collective self-defence necessarily involves an attacked state requesting military assistance in its defence.[75] As such, collective self-defence is a form of 'military assistance on request', at least where that label is used descriptively and not as a term of art.

In contrast, use of the more traditional term 'intervention by invention' would seem less likely to contribute to the blurring of the concepts. Describing the use of force in collective self-defence against a non-consenting state as being premised on the 'invitation' of another state would sit rather uncomfortably, given that the sovereignty of the non-consenting state is violated (albeit that this violation is excused by defensive necessity). However, using 'military assistance on request' as a term of art as distinguished from collective self-defence – as is done throughout this chapter – is difficult to justify as a matter of descriptive accuracy.

Whether this potential to add to the complexity of the relationship between collective self-defence and 'military assistance on request' is enough to abandon the latter term in favour of 'intervention by invitation' is debateable, however. As noted, there are other benefits that derive from employing the term 'military assistance on request'.[76] Nonetheless,

[72] IDI Rhodes Resolution, n.5; de Wet, n.3; Paddeu, n.34; Patrick M. Butchard, 'Territorial Integrity, Political Independence, and Consent: The Limitations of Military Assistance on Request under the Prohibition of Force' (2020) 7 *Journal on the Use of Force and International Law* 35; ILA, Use of Force Committee, Interim Report, n.5, section III.B.

[73] Visser, n.3, 652–653.

[74] Gerhard Hafner, *l'Institut de droit international*, 10th Commission, 'Present Problems of the Use of Force in International Law Sub-group: Intervention by Invitation' (2009) 73 *Annuaire de l'Institut de droit international* 299, 310–311.

[75] See Chapter 4.

[76] See nn.73–74 and accompanying text.

given that the aim of this chapter is to map out the relationship between the two concepts, particularly so as to better delineate the concept of collective self-defence, this terminological issue is worth keeping in mind.

8.5 Armed Attack and the Possibility of an Equivalent for Counter-Intervention

8.5.1 No Threshold Trigger for Military Assistance on Request

It was established in Chapter 3 that an 'armed attack' acts as the key trigger for the lawful exercise of collective self-defence in the same way that it does for individual self-defence. This is confirmed in case law and state practice and need not be revisited again here.[77]

Military assistance on request, in contrast to collective self-defence, does not have an equivalent 'trigger' to the armed attack requirement, at least not per se. This can be demonstrated relatively easily by the fact that a state can consent, for example, to the peacetime stationing of another state's troops on its territory – something that would be an unlawful use of force without that consent,[78] but which is clearly not legally premised on any trigger or threshold. Thus, a distinction that can be made between collective self-defence and military assistance on request is the existence of the armed attack criterion for the former. An armed attack is a very particular (grave) use of force that acts as a necessary legal trigger; military assistance on request can be actioned absent any such trigger, grave, or otherwise.[79]

8.5.2 The Particular Case of 'Counter-Intervention': An 'External Intervention' Requirement?

While military assistance on request per se does not have a threshold trigger equivalent to the armed attack requirement, however, it is notable

[77] See Section 3.2.

[78] See UNGA Res. 3314 (XXIX), UN Doc. A/RES/3314 (14 December 1974), annex, Article 3(e); James A. Green, 'The Annexation of Crimea: Russia, Passportisation and the Protection of National Revisited' (2014) 1 *Journal on the Use of Force and International Law* 3, 5–6.

[79] Visser, n.4, 308 ('no threshold requirement exists in general for an intervention by invitation, let alone the requirement of an armed attack'); Petra Perišić, 'Intervention by Invitation – When Can Consent from a Host State Justify Foreign Military Intervention?' (2019) 7 *Russian Law Journal* 4, 26 (military assistance on request 'clearly has to be differentiated from collective self-defense, as the latter includes the existence of an unlawful armed attack in terms of Article 51 of the U.N. Charter, while the former necessarily does not').

that counter-interventions – again, being a particular 'species' of military assistance on request – *are* premised on a response to some measure of 'external intervention'[80] in the requesting state. By definition, counter-interventions are situations where a state requests aid from another in response to a preceding intervention against it. This preceding intervention could, perhaps, be equated to an armed attack, meaning that this manifestation of military assistance on request might look especially similar to collective self-defence.[81] Indeed, some commentators have taken the view, presumably (although not explicitly) on this basis, that collective self-defence and counter-intervention are effectively one and the same thing.[82]

However, 'armed attack' and 'external intervention' cannot necessarily be equated. As noted, armed attack is unquestionably an essential legal trigger for the exercise of collective self-defence. But whether 'external intervention', too, is viewed as a 'legal trigger' largely depends on whether one subscribes to the so-called negative equality principle.[83] For those who take the view that international law prohibits intervention in support of any party to a civil war (i.e. negative equality), counter-

[80] See Erika de Wet, 'The (Im)permissibility of Military Assistance on Request During a Civil War' (2020) 7 *Journal on the Use of Force and International Law* 26, 30 (although de Wet uses the term 'counter-interference'). It is worth noting that use of the term 'intervention' in this context does not necessarily correspond to the wider concept as prohibited by the 'principle of non-intervention' under customary international law (e.g. because counter-intervention need not always be in response to 'intervention' *by a state*, see nn.92–95 and accompanying text), although it is likely to do so in most cases. On the principle of non-intervention, see *Nicaragua* (merits), n.3, para. 205; UNGA Res. 2625 (XXV), UN Doc. A/RES/25/2625 (24 October 1970), annex; UNGA Res. 31/91, UN Doc. A/RES/31/91 (14 December 1976), particularly paras. 1, 3, 4; UNGA Res. 36/103, UN Doc. A/RES/36/103 (9 December 1981), paras. 1, 2.

[81] See Henderson, n.60, especially 62–63; Hasar, n.3, 294–295; Perkins, n.7 (referring to the similarities between collective self-defence and counter-intervention throughout).

[82] See, for example, Perkins, n.7, 206 ('[a]ction taken by a third state in the right of "collective" self-defense when an armed attack occurs *is a form of counterintervention*', emphasis added); Oscar Schachter, 'Self-Defense and the Rule of Law' (1989) 83 *American Journal of International Law* 259, 267, 271; Thomas M. Franck, 'Who Killed Article 2(4)? Or: Changing Norms Governing the Use of Force by States' (1970) 64 *American Journal of International Law* 809, 814 (discussing the exercise of 'counter-intervention by way of collective self-defence'). See also R. St. J. MacDonald, 'The *Nicaragua* Case: New Answers to Old Questions' (1986) 24 *Canadian Yearbook of International Law* 127, 157–158 (arguing that *the ICJ* conflated collective self-defence and counter-intervention in its *Nicaragua* decision, albeit not himself necessarily subscribing to that conflation).

[83] For the classic statement of the 'negative equality' principle, see, generally, IDI Wiesbaden Resolution, n.5.

intervention is commonly recognised as an exception to that prohibition.[84] Here, external support for a non-state party to a civil war acts as a necessary legal trigger, effectively 'reinstating' the state's presumptive right to request external assistance in response. The existence of 'external intervention' is, on this basis, legally essential (as is also true for collective self-defence). Even for proponents of negative equality, however, significant uncertainty remains as to the point at which this legal requirement would 'kick in' – recognition of belligerency, non-international armed conflict, etc. – with the answer being dependent on where one considers the outer limits of 'negative equality' to be located.[85]

All of this is, of course, premised on the existence of the 'negative equality' principle as a matter of *lex lata*, which is something that is very much disputed.[86] Avoiding engaging here with deep-rooted debates on the question, which run beyond the scope of this book, it suffices to say that this author is not convinced as to the legal basis of the negative equality principle as a restriction on military assistance on request. This is not least (although not solely) because of the fact that state practice/*opinio juris* does not support its existence.[87] For those who share this view and see, for good or ill, the presumptive legality of a state's right to request outside military assistance as extending into the civil war context, the 'external intervention' aspect of counter-interventions becomes merely descriptive rather than legally determinative. This, of course, would be in stark contrast to the armed attack requirement for collective self-defence.

Whether or not one sees the 'external inference' trigger for counter-intervention to be descriptive/politically persuasive or legally essential, it is also worth noting that state practice does not appear to support any particular gravity threshold for such intervention. While some claimed counter-interventions have been based on an intervention that would

[84] *Ibid*, Article 5. See also Gray, n.10, 95–100.

[85] Fox, n.70, 827–828 (usefully summarising different approaches and the difficulty involved in identifying the necessary 'civil war' threshold).

[86] *Ibid*, 828–829.

[87] See de Wet, n.3, 83–124 (setting out relevant practice in significant detail, and – for this author – making a compelling case that the negative equality principle cannot be identified as a matter of customary international law). See also Gerhard Hafner, *l'Institut de droit international*, 10th Commission, 'Present Problems of the Use of Force in International Law Sub-group: Intervention by Invitation: Final Report' (2011) 74 *Annuaire de l'Institut de droit international* 359, paras. 9–28.

(seemingly) be of sufficient scale to qualify as an armed attack,[88] other such interventions have been based on much lower-level forms of intervention,[89] and yet still have received support from other states.[90] This would be in contrast to the armed attack criterion, for which a required – if perhaps not especially well-defined – level of gravity is established in state practice.[91]

It is also relatively clear that the 'external intervention' element to counter-interventions need not amount to intervention by a *state*. This is said to be on the normative basis that if non-state groups come from abroad or are supported by external private actors, such external intervention will go against the will of the state's people, irrespective of whether or not another state is involved – thus counter-intervention still can be undertaken.[92] Importantly, accepted responses to external intervention by non-state actors can also be seen to be a feature of state practice.[93] In a measure of contrast, there exists well-known and significant disagreement as to whether an armed attack can be perpetrated by a non-state actor absent any attribution of its actions to another state.[94]

[88] One might, for example, note the action by France in Comoros in 1995, to reverse a coup supported by external mercenary forces. Those forces overthrew the incumbent government, which – although involving numerically small forces – would seemingly have the necessary 'scale and effects' to amount to an 'armed attack'. See UNESC, Report on the Question of the Use of Mercenaries as a Means of Violating Human Rights and Impeding the Exercise of the Right of Peoples to Self-Determination, submitted by Mr. Enrique Bernales Ballesteros, Special Rapporteur, pursuant to Commission resolution 1995/5 and Economic and Council resolution 1995/254, UN Doc. E/CN.4/1996/27 (17 January 1996), paras. 48–61.

[89] See, for example, the Gulf Cooperation Council (GCC)'s avowed counter-intervention in Bahrain in 2011. This was undertaken in response to Iranian support for internal civil agitation – something that would fall well below the threshold of an armed attack. See GCC, Secretary-General of the Cooperation Letter, Riyadh (23 March 2011), translated from Arabic and quoted in Agatha Verdebout, 'The Intervention of the Gulf Cooperation Council in Bahrain – 2011', in Tom Ruys and Olivier Corten (with Alexandra Hofer) (eds.), *The Use of Force in International Law: A Case-Based Approach* (Oxford, Oxford University Press, 2018), 793, 797.

[90] Tellingly, for example, the GCC met with general support for its action in Bahrain in 2011, including explicitly from the Arab League. See *ibid*, 798.

[91] See Section 3.2.2.

[92] Olivier Corten, 'Intervention by Invitation: The Expanding Role of the Security Council', in Olivier Corten, Gregory H. Fox and Dino Kritsiotis, *Armed Intervention and Consent*, Max Planck Trialogues on the Law of Peace and War (Anne Peters and Christian Marxsen, series eds.), vol. IV (Cambridge, Cambridge University Press, 2023), 101, 114–115.

[93] *Ibid*, 115.

[94] See Section 3.2.4.

Without opening that particular can of worms again here,[95] the disagreement in itself is enough to distinguish collective self-defence from counter-intervention to some extent, given that there seems to be no corresponding disagreement in relation to the legality of counter-interventions against non-state actors.

Overall, one can conclude that a distinction can be drawn between collective self-defence and military assistance on request, based on the armed attack requirement for the former and the absence of an equivalent trigger for the latter. This distinction still holds true – although perhaps becomes less of a 'bright line' – when one compares collective self-defence specifically to instances of counter-intervention.

8.6 Necessity and Proportionality

As with the armed attack criterion, the customary international law requirements of necessity and proportionality apply equally to collective, as well as individual, self-defence.[96] When it comes to military assistance on request, whether (and, if so, the extent to which) the provision of assistance is legally limited by requirements of necessity and proportionality is far less clear than is the case for collective self-defence. Various arguments have, admittedly, been advanced to support the legal status of these requirements specifically for military assistance on request. These include the argument that necessity and proportionality exist as general principles of law and thus are inherently applicable to any and all uses of force.[97] Another argument advanced in support of these requirements applying to military assistance on request is based on an analogy to collective self-defence and/or countermeasures, being other forms of 'self-help'.[98]

In instances of 'counter-intervention'[99] in particular, the proportionality criterion can be viewed as being especially appropriate, partly because it is relatively clear what one can factor into the calculation – the prior 'external intervention' and the response.[100] For those who view

[95] See *ibid.*

[96] See Section 3.3.

[97] Mary Ellen O'Connell, 'Necessity and Assistance' (2022), background paper for the International Law Association, Use of Force: Military Assistance on Request Committee (unpublished, on file with author), particularly at 2.

[98] Ruys and Ferro, n.34, 93.

[99] See, generally, Perkins, n.7.

[100] Oscar Schachter, 'The Right of States to Use Armed Force' (1984) 82 *Michigan Law Review* 1620, 1644.

counter-intervention as an exception to the negative equality principle,[101] there is an especially important role for proportionality to play.[102] This is because if the only lawful purpose of a counter-intervention is to redress the balance of the 'scales' of a self-determination struggle – tipped unjustly by the initial external intervention – then any action that was disproportional to the goal of redressing that balance would become unlawful.[103]

However, as was discussed in Section 8.5, the negative equality principle is disputed as a matter of law, meaning that, for some – including the present author – this rationale for the proportionality requirement's existence as a legal restriction on the exercise of military assistance on request will not be entirely convincing.

Unlike with collective self-defence, it is extremely difficult to identify a basis for the applicability of necessity and proportionality to military assistance on request in state practice.[104] States do not tend to include reference to these requirements when making a claim to be providing military assistance on request (including counter-intervention claims) in the same way that they often do when claiming to be acting in self-defence. It also appears to be the case, at least so far as this author can tell, that – despite the fact that counter-interventions are, on occasion, widely condemned by other states – such condemnation does not seem to have been on the basis of a failure to comply with necessity or proportionality requirements. One might note, as a recent example, the wide-ranging condemnation of Turkey's actions in Libya in 2020.[105]

In addition, there are practical concerns. In cases of counter-intervention (actual and/or avowed), it may be difficult to ensure that there is true equivalence between the initial external intervention and the response, to the point that even 'rough equivalence may be very difficult to achieve'.[106] Ensuring *any degree* of equivalence also assumes that the requesting and responding states know the scale of the external intervention that they are acting against, which may well not be the case.[107] While these practical issues are pertinent, however, they are not, perhaps, all that different from the practical problems that regularly beset the

[101] See Section 8.5.3.
[102] Ruys and Ferro, n.34, 93–94.
[103] *Ibid*; Hasar, n.3, 295.
[104] See Schachter, n.100, 1644.
[105] As set out in Ferro, n.43, 18–20.
[106] Kritsiotis, n.13, 85.
[107] *Ibid*; Hasar, n.3, 295.

application of the proportionality requirement to instances of the exercise of the right of self-defence,[108] which would not be seen by anyone as reason to conclude that the self-defence proportionality requirement does not exist or was undesirable.

In other manifestations of military assistance on request beyond counter-intervention, though, problems of application become more acute. Take, for example, the peacetime stationing of troops with consent.[109] Against what, exactly, is one to measure the 'proportionality' of the action? Would such troop stationing be considered 'necessary' simply by virtue of the request itself?

Overall, a case can be made that necessity and proportionality apply, as a matter of law, to military assistance on request operations, or, at least, specifically to counter-intervention operations. That case is far from watertight, however, and how far one accepts it is likely to depend on what stock one puts in the negative equality principle and/or in the need for supporting state practice and *opinio juris*. Ultimately, the present author is unconvinced that the applicability of these principles to military assistance on request has been established as a matter of law. This is in contrast to collective self-defence, where necessity and proportionality are unquestionably required in law.

8.7 Reporting

As was discussed in Chapter 3, Article 51 of the UN Charter provides that '[m]easures taken by members in exercise of this right of self-defence shall be immediately reported to the Security Council. . .'[110] This applies to collective self-defence just as it does to its individual counterpart, albeit that – in both cases – a failure to report is generally seen as evidential in relation to illegality rather than legally determinative in isolation.[111]

As regards military assistance on request, one might note that the 2011 Rhodes resolution of the Institut de droit international (IDI) asserted that '[a]ny request that is followed by military assistance shall

[108] See Richard R. Baxter, 'The Legal Consequences of the Unlawful Use of Force under the Charter' (1968) 62 *American Society of International Law Proceedings* 68, 74 (discussing the inherent uncertainties in applying the necessity and proportionality criteria for self-defence).

[109] See n.78 and accompanying text.

[110] UN Charter, n.17, Article 51.

[111] See Section 3.4.

be notified to the Secretary-General of the United Nations'.[112] It is not entirely clear why the Secretary-General was identified by the IDI as the necessary recipient of such reports, as opposed to the Security Council (which Article 51, of course, designates as the recipient of self-defence reports). It has been suggested, however, that this may have been because the Secretary-General was a more politically neutral choice.[113] In any event, the IDI is not alone in identifying a form of 'military assistance on request reporting requirement', with some scholars arguing that such a requirement exists, or, at least, that it might be emerging in customary international law.[114]

However, these claims are largely based on the desirability of such a requirement[115] and/or an analogy to collective self-defence.[116] Notwithstanding that the public reporting of military actions is, indeed, likely to be desirable in most cases, neither that nor the existence of the self-defence reporting requirement are sufficient, in themselves, to establish a legal requirement to report instances of military assistance on request.

With no treaty-based equivalent to Article 51's reporting requirement, any obligation to report instances of military assistance on request can only be created in customary international law, based on sufficient state practice and *opinio juris*.[117] States do at times 'report' (or, at least, publicly notify the Security Council of) their provision of military assistance premised on the consent of the territorial state.[118] There equally, though, have been a notable number of examples of military assistance on request that went unreported.[119] Such 'reporting' practice certainly has been much more sporadic than has been the case for collective self-

[112] IDI Rhodes Resolution, n.5, Article 4(4).

[113] Larissa van den Herik, 'Article 51's Reporting Requirement as a Space for Legal Argument and Factfulness', in Claus Kreß and Robert Lawless (eds.), *Necessity and Proportionality in International Peace and Security Law* (Oxford, Oxford University Press, 2021), 221, 237.

[114] See, for example, van den Herik, n.39; Karine Bannelier and Theodore Christakis, 'Under the UN Security Council's Watchful Eyes: Military Intervention by Invitation in the Malian Conflict' (2013) 26 *Leiden Journal of International Law* 855, 869–870.

[115] van den Herik, n.39.

[116] *Ibid*; Bannelier and Christakis, n.114, 869–870.

[117] van den Herik, n.113, 237.

[118] See, for example, UN Doc. S/26110, n.42; UN Doc. S/2013/17, n.42; Letter dated 15 October 2016 from the Permanent Representative of the United States of America to the United Nations addressed to the President of the Security Council, UN Doc. S/2016/869 (17 October 2016).

[119] Corten, n.92, 177.

defence. In any event, to the extent that there is relevant *opinio juris* – which is very little – it points in the other direction. In relation to its interventions in Yemen, for example, the United States was explicit in 2016 that its:

> actions were taken with the consent of the Government of Yemen. Although the United States therefore does not believe notification pursuant to Article 51 of the Charter of the United Nations is necessary in these circumstances, the United States nevertheless wishes to inform the Council that these actions were taken consistent with international law.[120]

Therefore, the reporting requirement for collective self-defence would seem to be another distinction between the concept and military assistance on request (which, it is argued here, has no such legal requirement). However, this is perhaps not an especially notable distinction, given that 1) states are increasingly choosing to report acts of military assistance (albeit without feeling obliged); 2) the legal consequences of a failure to comply with the self-defence reporting requirement are generally considered to be relatively limited; and 3) self-defence reports still tend to be quite cursory and thus of questionable value in any event.[121]

8.8 Location and Simultaneousness

8.8.1 Questions of Location and Simultaneousness in Scholarship

In one of the few scholarly works seriously to examine the relationship between collective self-defence and military assistance on request, Visser has argued that the fundamental distinction between the two concepts, and primary means of distinguishing them in practice, is the territory upon which the use of force occurs:

> [M]ost strikingly … the key difference between the two concepts is the territorial location of the force used. With intervention by invitation, the force is used in the requesting state's own territory. … With collective self-defence the force is used outside the attacked state's territory and in the territory of the attacking state[122]

If Visser is correct in this regard, then the distinction between collective self-defence and military assistance on request might actually be quite

[120] UN Doc. S/2016/869, n.118.
[121] See Chapter 3, n.199 and accompanying text.
[122] Visser, n.4, argued throughout, quoted at 315.

straightforward. Where military assistance occurs on the territory of the requesting state, it is military assistance on request; if it takes place on another state's territory, it is collective self-defence. Any other differences – for example, whether an armed attack is required, reporting obligations, etc. – all become applicable (or not) to any given action dependant wholly on an initial determination of which side of the line (literally, the territorial border) force is used. A distinction based on territorial location is thus hugely appealing in its simplicity.

It also certainly holds true on one side of the equation. Military assistance on request unquestionably must be confined to the territory of the requesting state. A state cannot consent to conduct by another state that it would not itself lawfully be able to undertake.[123] This is why a state cannot consent to another state perpetrating human rights violations or breaches of the requirements of the *jus in bello* on its territory,[124] but it also means, very obviously, that a state cannot 'consent' to the violation of another (non-consenting) state's territorial integrity. Military assistance on request must *always* be confined to the territory of the requesting state (or states, if more than one state consents).[125] Thus, one 'half' of Visser's distinction is easily confirmed.

The reverse proposition, though, is more debatable. Visser argues that, just as military assistance on request is limited to the territory of the requesting state, collective self-defence is limited to occurring on the territory of the aggressor state (or, perhaps, the territory from which a non-state aggressor is based).[126] She reaches this conclusion on the basis that an armed attack necessarily must have a 'cross-border element', and therefore that the 'mirror image' of this is that collective self-defence actions must occur in the territory of a state other than the one requesting aid.[127]

[123] See, for example, Ashley S. Deeks, 'Consent to the Use of Force and International Law Supremacy' (2013) 54 *Harvard International Law Journal* 1, 35; Schmitt, n.3, 315.

[124] Byrne, n.2, 120–124.

[125] See, for example, United Kingdom, Summary of the Government Legal Position on Military Action in Iraq against ISIL, Policy paper (25 September 2014), www.gov.uk/government/publications/military-action-in-iraq-against-isil-government-legal-position/summary-of-the-government-legal-position-on-military-action-in-iraq-against-isil (arguing that the prohibition on the use of force 'does not apply to the use of military force by one State *on the territory of another if the territorial State* so requests or consents', emphasis added).

[126] On the controversial question of collective self-defence against attacks by non-state actors, see Section 3.2.4.

[127] Visser, n.4, 304.

With regard to armed attacks requiring a 'cross-border element', the ICJ's designation of such an attack as 'the most grave form of the use of force'[128] indicates that an armed attack must itself be a violation of the prohibition in Article 2(4),[129] and, given that the prohibition therein only relates to *inter*state uses of force,[130] this would suggest that armed attacks must also necessarily be cross-border acts. However, it perhaps is a little simplistic to conclude that armed attacks must have a 'cross-border element', given that it is evident that attacks on state embassies, vessels, and nationals have all been considered to qualify as armed attacks, even though they do not necessarily cross a state border.[131]

Equally, it is correct that armed attacks cannot be wholly 'internal' and, to be fair, Visser also uses a different phrase that accurately captures this nuance: this is that armed attacks 'must have an external *component*'.[132] Their occurrence need not necessarily be transboundary, but if they both originate and occur within the territory of the state against which they are directed without any external input, they are not 'armed attacks' giving rise to the right of self-defence.[133]

[128] *Nicaragua* (merits), n.3, para. 191; *Case concerning Oil Platforms (Islamic Republic of Iran v. United States of America)* (merits) [2003] ICJ Rep. 161, para. 51.

[129] James A. Green, *The International Court of Justice and Self-Defence in International Law* (Oxford, Hart, 2009), 32.

[130] UN Charter, n.17, Article 2(4) is clearly addressed to 'states' (specifically, members of the United Nations) with regard to actions undertaken in the context of their 'international relations', against 'any state'. See Christian Henderson and James A. Green, 'The *Jus ad Bellum* and Entities Short of Statehood in the Report on the Conflict in Georgia' (2010) 59 *International and Comparative Law Quarterly* 129, 131–134; Dinstein, n.10, 89–90.

[131] See Henderson, n.3, 212–213 (providing relevant examples from practice and case law).

[132] Visser, n.4, 304 (emphasis added). See also Henderson, n.3, 212–213 (arguing that armed attacks must be directed at a 'manifestation' of the state, not necessarily against its territory); Marko Svicevic, 'Collective Self-Defence or Regional Enforcement Action: The Legality of a SADC Intervention in Cabo Delgado and the Question of Mozambican Consent' (2022) 9 *Journal on the Use of Force and International Law* 138, 149 (arguing that an armed attack '*ordinarily* consists of a cross border use of force', emphasis added).

[133] See *Legal Consequences of the Construction of a Wall in the Occupied Palestinian Territory* (advisory opinion) [2004] ICJ Rep. 135, para. 139 (noting that 'Israel exercises control in the Occupied Palestinian Territory and that, as Israel itself states, the threat which it regards as justifying the construction of the wall originates within, and not outside, that territory ... [as such] Article 51 of the Charter has no relevance in this case'); Statement by the North Atlantic Council, *North Atlantic Treaty Organisation*, Press Release (2001)124 (12 September 2001) (NATO 'agreed that if it is determined that this attack [9/11] was directed from abroad against the United States, it shall be regarded as an action covered by Article 5 of the Washington Treaty, which states that an armed attack against one or more of the Allies in Europe or North America shall be considered

In any event, it is unclear why the 'external element' required for an armed attack establishes, in itself, a requirement that *the response to such an attack* must take place in the territory of another state or states. The latter is not necessarily a logical consequence of the former. Similarly, the corollary of the finding that military assistance on request must be restricted to the territory of the requesting state is that force used in the territory of a non-consenting state must be an act of self-defence (absent Security Council authorisation), which is not the same as concluding that an act of collective self-defence must exclusively take place on the territory of a non-consenting state.

Self-defence functions to excuse a violation of the prohibition of the use of force specifically.[134] This means that a state acting in individual self-defence must be engaged in an extra-territorial defensive response, because otherwise it is not using 'force' in the sense of Article 2(4) and therefore self-defence will not be relevant to its actions as they will not have triggered the *ad bellum* prohibition. But in cases of collective self-defence, where an 'internal' response would actually involve the co-defending state acting on the territory of the defending state, then that act in itself (absent consent) would constitute an unlawful extra-territorial use of force. Thus, self-defence is a relevant defence even if the co-defending state does not venture into the territory of the non-consenting aggressor state.

Therefore, however appealingly straightforward it may be as a distinction, it is unclear, legally, why acts within the territory of the requesting state are necessarily excluded from the scope of collective self-defence. Indeed, to require this may lead to problems. One might, for example, consider a 'classic' collective self-defence scenario. State A's regular forces launch an armed attack against State B, invading its territory. State B requests aid from State C. In such circumstances, State C would be very likely to begin its defensive operation within State B's territory, to help it repel the invader. To begin by using force on the territory of State C would likely be operationally unwise and also may well fall foul of the self-defence necessity criterion.[135]

At the same time, it will be recalled that the proportionality criterion for self-defence does not require that a defending or co-defending state

an attack against them all', emphasis added). See also Ruys and Ferro, n.34, 72–74; Ferro, n.43, 10.

134 See Chapter 1, nn.172–173 and accompanying text.

135 See Section 3.3.

necessarily stops its response the instant that the aggressor is pushed back to the territorial border: the defensive action can continue into the territory of the aggressor, so long as it remains proportionate to the established defensive necessity.[136] Yet, a sharp 'location distinction' between collective self-defence and military assistance on request would suggest that, when the action to repel the aggressor reached the territorial boundary, the legal basis for that action would have to change. This would be artificial, and likely unworkable. It would mean that State C is, first, providing military assistance on request, and then, once the action crossed the border, it would be acting in collective self-defence. This would come with sudden imposition of all of the different legal requirements for collective self-defence for the continuance of the same action.

Moreover, fighting will not always cross a territorial boundary all at once, in a neat location shift. When an aggressor's forces are pushed back to the territorial border and then across it, it is quite possible that the *same* operative use of force could be simultaneously occurring on both sides of the border, with the fighting spread across it. Here, an absolute 'location distinction' would require that an *operationally singular* use of force be legally 'severed' into two different uses of force, with different rules applying to different parts of it. Again, this seems artificial and probably unworkable.

One conclusion that Visser draws from the 'location distinction' is that the same action cannot simultaneously be both collective self-defence and military assistance on request, because the use of force will be located in one territory or another, and its location designates its legal character.[137] However, while many uses of force – take, for example, localised counter-terrorism operations – will indeed occur wholly within a single state's territory, this will certainly not always be the case.

It is worth noting that another reason beyond the 'location distinction' has been advanced to support the view that both military assistance on request and self-defence cannot be available as potential justifications for the same use of force. This is on the basis that military assistance on request preserves the sovereign integrity of all the involved states, meaning that wherever it is available as an option it takes primacy over self-defence, which *overrides* sovereign will for the aggressor state.[138] A more

[136] See Chapter 3, nn.141–143 and accompanying text.

[137] Visser, n.4, 311.

[138] Couzigou, n.13. See also nn.28–32 and accompanying text (discussing the differently implicated rights for collective self-defence and military assistance on request).

specific version of this argument focuses on the self-defence necessity requirement: the point being that where consent is given, military assistance on request will suffice to allow for any required action (rendering self-defence unnecessary, and thus unlawful).[139] As Kreß has phrased this:

> If the goal to end a non-State armed attack can be effectively achieved through coordinated military action with the territorial State, then, in principle, this avenue must be pursued because it reconciles the needs to protect the sovereignty both of the victim and the territorial State. It follows, that, again in principle, the right of collective self-defense in case of a non-State attack is subsidiary to 'intervention by invitation'.[140]

This analysis is surely correct. However, it is dependant, as Kreß acknowledges, on context: '[*i*]*f* the goal to end a non-State armed attack *can be effectively achieved* . . .'[141] At least at the margins, it certainly is possible – even where consent is provided – that limits placed on the scope of that consent mean that it does not provide sufficient scope to achieve the alleviation of the defensive necessity of the requesting state.[142]

More importantly for the purposes of this chapter, this analysis is focused on situations where consent is given by the state from the territory of which an armed attack by non-state actors emanates. But in cases where the aggressor/'host' state does not provide consent, but the *defending state does*, it is unclear why the necessity criterion would preclude the exercise of collective self-defence solely on the territory of the consenting state, or preclude the simultaneous lawfulness of collective self-defence and military assistance on request. In such a situation, collective self-defence would not override sovereign will, as consent would exist, and if an armed attack had occurred, it may well be equally 'necessary' to use force in either self-defence or military assistance on request.

Where force is limited to the territory of the requesting state, and where the other requirements for both claims are met, there seems no reason why a state cannot choose which claim it wishes to advance (or,

139 Hasar, n.3, 296 (albeit not ultimately taking this view); Dapo Akande and Thomas Liefländer, 'Clarifying Necessity, Imminence, and Proportionality in the Law of Self-Defense' (2013) 107 *American Journal of International Law* 563, 566.

140 Kreß, n.13.

141 *Ibid.* See also Akande and Liefländer, n.139, 566 ('there is no need to violate the territorial sovereignty of another state and to resort to a self-defense justification where *effective action* can be taken with the consent of the host state', emphasis added).

142 Hasar, n.3, 296–297.

indeed, advance *both* – unhelpful as this may be for mapping their differences).[143] A reason that a state might 'pick' collective self-defence in such circumstances is that it might be keeping in mind that (but not yet know whether) the defensive necessity that it is acting to alleviate may *later* require it to use force in the territory of a non-consenting state: starting with a self-defence claim future proofs against the need to change the legal basis artificially, should the defensive response ultimately need to move into the aggressor's territory.[144]

8.8.2 *Questions of Location and Simultaneousness in State Practice*

The relatively common practice of states arguing both collective self-defence and military assistance on request in relation to the same use of force, as discussed in Section 8.3, would certainly indicate that states in the UN era have felt that collective self-defence and military assistance on request can be simultaneously applicable to the same circumstances, which necessarily must be instances where force is used on the territory of the requesting state (again, given that military assistance on request undoubtedly cannot provide a legal basis for the use of force in the territory of another state).

Moreover, claims of collective self-defence in relation to forcible action that was wholly confined to the territory of the requesting state – whether or not accompanied by a simultaneous military assistance on request claim – have been common. In fact, they have been *more* common in the UN era than instances where the force used has ventured into the territory of a non-consenting state.[145]

As a classic example, one might note the United Kingdom's dispatch of troops to Jordan in 1958, in relation to a formal request by Jordan for states to 'come to its immediate aid', in response to an alleged threat from the United Arab Republic (UAR).[146] The presence of British troops was limited to Jordanian territory. While the United Kingdom was somewhat ambiguous with regard to the legal basis for this, referring to it as 'a Government . . . asking a friendly Government for military assistance as a

[143] See Section 8.3.

[144] As previously noted, another reason may be domestic constitutional requirements for the authorisation to use force internationally. See nn.45–46 and accompanying text.

[145] Gray, n.10, 177.

[146] UNSC Verbatim Record, UN Doc. S/PV.831 (17 July 1958), para. 24.

defensive measure',[147] Jordan itself was very clear that it viewed the support it received from the United Kingdom as an exercise of collective self-defence.[148] More importantly, both the states that supported the presence of British troops in Jordan and those that opposed it framed its legality through the requirements for self-defence. China, for example, asserted that the situation amounted to a 'legitimate exercise of Jordan's inherent right of self-defence',[149] whereas the USSR strongly argued that the action was unlawful on the basis that there had been no armed attack against Jordan from the UAR.[150] The USSR therefore seemingly accepted in principle that collective self-defence could be exercised solely on the territory of the requesting state and simply felt that the required criteria had not been met in this case.

The same view – that collective self-defence actions can occur wholly on the territory of the requesting state, would also seem to be supported by the conflict in the Democratic Republic of Congo (DRC) that became known as 'The Great African War' (1998–2003), which involved at least seven different states.[151] With regard to the states that intervened on the side of the incumbent DRC government (Angola, Zimbabwe, Namibia, and Chad), their support would seem, relatively uncontroversially, to qualify as military assistance on request, in the form of counter-intervention.[152] However, the states themselves were clear that they were acting in collective self-defence, at the request of the DRC and pursuant to Article 51.[153] The DRC, too, was explicit that these states were

[147] *Ibid*, para. 29.

[148] *Ibid*, para. 24.

[149] *Ibid*, para. 99. See also *ibid*, para. 35 (the US, expressing a similar view).

[150] *Ibid*, paras. 65–68.

[151] See James A. Green, 'The Great African War and the Intervention by Uganda and Rwanda in the Democratic Republic of Congo – 1998–2003', in Tom Ruys and Olivier Corten (with Alexandra Hofer) (eds.), *The Use of Force in International Law: A Case-Based Approach* (Oxford, Oxford University Press, 2018), 575.

[152] See, for example, Ben Chigara, 'Operation of the SADC Protocol on Politics, Defence and Security in the Democratic Republic of Congo' (2000) 12 *African Journal of International and Comparative Law* 58, particularly at 64–65.

[153] Thus, Zimbabwe contended, on behalf of all of the states that intervened in support of the government of the DRC, that these states were acting 'in line with Article 51 of the Charter of the United Nations regarding the right of a State to ask for military assistance when its security, sovereignty and territorial integrity are threatened'. See Letter dated 23 September 1998 from the Permanent Representative of Zimbabwe to the United Nations addressed to the President of the Security Council (25 September 1998) UN Doc. S/1998/891, 3. See also UNGA Verbatim Record (23 March 1999) UN Doc. A/53/PV.95, 20 (Namibia).

supporting it 'en vertu de l'exercice du droit de légitime défense individuelle et collective prévu par l'article 51 de la Charte de l'ONU'.[154] Yet, the military action taken by Angola *et al.* was notably confined to the territory of the DRC.[155] Collective self-defence was, indeed, explicitly asserted regarding action 'to repel the Ugandan-Rwandan aggression . . . *within the country*'.[156]

Leaving aside the fact that their actions were confined to the territory of the DRC, it seems relatively clear[157] that Angola *et al.* complied with the requirements for collective self-defence, that is, a response to an armed attack, at the request of the state attacked, undertaken in a necessary and proportional manner.[158] It has been argued[159] that the UN Security Council endorsed the collective self-defence claims made by the pro-DRC states when it explicitly emphasised the individual and *collective* right of self-defence in resolution 1234.[160] This is possible, although this equally could just have amounted to a rote reiteration of the wording of Article 51. With similar caveats, one might also note resolution 1304, in which the Council demanded the withdrawal of Ugandan and Rwandan troops from the DRC, while remaining silent on the interventions of Angola *et al.*[161] As this author has suggested in previous writings, this unusually partisan resolution is a strong indicator that the Council viewed the actions of Angola *et al.* as lawful,[162] although

154 *Armed Activities on the Territory of the Congo (Democratic Republic of the Congo v. Uganda)* (mémoire de la Republique Démocratique du Congo) (6 July 2000), para. 2.38. See also Letter dated 31 August 1998 from the Permanent Representative of the Democratic Republic of the Congo to the United Nations addressed to the President of the Security Council, UN Doc. S/1998/827 (2 September 1998), para. 81.

155 One might note that Uganda, for its part, did allege that cross-border uses force had occurred, in that it claimed that the DRC (and some other states, notably Sudan) had supported insurgents within Ugandan territory. See, for example, *Armed Activities on the Territory of the Congo (Democratic Republic of the Congo v. Uganda)* (counter-memorial submitted by Uganda) (21 April 2001), paras. 11–47. This was never established, however. See *Armed Activities* (merits), n.3, paras. 297–301. Moreover, it was never alleged of the states claiming to support the DRC in collective self-defence.

156 UN Doc. S/1998/827, n.154, para. 81 (emphasis added).

157 Nina Wilén, *Justifying Interventions in Africa: (De)Stabilizing Sovereignty in Liberia, Burundi and the Congo* (London, Palgrave Macmillan, 2012), 102.

158 Martin R. Rupiya, 'A Political and Military Review of Zimbabwe's Involvement in the Second Congo War', in John F. Clark (ed.), *The African Stakes of the Congo War* (New York, Palgrave Macmillan, 2002), 93, 96–97.

159 Wilén, n.157, 106; Gray, n.10, 80 (albeit only implicitly).

160 UNSC Res. 1234, UN Doc. S/RES/1234 (9 April 1999) (emphasis added).

161 UNSC Res. 1304, UN Doc. S/RES/1304 (16 June 2000).

162 See Green, n.151, 584.

whether it can be read as indicating that the Council saw those actions as lawful based specifically on the exercise of collective self-defence, as those states advanced, is less clear.[163]

A more recent example of intra-territorial collective self-defence is the US airstrikes in Somalia in July and August 2021. Following the first strike, near Galkayo, the US Africa Command deputy director of operations was very clear that it 'was conducted under collective self-defense authority and targeted al-Shabaab fighters engaged in active combat with our Somali partners'.[164] Similarly, after the second strike a few days later, which occurred near Galmudug, a Pentagon statement reiterated that 'US forces are authorized to conduct strikes in support of combatant commander designated partner forces under collective self-defense'.[165] While al-Shabaab certainly has a cross-border presence,[166] whether there was indeed an 'imminent threat' of armed attack against Somalia's 'Danab' force, as was asserted, can be questioned on the facts.[167]

In any event, the US strikes themselves were confined to Somali territory. While the collective self-defence claim received a (limited) degree of domestic criticism,[168] other states were effectively silent on the matter. For example, in a meeting of the Security Council in

[163] It is worth noting that the 2005 merits decision of the ICJ in *Armed Activities on the Territory of the Congo* did not pronounce on the lawfulness of the actions of the states acting in support of the DRC, as this was not directly at issue. Uganda's counterclaims focused instead on the alleged responsibility for, *inter alia*, a breach of Article 2(4) *by the DRC*. See *Armed Activities* (counter-memorial of Uganda), n.155, paras. 379–386. However, the very name of the case itself neatly acts as a reminder of where the 'activity' – which was generally accepted to be the lawful exercise of collective self-defence on the part of multiple co-defending states – took place: 'on the territory of the Congo'.

[164] US Africa Command, 'U.S. Africa Command Conducts Strike against al-Shabaab' (20 July 2021), www.africom.mil/pressrelease/33893/us-africa-command-conducts-strike-against-al-shabaab. See also 'US launches air strike targeting Al Shabaab in Somalia', *The Defense Post* (21 July 2021), www.thedefensepost.com/2021/07/21/us-air-strike-somalia.

[165] Idrees Ali and Phil Stewart, 'US Military Carries out Second Strike in Somalia This Week', *Reuters* (23 July 2021), www.reuters.com/world/africa/us-military-carries-out-second-strike-somalia-this-week-2021-07-23.

[166] See, generally, Claire Felter, Jonathan Masters and Mohammed Aly Sergie, 'Al-Shabab', *Council on Foreign Relations* (last updated 19 May 2021), www.cfr.org/backgrounder/al-shabab.

[167] Hathaway and Hartig, n.45.

[168] See, for example, Ryan Grim and Sara Sirota, 'Rep. Ilhan Omar Questions Biden's First Airstrike on Somalia', *The Intercept* (23 July 2021), https://theintercept.com/2021/07/23/ilhan-omar-biden-somalia-airstrike.

September 2021, which included wide-ranging discussions on peace and security in Somalia, the strikes were not even raised.[169] Of course, one must be careful not necessarily to read silence as endorsement,[170] but it can at least be noted that the US collective self-defence claim met with no explicit criticism from other states, even in the context of a clear opportunity to do so, irrespective of the fact that the strikes were limited to Somali territory.[171]

These examples – Jordan (1958), the DRC (1998–2003), and Somalia (2021) – are representative of wider state practice across the period that they span. Admittedly, one might note that there are some instances where states have explicitly 'switched' or 'severed' their justifications between collective self-defence and military assistance on request in that same period. The most obvious example of this is the arguments presented by a number of states in relation to their uses of force against the entity known as 'Islamic State' in Iraq and Syria.[172] These states generally justified their actions within Iraqi territory as being based on Iraq's consent, and characterised this as military assistance on request,[173] whereas they were careful to invoke collective self-defence in defence of Iraq, in relation to their uses of force that have occurred within Syria.[174] This would suggest that these states drew a clear distinction based on

[169] UNSC Verbatim Record, UN Doc. S/PV.8867 (28 September 2021).

[170] See, generally, Paulina Starski, 'Silence within the Process of Normative Change and Evolution of the Prohibition on the Use of Force: Normative Volatility and Legislative Responsibility' (2017) 4 *Journal on the Use of Force and International Law* 14.

[171] It is perhaps worth noting that the Security Council's Panel of Experts on the situation in Somalia, while noting that the airstrikes had occurred, took no issue with the US collective self-defence claim in its extensive October 2021 report. See Letter dated 5 October 2021 from the Chair of the Security Council Committee pursuant to resolution 751 (1992) concerning Somalia addressed to the President of the Security Council, UN Doc. S/2021/849 (6 October 2021), para. 20.

[172] Indeed, this was the example used by Visser to support the 'location distinction'. See Visser, n.4, 304–306.

[173] See, for example, United Kingdom, Military Action in Iraq, n.125; United States, Background Briefing by Senior Administration Officials on Iraq (via conference call), White House, Office of the Press Secretary (8 August 2014), https://obamawhitehouse.archives.gov/the-press-office/2014/08/08/background-briefing-senior-administration-officials-iraq; France, Travaux parlementaires, Engagement des forces armées en Irak, Déclaration du Gouvernement suivie d'un débat (M. Jean-Yves Le Drian, ministre de la défense) (24 September 2014), www.senat.fr/seances/s201409/s20140924/s20140924001.html.

[174] See the various letters cited at Introduction, n.21.

territory.[175] However, this does not establish that these states felt that they had no option but to invoke military assistance on request for their action within Iraq. It simply could be that having exercised a choice to invoke military assistance on request for action in Iraq, they then had no choice but later to invoke collective self-defence once their action against Islamic State moved into Syria.

8.8.3 *Conclusion on Questions of Location and Simultaneousness*

Overall, commentators do not seem to view the 'location distinction' as absolute in relation to collective self-defence. For example, Corten argues that, when exercising collective self-defence, states have 'grounds to act *not only* in the territory of the [requesting] state ... but *also* in the territory of the state to which an armed attack can be imputed ...'[176] Perhaps most tellingly, in previous writing, Visser herself has taken the view that, if State X suffers an armed attack by State Y, and 'state X requests state Z to assist it, then state Z *can not only use force on X's territory* to repel state Y, but also on Y's territory, provided that the requirements for collective self-defence are met'.[177]

Given the problems that drawing an absolute territorial distinction between collective self-defence and military assistance on request – which would outweigh the benefits of any clarity that so doing would bring – it seems evident that such a distinction is not desirable. It is also not the law, as can be seen from the state practice to the contrary.

Military assistance on request must be confined to the territory of the requesting state. In contrast, collective self-defence can occur in the territory of the requesting state(s), the territory of a non-consenting aggressor (or, perhaps, harbouring) state(s), or both. This means that it is possible – assuming the requirements for both collective self-defence and military assistance on request are met and action stays within the requesting state's territory – for both to be available bases of legality, simultaneously.[178]

175 Indeed, some of them made this explicit. See, for example, Prime Minister of Australia, 'Interview with Fran Kelly', n.40.
176 Corten, n.92, 114 (emphasis added).
177 Visser, n.3, 28 (emphasis added).
178 de Wet, n.3, 122, 182.

8.9 Conclusion

This chapter has argued that collective self-defence and military assistance on request (used herein as a term of art) have numerous similarities. The most notable of these is the condition of a 'request'. Although there may arguably be a degree of difference in determining the legitimate government that can make that request, this is far from clear. The shared request requirement has led to a notable mixing by states of collective self-defence and military assistance on request arguments, which, in turn, has made untangling these two claims difficult.

However, while there is something of a blurred boundary between collective self-defence and military assistance on request, this cannot be viewed as an invitation to conflate the two concepts or to try to merge them further together in theory or practice. They have different doctrinal bases and, more importantly, different requirements. The most important of these are that 1) collective self-defence is premised on the occurrence of an armed attack, whereas military assistance on request is not and 2) military assistance on request is restricted to action within the territory of the requesting state, whereas collective self-defence is not. Beyond these 'headline' differences, this chapter has attempted to map out more subtle differences, while also recognising where clear distinctions between the concepts do not exist.

Ultimately, while the concepts can be distinguished in many respects, '[t]he line between collective self-defence and military assistance on request is . . . nowhere near as clear as one might hope'.[179] This is not a reason not to attempt further to clarify the features of the concepts, and to untangle them wherever possible. Nor, conversely, does it justify the imposition of artificial 'bright lines' around them, which cannot actually be found in *lex lata*. Such clarity is to be aspired to and worked towards, but it should not be the product of legal alchemy.

[179] James A. Green, Christian Henderson and Tom Ruys, 'Russia's Attack on Ukraine and the *Jus ad Bellum*' (2022) 9 *Journal on the Use of Force and International Law* 4, 22. See also Kritsiotis, n.13, 80 ('[t]here is . . . a "fine line" to be drawn from the legal standpoint between the consent offered for collective self-defence and that offered for an "intervention by invitation" . . .').

Conclusion

Self-defence is a crucial feature of international law, amounting as it does to the only lawful basis for the unilateral use of military force in the modern world.[1] It is not surprising, then, that a vast literature has developed regarding the nature and parameters of the exercise of self-defence in international law.[2] However, there has been relatively little consideration of the specific concept of collective self-defence. This is true not just in scholarship[3] but also in terms of the way that states discuss or debate self-defence in a general sense.[4] Marginalisation of the topic in this way perhaps has been due to the common perception that collective self-defence was effectively 'invented' by the drafters of the United Nations (UN) Charter,[5] and the view that states have exercised it only very rarely since.[6]

Collective self-defence actually has a long history, particularly since the seventeenth century when a number of common elements of the modern concept began to emerge in writings and in the practice of states in the

1 See Patrick M. Butchard, 'Back to San Francisco: Explaining the Inherent Contradictions of Article 2(4) of the UN Charter' (2018) 23 *Journal of Conflict and Security Law* 229, 262–264.

2 See Christopher Greenwood, 'Self-Defence', in Rüdiger Wolfrum (ed.), *Max Planck Encyclopaedia of Public International Law*, vol. IX (Oxford, Oxford University Press, 2012), 103, 113, para. 52 (providing a useful select bibliography of some of the key works).

3 See Introduction, nn.30–34 and accompanying text.

4 See *ibid*, nn.35–39 and accompanying text.

5 See, for example, *Military and Paramilitary Activities in and against Nicaragua* (*Nicaragua v. United States of America*) (merits) [1986] ICJ Rep. 14, dissenting opinion of Judge Jennings, 530–531; R. St. J. MacDonald, 'The *Nicaragua* Case: New Answers to Old Questions' (1986) 24 *Canadian Yearbook of International Law* 127, 143, 146; Rosalyn Higgins, *The Development of International Law through the Political Organs of the United Nations* (London, Oxford University Press, 1963), 208.

6 See, for example, Christine Gray, *International Law and the Use of Force* (Oxford, Oxford University Press, 4th ed., 2018), 176; Christine Chinkin and Mary Kaldor, *International Law and New Wars* (Cambridge, Cambridge University Press, 2017), 140.

form of treaty-based military alliances.[7] It is also the case that states have exercised collective self-defence – or, at least, have advanced it as a legal claim in relation to their uses of force – far more often since 1945 than is commonly supposed. Moreover, there has been a significant increase in such invocations over the last decade, perhaps most notably in the context of uses of force in Syria.[8] Against the backdrop of collective self-defence being appealed to more than ever before, this book has aimed to provide its readers with the most detailed and extensive account of the concept to date.

One important goal for the work has been extensively to theorise the concept of collective self-defence. This has not been for the mere sake of conceptual ordering: the theorisation of collective self-defence has practical implications for its operation in practice. It is concluded herein that collective self-defence is not '*self*-defence' at all, but instead involves the 'defence of another'.[9] This is hardly a revelatory finding, because this understanding already represents the majority view,[10] but it is important to have reached this conclusion based on a detailed examination of practice, given the competing assertions that have been made in scholarship to the effect that some measure of 'interest' is required on the part of the co-defending state.[11] This is not the case, and confirming that conclusion is valuable because it helps to determine who can act in collective self-defence and when. For good or ill, a state seeking to defend another need not concern itself with its own relationship to that state (beyond the need for that state to have requested aid, or if a relevant treaty arrangement exists between them). Nor need it concern itself with the implications *for itself* of the attack that it seeks to respond to.

It can also be concluded that collective self-defence is an inherent right not just for the defending state but also for the co-defending state(s). That may, again, seem a somewhat anodyne conclusion given that Article 51 of the UN Charter explicitly proclaims that collective self-defence is an 'inherent right'.[12] However, there is no reason why the use of this phrase in Article 51 could not be a reference to a right held only by the defending state: it is not necessarily inconsistent with Article 51 to consider collective

[7] See Chapter 2, particularly Sections 2.2 and 2.3.
[8] See Introduction, nn.21–29 and accompanying text.
[9] See Section 1.2.
[10] See sources cited at n.118.
[11] See Chapter 1, Section 1.2.
[12] Charter of the United Nations (1945) 1 UNTS XVI (UN Charter), Article 51.

self-defence not to be a right of the co-defending state(s) that are coming to the defending state's aid. Indeed, conceptually, the idea that a state that has not been attacked (and that need not have any direct interest in abating an attack against another) has a 'right' – let alone an 'inherent' one – to use military force against another sovereign nation is counterintuitive. Yet, states themselves have been clear as to the status of collective self-defence as a right for both defending and co-defending states, to the extent that it is difficult to conceive of it otherwise. This is also the predominant view in scholarship.[13] There is notable danger in reaching the conclusion that the right of collective self-defence is 'inherent' for the co-defending state, however. Such a perception on the part of states might suggest *carte blanche* to exercise their 'inherent right' with harmful and potentially abusive results.[14]

It is therefore crucial to be clear that collective self-defence is a legally *qualified* right. Inherence is not the same thing as immutability. As Schachter argued in 1991:

> Since collective self-defense may well be the legal basis for future collective security actions, it becomes important to remind states that the conditions for self-defense, collective and individual, are imposed by international law. The states claiming the right to use force in collective self-defense cannot be the final arbiters of its legality.[15]

Reminding states of this remains just as important – indeed, arguably more so – today. International law dictates compliance with a number of requirements for the lawful exercise of collective self-defence. Most of these criteria are well known, as are both their contours and controversies, because they are criteria that are shared with individual self-defence and have thus been examined in detail in that context. It is evident that, just as with individual self-defence, the exercise of collective self-defence must be undertaken in response to an armed attack (i.e. a grave use of force).[16] There is also state practice and evidence of *opinio juris* supporting the view that collective self-defence specifically can be exercised in relation to a demonstrably imminent armed attack – not solely one that has occurred – and that the author of the armed attack can be a non-state

[13] See Section 1.3.

[14] John S. Gibson, 'Article 51 of the Charter of the United Nations' (1957) 13 *India Quarterly* 121, 128.

[15] Oscar Schachter, 'United Nations in the Gulf Conflict' (1991) 85 *American Journal of International Law* 452, 471.

[16] See Sections 3.2.1 and 3.2.2.

actor. However, whether there is *sufficient* state practice and evidence of *opinio juris* to alter the legal parameters of the *jus ad bellum* regarding these entrenched points of contention is debatable in the collective context (again, just as with individual self-defence). This is especially the case in relation to the exercise of collective self-defence against non-state actors, which remains extremely legally controversial even following the invocation of the right at notable scale in relation to recent uses of force directed against the 'Islamic State of Iraq and the Levant' in Syria. Ultimately, it can be said that the same controversies that plague individual self-defence also exist in the collective context.

The customary international law requirements of necessity and proportionality unquestionably apply to collective self-defence.[17] In relation to collective action, though, it is worth noting that there is no clear evidence of *opinio juris* to establish any legal prescription as to which state(s) need to make these calculations. A co-defending state therefore can rely, for example, on the determination of another co-defending state acting with it in coalition as to compliance with the necessity and proportionality criteria. However, in practice, states would be wise to make their own determination, especially given that the exercise of collective self-defence increases the potential for disagreement between states as to the correct application of these criteria.[18] Yet, while co-defending states would be well advised to make necessity and proportionality calculations individually, it is important to note that proportionality, at least, is ultimately to be assessed by reference to the aggregate overall use of force in collective self-defence. Thus, states acting in concert must be careful to ensure that their shared action remains within the bounds of what is required to alleviate the defensive necessity of the defending state.[19]

A large proportion of this book has been dedicated to the examination and analysis of a crucial requirement for the exercise of collective self-defence that is *not* shared with individual self-defence: the request criterion. It will be recalled that the International Court of Justice (ICJ) famously identified that requirement as an element of customary international law in its 1986 *Nicaragua* judgment.[20] Despite some suggestions

[17] See Section 3.3.
[18] See *ibid.*
[19] See *ibid.*
[20] See *Nicaragua* (merits), n.5, particularly paras. 165–166, 195, 199, 231.

to the contrary,[21] there is no question that the request requirement does indeed exist in custom and is a legal prerequisite for any action taken in collective self-defence.[22] However, the other purported requirement that the ICJ identified in *Nicaragua* – that the defending state formally 'declare' that it has suffered an armed attack – has no basis in the law.[23]

That the request requirement exists as a matter of customary international law is fairly uncontentious today (although that was not the case when the Court identified it in the mid-1980s).[24] However, there has been very little consideration of how the request requirement in particular is to be applied. This is something this book has attempted to (begin) to remedy.

It is evident that only states have the legal capacity to issue a request for aid in collective self-defence.[25] However, contrary to some assertions,[26] there is no requirement that the requester be a UN member state.[27] The authority empowered to make a collective self-defence request on behalf of the state is its de jure government.[28] Yet, identifying the de jure government in instances where this is unclear or disputed can be extremely difficult.[29] While the effective control of territory is the traditional starting point for the recognition of governments in international law generally, this does not appear to be the test for identifying a collective self-defence requester. Or, at least, it is not the primary or determinative test.[30] Other factors are crucial, including the democratic credentials of the requester (actual or at least purported), external recognition, and compliance with internal constitutional (or other formal) processes.[31] The extent to which these factors are considered and applied is context specific. There is insufficient evidence of *opinio juris* to establish binding criteria in customary international law for determining the government for the purposes of issuing a collective self-defence request.[32] That said, it is evident that a combination of the factors identified is

[21] See Section 4.3.1.
[22] See, generally, *ibid.*
[23] See *ibid.*
[24] See Section 4.3.1.
[25] See Section 5.2.
[26] See Chapter 5, nn.48–49 and accompanying text.
[27] See Section 5.3.
[28] See Section 5.4.
[29] See Section 5.5.
[30] See *ibid.*
[31] See *ibid.*
[32] See *ibid.*

highly likely to influence the (political) decision of other states as to whether a collective self-defence 'requester' is indeed competent to issue a request on behalf of the defending state.[33]

It can also be concluded that the request need not be directed specifically at the state or states that ultimately respond to it. Defending states can issue an 'open call' for aid in response to an armed attack, and this will be sufficient to meet the request criterion.[34] Indeed, there is no required format for collective self-defence requests.[35] They have been issued in a range of ways during the UN era, without this being considered problematic by other states.[36] There are no particular formalities required for the issuance of a request so long as it is sufficiently clear.

In fact, it is possible for the request to be inferred and even for it to be entirely private.[37] That said, given that the occurrence of a request itself is legally essential, if it has not been made explicitly there will be significant difficulties for the co-defending state in establishing that the request requirement has been complied with. States therefore would be wise to ensure that any collective self-defence action is premised upon a clear, explicit, public request. It is unsurprising that this is common practice, even though this approach cannot be established as a legal necessity. What *is* legally required is that the request is issued before the relevant use of force commences.[38] Moreover, a pre-existing collective defence treaty arrangement is insufficient to meet the request requirement.[39] While there is no need for states to 'declare' that they have suffered an armed attack, their request must be made specifically in relation to an armed attack: it cannot be general or abstract.

Overall, the detailed analysis of practice undertaken for this book indicates that states retain a great deal of flexibility in relation to the request requirement. The *issuance of* a request (or some form of approval) by the defending state is a legally essential prerequisite for the exercise of collective self-defence, but *how* requests are made and received remains largely ungoverned by international law. That flexibility has benefits in terms of prioritising the rationale for requests – sovereign

[33] See *ibid.*
[34] See Section 6.2.
[35] See Section 6.3.
[36] See Chapter 6, nn.39–46 and accompanying text.
[37] See Sections 6.2.3 and 6.4.
[38] See Section 6.5.1.
[39] See Section 6.5.2.

autonomy and protection against abuse[40] – over technicalities of form, but it causes issues when it comes to certainty, and can be an invitation towards spurious invocations. Certainly, it may be said that such flexibility means that compliance with the request criterion is harder to test than one might initially suppose.

Beyond its assessment of the criteria for the operation of collective self-defence, this book also sought to map out the nature and scope of the hundreds of collective self-defence treaty arrangements that have emerged in the UN era. These arrangements have a facilitating function, meaning that states have notable freedom in the way they have created them, albeit that ultimately all such arrangements must only provide for action that complies with Article 51 and the relevant customary international law governing collective self-defence.

A notable – and perhaps surprising – feature of collective self-defence treaty arrangements is that they inevitably entail only 'weak' or 'soft' obligations.[41] They can also be problematic for their parties for a range of reasons: multiple memberships resulting in overlapping but different legal commitments,[42] tensions between members,[43] complex decision-making,[44] and a tendency towards regionalism and other self-imposed geographical limitations.[45] The *value* of these treaty arrangements thus is primarily to be found in their deterrent effect rather than their actual activation.[46] Nonetheless, collective self-defence treaty arrangements have continued to play an important role after the end of the Cold War and, indeed, there has been something of a renewed sense of their importance at the time of writing, given East–West tensions over, in particular, Russia's full-scale invasion of Ukraine that began in February 2022.[47]

The final goal of this book is to unpick the relationship between collective self-defence and so-called military assistance on request (also known as 'intervention by invitation'). Both concepts are premised on the requirement of a valid 'request' for military aid and – on their face – appear strikingly similar. As such, states have tended to blur them when

[40] See Chapter 4, nn.38–40 and accompanying text.
[41] See Section 7.3.
[42] See Section 7.4.
[43] See *ibid.*
[44] See Chapter 7, nn.29–37 and accompanying text.
[45] See Section 7.5.1.
[46] See Section 7.6.
[47] See *ibid.*

making legal arguments about the use of force,[48] to the point that it is important that they be carefully distinguished so that they can be appropriately assessed against their respective legal requirements. Collective self-defence and military assistance on request have different doctrinal bases and different underpinning rationales.[49] They can also be distinguished in a number of ways in terms of the respective criteria for their operation. Most crucially, collective self-defence is limited by the requirement of an armed attack, whereas military assistance on request is not,[50] and military assistance on request is restricted to action within the territory of the requesting state, whereas collective self-defence is not.[51]

Overall, this book has aimed to contribute to the theorisation and delineation of collective self-defence in international law. More importantly, it has sought to provide increased clarity regarding how the legal requirements for collective self-defence are to be *applied*. This, in turn, is intended both to reduce the scope for abusive invocation of collective self-defence and to provide states with more data to ensure that they are able lawfully to act in the genuine defence of another state that has been attacked. It must be said that these goals have only been partially achieved. Much of the relevant law is customary in nature, and the investigation of the right of collective self-defence undertaken for this book – perhaps unsurprisingly – at times acts to highlight the room for contestation inherent in attempts to identify customary international law[52] rather than providing 'clarity'.

There are a number of fundamental issues that remain unsettled in the law governing collective self-defence. Some of these are well known, as they are replicated in the context of individual self-defence: most notably, issues of preventative defensive action and the perennial question of the (un)lawful use of force in self-defence in response to attacks by non-state actors. However, this book has also revealed other areas of uncertainty specific to collective self-defence, especially in relation to the request requirement. This requirement is crucial for the prevention of abuse,

[48] See Section 8.3.
[49] See Section 8.2.
[50] See Section 8.5.
[51] See Section 8.8.
[52] See, for example, Fernando R. Tesón, 'Fake Custom', in Brian D. Lepard (ed.), *Reexamining Customary International Law* (Cambridge, Cambridge University Press, 2017), 86; Daniel Joyner, 'Why I Stopped Believing in Customary International Law' (2019) 9 *Asian Journal of International Law* 31, 38; Maurice Mendelson, 'Practice, Propaganda and Principle in International Law' (1989) 42 *Current Legal Problems* 1, 12.

but there exists substantial flexibility in terms of the way that states can comply with it. For many of the factors that influence how states apply the request requirement in practice, there seems to be insufficient evidence of *opinio juris* to conclude that they are legally binding. That said, the identification of those factors is, in itself, valuable: more work needs to be done in terms of developing the parameters that they imply, and the strengthening of those parameters in *legal* terms through engagement with states. The request requirement is ultimately fundamental to finding a balance between states being able to support each other in genuine acts of defence against aggression and opportunistic and abusive uses of force in the name of collective self-defence. Without this requirement, and without a true sense of how it correctly must be applied, 'the way would be open to unlimited aggression'.[53]

For all the uncertainty that remains regarding collective self-defence, this book has also confirmed its continued importance in the post–Cold War world, both in relation to the fundamental deterrent effect of treaty arrangements (small and, especially, large) and as an ad hoc basis for military action. Collective self-defence is a right that is particularly susceptible to invocation as a pretext, as it involves at least one third party that need not be 'invested' in the *defensive* nature of the military action it undertakes. This introduction of a third party (or third parties) into the self-defence mix also undoubtedly increases the potential for the escalation of uses of force.[54]

This understandably means that, as Åkermark has remarked, 'opinions are divided as to whether collective self-defence is a valuable safeguard for small states or a dangerous doctrine justifying intervention by powerful states'.[55] The reality is, of course, that it can be either. It is thus important that international lawyers 'hold the line' with respect to the crucial requirements of armed attack, necessity, proportionality, and request, especially when one considers the combined contexts of the high number of dubious invocations of collective self-defence that have occurred throughout the UN era and the unprecedented increase in the number of invocations of collective self-defence that have occurred specifically in the last decade.

[53] Quincy Wright, 'United States Intervention in the Lebanon' (1959) 53 *American Journal of International Law* 112, 118.

[54] On the potential for escalation in the context of collective self-defence actions, see, generally, Chapter 3, nn.32–33 and accompanying text.

[55] Sia Spiliopoulou Åkermark, 'The Puzzle of Collective Self-Defence: Dangerous Fragmentation or a Window of Opportunity? An Analysis with Finland and the Åland Islands as a Case Study' (2017) 22 *Journal of Conflict and Security Law* 249, 262.

BIBLIOGRAPHY

Books

Alder, Murray Colin, *The Inherent Right of Self-Defence in International Law* (Dordrecht, Springer, 2013)

Alexandrov, Stanimir A., *Self-Defence against the Use of Force in International Law* (The Hague, Kluwer Law International, 1996)

Arend, Anthony Clark, and Beck, Robert J., *International Law and the Use of Force* (London, Routledge, 1993)

Armstrong, David, Farrell, Theo, and Maiguashca, Bice (eds.), *Force and Legitimacy in World Politics* (Cambridge, Cambridge University Press, 2005)

Aronsson-Storrier, Marie, *Publicity in International Law-Making: Covert Operations and the Use of Force* (Cambridge, Cambridge University Press, 2020)

Beckett, W. Eric, *The North Atlantic Treaty, the Brussels Treaty, and the Charter of the United Nations* (London, Stevens & Sons, 1950)

Bhuta, Nehal, and Vallejo, Rodrigo (eds.), *Global Governance and Human Rights* (Collected Courses of the Academy of European Law) (Oxford, Oxford University Press, in press)

Blackstone, William, *Commentaries on the Laws of England* (Oxford, Clarendon Press, 1765–1769)

Bowett, Derek W., *Self-Defense in International Law* (Manchester, Manchester University Press, 1958)

Brecher, Michael, *A Century of Crisis and Conflict in the International System* (Cham, Palgrave Macmillan, 2017)

Briggs, Asa, and Clavin, Patricia, *Modern Europe, 1789–Present* (London, Routledge, 2nd ed., 2013)

Bronitt, Simon, Gani, Miriam, and Hufnagel, Saskia (eds.), *Shooting to Kill: Socio-legal Perspectives on the Use of Lethal Force* (Oxford, Hart, 2012)

Brownlie, Ian, *International Law and the Use of Force by States* (Oxford, Oxford University Press, 1963)

Buchan, Russell, and Tsagourias, Nicholas, *Regulating the Use of Force in International Law: Stability and Change* (Cheltenham, Edward Elgar, 2021)

Casey-Maslen, Stuart, *Jus ad Bellum: The Law on Inter-state Use of Force* (Oxford, Hart, 2020)

Cassese, Antonio (ed.), *The Current Legal Regulation of the Use of Force* (Leiden, Martinus Nijhoff, 1986)

Chen, Albert H. Y. (ed.), *Constitutionalism in Asia in the Early Twenty-First Century* (Cambridge, Cambridge University Press, 2014)

Chinkin, Christine, and Kaldor, Mary, *International Law and New Wars* (Cambridge, Cambridge University Press, 2017)

Clark, John F. (ed.), *The African Stakes of the Congo War* (New York, Palgrave Macmillan, 2002)

Constantinou, Avra, *The Right of Self-Defence under Customary International Law and Article 51 of the UN Charter* (Brussels, Bruylant, 2000)

Corten, Olivier, *The Law against War: The Prohibition on the Use of Force in Contemporary International Law* (Oxford, Hart, 2nd ed., 2021)

Corten, Olivier, Fox, Gregory H., and Kritsiotis, Dino, *Armed Intervention and Consent*, Max Planck Trialogues on the Law of Peace and War (Anne Peters and Christian Marxsen, series eds.), vol. IV (Cambridge, Cambridge University Press, 2023)

Cunningham, Anne C., *Critical Perspectives on Government-Sponsored Assassinations* (New York, Enslow, 2018)

Damrosch, Lori Fisler, and Scheffer, David J. (eds.), *Law and Force in the New International Order* (Boulder, Westview Press, 1991)

de Nooy, Gert (ed.), *The Role of European Naval Forces after the Cold War* (The Hague, Kluwer Law International, 1996)

de Vattel, Emer, *The Law of Nations (Droit des gens)* (Béla Kapossy and Richard Whatmore, eds., Thomas Nugent, trans., Indianapolis, Liberty Fund, 2008 (1758))

de Wet, Erika, *Military Assistance on Request and the Use of Force* (Oxford, Oxford University Press, 2020)

Dinstein, Yoram, *War, Aggression and Self-Defence* (Cambridge, Cambridge University Press, 6th ed., 2017)

Djalili, Mohammad-Reza, Grare, Frédéric, and Akiner, Shirin (eds.), *Tajikistan: The Trials of Independence* (Richmond, Curzon Press, 1998)

Eichler, Jan, *NATO's Expansion after the Cold War: Geopolitics and Impacts for International Security* (Cham, Springer, 2021)

Eyffinger, Arthur, Stephens, Alan, and Muller, Sam (eds.), *Self-Defence as a Fundamental Principle* (The Hague, Hague Academic Press, 2009)

Fitzmaurice, Malgosia, Elias, Olufemi, and Merkouris, Panos (eds.), *Treaty Interpretation and the Vienna Convention on the Law of Treaties: 30 Years On* (Leiden, Martinus Nijhoff, 2010)

Fletcher, George, and Ohlin, Jens, *Defending Humanity: When Force Is Justified and Why* (Oxford, Oxford University Press, 2008)

Forcese, Craig, *Destroying the* Caroline: *The Frontier Raid that Reshaped the Right to War* (Toronto, Irwin Law, 2018)

Franck, Thomas M., *Recourse to Force: State Action against Threats and Armed Attacks* (Cambridge, Cambridge University Press, 2002)

Frankel, Josepeh, *National Interest* (London, Pall Mall Press, 1970)

Friman, Johanna, *Revisiting the Concept of Defence in the Jus ad Bellum: The Dual Face of Defence* (Oxford, Hart, 2017)

Gardam, Judith, *Necessity, Proportionality and the Use of Force by States* (Cambridge, Cambridge University Press, 2004)

Gazzini, Tarcisio, *The Changing Rules on the Use of Force in International Law* (Manchester, Manchester University Press, 2005)

Goodrich, Leland M., Simons, Anne Patricia, and Hambro, Edvard, *Charter of the United Nations: Commentary and Documents* (New York, Columbia University Press, 3rd ed., 1969)

Gray, Christine, *International Law and the Use of Force* (Oxford, Oxford University Press, 4th ed., 2018)

Green, James A., *The International Court of Justice and Self-Defence in International Law* (Oxford, Hart, 2009)

(ed.), *Cyber Warfare: A Multidisciplinary Analysis* (Abingdon, Routledge, 2015)

Green, James A., and Waters, Christopher P. M. (eds.), *Conflict in the Caucasus: Implications for International Legal Order* (Basingstoke, Palgrave Macmillan, 2010)

Grotius, Hugo, *On the Law of War and Peace (De juri belli ac pacis libri tres)* (Richard Tuck, ed. / Jean Barbeyrac, original ed. & French trans., John Morrice, English trans., Indianapolis, Liberty Fund, 2005 (1625))

Hasar, Seyfullah, *State Consent to Foreign Military Intervention during Civil Wars* (Leiden, Brill Nijhoff, 2022)

Hathaway, Oona A., and Shapiro, Scott J., *The Internationalists* (London, Penguin Books, 2018)

Heathcote, Gina, *The Law on the Use of Force: A Feminist Analysis* (Abingdon, Routledge, 2012)

Henderson, Christian, *The Persistent Advocate and the Use of Force: The Impact of the United States upon the Jus ad Bellum in the Post-Cold War Era* (Farnham, Ashgate, 2010)

The Use of Force and International Law (Cambridge, Cambridge University Press, 2018)

Higgins, Rosalyn, *The Development of International Law through the Political Organs of the United Nations* (London, Oxford University Press, 1963)

Problems and Process: International Law and How We Use It (Oxford, Oxford University Press, 1994)

Ismay (Lord), *NATO: The First Five Years, 1949–1954* (Paris, North Atlantic Treaty Organisation, 1955)

Jackson, Miles, *Complicity in International Law* (Oxford, Oxford University Press, 2015)

Kassimeris, George, and Buckley, John (eds.), *The Ashgate Research Companion to Modern Warfare* (Farnham, Ashgate, 2010)

Koskenniemi, Martti, *From Apology to Utopia: The Structure of International Legal Argument* (Cambridge, Cambridge University Press, 2005 reissue)

Koutrakos, Panos (ed.), *European Foreign Policy: Legal and Political Perspectives* (Cheltenham, Edward Elgar, 2011)

The EU Common Security and Defence Policy (Oxford, Oxford University Press, 2013)

Lanovoy, Vladyslav, *Complicity and Its Limits in the Law of International Responsibility* (Oxford, Hart, 2016)

Lawson, Ruth C., *International Regional Organizations: Constitutional Foundations* (New York, Praeger, 1962)

Lepard, Brian D. (ed.), *Reexamining Customary International Law* (Cambridge, Cambridge University Press, 2017)

Lieblich, Eliav, *International Law and Civil Wars: Intervention and Consent* (Abingdon, Routledge, 2013)

Lubell, Noam, *Extraterritorial Use of Force against Non-State Actors* (Oxford, Oxford University Press, 2010)

Martin, Andrew, *Collective Security: A Progress Report* (Paris, United Nations (UNESCO), 1952)

Matsui, Shigenori, *The Constitution of Japan: A Contextual Analysis* (London, Hart, 2011)

McDermott, Kevin, and Stibbe, Matthew (eds.), *Eastern Europe in 1968* (Cham, Palgrave Macmillan, 2018)

McDougal, Myres S., and Feliciano, Florentino P., *Law and Minimum World Public Order: The Legal Regulation of International Coercion* (New Haven, Yale University Press, 1961)

McWhinney, Edward, *The September 11 Terrorist Attacks and the Invasion of Iraq in Contemporary International Law: Opinions on the Emerging New World Order System* (Leiden, Martinus Nijhoff, 2004)

Meiertöns, Heiko, *The Doctrines of US Security Policy: An Evaluation under International Law* (Cambridge, Cambridge University Press, 2010)

Moir, Lindsay, *Reappraising the Resort to Force* (Oxford, Hart, 2010)

Morgenthau, Hans J., *Politics among Nations: The Struggle for Power and Peace* (New York, McGraw-Hill, 7th ed., revised by Kenneth W. Thompson and W. David Clinton, 2005)

Mori, Tadashi, *Origins of the Right of Self-Defence in International Law: From the* Caroline *Incident to the United Nations Charter* (Leiden, Brill Nijhoff, 2018)

Neff, Stephen C., *War and the Law of Nations: A General History* (Cambridge, Cambridge University Press, 2005)

Notter, Harley A., *Postwar Foreign Policy Preparation, 1939–1945* (Washington DC, Greenwood Press, 1975)

O'Connell, Mary Ellen, Tams, Christian J., and Tladi, Dire, *Self-Defence against Non-State Actors*, Max Planck Trialogues on the Law of Peace and War (Anne Peters and Christian Marxsen, series eds.), vol. I (Cambridge, Cambridge University Press, 2019)

O'Meara, Chris, *Necessity and Proportionality and the Right of Self-Defence in International Law* (Oxford, Oxford University Press, 2021)

Okimoto, Keiichiro, *The Distinction and Relationship between Jus ad Bellum and Jus in Bello* (Oxford, Hart, 2011)

Orakhelashvili, Alexander, *Peremptory Norms in International Law* (Oxford, Oxford University Press, 2006)

Collective Security (Oxford, Oxford University Press, 2011)

Paddeu, Federica, *Justification and Excuse in International Law: Concept and Theory of General Defences* (Cambridge, Cambridge University Press, 2018)

Piris, Jean-Claude, *The Lisbon Treaty: A Legal and Political Analysis* (Cambridge, Cambridge University Press, 2010)

Powell, Nathaniel K., *France's Wars in Chad: Military Intervention and Decolonisation in Africa* (Cambridge, Cambridge University Press)

Ragazzi, Maurizio, *The Concept of International Obligations Erga Omnes* (Oxford, Clarendon Press, 1997)

Redaelli, Chiara, *Intervention in Civil Wars: Effectiveness, Legitimacy, and Human Rights* (Oxford, Hart, 2021)

Redslob, Robert, *Traité de droit des gens: l'évolution historique, les institutions positives, les idées de justice, le droit nouveau* (Paris, Recueil Sirey, 1950)

Rotelle, John E. (ed.), *The Works of Saint Augustine: A Translation for the 21st Century, Part II – Letters, vol. 1*, Letters 1–99 (Hyde Park, NY, New City Press, 2001) (398 AD) (Roland Teske, trans. & notes)

Roth, Brad R., *Governmental Illegitimacy in International Law* (Oxford, Oxford University Press, 1999)

Rozanov, Anatoliy A., and Douhan, Alena F., *Collective Security Treaty Organisation, 2002–2012* (Geneva/Minsk, The Geneva Centre for the Democratic Control of Armed Forces, 2013)

Ruys, Tom, *'Armed Attack' and Article 51 of the UN Charter: Evolutions in Customary Law and Practice* (Cambridge, Cambridge University Press, 2010)

Ruys, Tom, and Corten, Olivier (with Hofer, Alexandra) (eds.), *The Use of Force in International Law: A Case-Based Approach* (Oxford, Oxford University Press, 2018)

Schachter, Oscar, *International Law in Theory and Practice* (Dordrecht, Martinus Nijhoff, 1991)

Schelling, Thomas, *Arms and Influence* (New Haven, Yale University Press, 1966 (Veritas paperback ed., 2020))

Simma, Bruno, Khan, Daniel-Erasmus, Nolte, Georg, Paulus, Andreas, and Wessendorf, Nikolai (eds.), *The Charter of the United Nations: A Commentary*, vol. II (Oxford, Oxford University Press, 3rd ed., 2012)

Stallybrass, W. T. S., *Salmond's Law of Torts* (London, Sweet and Maxwell, 10th ed., 1945)

Stone, Julius, *Aggression and World Order* (Berkeley and Los Angeles, University of California Press, 1958)

Legal Controls of International Conflict: A Treatise on the Dynamics of Disputes and War-Law, second impression, revised with supplement 1953–1958 (Sydney, Maitland Publications, 1959)

Talmon, Stefan, *Recognition of Governments in International Law: With Particular Reference to Governments in Exile* (Oxford, Clarendon Press, 1998)

Tanca, Antonio, *Foreign Armed Intervention in Internal Conflict* (Dordrecht, Martinus Nijhoff, 1993)

Tibori-Szabó, Kinga, *Anticipatory Action in Self-Defence: Essence and Limits under International Law* (The Hague, TMC Asser Press, 2011)

Tsagourias, Nicholas, and White, Nigel D., *Collective Security: Theory, Law and Practice* (Cambridge, Cambridge University Press, 2013)

Tzouvala, Ntina, *Capitalism as Civilisation: A History of International Law* (Cambridge, Cambridge University Press, 2020)

Upcher, James, *Neutrality in Contemporary International Law* (Oxford, Oxford University Press, 2020

van Oudenaren, John, *Détente in Europe: The Soviet Union and the West Since 1953* (Durham, Duke University Press, 1991)

von Pufendorf, Samuel, *The Whole Duty of Man According to the Law of Nature (De officio hominis & civis juxta legem naturalem libri duo)* (Ian Hunter and David Saunders, eds. / Jean Barbeyrac, original ed. & French trans., Andrew Tooke, English trans., Indianapolis, Liberty Fund, 2003 (1673))

Weller, Marc (ed.), *The Oxford Handbook of the Use of Force in International Law* (Oxford, Oxford University Press, 2015)

Westra, Joel H., *International Law and the Use of Armed Force: The UN Charter and the Major Powers* (Abingdon, Routledge, 2007)

White, Nigel D., and Henderson, Christian (eds.), *Research Handbook on International Conflict and Security Law: Jus ad Bellum, Jus in Bello and Jus Post Bellum* (Abingdon, Routledge, 2013)

Wilén, Nina, *Justifying Interventions in Africa: (De)Stabilizing Sovereignty in Liberia, Burundi and the Congo* (London, Palgrave Macmillan, 2012)

Williams, Kieran, *The Prague Spring and Its Aftermath: Czechoslovak Politics, 1968–1970* (Cambridge, Cambridge University Press, 1997)

Williamson, Myra, *Terrorism, War and International Law: The Legality of the Use of Force against Afghanistan in 2001* (Farnham, Ashgate, 2009)

Wolfrum, Rüdiger (ed.), *Max Planck Encyclopaedia of Public International Law* (Oxford, Oxford University Press, 2012) (online version, https://opil.ouplaw.com/home/mpil)

Wolfrum, Rüdiger, and Philipp, Christiane E. (eds.), *United Nations: Law, Policies and Practice*, vol. II (Dordrecht, Martinus Nijhoff, 1995)

Wouters, Jan, Hoffmeister, Frank, de Baere, Geert, and Ramopoulos, Thomas, *The Law of EU External Relations: Cases, Materials, and Commentary on the EU as an International Legal Actor* (Oxford, Oxford University Press, 3rd ed., 2021)

[no designated editor] *Right v. Might* (New York, Council on Foreign Relations Press, 1991)

Book Chapters

Besson, Samantha, 'Sovereignty', in Rüdiger Wolfrum (ed.), *Max Planck Encyclopaedia of Public International Law*, vol. IX (Oxford, Oxford University Press, 2012), 366

Bothe, Michael, 'Neutrality, Concept and General Rules', in Rüdiger Wolfrum (ed.), *Max Planck Encyclopaedia of Public International Law*, vol. VII (Oxford, Oxford University Press, 2012), 617

Brown, Bess A., 'The Civil War in Tajikistan, 1992–1993', in Mohammad-Reza Djalili, Frédéric Grare, and Shirin Akiner (eds.), *Tajikistan: The Trials of Independence* (Richmond, Curzon Press, 1998), 86

Byers, Michael, 'Geopolitical Change and International Law', in David Armstrong, Theo Farrell, and Bice Maiguashca (eds.), *Force and Legitimacy in World Politics* (Cambridge, Cambridge University Press, 2005), 51

Chayes, Abram, 'The Use of Force in the Persian Gulf', in Lori Fisler Damrosch and David J. Scheffer (eds.), *Law and Force in the New International Order* (Boulder, Westview Press, 1991), 3

Cliteur, Paul, 'Self-Defence and Terrorism', in Arthur Eyffinger, Alan Stephens, and Sam Muller (eds.), *Self-Defence as a Fundamental Principle* (The Hague, Hague Academic Press, 2009), 67

Corten, Olivier, 'Intervention by Invitation: The Expanding Role of the Security Council', in Olivier Corten, Gregory H. Fox, and Dino Kritsiotis, *Armed Intervention and Consent*, Max Planck Trialogues on the Law of Peace and War (Anne Peters and Christian Marxsen, series eds.), vol. IV (Cambridge, Cambridge University Press, 2023), 101

Daniel, Donald, and Hayes, Bradd, 'Toward a West European Navy: Organizational and Operational Issues', in Gert de Nooy (ed.), *The Role of European Naval Forces after the Cold War* (The Hague, Kluwer Law International, 1996), 73

Deeks, Ashley S., 'Taming the Doctrine of Pre-emption', in Marc Weller (ed.), *The Oxford Handbook of the Use of Force in International Law* (Oxford, Oxford University Press, 2015), 661

Eyffinger, Arthur, 'Self-Defence or the Meanderings of a Protean Principle', in Arthur Eyffinger, Alan Stephens, and Sam Muller (eds.), *Self-Defence as a Fundamental Principle* (The Hague, Hague Academic Press, 2009), 103

Fox, Gregory H., 'Intervention by Invitation', in Marc Weller (ed.), *The Oxford Handbook of the Use of Force in International Law* (Oxford, Oxford University Press, 2015), 816

'Invitations to Intervene after the Cold War: Toward a New Collective Model', in Olivier Corten, Gregory H. Fox, and Dino Kritsiotis, *Armed Intervention and Consent*, Max Planck Trialogues on the Law of Peace and War (Anne Peters and Christian Marxsen, series eds.), vol. IV (Cambridge, Cambridge University Press, 2023), 179

Gardner, Richard N., 'Commentary on the Law of Self-Defence', in Lori Fisler Damrosch and David J. Scheffer (eds.), *Law and Force in the New International Order* (Boulder, Westview Press, 1991), 49

Green, James A., 'Passportisation, Peacekeepers and Proportionality: The Russian Claim of the Protection of Nationals Abroad in Self-Defence', in James A. Green and Christopher P. M. Waters (eds.), *Conflict in the Caucasus: Implications for International Legal Order* (Basingstoke, Palgrave Macmillan, 2010), 54

'The Regulation of Cyber Warfare under the *Jus ad Bellum*', in James A. Green (ed.), *Cyber Warfare: A Multidisciplinary Analysis* (Abingdon, Routledge, 2015), 96

'The Great African War and the Intervention by Uganda and Rwanda in the Democratic Republic of Congo – 1998–2003', in Tom Ruys and Olivier Corten (with Alexandra Hofer) (eds.), *The Use of Force in International Law: A Case-Based Approach* (Oxford, Oxford University Press, 2018), 575

Greenwood, Christopher, 'Self-Defence', in Rüdiger Wolfrum (ed.), *Max Planck Encyclopaedia of Public International Law*, vol. IX (Oxford, Oxford University Press, 2012), 103

Haggenmacher, Peter, 'Self-Defence as a General Principle of Law and Its Relation to War', in Arthur Eyffinger, Alan Stephens, and Sam Muller (eds.), *Self-Defence as a Fundamental Principle* (The Hague, Hague Academic Press, 2009), 3

Heathcote, Gina, 'Feminist Perspectives on the Law on the Use of Force', in Marc Weller (ed.), *The Oxford Handbook of the Use of Force in International Law* (Oxford, Oxford University Press, 2015), 114

Henkin, Louis, 'The Use of Force: Law and US Policy', in *Right v Might* (New York, Council on Foreign Relations Press, 1991), 45

Higgins, Rosalyn, 'The Attitudes of Western States towards Legal Aspects of the Use of Force', in Antonio Cassese (ed.), *The Current Legal Regulation of the Use of Force* (Leiden, Martinus Nijhoff, 1986), 435

Kenny, Kevin C., 'Self-Defence', in Rüdiger Wolfrum and Christiane E. Philipp (eds.), *United Nations: Law, Policies and Practice*, vol. II (Dordrecht, Martinus Nijhoff, 1995), 1162

Koutrakos, Panos, 'The Role of Law in Common Security and Defence Policy: Functions, Limitations and Perceptions', in Panos Koutrakos (ed.), *European Foreign Policy: Legal and Political Perspectives* (Cheltenham, Edward Elgar, 2011), 235

Kritsiotis, Dino, 'A Study of the Scope and Operation of the Rights of Individual and Collective Self-Defence under International Law', in Nigel D. White and Christian Henderson (eds.), *Research Handbook on International Conflict and Security Law: Jus ad Bellum, Jus in Bello and Jus Post Bellum* (Abingdon, Routledge, 2013), 170

'Intervention and the Problematisation of Consent', in Olivier Corten, Gregory H. Fox, and Dino Kritsiotis, *Armed Intervention and Consent*, Max Planck Trialogues on the Law of Peace and War (Anne Peters and Christian Marxsen, series eds.), vol. IV (Cambridge, Cambridge University Press, 2023), 26

Lalaj, Ana, '1968: The Prague Spring and the Albanian "Castle"', in Kevin McDermott and Matthew Stibbe (eds.), *Eastern Europe in 1968* (Cham, Palgrave Macmillan, 2018), 235

Lieblich, Eliav, 'The Soviet Intervention in Hungary – 1956', in Tom Ruys and Olivier Corten (with Alexandra Hofer) (eds.), *The Use of Force in International Law: A Case-Based Approach* (Oxford, Oxford University Press, 2018), 48

'Self-Defense against Non-State Actors and the Myth of the Innocent State', in Nehal Bhuta and Rodrigo Vallejo (eds.), *Global Governance and Human Rights* (Collected Courses of the Academy of European Law) (Oxford, Oxford University Press, in press), *SSRN* version (13 May 2019), https://papers.ssrn.com/sol3/papers.cfm?abstract_id=3364163

Lubell, Noam, 'The Problem of Imminence in an Uncertain World', in Marc Weller (ed.), *The Oxford Handbook of the Use of Force in International Law* (Oxford, Oxford University Press, 2015), 697

Merkouris, Panos, 'Introduction: Interpretation Is a Science, Is an Art, Is a Science', in Malgosia Fitzmaurice, Olufemi Elias, and Panos Merkouris (eds.), *Treaty Interpretation and the Vienna Convention on the Law of Treaties: 30 Years On* (Leiden, Martinus Nijhoff, 2010), 1

Müllerson, Rein, 'Self-Defence in the Contemporary World', in Lori Fisler Damrosch and David J. Scheffer (eds.), *Law and Force in the New International Order* (Boulder, Westview Press, 1991), 13

Nolte, Georg, and Randelzhofer, Albrecht, 'Article 51', in Bruno Simma, Daniel-Erasmus Khan, Georg Nolte, Andreas Paulus, and Nikolai Wessendorf (eds.), *The Charter of the United Nations: A Commentary*, vol. II (Oxford, Oxford University Press, 3rd ed., 2012), 1397

O'Connell, Mary Ellen, 'Unlawful Killing with Combat Drones: A Case Study of Pakistan, 2004–2009', in Simon Bronitt, Miriam Gani, and Saskia Hufnagel (eds.), *Shooting to Kill: Socio-Legal Perspectives on the Use of Lethal Force* (Oxford, Hart, 2012), 263

Peters, Anne, 'Armed Intervention and Consent: Principle and Practice', in Olivier Corten, Gregory H. Fox, and Dino Kritsiotis, *Armed Intervention and Consent*, Max Planck Trialogues on the Law of Peace and War (Anne Peters and Christian Marxsen, series eds.), vol. IV (Cambridge, Cambridge University Press, 2023), 1

Rupiya, Martin R., 'A Political and Military Review of Zimbabwe's Involvement in the Second Congo War', in John F. Clark (ed.), *The African Stakes of the Congo War* (New York, Palgrave Macmillan, 2002), 93

Sakaguchi, Shojiro, 'Major Constitutional Developments in Japan in the First Decade of the Twenty-First Century', in Albert H. Y. Chen (ed.), *Constitutionalism in Asia in the Early Twenty-First Century* (Cambridge, Cambridge University Press, 2014), 52

Salmon, Jean, 'Representatives of States in International Relations', in Rüdiger Wolfrum (ed.), *Max Planck Encyclopaedia of Public International Law*, vol. VIII (Oxford, Oxford University Press, 2012), 919

Tams, Christian J., 'Self-Defence against Non-State Actors: Making Sense of the "Armed Attack" Requirement', in Mary Ellen O'Connell, Christian J. Tams, and Dire Tladi, *Self-Defence against Non-State Actors*, Max Planck Trialogues on the Law of Peace and War (Anne Peters and Christian Marxsen, series eds.), vol. I (Cambridge, Cambridge University Press, 2019), 90

Tesón, Fernando R., 'Fake Custom', in Brian D. Lepard (ed.), *Reexamining Customary International Law* (Cambridge, Cambridge University Press, 2017), 86

Verdebout, Agatha, 'The Intervention of the Gulf Cooperation Council in Bahrain – 2011', in Tom Ruys and Olivier Corten (with Alexandra Hofer) (eds.), *The Use of Force in International Law: A Case-Based Approach* (Oxford, Oxford University Press, 2018), 793

Waters, Christopher P. M., and Green, James A., 'International Law: Military Force and Armed Conflict', in George Kassimeris and John Buckley (eds), *The Ashgate Research Companion to Modern Warfare* (Farnham, Ashgate, 2010), 289

White, Nigel D., 'The Korean War – 1950–53', in Tom Ruys and Olivier Corten (with Alexandra Hofer) (eds.), *The Use of Force in International Law: A Case-Based Approach* (Oxford, Oxford University Press, 2018), 17

Wood, Michael, 'Self-Defence and Collective Security', in Marc Weller (ed.), *The Oxford Handbook of the Use of Force in International Law* (Oxford University Press, 2015), 649

Journal Articles and Other Major Research Papers

Acevedo, Domingo E., 'Collective Self-Defense and the Use of Regional or Subregional Authority as Justification for the Use of Force' (1984) 78 *American Society of International Law Proceedings* 69

Akande, Dapo, and Liefländer, Thomas, 'Clarifying Necessity, Imminence, and Proportionality in the Law of Self-Defense' (2013) 107 *American Journal of International Law* 563

Åkermark, Sia Spiliopoulou, 'The Puzzle of Collective Self-Defence: Dangerous Fragmentation or a Window of Opportunity? An Analysis with Finland and the Åland Islands as a Case Study' (2017) 22 *Journal of Conflict and Security Law* 249

Alvarez, Alejandro, 'The Monroe Doctrine from the Latin-American Point of View' (1917) 2 *St. Louis Law Review* 135

Antonopoulos, Constantine, 'The Unilateral Use of Force by States after the End of the Cold War' (1999) 4 *Journal of Armed Conflict Law* 117

'Some Thoughts on the NATO Position in Relation to the Iraqi Crisis' (2004) 17 *Leiden Journal of International Law* 171

'Force by Armed Groups as Armed Attack and the Broadening of Self-Defence' (2008) 55 *Netherlands International Law Review* 159

Azubuike, Eustace Chikere, 'Probing the Scope of Self Defense in International Law' (2011) 17 *Annual Survey of International and Comparative Law* 129

Bakhashab, Omar Abubakar, 'The Relationship between the Right of Self-Defence on the Part of States and the Powers of the Security Council' (1996) 9 *Journal of King Abdulaziz University: Economics and Administration* 3

Bakircioglu, Onder, 'The Right to Self-Defence in National and International Law: The Role of the Imminence Requirement' (2009) 19 *Indiana International and Comparative Law Review* 1

Bannelier, Karine, and Christakis, Theodore, 'Under the UN Security Council's Watchful Eyes: Military Intervention by Invitation in the Malian Conflict' (2013) 26 *Leiden Journal of International Law* 855

Bannelier-Christakis, Karine, 'Military Interventions against ISIL in Iraq, Syria and Libya, and the Legal Basis of Consent' (2016) 29 *Leiden Journal of International Law* 74

Bassett Moore, John, 'The New Isolation' (1933) 27 *American Journal of International Law* 607

Baxter, Richard R., 'The Legal Consequences of the Unlawful Use of Force under the Charter' (1968) 62 *American Society of International Law Proceedings* 68

Bellamy, Alex, 'International Law and the War with Iraq' (2003) 4 *Melbourne Journal of International Law* 497

Blank, Laurie R., 'Irreconcilable Differences: The Thresholds for Armed Attack and International Armed Conflict' (2020–2021) 96 *Notre Dame Law Review* 249

Bowett, Derek W., 'Collective Self-Defence under the Charter of the United Nations' (1955–1956) 32 *British Yearbook of International Law* 130

Boyle, Joe, 'Making Sense of Self-Defence in the War on Terror' (2014) 1 *Journal on the Use of Force and International Law* 55

Brookman-Byrne, Max, 'Intervention by (Secret) Invitation: Searching for a Requirement of Publicity in the International Law on the Use of Force with Consent' (2020) 7 *Journal on the Use of Force and International Law* 74

Brzezinski, Zbigniew, 'An Agenda for NATO – Toward a Global Security Web' (2009) 88 *Foreign Affairs* 2

Buchan, Russell, 'Non-Forcible Measures and the Law of Self-Defence' (2023) 72 *International and Comparative Law Quarterly* 1

Butchard, Patrick M., 'Back to San Francisco: Explaining the Inherent Contradictions of Article 2(4) of the UN Charter' (2018) 23 *Journal of Conflict and Security Law* 229, 262–264.

'Territorial Integrity, Political Independence, and Consent: The Limitations of Military Assistance on Request under the Prohibition of Force' (2020) 7 *Journal on the Use of Force and International Law* 35

Byers, Michael, 'Terrorism, the Use of Force and International Law after 11 September' (2002) 51 *International and Comparative Law Quarterly* 401

'Still Agreeing to Disagree: International Security and Constructive Ambiguity' (2021) 8 *Journal on the Use of Force and International Law* 91

Byrne, Max, 'Consent and the Use of Force: An Examination of "Intervention by Invitation" as a Basis for US Drone Strikes in Pakistan, Somalia and Yemen' (2016) 3 *Journal on the Use of Force and International Law* 97

Cannizzaro, Enzo, and Rasi, Aurora, 'Europe at War' (2022), (2021) 6 *European Papers* 1523

Caserta, Salvatore, 'Western Centrism, Contemporary International Law, and International Courts' (2021) 34 *Leiden Journal of International Law* 32

Cavandoli, Sofia, and Wilson, Gary, 'Distorting Fundamental Norms of International Law to Resurrect the Soviet Union: The International Law Context of Russia's Invasion of Ukraine' (2022) 69 *Netherlands International Law Review* 383

Chen, Jie, *et al.*, 'The Primacy of the Individual Versus the Collective Self: Evidence from an Event-Related Potential Study' (2013) 535 *Neuroscience Letters* 30

Chigara, Ben, 'Operation of the SADC Protocol on Politics, Defence and Security in the Democratic Republic of Congo' (2000) 12 *African Journal of International and Comparative Law* 58

Couzigou, Irène, 'Respect for State Sovereignty: Primacy of Intervention by Invitation over the Right to Self-Defence' (2019) 79 *Zeitschrift für Ausländisches Öffentliches Recht und Völkerrecht* 695

d'Aspremont, Jean, 'Legitimacy of Governments in the Age of Democracy' (2006) 38 *New York University Journal of International Law and Politics* 877

'Mapping the Concepts behind the Contemporary Liberalization of the Use of Force in International Law' (2010) 31 *University of Pennsylvania Journal of International Law* 1089

de Wet, Erika, 'The (Im)permissibility of Military Assistance on Request during a Civil War' (2020) 7 *Journal on the Use of Force and International Law* 26

'Military Assistance Based on Ex-Ante Consent: A Violation of Article 2(4) UN Charter?' (2020) 93 *Die Friedens-Warte* 413

Deeks, Ashley S., 'Consent to the Use of Force and International Law Supremacy' (2013) 54 *Harvard International Law Journal* 1

Delanis, James A., '"Force" under Article 2(4) of the United Nations Charter: The Question of Economic and Political Coercion' (1979) 12 *Vanderbilt Journal of Transnational Law* 101

Deutsch, Eberhard P., 'The Legality of the United States Position in Vietnam' (1966) 52 *American Bar Association Journal* 436

Diab, Nader Iskandar, 'Enforcement Action by Regional Organisations Revisited: The Prospective Joint Arab Forces' (2017) 4 *Journal on the Use of Force and International Law* 86

Dinstein, Yoram, 'The Jurisprudence of the Court in the *Nicaragua* Decision: Remarks' (1987) 81 *American Society of International Law Proceedings* 266

Doswald-Beck, Louise, 'The Legal Validity of Military Intervention by Invitation of the Government' (1985) 56 *British Yearbook of International Law* 189

Dris Aït-Hamadouche, Louisa, and Zoubir, Yahia H., 'The US–Saudi Relationship and the Iraq War: The Dialectics of a Dependent Alliance' (2007) 24 *Journal of Third World Studies* 109

Egan, Patrick T., 'The Kosovo Intervention and Collective Self-Defence' (2001) 8 *International Peacekeeping* 39

Emanuel, Lia, *et al.*, 'Who am I? Representing the Self Offline and in Different Online Contexts' (2014) 41 *Computers in Human Behavior* 146

Etezazian, Sina, 'The Nature of the Self-Defence Proportionality Requirement' (2016) 3 *Journal on the Use of Force and International Law* 260

Ezechi, K. C., Onyishi, A. U., Okonkwo, W. O., and Ogbuka, Ikenna, 'Maintenance of International Peace and Security and Great Power Hypocrisy: Insights from the Iraqi and Ukrainian Invasions' (2022) 4 *Sapientia Foundation Journal of Education, Sciences and Gender Studies* 237

Falk, Richard A., 'International Law and the United States Role in the Viet Nam War' (1966) 75 *Yale Law Journal* 1122

'The Cambodian Operation and International Law' (1971) 65 *American Journal of International Law* 1

Farer, Tom J., 'Political and Economic Coercion in Contemporary International Law' (1985) 79 *American Journal of International Law* 40

'Drawing the Right Line' (1987) 81 *American Journal of International Law* 112

Fawcett, J. E. S., The Legal Character of International Agreements' (1953) 30 *British Yearbook of International Law* 381

'Intervention in International Law: A Study of Some Recent Cases' (1961) 103 *Recueil des cours* 343

Fenwick, Charles G., 'The Monroe Doctrine and the Declaration of Lima' (1939) 33 *American Journal of International Law* 257

Ferro, Luca, 'The Doctrine of "Negative Equality" and the Silent Majority of States' (2021) 8 *Journal on the Use of Force and International Law* 4

Fisher, Ryan M., 'Defending Taiwan: Collective Self-Defense of a Contested State' (2020) 32 *Florida Journal of International Law* 101

Flasch, Olivia, 'The Legality of the Air Strikes against ISIL in Syria: New Insights on the Extraterritorial Use of Force against Non-State Actors' (2016) 3 *Journal on the Use of Force and International Law* 37

Franck, Thomas M., 'Who Killed Article 2(4)? or Changing the Norms Governing the Use of Force by States' (1970) 64 *American Journal of International Law* 809

'Terrorism and the Right of Self-Defence' (2001) 95 *American Journal of International Law* 839

Gaertner, Lowell, *et al.*, 'A Motivational Hierarchy Within: Primacy of the Individual Self, Relational Self, or Collective Self?' (2012) 48 *Journal of Experimental Social Psychology* 997

Garwood-Gowers, Anthony, 'Israel's Airstrike on Syria's Al-Kibar Facility: A Test Case for the Doctrine of Preemptive Self-Defence?' (2011) 16 *Journal of Conflict and Security Law* 263

Gehrke, William, 'The Mozambique Crisis: A Case for United Nations Military Intervention' (1991) 24 *Cornell International Law Journal* 135

Gerges, F. A., 'The Lebanese Crisis of 1958: The Risks of Inflated Self-Importance' (1993) 5 *Beirut Review* 83

German, Robert K., 'Norway and the Bear: Soviet Coercive Diplomacy and Norwegian Security Policy' (1982) 7 *International Security* 55

Gibson, John S., 'Article 51 of the Charter of the United Nations' (1957) 13 *India Quarterly* 121

Gill, Terry D., 'The Law of Armed Attack in the Context of the *Nicaragua* Case' (1988) 1 *Hague Yearbook of International Law* 30

'The Second Gulf Crisis and the Relation between Collective Security and Collective Self-Defense' (1989) 10 *Grotiana* 47

'The *Jus ad Bellum* and Russia's "Special Military Operation" in Ukraine' (2022) 25 *Journal of International Peacekeeping* 121

Gill, Terry D., and Tibori-Szabó, Kinga, 'Twelve Key Questions on Self-Defense against Non-State Actors' (2019) 95 *International Law Studies* 467

Glennon, Michael J., 'United States Mutual Security Treaties: The Commitment Myth' (1986) 24 *Columbia Journal of Transnational Law* 509

Goldberg, Michael A., 'Mirage of Defense: Reexamining Article Five of the North Atlantic Treaty after the Terrorist Attacks on the United States' (2003) 26 *Boston College International and Comparative Law Review* 77

Goodhart, A. L., 'The North Atlantic Treaty of 1949' (1951) 79 *Recueil des cours* 182

Grady, Broderick C., 'Article 5 of the North Atlantic Treaty: Past, Present, and Uncertain Future' (2002) 31 *Georgia Journal of International and Comparative Law* 167

Gray, Christine, 'The US National Security Strategy and the New "Bush Doctrine" on Pre-Emptive Self-Defence' (2002) 1 *Chinese Journal of International Law* 437

Green, James A., 'Docking the *Caroline*: Understanding the Relevance of the Formula in Contemporary Customary International Law Concerning Self-Defence' (2006) 14 *Cardozo Journal of International and Comparative Law* 429

'Fluctuating Evidentiary Standards for Self-Defence in the International Court of Justice' (2009) 58 *International and Comparative Law Quarterly* 163

'The Annexation of Crimea: Russia, Passportisation and the Protection of National Revisited' (2014) 1 *Journal on the Use of Force and International Law* 3

'The Article 51 Reporting Requirement for Self-Defense Actions' (2015) 55 *Virginia Journal of International Law* 463

'The *Ratione Temporis* Elements of Self-Defence' (2015) 2 *Journal on the Use of Force and International Law* 97

'The "Additional" Criteria for Collective Self-Defence: Request but Not Declaration' (2017) 4 *Journal on the Use of Force and International Law* 4

'The Provision of Weapons and Logistical Support to Ukraine and the *Jus ad Bellum*' (2023) 10 *Journal on the Use of Force and International Law* 3

Green, James A., and Grimal, Francis, 'The Threat of Force as an Action in Self-Defense under International Law' (2011) 44 *Vanderbilt Journal of Transnational Law* 285

Green, James A., Henderson, Christian, and Ruys, Tom, 'Russia's Attack on Ukraine and the *Jus ad Bellum*' (2022) 9 *Journal on the Use of Force and International Law* 4

Greenwood, Christopher, 'International Law and the Pre-Emptive Use of Force: Afghanistan, Al-Qaida, and Iraq' (2003) 4 *San Diego International Law Journal* 7

Greig, D. W., 'Self-Defence and the Security Council: What Does Article 51 Require?' (1991) 40 *International and Comparative Law Quarterly* 366

Hafner, Gerhard, *l'Institut de droit international*, 10th Commission, 'Present Problems of the Use of Force in International Law Sub-group: Intervention by Invitation' (2009) 73 *Annuaire de l'Institut de droit international* 299

Halberstam, Malvina, 'The Right to Self-Defense Once the Security Council Takes Action' (1996) 17 *Michigan Journal of International Law* 229

Hamid, Abdul Ghafur, and Sein, Khin Maung, 'Combating Terrorism and the Use of Force against a State: A Relook at the Contemporary World Order' (2015) 8 *Journal of East Asia and International Law* 107

Hamilton, Tomas, 'Defending Ukraine with EU Weapons: Arms Control Law in Times of Crisis' (2022) 1 *European Law Open* 635

Haque, Adil Ahmad, 'The Use of Force against Non-State Actors: All over the Map' (2021) 8 *Journal on the Use of Force and International Law* 278

Hargrove, John Lawrence, 'The *Nicaragua* Judgment and the Future of the Law of Force and Self-Defence' (1987) 81 *American Journal of International Law* 135

Heindel, Richard H., Kalijarvi, Thorsten V., and Wilcox, Francis O., 'The North Atlantic Treaty in the United States Senate' (1949) 43 *American Journal of International Law* 633

Heller, Kevin Jon, 'The Unlawfulness of a "Bloody Nose Strike" on North Korea' (2020) 96 *International Law Studies* 1, 15

Heller, Kevin Jon, and Trabucco, Lena, 'The Legality of Weapons Transfers to Ukraine under International Law' (2022) 13 *Journal of International Humanitarian Legal Studies* 251

Henderson, Christian, 'The 2006 National Security Strategy of the United States: The Pre-Emptive Use of Force and the Persistent Advocate' (2007–2008) 15 *Tulsa Journal of Comparative and International Law* 1

'Contested States and the Rights and Obligations of the *Jus ad Bellum*' (2013) 21 *Cardozo Journal of International and Comparative Law* 367

'A Countering of the Asymmetrical Interpretation of the Doctrine of Counter-Intervention' (2021) 8 *Journal on the Use of Force and International Law* 34

'Book Review: Erika de Wet, Military Assistance on Request and the Use of Force' (2022) 33 *European Journal of International Law* 1037

Henderson, Christian, and Green, James A., 'The *Jus ad Bellum* and Entities Short of Statehood in the Report on the Conflict in Georgia' (2010) 59 *International and Comparative Law Quarterly* 129

Higgins, Rosalyn, 'The Legal Limits to the Use of Force by Sovereign States: United Nations Practice' (1961) 37 *British Yearbook of International Law* 269

Himes, Annie, and Kim, Brian J., 'Self-Defense on Behalf of Non-State Actors' (2021) 43 *University of Pennsylvania Journal of International Law* 241

Hoffmann, Tamás, 'The International Legal Aspects of the Georgia–Russia Conflict' (December 2008) *Foreign Policy Review* 80

Hofmann, Rainer, 'International Law and the Use of Military Force against Iraq' (2002) 45 *German Yearbook of International Law* 9

Holder, William E., 'The Legality of United States Participation in Vietnam: An Appraisal' (1966) 2 *Australian Yearbook of International Law* 67

Hughes, Charles E., 'Observations on the Monroe Doctrine' (1923) 17 *American Journal of International Law* 611

Hursh, John, 'International Humanitarian Law Violations, Legal Responsibility, and US Military Support to the Saudi Coalition in Yemen: A Cautionary Tale' (2020) 7 *Journal on the Use of Force and International Law* 122

Ikejiaku, Brian-Vincent, 'International Law Is Western Made Global Law: The Perception of Third-World Category' (2013) 6 *African Journal of Legal Studies* 337

Jacewicz, Andrzej, 'The Concept of Force in the United Nations Charter' (1977–1978) 9 *Polish Yearbook of International Law* 137

Jain, Abhimanyu George, 'Rationalising International Law Rules on Self-Defence: The Pin-Prick Doctrine' (2014) 14 *Chicago-Kent Journal of International and Comparative Law* 23

Joffe, George, 'Turmoil in Chad' (1990) 89 *Current History* 157

Joyner, Daniel, 'Why I Stopped Believing in Customary International Law' (2019) 9 *Asian Journal of International Law* 31

Kahn, Paul W., 'From Nuremburg to The Hague: The United States Position in *Nicaragua v. United States* and the Development of International Law' (1987) 12 *Yale Journal of International Law* 1

Kammerhofer, Jörg, 'Uncertainty in the Formal Sources of International Law: Customary International Law and Some of Its Problems' (2004) 15 *European Journal of International Law* 523

Kelsen, Hans, 'Collective Security and Collective Self-Defense under the Charter of the United Nations' (1948) 42 *American Journal of International Law* 783

'The Future of Collective Security' (1951) 21 *Revista Juridica de la Universidad de Puerto Rico* 83

'Is the North Atlantic Treaty a Regional Arrangement?' (1951) 45 *American Journal of International Law* 162

Khater, Maya, 'The Legality of the Russian Military Operations against Ukraine from the Perspective of International Law' (2022) 3 *Access to Justice in Eastern Europe* 1

Kleczkowska, Agata, 'The Misconception about the Term "Intervention by Invitation"' (2019) 79 *Zeitschrift für Ausländisches Öffentliches Recht und Völkerrecht* 1

'The Meaning of Treaty Authorisation and Ad Hoc Consent for the Legality of Military Assistance on Request' (2020) 7 *Journal on the Use of Force and International Law* 270

Kopel, David B., Gallant, Paul, and Eisen, Joanne D., 'The Human Right of Self-Defense' (2007) 22 *Brigham Young University Journal of Public Law* 43

Kreß, Claus, 'The Ukraine War and the Prohibition of the Use of Force in International Law' (2022) *Torkel Opsahl Academic EPublisher*, Occasional Paper Series No. 13, 1

Kritsiotis, Dino, 'Arguments of Mass Confusion' (2004) 15 *European Journal of International Law* 233

Kufuor, Kofi Oteng, 'The OAU and the Recognition of Governments in Africa: Analyzing its Practice and Proposals for the Future' (2002) 17 *American University International Law Review* 369

Kulski, W. W., 'The Soviet System of Collective Security Compared with the Western System' (1950) 44 *American Journal of International Law* 453

Kunz, Joseph L., 'Individual and Collective Self-Defence under Article 51 of the Charter of the United Nations' (1947) 41 *American Journal of International Law* 872

Kwiecień, Roman, 'The *Nicaragua* Judgment and the Use of Force – 30 Years Later' (2016) 36 *Polish Yearbook of International Law* 21

Land, Kristi, 'Legal Aspects of the Conflict in Georgia and Post-Conflict Developments' (2008–2009) *Estonian Ministry of Foreign Affairs Yearbook* 49

Lauterpacht, Hersch, 'Recognition of States in International Law' (1944) 53 *Yale Law Journal* 385

'Recognition of Governments: I' (1945) 45 *Columbia Law Review* 815

Le Mon, Christopher J., 'Unilateral Intervention by Invitation in Civil Wars: The Effective Control Test Tested' (2003) 35 *New York University Journal of International Law and Politics* 741

Lee, Jaemin, 'Collective Self-Defense or Collective Security: Japan's Reinterpretation of Article 9 of the Constitution' (2015) 8 *Journal of East Asia and International Law* 373

Lieblich, Eliav, 'Internal *Jus ad Bellum*' (2016) 67 *Hastings Law Journal* 687

Linderfalk, Ulf, 'Is Treaty Interpretation an Art or a Science? International Law and Rational Decision Making' (2015) 26 *European Journal of International Law* 169

Lotrionte, Catherine, 'The Just War Doctrine and Covert Responses to Terrorism' (2002) 3 *Georgetown Journal of International Affairs* 85

Lott, Alexander, 'The Tagliavini Report Revisited: *Jus ad Bellum* and the Legality of the Russian Intervention in Georgia' (2012) 28 *Merkourios – International and European Security Law* 4

MacDonald, R. St. J., 'The *Nicaragua* Case: New Answers to Old Questions' (1986) 24 *Canadian Yearbook of International Law* 127

Mahmoudi, Said, 'Self-Defence and "Unwilling or Unable" States' (2021) 422 *Recueil des cours* 249

Martin, Craig, 'Challenging and Refining the "Unwilling or Unable" Doctrine' (2019) 52 *Vanderbilt Law Review* 387

McWhinney, Edward, 'President Bush and the New U.S. National Security Strategy: The Continuing Relevance of the Legal Advisor and International Law' (2002) 1 *Chinese Journal of International Law* 421

Meeker, Leonard C., 'The Legality of United States Participation in the Defense of Viet-Nam' (1966) 54 *Department of State Bulletin* 474

Meiβner, Berhard, 'Ancient Greek Coalition Warfare: Classical and Hellenistic Examples' (2012) 14 *Journal of Military and Strategic Studies* 1

Mendelson, Maurice, 'Practice, Propaganda and Principle in International Law' (1989) 42 *Current Legal Problems* 1

Meyer, Jane A., 'Collective Self-Defense and Regional Security: Necessary Exceptions to a Globalist Doctrine' (1993) 11 *Boston University International Law Journal* 391

Michael, Helen, 'Covert Involvement in Essentially Internal Conflicts: United States Assistance to the Contras under International Law' (1990) 23 *Vanderbilt Journal of Transnational Law* 539

Miles, William F. S., 'Tragic Tradeoffs: Democracy and Security in Chad' (1995) 33 *The Journal of Modern African Studies* 53

Miller, Edward, 'Self-Defence, International Law and the Six Day War' (1985) 20 *Israeli Law Review* 49

Mills, Claire, 'Military Assistance to Ukraine since the Russian Invasion', *House of Commons Library*, Research Briefing (17 October 2022)

Minai, Keisuke, 'What Legal Interest Is Protected by the Right of Collective Self-Defense: The Japanese Perspective' (2016) 24 *Willamette Journal of International Law and Dispute Resolution* 105

Modabber, Zia, 'Collective Self-Defense: *Nicaragua v. United States*' (1988) 10 *Loyola of Los Angeles International and Comparative Law Journal* 449

Mori, Tadashi, 'Collective Self-Defence in International Law and in the New Japanese Legislation for Peace and Security (2015)' (2017) 60 *Japanese Yearbook of International Law* 158

Morrison, Fred L., 'Legal Issues in the *Nicaragua* Opinion' (1987) 81 *American Journal of International Law* 160

Mrázek, Josef, 'Prohibition of the Use and Threat of Force: Self-Defence and Self-Help in International Law' (1989) 27 *Canadian Yearbook of International Law* 81

Mulgan, Aurelia George, 'Japan's Defence Dilemma' (2005) 1 *Security Challenges* 59

Murphy, Sean D., 'Self-Defence and the *Israeli Wall* Advisory Opinion: An *Ipse Dixit* from the ICJ?' (2005) 99 *American Journal of International Law* 62

'The International Legality of US Military Cross-border Operations from Afghanistan into Pakistan' (2009) 85 *International Legal Studies* 109

Mushkat, Roda, 'Who May Wage War – An Examination of an Old/New Question' (1987) 2 *American University Journal of International Law and Policy* 97

Nagan, Winston P., and Hammer, Craig, 'The Changing Character of Sovereignty in International Law and International Relations' (2004) 43 *Columbia Journal of Transnational Law* 141

Norton Moore, John, 'The Secret War in Central America and the Future of World Order' (1986) 80 *American Journal of International Law* 43

'The *Nicaragua* Case and the Deterioration of World Order' (1987) 81 *American Journal of International Law* 151

Norton Moore, John, and Underwood, James L., 'The Lawfulness of United States Assistance to the Republic of Viet Nam' (1966) 5 *Duquesne Law Review* 235

Nußberger, Benjamin, 'Military Strikes in Yemen in 2015: Intervention by Invitation and Self-Defence in the Course of Yemen's "Model Transitional Process"' (2017) 4 *Journal on the Use of Force and International Law* 110

O'Connell, Mary Ellen, 'Review: Necessity, Proportionality and the Use of Force by States by Judith Gardam' (2006) 100 *American Journal of International Law* 973

'Rules of Evidence for the Use of Force in International Law's New Era' (2006) 100 *American Society of International Law Proceedings* 44

'Preserving the Peace: The Continuing Ban on War between States' (2007) 38 *California Western International Law Journal* 41

'The True Meaning of Force' (2014) 108 *AJIL Unbound* 141

'The True Meaning of Force: A Further Response to Tom Ruys in the Interest of Peace' (2014) 108 *AJIL Unbound* 153

O'Connor, Laurie, 'Legality of the Use of Force in Syria against Islamic State and the Khorasan Group' (2016) 3 *Journal on the Use of Force and International Law* 70

Ochoa-Ruiz, Natalia, and Salamanca-Aguado, Esther, 'Exploring the Limits of International Law relating to the Use of Force in Self-Defence' (2005) 16 *European Journal of International Law* 499

Oliver, Covey, 'International Law and the Quarantine of Cuba: A Hopeful Prescription for Legal Writing' (1963) 57 *American Journal of International Law* 373

Orford, Anne, 'Regional Orders, Geopolitics, and the Future of International Law' (2021) 74 *Current Legal Problems* 149

Österdahl, Inger, 'Sweden's Collective Defence Obligations or This Is Not a Collective Defence Pact (or Is It?): Considerations of International and Constitutional Law' (2021) 90 *Nordic Journal of International Law* 127

Paddeu, Federica, 'Use of Force against Non-State Actors and the Circumstance Precluding Wrongfulness of Self-Defence' (2017) 30 *Leiden Journal of International Law* 93

Paddeu, Federica I., 'Military Assistance on Request and General Reasons against Force: Consent as a Defence to the Prohibition of Force' (2020) 7 *Journal on the Use of Force and International Law* 227

Padmanabhan, Aadhithi, and Shih, Michael, 'Collective Self-Defense: A Report of the Yale Law School Center for Global Legal Challenges' (10 December 2012), https://law.yale.edu/sites/default/files/documents/pdf/cglc/GLC_Collective_SelfDefense.pdf

Perišić, Petra, 'Intervention by Invitation – When Can Consent from a Host State Justify Foreign Military Intervention?' (2019) 7 *Russian Law Journal* 4

Perkins, John A., 'The Right of Counterintervention' (1987) 17 *Georgia Journal of International and Comparative Law* 171

Perot, Elie, 'The Art of Commitments: NATO, the EU, and the Interplay between Law and Politics within Europe's Collective Defence Architecture' (2019) 28 *European Security* 40

Peters, Anne, 'Intervention by Invitation: Impulses from the Max Planck Trialogues on the Law of Peace and War' (2019) 79 *Zeitschrift für Ausländisches Öffentliches Recht und Völkerrecht* 635

Pijpers, Peter B. M. J., Boddens Hosang, Hans J. F. R., and Ducheine, Paul A. L., 'Collective Cyber Defence – The EU and NATO Perspective on Cyber Attacks' (2021) *Amsterdam Law School Legal Studies* Research Paper No. 2021-37, Amsterdam Center for International Law No. 2021-13

Powell, Russell, 'The Law and Philosophy of Preventive War: An Institution-Based Approach to Collective Self-Defence' (2007) 32 *Australian Journal of Legal Philosophy* 67

Reichler, Paul S., and Wippman, David, 'United States Armed Intervention in *Nicaragua*: A Rejoinder' (1986) 11 *Yale Journal of International Law* 462

Reisman, W. Michael, 'International Incidents: Introduction to a New Genre in the Study of International Law' (1984–1985) 10 *Yale Journal of International Law* 1

'Old Wine in New Bottles: The Reagan and Brezhnev Doctrines in Contemporary International Law and Practice' (1988) 13 *Yale Journal of International Law* 171

'Sovereignty and Human Rights in Contemporary International Law' (1990) 84 *American Journal of International Law* 866

Parra, Paola Diana Reyes, 'Self-Defence against Non-State Actors: Possibility or Reality?' (2021) 9 *Revista de la Facultad de Jurisprudencia* 151

Rohlik, Josef, 'Some Remarks on Self-Defense and Intervention: A Reaction to Reading Law and Civil War in the Modern World' (1976) 6 *Georgia Journal of International and Comparative Law* 395

Rondos, Alex, 'Civil War and Foreign Intervention in Chad' (1985) 84 *Current History* 209

Roscini, Marco, 'On the "Inherent" Character of the Right of States to Self-Defence' (2015) 4 *Cambridge Journal of International and Comparative Law* 634

Ross, Simona, 'U.S. Justifications for the Use of Force in Syria through the Prism of the Responsibility to Protect' (2021) 8 *Journal on the Use of Force and International Law* 233

Rostow, Eugene V., 'Until What? Enforcement Action or Collective Self-Defense' (1991) 85 *American Journal of International Law* 506

Rostow, Nicholas, '*Nicaragua* and the Law of Self-Defense Revisited' (1986) 11 *Yale Journal of International Law* 437

Roth, Brad R., 'The Enduring Significance of State Sovereignty' (2004) 56 *Florida Law Review* 1017

Roucounas, Emmanuel, *l'Institut de droit international*, 10th Commission, 'Present Problems of the Use of Force in International Law Sub-group: Self-Defence' (2007) 72 *Annuaire de l'Institut de droit international* 75

Rowles, James P., 'Secret Wars, Self-Defense and the Charter – A Reply to Professor Moore' (1986) 80 *American Journal of International Law* 568

Rumpf, Helmut, 'The Concepts of Peace and War in International Law' (1984) 27 *German Yearbook of International Law* 429

Ruys, Tom, 'The "Protection of Nationals" Doctrine Revisited' (2008) 13 *Journal of Conflict and Security Law* 233

'The Meaning of Force and the Boundaries of the *Jus ad Bellum*: Are Minimal Uses of Force Excluded from UN Charter Article 2(4)' (2014) 108 *American Journal of International Law* 159

'The True Meaning of Force: A Reply to Mary Ellen O'Connell' (2014) 108 *AJIL Unbound* 148

Ruys, Tom, and Ferro, Luca, 'Weathering the Storm: Legality and Legal Implication of the Saudi-Led Military Intervention in Yemen' (2016) 65 *International and Comparative Law Quarterly* 61

Salvin, Marina, 'The North Atlantic Pact' (1949) 27 *International Conciliation* 375

Sapiro, Miriam, 'Iraq: The Shifting Sands of Pre-Emptive Self-Defense' (2003) 97 *American Journal of International Law* 599

Sari, Aurel, 'The Mutual Assistance Clauses of the North Atlantic and EU Treaties: The Challenge of Hybrid Threats' (2019) 10 *Harvard National Security Journal* 405

Scarfi, Juan Pablo, 'Denaturalizing the Monroe Doctrine: The Rise of Latin American Legal Anti-Imperialism in the Face of the Modern US and Hemispheric Redefinition of the Monroe Doctrine' (2020) 33 *Leiden Journal of International Law* 541

Schachter, Oscar, 'The Right of States to Use Armed Force' (1983–1984) 82 *Michigan Law Review* 1620

'Self-Defense and the Rule of Law' (1989) 83 *American Journal of International Law* 259

'United Nations in the Gulf Conflict' (1991) 85 *American Journal of International Law* 452

'Implementing Limitations on the Use of Force: The Doctrine of Proportionality and Necessity: Remarks' (1992) 86 *American Society of International Law Proceedings* 39

Schmitt, Michael N., 'Computer Network Attack and the Use of Force in International Law: Thoughts on a Normative Framework' (1999) 37 *Columbia Journal of Transnational Law* 885

'Drone Attacks under the *Jus as Bellum* and *Jus in Bello*: Clearing the "Fog of Law"' (2010) 13 *Yearbook of International Humanitarian Law* 311

Schuit, Anne, 'Recognition of Governments in International Law and the Recent Conflict in Libya' (2012) 14 *International Community Law Review* 381

Scobbie, Iain, 'Words My Mother Never Taught Me: In Defence of the International Court' (2005) 99 *American Journal of International Law* 76

Shah, Niaz A., 'Self-Defence, Anticipatory Self-Defence and Pre-Emption: International Law's Response to Terrorism' (2007) 12 *Journal of Conflict and Security Law* 95

Shteynberg, Garriy, *et al.*, 'Agency and Identity in the Collective Self' (2022) 26 *Personality and Social Psychology Review* 35

Simma, Bruno, 'NATO, the UN and the Use of Force: Legal Aspects' (1999) 10 *European Journal of International Law* 1

Sofaer, Abraham D., 'On the Necessity of Pre-Emption' (2003) 14 *European Journal of International Law* 209

Sohn, Louis B., 'Western European Treaty for Collaboration and Collective Self-Defence' (1948) 34 *American Bar Association Journal* 406

'How New Is the New International Legal Order?' (1992) 20 *Denver Journal of International Law and Policy* 205

Spagnolo, Andrea, 'The Armed Attack against Ukraine and the Italian Reaction from a *Ius ad Bellum* Perspective' (2022) 2 *The Italian Review of International and Comparative Law* 443

Starski, Paulina, 'Silence within the Process of Normative Change and Evolution of the Prohibition on the Use of Force: Normative Volatility and Legislative Responsibility' (2017) 4 *Journal on the Use of Force and International Law* 14

Svicevic, Marko, 'Collective Self-Defence or Regional Enforcement Action: The Legality of a SADC Intervention in Cabo Delgado and the Question of Mozambican Consent' (2022) 9 *Journal on the Use of Force and International Law* 138

Szpak, Agnieszka, *et al.*, 'Reaction to the Russian Aggression against Ukraine: Cities as International Standards' Supporters' (2022) *Journal of Contemporary European Studies*, advance access version, www.tandfonline.com/doi/full/10.1080/14782804.2022.2126445

Taft IV, William H., 'Self-Defence and the Oil Platforms Decision' (2004) 29 *Yale Journal of International Law* 295

Talmon, Stefan, 'Changing Views on the Use of Force: The German Position' (2005) 5 *Baltic Yearbook of International Law* 41

Terry, Patrick C. R., 'Afghanistan's Civil War (1979–1989): Illegal and Failed Foreign Interventions' (2011) 31 *Polish Yearbook of International Law* 107

Terry, Patrick, 'Germany Joins the Campaign against ISIS in Syria: A Case of Collective Self-Defence or Rather the Unlawful Use of Force?' (2016) 4 *Russian Law Journal* 26

Tertrais, Bruno, 'Article 5 of the Washington Treaty: Its Origins, Meaning and Future' (2016) *NATO Defense College*, Research Paper No. 130

Thomas Jr., A. J., and Van Wynen Thomas, Ann, 'The Organization of American States and Collective Security' (1959) 13 *Southwestern Law Journal* 177

Trapp, Kimberley N., 'Back to Basics: Necessity, Proportionality and the Right of Self-Defence against Non-State Terrorist Actors' (2007) 56 *International and Comparative Law Quarterly* 141

Tucker, Robert W., 'The Interpretation of War under Present International Law' (1951) 4 *International Law Quarterly* 11

Tzouvala, Ntina, 'TWAIL and the "Unwilling or Unable" Doctrine: Continuities and Ruptures' (2015) 109 *AJIL Unbound* 266

Ulfstein, Geir, and Christiansen, Hege Føsund, 'The Legality of the NATO Bombing in Libya' (2013) 62 *International and Comparative Law Quarterly* 159

van den Herik, Larissa, 'Replicating Article 51: A Reporting Requirement for Consent-Based Use of Force?' (2019) 79 *Zeitschrift für Ausländisches Öffentliches Recht und Völkerrecht* 707

van der Steenhoven, Nick, 'Conduct and Subsequent Practice by States in the Application of the Requirement to Report under UN Charter Article 51 (2019) 6 *Journal on the Use of Force and International Law* 242

van der Vyver, Johan D., 'Military Intervention in Syria: The American, British and French Alternatives and the Russian Option' (2015) 48 *De Jure* 36

Verdross, Alfred, 'Austria's Permanent Neutrality and the United Nations Organization' (1956) 50 *American Journal of International Law* 61

Visser, Laura, 'May the Force Be with You: The Legal Classification of Intervention by Invitation' (2019) 66 *Netherlands International Law Review* 21

'What's in a Name? The Terminology of Intervention by Invitation' (2019) 79 *Zeitschrift für Ausländisches Öffentliches Recht und Völkerrecht* 651

'Intervention by Invitation and Collective Self-Defence: Two Sides of the Same Coin?' (2020) 7 *Journal on the Use of Force and International Law* 292

Waldock, C. H. M., 'The Regulation of the Use of Force by Individual States in International Law' (1952) 81 *Recueil des cours* 451

Walker, George K., 'Anticipatory Collective Self-Defense in the Charter Era: What the Treaties Have Said' (1998) 31 *Cornell International Law Journal* 321

Warren, Patrick T., 'Alliance History and the Future NATO: What the Last 500 Years of Alliance Behavior Tells Us about NATO's Path Forward',

21st Century Defense Initiative Policy Paper, Foreign Policy at Brookings (30 June 2010), www.brookings.edu/wp-content/uploads/2016/06/0630_nato_alliance_warren.pdf

Wedgwood, Ruth, 'Proportionality and Necessity in American National Security Decision Making' (1992) 86 *American Society of International Law Proceedings* 58

'Responding to Terrorism: Strikes against bin Laden' (1999) 24 *Yale Journal of International Law* 559

'The ICJ Advisory Opinion on the Israeli Security Fence and the Limits of Self-Defence' (2005) 99 *American Journal of International Law* 52

Weightman, M. A., 'Self-Defense in International Law' (1951) 37 *Virginia Law Review* 1095

Wigmore, John H., 'The Work of the Fourth Assembly (1923) of the League of Nations: A Legislative Summary' (1924) 9 *The Virginia Law Register* 887

Willard, Andrew R., 'Incidents: An Essay in Method' (1984–1985) 10 *Yale Journal of International Law* 21

Wilmshurst, Elizabeth (ed.), 'The Chatham House Principles of International Law on the Use of Force by States in Self-Defence' (2006) 55 *International and Comparative Law Quarterly* 963

Wingfield, Thomas C., 'Forcible Protection of Nationals Abroad' (1999–2000) 104 *Dickinson Law Review* 447

Wilson, Gary, 'The Legal, Military and Political Consequences of the "Coalition of the Willing" Approach to UN Military Enforcement Action' (2007) 12 *Journal of Conflict and Security Law* 295

Wilson, Larry C., 'The Defence of Others – Criminal Law and the Good Samaritan' (1988) 33 *McGill Law Journal* 756

Wippman, David, 'Military Intervention, Regional Organizations, and Host-State Consent' (1996) 7 *Duke Journal of Comparative and International Law* 209

Wood, Michael, 'International Law and the Use of Force: What Happens in Practice?' (2013) 53 *Indian Journal of International Law* 345

Wrange, Päl, 'Law, Force and Contingency – Notes on a Bold Monograph on Article 2(4) and the Problems of Finding a Proper Basis for International Legal Reasoning' (1992–1993) 61 *Nordic Journal of International Law* 83

Wright, Quincy, 'United States Intervention in the Lebanon' (1959) 53 *American Journal of International Law* 112

'Legal Aspects of the Viet-Nam Situation' (1966) 60 *American Journal of International Law* 750

Wyse, Christian, 'The African Union's Right of Humanitarian Intervention as Collective Self-Defense' (2018) 19 *Chicago Journal of International Law* 295

Yoo, John, 'International Law and the War in Iraq' (2003) 97 *American Journal of International Law* 563

Yost, David S., 'NATO and the Anticipatory Use of Force' (2007) 83 *International Affairs* 39

Zamani, Masoud, and Nikouei, Majid, 'Intervention by Invitation, Collective Self-Defence and the Enigma of Effective Control' (2017) 16 *Chinese Journal of International Law* 663

Blog Posts

Benton, Tim, Froggatt, Antony, and Wellesley, Laura, 'Ukraine Crisis Could Trigger Cascading Risks Globally', *Chatham House* (16 March 2022), www.chathamhouse.org/2022/03/ukraine-crisis-could-trigger-cascading-risks-globally

Christakis, Theodore, and Bannelier, Karine, 'French Military Intervention in Mali: It's Legal but . . . Why? Part I', *EJIL:Talk!* (24 January 2013), www.ejiltalk.org/french-military-intervention-in-mali-its-legal-but-why-part-i

Constantinou, Costas M., 'Revising the Treaty of Guarantee for a Cyprus Settlement', *EJIL:Talk!* (21 June 2017), www.ejiltalk.org/revising-the-treaty-of-guarantee-for-a-cyprus-settlement/#:~:text=The%20existing%20Treaty%20of%20Guarantee,led%20military%20coup%20in%201974

Doubek, Pavel, 'War in Ukraine: Time for a Collective Self-Defense?' *Opinio Juris* (29 March 2022), http://opiniojuris.org/2022/03/29/war-in-ukraine-time-for-a-collective-self-defense

Gorenburg, Dmitry, 'Russia and Collective Security: Why CSTO Is No Match for Warsaw Pact', *Russia Matters* (27 May 2020), www.russiamatters.org/analysis/russia-and-collective-security-why-csto-no-match-warsaw-pact

Haque, Adil Ahmad, 'On the Precipice: The U.S. and Russia in Syria', *Just Security* (19 June 2017), www.justsecurity.org/42297/precipice-u-s-russia-syria

Hasar, Seyfullah, 'Kazakhstan: Another Intervention by Invitation that Played Out as Expected', *Opinio Juris* (7 February 2022), http://opiniojuris.org/2022/02/07/kazakhstan-another-intervention-by-invitation-that-played-out-as-expected

Hathaway, Oona, and Hartig, Luke, 'Still at War: The United States in Somalia', *Just Security* (31 March 2022), www.justsecurity.org/80921/still-at-war-the-united-states-in-somalia

Heller, Kevin Jon, 'The Coming Attack on Syria Will Be Unlawful', *Opinio Juris* (12 April 2018), http://opiniojuris.org/2018/04/12/the-coming-attack-on-syria-will-be-unlawful

Kreß, Claus, 'The Fine Line between Collective Self-Defense and Intervention by Invitation: Reflections on the Use of Force against "IS" in Syria', *Just Security* (17 February 2015), www.justsecurity.org/20118/claus-kreb-force-isil-syria

Lukyanov, Fyodor A., 'Kazakhstan Intervention Sees Russia Set a New Precedent', *Russia in Global Affairs* (7 January 2022), https://eng.globalaffairs.ru/articles/kazakhstan-new-precedent

Martin, Craig, 'Japan's Definition of Armed Attack and "Bloody Nose" Strikes against North Korea', *Just Security* (1 February 2018), www.justsecurity.org/51678/japans-definition-armed-attack-bloody-nose-strikes-north-korea

Milanovic, Marko, 'The Clearly Illegal US Missile Strike in Syria', *EJIL:Talk!* (7 April 2017), www.ejiltalk.org/the-clearly-illegal-us-missile-strike-in-syria

Nevitt, Mark, 'The Operational and Legal Risks of a No-Fly Zone over Ukrainian Skies', *Just Security* (10 March 2022), www.justsecurity.org/80641/the-operational-and-legal-risks-of-a-no-fly-zone-over-ukrainian-skies

Paddeu, Federica, 'The Rio Treaty: Paving the Way for Military Intervention in Venezuela?', *Just Security* (29 October 2019), www.justsecurity.org/66758/the-rio-treaty-paving-the-way-for-military-intervention-in-venezuela

Pothelet, Elvina, 'U.S. Military's "Collective Self-Defense" of Non-State Partner Forces: What Does International Law Say?', *Just Security* (26 October 2018), www.justsecurity.org/61232/collective-self-defense-partner-forces-international-law-say

Sari, Aurel, and Nasu, Hitoshi, 'Collective Self-Defense and the "Bloody Nose Strategy": Does It Take Two to Tango?', *Just Security* (26 January 2018), www.justsecurity.org/51435/collective-self-defense-bloody-nose-strategy-tango

Schmitt, Michael N., 'Providing Arms and Materiel to Ukraine: Neutrality, Co-Belligerency, and the Use of Force', *Articles of War* (7 March 2022), https://lieber.westpoint.edu/ukraine-neutrality-co-belligerency-use-of-force

Schönleben, Ella, 'Collective Self-Defence or Just Another Intervention?: Some Thoughts on Turkey Allegedly Sending Syrian Mercenaries to Nagorno-Karabakh', *Völkerrechtsblog* (2 November 2020), https://voelkerrechtsblog.org/de/collective-self-defence-or-just-another-intervention

Tibori-Szabó, Kinga, 'The Downing of the Syrian Fighter Jet and Collective Self-Defence', *Opinio Juris* (23 June 2017), http://opiniojuris.org/2017/06/23/the-downing-of-the-syrian-fighter-jet-and-collective-self-defence

van Wilgenburg, Wladimir, 'Syrian Democratic Forces (Syria)', in Guns and Governance: How Europe Should Talk with Non-State Armed Groups in The Middle East the Middle East and North Africa', *European Council on Foreign Relations*, https://ecfr.eu/special/mena-armed-groups/syrian-democratic-forces-syria

Vermeer, Zachary, 'The *Jus ad Bellum* and the Airstrikes in Yemen: Double Standards for Decamping Presidents?', *EJIL:Talk!* (30 April 2015), www.ejiltalk.org/the-jus-ad-bellum-and-the-airstrikes-in-yemen-double-standards-for-decamping-presidents

Weller, Marc, 'Options for a Peace Settlement for Ukraine: Option Paper I – Neutrality and Related Concepts', *Opinio Juris* (31 March 2022), https://opiniojuris.org/2022/03/31/options-for-a-peace-settlement-for-ukraine-option-paper-i-neutrality-and-related-concepts

Wentker, Alexander, 'At War: When Do States Supporting Ukraine or Russia Become Parties to the Conflict and What Would that Mean?', *EJIL:Talk!*

(14 March 2022), www.ejiltalk.org/at-war-when-do-states-supporting-ukraine-or-russia-become-parties-to-the-conflict-and-what-would-that-mean

Wilmshurst, Elizabeth, 'Ukraine: Debunking Russia's Legal Justifications', *Chatham House* (24 February 2022), www.chathamhouse.org/2022/02/ukraine-debunking-russias-legal-justifications

INDEX

9/11
  anticipatory response to, 115
  NATO and, 269
  non state actors and, 120
  support for US-led operation following (2001), 33, 34, 38, 55

Abkhazia, 174–176
Act of Chapultepec (1945), 66, 82, 86
Afghanistan
  re USSR (1979), 157, 225
African Union (AU), 132
aggression, 37, 41, 79–80, 106, 154, 158, 165, 242–243
'alter ego rule', the, 90
Angola
  re Cuba (from 1975), 34, 191–193
anticipatory self-defence, 28, 108–116, 314, 319
ANZUS Treaty, 33, 34, 237
apologist/utopian dilemma, 11
Arab League, the, 200, 240
Armed Activities case
  armed attack, 100
  non-state actors and self-defence, 116
  request requirement, 144, 171
armed attack, 19, 62, 100–108, 218, 253, 292, 301, 314, 319
Armenia
  re Azerbaijan (2008), 213
  re CSTO (2022), 5, 274
Article 51 of the UN Charter
  collective self-defence treaties and, 239
  collective self-defence, inclusion of, 1, 10, 29, 68, 84–89
  conjoining of individual and collective self-defence, 68, 89–94, 98, 106
  differences between authoritative languages, 45–46, 47, 88, 110
  drafting of, 84–89, 94
  regional arrangements and, 262, 264
  UN membership and, 178
Athens-Boeotia-Locris alliance (395 BCE), 70
'attack on one = attack on all', 82, 89, 246
Augustine of Hippo, 69
Australia
  re 9/11 (2001), 33
  re ISIL (2015), 120, 160
  views on collective self-defence, 271
Azerbaijan
  re Armenia (2008), 213
  re Turkey (2020), 5

Baghdad Pact, the (1955), 244, 248
Bahrain
  re UK (1990), 115, 158
  re Yemen (since 2015), 134
Belgium
  re ISIL (2016), 128, 160
Bowett, Derek, 27–28, 29, 87
Brussels Treaty, the (1948), 254

Cambodia
  re US (1970), 124, 214
  re Vietnam War, the (1964), 183
Canada
  Criminal Code, 37
  'defence of others' concept and, 36
  re 9/11 (2001), 55

Canada (cont.)
re Czechoslovakia (1968), 156, 190
re ISIL (2015), 161
re Lebanon (1958), 137
Caroline incident (1837), 122
casus fœderis, 71, 74, 78–80, 242–244, 247, 248, 252
Chad
re various interventions (1979–1986), 107, 193–195, 209, 219, 221
Charter of the United Nations
Article 2(4), 56, 60, 104, 243, 252, 268, 301
Article 51. *See* Article 51 of the UN Charter
Article 52, 267
Article 53, 241, 262
Article 54, 265
Article 103, 239, 241
Chapter VII, 78
Chapter VIII, 85, 262
drafting of the, 84–89
China
re Czechoslovakia (1968), 191
co-belligerency, 63
Cold War, the, 14–15, 269, 271, 273
Collective Security Treaty Organisation. *See* CSTO
collective self-defence
seventeenth-/eighteenth-century writings on, 70–72
definition, 1–2, 23, 56
duty to act in, 41–43, 71
existing literature, summary of, 6–7
novelty of the concept of, 66–67, 68
terminology, 18, 23–24, 26–27, 28, 46–47, 87–89, 96
Colombia
views on collective self-defence, 89, 91
Commission to Study the Organisation of Peace, 135, 153
Commonwealth of Independent States (CIS)
re Tajikistan (1993), 196
complicity, 130
covert uses of force, 215–222
Covid-19 pandemic, 40, 233
CSTO
membership, 259
re Armenia (2022), 5, 274
re Kazakhstan (2022), 5, 30–31, 243, 274
relationship to Uzbekistan, 257
trigger for collective defence mechanism, 249
Cuba
re Angola (from 1975), 34, 191–193
re Kuwait (1990), 159
views on collective self-defence, 266
cyber force, 56
Czechoslovakia
re USSR (1968), 32, 102, 124, 156, 189–191

de minimis threshold, 57
Declaration of Havana (1940), 82
Declaration of Panama (1939), 81
declaration requirement
case law, found in, 142–147
lack of legal basis for, 166, 316
state practice, found in, 153–163
'defence of others' concept, 36, 44, 69, 90, 313
Denmark
re Czechoslovakia (1968), 156
re ISIL (2016), 55, 108, 128
derivative right
collective self-defence as a, 52–53, 92, 98
Donetsk, 11, 161–163, 176–178
DRC/Zaire
ICJ proceedings. *See Armed Activities* case
re Chad (1979–1986), 107, 193–195, 210
re Great African War, the, 306–308
Dubček, Alexander, 189–191
Dumbarton Oaks proposals (1944), 92

Economic Community of West African States (ECOWAS), 242
effective control test, 185–187, 195, 201–202, 287, 316
Ethiopia
re Angola (from 1975), 34

European Union (EU), 60, 145, 235
  relationship to NATO, 255–256, 261
  TEU Article 42(7), 242, 250, 261, 273

Falklands/Malvinas conflict (1982), 60, 261
'force', *jus ad bellum* meaning of, 56–57, 302
France
  re Chad (1979–1986), 193–195
  re Hungary (1956), 225
  re Mali (2013), 197–198
  re Paris attacks (2015), 273
  re Sardinia (1858), 76
Friendly Relations Declaration (1970), 60

General Assembly, 7, 43, 44, 54, 135, 260, 271
Georgia
  re Russia (2008), 145, 174–176, 226–227
Germany
  re NATO membership, 180
  re Ukraine (2022), 63
Ghana
  views on collective self-defence, 53–54
Greece
  Ancient, defensive alliances in, 69–70
  relationship with Turkey, 257
Grotius, Hugo, 70–71, 72, 75, 76
guarantee, treaties of, 244–246

Habré, Hissène, 193–195
Hadi, Abdo Rabbo Mansour, 198–201
Honduras
  re US (1988), 107, 124, 158, 222
Hungary
  re USSR (1956), 154–155, 187–189, 225, 229

imminence requirement. *See* anticipatory self-defence
Independent International Fact-Finding Mission on the Conflict in Georgia, 145, 172, 175, 213, 227, 278
India
  views on collective self-defence, 54
inherent right
  collective self-defence as an, 1, 24, 71, 92, 280, 313
  customary international law, relationship to, 50
  individual self-defence as an, 48, 81, 86, 92
  legal basis, 53
  military assistance on request as an, 280
  natural law, relationship to, 48–49
  sovereignty, relationship to, 49–50
Institut de droit international
  Resolution on self-defence (2007), 166
  Rhodes resolution (2011), 297
International Humanitarian Law, 63, 72, 300
intervention by invitation. *See* military assistance on request
Iraq
  re ISIL (since 2014), 4, 54, 124, 134, 210, 220, 309
  re Kuwait (1990), 137
ISIL, 4, 54, 159, 210, 315
Islamic State of Iraq and the Levant. *See* ISIL
Italy
  re Kuwait (1990), 196
  re NATO membership, 180

Japan
  Constitution, own interpretation of, 37, 55
Jordan
  re UK (1958), 34, 113–114, 119–120, 155, 225, 305–306
just war, 71, 75

Kazakhstan
  re CSTO (2022), 5, 30–31, 243, 274
Kellogg-Briand Pact, the (1928), 75, 81
Korean War, the, 153–154, 180–181, 207–208
Kuwait
  re US *et al.* (1990–1991), 127, 137, 193–196

League of Nations, 68, 77–78
Lebanon
  re US (1958), 29–30, 106, 114, 119–120, 136–137, 155–156, 221
Libya
  re Chad (1979–1986), 193–195
  re Turkey (2020), 296
Luhansk, 11, 161–163, 178

Malaysia
  re Afghanistan (1979), 226
Mali
  re France (2013), 197–198
medieval period, 69
Mexico
  Arria formula meeting (2021), 8
military assistance on request
  counter-intervention as an element of, 277, 288, 292
  inherent right, as an, 280
  mixed legal claims regarding, 15, 283–286
  necessity requirement for, 295–297
  'negative equality' principle and, 292, 296
  proportionality requirement for, 295–297
  reporting requirement for, 297–299
  request requirement for, 286–289
  terminology, 289–291
  territorial restriction on, 300
  trigger/armed attack requirement, lack of, 291
military bases, 236
minoris generis assistance, 58–60, 64
Monroe doctrine, 83–84
Mozambique
  re request for aid (1977), 54, 208
Mutual Defence Arrangement between France and Sardinia (1858), 76

Nagorno-Karabakh conflict, 5
Napoleon, 73
NATO, 180, 229, 230, 234, 257
  9/11 and, 269
  'attack on one = attack on all', 246
  consensus decision-making, 237
  membership, 260
  nature of obligation, 250
  nature of the organisation, 263
  relationship to EU, 255–256, 261
  relationship to WEU, 255
  response to invasion of Ukraine (2022), 5, 25, 61–64, 274
  role post–Cold War, 273
  trigger for collective defence mechanism, 249, 261
natural law, 48, 71, 93, 95, 96
necessity, 19, 41, 71, 218, 302, 315
  core concept, 121–122
  military assistance on request and, 295–297
  re Ukraine (2022), 62
  who makes determinations of, 126–127
negative equality principle. *See* military assistance on request
neutrality
  permanent neutrality, 51
New Zealand
  proposal on duty of collective defence (1945), 42
  re 9/11 (2001), 34, 55
Nicaragua
  re Honduras (1988), 107
Nicaragua case
  armed attack, 100, 104, 301
  assessing the legal claims of states, 12
  declaration requirement, 142–147
  'defence of others' concept and, 44
  funding, provision of, 59
  impact on collective self-defence, 15–16
  Judge Jennings, dissenting opinion of, 26, 44, 67
  Judge Ruda, separate opinion of, 146
  Judge Schwebel, dissenting opinion of, 216, 218
  military assistance on request, 281
  necessity, 123
  non-state actors and self-defence, 116
  overview of facts, claims, and decision, 16–17
  proportionality, 123
  reporting requirement for self-defence, 132

request requirement, 142–147, 205, 208, 211, 216, 223–224, 315
weapons and logistical support, provision of, 58
non-state actors and self-defence, 116–121, 294, 315, 319
Norway
re ISIL (2016), 160
re NATO membership, 230
nuclear powers, 63, 272

Oil Platforms case
armed attack, 100, 104
request requirement, 143–144, 146, 172, 205
Organisation of African Unity (OAU), 193–195
Organisation of American States (OAS), 263–264
Organisation of Eastern Caribbean States (OECS), 234, 238

Pakistan
views on collective self-defence, 54
Peru
re Honduras (1988), 107, 125
re Hungary (1956), 188
views on collective self-defence, 42, 44, 54
Poland
re 9/11 (2001), 55
Portugal
re NATO membership, 180
pre-emptive self-defence. *See* anticipatory self-defence
proportionality, 19, 41, 71, 218, 302, 315
core concept, 122–123
military assistance on request and, 295–297
re Ukraine (2022), 62
single vs cumulative application, 127–130
who makes determinations of, 127
psychology of 'the self', 24
Pufendorf, Samuel von, 71, 72, 76

Qatar
re Yemen (since 2015), 134

regional arrangements, 85, 262–268
reporting requirement for self-defence, 62, 115, 130–135, 216, 218–219, 266, 297
request requirement
addressee of, 204–211, 317
case law, found in, 142–147
collective self-defence as a right and, 50–52
consent, request as an expression of, 286
formalities for, 211–212
historical basis, 72
military assistance on request and the, 286–289
public nature of, 212–222, 317
re Ukraine (2022), 62
state practice, found in, 153–163
statehood and the, 170–178
timing of the request, 222–231
UN membership and the, 178–183

Rio Treaty (1948), 131, 151, 152, 249, 256, 260, 264
Roman law, 36, 69
Rome-Messina defence pact (241 BCE), 70
Roosevelt, Franklin D., 81
RSS (Caribbean treaty, 1996), 238, 259
Russia/USSR
post–Second World War treaties, 256
re Afghanistan (1979), 157, 225
re Czechoslovakia (1968), 32, 102, 124, 156, 189–191
re Georgia (2008), 145, 174–176, 226–227
re Hungary (1956), 154–155, 187–189, 225, 229
re ISIL (2014), 161
re Jordan (1958), 225
re Lebanon (1958), 102, 114, 136, 156
re Mozambique (1977), 208
re Tajikistan (1993), 196
re Ukraine (2022), 5, 61–64, 161–163, 177, 178, 275
re Vietnam War, the, 183

SADC Mutual Defence Pact (2003), 131, 234, 247, 249
Saudi Arabia
re UK (1990), 115, 158
re US (1990), 114, 158
re Yemen (since 2015), 134, 201
SEATO, 32, 37, 151, 241, 247, 260, 264
Security Council, 43, 62, 85, 86, 89, 136, 265, 267, 271
Arria formula meeting (2021), 8
self-determination, right of, 186, 188, 191, 192, 201, 288, 296
Senegal
re Czechoslovakia (1968), 190
Somalia
re US (2021), 308
South Africa
re Angola (from 1975), 34, 192
South Ossetia, 174–176, 226–227
Southeast Asia Treaty Organisation. *See* SEATO
Southern African Development Community. *See* SADC Mutual Defence Pact (2003)
Soviet Union. *See* Russia/USSR
state responsibility, law of, 117, 130, 223
Statute of the International Court of Justice
Article 38(1), 9
Sweden
re Lebanon (1958), 107
re TEU Article 42(7), 250
Syria
re ISIL (since 2014), 4, 39, 161
views on collective self-defence, 266
Syrian Democratic Forces (SDF), 173

Tajikistan
re Russia (1993), 196
the Netherlands
re ISIL (2016), 54, 160
threats of force, 56
Traoré, Dioncounda, 197–198
Treaty between Austria-Hungary/Romania (1883), 74
Treaty between Bulgaria/Servia (1912), 74
Treaty between France and Greece (2021), 235, 258
Treaty between France and Monaco (2002), 245
Treaty between Greece and Bulgaria (1912), 73
Treaty between the UK and Poland (1939), 79
Treaty between the United States and Japan (1951), 245
Treaty between the USSR and Estonia (1939), 79
Treaty of Alliance and Friendship (Britain/Austria/Prussia/Russia, 1815), 73, 74
Treaty of Alliance between Czechoslovakia and Romania (1921), 79
Treaty of Brotherhood and Alliance between Iraq and Transjordan (1947), 241
Treaty of Defence between Spain and Britain (1680), 73
Treaty of Dunkirk (1947), 235
Treaty of Friendship and Cooperation between Vietnam and the USSR (1978), 242
Treaty of Friendship, Alliance and Mutual Assistance (Sino-Soviet, 1950), 241
Treaty of Guarantee (Cyprus, 1960), 245
Treaty of Mutual Assistance between the USSR and France (1935), 79
Treaty of Mutual Assistance, draft of (1923), 80
Treaty of Triple Alliance (Austria-Hungary/Germany/Italy, 1882), 74
Trump, Donald, 273
Turkey
re Azerbaijan (2020), 5
re Libya (2020), 296
re Russia (2015), 257
relationship with Greece, 258

UK
re Bahrain (1990), 115
re Hungary (1956), 189

re ISIL (since 2014), 101, 160
re Jordan (1958), 34, 113–114, 119–120, 155, 225, 305–306
re Kuwait (1990), 138, 158, 196
re Saudi Arabia (1990), 115
views on collective self-defence, 44, 54, 55, 80, 260
Ukraine
re Russia (2022), 5, 61–64, 161–163, 177, 178, 275
United Arab Emirates
re Yemen (since 2015), 134
United Arab Republic
re Lebanon (1958), 106, 136
views on collective self-defence, 7, 239
United Kingdom. *See* UK
United Nations General Assembly. *See* General Assembly
United Nations Security Council. *See* Security Council
United States of America. *See* US
until clause, 135–138
Uruguay
views on collective self-defence, 266
US
Operational Law Handbook (2022), 98, 167, 185
re Cambodia (1970), 124, 214
re Czechoslovakia (1968), 156, 191
re Honduras (1988), 107, 124, 158, 222
re ISIL (2014), 108
re Korean War, the (1950), 153, 207
re Kuwait (1990), 138, 158, 196
re Lebanon (1958), 29–30, 119–120, 136–137, 155–156
re SDF (2017–2018), 173–174
re Somalia (2021), 308
re Ukraine (2022), 62
re Vietnam War, the, 32, 157, 181–183
re Yemen (2016), 299
statement on nature of peace, 43
views on collective self-defence, 55
USSR. *See* Russia/USSR
Uzbekistan
relationship to CSTO, 257

Vattel, Emer de, 71, 75, 93, 121
Vienna Convention on the Law of Treaties (1969), 150
Vietnam War, the, 32, 124, 157, 181–183, 214

Wall advisory opinion
Judge Higgins, separate opinion of, 117
non-state actors and self-defence, 116
Warsaw Pact, the, 32, 124, 156, 189, 190, 225, 229, 230, 240, 249, 263, 273, 274
weapons and logistical assistance, provision of, 58–60
Webster, Daniel, 122
Western European Union (WEU), 135, 247, 254, 260

Yemen
re Qatar *et al.* (since 2015), 134
re Saudi Arabia (since 2015), 198–201
re US (2016), 299
Yugoslavia
re Czechoslovakia (1968), 190
re Hungary (1956), 125

Zaire. *See* DRC/Zaire

CAMBRIDGE STUDIES IN INTERNATIONAL AND COMPARATIVE LAW

Books in the Series

184 *Collective Self-Defence in International Law*
James A. Green

183 *Weaponising Evidence: A History of Tobacco Control in International Law*
Margherita Melillo

182 *The Justice Factory: Management Practices at the International Criminal Court*
Richard Clements

181 *A Communitarian Theory of WTO Law*
Chi Carmody

180 *Drones and International Law: A Techno-Legal Machinery*
Mignot-Mahdavi

179 *The Necessity of Nature: God, Science and Money in 17th Century English Law of Nature*
Mónica García-Salmones

178 *Making the World Safe for Investment: The Protection of Foreign Property 1922–1959*
Andrea Leiter

177 *National Governance and Investment Treaties*
Josef Ostřanský and Facundo Pérez Aznar

176 *Who Owns Outer Space? International Law, Astrophysics, and the Sustainable Development of Space*
Michael Byers and Aaron Boley

175 *Intervening in International Justice: Third States before Courts and Tribunals*
Brian McGarry

174 *Reciprocity in Public International Law*
Arianna Whelan

173 *When Environmental Protection and Human Rights Collide*
Marie-Catherine Petersmann Drones and International Law

172 *The International Law of Sovereign Debt Dispute Settlement*
Kei Nakajima

171 *The Everyday Makers of International Law: From Great Halls to Back Rooms*
Tommaso Soave

170 *Virtue in Global Governance: Judgment and Discretion*
Jan Klabbers

169 *The Effects of Armed Conflict on Investment Treaties*
Tobias Ackermann

168 *Investment Law's Alibis: Colonialism, Imperialism, Debt and Development*
David Schneiderman

167 *Negative Comparative Law: A Strong Programme for Weak Thought*
Pierre Legrand

166 *Detention by Non-State Armed Groups under International Law*
Ezequiel Heffes

165 *Rebellions and Civil Wars: State Responsibility for the Conduct of Insurgents*
Patrick Dumberry

164 *The International Law of Energy*
Jorge Viñuales

163 *The Three Ages of International Commercial Arbitration*
Mikaël Schinazi

162 *Repetition and International Law*
Wouter Werner

161 *State Responsibility and Rebels: The History and Legacy of Protecting Investment Against Revolution*
Kathryn Greenman

160 *Rewriting Histories of the Use of Force: The Narrative of 'Indifference'*
Agatha Verdebout

159 *The League of Nations and the Protection of the Environment*
Omer Aloni

158 *International Investment Law and Legal Theory: Expropriation and the Fragmentation of Sources*
Jörg Kammerhofer

157 *Legal Barbarians: Identity, Modern Comparative Law and the Global South*
Daniel Bonilla Maldonado

156 *International Human Rights Law Beyond State Territorial Control*
Antal Berkes

155 *The Crime of Aggression under the Rome Statute of the International Criminal Court*
Carrie McDougall

154 *Minorities and the Making of Postcolonial States in International Law*
Mohammad Shahabuddin

153 *Preclassical Conflict of Laws*
Nikitas E. Hatzimihail

152 *International Law and History: Modern Interfaces*
Ignacio de la Rasilla

151 *Marketing Global Justice: The Political Economy of International Criminal Law*
Christine Schwöbel-Patel

150 *International Status in the Shadow of Empire*
Cait Storr

149 *Treaties in Motion: The Evolution of Treaties from Formation to Termination*
Edited by Malgosia Fitzmaurice and Panos Merkouris

148 *Humanitarian Disarmament: An Historical Enquiry*
Treasa Dunworth

147 *Complementarity, Catalysts, Compliance: The International Criminal Court in Uganda, Kenya, and the Democratic Republic of Congo*
Christian M. De Vos

146 *Cyber Operations and International Law*
François Delerue

145 *Comparative Reasoning in International Courts and Tribunals*
Daniel Peat

144 *Maritime Delimitation as a Judicial Process*
Massimo Lando

143 *Prosecuting Sexual and Gender-Based Crimes at the International Criminal Court: Practice, Progress and Potential*
Rosemary Grey

142 *Capitalism As Civilisation: A History of International Law*
Ntina Tzouvala

141 *Sovereignty in China: A Genealogy of a Concept Since 1840*
Adele Carrai

140 *Narratives of Hunger in International Law: Feeding the World in Times of Climate Change*
Anne Saab

139 *Victim Reparation under the Ius Post Bellum: An Historical and Normative Perspective*
Shavana Musa

138 *The Analogy between States and International Organizations*
Fernando Lusa Bordin

137 *The Process of International Legal Reproduction: Inequality, Historiography, Resistance*
Rose Parfitt

136 *State Responsibility for Breaches of Investment Contracts*
Jean Ho

135 *Coalitions of the Willing and International Law: The Interplay between Formality and Informality*
Alejandro Rodiles

134 *Self-Determination in Disputed Colonial Territories*
Jamie Trinidad

133 *International Law as a Belief System*
Jean d'Aspremont

132 *Legal Consequences of Peremptory Norms in International Law*
Daniel Costelloe

131 *Third-Party Countermeasures in International Law*
Martin Dawidowicz

130 *Justification and Excuse in International Law: Concept and Theory of General Defences*
Federica Paddeu

129 *Exclusion from Public Space: A Comparative Constitutional Analysis*
Daniel Moeckli

128 *Provisional Measures before International Courts and Tribunals*
Cameron A. Miles

127 *Humanity at Sea: Maritime Migration and the Foundations of International Law*
Itamar Mann

126 *Beyond Human Rights: The Legal Status of the Individual in International Law*
Anne Peters

125 *The Doctrine of Odious Debt in International Law: A Restatement*
Jeff King

124 *Static and Evolutive Treaty Interpretation: A Functional Reconstruction*
Christian Djeffal

123 *Civil Liability in Europe for Terrorism-Related Risk*
Lucas Bergkamp, Michael Faure, Monika Hinteregger and Niels Philipsen

122 *Proportionality and Deference in Investor-State Arbitration: Balancing Investment Protection and Regulatory Autonomy*
Caroline Henckels

121 *International Law and Governance of Natural Resources in Conflict and Post-Conflict Situations*
Daniëlla Dam-de Jong

120 *Proof of Causation in Tort Law*
Sandy Steel

119 *The Formation and Identification of Rules of Customary International Law in International Investment Law*
Patrick Dumberry

118 *Religious Hatred and International Law: The Prohibition of Incitement to Violence or Discrimination*
Jeroen Temperman

117 *Taking Economic, Social and Cultural Rights Seriously in International Criminal Law*
Evelyne Schmid

116 *Climate Change Litigation: Regulatory Pathways to Cleaner Energy*
Jacqueline Peel and Hari M. Osofsky

115 *Mestizo International Law: A Global Intellectual History 1842–1933*
Arnulf Becker Lorca

114 *Sugar and the Making of International Trade Law*
Michael Fakhri

113 *Strategically Created Treaty Conflicts and the Politics of International Law*
Surabhi Ranganathan

112 *Investment Treaty Arbitration As Public International Law: Procedural Aspects and Implications*
Eric De Brabandere

111 *The New Entrants Problem in International Fisheries Law*
Andrew Serdy

110 *Substantive Protection under Investment Treaties: A Legal and Economic Analysis*
Jonathan Bonnitcha

109 *Popular Governance of Post-Conflict Reconstruction: The Role of International Law*
Matthew Saul

108 *Evolution of International Environmental Regimes: The Case of Climate Change*
Simone Schiele

107 *Judges, Law and War: The Judicial Development of International Humanitarian Law*
Shane Darcy

106 *Religious Offence and Human Rights: The Implications of Defamation of Religions*
Lorenz Langer

105 *Forum Shopping in International Adjudication: The Role of Preliminary Objections*
Luiz Eduardo Salles

104 *Domestic Politics and International Human Rights Tribunals: The Problem of Compliance*
Courtney Hillebrecht

103 *International Law and the Arctic*
Michael Byers

102 *Cooperation in the Law of Transboundary Water Resources*
Christina Leb

101 *Underwater Cultural Heritage and International Law*
Sarah Dromgoole

100 *State Responsibility: The General Part*
James Crawford

99 *The Origins of International Investment Law: Empire, Environment and the Safeguarding of Capital*
Kate Miles

98 *The Crime of Aggression under the Rome Statute of the International Criminal Court*
Carrie McDougall

97 *'Crimes against Peace' and International Law*
Kirsten Sellars

96 *Non-Legality in International Law: Unruly Law*
Fleur Johns

95 *Armed Conflict and Displacement: The Protection of Refugees and Displaced Persons under International Humanitarian Law*
Mélanie Jacques

94 *Foreign Investment and the Environment in International Law*
Jorge E. Viñuales

93 *The Human Rights Treaty Obligations of Peacekeepers*
Kjetil Mujezinović Larsen

92 *Cyber Warfare and the Laws of War*
Heather Harrison Dinniss

91 *The Right to Reparation in International Law for Victims of Armed Conflict*
Christine Evans

90 *Global Public Interest in International Investment Law*
Andreas Kulick

89 *State Immunity in International Law*
Xiaodong Yang

88 *Reparations and Victim Support in the International Criminal Court*
Conor McCarthy

87 *Reducing Genocide to Law: Definition, Meaning, and the Ultimate Crime*
Payam Akhavan

86 *Decolonising International Law: Development, Economic Growth and the Politics of Universality*
Sundhya Pahuja

85 *Complicity and the Law of State Responsibility*
Helmut Philipp Aust

84 *State Control over Private Military and Security Companies in Armed Conflict*
Hannah Tonkin

83 *'Fair and Equitable Treatment' in International Investment Law*
Roland Kläger

82 *The UN and Human Rights: Who Guards the Guardians?*
Guglielmo Verdirame

81 *Sovereign Defaults before International Courts and Tribunals*
Michael Waibel

80 *Making the Law of the Sea: A Study in the Development of International Law*
James Harrison

79 *Science and the Precautionary Principle in International Courts and Tribunals: Expert Evidence, Burden of Proof and Finality*
Caroline E. Foster

78 *Transition from Illegal Regimes under International Law*
Yaël Ronen

77 *Access to Asylum: International Refugee Law and the Globalisation of Migration Control*
Thomas Gammeltoft-Hansen

76 *Trading Fish, Saving Fish: The Interaction between Regimes in International Law*
Margaret A. Young

75 *The Individual in the International Legal System: Continuity and Change in International Law*
Kate Parlett

74 *'Armed Attack' and Article 51 of the UN Charter: Evolutions in Customary Law and Practice*
Tom Ruys

73 *Theatre of the Rule of Law: Transnational Legal Intervention in Theory and Practice*
Stephen Humphreys

72 *Science and Risk Regulation in International Law*
Jacqueline Peel

71 *The Participation of States in International Organisations: The Role of Human Rights and Democracy*
Alison Duxbury

70 *Legal Personality in International Law*
Roland Portmann

69 *Vicarious Liability in Tort: A Comparative Perspective*
Paula Giliker

68 *The Public International Law Theory of Hans Kelsen: Believing in Universal Law*
Jochen von Bernstorff

67 *Legitimacy and Legality in International Law: An Interactional Account*
Jutta Brunnée and Stephen J. Toope

66 *The Concept of Non-International Armed Conflict in International Humanitarian Law*
Anthony Cullen

65 *The Principle of Legality in International and Comparative Criminal Law*
Kenneth S. Gallant

64 *The Challenge of Child Labour in International Law*
Franziska Humbert

63 *Shipping Interdiction and the Law of the Sea*
Douglas Guilfoyle

62 *International Courts and Environmental Protection*
Tim Stephens

61 *Legal Principles in WTO Disputes*
Andrew D. Mitchell

60 *War Crimes in Internal Armed Conflicts*
Eve La Haye

59 *Humanitarian Occupation*
Gregory H. Fox

58 *The International Law of Environmental Impact Assessment: Process, Substance and Integration*
Neil Craik

57 *The Law and Practice of International Territorial Administration: Versailles to Iraq and Beyond*
Carsten Stahn

56 *United Nations Sanctions and the Rule of Law*
Jeremy Matam Farrall

55 *National Law in WTO Law: Effectiveness and Good Governance in the World Trading System*
Sharif Bhuiyan

54 *Cultural Products and the World Trade Organization*
Tania Voon

53 *The Threat of Force in International Law*
Nikolas Stürchler

52 *Indigenous Rights and United Nations Standards: Self-Determination, Culture and Land*
Alexandra Xanthaki

51 *International Refugee Law and Socio-Economic Rights: Refuge from Deprivation*
Michelle Foster

50 *The Protection of Cultural Property in Armed Conflict*
Roger O'Keefe

49 *Interpretation and Revision of International Boundary Decisions*
Kaiyan Homi Kaikobad

48 *Multinationals and Corporate Social Responsibility: Limitations and Opportunities in International Law*
Jennifer A. Zerk

47 *Judiciaries within Europe: A Comparative Review*
John Bell

46 *Law in Times of Crisis: Emergency Powers in Theory and Practice*
Oren Gross and Fionnuala Ní Aoláin

45 *Vessel-Source Marine Pollution: The Law and Politics of International Regulation*
Alan Khee-Jin Tan

44 *Enforcing Obligations Erga Omnes in International Law*
Christian J. Tams

43 *Non-Governmental Organisations in International Law*
Anna-Karin Lindblom

42 *Democracy, Minorities and International Law*
Steven Wheatley

41 *Prosecuting International Crimes: Selectivity and the International Criminal Law Regime*
Robert Cryer

40 *Compensation for Personal Injury in English, German and Italian Law: A Comparative Outline*
Basil Markesinis, Michael Coester, Guido Alpa and Augustus Ullstein

39 *Dispute Settlement in the UN Convention on the Law of the Sea*
Natalie Klein

38 *The International Protection of Internally Displaced Persons*
Catherine Phuong

37 *Imperialism, Sovereignty and the Making of International Law*
Antony Anghie

36 *Principles of the Institutional Law of International Organizations*
C. F. Amerasinghe

35 *Necessity, Proportionality and the Use of Force by States*
Judith Gardam

34 *International Legal Argument in the Permanent Court of International Justice: The Rise of the International Judiciary*
Ole Spiermann

33 -

32 *Great Powers and Outlaw States: Unequal Sovereigns in the International Legal Order*
Gerry Simpson

31 *Local Remedies in International Law (second edition)*
Chittharanjan Felix Amerasinghe

30 *Reading Humanitarian Intervention: Human Rights and the Use of Force in International Law*
Anne Orford

29 *Conflict of Norms in Public International Law: How WTO Law Relates to Other Rules of International Law*
Joost Pauwelyn

28 -

27 *Transboundary Damage in International Law*
Hanqin Xue

26 -

25 *European Criminal Procedures*
Edited by Mireille Delmas-Marty, and J. R. Spencer

24 *Accountability of Armed Opposition Groups in International Law*
Liesbeth Zegveld

23 *Sharing Transboundary Resources: International Law and Optimal Resource Use*
Eyal Benvenisti

22 *International Human Rights and Humanitarian Law*
René Provost

21 *Remedies against International Organisations*
Karel Wellens

20 *Diversity and Self-Determination in International Law*
Karen Knop

19 *The Law of Internal Armed Conflict*
Lindsay Moir

18 *International Commercial Arbitration and African States: Practice, Participation and Institutional Development*
Amazu A. Asouzu

17 *The Enforceability of Promises in European Contract Law*
James Gordley

16 *International Law in Antiquity*
David J. Bederman

15 *Money Laundering: A New International Law Enforcement Model*
Guy Stessens

14 *Good Faith in European Contract Law*
Reinhard Zimmermann and Simon Whittaker

13 *On Civil Procedure*
J. A. Jolowicz

12 *Trusts: A Comparative Study*
Maurizio Lupoi and Simon Dix

11 *The Right to Property in Commonwealth Constitutions*
Tom Allen

10 *International Organizations before National Courts*
August Reinisch

9 *The Changing International Law of High Seas Fisheries*
Francisco Orrego Vicuña

8 *Trade and the Environment: A Comparative Study of EC and US Law*
Damien Geradin

7 *Unjust Enrichment: A Study of Private Law and Public Values*
Hanoch Dagan

6 *Religious Liberty and International Law in Europe*
Malcolm D. Evans

5 *Ethics and Authority in International Law*
Alfred P. Rubin

4 *Sovereignty over Natural Resources: Balancing Rights and Duties*
Nico Schrijver

3 *The Polar Regions and the Development of International Law*
Donald R. Rothwell

2 *Fragmentation and the International Relations of Micro-States: Self-Determination and Statehood*
Jorri C. Duursma

1 *Principles of the Institutional Law of International Organizations*
C. F. Amerasinghe